ACTS

OF THE APOSTLES.

Translated from the Greek,

ON THE BASIS OF THE COMMON ENGLISH VERSION.

WITH NOTES.
by
Alexander Campbell

He that hath my word, let him speak my word faithfully. What is the chaff to the wheat? saith Jehovah.

GOSPEL ADVOCATE
Nashville, Tenn.

THOMAS HOLMAN, Printer and Stereotyper, New York.

ADVERTISEMENT.

THE extraordinary delay, which has attended the issue of this revision, is readily accounted for by the distance of the reviser from the place of publication, and his occasional engagement in other duties, which compelled him to be absent from home, sometimes for long periods. The work itself has been prosecuted with an intense desire to make a faithful and perspicuous translation of the words of inspiration. Antiquated phraseology has been exchanged for the language of the present day. Errors in the Common English Version have been corrected, and obscurities removed. The most simple and appropriate terms have been sought, to give expression to the meaning of the original, and every effort has been employed to make the ordinary reader acquainted with the mind of the Holy Spirit.

The general principles, which have controlled the revision, are expressed in the following rules and instructions :—

"General Rules for the direction of Translators and Revisers employed by the American Bible Union.

"1. The exact meaning of the inspired text, as that text expressed it to those who understood the original scriptures at the time they were first written, must be translated by corresponding words and phrases, so far as they can be found, in the vernacular tongue of those for whom the version is designed, with the least possible obscurity or indefiniteness.

"2. Wherever there is a version in common use, it shall be made the basis of revision, and all unnecessary interference with the established phraseology shall be avoided; and only such alterations shall be made, as the exact meaning of the inspired text and the existing state of the language may require.

"3. Translations or revisions of the New Testament shall be made from the received Greek text, critically edited, with known errors corrected.

"*Special Instructions to the Revisers of the English New Testament.*

"1. The Common English Version must be the basis of the revision: the Greek Text, Bagster & Sons' octavo edition of 1851.

"2. Whenever an alteration from that version is made on any authority additional to that of the reviser, such authority must be cited in the manuscript, either on the same page or in an appendix.

"3. Every Greek word or phrase, in the translation of which the phraseology of the Common Version is changed, must be carefully examined in every other place in which it occurs in the New Testament, and the views of the reviser be given as to its proper translation in each place.

"4. As soon as the revision of any one book of the New Testament is finished, it shall be sent to the Secretary of the Bible Union, or such other person as shall be designated by the Committee on Versions, in order that copies may be taken and furnished to the revisers of the other books, to be returned with their suggestions to the reviser or revisers of that book. After being re-revised with the aid of these suggestions, a carefully prepared copy shall be forwarded to the Secretary."

There is no pretense or supposition, that this work is perfect. It is published to call forth criticism. The desire is that its faults should be detected, in order that they may be corrected. No one who really loves the truth, will prefer that a mistake or oversight of his should pass current for the word of God. To know and do His will, should constitute the sole aim of a disciple of the Divine Teacher. Whoever, by a just criticism, contributes his mite to the correction of a living translation of the Sacred Oracles, so as more clearly to bring out the truth, deserves more gratitude than the man who discovers a mine of gold or of diamonds.

ΠΡΑΞΕΙΣ ΤΩΝ ΑΠΟΣΤΟΛΩΝ.

ACTS OF THE APOSTLES*.

KING JAMES' VERSION.	GREEK TEXT.	REVISED VERSION.
CHAP. I.	CHAP. I.	CHAP. I.
THE former treatise have I made, O Theophilus, of all that	ΤΟΝ μὲν πρῶτον λόγον ἐποιησάμην περὶ πάντων ὦ Θεό-	THE former [a]Narrative, 1 [b]Theophilus, I [c]composed, of

* The common English title of this book is not truthful. There is no such book extant as "The Acts of the Apostles". The Acts, public or official, of not one of them are recorded. It is, indeed, more truthfully given in all the Greek copies which I have seen, "Acts of the Apostles". We cannot avoid saying of this book, that it contains *all the acts of all the Apostles, reported to us.* But while this may be its current value with us, still we should have it translated and presented just as it appears in the original—*Acts of the Apostles.* And this certainly is as true as the original, because true to it.

The text selected by the Bible Union, being our standard copy, we should have it "Acts of the Holy Apostles", *ΠΡΑΞΕΙΣ ΤΩΝ ΑΓΙΩΝ ΑΠΟΣΤΟΛΩΝ*, which lacks plenary authority. The Vulgate has *Actus Apostolorum*, more in accordance with truth. The Hebrew translation of the *Biblia Polyglotta* has also "Acts of the Apostles". See its translation of our common Greek into the Hebrew. S. Lee. S. T. B. London, 1831, Samuel Bagster. As there were no UNHOLY apostles, we cannot appreciate the propriety of the epithet HOLY, unless Judas be the exception.

---

[a] *Τον μεν πρωτον λογον.* The former treatise. *The former Narrative.* A *treatise* is rather a philosophical or a logical discussion of some thesis or topic—a logical and methodical discourse. Such is not this book of Acts. It is a *narrative* of certain sayings and doings of the Messiah, his Apostles, their associates and contemporaries.

The word *λογος* in the com. ver. is represented by *treatise, account, communication, speech, utterance, words, tidings, preaching,* and *saying.* But only in this place *treatise.* Account or narrative seems much more apposite to Luke's

Memoirs of Jesus Christ. He calls his gospel "*a declaration*" of the things concerning Christ. Cranmer, the Geneva and Rheims, in their respective versions, give *treatise,* merely followed in the com. ver. Murdock's ver. of the Syriac gives *book;* but this is no more pertinent. Wiclif gives *sermon.* Boothroyd gives *relation,* as also Granville Penn, Esq. The word treatise is appropriately followed by *upon.* Such a work Luke has not given to us.

[b] *Ω Θεοφιλε.*—Ω, exclamatory, is retained, or translated by *O,* and *Oh,* indicative of strong feeling or emotion; but in simple address it is not necessarily so, being merely the sign of the vocative. Hence Beza omits it, Wiclif also. Tyndale has given it a special sense, "*Dear friend*", and is followed by Cranmer, and the Rheims vers. The Geneva gives it no representation, nor even do the King's translators translate or transfer it, in ch. 27: 21, where we have *ω Ανδρες* translated Sirs, com. ver. To be consistent they ought not to have transferred it before *Θεοφιλε.* Luke in his Gospel having addressed him as "most excellent" (*Κρατιστε*), it seems enough, in his second dedication, simply and more familiarly to call him, Theophilus. The copy of Beza which I use was printed, London, 1581, and crowded with his critical notes and annotations. He was decidedly, by common consent, the most learned and able Latin and Greek critic of the sixteenth century.

[c] The aorist indicative is here better rendered by our imperfect, *composed,* which is really an aorist, or an indefinite, than by our perfect, *have composed.*

Ποιεω signifies, *to make, form, construct.* When applied to a *narrative* it is more congenial with our language to render it *composed,* as in this revision.

KING JAMES' VERSION.	GREEK TEXT.	REVISED VERSION.
Jesus began both to do and teach, 2 Until the day in which he was taken up, after that he through the Holy Ghost had given commandments unto the apostles whom he had chosen: 3 To whom also he shewed himself alive after his passion, by many infallible proofs, being seen of them forty days, and speaking of the things pertaining to the kingdom of God: 4 And being assembled together with *them*, commanded	φίλε, ὧν ἤρξατο ὁ Ἰησοῦς ποιεῖν τε καὶ διδάσκειν, ² ἄχρι ἧς ἡμέρας ἐντειλάμενος τοῖς ἀποστόλοις διὰ Πνεύματος Ἁγίου, οὓς ἐξελέξατο, ἀνελήφθη, ³ οἷς καὶ παρέστησεν ἑαυτὸν ζῶντα μετὰ τὸ παθεῖν αὐτὸν, ἐν πολλοῖς τεκμηρίοις, δὶ ἡμερῶν τεσσαράκοντα ὀπτανόμενος αὐτοῖς, καὶ λέγων τὰ περὶ τῆς βασιλείας τοῦ Θεοῦ. ⁴ καὶ συναλιζόμενος παρήγγειλεν αὐ-	all that Jesus ᵈbegan both to do and to teach, even to the day, ₂ on which he was taken up, after that he, through the ᵉHoly Spirit had given ᶠcommandment to the Apostles whom he had ᵍchosen; to whom also ₃ he showed himself alive, after his suffering, ʰin many convincing ⁱproofs, ʲduring forty days ᵏappearing to them, and speaking of the things pertaining to the Kingdom of God; and having convened them ₄ ˡtogether, he commanded them

ᵈ "*Began to do and teach*". "Performed and taught", Wakefield; "*did and taught*", Boothroyd. In vindication of this version he affirms, on considerable authority, "That the verb αρχομαι, with the infinitive of another verb, defines the time of the verb". But the fact, that all the Evangelists together did not relate all that Jesus did and taught, seriously impairs the value of the criticism. And the affirmation of John, "that the world could not contain the books that might have been written", had all his sayings and doings been recorded, seems to question the propriety, if not the validity, of his conclusion.

ᵉ *Holy Spirit* occurs in the com. ver. of the Old Testament seven times. In the New Test. *Holy Ghost* occurs ninety-one times; not once in the Old Test. Why the royal translators and some others so translated this word, I presume not dogmatically to affirm. Could it have been that they understood that the Holy Spirit of the former Dispensation was to become, and did become, the Holy Ghost, or the Holy Guest, of the New?

In our currency, we have almost exclusively given the title "ghost", to the spirit of a dead man. Unless by "Holy Ghost" our contemporaries understand Holy *Guest* much more suitable and intelligible to them, it will be better uniformly, in the New Testament as in the Old, to use, as its representative, Holy Spirit.

The transcendent glory of the New Constitution and Church of Jesus Christ is, that while Jesus, the Lord of glory, is its living head, the Holy Spirit is its Holy *Guest ;* and thus the New Constitution is written upon the fleshly tables of the heart, while the Old was written on granite or marble tables, and presented to the outward eye. How justly, in harmony with this view, does Paul say to the Corinthian Church, "You are the temple of the living God, as God has said, I will dwell in them, and I will be their God, and they shall be my people."

ᶠ *Εντειλαμενος—dedisset*, Beza; "having commanded",

Boothroyd; "after he had given a charge", Dodd.; "having given commandment", Wesley, Anonymous, London, 1836; "after giving his commands", Wakefield; "after giving a charge", Thom. Reference seems here to be had to Luke 24 : 48, to a specific command to wait for plenary power. There is no good reason why the com. ver. should assume the plural in this case. Either a special command or a general commission must be understood.

ᵍ *Εξελεξατο*. There is a general consent among translators and critics that reference is here had to the special call of apostles at the commencement of his public ministry; and, therefore, a pluperfect sense is given to the verb. Stuart's Grammar of the New Testament, p. 102.

ʰ *Εν πολλοις τεκμηριοις*. *In* or *by*—not *among*, in this case. His showing himself alive was not one *among* many signs or proofs—but during forty days' living, or appearing, among them, they had many opportunities of realizing and identifying his person.

ⁱ "Infallible proofs", com. ver. *Arguments*, Wiclif; *tokens*, Tyndale and Cranmer; "*infallible tokens*", Geneva; "many arguments", Rheims; "proofs", Wakefield; "plusieurs preuves", French; "*in multis argumentis*", Vulgate; Biblia Sacra Pol. S. Lee. S. T. B. London, 1831. To these, we prefer "*convincing proofs*", Wakefield. *Τεκμηριον* occurs but once in the N. T. "Many *convincing* manifestations", De Wette; "by numerous *signs*", Murdock's trans. of the Syriac Peshito version.

ʲ *Δια*, before words of time, means *during*.

ᵏ I take this participle in its active sense.

ˡ "And having assembled them together". "And being assembled together with them". "And when eating together". These three versions have been given to συναλιζομενος—arguments and versions have been adduced for each of them, and by critics, too, of high rank—translators and commentators. We shall first hear the versions. "And when he had eaten

KING JAMES' VERSION.	GREEK TEXT.	REVISED VERSION.
them that they should not depart from Jerusalem, but wait for the promise of the Father, which, *saith he*, ye have heard of me. 5 For John truly baptized	τοῖς ἀπὸ Ἱεροσολύμων μὴ χωρί-ζεσθαι, ἀλλὰ περιμένειν τὴν ἐπαγγελίαν τοῦ πατρὸς, ἣν ἠκούσατέ μου· 5 ὅτι Ἰωάννης μὲν ἐβάπτισεν ὕδατι, ὑμεῖς δὲ	not to depart from Jerusalem; but to await the gift ᵐpromised them by the Father, which, says he, you have heard from me: for John indeed ⁿimmersed 5

bread with them, he instructed them not to depart from Jerusalem ", Murdock's trans. of the Syr. Pesh. Et congregans eos, "And congregating them ", Beza, London Ed., 1581, with Junius and Tremellius. "And being assembled with them ", Granville Penn, Esq., London, 1836. "And eat with hem and commanded, that they shulden not departe, fro Jerusalem ", Wiclif, 1380. "And gaddered them togeder ", Tyndale, 1534. "And being assembled together with them ", Authorized version, 1611. "And gathered them together", Cranmer, 1539. "And gathering them together ", Geneva, 1557. "And eating with them ", Rheims, 1582. Boothroyd, with all these premises before him, renders the passage thus, "And then assembling them together, he commanded them not to depart, &c."

Prof. Hackett, for whose ability and candor I entertain a very high regard, in his recent very learned "Commentary on the Original Text of the Acts of the Apostles", Boston, 1852, says, " The active sense of this verb has not been proved ", and gives it " *being assembled* ", giving Meyer, Olshausen, and De Wette, as confirmatory of his conclusion. "Having assembled them together ", is, however, maintained by some distinguished scholars, I might say by many. Doddridge renders it, " having assembled them together ", stating, too, " that some critics, ancient and modern, particularly Chrysostom and Theophylact, understand the word συναλιζομενος as expressive of Christ's eating with his disciples during the forty days ". But he adds, " The notes of Elsner and Raphelius seem abundantly sufficient to justify the version I have given ". We have also συναυλιζομαι—*una commoror*, living together, in the same αυλη—hall, or court, which has been seized by some, in aid of their version of "eating together ". But, in our esteem, Leigh is our best authority. In his Critica Sacra, London, ed. 1650, on Acts 1 : 4, he gives *convescens, congregans—conversans*; and adds, Item, qua pastor dispersas oves sub tectum collegit; quæ significationes optime congruerent huic loco, quia Christus discipulos fugitivos velut dispersos oviculas iterum collegit, et ad spiritualem militiam armavit. There is nothing in "eating together ", relevant to a mission ; but there is something in congregating, or calling together a company of persons, in order to the better accomplishment of their mission, *or for commissioning them*. That such an assignation or appointment was made, we learn from Matthew 28 : 16, in connection with Matt. 26 : 32 — " I will go before you into Galilee, after I am risen again ". This appointment is fairly indicated in these passages with their context.

ᵐ Επαγγελια is here, by a metonomy, used for *the thing promised*. The promise itself having already been given, they could not be required to await it.

ⁿ Εβαπτισεν υδατι, υμεις δε βαπτισθησεσθε εν πνευματι αγιῳ. " *Immersed in water* "—"*Immersed in the Holy Spirit* ". The Βαπτω family, and the Βαπτιζω branch of it, have become famous through all Christendom. They are honorably descended from a very ancient family, in classic heraldry. They are descended from βαπ by an *onomatopœia*, "which coins a word from sound, by which alone its meaning may be ascertained ". It is self-interpretive. We have *dip* and *plunge* from the sound of any instrument or material variously brought into contact with water. *Dip, bap* and *plunge*, indicate the sounds made by variously applying any solid substance to water. The air echoes *plunge*, when a person is suddenly immersed in water—it echoes *dip* and *bap*, when persons or other solid substances are suddenly submerged.

Being words of *action*, and not of *mode*, *they can have but one literal and proper meaning*. Βαπτω occurs in the N. T. three times, always trans. com. ver. by *dip*. Βαπτιζω occurs eighty-one times, transferred seventy-eight times, thrice translated *wash*, by a metonymy of the effect for the cause. Βαπτισμος occurs only four times, once translated washing by the same figure. Βαπτιστης occurs fourteen times, exclusively applied to John, the Harbinger. Βαπτισμα is universally transferred in the com. ver. John, the Harbinger, is the only one called BAPTIST in King James' version.

In tracing their ancestral history up to Moses and his law of ceremonial observances, we find, on a grand occasion, the whole tribe of modes of wetting were convened, in Βαπτω, Ραινω, Χεω, Ῥαντιζω, on special duty, each one in his own official service, with his armor on. The priest was to *pour* oil into the palm of his left hand; he was then to *dip* his right forefinger in the oil that was in his left hand, and then to *sprinkle* of the oil seven times before the Lord.

Prof. Stuart, of Andover, affirms, that all lexicographers and critics of note agree that βαπτω and βαπτιζω indicate to *dip*, plunge, or immerse. Bib. Repository, 1833, p. 298. In support of which, he cites Lucian, in Timon, Plutarch, Strabo, Themestius, the Sybylline verse concerning the city of Athens, Josephus, Homer, Pindar, Aristotle, Aristophanes, Heraclides, Herodotus, Aratus, Xenophon, Diodorus Siculus, Plato, Epictetus, Hippocrates, Heliodorus, cum multis aliis.

To these we might add the testimony of Wall, Locke, Tillot-

KING JAMES' VERSION.	GREEK TEXT.	REVISED VERSION.
with water; but ye shall be baptized with the Holy Ghost not many days hence.	βαπτισθήσεσθε ἐν Πνεύματι Ἁγίῳ, οὐ μετὰ πολλὰς ταύτας	in water, but you shall be immersed in the Holy Spirit, not many days hence.

son, Secker, Samuel Clarke, Locke, the philosopher, Wall, Wells, Bishop Nicholson, Doddridge, Whitfield, Wesley, Macknight, and the Assembly of Divines, as concurring with this interpretation of the words of this family. So testifies also the whole Greek Church. The ancient versions—the Syriac, (both the Peshito, 2d century, and the Philoxenian, 6th century,) the Arabic Polyglott, 7th century, the Propaganda, A. D. 1671, all give the same family—"amada"—immerse, of which word the Greek representative is βαπτιζω.

° Πνευματι Ἁγιω. In v. 2 of this same chapter, we have Πνευματος Ἁγιου. In v. 8 we have τον Ἁγιον Πνευματος; v. 16 we again have το Πνευμα το Ἁγιον; and, again, another form ch. 2 : 4, Πνευματος Ἁγιου.

The Book of the Acts, or of Acts of Apostles by some of the Ancients was not inappropriately called "The Gospel of the Holy Spirit." He is, indeed, more frequently spoken of in this book than in the whole Four Gospels. His personal attributes, mission, and work, are more fully developed in the details of the apostolic mission than in any other portion of the Christian Scriptures. Speculative Theologians, in their metaphysics, have, indeed, been much perplexed in their versions and criticisms upon the anarthrous forms of this Divine person.

After a very special and protracted examination of his Divine personality and his work, we have much confidence in the result indicated in the following analysis and synthesis of the Christian oracles, and especially of this book; and because of its importance, and to prevent frequent allusions and references to the special positions and attitudes in which he appears, we judge it expedient, in the opening of this Book of Acts apostolic, to take a critical and full view of this *third personal* manifestation of Jehovah. We have *one Jehovah* in the person of the Father, in the person of the Son, or *word Incarnate*, and in the person of the Holy Spirit.

Πνευμα Ἁγιον is without the Greek article, though in rendering it, we are required to use the English definite article THE. The Greek ὁ, ἡ, το, commonly called the Greek article, must not be confounded with our definite English article, merely because they are called by the same name. Their uses, in the two languages, are by no means parallel. We are constrained, by the laws of the two languages, to employ the English article frequently, when it is not used in the Original, and *vice versa*. Each case must be considered with reference to the general principles of composition which obtain in the English and in the Greek respectively. We usually translate ὁ Θεος, simply *God*, not "*the God*." Yet it is, with but few exceptions, ὁ Θεος, "*the God*," in the Original. In Matt. 1 : 23, we correctly translate, Μεθ᾽ ἡμων ὁ Θεος, "*God* with us," and not "*the* God with us." So in

many places. Sometimes, however, we find the article omitted before Θεος, as in Matt. 22 : 32. In the first part of this verse, we have ὁ Θεος, and we translate properly, "I am *the* God of Abraham &c."—but in the latter clause we have ουκ εστιν ὁ Θεος, Θεος νεκρων αλλα ζωντων, literally, "*the* God is not God of dead, but of living," but properly, "God is not 'the' God of 'the' dead, but of 'the' living." Here, we not only omit the Greek article, where it is in the text, but supply the English article in three places, where there is no article in the original. In Mark 12 : 27 and Luke 20 : 38, we have the parallel passages, and the same construction. The use or omission of the Greek article, in these places, is governed by a very general principle of the Greek language, according to which they employed the article simply to distinguish between the subject and the predicate of a sentence. In the sublime and abstract language of John's introduction to his Gospel, we have a similar case. Εν αρχη, without an article, we translate, "in the beginning." But in the latter part of the 1st verse of this chapter, we have Θεος ην ὁ λογος. Why do we not translate, in the order of the Greek, and say, "God was the word"?—clearly, because ὁ λογος is shown to be the subject of the sentence, not only by the context, but by the use of the article before λογος, and its omission before Θεος. This principle of employing the Greek article or not, according as it is connected with the subject or predicate of a sentence, might be illustrated at great length, but it would be foreign to the purpose of this note to enter upon so extended a field of criticism.

This word πνευμα occurs very frequently in the scriptures, and with various adjuncts. We note, these five expressions πνευμα (spirit), το πνευμα (the spirit), πνευμα ἁγιον (spirit holy), το ἁγιον πνευμα (the holy spirit), and το πνευμα το ἁγιον (the spirit the holy). Let us consider first, the question, does the use or the omission of the article, in the Greek, determine the fact, whether it is the divine, that is, the infinite, or a finite spirit, which is spoken of? In Mark 9 : 20, "the spirit (το πνευμα) tare him." Here we have the article—but it is a demoniacal spirit, that is spoken of. So elsewhere. In Mark 1 : 10, "and the spirit (το πνευμα), like a dove," &c. Here we have the article, as before, but now it means the Holy Spirit or "the spirit of God" (το πνευμα του Θεου), as Matthew expresses it 3 : 16. In Luke 9 : 39, "Lo a spirit (πνευμα), taketh him," &c. Here there is no article, and it is a demoniacal spirit. In ch. 24 : 37, "They had seen a spirit (πνευμα), and v. 39, "a spirit (πνευμα), hath not flesh and bones," &c., without the article. But then, also, without the article, Jno. 3 : 5, "of water and of the spirit (πνευματος);" so frequently in the epistles; as in Gal. 5 : 25, "If we live in the spirit (πνευματι), let us also walk in the spirit (πνευματι);"

KING JAMES' VERSION.	GREEK TEXT.	REVISED VERSION.
6 When they therefore were come together, they asked of	ἡμέρας. [6] Οἱ μὲν οὖν συνελθόντες ἐπηρώτων αὐτὸν λέγοντες,	They now having come [p]together, [q]asked him, saying, 6

[p] This agrees with the command to "continue in Jerusalem", Luke 24 : 49. Some interpreters, with the concurrence of De Wette, construe the participle substantively, "They now, who came together". Grammatical enough, but not in accordance with the author of this book, in the case alluded to. So Olshausen judiciously remarks on this passage, when dissenting from De Wette, as quoted by Prof. Hackett, *Οἱ μεν ουν συνελθοντες; They now having come together.*

[q] *Επηρωτων,* literally *were asking,* tantamount to *asked,* and in most instances, in our idiom, represented by *asked.* Matt. 15 : 23. John 4 : 40; 8 : 7; 12 : 21, &c.

again Eph. 2 : 22, "Habitation of God through the spirit (*εν πνευματι*)"; and in 1 Tim. 3 : 16, "Justified in the spirit (*εν πνευματι*)."*

From these citations, it is clear, that the Greek article does not of itself, necessarily, indicate anything as to the quality, nature, or essence of the noun with which it stands connected but these must be ascertained from other sources. What other aids have we in respect to the word *πνευμα*? Besides the general scope of the context, there are both epithets and attributive or limiting clauses. Thus, to "*spirit,*" we have added, "unclean," "dumb," "deaf," "evil," "demoniacal," "pythonic," &c.—also "holy," "of God," "of Christ," "of the Lord," "of adoption," "of his son," &c. By these and such like tests, and not by the use or omission of the article, must we determine the quality, nature, or essence of the *πνευμα,* in any place. The article may or may not be used with any one of these expressions. This will depend upon its logical, that is, its syntactical relation in the thought of the speaker or writer. The article is in fact a contrivance of syntax to render words, however general, so individual, distinctive, or definite, as that they may be fitted to form the subject of a proposition; hence its introduction or omission will be governed by this general principle, and the same word, therefore, with precisely the same essential signification, will be found with or without the article, according to its syntactical relation in the context.

The uses of the word *πνευμα* afford ample illustrations of this ruling principle in the Greek language. It means, generally, *spirit*—neither *definite* nor *specific* in itself—but, by the use of some adjunct, it may be rendered so, and then it will take or reject the article according to the general rule of the language. Thus *πνευμα* becomes definite, because specific, by the adjunct *ἁγιον.* The adjective specifies *what spirit,* and, when placed after the noun, stands in the relation of the Hebrew genitive, and exerts, along with its qualifying sense, also a limiting and individualizing influence upon the noun. Therefore we find *πνευμα,* when succeeded by *ἁγιον,* uniformly without the article; yet always most specific and definite. There is no room for mistake. Thus (Luke 2 : 25, 26) it is said of Simeon, that the Holy Spirit was upon him. Here it is *πνευμα ἁγιον,* without the article. Yet in the next verse, in narrating the effect of this spirit, it is said, "It was revealed to him by the Holy Spirit," &c. (*απο του πνευματος του ἁγιου*), with the article before both *πνευμα* and *ἁγιον,* clearly because of the relation which this second introduction of the word sustains to the subject, as already introduced in *πνευμα ἁγιον.* The article does not introduce the idea of definiteness, or individuality, but simply demonstrates the *πνευμα* in the second place, as the *πνευμα,* already named, which was not simply *a* spirit, but a particular, that is *the Holy Spirit.* So in the next verse (27), the connection of thought being now clearly and closely established, the specific adjunct *ἁγιον* is dropt, as no longer necessary, and we have simply *τῳ πνευματι, the spirit,* that is, the spirit already referred to, known to be the Holy Spirit, not by the article simply, but by that to which the article refers, to wit, the *πνευμα ἁγιον,* first mentioned.

So far from the article being necessary to give definiteness or individuality to *πνευμα ἁγιον, it is its very definite and individual character that enables it to stand without the article.* It is a great mistake to suppose that *πνευμα ἁγιον* is an *abstract noun. Πνευμα* alone may be used as an abstract noun, but surely not with the qualifying and specific adjunct *ἁγιον.*

The Christian dispensation, being a dispensation of, or through the Holy Spirit, he is in the very beginning of the kingdom, as it was formally set up on the day of Pentecost, most appositely set forth in his individual, personal, and specific character, as *πνευμα ἁγιον*; not an influence of something else, an effect or product of some superior antecedent cause, but a concurring and self-acting personal divine agent, in consummating and completing the work of redemption. Therefore our Saviour said in his farewell discourse (Jno. 14 : 26), that the Father would send in his, the Son's, name "the advocate," the Holy Spirit, "who should teach them," &c. It is here *το πνευμα το ἁγιον,* and in this first chapter of Acts every thing is in perfect keeping with this divine distribution of the parts assigned to the Son and the Spirit respectively, in the salvation of man. In the first verse the commandments given to the apostles are referred to this promised (*πνευμα ἁγιον*) Holy Spirit, *ὁ παρακλητος.* In the 4th verse, the narrative represents the Saviour as commanding them to tarry at Jerusalem till this promise of the Father should be fulfilled—identifying it with the baptism in the Holy Spirit (*πνευμα ἁγιον*),—which had been promised by John, the

* In these critical notes, the common version is adopted, for convenience of reference simply.

KING JAMES' VERSION.	GREEK TEXT.	REVISED VERSION.
him, saying, Lord, wilt thou at this time restore again the king-dom to Israel?	Κύριε, εἰ ἐν τῷ χρόνῳ τούτῳ ἀποκαθιστάνεις τὴν βασιλείαν τῷ Ἰσραήλ; ⁷ Εἶπε δὲ πρὸς	Lord, dost thou at this time restore the kingdom to Israel?
7 And he said unto them, It		And he said to them, It is not 7

Baptist; and in the 8th verse, in reply to their questions concerning the restoration of the kingdom to Israel (v. 6), he tells them, "they shall receive power, after that the Holy Spirit (του ἁγιον πνευματος) shall have come upon them," &c. Here there can be no mistake. The το πνευμα το ἁγιον—promised in Jno. (14: 26)—is the πνευμα ἁγιον, in which the Harbinger promised, they should be immersed, the same πνευμα ἁγιον, for which the Saviour bid them to tarry at Jerusalem, and the το ἁγιον πνευμα, which was to come upon them, in order to endue them with power, &c., as found in v. 8. The identity of the subject indicated by the several expressions πνευμα ἁγιον, το πνευμα το ἁγιον, and το ἁγιον πνευμα, cannot be doubted. To those who think that the idea of the personality of the Spirit was not distinctly held by the Jews, and who yet contend that this idea is only properly and fully conveyed by the expression το πνευμα το ἁγιον, it may be suggested, that in the only places (three in all), where the expression "Holy Spirit" occurs in the Septuagint, this arrangement of the article with the noun and adjective is uniformly employed. The same form is also used by Peter (in Acts 1: 16), to designate the Spirit, prophesying by the mouth of David.

As to the use of the definite English article, the, always before Holy Spirit, it is found necessary in the fact, that we recognize the Spirit's agency always in relation to the Father, and to the Son. We may and do sometimes say "Father, Son, and Holy Spirit," but this rather to unify than to distinguish. Were there scriptural warrant for addressing the Holy Spirit directly, as is sometimes done, we would omit the English article.

Ὑδατι,—εν Πνευματι Ἁγιῳ. These baptisms, or immersions, are spoken of by Matt. 3: 11; Mark 1: 8; Luke 3: 16; Jno. 1: 33; and 1 Cor. 12: 13. In all these places the preposition εν is expressed both before ὑδατι and πνευματι, except that in Luke, where εν is omitted, as in this case, before ὑδατι. The insertion or omission, therefore, of the preposition does not alter the construction or the sense; in either case, the noun is the dative of the manner, or the way in which, or after which, or the place or medium in which, the action is performed. Both the preposition εν and the dative case-ending indicate the same primary thought, that of relative place. The Sanscrit has an "implementive or instrumental," a "dative" and a "locative" case, all of which are expressed, in the Greek, by the one, dative. But the primary and distinctive import of all these is "locative." This is also the import of the preposition εν, and, therefore, we find the case-ending of the dative, sometimes with, and sometimes without, the preposition, in precisely the same connection, and in the same sense. This is so common a liberty of the Greek language, that we need not illustrate it by other examples. As ὑδατι stands to the immersion by John, so precisely does εν πνευματι stand to the immersion by Christ. The relation, in both cases, is expressed by the dative or locative case, and is clearly that of where or in which the action was performed. It should be noted by those who speak of this connection, as the dative of instrument, that whilst the genitive is the whence-case, and the accusative the whither-case, the dative is strictly and properly the where-case, and can only be used to express instrumentality in a strictly passive sense. It is not properly employed to express concurrent action or co-agency. The action in this case is expressed by "immerse," the agents were John and Christ, the whither or object ὑμας, those addressed, and the place—that in which, in the action of John, ὑδατι, in water, and in the action of Christ, εν Πνευματι Ἁγιῳ, in the Holy Spirit.

There are five distinct conceptions of the Holy Spirit in the Holy Scriptures. The first is his nature, all Divine; the second, his person, distinct from that of the Father and the Son; the third, his office of illuminator and sanctifier; the fourth, his influence; the fifth, his work, peculiarly developed in creation, providence, and redemption.

1. In creation he "moved upon the face of the waters," impregnating them with life-giving power; Gen. 1: 6. "By his Spirit he has garnished the heavens;" "his hand has formed the crooked serpent;" the milky way; Job 26: 13. The Spirit of God has made me, Job 33: 4. "The Spirit gave the apostles utterance," Acts 2: 4.

2. In providence, annually renewing the face of the earth. "Thou sendest forth thy Spirit, and thou renewest the face of the earth." Psalm 104: 30. By the Holy Spirit the humanity of Jesus the Messiah was created out of the person of the Virgin Mary. The Holy Spirit (Πνευμα Ἁγιον) shall come upon thee, Luke 1: 35. Therefore she was found with child by the Holy Spirit, Matthew 1: 18. Hence the Christian church commenced by the direct and special influence, or creative power, of the Holy Spirit, Acts 2. The Father sent his Son into the world; the Son promised to send, and did send, with the concurrence of his Father, the Holy Spirit; and, by his gifts vouchsafed to the apostles, they instituted the Christian church, Christ's mystical body, of which he is the living, active, and efficient Spirit.

3. In redemption, He is the sanctifier, and comforter, or advocate, of the claims of Messiah, shedding abroad copiously, the love of God in the heart of his people; making intercessions for us with groanings inexpressible, which only he that searches the heart can interpret.

Such are the evangelical developments of the remedial dispensation, all found in the Divine essence and personalities.

KING JAMES' VERSION.

is not for you to know the times or the seasons which the Father hath put in his own power.

8 But ye shall receive power after that the Holy Ghost is come upon you: and ye shall be witnesses unto me, both in Jerusalem, and in all Judea, and in Samaria, and unto the uttermost part of the earth.

9 And when he had spoken these things, while they beheld, he was taken up; and a cloud received him out of their sight.

10 And while they looked steadfastly toward heaven as he went up, behold, two men stood by them in white apparel;

11 Which also said, Ye men of Galilee, why stand ye gazing up into heaven? this same Jesus which is taken up from you into heaven, shall so come in like manner as ye have seen him go into heaven.

12 Then returned they unto Jerusalem, from the mount called

GREEK TEXT.

αὐτοὺς, Οὐχ ὑμῶν ἐστι γνῶναι χρόνους ἢ καιροὺς οὓς ὁ Πατὴρ ἔθετο ἐν τῇ ἰδίᾳ ἐξουσίᾳ. ⁸ ἀλλὰ λήψεσθε δύναμιν, ἐπελθόντος τοῦ Ἁγίου Πνεύματος ἐφ' ὑμᾶς, καὶ ἔσεσθέ μοι μάρτυρες ἔν τε Ἱερουσαλὴμ καὶ ἐν πάσῃ τῇ Ἰουδαίᾳ καὶ Σαμαρείᾳ καὶ ἕως ἐσχάτου τῆς γῆς. ⁹ Καὶ ταῦτα εἰπὼν, βλεπόντων αὐτῶν ἐπήρθη, καὶ νεφέλη ὑπέλαβεν αὐτὸν ἀπὸ τῶν ὀφθαλμῶν αὐτῶν. ¹⁰ καὶ ὡς ἀτενίζοντες ἦσαν εἰς τὸν οὐρανὸν, πορευομένου αὐτοῦ, καὶ ἰδοὺ ἄνδρες δύο παρειστήκεισαν αὐτοῖς ἐν ἐσθῆτι λευκῇ, ¹¹ οἳ καὶ εἶπον, Ἄνδρες Γαλιλαῖοι, τί ἑστήκατε ἐμβλέποντες εἰς τὸν οὐρανόν; οὗτος ὁ Ἰησοῦς ὁ ἀναληφθεὶς ἀφ' ὑμῶν εἰς τὸν οὐρανὸν, οὕτως ἐλεύσεται ὃν τρόπον ἐθεάσασθε αὐτὸν πορευόμενον εἰς τὸν οὐρανόν. ¹² Τότε ὑπέστρεψαν εἰς Ἱερουσαλὴμ ἀπὸ ὄρους τοῦ καλουμένου Ἐλαιῶνος,

REVISED VERSION.

for you to know times or occasions, which the Father has reserved for his own ᵃdisposal. But you shall receive 8 ᵗpower, after that the Holy Spirit is come upon you: and you shall be witnesses for ᵘme, both in Jerusalem, and in all Judea, and in Samaria, and to the uttermost parts of the earth.

And when he had spoken 9 these things, while they beheld, he was taken ᵛup, and a cloud received him out of their sight. And while they were 10 gazing ᵂinto the heaven as he went up, behold, two men stood by them in white apparel; who also said, Galile- 11 ans, why stand you gazing into the heaven? This same Jesus, who is taken from you into the heaven, shall so come, in like manner, as you have seen him going into the heaven. Then they re- 12 turned into Jerusalem, from a mount called ˣOlivet, from

---

ʳ Χρονους ἡ καιρους, "times or occasions". "The seasons of time, or the exact time", Wakefield.

ˢ Εθετο εν τη ιδια εξουσια; "put in his own power", com. ver.; "appointed in his own authority". These, however literal, are not in the common currency of our present language. Men may place a matter in their own hands—in their own disposal. And by a very common figure, we speak of "reserved rights", we very seldom *put*, that which we possess, in our own hands. It is, therefore, a figurative expression, tantamount to—reserving or placing in one's own dispensation or disposal. It is, indeed, εξουσια, moral power, or authority of dispensation—at one's own disposal.

ᵗ Δυναμιν, not here εξουσια, moral power or authority, indicative of the powers of the Christian age—"the world that was to come". There was not only εξουσια, authority—or moral power—but also δυναμις, intellectual strength and miraculous power—equal to their day and work.

ᵘ Μου, for μοι, is substituted by the authority of Lachmann and Tischendorf (abbreviated Ln., Tf.). The difference between "my witnesses", and "witnesses for me" is considerable. My witnesses might depose against me, and not be "witnesses *for* me". I therefore, *a priori*, prefer the latter to the former—the *text* to the *emendation*.

ᵛ "Was taken up", επηρθη, not ανεληφθη, v. 2, indicating the commencement, not the completion of his ascent. He, it appears from the terminology here employed, gradually and with great dignity, ascended, not as a flash of lightning, nor as a meteor passes away, but slowly and with majesty, that they might clearly perceive and be assured of his return to his native heaven. Several of the old versions read, "And while they were looking steadfastly, as he was going towards heaven".

ᵂ Εις τον ουρανον; into the heaven. In vv. 10, 11, we have this precise formula four times, and, therefore, we must have it just as often in the version. We have also εις twice in vv. 12, 13, and should have *into* Jerusalem, and *into* the upper room, for in both instances they went not only *to*, or *unto*, but *into* Jerusalem, and *into* the upper room.

ˣ "Olivet", olive yard.

KING JAMES' VERSION.

Olivet, which is from Jerusalem a sabbath-day's journey.

13 And when they were come in, they went up into an upper room, where abode both Peter, and James, and John, and Andrew, Philip, and Thomas, Bartholomew, and Matthew, James *the son* of Alpheus, and Simon Zelotes, and Judas *the brother* of James.

14 These all continued with one accord in prayer and supplication, with the women, and Mary the mother of Jesus, and with his brethren.

15 And in those days Peter stood up in the midst of the disciples, and said, (the number of the names together were about an hundred and twenty,)

16 Men *and* brethren, this scripture must needs have been fulfilled, which the Holy Ghost by the mouth of David spake before concerning Judas, which was guide to them that took Jesus.

17 For he was numbered with us, and had obtained part of this ministry.

18 Now this man purchased a field with the reward of iniquity;

GREEK TEXT.

ὅ ἐστιν ἐγγὺς Ἱερουσαλὴμ, σαββάτου ἔχον ὁδόν·

13 Καὶ ὅτε εἰσῆλθον, ἀνέβησαν εἰς τὸ ὑπερῷον οὗ ἦσαν καταμένοντες, ὅ τε Πέτρος καὶ Ἰάκωβος καὶ Ἰωάννης καὶ Ἀνδρέας, Φίλιππος καὶ Θωμᾶς, Βαρθολομαῖος καὶ Ματθαῖος, Ἰάκωβος Ἀλφαίου καὶ Σίμων ὁ Ζηλωτὴς, καὶ Ἰούδας Ἰακώβου. 14 οὗτοι πάντες ἦσαν προσκαρτεροῦντες ὁμοθυμαδὸν τῇ προσευχῇ καὶ τῇ δεήσει, σὺν γυναιξὶ καὶ Μαρίᾳ τῇ μητρὶ τοῦ Ἰησοῦ, καὶ σὺν τοῖς ἀδελφοῖς αὐτοῦ.

15 ΚΑΙ ἐν ταῖς ἡμέραις ταύταις ἀναστὰς Πέτρος ἐν μέσῳ τῶν μαθητῶν εἶπεν· ἦν τε ὄχλος ὀνομάτων ἐπιτοαυτὸ ὡς ἑκατὸν εἴκοσιν· 16 Ἄνδρες ἀδελφοὶ, ἔδει πληρωθῆναι τὴν γραφὴν ταύτην, ἣν προεῖπε τὸ Πνεῦμα τὸ Ἅγιον διὰ στόματος Δαβὶδ, περὶ Ἰούδα τοῦ γενομένου ὁδηγοῦ τοῖς συλλαβοῦσι τὸν Ἰησοῦν· 17 ὅτι κατηριθμημένος ἦν σὺν ἡμῖν, καὶ ἔλαχε τὸν κλῆρον τῆς διακονίας ταύτης. 18 Οὗτος μὲν οὖν ἐκτήσατο χωρίον ἐκ τοῦ μισθοῦ τῆς ἀδικίας, καὶ πρηνὴς

REVISED VERSION.

Jerusalem, a sabbath-day's ᵍjourney. And when they had 13 entered, they went up into the upper room, where abode both Peter, and James, and John, and Andrew, Philip and Thomas, Bartholomew and Matthew, James, *son* of Alpheus, and Simon Zelotes, and Judas, *the brother* of James. These 14 were all ᵃpersevering with one consent, in prayer and supplication, with women, with Mary the mother of Jesus, and with his brothers.

And in those days Peter 15 stood up in the midst of the disciples, and said, (the number of the names together being about one hundred and twenty), ᵃBrethren, this scripture 16 must needs have been fulfilled, which the Holy Spirit, by the mouth of David, before spoke, concerning Judas, who was guide to them that seized Jesus. For he was numbered 17 with us, and had obtained part of this ministry. (Now a field 18 was purchased with the reward of his iniquity, and he,

---

ᵍ *Εχον*, *having*, not = *απεχον*, *distant*. Hackett, in loco., "*having from*"; *Sabbati habens iter*, Vulgate; "distant from", Syriac; "containing a saboth", Tyndale. So, also, the Geneva, "conteyning a sabboth dayes iorney". "Distant a sabbath day's journey", Rheims; "distant about seven furlongs", Syriac Version.

ᶻ *Προσκαρτερεω* signifies, *to persist in adherence to, to be intently engaged in, to attend constantly to*, Acts 2 : 42; Rom. 13 : 6, &c.; *to remain constantly*, Acts 2 : 46; *to attend constantly*, Mark 3 : 9; *to continue with*, Mark 8 : 13; 10 : 7.

ᵃ "Men brethren" occurs some eleven times in this book of Acts. A Hebraism, in our idiom, simply equivalent to *brethren*. Men, brethren and fathers, is a proper address, when three distinct classes are present; but "*men brethren*"

are not two classes, while men and brethren are. Without a conjunction between them, with us, they simply indicate brethren, which is more Anglo-Saxon than "men brethren". In a brother we always find a man, while sometimes we may find a man, but not in him a brother.

Men of Galilee, men of Judea, men of Israel, men of Cyprus, men of Macedonia, &c., &c., are, with us, Galileans, Jews, Israelites, Cyprians, Macedonians, &c., &c. Murdock's Syriac has *men*. The English Rheims ver. of the Vulgate has "you men brethren". Beza, London Ed., 1681, has *Viri fratres:* Boothroyd's London Ed., 1836, has simply "brethren"; our com. ver. follows Tyndale's; Thompson, "men brethren". We do not say, men and Virginians, men and Pennsylvanians, &c.

KING JAMES' VERSION.	GREEK TEXT.	REVISED VERSION.

and falling headlong, he burst asunder in the midst, and all his bowels gushed out.

19 And it was known unto all the dwellers at Jerusalem; insomuch as that field is called in their proper tongue, Aceldama, that is to say, The field of blood.

20 For it is written in the book of Psalms, Let his habitation be desolate, and let no man dwell therein: and, His bishoprick let another take.

21 Wherefore of these men which have companied with us, all the time that the Lord Jesus went in and out among us,

22 Beginning from the baptism of John, unto that same day that he was taken up from us, must one be ordained to be a witness with us of his resurrection.

23 And they appointed two, Joseph called Barsabas, who was surnamed Justus, and Matthias.

24 And they prayed, and said, Thou, Lord, which knowest the hearts of all *men*, shew whether of these two thou hast chosen,

25 That he may take part of this ministry and apostleship, from which Judas by transgression fell, that he might go to his own place.

26 And they gave forth their lots; and the lot fell upon Matthias; and he was numbered with the eleven apostles.

γενόμενος ἐλάκησε μέσος, καὶ ἐξεχύθη πάντα τὰ σπλάγχνα αὐτοῦ, ¹⁹ καὶ γνωστὸν ἐγένετο πᾶσι τοῖς κατοικοῦσιν Ἱερουσαλήμ, ὥστε κληθῆναι τὸ χωρίον ἐκεῖνο τῇ ἰδίᾳ διαλέκτῳ αὐτῶν Ἀκελδαμὰ, τουτέστι χωρίον αἵματος. ²⁰ γέγραπται γὰρ ἐν βίβλῳ Ψαλμῶν, Γενηθήτω ἡ ἔπαυλις αὐτοῦ ἔρημος, καὶ μὴ ἔστω ὁ κατοικῶν ἐν αὐτῇ, Καὶ, Τὴν ἐπισκοπὴν αὐτοῦ λάβοι ἕτερος. ²¹ Δεῖ οὖν τῶν συνελθόντων ἡμῖν ἀνδρῶν ἐν παντὶ χρόνῳ ἐν ᾧ εἰσῆλθε καὶ ἐξῆλθεν ἐφ' ἡμᾶς ὁ κύριος Ἰησοῦς, ²² ἀρξάμενος ἀπὸ τοῦ βαπτίσματος Ἰωάννου ἕως τῆς ἡμέρας ἧς ἀνελήφθη ἀφ' ἡμῶν, μάρτυρα τῆς ἀναστάσεως αὐτοῦ γενέσθαι σὺν ἡμῖν ἕνα τούτων. ²³ Καὶ ἔστησαν δύο, Ἰωσὴφ τὸν καλούμενον Βαρσαβᾶν, ὃς ἐπεκλήθη Ἰοῦστος, καὶ Ματθίαν. ²⁴ καὶ προσευξάμενοι εἶπον, Σὺ Κύριε καρδιογνῶστα πάντων, ἀνάδειξον ἐκ τούτων τῶν δύο ἕνα ὃν ἐξελέξω ²⁵ λαβεῖν τὸν κλῆρον τῆς διακονίας ταύτης καὶ ἀποστολῆς, ἐξ ἧς παρέβη Ἰούδας, πορευθῆναι εἰς τὸν τόπον τὸν ἴδιον. ²⁶ Καὶ ἔδωκαν κλήρους αὐτῶν, καὶ ἔπεσεν ὁ κλῆρος ἐπὶ Ματθίαν, καὶ συγκατεψηφίσθη μετὰ τῶν ἕνδεκα ἀποστόλων.

falling headlong, burst asunder in the midst, and all his bowels gushed out. And it 19 was known to all the dwellers in Jerusalem: insomuch as that field is called in their proper tongue Aceldama, that is to say, the field of blood.) For it 20 is written in the book of Psalms; Let his habitation be desolate, and let no man dwell in it, and his ᵇepiscopate let another take. Wherefore, of these men that 21 have accompanied us all the time that the Lord Jesus went in and out among us, begin- 22 ning from the immersion of John, to the day that he was taken up from us, must one be appointed to be witness with us of his resurrection. And they appointed ᶜtwo, Jo- 23 seph, called Barsabas, who was surnamed Justus, and Matthias. And they ᵈpraying 24 said: Thou Lord, who knowest the hearts of all men, show which of these two thou hast chosen, to take a part in this 25 ministry and an Apostleship, from which Judas by transgression fell, that he might go to his own place. And 26 they gave forth their lots; and the lot fell upon Matthias, and he was numbered ᵉtogether with the eleven Apostles.

ᵇ *Episcopate.* This term, being now canonized by Webster, is more apposite than any other word in our currency, to indicate the office of oversight or superintendency. The only question with us is, whether it would not be more intelligible to the masses to say "his office of Superintendant", or with Wiclif, "his bishoprick let another take". *Επισκοπη* = oversight.

ᶜ *Εστησαν δυο.* Literally "they placed two", but idiomatically, they nominated or appointed two.

ᵈ *Προσευξαμενοι ειπον·* "they praying said"

ᵉ *Συγκατεψηφισθη.* This indicates more than that he was numbered with. He was numbered *together* with, i. e. enrolled among them, Beza, Calvin, De Wette, Hackett. The fact here stated justifies the version given of v. 25, "a part in this ministry, and an Apostleship" from which Judas fell. He was a perfect and complete substitute, possessing all the qualifications equally with him. His treachery and fall are thus made to strengthen and complete the apostolic testimony.

KING JAMES' VERSION.	GREEK TEXT.	REVISED VERSION
CHAP. II.	CHAP. II.	CHAP. II.

AND when the day of Pente-cost was fully come, they were all with one accord in one place.

2 And suddenly there came a sound from heaven, as of a rush-ing mighty wind, and it filled all the house where they were sitting.

3 And there appeared unto them cloven tongues like as of fire, and it sat upon each of them.

4 And they were all filled with the Holy Ghost, and began to speak with other tongues, as the Spirit gave them utterance.

KAI ἐν τῷ συμπληροῦσθαι τὴν ἡμέραν τῆς Πεντηκοστῆς, ἦσαν ἅπαντες ὁμοθυμαδὸν ἐπιτοαυτό. ² καὶ ἐγένετο ἄφνω ἐκ τοῦ οὐρανοῦ ἦχος ὥσπερ φερομένης πνοῆς βιαίας, καὶ ἐπλήρωσεν ὅλον τὸν οἶκον οὗ ἦσαν καθήμενοι· ³ καὶ ὤφθησαν αὐτοῖς διαμεριζόμεναι γλῶσσαι ὡσεὶ πυρός, ἐκάθισέ τε ἐφ' ἕνα ἕκαστον αὐτῶν, ⁴ καὶ ἐπλήσθησαν ἅπαντες Πνεύματος Ἁγίου, καὶ ἤρξαντο λαλεῖν ἑτέραις γλώσσαις, καθὼς τὸ Πνεῦμα ἐδίδου αὐτοῖς ἀποφθέγγεσθαι. ⁵ Ἦσαν

WHEN the day of ᵃPentecost was fully ᵇcome, they were all with one accord in one place. And suddenly there came a sound ᶜout of heaven, as of a rushing mighty ᵈwind, and it filled all the house where they were sitting. And there appeared to them tongues ᵉdistributed, as of fire, and it sat upon every one of them. And they were all filled with the ᶠHoly Spirit, and they began to speak in other tongues, as the Spirit gave them ᵍutter-ance.

ᵃ *Πεντηκοστη*, from *πεντηκοστη = πεντηκοντη, fifty.*
The Pentecost commenced the fiftieth day from the first day of unleavened bread—on the morrow after the Paschal Lamb was offered.

ᵇ *Συμπληρουσθαι.* The verb *συμπληροω* occurs only three times, and exclusively in Luke's writings—twice in his Gospel and once here—"completely filled". The action of the verb (literally, to be completed) refers to the interval before his arrival. Olsh., Hackett. "And when the days of Pentecost were fully come"; Mur., Syriac Peshito Version. "The morrow after the seventh Sabbath". The Jews were on that day to celebrate a holy convocation according to the law.

ᶜ *Εκ του ουρανου,* literally *out of* heaven, usually represented *from* heaven.

ᵈ *Πνοης βιαιας,* a mighty blast; *φερομενης,* a rushing mighty wind; *φερεσθαι,* rapid and violent motion. *Ηχος* must be regarded here as the nom. case to *επληρωσεν.* The echo or sound filled the apartment in which they were assembled. Had it been in the temple it would doubtless have been named. No symbol of *spirit* known to mankind, is better than the wind. John 3 : 8.

ᵉ "Separate tongues as of fire, and it settled upon each of them", Thompson. "Distinct tongues as of fire, and it sat upon each of them", Wesley. "Tongues which were divided like flame, and they rested upon each of them", Murdock. "Divided tongues as of fire, and a tongue sat on each of them", Boothroyd. He adds, " Calvin, Heinrichs, and many of the older commentators render the participle *disparted,* or *cleft,* and suppose it to describe the flame as exhibiting in each instance a tongue-like, forked appearance". *Διαμεριζομεναι γλωσσαι. Διαμερίζομαι* occurs in the N. T. 12 times, 8 of which are in Luke's writings, translated com. ver. by di-

vided, 5 times ; *parted,* 6 times ; *cloven,* once, (in this passage only). Garments and property are " parted", kingdoms, families, and food, are *divided.* It would seem apropos, that one tongue was visible on the head of every apostle. Wake-field freely translates it, "And they saw, as it were, tongues of fire, distributing themselves and settling upon them ".

ᶠ *Πνευματος Ἁγιον*; we have *πνευμα, το πνευμα, πνευμα Ἁγιον, το Ἁγιον πνευμα,* and *το πνευμα το Ἁγιον* in the Christian Scriptures, and samples of each in the book of Acts. These, too, occasionally occur in connection with the third person of the Divinity, or Godhead.

That the same personality is occasionally indicated by each of them, is conceded by all learned men, so far as known to us. Our best Greek texts distinguish them, when supposed to refer to the Holy Spirit, by capital letters.

On a special examination of every passage in this book where these terms occur in Luke's writings, his gospel and his Acts, we find it with the article, *το πνευμα,* thirty-two times, with-out it nineteen times. In almost every case with the article, the Holy Spirit is intended, and sometimes without it.

Now, as there is but one Holy Spirit of a Divine conception in the Christian religion, we are constrained to think that when any one is said to be *filled with,* or led by *a* Holy Spirit whether with or without the article, the Spirit of God is in-tended and intimated. But that Spirit, now as formerly, dis-tributes or confers his graces as he wills, and especially in answer to the prayer of faith. It is God who works in us to will and to do, of his own benevolence—*το θελειν και το ενεργειν.* Phil. 2 : 13.

ᵍ *Αποφθεγγεσθαι* is found only in this book, and occurs but three times, chap. 2 : 14 : 26 : 25. In this place it inti-mates more than ordinary utterance. "As the Spirit gave

KING JAMES' VERSION.	GREEK TEXT.	REVISED VERSION.
5 And there were dwelling at Jerusalem Jews, devout men, out of every nation under heaven. 6 Now when this was noised abroad, the multitude came together, and were confounded, because that every man heard them speak in his own language. 7 And they were all amazed, and marvelled, saying one to another, Behold, are not all these which speak, Galileans? 8 And how hear we every man in our own tongue, wherein we were born? 9 Parthians, and Medes, and Elamites, and the dwellers in Mesopotamia, and in Judea, and Cappadocia, in Pontus, and Asia, 10 Phrygia, and Pamphylia, in Egypt, and in the parts of Libya about Cyrene, and strangers of Rome, Jews and proselytes, 11 Cretes and Arabians, we do	δὲ ἐν Ἰερουσαλὴμ κατοικοῦντες Ἰουδαῖοι ἄνδρες εὐλαβεῖς ἀπὸ παντὸς ἔθνους τῶν ὑπὸ τὸν οὐρανόν. ⁶ γενομένης δὲ τῆς φωνῆς ταύτης, συνῆλθε τὸ πλῆθος καὶ συνεχύθη· ὅτι ἤκουον εἷς ἕκαστος τῇ ἰδίᾳ διαλέκτῳ λαλούντων αὐτῶν. ⁷ ἐξίσταντο δὲ πάντες καὶ ἐθαύμαζον, λέγοντες πρὸς ἀλλήλους, Οὐκ ἰδοὺ πάντες οὗτοι εἰσιν οἱ λαλοῦντες Γαλιλαῖοι; ⁸ καὶ πῶς ἡμεῖς ἀκούομεν ἕκαστος τῇ ἰδίᾳ διαλέκτῳ ἡμῶν ἐν ᾗ ἐγεννήθημεν, ⁹ Πάρθοι καὶ Μῆδοι καὶ Ἐλαμῖται, καὶ οἱ κατοικοῦντες τὴν Μεσοποταμίαν, Ἰουδαίαν τε καὶ Καππαδοκίαν, Πόντον καὶ τὴν Ἀσίαν, ¹⁰ Φρυγίαν τε καὶ Παμφυλίαν, Αἴγυπτον καὶ τὰ μέρη τῆς Λιβύης τῆς κατὰ Κυρήνην, καὶ οἱ ἐπιδημοῦντες Ῥωμαῖοι, Ἰουδαῖοί τε καὶ προσήλυτοι, ¹¹ Κρῆτες καὶ Ἄραβες,	And there were dwelling 5 in Jerusalem Jews, [h]devout men, of every nation under heaven. Now when this was 6 noised abroad, the multitude came together, and were confounded, because [i]every one heard them speak in his own [j]tongue. And all were a-7 mazed, and marvelled, saying one to another, Behold, are not [k]all these who speak, Galileans? And how hear we, 8 every man in our own tongue, [l]in which we were born? Parthians, and Medes, and Elam-9 ites, and those [m]inhabiting Mesopotamia, —both [n]Judea and Cappadocia, Pontus and Asia, Phrygia and Pamphilia, 10 and the parts of Lybia about Cyrene, and Roman strangers —both Jews and Proselytes, 11 Cretes and Arabians, —we hear

them to make solemn addresses ", Thom.   Elsner, on this passage, quoting Diogenes Laertius, Iamblichus, and Kypke, shows that it is applied specially to indicate oracles or prophetic responses. So used by Josephus, Strabo, and Philo. —See Doddridge. "As the Spirit gave them utterance" has respect to the import of the communications rather than to the fact of their mere powers of speaking, or of expressing themselves.

[h] Εὐλαβεῖς occurs but three times in N. T., always rendered *devout*. Its whole family—*ευλαβεια* and *ευλαβεομαι* are found but seven times. It is only in Hellenistic Greek found in this usage. The *pious* Eneas and the *devout* Greeks correspond with this use of it. It is probable that the Jews, then sojourners in all nations, were represented in this great anniversary of the giving of their law by men the most pious and devout in their nation.

[i] Εἰς ἕκαστος: literally *each one*, but in our usage, *every one*, is more congenial. In some eighty occurrences in the N. T. it is, with some few exceptions, translated by *every one*.

[j] Τῇ διαλέκτῳ: literally *dialect*. This word in the Christian scriptures is found but six times, and these are found in "The

Acts." It is with us more familiarly rendered *tongue*. This, as in the case of *βαπτισμα*, we prefer to a mere transference.

[k] Πάντες is doubtful, and is rejected by Sch., Ln., and Tf. But Hackett and some others regard it as *emphatic*. It is, indeed, if genuine, a figure of amplification.

[l] Εν ᾗ—in which, not, "wherein".

[m] For *the dwellers*, now also obsolete, substitute *those inhabiting*, as not only more modern, but more indicative of the regimen and more in harmony with it. *Inhabit*, in our vernacular, is both transitive and intransitive.

[n] "Judea". Some eminent critics, such as Dr. Bloomfield and Granville Penn, Esq., regard this as a vitiation of the common reading. "Idumea exactly fits the geographical order of the countries named, Judea does not—Parthians, and Medes, and Elamites; those who inhabit Mesopotamia and Idumea". Besides, it is not likely that, in such a collation of countries, Judea, in which they were assembled, would be named—and named, too, out of its proper place. But Bagster's text, being the standard text, renders this position gratuitous. Otherwise we strongly incline to Idumea.

KING JAMES' VERSION.

hear them speak in our tongues
the wonderful works of God.

12 And they were all amazed,
and were in doubt, saying one to
another, What meaneth this?

13 Others mocking, said, These
men are full of new wine.

14 But Peter, standing up
with the eleven, lifted up his
voice, and said unto them, Ye
men of Judea, and all *ye* that
dwell at Jerusalem, be this
known unto you, and hearken
to my words·

15 For these are not drunken,
as ye suppose, seeing it is *but*
the third hour of the day.

16 But this is that which was
spoken by the prophet Joel

17 And it shall come to pass
in the last days, saith God, I will
pour out of my Spirit upon all
flesh: and your sons and your
daughters shall prophesy, and
your young men shall see visions,
and your old men shall dream
dreams:

GREEK TEXT.

ἀκούομεν λαλούντων αὐτῶν ταῖς
ἡμετέραις γλώσσαις τὰ μεγαλεῖα
τοῦ Θεοῦ; 12 Ἐξίσταντο δὲ
πάντες καὶ διηπόρουν, ἄλλος
πρὸς ἄλλον λέγοντες, Τί ἂν θέλοι
τοῦτο εἶναι; 13 Ἕτεροι δὲ χλευ-
άζοντες ἔλεγον, Ὅτι γλεύκους
μεμεστωμένοι εἰσί.

14 Σταθεὶς δὲ Πέτρος σὺν τοῖς
ἕνδεκα, ἐπῆρε τὴν φωνὴν αὐτοῦ,
καὶ ἀπεφθέγξατο αὐτοῖς, Ἄνδρες
Ἰουδαῖοι, καὶ οἱ κατοικοῦντες
Ἱερουσαλὴμ ἅπαντες, τοῦτο ὑμῖν
γνωστὸν ἔστω, καὶ ἐνωτίσασθε
τὰ ῥήματά μου. 15 οὐ γὰρ ὡς
ὑμεῖς ὑπολαμβάνετε, οὗτοι με-
θύουσιν· ἔστι γὰρ ὥρα τρίτη τῆς
ἡμέρας· 16 ἀλλὰ τοῦτό ἐστι τὸ
εἰρημένον διὰ τοῦ προφήτου
Ἰωὴλ, 17 Καὶ ἔσται ἐν ταῖς
ἐσχάταις ἡμέραις, λέγει ὁ Θεὸς,
ἐκχεῶ ἀπὸ τοῦ πνεύματός μου
ἐπὶ πᾶσαν σάρκα, καὶ προφητεύ-
σουσιν οἱ υἱοὶ ὑμῶν καὶ αἱ θυγατέρες ὑμῶν· καὶ οἱ νεανίσκοι
ὑμῶν ὁράσεις ὄψονται, καὶ οἱ
πρεσβύτεροι ὑμῶν ἐνύπνια ἐνυ-

REVISED VERSION.

them speaking in our own
tongues the [o]majestic works
of God. And they were all 12
amazed and perplexed, saying
one to another, What means
this? Others (mocking) said, 13
[p]They are full of [q]sweet
wine. But Peter, standing up 14
with the eleven, raised his
voice, and said to them, [r]Jews,
and all you that reside in Jerusalem, be this known to you,
and hearken to my words: for 15
these men are not drunk, as
you suppose, seeing it is but
the third [s]hour of the day.
But this is that which was 16
spoken [t]through the prophet
Joel, And it shall come to 17
pass, in [u]the last days, that
I will pour out of my Spirit
upon all flesh, and they shall
prophesy. Your young men
shall see visions, and your old
men shall dream [v]in dreams:

---

[o] *Τα μεγαλεια* is more than *mighty*, or *wonderful*. *Την μεγαλειοτητα* is rendered *magnificence*, Acts 19 : 27; *majesty*, 2 Peter 1 : 16. In this context, its full import of grandeur is called for. "Wonderful dispensations of God", Thompson; "Wonderful works of God", Wakefield, Boothroyd, Wesley; "Wonders of God", Mur. Syriac.

[p] *Men* is supplied in com. vers. *Χλευαζοντες* is repudiated by Gb., Sch., Ln., and Tf., and *διαχλευαζοντες* substituted.

[q] *Γλευκους*, mustum vinum recens ex uvis expressum et synecdochice, quivis dulcis potus quasi, a sweet wine.—Stockius, Wesley, Thompson, Geneva, Rheims. *Musto*, Vulgate, Wickliff. *New wine*, Murdock, cum multis aliis. The Pentecost occurred in June, the First Vintage in August. Consequently, it could not be new wine.

[r] *Ανδρες Ιουδαιοι*, Jews; born in Jerusalem, *οἱ κατοικουντες*. "Jews, and Jewish converts, or Jews born in Jerusalem, and Foreign Jews." Hackett, cum multis aliis.

[s] Nine o'clock in the morning.

[t] *Δια, through*, not *by*. V. 16. *Ὑπο* frequently indicates *by*, as an *author*; but *δια, through*, as an agent, or messenger. So Vigerius, p. 670, Sec. 6, "cum dativo, ut plurimum redditur *sub*".

[u] In these writings, "*the last days*" generally, if not always, indicate the Christian age. Indeed, the conclusion of the Jewish dispensation was the commencement of the Christian. As the morning star sets in day, so did the Harbinger decrease as the sun of righteousness arose with healing in his wings. Jesus Christ is, in this view of the premises, properly said to have "Appeared in the end of the world", to put away sin-offerings by the sacrifice of himself.

[v] "Shall dream dreams", or dream with dreams; for *ενυπνιοις* Mill gives *ενυπνια*. With Prof. Hackett and some other translators, we, in this case, prefer Griesbach's text.

KING JAMES' VERSION.	GREEK TEXT.	REVISED VERSION.
18 And on my servants, and on my hand-maidens, I will pour out in those days of my Spirit; and they shall prophesy:	πνιασθήσονται. ¹⁸ καί γε ἐπὶ τοὺς δούλους μου καὶ ἐπὶ τὰς δούλας μου, ἐν ταῖς ἡμέραις ἐκείναις ἐκχεῶ ἀπὸ τοῦ πνεύματός μου, καὶ προφητεύσουσι.	and on my man servants, and 18 my maid servants, in those days I will pour out of my Spirit, and they shall prophesy. And 19
19 And I will shew wonders in heaven above, and signs in the earth beneath; blood, and fire, and vapour of smoke:	¹⁹ καὶ δώσω τέρατα ἐν τῷ οὐρανῷ ἄνω, καὶ σημεῖα ἐπὶ τῆς γῆς κάτω, αἷμα καὶ πῦρ καὶ ἀτμίδα καπνοῦ.	I will show wonders in the heavens ʷabove, and signs on the earth beneath—blood and fire, and smoky ˣvapor. The 20
20 The sun shall be turned into darkness, and the moon into blood, before that great and notable day of the Lord come.	²⁰ ὁ ἥλιος μεταστραφήσεται εἰς σκότος, καὶ ἡ σελήνη εἰς αἷμα, πρὶν ἢ ἐλθεῖν τὴν ἡμέραν κυρίου τὴν μεγάλην καὶ ἐπιφανῆ.	sun shall be turned into darkness, and the moon into blood, before that great and illustrious day of the Lord come.
21 And it shall come to pass, *that* whosoever shall call on the name of the Lord, shall be saved.	²¹ καὶ ἔσται, πᾶς ὃς ἂν ἐπικαλέσηται τὸ ὄνομα κυρίου, σωθήσεται.	And it shall come to pass, that 21 every one who shall call upon the name of the Lord, shall be ʸsaved. Israelites, hear these 22
22 Ye men of Israel, hear these words; Jesus of Nazareth, a man approved of God among you by miracles, and wonders, and signs, which God did by him in the midst of you, as ye yourselves also know:	²² Ἄνδρες Ἰσραηλῖται, ἀκούσατε τοὺς λόγους τούτους· Ἰησοῦν τὸν Ναζωραῖον, ἄνδρα ἀπὸ τοῦ Θεοῦ ἀποδεδειγμένον εἰς ὑμᾶς δυνάμεσι καὶ τέρασι καὶ σημείοις, οἷς ἐποίησε δι᾽ αὐτοῦ ὁ Θεὸς ἐν μέσῳ ὑμῶν, καθὼς καὶ αὐτοὶ οἴδατε,	words: Jesus, the Nazarene, a man approved of God among you, by miracles, and wonders, and signs, which God did by him, in the midst of you (as you, yourselves also know)—
23 Him, being delivered by the determinate counsel and	²³ τοῦτον τῇ ὡρισμένῃ βουλῇ καὶ προγνώσει τοῦ	him having seized, who, by the 23 ᶻdeclared counsel and fore-

ʷ Peter inserts ανω, σημεια, κατω, not in the Hebrew.

ˣ "Smoky vapor", Thompson. "Clouds of smoke". The τερατα και σημεια have placed in apposition to them, αἱμα, πυρ, ατμιδα καπνου, i. e. the prodigies and signs are blood, fire, and smoky vapor. These are but the portents of the destiny, and not the desolations of the Jerusalem that then was. Such are the τερατα εν τω ουρανω, and the σημεια επι της γης.

ʸ Σωθησεται, shall be saved from the then impending judgments. The context gives it this meaning in this place, though usually in this Book of Acts, it refers to the future and eternal salvation.

ᶻ Ωρισμενη βουλη και προγνωσει Θεου. In this phrase ὀριζω is emphatic and important. It is defined by the words *determine, ordain, declare, limit,* in our com. ver., Luke 22 : 22; Acts 10 : 42. Which of these four shall be selected in any given passage is, of course, according to the context, in the judgment of the translator; and that, generally, is according to his analogy of faith. But to these four definitions may be added—*termino, finio, definio, do definitionem rei,* Aristotle, Scapula, Robertson. To *define,* and to *declare,* are its most etymological and general acceptations.

That the person, mission, and work of the Lord Jesus Christ was *declared, promulged, marked out* and *defined,* in the Law, the Prophets, and the Psalms, no enlightened Christian can or will deny. In cases of this sort, our rule in translation is to give, not a particular, or a private interpretation, but either a generic, or a specific one, as the case may clearly indicate. We have the genus, the species, and the individual in words, and their acceptations, as we have in animals or plants. Where there is no reasonable doubt, we prefer the precise *individual* meaning, clearly indicated in the context; next to this, the *specific*; and when neither is clearly indicated, the *generic* sense; thus giving an equal chance to every one to form his own judgment of the word or sentence, as to the meaning of the Spirit.

Christ Jesus being the centre and circumference of the Bible, the Alpha and the Omega of the whole volume of God, of whom Moses in the Law, and all the Prophets, the Evangelists, and the Apostles, spoke and wrote, the sun of the spiritual and the moral universe, the testimony which God the Father has given of him, is the spirit of the whole oracle or testimony of God. Rev. 19 : 10.

Ὁριζω occurs eight times in the N. T. represented by *determinate,* Luke 22 : 22; *ordain, declare, limit.* See Acts 10 : 42; 11 : 29; 17 : 26, 31; Romans 1 : 4; Heb. 4 : 7.

KING JAMES' VERSION.	GREEK TEXT.	REVISED VERSION.

foreknowledge of God, ye have taken, and by wicked hands have crucified and slain:

24 Whom God hath raised up, having loosed the pains of death: because it was not possible that he should be holden of it.

25 For David speaketh concerning him, I foresaw the Lord always before my face; for he is on my right hand, that I should not be moved:

26 Therefore did my heart rejoice, and my tongue was glad; moreover also, my flesh shall rest in hope:

27 Because thou wilt not leave my soul in hell, neither

Θεοῦ ἔκδοτον λαβόντες, διὰ χειρῶν ἀνόμων προσπήξαντες ἀνείλετε· 24 ὃν ὁ Θεὸς ἀνέστησε, λύσας τὰς ὠδῖνας τοῦ θανάτου, καθότι οὐκ ἦν δυνατὸν κρατεῖσθαι αὐτὸν ὑπ᾽ αὐτοῦ. 25 Δαβὶδ γὰρ λέγει εἰς αὐτὸν, Προωρώμην τὸν Κύριον ἐνώπιόν μου διὰ παντός· ὅτι ἐκ δεξιῶν μου ἐστὶν, ἵνα μὴ σαλευθῶ· 26 διὰ τοῦτο εὐφράνθη ἡ καρδία μου, καὶ ἠγαλλιάσατο ἡ γλῶσσά μου· ἔτι δὲ καὶ ἡ σάρξ μου κατασκηνώσει ἐπ᾽ ἐλπίδι. 27 ὅτι οὐκ ἐγκαταλείψεις τὴν ψυχήν μου εἰς ᾅδου,

[a]knowledge of God was yielded [b]up, you have, by wicked hands, crucified and slain, 24 whom God has raised up, having loosed the [c]bands of death, because it was impossible that he should be held under it. For David speaks for 25 [d]him: I have always regarded the Lord, as before my face; for he is on my right hand, that I should not be moved. Therefore did my heart re- 26 joice, and my tongue was glad: moreover my flesh shall rest in hope, [e]that thou wilt 27 not leave my soul among the [f]dead, neither wilt thou suffer

---

[a] *Προγνωσις* occurs but twice in the Christian scriptures. In both cases it refers to God's foreknowledge. This, indeed, in condescension to our modes of viewing events. To a being inhabiting eternity—to whom all things past, present, and to come are ever and alike present—foreknowledge or past knowledge applies not. Eternity past and future are a *nunc stans*, an everlasting now. Does not he "inhabit eternity"? Is. 57 : 15.

[b] *Εχδοτον—deditus*, yielded up. This is literal, but, being a much litigated passage, we prefer being literal to a fault.

[c] *Bonds, bands, cords, pangs*, have been by divers translators and critics regarded as appropriate representatives of *ωδινας*. With much probability Beza conjectures that as the Hebrew חבלי, with the variation of one little point, may indifferently signify *pains* or *bonds*, the former is here preferred, because agreeing best with the connection—else it must signify the confinement to which the pains of death had brought him. Dodd., compare Matth. 24 : 15. Rev. 17 : 1.—But as the bands of death better agree with what follows we prefer it. Again there seems to be an allusion to David's triumph over the Philistines, or over Saul, supposed to be described, Ps. 18 : 5. in these words :—

The cords of Hades enclosed me,
The snares of death were laid for me,
In my distress I called upon Jehovah,
——Then the earth shook and trembled,
The foundation of the mountains rocked.

We prefer this view of it, as appropriate to Christ's resurrection.

[d] *Εις αυτον* :—*for him*, or in reference to him, impersonating him.

[e] *Οτι* com. ver. is frequently rendered by *for, that, because*, "because that". The last of these is as redundant as *for to*.

That is most generally adapted to declare its full sense, and in better taste than *because*, or because that. Vigerius on ὅτι and τοινυν, p. 547. London, 1824.

[f] *Εις ᾅδου*. Such is the reading of the selected Gr. text. But, although in the main we regard it as the best Ed. of the N. T., we cannot uniformly conform to it. In this case we prefer εις ᾅδην, the marginal reading adopted by Griesbach, Lachmann, and Tischendorf. The object of this hope was, that his soul or life would not be lost among the dead. "In hope *that* thou wilt not leave, &c., not "*because*".

Ἅδης is by Romanists and some Protestants frequently rendered *hell*. The king's translators of the Bible render שְׁאוֹל, *sheol*, in the Old Testament, *hell*. Yet, says Leigh, in his Critica Sacra, "All learned men know that *grave* is more proper than *hell*. The Hebrews had no word proper to indicate *hell*, as Christians understand it. They had Tophet and Gehinnom. The Hebrew *Sheol* signifies a place dark and obscure, where nothing can be seen. Job calls it "the land of darkness". The Romans had their infernal, as well as their supernal regions, their *Orcus* and their *Plutonic* realms.

Christians believe and teach, that there is a *Heaven*, a *Hades*, and a *Gehenna*. Their *Hades* is a state of separation of body and spirit. The body returns to the earth whence it was created, and the spirit returns to God who gave it. This separation continues till the Resurrection of the dead. Then the wicked dead shall be turned into Gehenna, and the righteous shall ascend to their Father and their Savior, and continue forever with them. The Apostolic use of this word, and their application of the saying of our Lord, "Thou wilt not leave my soul in *hades*, nor suffer thy Holy One to see corruption", indicate that Jesus, the Messiah, was not in his body to perish, not even to decompose; and though really dead, and his body interred, should see no corruption; but, as from a

KING JAMES' VERSION.

wilt thou suffer thine Holy One to see corruption.

28 Thou hast made known to me the ways of life; thou shalt make me full of joy with thy countenance.

29 Men *and* brethren, let me freely speak unto you of the patriarch David, that he is both dead and buried, and his sepulchre is with us unto this day.

30 Therefore being a prophet, and knowing that God had sworn with an oath to him, that of the fruit of his loins, according to the flesh, he would raise up Christ to sit on his throne;

31 He seeing this before, spake of the resurrection of Christ, that his soul was not left in hell, neither his flesh did see corruption.

GREEK TEXT.

οὐδὲ δώσεις τὸν ὅσιόν σου ἰδεῖν διαφθοράν. 28 ἐγνώρισάς μοι ὁδοὺς ζωῆς· πληρώσεις με εὐφροσύνης μετὰ τοῦ προσώπου σου. 29 Ἄνδρες ἀδελφοί, ἐξὸν εἰπεῖν μετὰ παρρησίας πρὸς ὑμᾶς περὶ τοῦ πατριάρχου Δαβὶδ, ὅτι καὶ ἐτελεύτησε καὶ ἐτάφη, καὶ τὸ μνῆμα αὐτοῦ ἐστιν ἐν ἡμῖν ἄχρι τῆς ἡμέρας ταύτης. 30 προφήτης οὖν ὑπάρχων, καὶ εἰδὼς ὅτι ὅρκῳ ὤμοσεν αὐτῷ ὁ Θεὸς, ἐκ καρποῦ τῆς ὀσφύος αὐτοῦ τὸ κατὰ σάρκα ἀναστήσειν τὸν Χριστὸν, καθίσαι ἐπὶ τοῦ θρόνου αὐτοῦ, 31 προϊδὼν ἐλάλησε περὶ τῆς ἀναστάσεως τοῦ Χριστοῦ, ὅτι οὐ κατελείφθη ἡ ψυχὴ αὐτοῦ εἰς ᾅδου, οὐδὲ ἡ σὰρξ αὐτοῦ εἶδε

REVISED VERSION.

thy Holy One to see corruption. Thou hast made 28 known to me the ways of life: thou wilt make me full of joy with thy presence. Brethren, let me freely speak 29 to you of the Patriarch David, that he is both dead and buried, and his sepulchre is with us to this day. But 30 being a prophet, and ᵍknowing that God had ʰsworn to him, that of the fruit of his ⁱloins he would raise up the Christ, to sit on his throne; he, ʲforeseeing this, spoke of 31 the resurrection of the ᵏChrist, that his ˡsoul should not be left among the ᵐdead, nor his

---

state of suspended animation, would awaken and resume his whole personality. He was, therefore, but some thirty-seven hours in the grave, portions of three days and three nights.

ᵍ Εἰδως, active, De Wette; *knowing*, Hackett.

ʰ Ορκω ωμοσεν: literally, had sworn with an oath, covenanted with David.—Covenants and oaths are, in the ancient Jews' usage, in reference to God and man, used as equivalents. Ps. 89 : 3. "I have made a *covenant* with my chosen, I have *sworn* to David." Still, in an exact version, the latter is to be preferred to the former.

ⁱ Το κατα σαρκα αναστησειν τον Χριστον seem to be redundant after οσφυος αυτου—they are, however, retained by Scholz, and in the selected text of Mill, Bagster's Edition. A majority of Editors omit them.

The whole answer to the whole question given by Peter, to whom were vouchsafed " the keys " of the kingdom, or reign of heaven, commands the profound regard of all mankind. Being honored by the great Master with such a conspicuous position, does not his whole conduct in the premises merit the most profound respect for the answer he gave under this plenary inspiration and direction ?

ʲ Προϊδων: He *foreseeing* this. It is thus rendered, Gal. 3 : 8, com. ver. And the scripture *foreseeing* that, com. ver., *foreseeing* this, Dodd., Booth., Rheims.—He spoke *prophetically*, Thom. And he *foresaw*, Mur. He *saw before*, Tyndal.

—both official and perfect equivalents in their respective tongues. It is not *a* Christ nor *a* Messiah. And as both titles belong to one and the same person, it behoves that he stand in the same rank in both. Although there were many *Christs*, or anointed kings and priests, that preceded and prefigured him, still he alone is *the* Christ of God. He was promised and prefigured as *the prophet, the High Priest, and the King of Zion*, equally the son and the Lord of David. The Jews and the Christians so received and represented the Messiah. The controversy was, *Is Jesus of Nazareth the Messiah—the Christ of God ?* To maintain this was the main drift of all apostolic preaching and teaching. So important is it, then, that it should stand before all men in the proper attitude. In reading the five historical books of the Christian religion, every intelligent reader must have observed that the issue concerning Jesus of Nazareth is, *Is he, or is he not, the Christ of whom Moses in the law, and all the prophets wrote ?*

ˡ Πνευμα is found some 400 times, but *never represented* by soul, or life. A man may lose his *soul* or *life*, but can never lose his spirit. Hence no such intimation as the loss of a spirit is found in the Bible. The spirit is, indeed, the man proper, and never can die, any more than an angel spirit. There will be spiritual bodies for human spirits; "for there is a spiritual body as well as animal body." It is worthy of notice here, v. 31, that ἡ ψυχη αυτου is rejected from the text by the celebrated collators, Griesbach, Lachmann, and Tischendorf.

ᵐ Εις ᾅδου—η ψυχη αυτου: "That he" (Christ) "was not left

KING JAMES' VERSION.

32 This Jesus hath God raised up, whereof we all are witnesses.

33 Therefore being by the right hand of God exalted, and having received of the Father the promise of the Holy Ghost, he hath shed forth this, which ye now see and hear.

34 For David is not ascended into the heavens, but he saith himself, The LORD said unto my Lord, Sit thou on my right hand,

35 Until I make thy foes thy footstool.

36 Therefore let all the house of Israel know assuredly, that God hath made that same Jesus whom ye have crucified, both Lord and Christ.

37 Now when they heard *this*, they were pricked in their heart, and said unto Peter and to the rest of the apostles, Men *and* brethren, what shall we do?

38 Then Peter said unto them, Repent, and be baptized every

GREEK TEXT.

διαφθοράν. ³² τοῦτον τὸν Ἰη-σοῦν ἀνέστησεν ὁ Θεός, οὗ πάν-τες ἡμεῖς ἐσμεν μάρτυρες. ³³ τῇ δεξιᾷ οὖν τοῦ Θεοῦ ὑψωθεὶς, τήν τε ἐπαγγελίαν τοῦ Ἁγίου Πνεύ-ματος λαβὼν παρὰ τοῦ πατρὸς, ἐξέχεε τοῦτο ὃ νῦν ὑμεῖς βλέπετε καὶ ἀκούετε. ³⁴ οὐ γὰρ Δαβὶδ ἀνέβη εἰς τοὺς οὐρανοὺς, λέγει δὲ αὐτὸς, Εἶπεν ὁ Κύριος τῷ κυρίῳ μου, Κάθου ἐκ δεξιῶν μου· ³⁵ ἕως ἂν θῶ τοὺς ἐχθρούς σου ὑποπό-διον τῶν ποδῶν σου. ³⁶ Ἀσφαλῶς οὖν γινωσκέτω πᾶς οἶκος Ἰσραὴλ, ὅτι κύριον καὶ Χριστὸν αὐτὸν ὁ Θεὸς ἐποίησε, τοῦτον τὸν Ἰησοῦν ὃν ὑμεῖς ἐσταυρώσατε.

³⁷ Ἀκούσαντες δὲ κατενύγη-σαν τῇ καρδίᾳ, εἶπόν τε πρὸς τὸν Πέτρον καὶ τοὺς λοιποὺς ἀπο-στόλους, Τί ποιήσομεν, ἄνδρες ἀδελφοί; ³⁸ Πέτρος δὲ ἔφη πρὸς αὐτοὺς, Μετανοήσατε, καὶ βαπ-

REVISED VERSION.

flesh see corruption. This 32 Jesus has ⁿGod raised up, of which we are all °witnesses. Therefore, being exalted by 33 the right ᴾhand of God, and hav-ing received of the Father the promise of the Holy Spirit, he was shedding ᑫforth this which you now see and near. For 34 David is not ascended into the heavens; but he himself says, The Lord said to my Lord: Sit thou on my right hand, till 35 I make thy foes thy footstool. Let all the house of Israel, 36 therefore, assuredly know, that God has constituted that same Jesus, whom you have ʳcruci-fied, Lord and Christ. Now 37 when they heard this, they were pierced to the heart, and said to Peter, and to the other Apostles, Brethren, what shall we do? Then Peter 38 said to them, ˢReform and be

---

Wakefield, "not left in the mansion of the dead," Thom., "his soul should not be left in the unseen world," Dodd., "that his soul should not be left in hell," Rheims. "Not left in Death," Penn. The words "his soul" are omitted by A.B.C.D, Syriac, Coptic, Æthiopic, and Vulgate. Adam Clark. But ἡ ψυχη is found in the text, selected as the most approved

Ἡ ψυχη is 110 times, translated *life* and *soul*, once *mind*, and once *heart*, and *heartily*.

ⁿ God is never called a ψυχη. But he is emphatically called by his own son—Πνευμα. Not *a* spirit but SPIRIT. God is never called *a* Holy Ghost, but there is a Holy WORD and a Holy SPIRIT of equal divinity, power, and glory, with himself. There is Jehovah God, the Father, and Jehovah God, the Son, and Jehovah God, the Holy Spirit, in the Christian revelations. Such were not the Jewish; but such are the Christian reve-lations and manifestations of Jehovah Elohim.

The following profound note on אֱלֹהַ Deus—El, Eloah, Elohim, is worthy of a place here:—Duo haec nomina conjuncta distin-guunt verum Deum a falso nominatis Diis, Deut. 10: 17; Dan. 2: 47; 11: 36.—Elohim significat relationem quandam Dei ad creaturas, designat, nomen, dominium, et potentiam Dei, auctoritatem et vim quam exerit in mundo. Critici Sacri, p. 11. Printed, London, 1650. A. D.

° Οὐ παντες &c. of which (fact) we all are witnesses. The resurrection of Jesus, being the consummating act of approval of his innocence of the charges alleged against him, is here made conspicuous, being affirmed by all the apostles present from the sensible demonstrations which they had of it.

ᴾ Τῃ δεξιᾳ: Dative of the *instrument*. By the right hand of God exalted.

Some versions have *to* the right hand of God. Booth., Dodd. Penn.—*at* the right hand of God—Wakefield, Thompson.—*By* the right hand of God. Wic., Tyndale, Cran., Gen., Rheims Murd.

ᑫ Εξεχεε: "sent forth this gift", Murd. "*Shed forth*", Tyn-dale, Cranmer. Geneva, Dodd. It is well represented by shed or, rather, "was shedding." by some regarded as here indi-cative of a continued act—at the time of his speaking. For it occurred while he was yet speaking.

ʳ "*Both*" appears to be redundant—for "*made* that same Jesus"—we prefer "*constituted*" that same Jesus Lord and Christ.

ˢ Μετανοησατε καὶ βαπτισθητω ἑκαστος ὑμων. *Reform*, not *repent*, is the first part of the response, or the first step *after* *faith*. No apostle ever employs any part of the verb μετα-μελομαι, literally indicating *repent*, in any exhortation to saint

KING JAMES' VERSION.	GREEK TEXT.	REVISED VERSION.
one of you in the name of Jesus Christ, for the remission of sins, and ye shall receive the gift of the Holy Ghost. 39 For the promise is unto you, and to your children, and to all that are afar off, *even as* many as the Lord our God shall call.	τισθήτω ἕκαστος ὑμῶν ἐπὶ τῷ ὀνόματι Ἰησοῦ Χριστοῦ εἰς ἄφεσιν ἁμαρτιῶν· καὶ λήψεσθε τὴν δωρεὰν τοῦ Ἁγίου Πνεύματος. 39 ὑμῖν γάρ ἐστιν ἡ ἐπαγγελία καὶ τοῖς τέκνοις ὑμῶν, καὶ πᾶσι τοῖς εἰς μακρὰν, ὅσους ἂν προσκαλέσηται κύριος ὁ Θεὸς ἡμῶν.	ᵗimmersed, every one of you, in the ᵘname of Jesus Christ, ᵛfor the remission of sins, and you shall receive the ʷgift of the Holy Spirit. For the 39 promise is to you, and to your children, and to all those that are afar off, even as many as the Lord our God shall call.

or sinner, in the whole of their reported labors in the N. Testament. Yet that word is found in the Christian Scriptures as in use by Paul and Matthew. They never used it in preaching the gospel. They commanded all men everywhere to reform— " to *turn to God* "—" to do the first works "—" To cease to do evil " ; to bring forth works meet for faith ; a change of views, a change of heart, and a new life. The μετανοια family appear *fifty-eight times*, in the New Testament, and the μεταμελομαι family only *five times!!* There is, indeed, an outward reformation of life, not proceeding from evangelical faith, of considerable value in a worldly point of view, but which is not akin to that reformation, or repentance into life, preached and expounded in the Christian Scriptures.

Evangelical repentance is summed up Acts 2 : 38–41. Principles lie aback of these acts, which are developed, or perfected in the details given. And specially the question propounded in some particular cases applies to every Christian or immersed person. "*Into what* were you immersed ? " Acts 19 : 3–5. They responded, Εις το Ιωαννου βαπτισμα, *Into John's baptism.* He preached to them the gospel. They now understood and believed it. And what then ? Εβαπτισθησαν εις το ονομα του Κυριου Ιησου, *They were immersed into the name of the Lord Jesus.*

Reform, and be immersed. Μετανοητατε. Μετανοεω, the verb, and μετανοια, the noun, occur frequently in the Christian Scriptures, the former 34 times, the latter 24 times. They are uniformly translated in the com. ver. by one and the same word—the verb by *repent*, and the noun by *repentance*. This is manifestly wrong, inasmuch as we, in so doing, stultify the Spirit of inspiration by employing one word, when he employs two. He uses μεταμελομαι as well as μετανοεω. The Holy Spirit in commanding sinners, always employs μετανοεω. In speaking of evangelical repentance, he never uses μεταμελομαι; this word is found only five times in the N. T. It is used in the case of Judas, who repented without reformation, but never occurs in any case of conversion or change of moral conduct. Christians are said to repent, in the sense of μεταμελομαι, when they merely grieve, or are sorry for something done. Paul in this sense repented. " I do not repent, said he, though I did repent ", that I wrote to you.

In preaching what is usually called *repentance*, no inspired person ever used μεταμελομαι, but always μετανοεω. The former indicating only painful retrospections of the past, accompanied with fearful anticipations of the future. A change of views, a change of feelings, or of the affections, and a change of life, or of conduct, are all implied and commanded by John, by Jesus and his apostles, in preaching repentance, or rather, a reformation of purpose, of affections, and of conduct towards God, all of which are indicated and implied in μετανοια.

Μεταμελεια is not found at all in the Christian Scriptures. The verb is only used five times in the Greek text of the Christian oracles, and one of these in reference to Judas, when he returned to the Chief Priests and Elders the price of the betrayal of his master.

ᵗ See N. j, 1 : 5.

ᵘ Επι τω ονοματι: This indicates authority ; and in such cases is well represented by our prepositions *in* or *upon* ; in the name, or upon the name of the Lord be immersed every one of you—εις, immediately following, intimates transition into a new state, or relation ; such as matrimony, citizenship, servitude, or freedom.

ᵛ *Eis* is found some 1700 times in the N. Test. translated by *into, unto, for, to, in order to* ; its most common version, cum verbis significantibus motum. We have the phrase εις ἁδου but this only as an abbreviated formula for εις οικον ἁδου, Scapula. V. 37. Εις αφεσιν. We enter into contracts, states, conditions—into marriage, into servitude, into freedom, into Christ, into the church, into heaven. Εις and εν can never be substituted the one for the other. As any one *in* any state cannot enter *into* it, so he that is commanded to repent, or to reform, or to be baptized εις—*for, in order to*, or into any state, condition, or relation, cannot be supposed to be already in that state, condition, or relation, into which he is commanded to enter ; or for which, as a subject, he is to become, he is to do, or he is to suffer, anything. Hence those immersed by Peter were immersed into Christ, into a relation, and into privileges not secured to them before.

Εις immediately following and indicating transition, not rest, like εν, intimates an important change, if not in the character, at least in the *state* of the proper subject of this Divine Law, or Ordinance of admission.

ʷ Την δωρεαν του Ἁγιου Πνευματος. Δωρεα indicates the freest and most benignant gifts ; while δωρον means a legal gift or offering, which law or custom enacts. So witness our most estimable lexicographers and concordances.

KING JAMES' VERSION.

40 And with many other words did he testify and exhort, saying, Save yourselves from this untoward generation.

41 Then they that gladly received his word, were baptized: and the same day there were added *unto them* about three thousand souls.

42 And they continued steadfastly in the apostles' doctrine and fellowship, and in breaking of bread, and in prayers.

43 And fear came upon every soul: and many wonders and signs were done by the apostles.

44 And all that believed were together, and had all things common;

45 And sold their possessions and goods, and parted them to all *men*, as every man had need.

46 And they, continuing daily with one accord in the temple, and breaking bread from house to house, did eat their meat with gladness and singleness of heart,

47 Praising God, and having

GREEK TEXT.

40 Ἑτέροις τε λόγοις πλείοσι διεμαρτύρετο καὶ παρεκάλει λέγων, Σώθητε ἀπὸ τῆς γενεᾶς τῆς σκολιᾶς ταύτης. 41 Οἱ μὲν οὖν ἀσμένως ἀποδεξάμενοι τὸν λόγον αὐτοῦ ἐβαπτίσθησαν· καὶ προσετέθησαν τῇ ἡμέρᾳ ἐκείνῃ ψυχαὶ ὡσεὶ τρισχίλιαι.

42 Ἦσαν δὲ προσκαρτεροῦντες τῇ διδαχῇ τῶν ἀποστόλων καὶ τῇ κοινωνίᾳ καὶ τῇ κλάσει τοῦ ἄρτου καὶ ταῖς προσευχαῖς. 43 ἐγένετο δὲ πάσῃ ψυχῇ φόβος, πολλά τε τέρατα καὶ σημεῖα διὰ τῶν ἀποστόλων ἐγίνετο. 44 πάντες δὲ οἱ πιστεύοντες ἦσαν ἐπὶ τὸ αὐτὸ, καὶ εἶχον ἅπαντα κοινὰ, 45 καὶ τὰ κτήματα καὶ τὰς ὑπάρξεις ἐπίπρασκον, καὶ διεμέριζον αὐτὰ πᾶσι, καθότι ἄν τις χρείαν εἶχε· 46 καθ' ἡμέραν τε προσκαρτεροῦντες ὁμοθυμαδὸν ἐν τῷ ἱερῷ, κλῶντές τε κατ' οἶκον ἄρτον, μετελάμβανον τροφῆς ἐν ἀγαλλιάσει καὶ ἀφελότητι καρδίας, 47 αἰνοῦντες τὸν

REVISED VERSION.

And with many other words 40 he testified, and exhorted, saying, Save yourselves from this froward generation.

They, therefore, having 41 gladly received the ˣword, were ʸimmersed; ˙and the same day there were ᶻadded about three thousand souls. And they perseveringly con- 42 tinued in the Apostle's teaching, and in the ᵃcontribution, and in the breaking of the loaf, and in the prayers. And fear came upon every 43 soul; and many wonders and signs were done by the Apostles. And all that be- 44 lieved were together, and had all things common, and sold 45 their possessions and goods, and distributed them to all, as any one had need. And 46 they, continuing daily with one accord in the temple, and breaking bread from house to house, did eat their food with gladness and singleness of heart. praising God, and hav- 47

ˣ *Tov λογον*: The *word*—the *message*. See chap. 1, v. 1, of this book: "The message", "the *gospel*", or "the *word of life*" is generally presented in, or by this term, often expressive of the *To Ευαγγελιον*.

ʸ See N. j, 1 : 5.

ᶻ The supplement *to them* is pleonastic, and better omitted. It is *italicised* by Wesley, omitted by Wakefield and others.

ᵃ *Κοινωνια* occurs in the N. T. 20 times; translated *fellowship* 12 times, *communion* 4 times, *contribution* and *distribution*, *communication* and *communicate* severally once. There is communion in all acts of social worship, in observing not the Lord's supper alone, but in prayer, praise, the meeting on the Lord's day, and in contributions for the poor saints, or in contributions to a Missionary fund—the Bible Union, or to any grand humane enterprise. See Rom. 15 : 26 ; 2 Cor. 9 : 13. The contribution of money for the wants of the brotherhood, appears to be its import in this passage as in Rom. 15 : 16. Paul desired Philemon to have communion with him in aid of Onesimus, a servant.

"The English version unites αποστολων with both nouns:

The Apostles' doctrine and fellowship. With that combination, we should have had, regularly, the genitive after the second noun, without a repetition of the article. See W., §18, 4. Some (Vulg., Bloomf.,) assume a hendiadys: the communion in the breaking of bread. The analysis is not only awkward, but opposed by *τη* before *κλασει*.—*τη κλασει τον αρτον* denotes the breaking of the bread, as performed at the Lord's Supper". See 20 : 7, 11 ; 1 Cor. 10 : 16. The expression itself may designate an ordinary meal, as in Luke 24 : 35 ; but that here would be an unmeaning notice. There can be no doubt that the Eucharist, at this period, was preceded uniformly by a common repast, as was the case when the ordinance was instituted. Most scholars hold that this was the prevailing usage in the first centuries after Christ. We have traces of that practice in 1 Cor. 11, 20, sq., and, in all probability, in v. 46 below. The *bread* only being mentioned here, the Catholics appeal to this passage as proving that their custom of distributing but one element (the cup they withhold from the laity) is the Apostolic one. It is a case obviously in which the leading act of the transaction gives name to the transaction itself".—*Hackett*.

KING JAMES' VERSION.

favour with all the people. And the Lord added to the church daily such as should be saved.

CHAP. III.

Now Peter and John went up together into the temple, at the hour of prayer, *being* the ninth *hour*.

2 And a certain man lame from his mother's womb was carried, whom they laid daily at the gate of the temple which is called Beautiful, to ask alms of them that entered into the temple;

3 Who, seeing Peter and John

GREEK TEXT.

Θεὸν καὶ ἔχοντες χάριν πρὸς ὅλον τὸν λαόν. Ὁ δὲ κύριος προσετίθει τοὺς σωζομένους καθ' ἡμέραν τῇ ἐκκλησίᾳ.

CHAP. III.

ΕΠΙ τὸ αὐτὸ δέ Πέτρος καὶ Ἰωάννης ἀνέβαινον εἰς τὸ ἱερὸν ἐπὶ τὴν ὥραν τῆς προσευχῆς τὴν ἐννάτην. ² καί τις ἀνὴρ χωλὸς ἐκ κοιλίας μητρὸς αὐτοῦ ὑπάρχων ἐβαστάζετο· ὃν ἐτίθουν καθ' ἡμέραν πρὸς τὴν θύραν τοῦ ἱεροῦ τὴν λεγομένην Ὡραίαν, τοῦ αἰτεῖν ἐλεημοσύνην παρὰ τῶν εἰσπορευομένων εἰς τὸ ἱερόν. ³ ὃς

REVISED VERSION.

ing favor with all the people. And the Lord daily added the [b]saved to the [c]congregation.

CHAP. III.

Now Peter and John went 1 up together into the temple, at the hour of [d]prayer—the ninth hour. And a certain 2 man, lame from his birth, [e]was carried thither, whom they daily [f]laid at the gate of the temple, which is called [g]Beautiful, [h]to ask alms of those [i]entering into the temple, [j]who, 3

---

[b] Τους σωζομενους. "The Greek asserts not a purpose but a fact", Hackett. They *were* actually saved, not *to be* saved. Τους σωζομενους. "The saved", those that "were saved", Boothroyd; "That were cured", Thom.; "who were saved", Dodd.

[c] Εκκλησια is represented in the com. ver. by *Church*, singular and plural, 112 times; by *assembly*, three times, neither of which in our tongue exactly represents the word, which etymologically indicates *the called out*, or a community called out from the world, while, living in it; *Church*, being a compound of κυριος and οικος = κυριοικ compounded: whence *Kyrke*, is applicable to a material building for the Lord, as well as to the community which meets in it. The word *Congregation* is also too vague, for it indicates merely an assembly. Still in the appropriated currency of our day and people, and because of its indicating a community assembled, or a congregation in one place, it, better than any other word in our currency, intimates its evangelical significance. We, therefore, after much reflection, give it our suffrage, and would so have it represented in all the Christian Scriptures. Add to N. v., p. 17.—For εις we prefer *for* to any other representative in this language, because of its present use; inasmuch as to, into and unto, its other representatives, would not more fully or clearly represent it with the article here found—"for the remission of sins". The word occurs over 1750 times in the Christian Scriptures, represented in the N. T. by to, into, unto, for, at. When indicating any means to any end, *for* is its generally current value. Hence we find—"for a testimony", "for a memorial", "for a sign", "for a journey", "for a witness", "for remission", "for a possession", &c., &c.

[d] "And Peter and John were going up to the temple at the last hour of prayer", Penn's Ver., London, 1836; "at the

hour of prayer, the ninth hour", Wesley; "being at the ninth hour", Dod.; "at the ninth hour", Wiclif; "ninth hour of prayer", Rheims, Tyndale, Cranmer, Geneva; "being the ninth hour", Murdock; "at that hour of prayer", Wakefield; "now at the same time, that Peter and John, were going up to the temple, at the hour of prayer, at the ninth hour", Thompson; "at the last hour of prayer".—The Vatican Manuscript alone reads "*last*".—Not noticed by Wetstein, Granville Penn, London, 1837.

Την εννατην. The believing Jews, not being yet separated from their Jewish brethren religiously, respected their institutions. Regarding six o'clock as their sunrise, or first hour of the day, the *ninth* hour, here named, corresponds with our three o'clock P.M. This hour was consecrated to their evening sacrifice. The Jewish converts to Jesus Christ, for some considerable time religiously observed some of their own peculiar institutions.

[e] Βαστάζω, com. ver. renders by *carry, bear, take up*. The verb being here found in the imperfect tense indicates an imperfect act. He was being carried not there—but *thither*.

[f] Ἐτίθουν is also imperfect, because it states what is customary.

[g] "Beauty Gate", Ωραιαν, Thompson; "specious", Rheims. —Την λεγομενην ωραιων—called Beautiful. This gate was on the East side of the temple. Its immense folding doors —of Corinthian brass—some 75 feet high and 60 broad covered with plates of Gold and Silver, were, at the rising sun, most beautiful—indeed, beyond description.

[h] του αιτειν—is usually called a Telic infinitive, denoting the purpose or final cause—equivalent to ινα, οπως, in order to ask.

[i] Παρα των εισπορευομενων, from those in the act of entering, not yet entered into the temple.

[j] Ος here, as elsewhere, often stands for ουτος—this one.

KING JAMES' VERSION.	GREEK TEXT.	REVISED VERSION.
about to go into the temple, asked an alms. 4 And Peter fastening his eyes upon him with John, said, Look on us. 5 And he gave heed unto them, expecting to receive something of them. 6 Then Peter said, Silver and gold have I none; but such as I have give I thee: In the name	ἰδὼν Πέτρον καὶ Ἰωάννην μέλλοντας εἰσιέναι εἰς τὸ ἱερὸν, ἠρώτα ἐλεημοσύνην λαβεῖν. ⁴ ἀτενίσας δὲ Πέτρος εἰς αὐτὸν σὺν τῷ Ἰωάννῃ, εἶπε, Βλέψον εἰς ἡμᾶς. ⁵ Ὁ δέ ἐπεῖχεν αὐτοῖς, προσδοκῶν τι παρ᾽ αὐτῶν λαβεῖν. ⁶ εἶπε δὲ Πέτρος, Ἀργύριον καὶ χρυσίον οὐχ ὑπάρχει μοι· ὃ δὲ ἔχω, τοῦτό σοι δίδωμι.	seeing Peter and John about to go into the temple, asked ᵏalms. And Peter, ˡearnest- 4 ly looking upon him with John, said, Look on us. And 5 he gave heed to them, expecting to receive something from them. Then Peter said: Silver 6 and gold I have ᵐnot, but ⁿwhat I have, I give you. ᵒIn

ᵏ Ἠρώτα ἐλεημοσύνην λαβεῖν, literally "asked to receive alms"; "begged to receive alms", Anonymous; "an alms", Thompson, Wesley; "to ask alms", Doddridge; "asked to receive alms", Rheims; les pria delui donner l'aumone, French com. Fest.

ˡ Ἀτενίσας. Fixing, or having fixed, his eyes upon him;—defined in Latin by *defigo*, indicating intensity of action; in our idiom happily expressed by *earnestly looking*.

ᵐ "Silver and gold I have not". However use may have sanctioned the phrase—"Silver and gold I have none", it cannot be justified. "None", is an abbreviation of "not one," which does not apply to these metals named, in the form of money. "Silver and gold I have not", was strictly true in his case, and more eloquent than to say he had not an obolus or a denarius.

ⁿ Ὁ δε ἔχω, literally *that which I have;* but in our language, *what I have* is its present currency, and tantamount in value. So Wakef., Mur. Syriac ver., Dodd., Thomp. cum multis aliis.

ᵒ Εν τω ονοματι,—and εις το ονομα, are two formulas, wholly incommutable, and well marked, in this book of Acts. No person in the annals of the Bible, till the close of its canon, was baptized or immersed "in the name of the Father, the Son, or the Holy Spirit"—nor *in* any name whatever. They were all baptized *into* the name of the Father, the Son, and the Holy Spirit. These are very important fixtures in the Greek of the New Testament. In all cases of authority we have εν τω ονοματι, never εις το ονομα.

We have in the Book of Acts four prepositions occasionally found in connection with ονομα, which has itself three forms in Grecian usage.—The poets sometimes prefer ουνομα, the Aeolians ονυμα, indicative of name, fame, celebrity, and pretext. It is, in "Critica Sacra"—philosophically defined, "quasi ονεομα, a *juvando* ut cujus usuram agnosceres. Nomen quasi *notamen*—Acts 1 : 15. "The number of *names*"—indicative of *persons*.

In connection with ονομα, we find in this single book of Acts εις, εν, επι, and διὰ, indicative of, at least as many shades

and varieties of thought, modes of action, passion, and dependence.

We have εἰς τὸ ονομα, *into the name; εν το ονοματι, in the name; επι το ονομα, upon* the name; and *δια του ονοματος, through* the name, or *by* the name. These, historically considered, indicate four distinct ideas, in reference to certain public acts.—E. g. An alien becomes a citizen, 1st by immigrating *into* a country; 2nd by adopting, *in* the name of God, its constitution and renouncing all former allegiance; 3rd by calling *upon* God to witness and attest his sincerity; and all these *through* the officers of state, or courts appointed for such solemnities. Such is the use of these prepositions, in the affairs pertaining to the kingdom of Grace, over which, presides his Divine Majesty—Jesus, the King of kings, and the Lord of lords.

"In the name of the Lord", equivalent to *by the authority of the Lord.* Ever since his coronation in the heavens, he is the only *authority* for any Christian act, observance, or institution. Nothing is ever done, or commanded to be done, *in the name of the Father,* or *in the name of the Holy Spirit,* from the commencement of the Acts of the Apostles to the end of the Apocalypse.

The reason is obvious.—On his ascension into the Heavens, and formal investiture with the government, management, and ultimate judgment of Angels and of men—all things are to be done *in his name,* or by his authority.—Hence in Christian Baptism, as enacted by himself, he commands all converts to be immersed not *in,* but "*into* (εις) the name of the Father, and of *the Son,* and of the Holy Spirit." This is purely a *Christian* Institution—not of Moses nor of the prophets.—Hence the Formula is a perfectly original and unprecedented institution. There had been washings, cleansings, and purifyings amongst Jews, Samaritans, and Gentiles, by various authorities and enactments. But not one like this;—*into the name of the Father, into the name of the Son,* and *into the name of the Holy Spirit.* Therefore—IN THE NAME—and INTO THE NAME indicate two distinct and *inconvertible* acts which no grammar nor dictionary in the civilized world can equivalence or synonymize.

KING JAMES' VERSION.

of Jesus Christ of Nazareth, rise up and walk.

7 And he took him by the right hand, and lifted *him* up: and immediately his feet and ancle-bones received strength.

8 And he, leaping up, stood, and walked, and entered with them into the temple, walking, and leaping, and praising God.

9 And all the people saw him walking and praising God:

10 And they knew that it was he which sat for alms at the Beautiful gate of the temple: and they were filled with wonder and amazement at that which had happened unto him.

11 And as the lame man which was healed held Peter and John, all the people ran together unto them in the porch that is called Solomon's, greatly wondering.

GREEK TEXT.

ἐν τῷ ὀνόματι Ἰησοῦ Χριστοῦ τοῦ Ναζωραίου, ἔγειραι καὶ περιπάτει. [7] Καὶ πιάσας αὐτὸν τῆς δεξιᾶς χειρὸς ἤγειρε· παραχρῆμα δὲ ἐστερεώθησαν αὐτοῦ αἱ βάσεις καὶ τὰ σφυρά, [8] καὶ ἐξαλλόμενος ἔστη καὶ περιεπάτει, καὶ εἰσῆλθε σὺν αὐτοῖς εἰς τὸ ἱερὸν, περιπατῶν καὶ ἁλλόμενος καὶ αἰνῶν τὸν Θεόν. [9] καὶ εἶδεν αὐτὸν πᾶς ὁ λαὸς περιπατοῦντα καὶ αἰνοῦντα τὸν Θεόν· [10] ἐπεγίνωσκόν τε αὐτὸν ὅτι οὗτος ἦν ὁ πρὸς τὴν ἐλεημοσύνην καθήμενος ἐπὶ τῇ Ὡραίᾳ πύλῃ τοῦ ἱεροῦ· καὶ ἐπλήσθησαν θάμβους καὶ ἐκστάσεως ἐπὶ τῷ συμβεβηκότι αὐτῷ.

[11] Κρατοῦντος δὲ τοῦ ἰαθέντος χωλοῦ τὸν Πέτρον καὶ Ἰωάννην, συνέδραμε πρὸς αὐτοὺς πᾶς ὁ λαὸς ἐπὶ τῇ στοᾷ τῇ καλουμένῃ Σολομῶντος, ἔκθαμβοι. [12] ἰδὼν

REVISED VERSION.

the name of Jesus Christ of Nazareth rise up and walk. And seizing him by the right 7 hand, he lifted him up; and immediately his feet and [p]ankles received strength. And 8 [q]leaping forth, he stood, and walked, and entered with them into the temple, walking, and leaping, and praising God. And all the people saw him 9 walking and praising God: and they [r]well knew that it 10 was he, who sat for alms, [s]at the Beautiful gate of the temple: and they were filled with wonder and amazement, at that which had happened to him.

And while the lame man, 11 who was healed, [t]held fast Peter and John, all the people ran together to them, [u]upon [v]the porch, called Solomon's, greatly wondering. And when 12

---

[p] *His feet and ankles.* "Bones" is, com. ver., a supplement unnecessary. It was rather his ankle *joints* that were strengthened.

[q] Εξ αλλομενος. This would indicate leaping forward, rather than leaping up. He was sitting, as intimated by καθημενος.

[r] Ὅτι οὗτος, very definitely indicates the person alluded to —the identical person that sat begging.

And they well knew—επεγίνωσκόν. They *recognized*, may not be forcible enough. It is, however, in our present currency indicative of an effort. But no effort was here necessary—at the first glance they seem to have known him as a familiar person.

[s] Επι τη πύλη—in this context would indicate that he sat *upon* the gate. Επί is found in the N. Test. in company with *three* cases, and this fact makes it a *hard case*, on some occasions, to give a decided preference. *Upon* is decidedly its most distinctive, and probably its most etymological and common import. It is found in construction with genitive, dative, and accusative, occasionally translated by *upon*. And very frequently so found in Luke's and Paul's writings. *At* is a sort of compromized representative of it, in Luke's and Paul's departments of the Christian Scriptures. This is a happy expedient, and places the English reader in the same predicament

with a Jew or a Greek. The context, thereiore, must, *in all cases,* decide; and that is our special umpire in all ambiguous cases. Nothing essentially *doctrinal* is in jeopardy—but perspicuity being the desideratum, that will be better secured in this case by the context than by either dictionary or grammar.

[t] Κρατοῦντος—αυτους—Gb., Sch., Ln., Tf. Holding them fast; or, "as he held them fast"—or, "kept near to them". De Wette, Meyer, Hackett concur in the former meaning, and in our judgment with satisfactory evidence.

[u] Επι τῇ στοᾷ—for the preceding reasons given, we have here preferred "*upon the porch* called Solomon's."

[v] Στοᾷ Σολομωντος. This porch is named twice in this book —here and in ch. 5 : 12. Again once in John 10 : 23. This portico, or hall, was in the court of the heathen on tne Eastern side of the temple. The common opinion has long been and yet is—that, being placed on the spot where Solomon had made the entrance into the old Temple, it still retained his name. There are not wanting some distinguished moderns who think that it was the identical porch that Solomon himself reared.

Josephus calls this porch Εργον Σαλομωντος. Hackett, Tholuck. Lightfoot affirms the conviction that the Jews indicated the court of the Gentiles by this name.

KING JAMES' VERSION.	GREEK TEXT.	REVISED VERSION.

KING JAMES' VERSION.

12 And when Peter saw *it*, he answered unto the people, Ye men of Israel, why marvel ye at this? or why look ye so earnestly on us, as though by our own power or holiness we had made this man to walk?

13 The God of Abraham, and of Isaac, and of Jacob, the God of our fathers hath glorified his Son Jesus; whom ye delivered up, and denied him in the presence of Pilate, when he was determined to let *him* go.

14 But ye denied the Holy One, and the Just, and desired a murderer to be granted unto you;

15 And killed the Prince of life, whom God hath raised from the dead; whereof we are witnesses.

16 And his name, through faith in his name, hath made this man strong, whom ye see and know: yea, the faith which is by him, hath given him this perfect soundness in the presence of you all.

GREEK TEXT.

δὲ Πέτρος ἀπεκρίνατο πρὸς τὸν λαὸν, Ἄνδρες Ἰσραηλῖται, τί θαυμάζετε ἐπὶ τούτῳ, ἢ ἡμῖν τί ἀτενίζετε, ὡς ἰδίᾳ δυνάμει ἢ εὐσεβείᾳ πεποιηκόσι τοῦ περιπατεῖν αὐτόν; ¹³ ὁ Θεὸς Ἀβραὰμ καὶ Ἰσαὰκ καὶ Ἰακὼβ, ὁ Θεὸς τῶν πατέρων ἡμῶν, ἐδόξασε τὸν παῖδα αὐτοῦ Ἰησοῦν· ὃν ὑμεῖς παρεδώκατε, καὶ ἠρνήσασθε αὐτὸν κατὰ πρόσωπον Πιλάτου, κρίναντος ἐκείνου ἀπολύειν. ¹⁴ ὑμεῖς δὲ τὸν ἅγιον καὶ δίκαιον ἠρνήσασθε, καὶ ᾐτήσασθε ἄνδρα φονέα χαρισθῆναι ὑμῖν, ¹⁵ τὸν δὲ ἀρχηγὸν τῆς ζωῆς ἀπεκτείνατε· ὃν Θεὸς ἤγειρεν ἐκ νεκρῶν, οὗ ἡμεῖς μάρτυρές ἐσμεν. ¹⁶ καὶ ἐπὶ τῇ πίστει τοῦ ὀνόματος αὐτοῦ, τοῦτον ὃν θεωρεῖτε καὶ οἴδατε, ἐστερέωσε τὸ ὄνομα αὐτοῦ· καὶ ἡ πίστις ἡ δι᾽ αὐτοῦ ἔδωκεν αὐτῷ τὴν ὁλοκληρίαν ταύτην ἀπέναντι πάντων ὑμῶν.

REVISED VERSION.

Peter saw it, he addressed the people;—Israelites, why marvel at this? or why look so earnestly on us, as though, by our own ʷstrength, or ˣpiety, we had caused this man to walk? The God of Abraham, 13 and of Isaac, and of Jacob, the God of our fathers, glorified his ʸservant Jesus, whom you delivered up, and disowned, in presence of Pilate, when he was determined to ᶻacquit him. But you dis- 14 owned the Holy and the Just One, and desired a murderer to be granted to you: and killed 15 the Author of ᵃthe Life, whom God raised from the dead: whose witnesses we are. And 16 upon the faith in his name, he has made this man strong, whom you behold and know. Yes, his name, and the faith which is through him, has given him this perfect soundness, in presence of you all.

ʷ *Δυναμει* indicates physical *strength* or ability, and neither moral nor official power. Therefore to be apposite to the occasion and the fact, it is, in this case, more appropriately rendered *strength*, than *power*. On other occasions it may, without hazarding any ambiguity, be appropriately rendered *power*, as in chapter 4 : 33.

ˣ *Ευσεβεια,* occurs 15 times in the N. T.—It is fourteen times translated *godliness*—here *holiness*. There seems to be an impropriety in this change. Indeed *αγιοτης,* and *αγιωσυνη,* occur in the N. T. only 4 times, always translated *holiness.* Between these and *ευσεβεια* there is a difference. The latter usually denotes a quality of mind or heart. The former has respect to state or relation. In these there are no degrees of comparison. No person in matrimony or citizenship, is more married, or more a citizen than another.

To live in harmony with either state, more or less conjugally, or loyally, is conceiveable.—But piety is an attribute of man, himself, apart from all conventional, arbitrary, or legal arrangements. Leigh's Critica Sacra, Schrevelius, Doddridge, Wesley, Thompson, Geneva, and some others, "godliness".

ʸ *Παις* in the Hebrew Greek indicates—a *child,* a *servant,* a *son,* a *maid,* a *young man,* and is so found in N. T.

usage, com. ver.—Being in a quotation from Isaiah 42 : 1, by Matthew applied to Jesus—it should here be *servant,* not son. "Behold my *servant*—my elect, whom I uphold, in whom my soul delights &c." Again v. 26, 27. The com. ver. more frequently renders it *servant,* than *child.*

Παιδα, servant. Παις occurs in this book of Acts applied to Jesus Christ four times, translated com. ver., twice *son* and twice *child.* With us *child* is common gender. It is, therefore, once translated *maid,* Luke 8 : 24, once *maiden,* Luke 8 : 51—also by *servant*—Jesus was *personally* a son—*officially* a *servant,* v. 13.

ᶻ *Απολυω* is, in this book, suitably represented by the words to *put away, release, forgive, dismiss, depart, set at liberty.* To *acquit* in a case of trial before a magistrate is, in our present currency of courts, preferable to *put away, release, depart,* or *to set at liberty.*

ᵃ *The life.* In this association of ideas—it is due to the original, and to the reader—that as it is definitely *τῆς ζωῆς,* and connected with *Αρχηγον,* the Prince or Author of it should be rendered *The Prince of the Life*—of all life, indeed, but here especially, *The Life Eternal.*

KING JAMES' VERSION.

17 And now, brethren, I wot that through ignorance ye did *it*, as *did* also your rulers.

18 But those things which God before had shewed by the mouth of all his prophets, that Christ should suffer, he hath so fulfilled

19 Repent ye therefore, and be converted, that your sins may be blotted out, when the times of refreshing shall come from the presence of the Lord;

20 And he shall send Jesus Christ, which before was preached unto you:

21 Whom the heaven must receive, until the times of resti-

GREEK TEXT.

17 καὶ νῦν, ἀδελφοὶ, οἶδα ὅτι κατὰ ἄγνοιαν ἐπράξατε, ὥσπερ καὶ οἱ ἄρχοντες ὑμῶν· 18 ὁ δὲ Θεὸς ἃ προκατήγγειλε διὰ στόματος πάντων τῶν προφητῶν αὐτοῦ παθεῖν τὸν Χριστὸν, ἐπλήρωσεν οὕτω. 19 μετανοήσατε οὖν καὶ ἐπιστρέψατε, εἰς τὸ ἐξαλειφθῆναι ὑμῶν τὰς ἁμαρτίας, ὅπως ἂν ἔλθωσι καιροὶ ἀναψύξεως ἀπὸ προσώπου τοῦ κυρίου, 20 καὶ ἀποστείλῃ τὸν προκεκηρυγμένον ὑμῖν Ἰησοῦν Χριστὸν, 21 ὃν δεῖ οὐρανὸν μὲν δέξασθαι ἄχρι χρόνων ἀποκαταστάσεως

REVISED VERSION.

And now brethren, I know 17 that [b]you acted in ignorance, as also did your rulers. But 18 God has thus accomplished those things which he had formerly announced by the mouth of all his prophets, [c]that the Christ should suffer. Reform, then, and [d]turn, 19 that your sins may be blotted out, and that seasons of refreshing may come from the presence of the Lord: and 20 that he may send [e]Jesus Christ, the one before [f]prepared for you, whom the heavens must, 21 indeed, [g]retain until the times of the [h]completion of all things,

---

[b] Κατὰ ἄγνοιαν ἐπράξατε, you acted in ignorance, is better than "through ignorance you did it"—or "you acted according to ignorance,"—though it be more literal. A "zeal according to knowledge" is also too literal—an intelligent zeal is in better keeping with our present vernacular, and equally true to the original.

[c] Παθεῖν τον Χριστον—That the Christ—not Christ—should suffer. It was not of a Christ—but of *the* Christ the prophets spoke, as here alluded to.

[d] Επιστρεψατε—is fully represented by *turn*, or "turn to him," Wakef., Dodd., Tyndale, Geneva. Return, Thompson. In the com. ver. of the Acts it is translated by *turn* eight times; and in Luke's Gospel turn and return five times. "Turn from your present course, or character."—*Hackett.*

[e] Τὸν, in this verse should, in our conception of it, be placed before Jesus Christ, if the reading we prefer be adopted. Gb., Sch., Ln., Tf., Προκεχειρισμενον, "And that he may send *the* Jesus Christ before announced to you" whom the Heaven must retain &c.

[f] Προκεχειρισμενον (Gb., Sch., Ln.. Tf.) is by distinguished critics preferred to προκεκηρυγμενον, the former represented by *before appointed* or *before prepared*, the latter by *before announced*. The former, we presume, to be the genuine reading. But as to the significance they are materially the same. It is an unquestionable fact, that his mission or work was previously announced and prepared—as Christ himself is the Lamb that was slain from the foundation of the world, in all the proceedings of redeeming grace—and also that he will appear a *second* time without a sin-offering, at the consummation of the mediatorial interposition.

[g] Almost all the modern versions, have *receive.* Yet with Murdock, I prefer *retain.* Reception and retention are with us, now very distinguishable acts and ideas. It is true, in fact, that the heavens must retain the Messiah, our Lord, until the final consummation of this drama of humanity.

Hackett and some others would have *receive* still retained in the text. We concur with him that δεχομαι by itself is no where rendered *retain*, but we connect it with αχρι, as fully indicative, in our currency, of, *to retain.* Is not "to receive a person into our house *until* any specified time— to *retain* him till that time arrive!" How, otherwise, could the heavens *retain* him until? The most literal rendition in this case is, therefore, equivalent to that proposed. But in either case there is no difference in the sense. He must continue in the heavens till the consummation of all the promises concerning his church.

"To *receive*" indicates a special act—but to *retain* a continued act—and this αχρι, imports.—In any case—he must continue in the heavens, till the consummation of all the promises touching the earthly career of his church.

[h] Αχρι ... παντων, "*until the times of the restoration of all things*," to primitive order and felicity. This seems to be an allusion to the Καιροι αναψυξεως—the restoration of primeval rectitude and felicity, contemplated in the triumphant epoch of Christ's reign.

Αποκαταστασεως. This is one of the *hapax legomena—completion*, Boothroyd, Murdock; *restoration*, Wakefield; *consummation*, Thomp; *restitution*, Wesley, Rheims, Wickliff; all things be *restored again*, Tyndale, Geneva, Cranmer; *regulation* of all things, Dodd. We yet prefer *completion*, because more generic, as the full sense of all the prophetic oracles. Leigh's Critica Sacra, while giving *restitutio*—observes;—Astronomis, Reversio Stellae ad eum locum unde discesserat.

Referring to Moses and all the prophets concerning the times of the Messiah, as Peter now does, it would seem to us

KING JAMES' VERSION.	GREEK TEXT.	REVISED VERSION.
tution of all things, which God hath spoken by the mouth of all his holy prophets, since the world began.	πάντων, ὧν ἐλάλησεν ὁ Θεὸς διὰ στόματος πάντων ἁγίων αὐτοῦ προφητῶν ἀπ᾽ αἰῶνος.	which God has spoken through the mouth of all his holy prophets, since the world began.
22 For Moses truly said unto the fathers, A Prophet shall the Lord your God raise up unto you, of your brethren, like unto me; him shall ye hear in all things, whatsoever he shall say unto you.	²² Μω-σῆς μὲν γὰρ πρὸς τοὺς πατέρας εἶπεν, Ὅτι προφήτην ὑμῖν ἀνα-στήσει Κύριος ὁ Θεὸς ὑμῶν ἐκ τῶν ἀδελφῶν ὑμῶν, ὡς ἐμέ· αὐ-τοῦ ἀκούσεσθε κατὰ πάντα ὅσα ἂν λαλήσῃ πρὸς ὑμᾶς.	For Moses, indeed, said to the 22 Fathers, That a prophet shall the Lord your God ¹raise up for you, from among your brethren, as he raised me up; him shall you hear in all things, whatever he shall say to you.
23 And it shall come to pass, *that* every soul which will not hear that Prophet, shall be destroyed from among the people.	²³ ἔσται δὲ, πᾶσα ψυχὴ, ἥτις ἂν μὴ ἀκού-σῃ τοῦ προφήτου ἐκείνου, ἐξολο-θρευθήσεται ἐκ τοῦ λαοῦ.	And every soul who will not 23 hear that prophet, shall be destroyed from among the people.
24 Yea, and all the prophets from Samuel, and those that follow after, as many as have spoken, have likewise foretold of these days.	²⁴ Καὶ πάντες δὲ οἱ προφῆται ἀπὸ Σα-μουὴλ καὶ τῶν καθηξῆς, ὅσοι ἐλάλησαν, καὶ προκατήγγειλαν τὰς ἡμέρας ταύτας.	And, indeed, all the 24 prophets, from Samuel and those following in order, as many as have spoken, have also foretold these days.
25 Ye are the children of the prophets, and of the covenant which God made with our fathers, saying unto Abraham, And in thy seed shall all the kindreds of the earth be blessed.	²⁵ ὑμεῖς ἐστε υἱοὶ τῶν προφητῶν, καὶ τῆς δια-θήκης ἧς διέθετο ὁ Θεὸς πρὸς τοὺς πατέρας ἡμῶν, λέγων πρὸς Ἀβραάμ, Καὶ τῷ σπέρματί σου ἐνευλογηθήσονται πᾶσαι αἱ πα-τριαὶ τῆς γῆς.	You are ¹the sons of the pro- 25 phets, and of the covenant which God made with our fathers, saying, to Abraham, "And in thy seed shall all the kindreds of the earth be blessed." God having raised 26
26 Unto you first, God hav-ing raised up his Son Jesus, sent him to bless you, in turning away every one of you from his iniquities.	²⁶ Ὑμῖν πρῶτον ὁ Θεὸς ἀναστήσας τὸν παῖδα αὐ-τοῦ Ἰησοῦν, ἀπέστειλεν αὐτὸν εὐλογοῦντα ὑμᾶς, ἐν τῷ ἀποστρέ-φειν ἕκαστον ἀπὸ τῶν πονηριῶν ὑμῶν.	ed up his ᵏservant Jesus, sent him first to you, to bless you in turning away, every one of you, from his iniquities.

---

that the *completion* of the ancient oracles respecting Messiah and his kingdom covers the whole area of his premises; and, therefore, meets all the demands of the case better than *restitution, restoration, regulation,* or *consummation:* whether promises or predictions, (and these include the whole prophetic school,) *completion* is quite apposite.

¹ Ἀναστήσει = יָקִים, *will raise up*—cause to appear *ὡς ἐμε, like me.* Hence a rendition quite as peculiar as the former —not like to me—but like as he raised me up.

ʲ Υἱοι . . . . . Τῆς διαθηκης, sons of the covenant, or institution—υἱοί here Hebraistically indicates *heirs;* parti-cipators—still the sons of the prophets is the proper expres-sion of the original. All believers—all Christians are heirs in common of all the spiritual blessings promised in the seed of Abraham.

Sons, rather than *children,* of the prophets—inheritors of the blessings which the prophets foretold—heirs of covenanted

mercies. On these promises he urges their right ānd duty to accept these promised blessings.

ᵏ Τον παιδα Ιησουν.—Ιησουν is, in this case, rejected as spurious by Gb., Sch., Ln. and Tf.—Παις is found applied to Jesus only *once* in Matthew as a *servant,* and in Luke's writings *five* times;—once in his Gospel, referring to him where literally a *child,* ch. 2:43; and in his Acts four times;— twice rendered in com. ver., *son* Jesus, and twice *child* Jesus. This is an anomalous license. It is most generally, in other cases, rendered *servant.* The Jews are called "*sons of the Prophets,*" not merely of the four *major* prophets, or of the twelve *minor* prophets, as the Jews call them in distinction from the *Patriarcha!* prophets. They were educated by these sixteen Jewish Prophets, being weekly read in their syna-gogues. Hence, we presume, they were called "sons of the prophets;" and, therefore, ought to have recognized and acknowledged their own Messiah.

KING JAMES' VERSION.	GREEK TEXT.	REVISED VERSION.
CHAP. IV.	CHAP. IV.	CHAP. IV.

AND as they spake unto the people, the priests, and the captain of the temple, and the Sadducees came upon them.

2 Being grieved that they taught the people, and preached through Jesus the resurrection from the dead.

3 And they laid hands on them, and put *them* in hold unto the next day: for it was now even-tide.

4 Howbeit, many of them which heard the word, believed; and the number of the men was about five thousand

5 And it came to pass on the morrow, that their rulers, and elders, and scribes,

6 And Annas the high priest, and Caiaphas, and John, and Alexander, and as many as were of the kindred of the high priest, were gathered together at Jerusalem.

7 And when they had set them in the midst, they asked, By what power, or by what name have ye done this?

8 Then Peter, filled with the Holy Ghost, said unto them, Ye rulers of the people, and elders of Israel,

9 If we this day be examined of the good deed done to the

ΛΑΛΟΥΝΤΩΝ δὲ αὐτῶν πρὸς τὸν λαὸν, ἐπέστησαν αὐτοῖς οἱ ἱερεῖς καὶ ὁ στρατηγὸς τοῦ ἱεροῦ καὶ οἱ Σαδδουκαῖοι, ² διαπονούμενοι διὰ τὸ διδάσκειν αὐτοὺς τὸν λαὸν, καὶ καταγγέλλειν ἐν τῷ Ἰησοῦ τὴν ἀνάστασιν τὴν ἐκ νεκρῶν· ³ καὶ ἐπέβαλον αὐτοῖς τὰς χεῖρας, καὶ ἔθεντο εἰς τήρησιν εἰς τὴν αὔριον· ἦν γὰρ ἑσπέρα ἤδη. ⁴ πολλοὶ δὲ τῶν ἀκουσάντων τὸν λόγον ἐπίστευσαν· καὶ ἐγενήθη ὁ ἀριθμὸς τῶν ἀνδρῶν ὡσεὶ χιλιάδες πέντε. ⁵ Ἐγένετο δὲ ἐπὶ τὴν αὔριον συναχθῆναι αὐτῶν τοὺς ἄρχοντας καὶ πρεσβυτέρους καὶ γραμματεῖς εἰς Ἱερουσαλὴμ, ⁶ καὶ Ἄνναν τὸν ἀρχιερέα καὶ Καϊάφαν καὶ Ἰωάννην καὶ Ἀλέξανδρον, καὶ ὅσοι ἦσαν ἐκ γένους ἀρχιερατικοῦ. ⁷ καὶ στήσαντες αὐτοὺς ἐν τῷ μέσῳ, ἐπυνθάνοντο, Ἐν ποίᾳ δυνάμει ἢ ἐν ποίῳ ὀνόματι ἐποιήσατε τοῦτο ὑμεῖς; ⁸ Τότε Πέτρος πλησθεὶς Πνεύματος Ἁγίου, εἶπε πρὸς αὐτούς, Ἄρχοντες τοῦ λαοῦ καὶ πρεσβύτεροι τοῦ Ἰσραὴλ, ⁹ εἰ ἡμεῖς σήμερον ἀνακρινόμεθα ἐπὶ εὐεργε-

AND while they were speaking to the people, the priests, and the captain of the temple guard, and the Sadducees came upon them, being ¹indignant 2 that they taught the people, and preached, that through Jesus is the resurrection from the dead. And they laid hands 3 on them, and put them in prison, until the next day: for it was already evening. But many of those who heard 4 the ᵐword believed; and the number of the men became about five thousand.

And it came to pass, on the 5 morrow, that their rulers, and elders, and scribes, and Annas 6 the High Priest, and Caiaphas, and John, and Alexander, and as many as were of the ⁿpontifical family, were gathered together in Jerusalem. And 7 ᵒplacing them in the midst, they asked, ᵖIn what strength, or in what name, have you done this? Then Peter, filled with 8 the Holy Spirit, said to them, Rulers of the people, and Elders of Israel, if we be ex- 9 examined this day concerning a good deed done to an infirm

---

¹ *Διαπονουμενοι*, "being grieved," is not indicative of the feeling of the Apostle Paul, in witnessing the malice of a wicked spirit, reported in Acts 16 : 18. In that case Paul was *indignant.* In this case the Saducees and the priesthood could be no less *indignant,* while witnessing the power of the Apostles' doctrine, in stultifying their doctrine of no resurrection of the dead. We, therefore, prefer "indignant" to "grieved", as more truly indicative of their feelings on this occasion. The word is found only in these two cases in the Apostolic Scriptures.

ᵐ *Τον λογον,* the word. This has exclusive reference to the gospel of the resurrection of Jesus Christ. It was the special message of the day.

ⁿ *Εκ γενους αρχιερατικου. Pontifical family* is, in our currency, more definite and perspicuous than the "kindred of the High Priest," which might comprehend more than were personally interested in the premises. Those specially interested were, doubtless, present.

ᵒ "When they had set them." *Placing them,* indicates the whole work comprehended in *στησαντες αυτους.*

ᵖ *Ποια δυναμει,* not *ποια εξουσια*—physical strength. In what strength—in what name? There was *strength* and *authority* also in the name of the Lord. But as to the spectators —in this case of physical infirmity—their attention was absorbed in the *strength* put forth.

KING JAMES' VERSION.

impotent man, by what means he is made whole;

10 Be it known unto you all, and to all the people of Israel, that by the name of Jesus Christ of Nazareth, whom ye crucified, whom God raised from the dead, *even* by him doth this man stand here before you whole.

11 This is the stone which was set at naught of you builders, which is become the head of the corner.

12 Neither is there salvation in any other: for there is none other name under heaven given among men, whereby we must be saved.

13 Now when they saw the boldness of Peter and John, and perceived that they were unlearned and ignorant men, they marvelled; and they took knowledge of them, that they had been with Jesus.

14 And beholding the man which was healed standing with them, they could say nothing against it.

GREEK TEXT.

σία ἀνθρώπου ἀσθενοῦς, ἐν τίνι οὗτος σέσωσται· ¹⁰ γνωστὸν ἔστω πᾶσιν ὑμῖν καὶ παντὶ τῷ λαῷ Ἰσραὴλ, ὅτι ἐν τῷ ὀνόματι Ἰησοῦ Χριστοῦ τοῦ Ναζωραίου, ὃν ὑμεῖς ἐσταυρώσατε, ὃν ὁ Θεὸς ἤγειρεν ἐκ νεκρῶν, ἐν τούτῳ οὗτος παρέστηκεν ἐνώπιον ὑμῶν ὑγιής. ¹¹ οὗτός ἐστιν ὁ λίθος ὁ ἐξουθενηθεὶς ὑφ᾽ ὑμῶν τῶν οἰκοδομούντων, ὁ γενόμενος εἰς κεφαλὴν γωνίας. ¹² καὶ οὐκ ἔστιν ἐν ἄλλῳ οὐδενὶ ἡ σωτηρία· οὔτε γὰρ ὄνομά ἐστιν ἕτερον ὑπὸ τὸν οὐρανὸν τὸ δεδομένον ἐν ἀνθρώποις, ἐν ᾧ δεῖ σωθῆναι ἡμᾶς.
¹³ Θεωροῦντες δὲ τὴν τοῦ Πέτρου παρρησίαν καὶ Ἰωάννου, καὶ καταλαβόμενοι ὅτι ἄνθρωποι ἀγράμματοί εἰσι καὶ ἰδιῶται, ἐθαύμαζον, ἐπεγίνωσκόν τε αὐτοὺς ὅτι σὺν τῷ Ἰησοῦ ἦσαν·
¹⁴ τὸν δὲ ἄνθρωπον βλέποντες σὺν αὐτοῖς ἑστῶτα τὸν τεθεραπευμένον, οὐδὲν εἶχον ἀντειπεῖν.

REVISED VERSION.

man, in what ᵑname he is made whole, be it known to you 10 all, and to all the people of Israel, that in the name of Jesus Christ, the Nazarene— whom you crucified—whom God raised from the dead, by him does this man stand before you sound. This is 11 the stone which was set at nought by you, the builders, which is ʳmade the head of the corner. And ˢthe salvation is 12 not in another person; for there is not another name under the heaven, given among men, by which it ᵗbehooves us to be saved.

Now, ᵘconsidering the ᵛfree- 13 dom of speech, of Peter and John, and having ʷperceived that they were ˣilliterate, and persons in private life, they marveled; and they knew them well, that they ʸused to be with Jesus. And beholding the man who was 14 healed, standing with them, they ᶻhad nothing to say

---

ᑫ *Ἐν τίνι*—reference is here to *ὄνομα*, as the answer given clearly intimates—In the name of Jesus Christ.

ʳ *Ὁ γενόμενος*—made *εἰς κεφαλήν.*

ˢ The common version does not indicate the fullness of the original. It is in the original *ἡ σωτηρία*—not salvation in general, but the salvation which the gospel brings—not a salvation of the body, of the soul, or of the spirit, but of *the man*. —*Οὐδενί*, no person; *ἄλλῳ οὐδενί*, not another person.

ᵗ *Δεῖ, behooves.*—Nor is it presented with a *must be*, as a fatal necessity; nor with a *may be*, as of doubtful import; but as claiming, commanding, behooving, us to embrace it, which latter word is inclusive of all *its* claims, and of all *our* wants. It is necessary, expedient, blissful.

Δεῖ fully indicates this, by three of its current acceptations —*must, should, ought.* No one word fills its area so well as *behoove*, which word is selected in Luke to indicate all the causes concurring in the death of Christ. Thus it *behooved* Christ to suffer &c., Luke 24 : 7, 26, 46, where all these terms —must, ought, behoove, occur.

ᵘ *Θεωροῦντες, considering*, not merely seeing, or looking at it, but contemplating upon it—considering it. To theorize on

premises implies more than seeing them, or even looking at them.

ᵛ *Παρρησία*, boldness of speech, 2 Cor. 7 : 4. The dative of this word is used adverbially, and indicates speaking, writing, acting boldly, or with much freedom. Here, contextually viewed, it indicates a *freedom of speech* which they could not reconcile with the apparent condition, education and circumstances of men in private stations of life. *Freedom of speech*, in all the associations of this scene, best harmonizes with the circumstances, and the terms employed.

ʷ *Καταλαβόμενοι*, "when they saw", Wakefield; "when they observed", Boothroyd. "*Having perceived*", Hackett. The tense differs from that of the other participle.

ˣ *Ἀγράμματοι καὶ ἰδιῶται*, "illiterate and obscure", Hack.; "unlearned and obscure", Booth.; "unlearned and common men", Wakefield; "sans lettres, du commun peuple", French. So in most modern versions. S. Lee, Polyglott.

ʸ *Ὅτι σὺν τῷ Ἰησοῦ ἦσαν* indicates more than a casual interview. They were wont to be with Jesus.

ᶻ *Ἀντειπεῖν*—to contradict, to speak against—literally, they had nothing to speak against it, or, they could say nothing against it.

KING JAMES' VERSION.

15 But when they had commanded them to go aside out of the council, they conferred among themselves.

16 Saying, What shall we do to these men? for that indeed a notable miracle hath been done by them is manifest to all them that dwell in Jerusalem, and we cannot deny it.

17 But that it spread no further among the people, let us straitly threaten them, that they speak henceforth to no man in this name.

18 And they called them, and commanded them not to speak at all, nor teach in the name of Jesus.

19 But Peter and John answered and said unto them, Whether it be right in the sight of God to hearken unto you more than unto God, judge ye.

20 For we cannot but speak the things which we have seen and heard.

21 So when they had further threatened them, they let them go, finding nothing how they might punish them, because of the people: for all *men* glorified God for that which was done.

22 For the man was above

GREEK TEXT.

15 κελεύσαντες δὲ αὐτοὺς ἔξω τοῦ συνεδρίου ἀπελθεῖν, συνέβαλον πρὸς ἀλλήλους, 16 λέγοντες, Τί ποιήσομεν τοῖς ἀνθρώποις τούτοις; ὅτι μὲν γὰρ γνωστὸν σημεῖον γέγονε δι' αὐτῶν, πᾶσι τοῖς κατοικοῦσιν Ἱερουσαλὴμ φανερὸν, καὶ οὐ δυνάμεθα ἀρνήσασθαι· 17 ἀλλ' ἵνα μὴ ἐπὶ πλεῖον διανεμηθῇ εἰς τὸν λαὸν, ἀπειλῇ ἀπειλησώμεθα αὐτοῖς μηκέτι λαλεῖν ἐπὶ τῷ ὀνόματι τούτῳ μηδενὶ ἀνθρώπων. 18 Καὶ καλέσαντες αὐτοὺς, παρήγγειλαν αὐτοῖς τὸ καθόλου μὴ φθέγγεσθαι μηδὲ διδάσκειν ἐπὶ τῷ ὀνόματι τοῦ Ἰησοῦ. 19 ὁ δὲ Πέτρος καὶ Ἰωάννης ἀποκριθέντες πρὸς αὐτοὺς εἶπον, Εἰ δίκαιόν ἐστιν ἐνώπιον τοῦ Θεοῦ, ὑμῶν ἀκούειν μᾶλλον ἢ τοῦ Θεοῦ, κρίνατε. 20 οὐ δυνάμεθα γὰρ ἡμεῖς, ἃ εἴδομεν καὶ ἠκούσαμεν, μὴ λαλεῖν. 21 Οἱ δὲ προσαπειλησάμενοι ἀπέλυσαν αὐτοὺς, μηδὲν εὑρίσκοντες τὸ πῶς κολάσωνται αὐτοὺς, διὰ τὸν λαὸν, ὅτι πάντες ἐδόξαζον τὸν Θεὸν ἐπὶ τῷ γεγονότι. 22 ἐτῶν γὰρ ἦν πλειόνων τεσ-

REVISED VERSION.

against it. But having com- 15 manded them to withdraw from the council, they conferred with one another, saying, What shall we do to these 16 men? for, that, indeed, a ᵃnotorious miracle has been wrought by them, is manifest to all those who dwell at Jerusalem, and we cannot deny it. But, that it may ᵇbe spread no 17 further among the people, let us strictly threaten them, that they speak, henceforth, to no man ᶜupon this name. And 18 they called them, and commanded them not to speak at all, nor to teach, upon the name of Jesus.

But Peter and John answer- 19 ed, and said to them, Whether it be right in the sight of God, to hearken to you, rather than to God, judge. For we 20 cannot but speak the things which we have seen and heard. So, when they had further 21 threatened them, they discharged them, finding no means of punishing them, because of the people; for all were glorifying God, for that which had been done. ᵈFor the 22

ᵃ Γνωστον, "signal", Booth., Doddridge; *notorious*, Rheims; manifest sign, Murdock.

ᵇ Διανεμηθη being passive, we prefer, on all the premises, to retain the passive form—*that it may be spread.*

ᶜ Επι and εν τῳ ονοματι τουτῳ. These are not identical expressions. To *speak upon* a name, and to teach *in* a name, are not equivalent enunciations. The latter has respect to authority, and the former to a topic, or subject. The mysteries of this name constituted the secret of their power with the people.

Επι τῳ ονοματι του Ιησου. In as much as we have in the original Scriptures three forms of expression connected with ονομα του Ιησου Χριστου, of very different import, it seems to me not merely expedient, but obligatory, that we should give to an English reader three corresponding formulas in our

language, such as "*in the name of*"—"*upon the name of*"— and "*into the name of*". These three formulas are as distinct in sense as in form. The first indicates authority, viz., *in the name of* the king, or commonwealth. The second indicates the subject, *on which* the authority terminates, the citizens of the commonwealth, and the third the reason why, or *object for which*, the action is performed. *By the authority of* the government, I, A. B. will speak to you *upon* American citizenship, and then I will introduce you *into* the possession of it.

In this agree, so far as I know, all Grammarians and Lexicographers. So we find it in the Apostolic commission. *In the name of* the Lord, I baptize you *into the name of* the Father, the Son, and the Holy Spirit, *for*, or *in order to* introduction into his kingdom.

ᵈ In conformity with the order and arrangement of words in the Greek text we might, grammatically, render this verse

KING JAMES' VERSION.	GREEK TEXT.	REVISED VERSION.

forty years old on whom this miracle of healing was shewed.

23 And being let go, they went to their own company, and reported all that the chief priests and elders had said unto them.

24 And when they heard that, they lifted up their voice to God with one accord, and said, Lord, thou *art* God, which hast made heaven, and earth, and the sea, and all that in them is;

25 Who, by the mouth of thy servant David hast said, Why did the heathen rage, and the people imagine vain things?

26 The kings of the earth stood up, and the rulers were gathered together against the Lord, and against his Christ.

27 For of a truth against thy holy child Jesus, whom thou

σαράκοντα ὁ ἄνθρωπος ἐφ᾽ ὃν ἐγεγόνει τὸ σημεῖον τοῦτο τῆς ἰάσεως.

²³ Ἀπολυθέντες δὲ ἦλθον πρὸς τοὺς ἰδίους, καὶ ἀπήγγειλαν ὅσα πρὸς αὐτοὺς οἱ ἀρχιερεῖς καὶ οἱ πρεσβύτεροι εἶπον. ²⁴ οἱ δὲ ἀκούσαντες, ὁμοθυμαδὸν ἦραν φωνὴν πρὸς τὸν Θεὸν, καὶ εἶπον, Δέσποτα, σὺ ὁ Θεὸς ὁ ποιήσας τὸν οὐρανὸν καὶ τὴν γῆν καὶ τὴν θάλασσαν καὶ πάντα τὰ ἐν αὐτοῖς, ²⁵ ὁ διὰ στόματος Δαβὶδ τοῦ παιδός σου εἰπὼν, Ἱνατί ἐφρύαξαν ἔθνη, καὶ λαοὶ ἐμελέτησαν κενά; ²⁶ παρέστησαν οἱ βασιλεῖς τῆς γῆς, καὶ οἱ ἄρχοντες συνήχθησαν ἐπὶ τὸ αὐτὸ κατὰ τοῦ κυρίου, καὶ κατὰ τοῦ Χριστοῦ αὐτοῦ. ²⁷ Συνήχθησαν γὰρ ἐπ᾽ ἀληθείας ἐπὶ τὸν ἅγιον παῖδά σου, Ἰη-

man on whom this miracle of the healing was wrought, was more than forty years old.

And now, having been dis- 23 charged, they went to their own ᵉfriends, and announced all that the priests and elders had said to them. And they, ᶠhearing, raised a 24 voice to God, with one accord, and said, ᵍSovereign Lord, thou art the God who hast made the heavens, and the earth, and the sea, and all that is in them; who by thy servant David's 25 mouth hast said, ʰWhy did nations rage, and people imagine a vain thing? The 26 kings of the earth presented themselves, and the Princes were gathered together against the Lord, and against his A-nointed. For, of a truth, in this 27 ᶦcity, against thy holy ʲson, Je-

---

as follows—"of years, for was of more than forty the man on whom had had the miracle this of the healing." This is exactly according to the order and meaning of the words in the Greek text before me. Nor could all the rules of grammar, alone, or without a knowledge of the subject, as well as of the verbiage in which it is clothed, enable any one to give the exact ideas, contained in the original oracle of the inspired writer. This fact, incontrovertible as it is, demonstrates, how much depends upon a translator's knowledge of the subject, as well as of the language from which, and of the language into which, he transfers the ideas which existed in the mind of the original writer or speaker.

ᵉ Πρὸς τους ιδιους, *to their own friends*, not especially to the Apostles.

ᶠ Οἱ δε ακουσαντες. It seems better to preserve the participial construction here, and to render the οἱ, *they*.

ᵍ Δεσποτα. This title is given to the Messiah, 2 Pet. 2 : 1; Judas 4. It occurs ten times in the New Testament—five times indicative of our Master in heaven, and five times of masters, or proprietors of men. Here it seems fitting to give to it all its grandeur, and therefore, we render it Sovereign Lord. This is warranted by the current difference between δεσποτης and κυριος. This the spirit of the context seems to require. It is found five times indicative of supreme power or authority. Judas 4, Our only sovereign God and Lord.

ʰ Ἱνατι, an abbreviation of ινα τι γενηται, *why*, or in order to which might be—*Hackett.*

ᶦ Εν τη πολει ταυτη, after αληθειας is found in many ancient copies, but rejected by Bloomfield, though resting on good authority—*Hackett.* It is found in most ancient manuscripts, (Vul.) the two uncial Mss. Codd., Clermont, Augiensis, and the Codex Alex., which last after σου adds πολει. So also reads the Latin with the Coptic, Arm., Ethiop. versions, Irenaeus, Cyril, Tertullian, and other fathers.

There can be no just ground of supposing the clause an addition in the oldest copies extant, until a still older copy can be produced, which has not the clause. See Ann. to the Book of the New Covenant, London Ed., 1807. By Granville. Penn, Esq., Hackett.—On the authority of Griesbach, Scholz, Lachmann, and Tischendorf, I would restore this clause.

Penn's work, now lying before me, is, in my judgment, a work of much learning, ingenuousness and real merit. His version is dedicated to the Universal Church. London, 1837, two vols. octavo. He renders the passage thus, v. 27: For, of a truth, both Herod and Pontius Pilate, with the Gentiles and people of Israel, were gathered together *in this city*, against thy Holy child Jesus, whom thou hast anointed.—This was certainly true in fact.

ʲ Παις is applied to Jesus only six times in the Christian Scriptures—four times in the Acts, once in Luke's Testimony, and once quoted from the Septuagint, Matt. 12 : 18. It is translated, com. ver., *servant* ten times, *child* twice. In other cases, and once. on allusion to the Lord Jesus, when he is

KING JAMES' VERSION.

hast anointed, both Herod, and Pontius Pilate, with the Gentiles, and the people of Israel, were gathered together,

28 For to do whatsoever thy hand and thy counsel determined before to be done.

29 And now, Lord, behold their threatenings: and grant unto thy servants, that with all boldness they may speak thy word,

30 By stretching forth thy hand to heal; and that signs and wonders may be done by the name of thine holy child Jesus.

31 And when they had prayed, the place was shaken where they were assembled together; and they were all filled with the Holy Ghost, and they spake the word of God with boldness.

32 And the multitude of them that believed were of one heart, and of one soul: neither said any *of them* that ought of the things which he possessed was his own; but they had all things common.

33 And with great power gave the apostles witness of the resurrection of the Lord Jesus: and great grace was upon them all.

34 Neither was there any among them that lacked: for as many as were possessors of lands or houses sold them, and brought the prices of the things that were sold,

35 And laid *them* down at the apostles' feet: and distribution

GREEK TEXT.

σοῦν, ὃν ἔχρισας, Ἡρώδης τε καὶ Πόντιος Πιλάτος, σὺν ἔθνεσι καὶ λαοῖς Ἰσραὴλ, 28 ποιῆσαι ὅσα ἡ χείρ σου καὶ ἡ βουλή σου προώρισε γενέσθαι. 29 καὶ τὰ νῦν, κύριε, ἔπιδε ἐπὶ τὰς ἀπειλὰς αὐτῶν, καὶ δὸς τοῖς δούλοις σου μετὰ παρρησίας πάσης λαλεῖν τὸν λόγον σου, 30 ἐν τῷ τὴν χεῖρά σου ἐκτείνειν σε εἰς ἴασιν, καὶ σημεῖα καὶ τέρατα γίνεσθαι διὰ τοῦ ὀνόματος τοῦ ἁγίου παιδός σου Ἰησοῦ. 31 Καὶ δεηθέντων αὐτῶν ἐσαλεύθη ὁ τόπος ἐν ᾧ ἦσαν συνεγμένοι, καὶ ἐπλήσθησαν ἅπαντες Πνεύματος Ἁγίου, καὶ ἐλάλουν τὸν λόγον τοῦ Θεοῦ μετὰ παρρησίας.

32 ΤΟΥ δὲ πλήθους τῶν πιστευσάντων ἦν ἡ καρδία καὶ ἡ ψυχὴ μία· καὶ οὐδὲ εἷς τι τῶν ὑπαρχόντων αὐτῷ ἔλεγεν ἴδιον εἶναι, ἀλλ᾽ ἦν αὐτοῖς ἅπαντα κοινά. 33 καὶ μεγάλῃ δυνάμει ἀπεδίδουν τὸ μαρτύριον οἱ ἀπόστολοι τῆς ἀναστάσεως τοῦ Κυρίου Ἰησοῦ, χάρις τε μεγάλη ἦν ἐπὶ πάντας αὐτούς. 34 οὐδὲ γὰρ ἐνδεής τις ὑπῆρχεν ἐν αὐτοῖς· ὅσοι γὰρ κτήτορες χωρίων ἢ οἰκιῶν ὑπῆρχον, πωλοῦντες ἔφερον τὰς τιμὰς τῶν πιπρασκομένων, 35 καὶ ἐτίθουν παρὰ τοὺς πόδας τῶν ἀποστόλων· διεδίδοτο δὲ

REVISED VERSION.

sus, whom thou hast anointed, both Herod and Pontius Pilate, with the Gentiles and the people of Israel, were assembled, to do whatever thy hand, and 28 thy counsel had before ᵏdetermined to be done. And now, 29 Lord, behold their threatenings, and grant to thy servants, that, with all boldness, they may speak thy word, by 30 stretching out thy hand to heal; and that signs and wonders may be done, by the name of thy holy son, Jesus.

And, they having prayed, the 31 place in which they were assembled together was shaken, and they were all filled with the Holy Spirit, and spoke the word of God with boldness. And the multitude of those 32 that believed were of one heart and of one soul, neither did any of them say, that any of the things which he possessed was his own; but they had all things common. And with 33 great ˡpower the Apostles gave testimony concerning the resurrection of the Lord Jesus: and great grace was upon them all. For neither was there any 34 among them who lacked; for as many as were possessors of lands, or of houses, sold them, and brought the prices of the things sold, and laid them down at the Apostles' feet. And ᵐit was distributed to 35

---

found in the temple answering questions, it is properly translated *child*. In the Acts, it is twice translated *son*, and twice *child*. In this case, we think, in all dignity and propriety, it should be translated *son*.

ᵏ Προορίζω, occurs 8 times in N. T. rendered by *determined, ordained, declared*, Rom. 1 : 4, *limiteth*. Luke uses ὁρίζω, six times out of its eight occurrences. Translated *determined, ordained, determinate*. Paul uses προορίζω five times out of its six occurrences. Etymologically, it indicates, *to mark*

out before, to bound or to limit before. Hence, Heb. 4 : 7, " He limiteth a certain day". Whether used to indicate a purpose, a delineation, description or prediction, as respects the Divine knowledge, or will, it equally involves one and the same radical idea. With God there is nothing past, present or future. He fills, he inhabits eternity.

ˡ Μεγαλη δυναμει, with great power, i. e. physical demonstration, not εξουσια, authority.

ᵐ Διεδιδοτο, being impersonal—*it was distributed*.

KING JAMES' VERSION.

was made unto every man according as he had need.

36 And Joses, who by the apostles was surnamed Barnabas, (which is, being interpreted, The son of consolation,) a Levite, *and* of the country of Cyprus,

37 Having land, sold *it*, and brought the money, and laid *it* at the apostles' feet.

CHAP. V.

But a certain man named Ananias, with Sapphira his wife, sold a possession,

2 And kept back *part* of the price, (his wife also being privy *to it*,) and brought a certain part, and laid *it* at the apostles' feet.

3 But Peter said, Ananias, why hath Satan filled thine heart to lie to the Holy Ghost, and to keep back *part* of the price of the land?

4 While it remained, was it not thine own? and after it was

GREEK TEXT.

ἑκάστῳ καθότι ἄν τις χρείαν εἶχεν. ³⁶ Ἰωσῆς δὲ ὁ ἐπικληθεὶς Βαρνάβας ὑπὸ τῶν ἀποστόλων, ὅ ἐστι μεθερμηνευόμενον, υἱὸς παρακλήσεως, Λευΐτης, Κύπριος τῷ γένει, ³⁷ ὑπάρχοντος αὐτῷ ἀγροῦ, πωλήσας ἤνεγκε τὸ χρῆμα, καὶ ἔθηκε παρὰ τοὺς πόδας τῶν ἀποστόλων.

CHAP. V.

Ἀνὴρ δέ τις Ἀνανίας ὀνόματι, σὺν Σαπφείρῃ τῇ γυναικὶ αὐτοῦ, ἐπώλησε κτῆμα, ² καὶ ἐνοσφίσατο ἀπὸ τῆς τιμῆς, συνειδυίας καὶ τῆς γυναικὸς αὐτοῦ, καὶ ἐνέγκας μέρος τι παρὰ τοὺς πόδας τῶν ἀποστόλων ἔθηκεν. ³ εἶπε δὲ Πέτρος, Ἀνανία, διατί ἐπλήρωσεν ὁ Σατανᾶς τὴν καρδίαν σου, ψεύσασθαί σε τὸ Πνεῦμα τὸ Ἅγιον, καὶ νοσφίσασθαι ἀπὸ τῆς τιμῆς τοῦ χωρίου; ⁴ οὐχὶ μένον σοὶ ἔμενε, καὶ πραθὲν ἐν τῇ σῇ ἐξουσίᾳ

REVISED VERSION.

every one, according as any one had need.

Now Joses, who, by the 36 Apostles, was surnamed Barnabas (which is, being translated, Son of Consolation), a Levite, a Cyprian by birth, having land, sold it, and brought the money, and laid it at the Apostles' feet.

CHAP. V.

ᵇBut a certain man named 1 Ananias, with Sapphira his wife sold a possession, and 2 ᶜpurloined from the price (his wife also being privy to it), and brought a certain part, and laid it at the Apostles' feet. But Peter said, Ananias, 3 why has ᵖSatan ᵖpossessed your heart, to ᑫlie to the Holy Spirit, and to purloin from the price of the land? While 4 it ʳremained, was it not your

---

ᵃ Δε, *but*, in contrast with Barnabas.

ᶜ Ενοσφισατο, Ind. mid. *purloined*, took away for himself. The mid. voice is most apposite to this case, indicating the selfishness and hypocrisy of the man. *Purloin* is not obsolete, though not so much in use as formerly. It is found com. ver., Tit. 2 : 10. It is, in com. ver., twice represented in this book by " *kept back*." There is no absolute impropriety in *keeping back*; but there is always in *purloining*. This is a complex sin. It was not simply keeping back, but *feloniously* keeping back, with *intent to conceal*, associated with deliberate lying.

The Septuagint employs νοσφιζομαι, Josh. 7 : 1, in the case of Achan. It is well defined by Leigh in his *Critica Sacra: Non est totam rem auferre sed paululum tantummodo abstrahere*. Beza employs *intervertit*, which he interprets by *callide surripuit*. In our vernacular, to *embezzle*, to *filch*, most exactly represents it. We prefer *purloin*, because already familiarized in com. ver. "*Kept to himself*," Wakef. and Boothr.; "*carried away a part*," Murd., Syr.

Συνειδυιας, having been cognizant, having participated in ᵃ knowledge of it, being privy to it.

ᵖ Ὁ Σατανας, a proper name, and retainable here.

Επληρωσεν, literally *filled up*; in our more modern style *possessed* your heart. Πληροω, used here metaphorically, is taken from a ship sailing before the wind. "When a man is filled with the commandment, or with temptation, as the sail of a ship by the wind, he is said to be filled with it," Critica Sacra. It is found almost one hundred times in the N. T. Of these, some fifty times it is represented by *fulfill*, com. ver. It here indicates a full possession of the heart.

Possessed—literally *filled*. This is a bold figure in either case, to indicate a strong temptation. It is the language of earnestness or surprise.

ᑫ Ψευσασθαι, *to lie*, to deceive, not the Holy Spirit abstractly contemplated, but through the Apostles.

ʳ Ουχι μενον σοι εμενε. Literally, Remaining, did it not remain to you! And being sold, remained it not in your power? In our idiomatic currency, we would say : " While it remained

KING JAMES' VERSION.	GREEK TEXT.	REVISED VERSION.
sold, was it not in thine own power? why hast thou conceived this thing in thine heart? thou hast not lied unto men, but unto God.	ὑπῆρχε; τί ὅτι ἔθου ἐν τῇ καρδίᾳ σου τὸ πρᾶγμα τοῦτο; οὐκ ἐψεύσω ἀνθρώποις, ἀλλὰ τῷ Θεῷ.	own? and after it was sold, was it not in your own power? "Why have you ·conceived this thing in your ·heart? you have not lied to men "only, but to God. And Ananias hearing 5
5 And Ananias hearing these words, fell down, and gave up the ghost. And great fear came on all them that heard these things.	[5] Ἀκούων δὲ Ἀνανίας τοὺς λόγους τούτους, πεσὼν ἐξέψυξε· καὶ ἐγένετο φόβος μέγας ἐπὶ πάντας τοὺς ἀκούοντας ταῦτα.	"these words, "falling, expired; and great fear came on all that *heard these things. And the 6
6 And the young men arose, wound him up, and carried *him* out, and buried *him*.	[6] ἀναστάντες.δὲ οἱ νεώτεροι συνέστειλαν αὐτὸν, καὶ ἐξενέγκαντες ἔθαψαν.	young men ʸarose, wrapped him up, and ˙carrying him out, buried him. ˙Now an 7
7 And it was about the space of three hours after, when his wife, not knowing what was done, came in.	[7] Ἐγένετο δὲ ὡς ὡρῶν τριῶν διάστημα, καὶ ἡ γυνὴ αὐτοῦ μὴ εἰδυῖα τὸ γεγονὸς εἰσῆλθεν.	interval of about three hours occurred, and his wife, not knowing what was done, came in. And Peter said to her, Tell 8
8 And Peter answered unto her, Tell me whether ye sold the land for so much? And she said, Yea, for so much.	[8] ἀπεκρίθη δὲ αὐτῇ ὁ Πέτρος, Εἰπέ μοι, εἰ τοσούτου τὸ χωρίον ἀπέδοσθε; Ἡ δὲ εἶπε, Ναὶ, τοσούτου. [9] Ὁ δὲ Πέτρος	me whether you sold the land for so much? And she said verily, for so much. Then 9

was it not your own? And after it was sold, was it not in your own power, or at your own disposal?" We opine that the interrogative character of this sentence continues to its close, i. e. to ὑπηρχε.

Our reasons are two—It is so pointed in our most approved texts. And, again, because the impassioned speaker continues the same style of emotional feeling in another interrogation:—τι ότι εθου εν τη καρδια σου το πραγμα τουτο; why have you conceived this thing in your heart?

ᵇ *Τι ότι*, for τι`εστιν οτι, as in v. 9, what is this? Fritzsche, Meyer, De Wette.

ᶜ *Εθου*, aor. ind. mid. of τιθημι, literally, why have you placed, or deliberately machinated, this in your heart? The whole contour of the style indicates a deliberate design, calling forth a burst of feeling, bordering on excitement, on the part of the Apostle.

For a similar use of τιθημι see Luke 1 : 66; 21 : 14. Acts 19 : 21; 27 : 12. In Luke's currency τιθημι, in such cases, is indicative of settled design, fixedness of purpose, strong determination. Hence the aggravation of the sin of Ananias and his wife. They concealed, *with intent to lie*, for popularity.

ᵘ "Only" is supplied, but not called for. It is true *in fact* that he lied to men, and to God. And *therefore* it is implied. Modern translators differ. Hackett says it is logically correct to translate ουκ . . . αλλα, *not so much as*; but this is defective in form, and less forcible. Others, like Boothroyd, and Penn, supply *only*. It is therefore a matter of taste, or discretion.

ᵛ *Ταυτα*, after ακουντας, is of doubtful authority; rejected by some editors, wanting in the vulgate and some other versions. It is applied to a single event, Lachmann, Hackett, &c.

ʷ *Πεσων εξεψυξε*, falling, expired. This participial form,

when followed, as in this case, by an active verb in the aorist, may indicate that the act expressed in the verb was the result of that expressed by the participle, and, especially, when και is wanting between the participle and the verb.

ˣ "Who heard these" would be better than "that heard these things."—This is a matter of taste, and not of etymology.

ʸ And the young men—ανασταντες, arising, or having arisen, συνεστειλαν (as περιεστειλαν), wrapped him up, and εξενεγκαντες, 1st aor. part., having carried him out &c.

ᶻ *Εξενεγκαντες*, having carried him forth, out of the city. Most probably as the Jews did not usually bury within their city walls, and not in consequence of his judicial death.

ᵃ *Εγενετο και*, now it came to pass.—There was an interval of about three hours.—Then &c. " ὡς διαστημα is not here the subject of εγενετο, but forms a parenthetic clause and (see on 1 : 10) introduces the apodosis of the sentence. De Wette, Meyer, Fritzsche." So Hackett in loc. This Hebraistic use of και in the apodosis of a sentence, after an expression or idea of time, is frequent in the N. Testament. See Brud. Gr. Concord. p. 456. "Intercessit autem ferme horarum trium intervallum quum uxor quoque ipsius, nesciens quod factum, ingressa est." Beza. "Factum est autem quasi horarum trium spatium, et uxor ipsius, nesciens quod factum fuerat, introivit." Vulgate.

Δε, now; διαστημα, an interval of about three hours; εγενετο, occurred; και ἡ γυνη αυτου, and his wife. This prevents the necessity of the supply of the article, and the translation of και by "when," as in some versions. *Το γεγονος, what had occurred.* This agrees with the perfect tense of the participle, and with the active rather than with the passive sense. It was what had come to pass a providential act and not a mere act of Peter.

KING JAMES' VERSION.

9 Then Peter said unto her, How is it that ye have agreed together to tempt the Spirit of the Lord? behold the feet of them which have buried thy husband *are* at the door, and shall carry thee out.

10 Then fell she down straightway at his feet, and yielded up the ghost. And the young men came in, and found her dead, and carrying *her* forth, buried *her* by her husband.

11 And great fear came upon all the church, and upon as many as heard these things.

12 And by the hands of the apostles were many signs and wonders wrought among the people; (and they were all with one accord in Solomon's porch.

13 And of the rest durst no

GREEK TEXT.

εἶπε πρὸς αὐτὴν, Τί ὅτι συνεφωνήθη ὑμῖν πειράσαι τὸ πνεῦμα κυρίου; ἰδοὺ, οἱ πόδες τῶν θαψάντων τὸν ἄνδρα σου, ἐπὶ τῇ θύρᾳ, καὶ ἐξοίσουσί σε. 10 Ἔπεσε δὲ παραχρῆμα παρὰ τοὺς πόδας αὐτοῦ, καὶ ἐξέψυξεν· εἰσελθόντες δὲ οἱ νεανίσκοι εὗρον αὐτὴν νεκρὰν, καὶ ἐξενέγκαντες ἔθαψαν πρὸς τὸν ἄνδρα αὐτῆς. 11 καὶ ἐγένετο φόβος μέγας ἐφ᾽ ὅλην τὴν ἐκκλησίαν, καὶ ἐπὶ πάντας τοὺς ἀκούοντας ταῦτα.

12 Διὰ δὲ τῶν χειρῶν τῶν ἀποστόλων ἐγένετο σημεῖα καὶ τέρατα ἐν τῷ λαῷ πολλά· καὶ ἦσαν ὁμοθυμαδὸν ἅπαντες ἐν τῇ στοᾷ Σολομῶντος· 13 τῶν δὲ λοιπῶν οὐδεὶς ἐτόλμα κολλᾶσθαι

REVISED VERSION.

Peter said to her, [b]Why is it, that you have agreed together, to tempt the Spirit of the Lord? Behold the feet of these who have buried your husband are at the door, and shall carry you out. [c]Then she instant- 10 ly fell down at his feet and expired : and the young men came in and found her dead, and carrying her out, buried her by her husband. And 11 great fear came upon all the [d]congregation, and upon all those hearing these things.

And [e]through the hands of 12 the Apostles were many signs and wonders done among the people, (and [ee]they were all with one accord in Solomon's porch. And of the [g]rest durst 13

---

[b] Τί ὅτι, why is it that? Συνεφωνήθη, 3d pers. sing. aor. ind. pass.—it was concerted, ὑμῖν, by you—an instance well sustained of the dative after the passive, instead of the gen. with ὑπο.

[c] Επεσε δε, and she fell; παραχρημα, immediately, just then, as Peter pronounced the last word. Δε has merely a copulative sense. And the young men, εισελθοντες, coming in, found her dead. And carrying her out, εξενεγκαντες, they buried her, εθαψαν.

[d] And great fear came upon all the *congregation*, επι ὁλην την εκκλησιαν. Any assembly in this book being called an εκκλησια, and the word occurring 131 times in the Christian Scriptures it has been much in controversy, and consequently has caused much strife amongst Christians. It should be known and deliberated upon, that this word εκκλησια is represented in the Christian Scriptures by the following words, church, churches, assembly. It is, by apostolic use, indicative of any meeting or assembly of persons in any place, at any time, or for any purpose, with, or without a special call of those in authority. In the 19th chapter of Acts, com. v., it is thrice represented by the word assembly. Its etymological import is simply *called out*, or congregated. Hence assembly, concourse, or congregation, of any sort is indicated in and by the word εκκλησια.

[e] Δια, indicating *instrumentality*, is, in all books, and especially in the Christian Scriptures, interchangeably rendered *by*, or *through*. Whatever metaphysics may say, *by* and *through* are equally indicative of both Divine and human agency. We have many instances of this in the com. ver., such as Rom.

5 : 21: "Grace reign *through* (δια) righteousness *by* (δια) Jesus Christ our Lord." The condemnation *by*, or *through* Adam, and the righteousness *by* or *through* Christ are represented by one and the same δια, &c. Such also is our popular use of *by* and *through*. Where there is no established antithetical difference in the meaning or use of particles in the Christian Scriptures, we should not create it; and where there is, we should not annihilate it. All that God has done for man, since he created him, has been through (δια) agencies. Indeed, we are informed by Paul, Eph. 3 : 9, that God created all things (δια) through Jesus Christ. Moreover, *by*, and *through*, are used at the present time interchangeably.

[ee] Ἅπαντες, refers to the Apostles mentioned in the last clause. Olsh., De Wette, Mey., Bengel, extend it to all the believers. Hack.

[f] Ὁμοθυμαδὸν ἅπαντες ἐν τῃ στοᾳ Σολομωντος. Solomon's porch, being a place of much resort, and the disciples as yet being all Jews, and having a common national right to resort thither with their own nation, it was for them legitimate missionary ground; and there, with much boldness, they announced the claims of Jesus as the Messiah.

[g] "And of the rest." The sense of των λοιπων is explained by the last clause. Doddridge, Boothroyd, Hack. Dr. Lightfoot explains this "*of the rest*," "of the one hundred and twenty," from which Dr. Whitby dissents. Beza, would render κολλασθαι, in this passage, "to attack." This is too far fetched, and inappropriate to the contextual scope. They feared hypocritically to join them.

Τῶν δε λοιπων. Literally, *of the remainder*. Those yet

KING JAMES' VERSION.	GREEK TEXT.	REVISED VERSION.

KING JAMES' VERSION.

man join himself to them : but the people magnified them.

14 And believers were the more added to the Lord, multitudes both of men and women.)

15 Insomuch that they brought forth the sick into the streets, and laid *them* on beds and couches, that at the least the shadow of Peter passing by might overshadow some of them.

16 There came also a multitude *out* of the cities round about unto Jerusalem, bringing sick folks, and them which were vexed with unclean spirits; and they were healed every one.

17 Then the high priest rose up, and all they that were with him, (which is the sect of the Sadducees,) and were filled with indignation,

18 And laid their hands on the apostles, and put them in the common prison.

19 But the angel of the Lord by night opened the prison doors, and brought them forth, and said,

20 Go, stand and speak in the

GREEK TEXT.

αὐτοῖς, ἀλλ' ἐμεγάλυνεν αὐτοὺς ὁ λαός· ¹⁴ μᾶλλον δὲ προσετίθεντο πιστεύοντες τῷ κυρίῳ, πλήθη ἀνδρῶν τε καὶ γυναικῶν· ¹⁵ ὥστε κατὰ τὰς πλατείας ἐκφέρειν τοὺς ἀσθενεῖς, καὶ τιθέναι ἐπὶ κλινῶν καὶ κραββάτων, ἵνα ἐρχομένου Πέτρου κἂν ἡ σκιὰ ἐπισκιάσῃ τινὶ αὐτῶν. ¹⁶ συνήρχετο δὲ καὶ τὸ πλῆθος τῶν πέριξ πόλεων εἰς Ἰερουσαλήμ, φέροντες ἀσθενεῖς καὶ ὀχλουμένους ὑπὸ πνευμάτων ἀκαθάρτων, οἵτινες ἐθεραπεύοντο ἅπαντες.

¹⁷ Ἀναστὰς δὲ ὁ ἀρχιερεὺς καὶ πάντες οἱ σὺν αὐτῷ, ἡ οὖσα αἵρεσις τῶν Σαδδουκαίων, ἐπλήσθησαν ζήλου, ¹⁸ καὶ ἐπέβαλον τὰς χεῖρας αὐτῶν ἐπὶ τοὺς ἀποστόλους, καὶ ἔθεντο αὐτοὺς ἐν τηρήσει δημοσίᾳ. ¹⁹ ἄγγελος δὲ κυρίου διὰ τῆς νυκτὸς ἤνοιξε τὰς θύρας τῆς φυλακῆς, ἐξαγαγών τε αὐτοὺς εἶπε, ²⁰ Πορεύεσθε, καὶ σταθέντες λαλεῖτε ἐν

REVISED VERSION.

no man join himself to them, but the people ʰmagnified them. And believers were still more 14 added ᶦto the Lord, multitudes of men and also of women), insomuch that they brought 15 forth their sick into the streets, and laid them on beds and couches, that at the least, the shadow of Peter, passing by, might overshadow some of them. And the multitude of 16 the surrounding cities also came together into Jerusalem, bringing the sick and those harassed with unclean spirits. and they were every one healed.

But the High Priest aris- 17 ing, and all who were with him (being the party of the ʲSadducees), were filled with zeal, and ᵏthrew their 18 hands upon the Apostles, and put them in public ᵏcustody. But an ˡangel of the Lord, 19 under ᵐcover of the night, opened the prison doors, and bringing them forth, said, ⁿGo stand 20 and speak in the temple to the

---

unconverted dared not to associate themselves with them. The *remainder*, though an exact representation of των δε λοιπων, seems to be somewhat indefinite. The term, *λαος, people*, immediately after, is its best exponent. None could look upon these wonder-working men without fear and reverence. The fate of Ananias and his wife is as a fearful caveat against hypocrisy. If every one "glorified God for that which was done" (ch. 4 : 21), in the case of the impotent man, why should not these keep back from presumptuous sin, from the spectacle before them in the case of Ananias and his wife?

ʰ *Εμεγαλυνεν αυτους*, magnified them. The Apostles, at this time, were greatly exalted in the esteem of the multitude, as, in the sequel, still further appears.

As *quassare* is more than *quatere*, *taxare* than *tangere*, *jactare* than *jacere*, so *vexare* is more than *vehere*, yet not one of these, *shaken, troubled, terrified, strangled*, is so grievous as the feeling indicated in the text. According to Critica Sacra, "It is to be distracted hither and thither having no power of itself."

ᶦ *Τῳ κυριῳ*. This verse is evidently parenthetic.—Believers not added *in* the Lord, as some would have it, but *to* the Lord. Its case depends on the verb.

ʲ "Sadducees." The reason of their activity in this case, is happily illustrative of our indebtedness to sectarianism, at least in one respect; its eternal vigilance to guard proof texts against all violence. The Sadducees saw in Christ's resurrection the refutation of their system; and therefore they violently seized the Apostles, because their preaching that doctrine was fatal to their distinguishing tenets.

ᵏ *Επεβαλον*. This verb indicates strong violence. They fiercely threw their arms around them, or their hands upon them. *Τηρησει*, with us, *custody*.

ˡ *Αγγελος*. Why *an* angel should here become some particular angel is destitute of authority. Had some angel been named in the context, there might have been some reason for the definite article.

ᵐ *Δια, through* the night, or under cover of the night. More seems to be indicated than the escape by night—rather by *means* of the night—εξαγαγων τε αυτους ειπε, bringing them out, said.

ⁿ *Πορευεσθε,—σταθεντες*—go, and, standing in the Temple, speak. This form abounds in Luke's style.

KING JAMES' VERSION.	GREEK TEXT.	REVISED VERSION.

KING JAMES' VERSION.

temple to the people all the words of this life.

21 And when they heard *that*, they entered into the temple early in the morning, and taught. But the high priest came, and they that were with him, and called the council together, and all the senate of the children of Israel, and sent to the prison to have them brought.

22 But when the officers came, and found them not in the prison, they returned, and told,

23 Saying, The prison truly found we shut with all safety, and the keepers standing without before the doors: but when we had opened, we found no man within.

24 Now when the high priest, and the captain of the temple, and the chief priests heard these things, they doubted of them whereunto this would grow.

25 Then came one and told them, saying, Behold, the men whom ye put in prison are standing in the temple, and teaching the people.

26 Then went the captain with the officers, and brought them without violence: for they feared the people, lest they should have been stoned.

GREEK TEXT.

τῷ ἱερῷ τῷ λαῷ πάντα τὰ ῥήματα τῆς ζωῆς ταύτης. ²¹ Ἀκούσαντες δὲ εἰσῆλθον ὑπὸ τὸν ὄρθρον εἰς τὸ ἱερὸν, καὶ ἐδίδασκον. παραγενόμενος δὲ ὁ ἀρχιερεὺς καὶ οἱ σὺν αὐτῷ, συνεκάλεσαν τὸ συνέδριον καὶ πᾶσαν τὴν γερουσίαν τῶν υἱῶν Ἰσραὴλ, καὶ ἀπέστειλαν εἰς τὸ δεσμωτήριον, ἀχθῆναι αὐτούς. ²² οἱ δὲ ὑπηρέται παραγενόμενοι οὐχ εὗρον αὐτοὺς ἐν τῇ φυλακῇ· ἀναστρέψαντες δὲ ἀπήγγειλαν, ²³ λέγοντες, Ὅτι τὸ μὲν δεσμωτήριον εὕρομεν κεκλεισμένον ἐν πάσῃ ἀσφαλείᾳ, καὶ τοὺς φύλακας ἔξω ἑστῶτας πρὸ τῶν θυρῶν· ἀνοίξαντες δὲ, ἔσω οὐδένα εὕρομεν. ²⁴ Ὡς δὲ ἤκουσαν τοὺς λόγους τούτους ὅ τε ἱερεὺς καὶ ὁ στρατηγὸς τοῦ ἱεροῦ καὶ οἱ ἀρχιερεῖς, διηπόρουν περὶ αὐτῶν, τί ἂν γένοιτο τοῦτο. ²⁵ παραγενόμενος δέ τις ἀπήγγειλεν αὐτοῖς λέγων, Ὅτι ἰδοὺ οἱ ἄνδρες οὓς ἔθεσθε ἐν τῇ φυλακῇ, εἰσὶν ἐν τῷ ἱερῷ ἑστῶτες καὶ διδάσκοντες τὸν λαόν. ²⁶ Τότε ἀπελθὼν ὁ στρατηγὸς σὺν τοῖς ὑπηρέταις, ἤγαγεν αὐτούς, οὐ μετὰ βίας, ἐφοβοῦντο γὰρ τὸν λαόν, ἵνα μὴ λιθασθῶσιν. ²⁷ ἀγαγόν-

REVISED VERSION.

people, all the words of this life.

And when they heard that, 21 they entered into the temple °early in the morning, and were teaching. But the High Priest came, and those that were with him, and called the council together, and all the senate of the children of Israel, and sent into the prison to have them brought.

But when the officers came 22 and found them not in the prison, they returned and reported, saying: The prison in- 23 deed we found ᴾshut with all ᴾsecurity, and the guards, standing before the entrances; but on opening, we found not one within. ۹Now when the 24 High Priest, and the Captain of the temple, and the chief Priests, heard these words, they were in perplexity about them, what this might come to be. But ʳone came and report- 25 ed, saying, Behold, those whom you placed in the prison are standing in the temple and teaching the people. Then, 26 the Captain went, with the officers, and brought them without force (for they feared the people), that they ˢmight not be stoned.

° Ὑπὸ τὸν ὀρθρον. Literally, *under the dawn of day*. Ορθρος occurs but three times in the N. Test., and always represented by "*early in the morning*." Its use amongst the Greeks was equivalent to our "*dawn of day*," usually called "*the break of day*."

ᴾ Κεκλεισμενον, being the acc. sing. neut. perfect pass., indicates in all ασφαλεια, security, or *firmness* of defense, *impregnable*. Ὁτι, in this verse, is a pleonasm, because reciting the words of others. This is not unusual with Luke. And the guards standing (rather, being perfect participle, it is tantamount to our *having been placed*). Εξω, outside, is omitted by Gb., Sch., Ln. and Tf. Των θυρων, the *entrances* —doors, too specific.

۹ Now ὡς, as the High Priest &c.—*These words*, τους λογους τουτους. Διηπορουν, imp. *were being perplexed* = *in perplexity*; περι αυτων, *about them*—"*to what this might amount*."

ʳ Δε, but, in this perplexity; τις, a *certain one*; παραγενομενος, *having come* (aor. part.); reported, απηγγειλεν. Ὁτι, pleonastically used; ους εθεσθε, *those whom* you placed in τη φυλακη, the *prison*; εστωτες, perf. part., *having taken a stand* = *are standing*; και διδασκοντες τον λαον, and *teaching* the people.

ˢ The English translation, as well observed by Prof. Hack., here assumes an impossible connection, as, after verbs of fearing, μη, μηπως and the like do follow, but never ινα μη.

KING JAMES' VERSION.	GREEK TEXT.	REVISED VERSION.

KING JAMES' VERSION.

27 And when they had brought them, they set *them* before the council: and the high priest asked them,

28 Saying, Did not we straitly command you, that ye should not teach in this name? and behold, ye have filled Jerusalem with your doctrine, and intend to bring this man's blood upon us.

29 Then Peter and the *other* apostles answered and said, We ought to obey God rather than men.

30 The God of our fathers raised up Jesus, whom ye slew and hanged on a tree:

31 Him hath God exalted with his right hand *to be* a Prince and a Saviour, for to give repentance to Israel, and forgiveness of sins.

GREEK TEXT.

τες δὲ αὐτοὺς ἔστησαν ἐν τῷ συνεδρίῳ· καὶ ἐπηρώτησεν αὐτοὺς ὁ ἀρχιερεὺς, [28] λέγων, Οὐ παραγγελίᾳ παρηγγείλαμεν ὑμῖν μὴ διδάσκειν ἐπὶ τῷ ὀνόματι τούτῳ; καὶ ἰδοὺ πεπληρώκατε τὴν Ἱερουσαλὴμ τῆς διδαχῆς ὑμῶν, καὶ βούλεσθε ἐπαγαγεῖν ἐφ' ἡμᾶς τὸ αἷμα τοῦ ἀνθρώπου τούτου. [29] Ἀποκριθεὶς δὲ ὁ Πέτρος καὶ οἱ ἀπόστολοι εἶπον, Πειθαρχεῖν δεῖ Θεῷ μᾶλλον ἢ ἀνθρώποις. [30] ὁ Θεὸς τῶν πατέρων ἡμῶν ἤγειρεν Ἰησοῦν, ὃν ὑμεῖς διεχειρίσασθε κρεμάσαντες ἐπὶ ξύλου· [31] τοῦτον ὁ Θεὸς ἀρχηγὸν καὶ σωτῆρα ὕψωσε τῇ δεξιᾷ αὐτοῦ, δοῦναι μετάνοιαν τῷ Ἰσραὴλ καὶ ἄφεσιν ἁμαρτιῶν. [32] καὶ ἡμεῖς

REVISED VERSION.

And ᵗhaving led them away, 27 they placed them in the council: and the High Priest asked them;—Did we not 28 strictly command you not to teach ᵘupon this name? and, behold, you have filled up Jerusalem with your doctrine, and are intending to bring the blood of this man upon us.

But Peter and the Apostles 29 answering, said, We ought to obey God rather than men. The God of our fathers has rais- 30 ed up Jesus, whom you slew, having hanged him on a tree. This person has God exalted 31 to his right hand, a ᵛPrince and a Saviour, ʷto grant repentance to Israel, and forgiveness of

---

ᵗ *Αγαγοντες,* having *led them away,* i. e. from the Temple; *εστησαν, they caused them to stand,* they placed them.

ᵘ See v. 17. ch. 4.—This strict charge, on the part of the council, shows how much they dreaded the name of Jesus Christ. To speak *upon* it, or to speak *by* it, was to them "terrible as an army with banners."—They, therefore, prohibited a word *upon* that subject—from this view of the whole case, or premises, we concur with those who prefer *upon,* to *in* or *by.* Besides επι com. ver. is rendered some 150 times by *upon.*

ᵛ This verse is grammatically and logically in apposition. *Ιησουν τουτον, Αρχηγον, Σωτηρα,*—*Ιησουν* under the regimen of *ηγειρεν,* and *τουτον Αρχηγον Σωτηρα* under that of *υψωσε,* and in apposition with *Ιησουν,* as we must regard it. We then render it—"*This Prince and Saviour God has exalted to his right hand to grant reformation,*" or "*the benefit of reformation to Israel, even the remission of sins.*" Remission of sins is always, and in all cases, an act of *Sovereignty,* of pure grace. Hence it is not, in any case, ex merito, based upon any thought, volition, word, or deed of any sinner in the universe. Grace and merit are as incompatible as light and darkness, as good and evil. If of *grace,* it cannot be of *works,* of any work. If of works, or of any work, it cannot be of grace. Otherwise, grace and work cease to be of any difference. It is an act of grace, and all grace is sovereign. There is not, nor can there be, any grace that is not an act of absolute sovereignty. So the oracles of God, and so the oracles of man, of enlightened and cultivated reason, have always decided. This view of the

subject is not, at the bar of right reason, incompatible with making or propounding faith, repentance, baptism, or prayer, as means of *receiving* pardon. The beggar cannot think that the extending of his arm, or hand, to *receive* alms, annihilates the nature of alms, or converts the *receiving* of them into a work of merit. No more can common sense, unperverted by false views, imagine that pardon, based on any principle of faith, repentance, prayer, or baptism &c., annihilates the *nature,* or entrenches upon the *character,* of *grace,* even if crowded with the absurd prefixes of *free, sovereign,* and *special;* not one of which is found in Holy Writ.

By a special reference to Acts 11 : 18; Luke 1 : 74; Acts 14 : 3; Rom. 15 : 5; Eph. 3 : 16; 2 Tim. 2 : 18; Rev. 3 : 21 &c., com. ver., it will appear that *διδωμαι* is occasionally represented in Luke, Paul and John, by the words *grant, bestow,* and to *give, give gratuitously,* &c.

De Wette understands giving or granting repentance, in the sense of giving time or space for it. This may, in some cases, be equivalent to granting it, but to confine it to this view would stultify, or annihilate it, as properly a *gift.*

ʷ "To grant repentance." This indicates the benefit of repentance—the forgiveness of sins. Legally we do not grant to the lawless and disobedient, any benefit to repentance. God mercifully grants repentance, pardon and acceptance. Hence promises the most precious are annexed to faith and repentance. In Hebrew style, God grants repentance to life, by granting pardon and acceptance, through the sacrifice of the Lord Jesus, received by faith.

KING JAMES' VERSION.	GREEK TEXT.	REVISED VERSION.
32 And we are his witnesses of these things; and *so is* also the Holy Ghost, whom God hath given to them that obey him.	ἐσμὲν αὐτοῦ μάρτυρες τῶν ῥημά-των τούτων, καὶ τὸ Πνεῦμα δὲ τὸ Ἅγιον, ὃ ἔδωκεν ὁ Θεὸς τοῖς πειθαρχοῦσιν αὐτῷ.	sins. And we are his wit-32 nesses of these things; and so is also the ˣHoly Spirit, whom God has given to those who obey him. ʸNow those 33
33 When they heard *that*, they were cut *to the heart*, and took counsel to slay them.	³³ Οἱ δὲ ἀκούσαντες διεπρί-οντο, καὶ ἐβουλεύοντο ἀνελεῖν αὐτούς. ³⁴ ἀναστὰς δέ τις ἐν τῷ	hearing, were exasperated, and they were making up their mind to slay them. But a certain one, arising in 34
34 Then stood there up one in the council, a Pharisee, named Gamaliel, a doctor of the law, had in reputation among all the people, and commanded to put the apostles forth a little space;	συνεδρίῳ φαρισαῖος, ὀνόματι Γα-μαλιὴλ, νομοδιδάσκαλος τίμιος παντὶ τῷ λαῷ, ἐκέλευσεν ἔξω βραχύ τι τοὺς ἀποστόλους ποιῆ-σαι, ³⁵ εἶπε τε πρὸς αὐτούς,	the Sanhedrim, a Pharisee, Gamaliel by name, a teacher of law, ᶻhonored by all the people, commanded to put the Apostles out, for a little while, and said to them,
35 And said unto them, Ye men of Israel, take heed to your-selves what ye intend to do as touching these men:	Ἄνδρες Ἰσραηλῖται, προσέχετε ἑαυτοῖς ἐπὶ τοῖς ἀνθρώποις τού-τοις τί μέλλετε πράσσειν. ³⁶ πρὸ	ᵃIsraelites take heed to your-35 selves, what you ᵇexecute upon these men. For be-36
36 For before these days rose up Theudas, boasting himself to be somebody; to whom a num-ber of men, about four hundred, joined themselves: who was	γὰρ τούτων τῶν ἡμερῶν ἀνέστη Θευδᾶς, λέγων εἶναί τινα ἑαυτὸν, ᾧ προσεκολλήθη ἀριθμὸς ἀνδρῶν ὡσεὶ τετρακοσίων· ὃς ἀνῃρέθη,	fore these days Theudas arose, declaring himself to be some-body, to whom a number of men, about four hundred, ᶜat-tached themselves; who was

Δουναι μετανοιαν, i. e.—"the grace or disposition to exercise it." Compare 3 : 16 ; 18 : 27, John 16 : 7, 8. Hackett, De Wette, and others give this doctrinal view of it. When the Lord grants health or wealth &c., does he only grant the *dis-position* to acquire it? He grants the blessing at once; but it may be through *means*. But to Judas, he gave not repentance —though he did repent. But God gave no *benefit to his repent-ance.* Does not the phrase, or formula, indicate, that he gave them the avails or benefit of it?—namely pardon. Per-haps it is safer to say he gives both.

ˣ Και το πνευμα δε το Ἁγιον.—Δε is, in this case, exegetical as is evident from its position between πνευμα and Ἁγιον, the Spirit, viz. *the Holy one which* God has given to them that obey him; ὁ (neuter), *which,* εδωκεν (aorist), God gave to those, πειθαρχουσιν αυτῳ. This preserves the idiom.

ʸ Οἱ δε ακουσαντες, now those hearing; διεπριοντο (lit-erally), *were being sawn through.* This expression, in this *passive* form, indicated not what they were *doing,* nor *feeling,* but the *death blows* the Apostles were inflicting on them as opposers of the truth.

Εβουλευοντο, *and they were making up their minds.* It seems to have been the object of this historian to express not what was *done,* but what was *being done.* There was *much time* occupied by these events, and much *continuity* in all their affairs. The *continuative* force of the Greek imp. is beautifully exhibited in this narrative, all of which is entirely lost in the com. ver.

Ανελειν αυτους, *to put them aside.* The Greek and English are idiomatically the same here. In both the phrase is under-stood in the sense of to *kill,* but *to put them aside* is more literal, and therefore to be preferred.

ᶻ This gives the genuine meaning of τιμιος.

ᵃ Ανδρες Ισραηλιται—*Israelites,* is more forcible, as well as more in our usage, than men of Israel.—They stand in appo-sition. In such cases the common yields to the special and not the special to the common. Hence not *men,* nor *men of Israel,* but *Israelites.*

"Men of Israel" is more literal than Israelites; so is "men, brethren, and fathers," than "brethren and fathers," as we give it. This is measurably a matter of taste, and also of grammar.—Grammatically they stand in apposition, and not in regimen. Man, in our vernacular, is absorbed in all nationalities; because Virginians are *men of Virginia,* men of Israel are also Israelites. Being in one case in the original, we should, as far as idiom permits, place them in one case in our version. But the title Israelites is equal to men of Israel, and more in harmony with the spirit and feeling of the orator, especially when animated.

ᵇ Πρασσειν επι, *to execute upon;* more familiarly and literally expressed by *to do upon them.* But to *do officially,* in legal usage, is to *execute.*

ᶜ But if προσκλινω be preferred, as the true reading, of which, to me, the evidence is not satisfactory; then it would indicate only an *inclination* to him rather than an adhesion. There being nothing of real consequence in the matter, in either view of it, we are disposed to leave it *sub judice.*

KING JAMES' VERSION.

slain; and all, as many as obeyed him, were scattered, and brought to nought.

37 After this man rose up Judas of Galilee, in the days of the taxing, and drew away much people after him: he also perished; and all, *even* as many as obeyed him, were dispersed.

38 And now I say unto you, Refrain from these men, and let them alone: for if this counsel or this work be of men, it will come to nought:

39 But if it be of God, ye cannot overthrow it; lest haply ye be found even to fight against God.

40 And to him they agreed: and when they had called the apostles, and beaten *them*, they commanded that they should not speak in the name of Jesus, and let them go.

41 And they departed from the presence of the council, rejoicing that they were counted worthy to suffer shame for his name.

42 And daily in the temple, and in every house, they ceased not to teach and preach Jesus Christ.

GREEK TEXT.

καὶ πάντες ὅσοι ἐπείθοντω αὐτῷ, διελύθησαν καὶ ἐγένοντο εἰς οὐδέν. 37 μετὰ τοῦτον ἀνέστη Ἰούδας ὁ Γαλιλαῖος, ἐν ταῖς ἡμέραις τῆς ἀπογραφῆς, καὶ ἀπέστησε λαὸν ἱκανὸν ὀπίσω αὐτοῦ· κἀκεῖνος ἀπώλετο, καὶ πάντες ὅσοι ἐπείθοντο αὐτῷ διεσκορπίσθησαν. 38 καὶ τὰ νῦν λέγω ὑμῖν, ἀπόστητε ἀπὸ τῶν ἀνθρώπων, τούτων, καὶ ἐάσατε αὐτούς· ὅτι ἐὰν ᾖ ἐξ ἀνθρώπων ἡ βουλὴ αὕτη ἢ τὸ ἔργον τοῦτο, καταλυθήσεται· 39 εἰ δὲ ἐκ Θεοῦ ἐστιν, οὐ δύνασθε καταλῦσαι αὐτὸ, μήποτε καὶ θεομάχοι εὑρεθῆτε. 40 Ἐπείσθησαν δὲ αὐτῷ· καὶ προσκαλεσάμενοι τοὺς ἀποστόλους, δείραντες παρήγγειλαν μὴ λαλεῖν ἐπὶ τῷ ὀνόματι τοῦ Ἰησοῦ, καὶ ἀπέλυσαν αὐτούς. 41 Οἱ μὲν οὖν ἐπορεύοντο χαίροντες ἀπὸ προσώπου τοῦ συνεδρίου, ὅτι ὑπὲρ τοῦ ὀνόματος αὐτοῦ κατηξιώθησαν ἀτιμασθῆναι· 42 πᾶσάν τε ἡμέραν ἐν τῷ ἱερῷ καὶ κατ᾽ οἶκον οὐκ ἐπαύοντο διδάσκοντες καὶ εὐαγγελιζόμενοι Ἰησοῦν τὸν Χριστόν.

REVISED VERSION.

slain; and all, as many as obeyed him, were scattered and brought to nothing.

After this man, [d]Judas the 37 Galilean rose up, in the days of the [e]enrollment, and drew away sufficient people after him: and he utterly destroyed himself; and all, as many as were obedient to him, were dispersed. And now I 38 say to you, [ee]Withdraw from these men and let them alone; for if this purpose, or this work be of men, it will be destroyed; but if it be of God, you are not [f]able to destroy it, and [g]lest, perhaps, you be found 39 to fight against God. And they 40 were persuaded by him; and having called the Apostles, and [h]scourged them, they commanded that they should not speak [h]upon the name of Jesus, and released them. So 41 they departed from the presence of the council, rejoicing that they were esteemed worthy to be dishonored for [i] his name. And they did not 42 cease teaching every day, in the temple, and in every house, and [j]proclaiming Jesus the Christ.

---

[d] Judas the Galilean rose up in the days of the enrollment, λαον ικανον. I think that ικανον should be taken in its primitive sense; *sufficient*, or enough, λαοι πολλοι, is many people. He drew away sufficient people after him—κακεινος, by *crasis*, for και εκεινος, and he απωλετο, aor. mid. *utterly destroyed himself*, and all, as many as persuaded themselves to him επειθοντο (aor. mid.) αυτῳ (dat.) were dispersed, is here in the passive form of διεσκορ. I think the mid. and pass. forms used by this historian should be preserved.

[e] Others have it, "In the days of the registration"—having reference to the levying of the tax, εν ταις ημεραις απογραφης, Boothroyd, Wakefield, Hackett, Penn.

[ee] We presume the dual τα v. 38 refers to these two directions —"*Refrain from these men. Let them alone,*" equal to "I say these two things to you"—"withdraw from these men," and "let them alone." Καλαλυνθησεται, future ind. pass. of καταλνω, to loosen down. "It will be dissolved or destroyed;" or "It will come to nothing," is too far from the passive form, and withal a little too strong in its signification. It is rendered *destroy* and *dissolve* in the com. ver., but in this place only "come *to nought*."

[f] Ου δυνασθε καταλυσαι, you are not able to destroy it. This enables us to retain the infinitive form of καταλνω.

[g] The transposition of "lest perhaps" is sanctioned by De Wette and others. It is, however, a matter of taste.

[h] Literally, "having scourged them." Equivalent in our English idiom, to "*had scourged* them," which is more usual. Δερω, excorio.

[i] Αυτον is repudiated from the text by the best Manuscripts. Gb., Sch., Ln., Tf.

[j] The difference between *preaching* and teaching Jesus

KING JAMES' VERSION.	GREEK TEXT.	REVISED VERSION.
CHAP. VI.	CHAP. VI.	CHAP. VI.
AND in those days, when the number of the disciples was multiplied, there arose a murmuring of the Grecians against the Hebrews, because their widows were neglected in the daily ministration. 2 Then the twelve called the	'ΕΝ δὲ ταῖς ἡμέραις ταύταις πληθυνόντων τῶν μαθητῶν, ἐγένετο γογγυσμὸς τῶν 'Ελληνιστῶν πρὸς τοὺς 'Εβραίους, ὅτι παρεθεωροῦντο ἐν τῇ διακονίᾳ τῇ καθημερινῇ αἱ χῆραι αὐτῶν. ² προσκαλεσάμενοι δὲ οἱ δώδεκα	ᵏNow, in those days, the 1 number of the disciples being ᶫmultiplied, a murmuring of the ᵐHellenists against the ⁿHebrews occurred, because their own widows were °neglected in the daily ᵖministration. Then the Twelve, having 2

Christ, is very distinctly specified in this passage—It, in fact, pervades the narratives of the propagation of Christianity. The κηρυξ is but a herald, and his work is to *herald*, to *announce*, *proclaim*, or *preach*: but the διδασκαλος, from διδασκω, *teaches.* He simply addresses the *understanding* didactically. He may explain, or expound, or interpret a doctrine, or even a fact, or an event. But here his work ceases. But the preacher proclaims a person, or facts, or events, of public importance, and may herald his advent, and announce his mission. The Apostolic preaching had Jesus for its subject, and the Apostolic teaching had Christ for its subject. They preached Jesus as the Christ, and they taught Christ as the most grand and Divine official in the universe.

ᵏ *Δε* is here merely continuative and connective, not resumptive nor adversative. Either *and*, or *now* may, in this position, represent its full force. *Now*, in the beginning of a paragraph, is generally preferred, but, where intimate connection is indicated, *and*, for the most part, is to be preferred. Such is the case before us, in one point of view, but in another it may be regarded as the opening of a new scene, not *logically* related to the facts stated in the preceding narrative, and, therefore, we prefer *now.*

ᶫ *Πληθυνόντων.* *Πληθυνω*, found twelve times in N. T., is, with one exception, always translated by the word *multiply*, as more expressive of its import than our word *increase.* With only two exceptions, *πληθος* occurring thirty-two times in our com. ver. is rendered *multitude.* And what is the fact here? In a few days the disciples increased from 120 to 3120, in a few days more, to 5000. Acts 4 : 4, and 21 : 20. There were "many *myriads* of the Jews" that believed.

ᵐ Not Greeks, *Ἑλληνες*,—Hellenists. The "Greek Jews against the Hebrew Jews."

ⁿ *Προς τους Ἑβραιους, against* the Hebrews. While *προς* occurs some 750 times in the N. T., and is commonly rendered *to*, and *unto*, it is occasionally, necessarily rendered *against*, as well as *among*, because in appearing in certain attitudes, and in certain crises, or places, we appear *for*, or *against* certain purposes, persons, or undertakings. Jesus once spoke a parable—*προς τους γεωργους*—in reference to

certain husbandmen, and to their proper representatives, but in most English versions it is rendered "*against* them." See also Acts 6 : 1; 9 : 5; Mark 12 : 12. He spoke a parable "*against* them," com. ver., yet he spoke it to them. "Dash thy foot *against* a stone," *προς λιθον*, Luke 4 : 11. "Murmured *against* his disciples," Luke 5 : 30. "Kick *against* the goads," *προς κεντρα*, Acts 9 : 5.

° *Ὅτι παρεθεωρουντο.* Literally, *looked at* askance, impliedly with some degree of neglect. Widows were not universally neglected, but *αυτων*, of themselves, i. e. their own widows. *Παραθεωρουντο*, used to be "less regarded." This view is intimated in the radical conception of the verb *παραθεωρεω*— "to look at things side by side," hence comparatively to regard less. See Xen. Memorabilia 4, 87. Dem. 1414, 22. Diodorus Sic. Sect. 36. p. 218. In the N. T. this is an *απαξ λεγομενον.*

ᵖ *Εν τη διακονια.* Some prefer *administration* in this place. *Ministration*, Dodd., Tyndal ; Cranmer, *distribution;* Thompson, ministration or administration. *Διακονια* denotes all voluntary ministrations, from the humblest to the most august, from that of a church deacon to that of an apostle, even to that of the Lord Jesus Christ. Roman magistrates, the apostles, and the Lord himself are, in the N. T., represented under the word *διακονοι*, "*ministers of God.*" Sister Phœbe was a *διακονος*, a deaconess (com. gen.), or servant of the Church of Cenchrea, Rom. 16 : 1. By the same apostle and in the same epistle ch. 15 : 8, Jesus Christ is called a *διακονος*, a *deacon* or "*minister* of the circumcision."

We have our ministers of state, ordinary and extraordinary. So has God. He made his Son, his angels, his prophets, priests, and kings, his *διακονοι*, his deacons in the drama of Creation, Providence, moral government, and redemption.

It is of Rome, and her descendants, and especially of the Greeks, and not of Jesus Christ, to name one class of ecclesiastics *deacons*, to the exclusion of all others. It should also be noted of *διακονος* and *δουλος*, that *διακονια* and *δουλειαι* are never convertible terms. The same person may, indeed, be a *δουλος* and a *διακονος*, but the relation, or attitude, is not thereby changed.

KING JAMES' VERSION.

multitude of the disciples *unto them*, and said, It is not reason that we should leave the word of God, and serve tables.

3 Wherefore, brethren, look ye out among you seven men of honest report, full of the Holy Ghost and wisdom, whom we may appoint over this business.

4 But we will give ourselves continually to prayer, and to the ministry of the word.

5 And the saying pleased the whole multitude: and they chose Stephen, a man full of faith and of the Holy Ghost, and Philip, and Prochorus, and Nicanor, and Timon, and Parmenas, and Nicolas a proselyte of Antioch,

6 Whom they set before the apostles: and when they had prayed, they laid *their* hands on them.

GREEK TEXT.

τὸ πλῆθος τῶν μαθητῶν, εἶπον,
Οὐκ ἀρεστόν ἐστιν ἡμᾶς, κατα-
λείψαντας τὸν λόγον τοῦ Θεοῦ,
διακονεῖν τραπέζαις. [3] ἐπισκέ-
ψασθε οὖν, ἀδελφοὶ, ἄνδρας ἐξ
ὑμῶν μαρτυρουμένους ἑπτὰ, πλήρεις Πνεύματος Ἁγίου καὶ σο-
φίας, οὓς καταστήσομεν ἐπὶ τῆς
χρείας ταύτης· [4] ἡμεῖς δὲ τῇ
προσευχῇ καὶ τῇ διακονίᾳ τοῦ
λόγου προσκαρτερήσομεν. [5] Καὶ
ἤρεσεν ὁ λόγος ἐνώπιον παντὸς
τοῦ πλήθους· καὶ ἐξελέξαντο
Στέφανον, ἄνδρα πλήρη πίστεως
καὶ Πνεύματος Ἁγίου, καὶ Φίλιππον, καὶ Πρόχορον καὶ Νι-
κάνορα, καὶ Τίμωνα καὶ Παρμε-
νᾶν, καὶ Νικόλαον προσήλυτον
Ἀντιοχέα, [6] οὓς ἔστησαν ἐνώπιον τῶν ἀποστόλων· καὶ προσευξάμενοι ἐπέθηκαν αὐτοῖς τὰς

REVISED VERSION.

[q]called the multitude of the
disciples to them, said: [r]Re-
linquishing the word of God to
serve tables is not pleasing to
us. Wherefore, brethren, look 3
out among you seven men [s]of
attested character, full of the
Holy [t]Spirit and of wisdom,
whom we may appoint over this
[u]business; but we will give our- 4
selves [v]wholly to prayer, and to
the ministry of the word. And 5
the speech was pleasing in the
mind of all the people; and
they chose Stephen, a man full
of faith and of the Holy [t]Spirit,
and Philip, and Prochorus, and
Nicanor, and Timon, and Parmenas, and Nicholas, a proselyte of Antioch: whom they 6
presented before the Apostles;
and, [w]praying, they [ww]laid their

[q] Προσκαλεσαμενοι (1st aor. part. mid. of προσκαλεομαι, advoco), having called.

[r] Text—*Relinquishing the word of God to serve tables is not pleasing to us*, is in strict conformity to the Greek construction of the text as we judge, and better comports with the occasion and the feelings of the Apostles than any version of it we have seen, and has this preëminence that it impinges not in the least upon the grammatical construction and import of every word in the text. It is true it might be more literally read, Having relinquished the word of God, &c. But this evaporates the spirit of the response, and in the construction of the 1st aorist participle is not absolutely demanded.

[s] Μαρτυρουμενους, attested character, "good fame," Wiclif; "good testimony," Murd.; "of reputation," Thompson.

[t] Πληρεις πνευματος. Literally, "*full of Holy Spirit*," though there is no article in the original, yet we prefer to retain the usual form, "The Holy Spirit." It may be questionable, indeed, whether such a possession of the Holy Spirit as was given to the apostles, and by which they were enabled to work miracles, etc., was a special prerequisite, ih the case of these seven, more than in other members of the church. That they were to possess the influence and personal abiding of the Spirit of God; such a possession of the Holy Spirit manifested in such demonstrations of its sanctifying power, as to qualify them for a faithful discharge of their special duties, was all important to their office, and, therefore, in all similar cases, it should still be made an indispensable prerequisite.

[u] Επι της χρειας ταυτης, over this business, over this necessity. The latter is more in accordance with scriptural usage. It was, however, an *employment*, and they were to make it a *calling*, a *business*. It was a necessary employment, and being an employment it interfered with the Apostles' proper business; and viewed in this contextual light it falls under the character of a *business*, and is a *work* as much as was the special work lying upon the Apostles.

[v] Προσκαρτερεω, generally rendered by *continue*. It implies earnestness, urgency, a continued steadfastness, "instant in prayer." To persevere with strength, *Critica Sacra*.

[w] Προσευξαμενοι επεθηκαν αυτοις τας χειρας. This specially refers to the Apostles, while praying for these seven deacons elect, they placing their hands upon them solemnly set them apart to the work to which they had previously been elected by this great congregation. In pursuance of this solemnity, and the undivided attention of the Apostles to the preaching of the gospel, we are informed that the word of the Lord ηυξανε (increased) in its influence and power, insomuch that even of the priests a great multitude became obedient to the faith.

[ww] "They laid their hands upon them."—This Apostolic usage, in appointing to office, was indicative of the devotion

KING JAMES' VERSION.

7 And the word of God increased; and the number of the disciples multiplied in Jerusalem greatly; and a great company of the priests were obedient to the faith.

8 And Stephen, full of faith and power, did great wonders and miracles among the people.

9 Then there arose certain of the synagogue, which is called *the synagogue* of the Libertines, and Cyrenians, and Alexandrians, and of them of Cilicia, and of Asia, disputing with Stephen.

10 And they were not able to resist the wisdom and the spirit by which he spake.

11 Then they suborned men,

GREEK TEXT.

χεῖρας. ⁷ καὶ ὁ λόγος τοῦ Θεοῦ ηὔξανε, καὶ ἐπληθύνετο ὁ ἀριθμὸς τῶν μαθητῶν ἐν Ἱερουσαλὴμ σφόδρα, πολύς τε ὄχλος τῶν ἱερέων ὑπήκουον τῇ πίστει. ⁸ ΣΤΕΦΑΝΟΣ δὲ πλήρης πίστεως καὶ δυνάμεως ἐποίει τέρατα καὶ σημεῖα μεγάλα ἐν τῷ λαῷ. ⁹ ἀνέστησαν δέ τινες τῶν ἐκ τῆς συναγωγῆς τῆς λεγομένης Λιβερτίνων, καὶ Κυρηναίων καὶ Ἀλεξανδρέων, καὶ τῶν ἀπὸ Κιλικίας καὶ Ἀσίας, συζητοῦντες τῷ Στεφάνῳ· ¹⁰ καὶ οὐκ ἴσχυον ἀντιστῆναι τῇ σοφίᾳ καὶ τῷ πνεύματι ᾧ ἐλάλει. ¹¹ τότε ὑπέβαλον ἄνδρας λέγοντας, Ὅτι ἀκη-

REVISED VERSION.

hands upon them. And the 7 word of God ˣwas increasing, and the number of the disciples in Jerusalem was being greatly multiplied, and a ʸgreat crowd of the priests ᶻwas becoming submissive to ˣˣthe faith. And Stephen, full 8 of faith and power, did great wonders and miracles among the people.

ᵃThen there arose certain of 9 the Synagogue—of that composed of the freedmen—Cyrenians and Alexandrians, and of those from Cilicia, and of Asia, putting questions to Stephen; and they were not able 10 to resist the wisdom and the ᵇspirit by which he spoke. And they ᶜprivately procured 11

---

of the person to God—and to some specific service—also accompanied with prayer, indicating that, as the hands were laid upon him, God would impart to him the grace and the spirit of that office. *Επεθηκαν αυτοις τας χειρας.*

ˣ *Ηυξανε,* imperfect active, *was increasing.* This imperfect form of the verb happily illustrates a continued progressing influence upon the community, which our indefinite past tense does not express.

ʸ *Πολυς τε οχλος.* This is a bold representation of a great crowd of the priests, and intimates a great excitement, a tumult, an uproar.

ᶻ *Υπακουω* indicates a submissive hearing, especially in New Testament usage, but with a dative in the imperfect it means were becoming submissive, and clearly indicates the progress of the reformation of the priests.

ˣˣ "The faith"—here indicative of the Evangelical system. *Τη πιστει.*

ᵃ Then there arose certain persons of the Synagogue that is called Libertines, and Cyrenians, and Alexandrians, and of those from Cilicia and Asia, disputing with Stephen, and they were not able to resist the wisdom and the spirit by which he spoke. This is an awkward sentence grammatically contemplated, yet of easy interpretation. In his mind, he is about to say, "certain of the Libertines" (*των λιβερτινων*), *of the Freedmen,* but in the act of writing this, he throws in as explanatory (*εκ της συναγωγης της λεγομενης*) out of the Synagogue, that being called *the Libertines.* Still the sense is clear:—Then certain of the Synagogue, that being composed of freedmen, *της λεγομενης* (part. pr. pass. of *λεγω*), *to lay, to arrange together,* or, as we say of a discourse, *to compose.* The participle is also in the Gen. *Putting questions to*

Stephen is both better grammar and sense than disputing with Stephen, and is in harmony with the most radical meaning of *συζητεω, mutuo quæro,* alterior discepto. See Critica Sacra on this passage under *συζητεω, συζητειν, non solum significatum altero de re aliqua disquirere,* Acts 6 : 9, and 9 : 29. *Sed etiam rei alicujus novitate perculsum alterum interpellare,* Mark 1 : 27, and 9 : 16.

Λιβερτινων, denotes a class of Freedmen, both Cyrenians and Alexandrians. Critics have much debated this name, each with seeming probability, but without much assurance.— These *Freedmen,* if we so call them, being Jews, had their own language at Jerusalem. Had these three been distinct classes, regular usage would have called for *των,* before each of them. Pierce contends that they were inhabitants of a city, or district of Lybia, called Libertina. Quite probable, (Boothroyd), could we find such a place.

ᵇ *Ω ελαλει.* This being the dative of the cause, or instrument, or we must assign this defense to the immediate inspiration of the Holy Spirit. Hence the impregnability of his defense.

ᶜ *Υπεβαλον,* they suborned. We have been at considerable pains in tracing, in Greek literature, sacred and profane, the current acceptation of *υποβαλλω* to save these Jewish infidels from the imputation of bribery and murder. But it has been a fruitless effort. *Υποβαλλω* is to suborn, to hire or employ men to falsify, to swear a man's life away for a paltry reward. Subjicio and suborno are its whole area. To *suborn* is simply to put on a lie of any sort for a reward of any sort. It is found but this once in the Christian Scriptures. Stephen died for the truth through the falsehood and bribery of a corrupt priesthood.

KING JAMES' VERSION.

which said, We have heard him speak blasphemous words against Moses, and *against* God.

12 And they stirred up the people, and the elders, and the scribes, and came upon *him*, and caught him, and brought *him* to the council.

13 And set up false witnesses, which said, This man ceaseth not to speak blasphemous words against this holy place, and the law:

14 For we have heard him say, that this Jesus of Nazareth shall destroy this place, and shall change the customs which Moses delivered us.

15 And all that sat in the council, looking steadfastly on him, saw his face as it had been the face of an angel.

CHAP. VII.

THEN said the high priest, Are these things so?

2 And he said, Men, brethren, and fathers, hearken; The God

GREEK TEXT.

κόαμεν αὐτοῦ λαλοῦντος ῥήματα βλάσφημα εἰς Μωσῆν καὶ τὸν Θεόν. ¹² Συνεκίνησάν τε τὸν λαὸν καὶ τοὺς πρεσβυτέρους καὶ τοὺς γραμματεῖς, καὶ ἐπιστάντες συνήρπασαν αὐτὸν, καὶ ἤγαγον εἰς τὸ συνέδριον, ¹³ ἔστησάν τε μάρτυρας ψευδεῖς λέγοντας, Ὁ ἄνθρωπος οὗτος οὐ παύεται ῥήματα βλάσφημα λαλῶν κατὰ τοῦ τόπου τοῦ ἁγίου τούτου καὶ τοῦ νόμου. ¹⁴ ἀκηκόαμεν γὰρ αὐτοῦ λέγοντος, Ὅτι Ἰησοῦς ὁ Ναζωραῖος οὗτος καταλύσει τὸν τόπον τοῦτον, καὶ ἀλλάξει τὰ ἔθη ἃ παρέδωκεν ἡμῖν Μωϋσῆς. ¹⁵ Καὶ ἀτενίσαντες εἰς αὐτὸν ἅπαντες οἱ καθεζόμενοι ἐν τῷ συνεδρίῳ, εἶδον τὸ πρόσωπον αὐτοῦ ὡσεὶ πρόσωπον ἀγγέλου.

CHAP. VII.

Εἶπε δὲ ὁ ἀρχιερεύς, Εἰ ἄρα ταῦτα οὕτως ἔχει; ² Ὁ δὲ ἔφη, Ἄνδρες ἀδελφοὶ καὶ πατέρες,

REVISED VERSION.

men who said, We have heard him speaking reviling words against Moses and against God. And they ᵉex- 12 cited the people, and the elders, and the scribes, and came upon him, and seized, and brought him to the coun- cil, and set up false witnesses, 13 saying, This man ceases not to speak ᵈwords against this holy place, and the law: for ᶠwe 14 have heard him saying, that this Jesus, the Nazarene, will destroy this place, and change the customs which Moses de- livered us. And all ᵍwho sat in 15 the council, looking steadfastly on him, saw his face, as if it had been the face of an angel.

CHAP. VII.

THEN the ʰHigh Priest said, 1 Are these things so? And he 2 said, ⁱBrethren and fathers,

---

Ὑπεβαλον, ὑποβαλλω, v. 13; subjicio, suppono, as well as *suborno.*—To suborn—to procure privately, or by collusion— to procure by any indirect means. The connection here would indicate, not so much that they were foresworn, as pri- vately furnished with answers or instructions.

ᵈ Βλασφημα, is of doubtful authority, and repudiated by Griesbach, Sch., Ln., and Tf.—The Vatican, Ephrem, Beza, and Alexandrian MSS., and the most ancient versions, know not the reading.

Βλασφημα, in this place, which is a pleonastic supplement of a later age! for λαλων ῥηματα κατα as the first two manu- scripts read, and ῥηματα λαλων κατα as the last two, express the sense of βλασφημα, Granville Penn, Esq. London, 1837. This is, more than probably, a justifiable view of this read- ing.

ᵉ In this case, *they stirred up the people,* is too gross. The people were commoved, or put into commotion: elders, priests, scribes, and people were commoved; and they seized and brought Stephen into the Sanhedrim. They caused false witnesses to stand up saying, in the most definite language, The man, *this one, οὗτος,* does not restrain himself (indicative

middle) *λεγων,* saying, or from speaking, or from uttering slanders against τον τοπον τον ἁγιον τουτον, (most emphatic) *this, the consecrated place, and the law.*

ᶠ For we have heard *of him* ; no, but we have heard him saying, that this Jesus the Nazarene will demolish, καταλυσει τον τοπον τουτον, και αλλαξει τα εθη, will change the customs which Moses παρεδωκεν, gave over, ἡμιν, to us.

ᵍ And all these, καθεζομενοι, seating themselves in the Sanhedrim, ατενισαντες, *fixing their eyes* upon him, saw his face, ὡσει, used here in comparison, like the face of an angel.

ʰ Then the High Priest said—Then the Chief Priest said Some prefer the latter, some the former. Ὁ αρχιερευς never means the Chief Priest. We have Chief *Priests* some sixty or more times in com. ver., High Priest, some fifty times. In the singular number, ὁ αρχιερευς always indicates *the High Priest;* the plural, *Chief Priests,* never includes him.

ⁱ There appear but two classes addressed here, not men, and brethren, and fathers. Ανδρες, qualifies both nouns, and therefore, being not a distinct class, we absorb it in brethren and fathers. With this concur Prof. Hack. "Brethren and

KING JAMES' VERSION.	GREEK TEXT.	REVISED VERSION.
of glory appeared unto our father Abraham when he was in Mesopotamia, before he dwelt in Charran,	ἀκούσατε. ὁ Θεὸς τῆς δόξης ὤφθη τῷ πατρὶ ἡμῶν Ἀβραὰμ ὄντι ἐν τῇ Μεσοποταμίᾳ, πρὶν ἢ κατοικῆσαι αὐτὸν ἐν Χαῤῥὰν,	hearken: The God of ʲthe glory appeared to our father Abraham, when he was in Mesopotamia, before he dwelt in ᵏHaran, and said to him, "Go 3
3 And said unto him, Get thee out of thy country, and from thy kindred, and come into the land which I shall shew thee.	³ καὶ εἶπε πρὸς αὐτὸν, Ἔξελθε ἐκ τῆς γῆς σου καὶ ἐκ τῆς συγγενείας σου, καὶ δεῦρο εἰς γῆν ἣν ἄν σοι δείξω. ⁴ Τότε ἐξελ-	forth out of your country, and from your kindred, and come into a country that I will show you." Then he came 4
4 Then came he out of the land of the Chaldeans, and dwelt in Charran. And from thence, when his father was dead, he removed him into this land wherein ye now dwell.	θὼν ἐκ γῆς Χαλδαίων, κατῴκη-σεν ἐν Χαῤῥάν· κἀκεῖθεν μετὰ τὸ ἀποθανεῖν τὸν πατέρα αὐτοῦ, μετῴκισεν αὐτὸν εἰς τὴν γῆν ταύτην εἰς ἣν ὑμεῖς νῦν κατοι-κεῖτε·	out of the ˡland of the Chaldeans and dwelt in Haran; and thence, ᵐafter his father was dead, God caused him to remove into this land, in which you are now dwelling: but he did not ⁿgive 5
5 And he gave him none inheritance in it, no, not so much as to set his foot on: yet he promised that he would give it to him for a possession, and to his seed after him, when as yet he had no child.	⁵ καὶ οὐκ ἔδωκεν αὐτῷ κληρονομίαν ἐν αὐτῇ, οὐδὲ βῆμα ποδός· καὶ ἐπηγγείλατο αὐτῷ δοῦναι εἰς κατάσχεσιν αὐτὴν, καὶ τῷ σπέρματι αὐτοῦ μετ᾽ αὐτὸν, οὐκ ὄντος αὐτῷ τέκνου.	him an inheritance in it, not even a foot breadth. Yet he promised that he would give it to him, for a possession, and to his seed after him, when, as yet, he had no child. Then 6
6 And God spake on this wise, That his seed should sojourn in a strange land; and that they	⁶ ἐλά-λησε δὲ οὕτως ὁ Θεὸς, Ὅτι ἔσται τὸ σπέρμα αὐτοῦ πάροικον ἐν γῇ	God spoke thus to him: That his seed should be sojourners in a strange land, and that they

Fathers," Booth.—Viri fratres et patres, Vulgate. So also the Italian, Spanish, and French. Biblia Sacra Polyglot. Dr. Lee; also Adam Clark in loco.

ʲ *The God of* (τῆς δόξης) *the glory.* We have ἡ βασιλεία, ἡ δυναμις, καὶ ἡ δοξα, in the Lord's prayer. In the Acts we have δοξα four times, twice in this chapter, once *with*, and once *without*, the article, v. 55. Again we have it ch. 12: 23, εδωκε την δοξαν τῳ Θεῳ, and ch. 22: 11, απο της δοξης του φωτος εκεινου. There is a specific glory indicated in some of these cases, but not in all. In the case before us we see no special reason for the article, before glory, unless allusion be made to the call of Abraham out of Ur of the Chaldees, where God first appeared to him, which glorious appearance gave to that place the name ουρ, or *our*, contracted *Ur*, which in Chaldee means *light*. In Hebrew and Chaldee אוּר signifies *light* and *fire*. It is, therefore, highly probable that, as on other occasions, *Bethel, Beersheba, Gershom, Eliezer*, etc., commemorate Divine manifestations and interpositions; so Stephen here may allude to the special manifestations of Jehovah to the people of Abraham, and, therefore, prefixes *the article*, or those who interpreted his speech did so allusively; at all events, we should here insert it as we find it in this significant scene.

Ὁ Θεος της δοξης, literally, *the God of the glory*—כָּבוֹד—the light, or the visible splendor, in which he appeared to the Fathers of Israel. The symbol of his presence. Bloomf., De W., ωφθη, seen by, or appeared to, Abraham.—Εν Χαῤῥαν,

Charran, com. ver. Haran. From this place Abraham was called to the promised land. Stephen, by this allusion, seems to endeavor to subdue prejudices, by associations familiar and agreeable to his audience.

In the same felicitous manner, v. 3, he emphasizes on his call, εκ της γης σου, and εκ της συγγενειας σου,—forsake your country and your kindred—just what the martyr Stephen and his associates were virtually doing, in joining themselves to the Christian party.—Εκ της γης, out of *the* country of their kindred; εις γην, into *a* country. The power of the article and of the want of it is well exhibited here, out of *the* into *a* country.

ᵏ Χαῤῥαν, now the resort of wandering Arabs, is a monumental name. It was *Haran*, in Mesopotamia, monumental of the son of Terah, father of Abraham, Nahor, and *Haran*.

ˡ Here there is no article before γη. Yet we allow it because this land is already defined and made definite. In this we differ from, and excel, the Greeks who had only one article.

ᵐ *After*, rather than *when*, his father was dead. Μετα with Acc. *post*, after.

ⁿ Ουκ εδωκεν αυτω κληρονομιαν εν αυτη, he gave him not an inheritance in it, ουδε βημα ποδος, not even *a foot breadth*. How precisely the sense is here given by the absence of the article.

KING JAMES' VERSION.	GREEK TEXT.	REVISED VERSION.

KING JAMES' VERSION.

should bring them into bondage, and entreat *them* evil four hundred years.

7 And the nation to whom they shall be in bondage will I judge, said God: and after that shall they come forth, and serve me in this place.

8 And he gave him the covenant of circumcision. And so *Abraham* begat Isaac, and circumcised him the eighth day; and Isaac *begat* Jacob, and Jacob *begat* the twelve patriarchs.

9 And the patriarchs, moved with envy, sold Joseph into Egypt: but God was with him,

10 And delivered him out of all his afflictions, and gave him

GREEK TEXT.

ἀλλοτρίᾳ, καὶ δουλώσουσιν αὐτὸ καὶ κακώσουσιν, ἔτη τετρακόσια. 7 καὶ τὸ ἔθνος, ᾧ ἐὰν δουλεύσωσι, κρινῶ ἐγώ, εἶπεν ὁ Θεός· καὶ μετὰ ταῦτα ἐξελεύσονται, καὶ λατρεύσουσί μοι ἐν τῷ τόπῳ τούτῳ. 8 Καὶ ἔδωκεν αὐτῷ διαθήκην περιτομῆς· καὶ οὕτως ἐγέννησε τὸν Ἰσαάκ, καὶ περιέτεμεν αὐτὸν τῇ ἡμέρᾳ τῇ ὀγδόῃ· καὶ ὁ Ἰσαὰκ τὸν Ἰακώβ, καὶ ὁ Ἰακὼβ τοὺς δώδεκα πατριάρχας. 9 καὶ οἱ πατριάρχαι ζηλώσαντες τὸν Ἰωσὴφ ἀπέδοντο εἰς Αἴγυπτον· καὶ ἦν ὁ Θεὸς μετ᾽ αὐτοῦ, 10 καὶ ἐξείλετο αὐτὸν ἐκ πασῶν τῶν θλίψεων αὐτοῦ, καὶ ἔδωκεν

REVISED VERSION.

should enslave, and oppress them °four hundred years. And 7 the nation to whom they shall be in bondage, I will ᵖpunish, ˙said God, and after this they shall come forth and ᵠserve me in this place. And God gave Abraham a 8 ʳcovenant of circumcision; and so ˙he begat Isaac, and circumcised him the eighth day. ᵗAnd Isaac begat Jacob, and Jacob begat the twelve patriarchs. And the patriarchs, ᵘmoved 9 with envy, sold Joseph into Egypt. But God was with him, and delivered him out of 10 all his afflictions, and gave

---

° "*Four hundred years.*" This is a round sum, rather than a precise one. Paul, in a chronological argument concerning the superiority, in point of antiquity, of the *Promise*, to the giving of the Law, makes that interval four hundred and thirty years (Gal. 3 : 17), beginning with the calling of Abraham, at the age of 75 years. This event antedated the giving of the law 430 years—the interval which Paul computes, between the first promise made to Abraham, concerning *the Seed*, in whom all the families of the earth should be blessed. The whole period of the sojourning of Abraham and his seed, from the first promise to him, at 75, till the Exodus, was 430 years ; 215 before their descent into Egypt, and 215 years in it.—The covenant of the promised seed antedates the covenant of circumcision, consummated on the birth of Isaac, twenty-five years.

The sum of four hundred and thirty is computed as follows : From the promise to the birth of Isaac, 25 years. From the birth of Isaac to that of Jacob, 60 years, Gen. 25 : 26 ; Jacob was 130 years old, when he went down into Egypt. These added, give 215 years. And just as long time his children dwelt in Egypt, Gal. 3 : 17.—See Dr. Whitby, Dr. Adam Clark in loco.

ᵖ Κρινω εγω. Κρινω is represented by " *sue at law*," judge, *ordain, esteem, determine, condemn, decree, damn, avenge, punish.*

ᵠ Λατρευσουσι. Λατρευω, represented by *serve, seventeen* times ; *four* times by *worship*, com. ver. *Serve* is *generic, worship* is *specific* ; and, therefore, in this case we prefer the *genus* to the species, inasmuch as the Jews' religion was rather a fleshly service than a spiritual worship. They served

in the oldness of the letter, but Christians worship and serve God in newness of *spirit* and in *truth*, and not in the oldness of the letter.

ʳ Διαθηκην περιτομης, he gave him *a covenant* of circum cision, an institution of circumcision. Διαθηκη occurs 33 times in N. T., represented by *testament* 13 times. It properly indicates an *institution*, not a *testament*, only in the case of a *testator*. Generically, any institution proposed by one party. Συνθηκη with the Greeks indicated a *covenant* or contract between two parties, equal or confederate. But a διαθηκη is, or may be, absolute, and enacted by one party in power, to which submission and acquiescence may be due from another party. Such are all Divine institutions.

ˢ Οὑτως εγεννησε τον Ισαακ, και περιετεμεν. The οὑτως here has respect to the circumcising, as the context indicates, and yet it is not in our idiom so historically direct as we could wish. But, the point being so well understood by the Jews, he proceeds with the genealogy and not with the details of circumcision, which everybody understood.

ᵗ Και ὁ Ισαακ τον Ιακωβ. This is preceded by εγεννησε τον Ισαακ. Here, as in other cases, we have the article, to give eminence or special conspicuity, as in the same verse τους δωδεκα πατριαρχας—the twelve patriarchs—presuming that they were notorious persons.

ᵘ Ζηλωσαντες. Ζηλοω is used in four acceptations in the Christian Scriptures. It indicates simple *desire* and zeal. It is taken in *bonam partem* and in *malam partem*. I am jealous, I am zealous, I desire, I covet. " *Covet*," says Paul, " the best gifts," not for your own sake, but for the sake of others. Here it is taken in a bad sense, *in malam partem*, the patriarchs were moved with envy.

favour and wisdom in the sight of Pharaoh king of Egypt; and he made him governor over Egypt, and all his house.

11 Now there came a dearth over all the land of Egypt and Chanaan, and great affliction; and our fathers found no sustenance.

12 But when Jacob heard that there was corn in Egypt, he sent out our fathers first.

13 And at the second *time* Joseph was made known to his brethren : and Joseph's kindred was made known unto Pharaoh.

14 Then sent Joseph, and called his father Jacob to *him,* and all his kindred, three score and fifteen souls.

15 So Jacob went down into Egypt, and died, he, and our fathers,

16 And were carried over into Sychem, and laid in the sepulchre that Abraham bought for a sum of money of the sons of Emmor, *the father* of Sychem.

αὐτῷ χάριν καὶ σοφίαν ἐναντίον Φαραὼ βασιλέως Αἰγύπτου, καὶ κατέστησεν αὐτὸν ἡγούμενον ἐπ' Αἴγυπτον καὶ ὅλον τὸν οἶκον αὐτοῦ. 11 ἦλθε δὲ λιμὸς ἐφ' ὅλην τὴν γῆν Αἰγύπτου καὶ Χαναὰν, καὶ θλίψις μεγάλη· καὶ οὐχ εὕρισκον χορτάσματα οἱ πατέρες ἡμῶν. 12 ἀκούσας δὲ Ἰακὼβ ὄντα σῖτα ἐν Αἰγύπτῳ, ἐξαπέστειλε τοὺς πατέρας ἡμῶν πρῶτον. 13 καὶ ἐν τῷ δευτέρῳ ἀνεγνωρίσθη Ἰωσὴφ τοῖς ἀδελφοῖς αὐτοῦ, καὶ φανερὸν ἐγένετο τῷ Φαραὼ τὸ γένος τοῦ Ἰωσήφ. 14 ἀποστείλας δὲ Ἰωσὴφ μετεκαλέσατο τὸν πατέρα αὐτοῦ Ἰακὼβ, καὶ πᾶσαν τὴν συγγένειαν αὐτοῦ, ἐν ψυχαῖς ἑβδομηκονταπέντε. 15 κατέβη δὲ Ἰακὼβ εἰς Αἴγυπτον, καὶ ἐτελεύτησεν αὐτὸς καὶ οἱ πατέρες ἡμῶν· 16 καὶ μετετέθησαν εἰς Συχέμ, καὶ ἐτέθησαν ἐν τῷ μνήματι ὃ ὠνήσατο Ἀβραὰμ τιμῆς ἀργυρίου, παρὰ τῶν υἱῶν Ἐμμὸρ τοῦ Συχέμ.

him ᵛfavor and wisdom in the sight of Pharaoh, king of Egypt: and he made him governor over Egypt, and all his household.

Now there came a ʷfamine 11 upon all the land of Egypt and Canaan, and great affliction: and our fathers found no sustenance. But Jacob, 12 ˣhaving heard that there was ʸgrain in Egypt, ᶻfirst sent our fathers. And at the second 13 time, Joseph was ᵃmade known to his brethren ; and Joseph's kindred ᵇbecame well known to Pharaoh.

Then Joseph sent and 14 called his father Jacob to him ; and all ᶜhis kindred, ᵈseventy-five souls. So Jacob 15 went down into Egypt, and died, he and our fathers, and 16 were carried over into Shechem, and laid in a sepulchre—that which Abraham ᶠpurchased with a sum of money of Hamor, *father* of

---

ᵛ God gave to Joseph χαριν και σοφιαν—both anarthrous. But not *a* favor and *a* wisdom—this would have been only a special case. But it is unlimited, like Πνευμα Ἁγιον, not merely indefinite, but abstract or absolute, as the case may be. Like *grace,* or *favor,* it may be absolute and without measure, or it may be, in certain circumstances, a special grace, favor, or gift. It is, therefore, not *a* favor and *a* wisdom, nor *the* favor and *the* wisdom, but, superior to both, and more honorable, undefined favor and wisdom in the presence of Pharaoh, the king of Egypt.

ʷ Λιμος—θλιψις μεγαλη και ουχ χορτασματα—all indefinite, —famine, tribulation, no sustenance.

ˣ Ακουσας, part. aor., having heard, but quite as truthful and as tasteful, *when Jacob heard.*

ʸ Σιτος, fourteen times found in N. T., twelve times rendered *wheat,* twice *corn,* com. ver. *Frumentum* is its most general sense, *triticum,* often. *Grain* is a generic term, including all sorts, therefore preferable here.

ᶻ Πρωτον, adverb, *first, first time.* Εξαπεστειλε, they were literally his *apostles,* in quest of food.

ᵃ Ανεγνωρισθη—αναγνωριζομαι. This is an ἅπαξ λεγομενον, found only in this place in N. T. Joseph was made known, or revealed to his brethren. We need not pleonastically say he was again made known, but simply made known, never before having been made known.

ᵇ Φανερον το γενος, his kindred became well-known.

ᶜ Αυτου—omitted by Gb., Sch., Ln., Tf.—fairly, however, implied.

ᵈ These *"seventy-five souls"* must include the five sons of Ephraim and Manasseh—and probably other descendants of Joseph, to sustain the reading adopted; of which, however, we have never seen a wholly satisfactory vindication. We follow the text of Bagster. Πεντε is of doubtful authority.

ᵉ Ὁ ωνησατο—τιμης αργυριου, purchased with a sum of money, an estimate of silver. Παρα, *beside* of the sons of Hamor. Του Συχεμ—του εν Συχεμ, rejected by Ln.

ᶠ Παρα των υἱων Εμμορ του Συχεμ, near to. Dr. Clark's correction of the text here is plausible. Whether the purchase here mentioned was made by *Abraham* or by *Jacob* is litigated on manuscript authority. But as manuscripts are still

KING JAMES' VERSION.	GREEK TEXT.	REVISED VERSION.
17 But when the time of the promise drew nigh, which God had sworn to Abraham, the people grew and multiplied in Egypt,	¹⁷ Καθὼς δὲ ἤγγιζεν ὁ χρόνος τῆς ἐπαγγελίας ἧς ὤμοσεν ὁ Θεὸς τῷ Ἀβραὰμ, ηὔξησεν ὁ λαὸς καὶ ἐπληθύνθη ἐν Αἰγύπτῳ, ¹⁸ ἄχρις οὗ ἀνέστη βασιλεὺς ἕτερος, ὃς οὐκ ᾔδει τὸν Ἰωσήφ. ¹⁹ οὗτος κατασοφισάμενος τὸ γένος ἡμῶν, ἐκάκωσε τοὺς πατέρας ἡμῶν, τοῦ ποιεῖν ἔκθετα τὰ βρέφη αὐτῶν, εἰς τὸ μὴ ζωογονεῖσθαι. ²⁰ Ἐν ᾧ καιρῷ ἐγεννήθη Μωσῆς, καὶ ἦν ἀστεῖος τῷ Θεῷ· ὃς ἀνετράφη μῆνας τρεῖς ἐν τῷ οἴκῳ τοῦ πατρὸς αὐτοῦ. ²¹ ἐκτεθέντα δὲ αὐτὸν, ἀνείλετο αὐτὸν ἡ θυγάτηρ Φαραὼ, καὶ ἀνεθρέψατο αὐτὸν	Shechem. ᵍBut, according as the time of the promise, which God has sworn to Abraham, was drawing near, the people had grown and multiplied in Egypt, ʰtill another king arose, who had not known Joseph. ⁱThe same ʲhaving treated our race craftily, oppressed our fathers, that they might expose their ᵏinfants, in order that they might not be preserved alive. At this time Moses was born, and was ˡexceedingly beautiful; who was nourished in his father's house, three months. And, he being exposed, Pharaoh's daughter ᵐadopted him, and ⁿnourished him for her own
18 Till another king arose, which knew not Joseph.		17
19 The same dealt subtilly with our kindred, and evil-entreated our fathers, so that they cast out their young children, to the end they might not live.		18
20 In which time Moses was born, and was exceeding fair, and nourished up in his father's house three months:		19
21 And when he was cast out, Pharaoh's daughter took him up, and nourished him for her own son.		20
		21

accumulating we shall not enter into the merits of the question, on which there is not an element of faith or piety depending.

It is not a historic fact, that Abraham bought this field, or plot of ground.—This discrepancy is happily corrected by Adam Clark. His critical note on the passage we shall here quote in full.

"Two accounts seem here to be confounded. 1st. The purchase made by Abraham of the cave and field of Ephron, which was in the field of Machpelah; this purchase was made from the children of Heth, Gen. 23 : 3, 10, 17. 2nd. The purchase made by Jacob, from the sons of Hamor, or Emmor, of a sepulchre, in which the bones of Joseph were laid; this was in Sychem, or Shechem, Gen. 33 : 19; Josh. 14 : 32. The word Abraham, therefore, in this place, is certainly a mistake; and the word Jacob, which some have supplied, is, doubtless, more proper. Bp. Pearce supposes that Luke originally wrote, ὁ ὠνήσατο τιμῆς ἀργυρίου, which he bought for a sum of money; that is, which Jacob bought, who is the last person of the singular number spoken of in the preceding verse. Those who saw that the word ὠνήσατο, bought, had no nominative case joined to it, and did not know where to find the proper one, seem to have inserted Ἀβρααμ, Abraham, in the text, for that purpose, without sufficiently attending to the different circumstances of his purchase, from that of Jacob."—Acts 7 : 16.

Some think that Dr. Clark is not sufficient authority for correcting the text, against the authority of so many manuscripts. Some of which read "our father," without any proper name. But the Syriac—the oldest translation—retains the name Abraham. Murdock's Syriac reads it, "which Abraham bought with money of the sons of Emmor." And as we

have not all the ancient manuscripts, we shall retain this till we find some more plausible authority for repudiating it.

ᵍ But (καθως) according to the time of the promise which God (ὡμολογησεν, Ln., Tf., on the authority of A.B.C. vul. 15, 36, so Alf.) openly declared.

ʰ Αχρις ου ανεστη βασιλευς ἑτερος. Ln. and some others add επ Αιγυπτον, in Egypt.

ⁱ Οὑτος, this king, v. 18.

ʲ Κατασοφισαμενος το γενος ἡμων, having craftily treated. Ingeniosus adversus aliquem, Acts 7 : 19, Critica Sacra. It is worthy of notice, that this is the identical word found in the Septuagint, Exodus 1 : 10, as expressive of the wicked subtilty practiced upon the Israelites by the Egyptian despotism, well defined, "Sophismatis, et argutis fallaciis utor adversus aliquem, quasi falsis et sophisticis rationibus et cavillationibus redarguens. LXX. Interpretes utuntur hoc verbo. Ex. 1 : 10—Dealt subtilely, Penn. Mischievously politic, Thom. Unjustly, Wak., Wes. Craftily, Murd.

ᵏ Του ποιειν εκθετα τα βρεφη αυτων, by casting out, or exposing their babes that they might not live.

ˡ Και ην αστειος τω Θεω. He was exceeding beautiful, beautiful to God. The Hebrews, to express the superlative degree, were sometimes accustomed to add to their nouns the word God. Hence we read in Hebrew of "the cedars of God," "the mountains of God," indicative of lofty mountains and towering cedars. Moses then was beautiful to God, that is, superlatively beautiful. Πολις μεγαλη τω Θεω, Jonas 3 : 3, Sept., the same form of the Hebrew superlative.—Hack.

ᵐ Ανειλετο, not from the water, but tollere liberos, adopted.

ⁿ Ανεθρεψατο αυτον ἑαυτη εις υιον, nourished him; εις, in order to, or for a son to herself, for her own son. Αυτον with the participle is not an accusative absolute.

KING JAMES' VERSION.

GREEK TEXT.

REVISED VERSION.

22 And Moses was learned in all the wisdom of the Egyptians, and was mighty in words and in deeds.

23 And when he was full forty years old, it came into his heart to visit his brethren the children of Israel.

24 And seeing one *of them* suffer wrong, he defended *him*, and avenged him that was oppressed, and smote the Egyptian:

25 For he supposed his brethren would have understood how that God by his hand would deliver them: but they understood not.

26 And the next day he shewed himself unto them as they strove, and would have set them at one again, saying, Sirs, ye are brethren; why do ye wrong one to another?

27 But he that did his neighbour wrong, thrust him away, saying, Who made thee a ruler and a judge over us?

28 Wilt thou kill me, as thou didst the Egyptian yesterday?

29 Then fled Moses at this saying, and was a stranger in the land of Madian, where he begat two sons.

30 And when forty years were

ἑαυτῇ εἰς υἱόν. ²² καὶ ἐπαιδεύθη Μωσῆς πάσῃ σοφίᾳ Αἰγυπτίων· ἦν δὲ δυνατὸς ἐν λόγοις καὶ ἐν ἔργοις. ²³ Ὡς δὲ ἐπληροῦτο αὐτῷ τεσσαρακονταετὴς χρόνος, ἀνέβη ἐπὶ τὴν καρδίαν αὐτοῦ ἐπισκέψασθαι τοὺς ἀδελφοὺς αὐτοῦ τοὺς υἱοὺς Ἰσραήλ. ²⁴ καὶ ἰδών τινα ἀδικούμενον, ἠμύνατο καὶ ἐποίησεν ἐκδίκησιν τῷ καταπονουμένῳ, πατάξας τὸν Αἰγύπτιον. ²⁵ ἐνόμιζε δὲ συνιέναι τοὺς ἀδελφοὺς αὐτοῦ, ὅτι ὁ Θεὸς διὰ χειρὸς αὐτοῦ δίδωσιν αὐτοῖς σωτηρίαν· οἱ δὲ οὐ συνῆκαν. ²⁶ τῇ τε ἐπιούσῃ ἡμέρᾳ ὤφθη αὐτοῖς μαχομένοις, καὶ συνήλασεν αὐτοὺς εἰς εἰρήνην, εἰπών, Ἄνδρες, ἀδελφοί ἐστε ὑμεῖς· ἱνατί ἀδικεῖτε ἀλλήλους; ²⁷ Ὁ δὲ ἀδικῶν τὸν πλησίον, ἀπώσατο αὐτόν, εἰπών, Τίς σε κατέστησεν ἄρχοντα καὶ δικαστὴν ἐφ᾽ ἡμᾶς; ²⁸ μὴ ἀνελεῖν με σὺ θέλεις, ὃν τρόπον ἀνεῖλες χθὲς τὸν Αἰγύπτιον; ²⁹ Ἔφυγε δὲ Μωσῆς ἐν τῷ λόγῳ τούτῳ, καὶ ἐγένετο πάροικος ἐν γῇ Μαδιάμ, οὗ ἐγέννησεν υἱοὺς δύο. ³⁰ Καὶ πληρω-

son. And Moses was °educated 22 in all the wisdom of the Egyptians, and was ᴾmighty in his words and in ᑫhis actions.

And when he was full forty 23 years old, it came into his heart to look after his brethren, the children of Israel. And see- 24 ing one of them ʳwronged, he defended him, and avenged him who was oppressed, smiting the Egyptian. He 25 supposed, ˢindeed, his brethren would have understood that God, by his hand, would deliver them: but they did not understand. And the next 26 day, he ᵗshowed himself to them as they were quarreling, and would have ᵘcompelled them to peace, saying, You are brethren; why do you wrong one another? But he 27 who did his neighbor wrong, thrust him away, saying, Who made you a ruler and a judge over us? Will you kill me, as 28 you killed the Egyptian yesterday? Then Moses fled ᵛat this 29 saying, and was a stranger in ʷthe land of Midian, in which he begot two sons. And when 30

° Ἐπαιδεύθη πάσῃ σοφίᾳ, dative, not of the instrument, but of the *manner*. De Wette, Win., and some others, render it, *by the* wisdom of the Egyptians, as the instrument of his culture. "The accusative would be the ordinary case after this passive."—*Hack.*

ᴾ Δυνατὸς ἐν λόγοις, not so fluent as Aaron, but above him in strength, as his speeches fully attest.

ᑫ Αὐτοῦ should be added to ἐν λόγοις καὶ ἔργοις.—Gb., Sch., Ln., Tf. It is more definitive, and seems to be demanded.

ʳ Ἀδικούμενον, injured by violence, Ex. 2 : 11. Ἐποίησεν ἐκδίκησιν, avenged the wrong, or *wrought redress*. Πατάξας τὸν Αἰγύπτιον, smiting, killing the Egyptian.

ˢ Δὲ is frequently, in Luke's style, very elegantly rendered, *indeed*—*vero*, which in such cases as this, we conceive is in better taste than autem, *igitur, sed, tamen, quin,* or *porro.*

ᵗ Ὤφθη αὐτοῖς, showed himself, appeared—to them—two

of his countrymen. After ἐστε—ὑμεῖς is redundant. Ἱνατί, usually rendered *why*, is an abbreviation of three words, ἵνα τι γένηται, in order to what should it be = *why?*

ᵘ Συνήλασεν, drew together, compelled—would have compelled them to peace, as the sequel shows, but failed, through the acerbity of their temper. Only found in this passage N. T. Not by violence but by argument.

ᵛ Ἐν τῷ λόγῳ τούτῳ. This is superlatively definite, because it became a pregnant fact in his future history. Exodus 2 : 12. Pharaoh now sought his life.

ʷ Ἐν γῇ Μαδιάμ, in the land of Midian, or rather Madiam. It is common to omit the article before γῇ, "when any adjective or adjunct is connected immediately with it," just as in the case of Πνεῦμα, with Ἅγιον. Cases of special import not requiring it, the adjective itself being definitive. See v. 36; 13 : 19, ἐν γῇ Χαναάν.

KING JAMES' VERSION.	GREEK TEXT.	REVISED VERSION.
expired, there appeared to him in the wilderness of mount Sina, an angel of the Lord in a flame of fire in a bush. 31 When Moses saw *it*, he wondered at the sight; and as he drew near to behold *it*, the voice of the Lord came unto him, 32 *Saying*, I *am* the God of thy fathers, the God of Abraham, and the God of Isaac, and the God of Jacob. Then Moses trembled, and durst not behold. 33 Then said the Lord to him, Put off thy shoes from thy feet: for the place where thou standest is holy ground. 34 I have seen, I have seen	θέντων ἐτῶν τεσσαράκοντα, ὤφθη αὐτῷ ἐν τῇ ἐρήμῳ τοῦ ὄρους Σινᾶ ἄγγελος κυρίου ἐν φλογὶ πυρὸς βάτου. ³¹ ὁ δὲ Μωσῆς ἰδὼν ἐθαύμασε τὸ ὅραμα· προσερχομένου δὲ αὐτοῦ κατανοῆσαι, ἐγένετο φονὴ κυρίου πρὸς αὐτὸν, ³² Ἐγὼ ὁ Θεὸς τῶν πατέρων σου, ὁ Θεὸς Ἀβραὰμ καὶ ὁ Θεὸς Ἰσαὰκ καὶ ὁ Θεὸς Ἰακώβ. Ἔντρομος δὲ γενόμενος Μωσῆς οὐκ ἐτόλμα κατανοῆσαι. ³³ εἶπε δὲ αὐτῷ ὁ κύριος, Λῦσον τὸ ὑπόδημα τῶν ποδῶν σου· ὁ γὰρ τόπυς ἐν ᾧ ἕστηκας, γῆ ἁγία ἐστίν. ³⁴ ἰδὼν εἶδον τὴν κάκω-	forty years were expired, there appeared to him, in the wilderness of the mountain, Sinai, a ˣmessenger of the Lord, ʸin a flame of fire in a bush. And when 31 Moses saw it he wondered at the sight; and, as he drew near to ᶻcontemplate it, the voice of the Lord came ᵃto him, saying, I am the God of your fathers, 32 the God of Abraham, and the God of Isaac, and the God of Jacob. Then Moses trembled and durst not look. Then 33 the Lord said to him, Put off your ᵇshoes from your feet, for the place on which you stand is ᶜholy ground. ᵈTruly I have 34

ˣ "An angel of the Lord." Rather in this case, *a messenger* of the Lord. There does not appear to have been an angel here; for the Lord himself was here and spoke to Moses, in his own person. The supernatural fire was, in this case, a messenger of the Lord, to indicate his own presence. We are elsewhere told "He maketh the *winds* his angels, and a *flame of fire* his minister." Paul to the Hebrews, founds an argument in favor of the supreme Divinity of the Lord Messiah, on the name given to him, in contrast with that given to the higest rank of created spirits.

The Jews said the law was given by *angels*, and gloried in it. But says Paul, he gives this title and style to the *winds* and *lightnings* of heaven. But to the Son he saith: "Thy throne, O God, is for ever and ever, etc.—God thy God has *christed*—anointed thee *with the oil of joy*" above all coördinate functionaries. This beautiful and triumphant argument of the supreme Deity of the Lord Jesus is measurably lost in the com. ver. We, therefore, prefer to *translate angel* by *messenger*, especially when an argument depends upon it. All missionaries, whether spiritual or material, are properly styled angels. But all angels are not properly styled spirits.

It would seem expedient, in all such cases, either to transfer the word *angel*, or uniformly translate it *messenger*. And so of the words απστολος, διακονος, ευαγγελιστης, πρεσβυτερος, επισκοπος, Apostle, Deacon, Evangelist, Presbyter, Bishop. This class of words has a currency and a sense in the Apostolic writings, which they have not in their mere etymology. It is rather Hebraistic than Grecian, and can be ascertained only through a very strict analysis of New Testament usage. They ought all to

have been appositely translated or transferred in their original form. There is, however, no controversy as to their meaning.

ʸ Εν φογι πυρος βατου. Πυρος here supplies the place of an adjective, *in the fiery flame of a bush.* Comp. 9 : 15 ; 2 Thess. 1 : 8.

ᶻ Κατανοησαι, not to *behold*, nor to *observe* a *vision* (a rare work, indeed !) but to contemplate, to consider, *animadvert :* not in its present appropriated acceptation, but in its original etymological sense, *to turn the mind* to an object or subject. We find it well defined by an old critic long laid on the shelf. Non est, simpliciter *intelligere, inspicere, sed magno studio* mentem in rem intendere.—*Pareus on Hebrews 3 : l. Crit. Sacr.*

ᵃ Προς αυτον omitted by Ln., Tf., a probable omission with Griesb. Ὁ Θεος before Ισαακ and before Ιακωβ omitted by Ln. and Tf. The God of Abraham, Isaac, and Jacob is equipollent.

ᵇ Ὑποδημα, a distributive singular for the plural.—*Hackett.*

ᶜ Γη αγια εστιν, comparatively few of the Christian profession realize the full force of this family—Ἁγιος, ἁγιοτης, ἁγιωσυνη, ἁγιαζω, etc. Its root etymological is simply ἁγη, a negative or privative of γη, earth. We are aware that some derive it from αζω, colo, veneor, I *worship*, I *venerate ;* and a few from ἁγος, veneratio, a word of two very diverse significations—*in bonam et malam cadit significationem.* קדש, Kodesh, non rem sanctam, neque sanctitatur, sed Sanctuarium sive locum sanctum *significat,* Ps. 110 : 3 (ut Ps. 20 : 3, et 63 : 3) non quidem *Templum* sed vel urbem Hierosolyma, uti Kimchius voluit, vel potius arcem Sionis, Bootius Animadversiones. Sac. Lib. 2. Leigh, Holiness to the Lord, Separation to the Lord, is the radix, the tap-root of this tree of life everlasting.

ᵈ Ιδων ειδον = רָאֹה רָאִיתִי, truly I have seen. An infinitive absolute before a finite verb indicates the reality of an

KING JAMES' VERSION.	GREEK TEXT.	REVISED VERSION.
the affliction of my people which is in Egypt, and I have heard their groaning, and am come down to deliver them. And now come, I will send thee into Egypt. 35 This Moses, whom they refused, saying, Who made thee a ruler and a judge? the same did God send *to be* a ruler and a deliverer by the hand of the angel which appeared to him in the bush. 36 He brought them out, after that he had shewed wonders and signs in the land of Egypt, and in the Red sea, and in the wilderness forty years. 37 This is that Moses, which said unto the children of Israel, A prophet shall the Lord your God raise up unto you of your brethren, like unto me; him shall ye hear. 38 This is he, that was in the church in the wilderness with	σιν τοῦ λαοῦ μου τοῦ ἐν Αἰγύπτῳ, καὶ τοῦ στεναγμοῦ αὐτῶν ἤκουσα· καὶ κατέβην ἐξελέσθαι αὐτούς· καὶ νῦν δεῦρο, ἀποστελῶ σε εἰς Αἴγυπτον. ³⁵ Τοῦτον τὸν Μωϋσῆν ὃν ἠρνήσαντο εἰπόντες, Τίς σε κατέστησεν ἄρχοντα καὶ δικαστήν; τοῦτον ὁ Θεὸς ἄρχοντα καὶ λυτρωτὴν ἀπέστειλεν ἐν χειρὶ ἀγγέλου τοῦ ὀφθέντος αὐτῷ ἐν τῇ βάτῳ. ³⁶ οὗτος ἐξήγαγεν αὐτούς, ποιήσας τέρατα καὶ σημεῖα ἐν γῇ Αἰγύπτου καὶ ἐν ἐρυθρᾷ θαλάσσῃ, καὶ ἐν τῇ ἐρήμῳ ἔτη τεσσαράκοντα. ³⁷ Οὗτός ἐστιν ὁ Μωϋσῆς ὁ εἰπὼν τοῖς υἱοῖς Ἰσραὴλ, Προφήτην ὑμῖν ἀναστήσει κύριος ὁ Θεὸς ὑμῶν ἐκ τῶν ἀδελφῶν ὑμῶν ὡς ἐμέ· αὐτοῦ ἀκούσεσθε. ³⁸ Οὗτός ἐστιν ὁ γενόμενος ἐν τῇ ἐκκλησίᾳ ἐν	seen the affliction of my people, who are in Egypt, and have heard their groaning, and am come down to deliver them. And now, come, I will send you into Egypt. This Moses, whom 35 they had rejected, saying, Who made you a ruler and a judge? God sent ᵉthe same to be a ruler and a deliverer, by the hand of the messenger that appeared to him in the bush. He 36 brought them out, after showing wonders and signs, in the ᶠland of Egypt, and in the Red Sea, and in the wilderness, forty years. This is the Moses 37 who said to the children of Israel, The Lord your God will raise up a prophet for you, of your brethren, as he raised me up; you shall hear ᵍhim. This 38 is he who was in the ʰcongregation in the wilderness, with

act, or an effect of it in the highest degree. See Gesenius, Heb. Gram., § 128, 3. Some prefer ἀποστειλω to ἀποστελλω. The subjunctive could be used as future (W. § 42, 4), adopted probably from the Sept.—*Hackett.*

ᵉ Τουτον is here emphatic. Ηρνησαντο, one person's act, is here representative of the nation v. 27, τις σε κατεστησαν αρχοντα etc., who constituted you a captain *over us?*

Αρχοντα και δικαστην=λυτρωτην, they renounced Moses as a *Ruler* and a *Judge,* yet God constituted him their *Ruler* and *Redeemer;* and that, too, by the hand of an angel. Του οφθεντος, the one who *was seen by him,* or who appeared to him, in the unconsumed burning bush.

ᶠ Εν γη Αιγυπτου και εν ερυθρα θαλασση, not in a land of Egypt, nor in a Red Sea; for although anarthrous in form they are definite in the grammatical fact, that *adjectives* and *definitive* circumstances, dispense with the proper or peculiar use of the article. This further illustrates and confirms the fact that Πνευμα Άγιον is not grammatically *a* Holy Spirit, any more than γη Αιγυπτου is, grammatically, *a land* of Egypt.

ᵍ Αυτου ακουσεσθε is repudiated from the text by Gb., Sch., Ln., Tf., and so is κυριος and ὑμων by Gb.

ʰ This is a very definite verse. Ουτος εστιν ὁ γενομενος— τη εκκλησια—τη ερημω=του αγγελου—του λαλουντος, εν τω ορει=των πατερων. It settles the grammatical and historical import of εκκλησια beyond logical or grammatical debate. It was and is, and evermore shall be, *a people called out,* an

assembly; persons *convened by authority,* a people obedient to a Divine call. But λογια ζωντα are likewise anarthrous, yet not to be represented *living oracles,* but *the life-giving oracles.*

Εκκλησια. "In the church in the wilderness." "In the congregation in the wilderness." This term is found in the Christian Scriptures 115 times; of these, 111 times translated—com. ver.—*church,* and thrice, assembly. In the Septuagint version of O. Testament, we commonly find εκκλησια, where in the English we have *congregation:* while in the New, com. version, we find *congregation* once, and assembly once for the Greek εκκλησια, 115 times. With us the word "church" and meeting are most current. Of dissenting denominations it was said formerly they go to "*meeting,*" but now they all go to "*church,*" as the Jew goes to his synagogue.

A new and improved version should harmonize these denominational diversities. We, therefore, substitute the word "*congregation,*" as most appositely representing the original. True the words "called out," or "the called out," were it a current designation, would still more literally develope the import of εκκλησια. It is associated with πανηγορια, in Heb. 12 : 23, which is rendered the "General Assembly"— even the congregation of the "First Born." Κυριοκι, as an abbreviation of κυριου οικος, *a house of the Lord,* is not found in Ecclesiastic antiquity. The Scotch Kyrk, or kirk, or the Saxon *Cyric,* or circ, or the Danish *kirke,* was applied to the

KING JAMES' VERSION.	GREEK TEXT.	REVISED VERSION.
the angel which spake to him in the mount Sina, and *with* our fathers: who received the lively oracles to give unto us: 39 To whom our fathers would not obey, but thrust *him* from them, and in their hearts turned back again into Egypt, 40 Saying unto Aaron, Make us gods to go before us: for *as for* this Moses, which brought us out of the land of Egypt, we wot not what is become of him. 41 And they made a calf in those days, and offered sacrifice unto the idol, and rejoiced in the works of their own hands. 42 Then God turned, and gave them up to worship the host of heaven; as it is written in the book of the prophets, O ye house of Israel, have ye offered to me slain beasts and sacrifices *by the space of* forty years in the wilderness? 43 Yea, ye took up the tabernacle of Moloch, and the star	τῇ ἐρήμῳ μετὰ τοῦ ἀγγέλου τοῦ λαλοῦντος αὐτῷ ἐν τῷ ὄρει Σινᾶ καὶ τῶν πατέρων ἡμῶν, ὃς ἐδέξατο λόγια ζῶντα δοῦναι ἡμῖν. 39 ᾧ οὐκ ἠθέλησαν ὑπήκοοι γενέσθαι οἱ πατέρες ἡμῶν, ἀλλ᾽ ἀπώσαντο, καὶ ἐστράφησαν ταῖς καρδίαις αὐτῶν εἰς Αἴγυπτον, 40 εἰπόντες τῷ Ἀαρὼν, Ποίησον ἡμῖν θεοὺς οἳ προπορεύσονται ἡμῶν· ὁ γὰρ Μωσῆς οὗτος, ὃς ἐξήγαγεν ἡμᾶς ἐκ γῆς Αἰγύπτου, οὐκ οἴδαμεν τί γέγονεν αὐτῷ. 41 Καὶ ἐμοσχοποίησαν ἐν ταῖς ἡμέραις ἐκείναις, καὶ ἀνήγαγον θυσίαν τῷ εἰδώλῳ, καὶ εὐφραίνοντο ἐν τοῖς ἔργοις τῶν χειρῶν αὐτῶν. 42 Ἔστρεψε δὲ ὁ Θεὸς, καὶ παρέδωκεν αὐτοὺς λατρεύειν τῇ στρατιᾷ τοῦ οὐρανοῦ· καθὼς γέγραπται ἐν βίβλῳ τῶν προφητῶν, Μὴ σφάγια καὶ θυσίας προσηνέγκατέ μοι ἔτη τεσσαράκοντα ἐν τῇ ἐρήμῳ, οἶκος Ἰσραήλ; 43 καὶ ἀνελάβετε τὴν σκηνὴν τοῦ Μολὸχ, καὶ τὸ	the messenger that spoke to him in the mount Sinai, and with our fathers, who received the life-giving oracles to give to us: whom our fathers would 39 not obey, but ¹thrust him from them, and in their hearts turned back again into Egypt, saying to Aaron, Make 40 ʲgods to go before us: because, as for this Moses, who brought us out of the land of Egypt, we do not know what is become of him. And they ᵏmade a 41 calf in those days, and offered sacrifice to the idol, and ¹rejoiced in the work of their own hands. Then God ᵐturned and 42 gave them up to worship the ⁿarmy of heaven: as it is written in the book of the prophets; O house of Israel, have you offered to me slain beasts and sacrifices, during forty years in the wilderness? °You 43 even took up the tabernacle of Moloch, and the star of

house, in which Christians met for worship. In the Greek church, and in some Roman communities, κυριακα, included Ecclesiastic goods.—We cannot but regret the present currency of this indefinite term.—Any one can understand "congregation" a "*meeting* of the people," "an assembly ;" but how few know much, or anything, of "a *church*," as indicative of that in Greece, Rome, England, America, or that in ancient Jerusalem ?

ⁱ Απωσαντο (3 pers. plur. aor. 1 mid. from απωθεομαι), they thrust him from them ; so rendered, Acts 7 : 27, 39, twice rendered *cast away*, Rom. 11 : 1, 2 ; put away, 1 Tim. 1 : 19.

ʲ Θεους οἱ προπορευσονται, a literal translation of Exodus 32 : 8, pluralis excellentiæ. Aaron made but one calf, but they asked for gods, Θεοι, in the Hebrew אלהים. Οὑτος, *this* Moses, like *iste*, in Latin, is contemptuous—that Moses ! W. § 28.—*Hackett.*

ᵏ Εμοσχοποιησαν. The science and art of calfmaking are not found in any Greek extant. It was an Egyptian art. "The calf," like the ox at Memphis, called Apis, and that at Heliopolis, called *Mnevis.* Win., Realw. I. p. 644.—*Hackett.*

¹ Ευφραινοντο εν τοις εργοις. This festive celebration is mentioned Ex. 32 : 6. Τοις εργοις shows it to have been a conjoint operation of the people.

ᵐ Ὁ Θεος—εστρεψε—παρεδοκεν αυτους λατρευειν τη στρατιᾳ, God turned away from them—abandoned them to serve, or worship, the hosts—the stars of heaven.

ⁿ Στρατιᾳ, not στρατειᾳ. The latter is used only by Paul, and the former only by Luke, and is by him indicative of a *host*, and so found, Luke 2 : 13 ; Acts 7 : 42, the host of heaven. Τῃ στρατιᾳ του ουρανου, the army of heaven: sun, moon, and stars. "From the Hebrew this star-worship is called Sabaism, from צבא."—*Hackett.* Educated in Egypt the hot-bed of polytheism, the Jews were for ages the victims of creature-worship. It was the capital sin against the *theology* of the Jews, as *saint*-worship and *angel*-worship is the capital and soul-ruining sin of the *Roman apostasy.*

° "No, you apostatized and took up the tabernacle of your god Moloch," i. e. to carry it with them in their marches or in religious processions. The Tabernacle was, no doubt, intended to resemble the one consecrated to Jehovah. Stephen follows the Septuagint.—*Hackett.* The Seventy supply the name of

KING JAMES' VERSION.

of your God Remphan, figures which ye made to worship them: and I will carry you away beyond Babylon.

44 Our fathers had the tabernacle of witness in the wilderness, as he had appointed, speaking unto Moses, that he should make it according to the fashion that he had seen.

45 Which also our fathers, that came after, brought in with Jesus into the possession of the Gentiles, whom God drave out before the face of our fathers, unto the days of David;

46 Who found favour before God, and desired to find a tabernacle for the God of Jacob.

47 But Solomon built him an house.

48 Howbeit, the Most High dwelleth not in temples made with hands; as saith the prophet,

49 Heaven *is* my throne, and earth *is* my footstool: what house will ye build me? saith the Lord: or what *is* the place of my rest?

50 Hath not my hand made all these things?

51 Ye stiff-necked, and uncircumcised in heart and ears, ye do always resist the Holy Ghost: as your fathers *did*, so *do* ye.

52 Which of the prophets have not your fathers persecuted? and they have slain them

GREEK TEXT.

ἄστρον τοῦ θεοῦ ὑμῶν Ῥεμφὰν, τοὺς τύπους οὓς ἐποιήσατε προσκυνεῖν αὐτοῖς· καὶ μετοικιῶ ὑμᾶς ἐπέκεινα Βαβυλῶνος. 44 Ἡ σκηνὴ τοῦ μαρτυρίου ἦν ἐν τοῖς πατράσιν ἡμῶν ἐν τῇ ἐρήμῳ, καθὼς διετάξατο ὁ λαλῶν τῷ Μωσῇ, ποιῆσαι αὐτὴν κατὰ τὸν τύπον ὃν ἑωράκει· 45 ἣν καὶ εἰσήγαγον διαδεξάμενοι οἱ πατέρες ἡμῶν μετὰ Ἰησοῦ ἐν τῇ κατασχέσει τῶν ἐθνῶν, ὧν ἔξωσεν ὁ Θεὸς ἀπὸ προσώπου τῶν πατέρων ἡμῶν, ἕως τῶν ἡμερῶν Δαβίδ· 46 ὃς εὗρε χάριν ἐνώπιον τοῦ Θεοῦ, καὶ ᾐτήσατο εὑρεῖν σκήνωμα τῷ Θεῷ Ἰακώβ. 47 Σολομῶν δὲ ᾠκοδόμησεν αὐτῷ οἶκον. 48 Ἀλλ' οὐχ ὁ ὕψιστος ἐν χειροποιήτοις ναοῖς κατοικεῖ, καθὼς ὁ προφήτης λέγει, 49 Ὁ οὐρανός μοι θρόνος, ἡ δὲ γῆ ὑποπόδιον τῶν ποδῶν μου· ποῖον οἶκον οἰκοδομήσετέ μοι; λέγει κύριος· ἢ τίς τόπος τῆς καταπαύσεώς μου; 50 οὐχὶ ἡ χείρ μου ἐποίησε ταῦτα παντα;

51 Σκληροτράχηλοι, καὶ ἀπερίτμητοι τῇ καρδίᾳ καὶ τοῖς ὠσὶν, ὑμεῖς ἀεὶ τῷ Πνεύματι τῷ Ἁγίῳ ἀντιπίπτετε, ὡς οἱ πατέρες ὑμῶν καὶ ὑμεῖς. 52 τίνα τῶν προφητῶν οὐκ ἐδίωξαν οἱ πατέρες ὑμῶν; καὶ ἀπέκτειναν τοὺς προ-

REVISED VERSION.

your god Remphan, images
which you made to worship;
therefore, I will carry you away
beyond Babylon. Our fathers 44
had the [p]tabernacle of testimony
in the wilderness, as he had
appointed, speaking to Moses,
that he should make it according
to the pattern that he had
seen: which tabernacle also our 45
fathers having received, they
brought in with Joshua, into
the possession of the heathen,
whom God drove out before
the face of our fathers, until
the days of David; who found 46
favor before God, and desired
to find a tabernacle for the
God of Jacob. But Solomon 47
built him a house. Neverthe- 48
less, the Most High does not
dwell in temples made with
hands; as the prophet says:
The heaven is my throne, and 49
the earth is my footstool. What
house will you build for me?
says the Lord: or, what is the
place of my rest? [q]Did not 50
my hand make all these?

Stiffnecked and uncircum- 51
cised in heart and ears, you
are always resisting the Holy
Spirit: as your fathers did,
so you are doing. Which of 52
the prophets did not your fathers
persecute? They [r]even
slew those who [s]had pre-

the idol from tradition, but there is almost equal authority, says Baur, for reading מִלְכֹּם, Milkom, a proper name. The variation would bring the Greek into greater conformity to the Hebrew.—*Το αστρον του Θεου,* i. e. an image resembling, or representing a star worshiped by them as a god. By *Ρεμφαν* the Seventy express כִּיּוּן which, like most of the ancient translators, they took to be a proper name, some of the ablest modern scholars defend the correctness of that translation. In this case the Greek name must have sprung from a corrupt pronunciation of the Hebrew name. See Gesenius, Lex. p. 463.—*Hackett.*

p "Tabernacle of the Testimony"—so called because it contained the two tables of the constitution, or supreme law, given to the twelve Tribes.

q *Εποιησε,* is aor. 1, and should not be rendered by our perf. as in the Com. Vers. The supply of the word "things" is unnecessary, and is, therefore, omitted here.

r "Even they slew those" is the exact order of the original text. Still, as in our usage, They slew even those, is quite acceptable.

s Who *had previously announced,* who *showed before,* who

KING JAMES' VERSION.	GREEK TEXT.	REVISED VERSION.
which shewed before of the coming of the Just One; of whom ye have been now the betrayers and murderers;	καταγγείλαντας περὶ τῆς ἐλεύσεως τοῦ δικαίου, οὗ νῦν ὑμεῖς προδόται καὶ φονεῖς γεγένησθε·	viously announced the coming of the Just One, of whom you have now been the betrayers and murderers—you who have 53
53 Who have received the law by the disposition of angels, and have not kept it.	53 οἵτινες ἐλάβετε τὸν νόμον εἰς διαταγὰς ἀγγέλων, καὶ οὐκ ἐφυλάξατε.	received the law by the ᵘministration of angels, and have not kept it. When they heard 54
54 When they heard these things, they were cut to the heart, and they gnashed on him with their teeth.	54 Ἀκούοντες δὲ ταῦτα, διεπρίοντο ταῖς καρδίαις αὐτῶν, καὶ ἔβρυχον τοὺς ὀδόντας ἐπ᾿ αὐτόν.	these things, they were cut to the heart, and they gnashed on him with their teeth. But 55
55 But he, being full of the Holy Ghost, looked up steadfastly into heaven, and saw the glory of God, and Jesus standing on the right hand of God,	55 Ὑπάρχων δὲ πλήρης Πνεύματος Ἁγίου, ἀτενίσας εἰς τὸν οὐρανὸν, εἶδε δόξαν Θεοῦ, καὶ Ἰησοῦν ἑστῶτα ἐκ δεξιῶν τοῦ Θεοῦ,	he, being full of the Holy Spirit, looked up steadfastly ᵘinto the heaven, and saw the glory of God, and Jesus standing on the right hand of God, and
56 And said, Behold, I see the heavens opened, and the Son of man standing on the right hand of God.	56 καὶ εἶπεν, Ἰδοὺ, θεωρῶ τοὺς οὐρανοὺς ἀνεῳγμένους, καὶ τὸν υἱὸν τοῦ ἀνθρώπου ἐκ δεξιῶν ἑστῶτα τοῦ Θεοῦ.	said: Behold, I see the heaven 56 opened, and the ᵛSon of man standing on the right hand of God. Then they cried out 57
57 Then they cried out with a loud voice, and stopped their ears, and ran upon him with one accord,	57 Κράξαντες δὲ φωνῇ μεγάλῃ, συνέσχον τὰ ὦτα αὐτῶν, καὶ ὥρμησαν ὁμοθυμαδὸν ἐπ᾿ αὐτόν·	with a loud voice, and stopped their ears, and ran upon him with one consent, and cast him
58 And cast him out of the city, and stoned him: and the witnesses laid down their clothes at a young man's feet, whose name was Saul.	58 καὶ ἐκβαλόντες ἔξω τῆς πόλεως, ἐλιθοβόλουν. καί οἱ μάρτυρες ἀπέθεντο τὰ ἱμάτια αὐτῶν παρὰ τοὺς πόδας νεανίου καλουμένου Σαύλου,	out of the city, and stoned him. And the witnesses laid 58 off ᵂtheir garments at the feet of a young man, named Saul. And they stoned Ste- 59
59 And they stoned Stephen, calling upon God, and saying, Lord Jesus, receive my spirit.	59 καὶ ἐλιθοβόλουν τὸν Στέφανον, ἐπικαλούμενον καὶ λέγοντα, Κύριε Ἰησοῦ, δέξαι τὸ πνεῦμά μου. 60 Θεὶς	phen, ˣinvoking, and saying, Lord Jesus, receive my spirit.

foretold, are equally intelligible and equally exegetical of the word προκαταγγελλω. Αγγελος is transferred into our tongue, literally with us, an *angel*, a *messenger*, a *nuncio*. Nihil est absurdi si statuamus *nuncium eo loco angelum* dici. Crit. Sac.

Οἰτινες—εφυλαξατε—you yourselves have received the Law, and have not kept it.

ᵗ "Disposition of Angels," com. ver. εις διαταγας αγγελων, *ordinance* of Angels, Tyndale; *ministration* of Angels, Rheims; in-dispositione angelorum, Vulgate; par le ministere des anges, French. To me, it would seem, as if the tables were handed down through ranks of angels, as to persons standing on the rounds of a ladder, one below another in a line reaching from the threshold of heaven down to Moses.

This is indicated in the terms selected, in all the ancient and modern versions that we have seen.

ᵘ Εις τον ουρανον—*towards* heaven, Thomp., Doddridge, Murdock, Wakefield; *to* heaven, Wesley; *unto* heaven, Rheims; *into* heaven, com. ver., Boothroyd, Wickliffe, Tyndale, Cranmer, Geneva. It must literally have been *into*

heaven, because he saw the heavens opened and Jesus standing on the right hand of God. This case illustrates the looseness of translators and revisers, and, therefore, we so particularly notice it, and because of its bearings in more important cases.

ᵛ *Son* is found in the original with a small letter; still, in our style, I do not object to a capital S, provided only it be uniform in all other cases in the whole volume.

ᵂ Upper garments, Wakefield; "Clothes," Murd.

ˣ Επικαλουμενον και λεγοντα. Literally invoking and saying. "Calling on the Lord." In the Greek, calling on, and saying, Lord Jesus. The English requires the insertion of the object, who was "the Lord Jesus." We are, therefore, not to insert the word *God*, with our common version, which word it has retained from Wickliffe. "cloped God to help."

The Latin is correct, *invocantem et dicentem Domine Jesu*, Granville Penn in loco. This is the strongest evidence, in a given case, of the faith of Stephen, in the Divinity of Jesus Christ.

KING JAMES' VERSION.

60 And he kneeled down and cried with a loud voice, Lord, lay not this sin to their charge. And when he had said this, he fell asleep.

CHAP. VIII.

AND Saul was consenting unto his death. And at that time there was a great persecution against the church which was at Jerusalem; and they were all scattered abroad throughout the regions of Judea and Samaria, except the apostles.

2 And devout men carried Stephen *to his burial*, and made great lamentation over him.

3 As for Saul, he made havoc of the church, entering into every house, and haling men and women, committed *them* to prison.

4 Therefore they that were scattered abroad went every where preaching the word.

5 Then Philip went down to

GREEK TEXT.

δὲ τὰ γόνατα, ἔκραξε φωνῇ μεγάλῃ, Κύριε, μὴ στήσῃς αὐτοῖς τὴν ἁμαρτίαν ταύτην. Καὶ τοῦτο εἰπὼν ἐκοιμήθη.

CHAP. VIII.

Σαῦλος δὲ ἦν συνευδοκῶν τῇ ἀναιρέσει αὐτοῦ. Ἐγένετο δὲ ἐν ἐκείνῃ τῇ ἡμέρᾳ διωγμὸς μέγας ἐπὶ τὴν ἐκκλησίαν τὴν ἐν Ἱεροσολύμοις· πάντες τε διεσπάρησαν κατὰ τὰς χώρας τῆς Ἰουδαίας καὶ Σαμαρείας, πλὴν τῶν ἀποστόλων. ² συνεκόμισαν δὲ τὸν Στέφανον ἄνδρες εὐλαβεῖς, καὶ ἐποιήσαντο κοπετὸν μέγαν ἐπ' αὐτῷ. ³ Σαῦλος δὲ ἐλυμαίνετο τὴν ἐκκλησίαν, κατὰ τοὺς οἴκους εἰσπορευόμενος, σύρων τε ἄνδρας καὶ γυναῖκας παρεδίδου εἰς φυλακήν. ⁴ οἱ μὲν οὖν διασπαρέντες διῆλθον, εὐαγγελιζόμενοι τὸν λόγον.

⁵ ΦΙΛΙΠΠΟΣ δὲ κατελθὼν

REVISED VERSION.

And he kneeled down and 60 cried out, with a loud voice, Lord, lay not this sin to their charge. And when he had said this, he fell asleep. Now Saul was consenting to his death.

CHAP. VIII.

Now on that ʸday there 1 ᶻarose a great persecution against the congregation, which ᵃwas in Jerusalem; and they were all scattered abroad throughout the ᵇdistricts of Judea and Samaria, except the Apostles. Yet devout men 2 jointly bore ᶜaway Stephen to the grave, and made great lamentation over him. But Saul 3 ᵈwasted the congregation, entering into the houses, and ᵉdragging forth men and women, he committed them to prison. Nevertheless, the ᶠdispersed, passed along preach- 4 ing the ᵍword. Philip, indeed, 5

ʸ *Εν εκεινη τη ημερα.* And on that day. *In, on,* and *un* are derived from a Saxon verb signifying—*to come to, to meet, to pass.* Hence they all denote nearness, closeness, contiguity. Webster. "*In that day,*" with us, frequently indicates a length of time—a period of time, beyond a certain day—or a single day. Reference is here, obviously, to Stephen's Martyrdom, and the consequent dispersion of the Church that was in Jerusalem. This is confirmed by another reference to it, chap. 11 : 19; *οἱ μεν ουν διασπαρεντες απο της Θλιψεως της γενομενης επι Στεφανῳ,* making that very day the epoch of the dispersion of the Church.

ᶻ *Εγενετο. Γινομαι,* indicates *to come into existence,* or *to begin to be.* As more definite we may prefer *began to be*—to *there was.* In our currency they are nearly equal; still historical accuracy is better secured by the former than by the latter.

ᵃ *Την* after *εκκλησιαν* is demonstratively expletive—and justifies "that was in Jerusalem."

ᵇ *Τας χωρας*—*χωρα* in com. ver. is represented by *country, region, land, ground, field, coast,* occurring 27 times. *Territories* is here too large; *coasts,* too maritime; and *lands,* inapposite to the territory.—*District,* or *region,* is our remain-

ing choice. With us *district* is less Roman, and more popular than region.

ᶜ *Συνεκομισαν*—bore away together—to the grave, Hackett. Less ambiguous we prefer—*jointly bore away Stephen. Εκκομιζω* was appropriated to funeral pomp, like *offerre* with the Romans.

ᵈ *Λυμαινομαι,* is an *ἁπαξ λεγομενον.* Havoc is a Saxon word, and indicates a *hawk. He hawked the Church* would be hypercritical, and, therefore, inapposite.—"He made havoc" of it is little better. We prefer Milton's use of the term, or rendition of it—he *wasted* the Church. Being here the *imperfect* of *λυμαινομαι,* indicating a continuous devastation we would translate it.—But Saul wasted or was wasting the congregation entering into the houses of the disciples—*κατα τους οικους, εισπορευομενος συρων* &c., Meyer, Hack.

ᵉ *Συρων*—*εσυρον* as in com. ver. John 21 : 8, should here be represented by *dragging*—as fishes in a net.—So it is found in Acts 14 : 19, "after stoning Paul, they dragged (*εσυρον*) him out of the city."

ᶠ *Οἱ μεν ουν.* Nevertheless—" *They that were dispersed* " usually contracted into " *the dispersed;* " more sententious and equally grammatical.

ᵍ *Ευαγγελιζομενοι τον λογον,* literally, *evangelizing the word.*

KING JAMES' VERSION.

the city of Samaria, and preached Christ unto them.

6 And the people with one accord gave heed unto those things which Philip spake, hearing and seeing the miracles which he did.

7 For unclean spirits, crying with loud voice, came out of many that were possessed *with them*: and many taken with palsies, and that were lame, were healed.

8 And there was great joy in that city.

9 But there was a certain man, called Simon, which beforetime in the same city used sorcery, and bewitched the people of Samaria, giving out that himself was some great one:

10 To whom they all gave heed, from the least to the greatest, saying, This man is the great power of God.

11 And to him they had regard, because that of long time

GREEK TEXT.

εἰς πόλιν τῆς Σαμαρείας, ἐκήρυσσεν αὐτοῖς τὸν Χριστόν. ⁶ προσεῖχόν τε οἱ ὄχλοι τοῖς λεγομένοις ὑπὸ τοῦ Φιλίππου ὁμοθυμαδὸν, ἐν τῷ ἀκούειν αὐτοὺς καὶ βλέπειν τὰ σημεῖα, ἃ ἐποίει. ⁷ πολλῶν γὰρ τῶν ἐχόντων πνεύματα ἀκάθαρτα, βοῶντα μεγάλῃ φωνῇ ἐξήρχετο· πολλοὶ δὲ παραλελυμένοι καὶ χωλοὶ ἐθεραπεύθησαν. ⁸ καὶ ἐγένετο χαρὰ μεγάλη ἐν τῇ πόλει ἐκείνῃ. ⁹ Ἀνὴρ δέ τις ὀνόματι Σίμων προϋπῆρχεν ἐν τῇ πόλει μαγεύων καὶ ἐξιστῶν τὸ ἔθνος τῆς Σαμαρείας, λέγων εἶναί τινα ἑαυτὸν μέγαν· ¹⁰ ᾧ προσεῖχον πάντες ἀπὸ μικροῦ ἕως μεγάλου, λέγοντες, Οὗτός ἐστιν ἡ δύναμις τοῦ Θεοῦ ἡ μεγάλη. ¹¹ Προσεῖχον δὲ αὐτῷ, διὰ τὸ ἱκανῷ χρόνῳ ταῖς μαγείαις

REVISED VERSION.

having gone down to a city of Samaria, [h]was announcing the Christ to them: and the multitudes were, with one accord, giving heed to the things spoken by Philip, when they [i]heard and saw the miracles which he was doing: for, from [j]many who had unclean spirits, they were going out, crying with a loud voice; and many palsied and lame were healed. And there was great joy in that city.

But there was there, before, a certain man, named Simon, who formerly, in the same city, had practiced sorcery, and [k]astonished the people of Samaria, boasting that he was some great one. To whom they all gave heed, young and [l]old, saying, This man is the great power of God. And to him indeed they gave heed, because that for a long time, he

---

It first appears in the Christian oracles, Matthew 11:5.—In the passive sense "the poor are evangelized;" or it may be rendered "the poor have the gospel preached to them." But we have another Evangelical formula tantamount, in many instances, to this. It is first found Matt. 4:23, Jesus—*taught* (διδασκων) in the Synagogues of Galilee and *was* preaching (κηρυσσων) the gospel of the kingdom, το ευαγγελιον της βασιλειας. This subject merits a treatise rather than a note. We can only *note* the following facts.—1. Κηρυξ—a public herald—occurs but thrice in the Christian Scriptures, and is always rendered *preacher* com. ver.; literally, in Greek currency, it indicates a *public crier* and a *herald*, Critica Sacra.—The Septuagint use it for a word which signifies *clamare*, to cry aloud, Jonah 3:7; also for a word signifying *vocare*, to call; and *publicè profiteri*, Gen. 4:43; also for a word signifying *voce lata ac plena personare*, Hosea 5:8. "Blow the cornet in Gibeah, the trumpet in Ramah, cry aloud at Bethaven, after thee O Benjamin!" When used to denote preaching it is always used metaphorically, Critica Sacra. We *preach*, το ευαγγελιον, the gospel, we *teach*, η διδαχη, the doctrine of Christ. See note on v. 25.

[h] Κηρυσσω occurs 61 times; 5 times *publish, teach, proclaim,* and 54 times *preach.* We have of the same family κηρυξ, and κηρυγμα, the latter 8 times always rendered *preaching,* and κηρυξ, 3 times *preacher.* The whole family, then, appear in Holy Writ 72 times. Of these, 65 are *preach* and *preaching* and

preacher.—The διδασκω family, of six members, διδακτικος. διδακτος, διδασκαλια, διδασκαλος, διδαχη, occurs in the above members of it, in all 114 times; represented in our language by *teach, teaching, teacher,* or *Doctor, Doctrine, didactic,* or *apt to teach. Preach* and *teach* are therefore two distinct employments, never once confounded, or substituted, the one for the other, in all the oracles of God.

[i] Εν τω ακουειν—εν, with the infinitive, denotes, not the cause, but the occasion. Kühner's Greek Grammar, Hackett.

[j] Instead of "from many" we may read "out of many" without violating any law or reason; and also without any more precision of sense.

[k] Εξιστων. Imperfect active of εξιστημι and εξισταω, obstupefacio—to astonish, to amaze, to confound, to astound, to have no sense left—obstupuere animi, Virgil; extra se esse, to be out of one's self, Beza. Hence the word ecstasy. There is no one Latin word which doth sufficiently express that Greek word; for it signifieth—præ admiratione apud se non esse, et de statu mentis dejici, Mark 2:12, Vulgate. Miron, Beza; obstupesco, vel percellor: for the Greek word signifieth mentem alicujus veluti amovere, which the Latin percellor also doth, Beza, Critica Sacra. Astounded, that is—astonished to dumbness, Webster.

[l] "From young to old," is the exact rendering, if we change "from small to great." We repudiate unto as antiquated and out of use amongst our best writers.

KING JAMES' VERSION.	GREEK TEXT.	REVISED VERSION.
he had bewitched them with sorceries. 12 But when they believed Philip, preaching the things concerning the kingdom of God, and the name of Jesus Christ, they were baptized both men and women. 13 Then Simon himself believed also: and when he was baptized, he continued with Philip, and wondered, beholding the miracles and signs which were done. 14 Now when the apostles which were at Jerusalem heard that Samaria had received the word of God, they sent unto them Peter and John: 15 Who, when they were come down, prayed for them that they might receive the Holy Ghost: 16 (For as yet he was fallen upon none of them: only they were baptized in the name of the Lord Jesus.)	ἐξεστακέναι αὐτούς. 12 Ὅτε δὲ ἐπίστευσαν τῷ Φιλίππῳ εὐαγγελιζομένῳ τὰ περὶ τῆς βασιλείας τοῦ Θεοῦ καὶ τοῦ ὀνόματος τοῦ Ἰησοῦ Χριστοῦ, ἐβαπτίζοντο ἄνδρες τε καὶ γυναῖκες. 13 ὁ δὲ Σίμων καὶ αὐτὸς ἐπίστευσε, καὶ βαπτισθεὶς ἦν προσκαρτερῶν τῷ Φιλίππῳ· θεωρῶν τε σημεῖα καὶ δυνάμεις μεγάλας γινομένας, ἐξίστατο. 14 Ἀκούσαντες δὲ οἱ ἐν Ἱεροσολύμοις ἀπόστολοι, ὅτι δέδεκται ἡ Σαμάρεια τὸν λόγον τοῦ Θεοῦ, ἀπέστειλαν πρὸς αὐτοὺς τὸν Πέτρον καὶ Ἰωάννην· 15 οἵτινες καταβάντες προσηύξαντο περὶ αὐτῶν, ὅπως λάβωσι Πνεῦμα Ἅγιον. 16 οὔπω γὰρ ἦν ἐπ᾽ οὐδενὶ αὐτῶν ἐπιπεπτωκὸς, μόνον δὲ βεβαπτισμένοι ὑπῆρχον εἰς τὸ ὄνομα τοῦ Κυρίου Ἰησοῦ.	had astonished them with his [m]sorceries. But when they 12 [n]believed Philip, preaching the things concerning the kingdom of God, and the name of Jesus Christ, they were immersed, both men and women. Also Simon himself believed; 13 and when he was immersed, he constantly [o]adhered to Philip, and, beholding the miracles and signs which were done, he was astonished. Now when the Apostles 14 who were at Jerusalem, heard that Samaria had received the word of God, they sent to them Peter and John, who, when they had come 15 down, prayed for them, that they might receive the [p]Holy Spirit. For as yet, [q]he had 16 fallen upon none of them: only they had been immersed into the name of the Lord Jesus.

[m] Ταις μανειαις, with his sorceries. He is, therefore, properly called Simon the sorcerer.—One of the tribe that contended with Moses.

[n] Επιστευσαν τῳ Φιλιππῳ, literally, they believed in Philip preaching—in what he preached.

[o] Προσκαρτερων, semper adsum. He constantly adhered.

[p] Λαβωσι πνευμα Ἁγιον. That they might receive the Holy Spirit. This is literally a holy spirit or, as printed in our standard text, Holy Spirit. There are not wanting some who now, as formerly, have imagined that without the article, and without capital initials a holy spirit, or a holy temper is all that can be understood and expected in such cases. Fatal to such hypothesis is the fact, that, in our accredited originals, we have it, in both cases, with, and without the article, and with, and without capital initials. In the very next occurrence in the next verse and in the same Bagster's approved text, it is printed in capital initials. Το πνευμα το Ἁγιον, with the article, nor is this a solitary case. We have many such. See ch. 1 : 5, note o, and ch. 10 : 38, note

[q] He had fallen upon none of them. They had only been immersed into the name of the Lord Jesus. It may, indeed, be appropriately rendered, It had fallen upon none of them, but while gender is regarded, it must also be regarded and remembered, that the Spirit is appropriately personified by the Lord himself, and commissioned as his agent or missionary.—John reports his personal mission and work in a language and style most precise, definite, and unmistakable—under the commission of his personal ambassador or advocate, John 16. The mere Etymologist would translate the 16th verse as follows:—"because at that time it had fallen on not one of them." This would be apposite to a gust of wind, a shower of rain, or a flash of lightning. The ambiguity in some minds on this subject arises wholly, as we conceive, from the fact that there are no genders in heaven, nor amongst spirits, nor in the Θειοτης (an ἅπαξ λεγομενον), the Godhead. Again the Father, Son, and Holy Spirit are a special manifestation or revelation of Θειοτης, or Jehovah, in adaptation to a special emergency in the universe. Eternally it was Jehovah. In creation it was God, the Word, the Spirit. But the WORD that was in the beginning in or with God, and that was God, became a man, and therefore masculine, though embracing all humanity, no one personality; irrespective of sex or gender. Woman—or wombman, being created out of one person, became a second person in humanity, as the WORD was in Divinity.—Hence the Holy Spirit equally personal, proceeding from both, became a third person and though equally Divine was neither first nor second but third—hence neither and neuter are one in essence and constitute a third manifestation or personality of the absolute Jehovah. The pronominal neuter is a mere grammatical contingency growing out of the clumsiness and awkwardness of our composite language, an imperfect vehicle to introduce JEHOVAH ELOHIM into human head, human heart, or human tongue.

KING JAMES' VERSION.	GREEK TEXT.	REVISED VERSION.
17 Then laid they *their* hands on them, and they received the Holy Ghost. 18 And when Simon saw that through laying on of the apostles' hands the Holy Ghost was given, he offered them money. 19 Saying, Give me also this power, that on whomsoever I lay hands, he may receive the Holy Ghost. 20 But Peter said unto him, Thy money perish with thee, because thou hast thought that the gift of God may be purchased with money. 21 Thou hast neither part nor lot in this matter: for thy heart is not right in the sight of God. 22 Repent therefore of this thy wickedness, and pray God, if perhaps the thought of thine heart may be forgiven thee.	¹⁷ τότε ἐπετίθουν τὰς χεῖρας ἐπ᾽ αὐτοὺς, καὶ ἐλάμβανον Πνεῦμα Ἅγιον. ¹⁸ Θεασάμενος δὲ ὁ Σίμων, ὅτι διὰ τῆς ἐπιθέσεως τῶν χειρῶν τῶν ἀποστόλων δίδοται τ᾽ Πνεῦμα τὸ Ἅγιον, προσήνεγκεν αὐτοῖς χρήματα, ¹⁹ λέγων, Δότε κἀμοὶ τὴν ἐξουσίαν ταύτην, ἵνα ᾧ ἂν ἐπιθῶ τὰς χεῖρας, λαμβάνῃ Πνεῦμα Ἅγιον. ²⁰ Πέτρος δὲ εἶπε πρὸς αὐτὸν, Τὸ ἀργύριόν σου σὺν σοὶ εἴη εἰς ἀπώλειαν, ὅτι τὴν δωρεὰν τοῦ Θεοῦ ἐνόμισας διὰ χρημάτων κτᾶσθαι. ²¹ οὐκ ἔστι σοι μερὶς οὐδὲ κλῆρος ἐν τῷ λόγῳ τούτῳ. ἡ γὰρ καρδία σου οὐκ ἔστιν εὐθεῖα ἐνώπιον τοῦ Θεοῦ. ²² μετανόησον οὖν ἀπὸ τῆς κακίας σου ταύτης, καὶ δεήθητι τοῦ Θεοῦ, εἰ ἄρα ἀφεθήσεταί σοι ἡ ἐπίνοια τῆς καρδίας σου. ²³ εἰς γὰρ	Then they laid hands on them, 17 and they received the ʳHoly Spirit. And when Simon ˢsaw 18 that, through laying on of the Apostles' hands, the Holy Spirit was given, he offered them ᵗmoney, saying, Give to 19 me also this power, that on whomever I lay hands, he may receive the Holy Spirit. But Peter said to him, may your 20 silver go to destruction with you, because you have presumed to procure the gift of God through money. To ᵘyou 21 there is no part nor portion in this thing, for your heart is not right in the sight of God. Reform, therefore, from this your 22 wickedness, and pray ᵛthe Lord, if, perhaps, the ᵂdevice of your heart shall be forgiven

The great Teacher himself changed the *gender* of the Holy Spirit in his valedictory promise reported by the beloved disciple, who slept in his bosom; he christed, or christened him, ὁ παρακλητος.—Hence the new style πεμψω αυτον—εκεινος ελθων—εκεινος εμε δοξασει—του εμου ληψεται—εκ του εμου ληψεται, και αναγγελαι ὑμιν, John 16 : 12-15. I more than question the propriety of sacrificing a Divine impersonation, or a Divine personality, to the capricious etiquette of our *he, she, it*. *He* is our most worthy pronoun, and why fastidiously sacrifice the Παρακλητος, to our least worthy !!

ʳ Ελαμβανον πνευμα Ἁγιον. They received *the Holy Spirit*, or they received Holy Spirit—is equally *grammatical*—why not the latter rather than the former! Especially since in the next verse we find το πνευμα το Ἁγιον. But we shall be told in the latter case it is the subject of the proposition. It is, however, the same Holy Spirit whether the subject or the predicate of the proposition. But Simon when stipulating for this power, or authority of imparting the gift, uses the anarthrous form,—so we find it in John 20 : 22, after the same verb; but in Acts 10 : 47, in a similar attitude, we find the το πνευμα το Ἁγιον vouchsafed to the believing gentiles on the imposition of Paul's hands.

ˢ For θεασαμενος, read ιδων, Gb., Sch., Ln., Tf. : and Tf.'s Stereotype Ed., for το πνευμα το ἁγιον, simply το πνευμα.

ᵗ We have here χρηματα—riches—and in v. 20, το αργυριον—money or silver.

Αργυριον—properly indicates silver, and nine times in twenty occurrences is so rendered in the com. ver.; while χρημα in the plural number is always represented by *riches* or *money*, com. ver.

ᵘ " To you there is no part nor portion in this speech " is more literal—or grammatical—as λογος is sometimes so rendered in the com. ver.—Εν λογω τουτω, *in this word*, doctrine, or gospel, Ols., Neand. ; *in this thing*, viz., the gift of the Spirit, Ben., Mey., De Wette, as quoted by Hackett.

ᵛ Δεηθητι του θεου, com. text. Δεηθητι του κυριου, Ln., Tf.—Griesbach marks it as supported by great authorities. It is also more in harmony with the genius and spirit of that epoch—The Lord Jesus being then recognized as recently constituted the reigning sovereign—the head of the church—is in this case declared to be the immediate source of this special mission of the Spirit. " He has shed forth that which you now see and hear."

ᵂ Ει αρα επινοια. This word is only used once in N. T., and is not represented by the word *thought*.—Device or *machination* is its proper representative. The Vulgate and Erasmus give *cogitatio*. *Nimium dilute*, says Critica Sacra.—Επινοια, *pronsus hic respondet Hebrææ voci Zamam*. Beza in loc. Vide Drusium in loco, Crit. Sacra.

KING JAMES' VERSION.

23 For I perceive that thou art in the gall of bitterness, and *in* the bond of iniquity.

24 Then answered Simon, and said, Pray ye to the Lord for me, that none of these things which ye have spoken come upon me.

25 And they, when they had testified and preached the word of the Lord, returned to Jerusalem, and preached the gospel in many villages of the Samaritans.

26 And the angel of the Lord spake unto Philip, saying, Arise, and go toward the south, unto the way that goeth down from Jerusalem unto Gaza, which is desert.

27 And he arose, and went: and behold, a man of Ethiopia, an eunuch of great authority under Candace queen of the Ethiopians, who had the charge of all her treasure, and had come to Jerusalem for to worship,

GREEK TEXT.

χολὴν πικρίας καὶ σύνδεσμον ἀδικίας ὁρῶ σε ὄντα. ²⁴ Ἀποκριθεὶς δὲ ὁ Σίμων εἶπε, Δεήθητε ὑμεῖς ὑπὲρ ἐμοῦ πρὸς τὸν κύριον, ὅπως μηδὲν ἐπέλθῃ ἐπ' ἐμὲ ὧν εἰρήκατε.

²⁵ Οἱ μὲν οὖν διαμαρτυράμενοι καὶ λαλήσαντες τὸν λόγον τοῦ κυρίου, ὑπέστρεψαν εἰς Ἱερουσαλὴμ, πολλάς τε κώμας τῶν Σαμαρειτῶν εὐηγγελίσαντο.

²⁶ Ἄγγελος δὲ κυρίου ἐλάλησε πρὸς Φίλιππον, λέγων, Ἀνάστηθι καὶ πορεύου κατὰ μεσημβρίαν, ἐπὶ τὴν ὁδὸν τὴν καταβαίνουσαν ἀπὸ Ἱερουσαλὴμ εἰς Γάζαν· αὕτη ἐστὶν ἔρημος. ²⁷ καὶ ἀναστὰς ἐπορεύθη· καὶ ἰδοὺ, ἀνὴρ Αἰθίοψ εὐνοῦχος δυνάστης Κανδάκης τῆς βασιλίσσης Αἰθιόπων, ὃς ἦν ἐπὶ πάσης τῆς γάζης αὐτῆς, ὃς ἐληλύθει προσκυνήσων εἰς Ἱερουσαλὴμ,

REVISED VERSION.

you; for I perceive that you 23 are in the gall of bitterness, and in the bond of iniquity. Then 24 Simon, answering, said, Pray to the Lord for me that none of these things, which you have spoken, may come upon me. They therefore, when they had 25 testified and preached the word of the Lord, set out on their return to Jerusalem, and they preached the gospel in many ˣvillages of the Samaritans.

But an Angel of the Lord 26 spoke to Philip, saying, Arise, and go toward the south, to the way that goes down from Jerusalem to Gaza (which is the way through the desertʸ). And he arose and went; and 27 behold a man of Ethiopia, an ᶻofficer of great authority, under Candace, queen of the Ethiopians, who had the charge of all her treasure, and had come into Jerusalem to ᵃwor-

---

ˣ *Πολλας τε κωμας των Σαμαρειτων ευηγγελισαντο,* Aor. 1, mid. Villages being here the object of this verb, we must render it in grammatical harmony with this fact; and *they evangelized many villages of the Samaritans.*

Ευηγγελισαντο may state the result of their labors while they had been absent, or what took place on their return to Jerusalem, Kuin., De Wette. Mey. This latter view agrees best with the order of the narrative.

This verb, according to a later Grecism (Lob. ad Phryn. page 267) may take its object in the Accusative as well as in the Dative, Com. V. 40; 14 : 15, 21; 16 : 10; Luke 3 : 18; Gal. 1 : 9; W. § 32 : 1; Hackett, p. 125.

Dismissing the labors of Peter and John, he continues the narrative of Philip. They went to Jerusalem—and Philip towards Gaza.

"They went back to Jerusalem," or "returned to Jerusalem," is more in our modern style, if we do not regard the fact, that they did not immediately and straightforward prosecute their journey to Jerusalem—but we are informed, that on their return they communicated the glad tidings to many villages of the Samaritans.

ʸ *Ερημος,* being an adjective, is found as such fifteen times in the N. Test. This occurrence may, or may not be an ex-

ception—but it is the only one that is not obviously associated with a noun in concord, and here it may through *αυτη* qualify *οδος.* Some refer it to Gaza, sixty miles southwest of Jerusalem. Hence Hug, Scholtz, Meyer, and others suppose that this is the place here described by *ερημος,* desert. But Gaza was not destroyed A. D. 64 or 66, when this book was completed, and if even later it could not have received this name. There having been several ways, at least two, well known to history, we presume that the angel directed Philip to the course which he took in order to meet the officer of Queen Candace. Two roads actually exist to this day, one of which passes through the desert inhabited by nomadic Arabs. There was a plurality of queens of this name.

ᶻ This Eunuch is distinguished by the title—*δυναστης κανδακης της βασιλισσης Αιθιοπων*—Candace the queen of Ethiopians. Strabo and Dio name this queen as warring against the Romans in the 23d year of Augustus Cæsar.—Ethiopia was that portion of Africa south of Egypt. Pliny also names Candace a queen of the Ethiopians.

ᵃ *Προσκυνησων εις Ιερουσαλημ.* He not only came to Jerusalem to worship, but he came to worship, *εις Ιερουσαλημ,* into or within Jerusalem.—We find a different formula of worshiping at this centre. Paul in the *textus receptus*

KING JAMES' VERSION.	GREEK TEXT.	REVISED VERSION.

KING JAMES' VERSION.

28 Was returning; and sitting in his chariot, read Esaias the prophet.

29 Then the Spirit said unto Philip, Go near and join thyself to this chariot.

30 And Philip ran thither to *him*, and heard him read the prophet Esaias, and said, Understandest thou what thou readest?

31 And he said, How can I, except some man should guide me? And he desired Philip that he would come up, and sit with him.

32 The place of the scripture which he read was this, He was

GREEK TEXT.

28 ἦν τε ὑποστρέφων καὶ καθήμενος ἐπὶ τοῦ ἅρματος αὐτοῦ, καὶ ἀνεγίνωσκε τὸν προφήτην Ἡσαΐαν. 29 εἶπε δὲ τὸ πνεῦμα τῷ Φιλίππῳ, Πρόσελθε καὶ κολλήθητι τῷ ἅρματι τούτῳ. 30 Προσδραμὼν δὲ ὁ Φίλιππος ἤκουσεν αὐτοῦ ἀναγινώσκοντος τὸν προφήτην Ἡσαΐαν, καὶ εἶπεν, Ἆρά γε γινώσκεις ἃ ἀναγινώσκεις; 31 Ὁ δὲ εἶπε, Πῶς γὰρ ἂν δυναίμην, ἐὰν μή τις ὁδηγήσῃ με; Παρεκάλεσέ τε τὸν Φίλιππον ἀναβάντα καθίσαι σὺν αὐτῷ. 32 ἡ δὲ περιοχὴ τῆς γραφῆς ἣν ἀνεγίνωσκεν, ἦν αὕτη,

REVISED VERSION.

ship; and he was [b]returning, 28 and, sitting upon his chariot, he was reading Isaiah, the prophet. [c]Moreover the Spirit 29 said to Philip, Go near and [d]join yourself to this chariot. And Philip [e]having run up to 30 him, and heard him reading Isaiah, the prophet, said, Do you understand what you are reading? He replied, How can I, 31 except some one should [f]guide me? And he [g]invited Philip to come up and sit with him. Now the [h]passage of the Scrip- 32 ture, which he was reading,

---

says: ἀνέβην προσκυνήσων ἐν Ἰερουσαλήμ, Acts 24 : 11 The Eunuch went worshiping *into* Jerusalem; while Paul says, I went up worshiping *in* Jerusalem. We adjust this difference by repudiating the reading in the Textus Receptus in Acts 24 : 11, and by substituting εἰς for ἐν on the authority of Lachmann and Tischendorf in Bagsters' Improved Greek text. *Εἰς*, indeed, is grammatically and naturally associated with verbs indicative of motion or progress; while ἐν is appropriately connected with verbs intimating rest, repose, or cessation from action. It is a beautiful fact that προσκυνέω, occurring sixty times in the Christian Scriptures, is uniformly, in every case, represented by the word *worship*.

It is also another remarkable fact, and worthy of all commendation, that προσευχή, *prayer*, and προσεύχομαι, I *pray*, occurring in the Christian Greek Scriptures one hundred and twenty-three times, are invariably represented by *pray* and *prayer*. What an unspeakable blessing to the world—to Christendom especially, had the same law been observed in reference to *Baptize, Baptism, bishop, presbyter, deacon*, &c., &c.! There lives not the man who could compute the gain to the Church and to the world from such a fact.

A question on εἰς Ἰερουσαλήμ.—Did the Eunuch go to worship *within* Jerusalem, or go into Jerusalem to worship?—These are very different ideas or objects. If a Jewish proselyte he went to, or into Jerusalem to worship the God of the Jews as the God of the whole earth—the One only living and true God. But if he went merely to worship to, *into*, or unto, Jerusalem, or to do homage to the localities there, he had need to have propounded other and different questions than those he submitted to Philip.

But may not the idea embraced in the original be more appositely couched in the formula he had come to worship *within* Jerusalem—in the spirit of a pious Jew, as represented

in the songs of degrees, Ps. 122 : 3. To Jerusalem—" the Tribes go up, the Tribes of the Lord—to the testimony of Israel to give thanks to the name of the Lord. For there are placed the Thrones of Judgment—the thrones of the house of David.—Peace be within thee! Because of the house of the Lord our God I will seek thy good." This was the great attractive centre of all who recognized the God of the Jews, as the One only living and true God.

[b] Ἦν τε ὑποστρεφων καὶ καθημενος ἐπι.—And he *was returning*, &c., ἐπι, upon his chariot—*and he was reading*—a happy indication of the appositeness of the imperfect to express continuity of action.

[c] Δε, moreover, 1 Cor. 15 : 1. The Spirit said: *approach*, προσελθε και κολληθητι, and join yourself to that chariot.—" And do you understand what you do read?" said he; rather *are you understanding what you are reading?* A happy illustration of the *continuative force* of the present tense.

[d] Κολληθητι—κολλαω—to cleave to, to keep company, to join. In ten occurrences in Luke's and Paul's use of this word it is six times rendered *join*, com. ver.

[e] Προσδραμων. 2d Aor. part. Active of προστρεχω, curro, ran to him, having run up to him.

[f] Εαν μη ὁδηγησῃ—from ὁδος, a way, and αγω, I lead. Go before me, lead me.—So Homer, Od. 10 : 263; Xeno. Cyro. 4 : 5, 13; Mem. 3 : 2 4. A leader in war, to guide by leading the way.

[g] Παρεκαλεσε—invited him—καθισαι συν αυτῳ.

[h] Περιοχη της γραφης, the passage of Scripture, not the place. See Stobæus in Ecc. Phys. p. 164, a Dion. Hal. de Thuc. 25. Cic. ad Attic. 13 : 25.

KING JAMES' VERSION.	GREEK TEXT.	REVISED VERSION.

led as a sheep to the slaughter; and like a lamb dumb before his shearer, so opened he not his mouth:

33 In his humiliation his judgment was taken away: and who shall declare his generation? for his life is taken from the earth.

34 And the eunuch answered Philip, and said, I pray thee, of whom speaketh the prophet this? of himself, or of some other man?

35 Then Philip opened his mouth, and began at the same scripture, and preached unto him Jesus.

36 And as they went on *their* way, they came unto a certain water: and the eunuch said, See, *here is* water; what doth hinder me to be baptized?

37 And Philip said, If thou believest with all thine heart, thou mayest. And he answered and said, I believe that Jesus Christ is the Son of God.

Ὡς πρόβατον ἐπὶ σφαγὴν ἤχθη, καὶ ὡς ἀμνὸς ἐναντίον τοῦ κείροντος αὐτὸν ἄφωνος, οὕτως οὐκ ἀνοίγει τὸ στόμα αὐτοῦ. 33 ἐν τῇ ταπεινώσει αὐτοῦ ἡ κρίσις αὐτοῦ ἤρθη, τὴν δὲ γενεὰν αὐτοῦ τίς διηγήσεται; ὅτι αἴρεται ἀπὸ τῆς γῆς ἡ ζωὴ αὐτοῦ 34 Ἀποκριθεὶς δὲ ὁ εὐνοῦχος τῷ Φιλίππῳ εἶπε, Δέομαί σου, περὶ τίνος ὁ προφήτης λέγει τοῦτο; περὶ ἑαυτοῦ, ἢ περὶ ἑτέρου τινός; 35 Ἀνοίξας δὲ ὁ Φίλιππος τὸ στόμα αὐτοῦ, καὶ ἀρξάμενος ἀπὸ τῆς γραφῆς ταύτης, εὐηγγελίσατο αὐτῷ τὸν Ἰησοῦν. 36 ὡς δὲ ἐπορεύοντο κατὰ τὴν ὁδὸν, ἦλθον ἐπί τι ὕδωρ· καί φησιν ὁ εὐνοῦχος, Ἰδοὺ ὕδωρ· τί κωλύει με βαπτισθῆναι; 37 Εἶπε δὲ ὁ Φίλιππος, Εἰ πιστεύεις ἐξ ὅλης τῆς καρδίας, ἔξεστιν. Ἀποκριθεὶς δὲ εἶπε, Πιστεύω τὸν υἱὸν τοῦ Θεοῦ εἶναι τὸν Ἰησοῦν Χρι-

was this, "He was [i]led away as a sheep to slaughter: and as a lamb is [j]silent before the shearer, so [k]he opens not his mouth. In his humiliation, his 33 [l]condemnation was extorted; and who shall declare his generation? for his life is [m]violently taken from the earth." And 34 the officer, replying to Philip, said, I beg of you, of whom does the prophet speak this? of himself, or of some other person? And Philip opened 35 his mouth, and began at the same Scripture, and announced to him Jesus.

And as they were going 36 along the [n]road, they came [o]upon a certain water: and the officer said,—Behold water! What hinders my being immersed? And Philip said, If you 37 believe with all your heart, you may. And he answered, and said, I believe that Jesus Christ is the son of God. And he 38

---

[i] *Ηχθη*, he was led away. And, as a silent lamb—*αφωνος*, all lambs are dumb, but not silent. This Lamb of God was silent.

[j] *Εναντιον του κειραντος αυτον*, in sight of, before, in presence of the shearer—or devourer.

Κειραντος, specially claims attention. While *tondeo* in its mildest construction indicates simply to shear, it more literally and generally means to *destroy, consume, devour*. Represented in Latin by *depasci*, and in Homeric currency—to *consume*, to *devour*. Il. 11 : 560; Od. 11 : 578.

Επειρε πολυμεριον φονον. He slaughtered many a horned beast, Sophocles, Az. 55.

Shorn, or *shearing*, is not apposite to this case—too tame for the occasion. The idea here is slaughter, not lamb shearing.

[k] *Ουκ ανοιγει*. 3d per. sing. pres. Ind., he is not opening his mouth.

"His legal trial is taken away," Thompson. Through violence and punishment he was taken away, i. e. from life, De Wette. The Hebrew sustains this view. "The generation amongst whom he suffered who shall fully declare," Hackett. His judgment was taken away, might indicate in our style, that he was bereft of his reason.

[l] *Η κρισις αυτου ηρθη*. In com. ver. *κρισις* is represented by *judgment, damnation, condemnation, accusation*. His *condemnation was extorted*—They constrained him to witness against himself—and then exclaimed "*away with him*," "*crucify him*." So *αιρω* is occasionally understood; and in this case, it is more apposite than in any other known to us in Holy Scripture.

[m] Taken from the earth is too tame for this case. The Hebrew is מֵעֹצֶר וּמִמִּשְׁפָּט לֻקָּח tantamount to: *Through violence and punishment he was taken away*, from earth or from life. And his cotemporaries, or *generation*, who shall fully declare?—or exhibit, Meyer, Robinson, De Wette. Their wickedness was unparalleled.

"*Taken* from the earth" is, we repeat, too tame. It has in its concomitants the idea of violence—hence we prefer *violently taken* from the earth.

[n] *Κατα την οδον*—And as they were going along the road.

Behold water, *ιδου υδωρ*. There is here no supplement necessary. The exact Greek requires no supplement in this case; more especially because *τι υδωρ*—a certain water, or a water—immediately precedes.

[o] The phrase here is *επι τι υδωρ*—literally, *they came upon a certain water*, not *εις*, *to*, but *επι*, *upon* a certain water.

KING JAMES' VERSION.

38 And he commanded the chariot to stand still: and they went down both into the water, both Philip and the eunuch; and he baptized him.

39 And when they were come up out of the water, the Spirit of the Lord caught away Philip, that the eunuch saw him no more: and he went on his way rejoicing.

40 But Philip was found at Azotus: and passing through, he preached in all the cities, till he came to Cesarea.

CHAP. IX.

And Saul, yet breathing out threatenings and slaughter against the disciples of the Lord, went unto the high priest,

2 And desired of him letters to Damascus to the synagogues, that if he found any of this way,

GREEK TEXT.

στόν. ³⁸ Καὶ ἐκέλευσε στῆναι τὸ ἄρμα· καὶ κατέβησαν ἀμφότεροι εἰς τὸ ὕδωρ, ὅ τε Φίλιππος καὶ ὁ εὐνοῦχος· καὶ ἐβάπτισεν αὐτόν. ³⁹ ὅτε δὲ ἀνέβησαν ἐκ τοῦ ὕδατος, Πνεῦμα Κυρίου ἥρπασε τὸν Φίλιππον· καὶ οὐκ εἶδεν αὐτὸν οὐκέτι ὁ εὐνοῦχος, ἐπορεύετο γὰρ τὴν ὁδὸν αὐτοῦ χαίρων. ⁴⁰ Φίλιππος δὲ εὑρέθη εἰς Ἄζωτον· καὶ διερχόμενος εὐηγγελίζετο τὰς πόλεις πάσας, ἕως τοῦ ἐλθεῖν αὐτὸν εἰς Καισάρειαν.

CHAP. IX.

Ὁ ΔΕ Σαῦλος ἔτι ἐμπνέων ἀπειλῆς καὶ φόνου εἰς τοὺς μαθητὰς τοῦ κυρίου, προσελθὼν τῷ ἀρχιερεῖ, ² ᾐτήσατο παρ' αὐτοῦ ἐπιστολὰς εἰς Δαμασκὸν πρὸς τὰς συναγωγάς, ὅπως ἐάν τινας

REVISED VERSION.

commanded the chariot to stand still; and they both went down ᴾinto the water, Philip and the officer, and he immersed him. And when they 39 were come up out of the water, the Spirit of the Lord caught Philip away, that the officer saw him no more ; for he went on his journey rejoicing. But 40 Philip was found in Azotus: and, passing along, he announced the tidings in all the cities till his entrance into Cæsarea.

CHAP. IX.

ᑫBut Saul yet ʳbreathing 1 ˢout threatening and slaughter ᵗagainst the disciples of the Lord, went to the High Priest, and desired ᵘfrom him letters to 2 Damascus, to the ᵛSynagogues, that if he found any of ʷthat

---

ᴾ And they both went down *into*, εις—not επι. It is here κατεβησαν εις, they went down *into*, and again ανεβησαν εκ, they came up *out of*—the water.

ᑫ Δε and ετι, throw the reader back to ch. 8 : 3, and resume the history of Saul of Tarsus, who was merely introduced to us as a violent persecutor, and now further evidence of the fact is adduced. Therefore we prefer *but* to *and*, as the proper connective in this case.

ʳ Εμπνων—εν and πνεω, *flo*, spiro. The etymology of words, though not always an infallible index of their current value, or of their special import, in a given case, is, nevertheless, frequently of indispensable importance to a full appreciation of their proper significance.—To illustrate this fact and the case before us, we remark, that πνευμα, *spirit*, comes from πνεω, *spiro*, whose perfect passive is πεπνευμαι—whence πνευμα—a *breath*, a *spirit*. It is, therefore, an immediate product or effect of an oracle of God—of the breath or inspiration of God. So we read that God "breathed into his nostrils the breath of life," ורוח חיים—*ruach*, chaiyim—breath of lives, animal and spiritual. This was literal inspiration.

In the case before us Saul was breathing of threatenings and slaughter.—*Breathing of threatenings*, and *breaking of bread* are the same form, or formula of words.

ˢ Απειλης και φονου, governed by εμπνεω, spiro.

ᵗ Εις τους μαθητας, against the disciples. Εις is gram-

matically represented by inter, apud, pro, per, ad, usque ad, de, *adversus*, and by a Hebraism indicates the Dative. Piscator's Index of words. Critica Sacra. *Between, among, with, for, through, for to, even to, into, unto, concerning, against*, and *towards*. Such is its well-established currency. Of these, which is to be preferred, in any given case, must be decided by the subject and the context. It is essentially a particle of relations, and is associated with the idea of *motion, progress*, or change of position. While εν denotes both relative and absolute repose, εις represents relative and absolute motion or progress.

ᵘ Παρ' αυτον, from him, or from himself; προς τας συναγωγας, to the synagogues—not for himself, along the way—for their destiny is fixed, εις Δαμασκον. The local destination of the letters, Hack.—This settles his course and the end or object of it.

ᵛ The synagogues had their presbyteries, or presbyters ; and these had authority to commission Saul to defend their religion against the attacks of the disciples.

ʷ Της οδον, i. e., κατ' εξοχην, of the way, in regard to faith, manner of life, Hack.—The way which they call heresy, κατα την οδον, Acts 24 : 14; ch. 19 : 23; 22 : 4. This formula is frequent with Luke. Nusquam, in Novo Test. legem significat nisi quid adjiciatur ex quo, id possit intelligi, Critica Sacra. See Acts 24 : 22.

KING JAMES' VERSION.	GREEK TEXT.	REVISED VERSION.

whether they were men or women, he might bring them bound unto Jerusalem.

3 And as he journeyed, he came near Damascus: and suddenly there shined round about him a light from heaven:

4 And he fell to the earth, and heard a voice saying unto him, Saul, Saul, why persecutest thou me?

5 And he said, Who art thou, Lord? And the Lord said, I am Jesus whom thou persecutest. *It is* hard for thee to kick against the pricks.

6 And he trembling, and astonished, said, Lord, what wilt thou have me to do? And the Lord *said* unto him, Arise, and go into the city, and it shall be told thee what thou must do.

7 And the men which journeyed with him stood speechless, hearing a voice, but seeing no man.

8 And Saul arose from the earth; and when his eyes were opened, he saw no man: but they led him by the hand, and brought *him* into Damascus.

9 And he was three days with-

εὕρῃ τῆς ὁδοῦ ὄντας ἄνδρας τε καὶ γυναῖκας, δεδεμένους ἀγάγῃ εἰς Ἱερουσαλήμ. 3 ἐν δὲ τῷ πορεύεσθαι, ἐγένετο αὐτὸν ἐγγί-ζειν τῇ Δαμασκῷ, καὶ ἐξαίφνης περιήστραψεν αὐτὸν φῶς ἀπὸ τοῦ οὐρανοῦ· 4 καὶ πεσὼν ἐπὶ τὴν γῆν, ἤκουσε φωνὴν λέγου-σαν αὐτῷ, Σαοὺλ, Σαοὺλ, τί με διώκεις; 5 Εἶπε δὲ, Τίς εἶ, κύ-ριε; Ὁ δὲ κύριος εἶπεν, Ἐγώ εἰμι Ἰησοῦς ὃν σὺ διώκεις· σκληρόν σοι πρὸς κέντρα λακτί-ζειν. 6 Τρέμων τε καὶ θαμβῶν εἶπε, Κύριε, τί με θέλεις ποιῆ-σαι; Καὶ ὁ κύριος πρὸς αὐτὸν, Ἀνάστηθι καὶ εἴσελθε εἰς τὴν πόλιν, καὶ λαληθήσεταί σοι τί σε δεῖ ποιεῖν. 7 Οἱ δὲ ἄνδρες οἱ συνοδεύοντες αὐτῷ εἱστήκεισαν ἐννεοὶ, ἀκούοντες μὲν τῆς φωνῆς, μηδένα δὲ θεωροῦντες. 8 ἠγέρθη δὲ ὁ Σαῦλος ἀπὸ τῆς γῆς· ἀνε-ῳγμένων δὲ τῶν ὀφθαλμῶν αὐ-τοῦ, οὐδένα ἔβλεπε, χειραγωγοῦν-τες δὲ αὐτὸν εἰσήγαγον εἰς Δα-μασκόν. 9 καὶ ἦν ἡμέρας τρεῖς

way, whether they were men or women, he might bring them bound to Jerusalem. Now 3 ˣin the journey, he came near Damascus: and, suddenly, there flashed around him, a light from heaven, and ʸhaving 4 fallen upon the earth, he heard a voice saying to him, Saul, Saul, why do ᶻyou perse-cute me? And he said, who 5 art thou, Lord? ᵃAnd the Lord said, I am Jesus, whom you persecute; ᵇit is hard for you to kick against the goads. And he, trembling and aston- 6 ished, said, Lord, what wilt thou have me to do? And the Lord said to him, ᶜArise, and go into the city, and it shall be told you what you must do. And the men who were jour- 7 neying with him, ᵈhad stood speechless, hearing, indeed, the voice, but seeing no person. But Saul ᵉwas raised from the 8 earth; and, ᶠthough his eyes were opened, he saw no per-son: but they led him by the hand, and brought him into Damascus. And he was there 9

ˣ Ἐν δε τῳ πορευεσθαι, in the journey, or while he jour-neyed, Hack. Ἐγενετο αυτον εγγιζειν. This is a case of the Infinitive with the accusative as the subject.

Περιηστρψεν αυτον φως, light, not as a body, but as an element, *flashed* around him—as lightning.

ʸ And falling, having fallen, επι, upon the earth. The participial rendering requires not the supplementary *and* be-fore the Aorist ηκουσε.

ᶻ *Thou* and *thee* are yet regarded as the sacred style, but only retained in worship and worshipful style. We cannot as yet wholly repudiate this usage; but, with the exception of specific prayer or addresses to God, or in his addresses to any person, we presume to dispense with it as a mere spe-cimen of antiquity, no longer to be indulged.

ᵃ Ὁ δε κυριος ειπεν. The clause is omitted by Ln., Tf., and declared doubtful by Gries.—It is not needed. Indeed, all from σκληρον το αυτον is omitted by Gb., Knapp, Sch., Ln. Tf. following Erasmus. There is, indeed, nothing gained or lost

to truth, with or without it.—If retained, we omit the article, and render κεντρα, spurs or sharp points.

ᵇ From σκληρον, to λακτιζειν, has been transferred to this place from ch. 26 : 14, Hackett, Dodd., &c. Westen has pro-duced instances of this proverb from Greek and Roman authors. Κεντρα, a goad, Wakefield. Thompson, Wesley, Murdock. Griesbach regards this as a spurious reading.

ᶜ Αλλα αναστ. But rise up and enter into the city, and that which behooves you to do (to be doing). This verb ex-presses a continuous acting, not an act completed, Lidd. and Scott. Rob.

ᵈ And the men—journeying with him, ειστηκεισαν εννεοι—3d per. plural, pluperfect—*had stood speechless.*

ᵉ Εγερθη, aor. 1. ind. pass., *was raised up*, ab αγειρω.

ᶠ Ανεῳγμενον δε των οφθαλμων—perfect part. pass.; though his eyes were opened he saw no person; χειραγωγουντες, Paul; χειραγωγεω, manu duco, part. pres., ducentes manu, Beza.

out sight, and neither did eat nor drink.

10 And there was a certain disciple at Damascus, named Ananias; and to him said the Lord in a vision, Ananias. And he said, Behold, I *am here*, Lord.

11 And the Lord *said* unto him, Arise, and go into the street which is called Straight, and inquire in the house of Judas for *one* called Saul of Tarsus: for behold, he prayeth,

12 And hath seen in a vision a man named Ananias, coming in, and putting *his* hand on him, that he might receive his sight.

13 Then Ananias answered, Lord, I have heard by many of this man, how much evil he hath done to thy saints at Jerusalem:

14 And here he hath authority from the chief priests, to bind all that call on thy name.

15 But the Lord said unto him, Go thy way: for he is a chosen vessel unto me, to bear

μὴ βλέπων, καὶ οὐκ ἔφαγεν οὐδὲ ἔπιεν. 10 Ἦν δέ τις μαθητὴς ἐν Δαμασκῷ ὀνόματι Ἀνανίας, καὶ εἶπε πρὸς αὐτὸν ὁ κύριος ἐν ὁράματι, Ἀνανία. Ὁ δὲ εἶπεν, Ἰδοὺ ἐγώ, κύριε. 11 Ὁ δὲ κύριος πρὸς αὐτόν, Ἀναστὰς πορεύθητι ἐπὶ τὴν ῥύμην τὴν καλουμένην Εὐθεῖαν, καὶ ζήτησον ἐν οἰκίᾳ Ἰούδα Σαῦλον ὀνόματι, Ταρσέα. ἰδοὺ γὰρ προσεύχεται, 12 καὶ εἶδεν ἐν ὁράματι ἄνδρα ὀνόματι Ἀνανίαν εἰσελθόντα καὶ ἐπιθέντα αὐτῷ χεῖρα, ὅπως ἀναβλέψῃ. 13 Ἀπεκρίθη δὲ ὁ Ἀνανίας, Κύριε, ἀκήκοα ἀπὸ πολλῶν περὶ τοῦ ἀνδρὸς τούτου, ὅσα κακὰ ἐποίησε τοῖς ἁγίοις σου ἐν Ἱερουσαλήμ· 14 καὶ ὧδε ἔχει ἐξουσίαν παρὰ τῶν ἀρχιερέων, δῆσαι πάντας τοὺς ἐπικαλουμένους τὸ ὄνομά σου. 15 Εἶπε δὲ πρὸς αὐτὸν ὁ κύριος, Πορεύου, ὅτι σκεῦος ἐκλογῆς μοι ἐστὶν οὗτος, τοῦ

three days [g]without seeing, and did not eat nor drink.

Now, there was a certain 10 disciple at Damascus, named Ananias: and the Lord said to him in a vision, Ananias! And he said, Behold, I am here, Lord. And the Lord said to 11 him, Arise and go [h]upon the street which is called Straight, and inquire in the house of Judas for one called Saul, of Tarsus: for behold he is praying *to* [i]me, and has seen in a vision 12 a man named Ananias coming in, and putting his hand on him, that he might receive his sight. Then Ananias answer- 13 ed, Lord, I have heard, by many, of this man, how much evil he has done to thy saints who are in Jerusalem. And 14 here he has authority from the chief Priests, to bind all [j]those invoking thy name. But 15 the Lord said to him, [k]Go, for he is a chosen [l]instrument for

---

[g] And he was three days without seeing. *Μη βλεπων*, and eat not nor drank. To agree with drank it should be the imperfect and not the preterite, the imperfect is yet read *eat* as well as *ate*. We eat and drank is still in use amongst our best writers.

[h] *Επι την ῥυμην*, upon the street. Literally, as directions to find houses should be given—*Go up on the street called Straight*.

[i] Paul always prayed, as a Jew. Still I am not tenacious of supplements. It is a fact that he then prayed to Jesus, which he had never done before.

"For behold he prays."—Did Paul, who affirmed, that, "touching the righteousness that is in the law, he was blameless"—never before pray!! Certainly he prayed, else he could not have said this, or that he had, as a Jew, "lived in all good conscience before God," even to the day of his conversion.

I submit, therefore, that the facts in the case demand the supplement "*to me*." "For behold," said Jesus, "he prays to me, or in my name."

[j] *Τους επικαλουμενους*, thee calling on thy name. Who call, is more apposite to a class. All calling upon thy name—is not so specific—i. e., indicative of a class. These are professionally

—*habitually*, so employed. Hence, as indicative of a class rather than of an act, we prefer those that call, to those calling.

[k] *Πορευω—πορευομαι*, proficiscor—pergo, *iterfacio*; often used in this sense, Critica Sacra; go, Thomp., Wes., Penn, Wakefield; arise and go, Murd., Booth.

[l] *Σκευος εκλογης μοι*, a chosen vessel, Murd., Thomp., Booth., Penn, Wake.; *βαστασαι*, properly to bear up, to lift up, Jos. Ant. 7 : 11, 7 ; John 10 : 31—to exalt my name. We prefer to carry—"It signifieth only to carry," Crit. Sacra. It is rendered to *bear*, Murd., Wake., Penn, Wes., Thomp. To *bear* and *carry*, are used as synonyms in vessels or ships of burthen. *Ενωπιον*, in conspectu, coram.

Vessel, instrument. We prefer the latter. Vessel, now-a-days, is more appropriate to ships and seafaring life. *Σκευος*, indicates any kind of instrument.—The genitive use of *εκλογης* is rather Hebraistic than Grecian. It is a strong expression of the idea—an instrument of choice—rather than a chosen instrument. But we cannot legitimately think that there is any special reference to an eternal, or to a temporal choice, but to the admirable adaptation of the man to the work. However true that doctrine may be, it is not in the premises before us. Both truth and error are weakened by violence.

KING JAMES' VERSION.

my name before the Gentiles, and kings, and the children of Israel.

16 For I will show him how great things he must suffer for my name's sake.

17 And Ananias went his way, and entered into the house: and putting his hands on him, said, Brother Saul, the Lord (*even* Jesus that appeared unto thee in the way as thou camest) hath sent me that thou mightest receive thy sight, and be filled with the Holy Ghost.

18 And immediately there fell from his eyes as it had been scales: and he received sight forthwith, and arose, and was baptized.

19 And when he had received meat, he was strengthened. Then was Saul certain days with the disciples which were at Damascus.

20 And straightway he preached Christ in the synagogues, that he is the Son of God.

GREEK TEXT.

βαστάσαι τὸ ὄνομά μου ἐνώπιον ἐθνῶν καὶ βασιλέων, υἱῶν τε Ἰσραήλ. 16 ἐγὼ γὰρ ὑποδείξω αὐτῷ, ὅσα δεῖ αὐτὸν ὑπὲρ τοῦ ὀνόματός μου παθεῖν.

17 Ἀπῆλθε δὲ Ἀνανίας καὶ εἰσῆλθεν εἰς τὴν οἰκίαν, καὶ ἐπιθεὶς ἐπ' αὐτὸν τὰς χεῖρας εἶπε, Σαοὺλ ἀδελφέ, ὁ Κύριος ἀπέσταλκέ με, Ἰησοῦς ὁ ὀφθείς σοι ἐν τῇ ὁδῷ ᾗ ἤρχου, ὅπως ἀναβλέψῃς καὶ πλησθῇς Πνεύματος Ἁγίου. 18 Καὶ εὐθέως ἀπέπεσον ἀπὸ τῶν ὀφθαλμῶν αὐτοῦ ὡσεὶ λεπίδες, ἀνέβλεψέ τε παραχρῆμα, καὶ ἀναστὰς ἐβαπτίσθη, 19 καὶ λαβὼν τροφὴν ἐνίσχυσεν. Ἐγένετο δὲ ὁ Σαῦλος μετὰ τῶν ἐν Δαμασκῷ μαθητῶν ἡμέρας τινάς· 20 καὶ εὐθέως ἐν ταῖς συναγωγαῖς ἐκήρυσσε τὸν Χριστὸν, ὅτι οὗτός ἐστιν ὁ υἱὸς τοῦ Θεοῦ. 21 ἐξί-

REVISED VERSION.

me, to bear my name before
the Gentiles, and kings, and
the children of Israel: for I 16
will [m]indicate to him how great
things he must suffer on account of my name.

And Ananias [n]went away and 17
entered into the house, and having laid his hands on him, said, Brother Saul, [o]the Lord, even Jesus, who appeared to you in the way as you came, has sent me, that you may receive sight, and be [p]filled
with the Holy Spirit. And 18
immediately there fell from his eyes, as it were scales: and he received sight [q]forthwith, and arose, and was immersed: and having taken food 19
he was strengthened. Then [r]Paul was some days with the disciples who were at Damascus. And immediately he 20
[s]proclaimed Christ in the synagogues, that this is the Son

---

[m] *Ὑποδειξω—ὑποδεικνυμι,* premonstro—*indico.* I *will show* him, or *indicate to him*—is more in harmony with our style.

[n] *Απηλθε,* went away, *επιθεις—χειρας*—and "*put* his hands" on him, Wake.; "*laid* his hands," Murd.; "*having laid* his hands," Thomp.; "laying his hands," Penn; "*putting* his hands," Wes.; when *he had put* his hands, Booth.; and put his hands, Geneva, Cranmer; imposing hands, Rheims; and laid on him his hands, Wiclif.

[o] *Ιησους ὁ οφθεις—ὁ κυριος,* per apposition—the Lord Jesus, Wakefield; our Lord Jesus, Murd.; the Lord, even Jesus, Thomp.; the Lord Jesus, Murd.; "*the Lord has sent me,* Jesus who appeared to thee," Wesley. We prefer, *the Lord, even Jesus* who appeared, &c.

[p] Filled with Holy Spirit—with capitals *Holy Spirit* does not at any time denote a mere spiritual *influence*, and, in the case of Paul, it was not an ordinary influence that was vouchsafed to him. He was *Apostolically* a *temple* of the Holy Spirit, and not merely, as all Christians are, possessed of its sanctifying, comforting influence. But theologically we do not discuss this subject, but only say that according to the text before us it is printed as *the* Holy Spirit, although *anarthrous,* and doubtless has reference to his personal abiding.

[q] *Παραχρημα,* is omitted by Gb., Ln., Tf.; *και αναστας,* is not necessarily rendered *having risen.* It is by the highest authorities *exsurgens.* See Thesauros Græcæ Linguæ *Redactus* secundum Constantini Methodum et Schrevellii Reseratus—Concinatus &c. Gulielmi Robertson, An. Dom. 1676. *And arose and was immersed*—"on this Hebraistic use of the word see Gesen. Lex. p. 919"—Hack. *Λαβων τροφην,* having taken food.

[r] *Ὁ Σαυλος.* Gb., Sch., Ln., and Tf. omit *ὁ Σαυλος* in this place.

[s] *Εκηρυσσε.* He proclaimed Jesus (*τον Ιησουν,* Gries., Sch., Ln., and Tf.) that he is—or that himself *is* the Son of God.

"He preached Christ, that he was the Son of God"—That "Jesus is the Christ"—and that "the Christ, is the Son of God," are two forms of the great apostolic proposition, announced, debated, and established in that age. To *preach* thus, was to announce it, with all evidence, and with all authority. Paul having formerly denied this fact, gave great prominence and weight to it in his annunciations of it.

"To *teach*" and "to preach" Christ, were technical or professional phrases in that age. They were then regarded as different works; as enlisting soldiers and training them. The *κηρυσσω* and the *διδασκω* families have neither consanguinity nor affinity. The latter is always *teach,* the former is always *preach, publish,* or *proclaim.* They never ought to be con-

KING JAMES' VERSION.	GREEK TEXT.	REVISED VERSION.

KING JAMES' VERSION.

21 But all that heard *him* were amazed, and said, Is not this he that destroyed them which called on this name in Jerusalem, and came hither for that intent, that he might bring them bound unto the chief priests?

22 But Saul increased the more in strength, and confounded the Jews which dwelt at Damascus, proving that this is very Christ.

23 And after that many days were fulfilled, the Jews took counsel to kill him.

24 But their laying wait was known of Saul. And they watched the gates day and night to kill him.

25 Then the disciples took

GREEK TEXT.

σταντο δὲ πάντες οἱ ἀκούοντες καὶ ἔλεγον, Οὐχ οὗτός ἐστιν ὁ πορθήσας ἐν Ἰερουσαλὴμ τοὺς ἐπικαλουμένους τὸ ὄνομα τοῦτο, καὶ ὧδε εἰς τοῦτο ἐλήλυθει ἵνα δεδεμένους αὐτοὺς ἀγάγῃ ἐπὶ τοὺς ἀρχιερεῖς; ²² Σαῦλος δὲ μᾶλλον ἐνεδυναμοῦτο, καὶ συνέχυνε τοὺς Ἰουδαίους τοὺς κατοικοῦντας ἐν Δαμασκῷ, συμβιβάζων ὅτι οὗτός ἐστιν ὁ Χριστός. ²³ ὡς δὲ ἐπληροῦντο ἡμέραι ἱκανεὶ, συνεβουλεύσαντο οἱ Ἰουδαῖοι ἀνελεῖν αὐτόν· ²⁴ ἐγνώσθη δὲ τῷ Σαύλῳ ἡ ἐπιβουλὴ αὐτῶν. παρετήρουν τε τὰς πύλας ἡμέρας τε καὶ νυκτὸς, ὅπως αὐτὸν ἀνέλωσι· ²⁵ λαβόντες δὲ αὐτὸν οἱ μαθηταὶ

REVISED VERSION.

of God. But all that heard 21 him were amazed, and said, Is not this he who destroyed those who invoked this name in Jerusalem, and came hither for this purpose, that he might bring them bound to the chief Priests? But Saul increased 22 the more in strength, and ᵘconfounded the Jews who dwelt in Damascus, ᵛproving that this person is the Christ. Now 23 when many days were accomplished, the Jews consulted to ʷkill him. But their ˣconspiracy was ʸknown to Saul, and they watched the gates, day and night, that they might kill him. Then the disciples ᶻtook him 25

---

founded or substituted one for the other. The *teacher* is a διδασκαλος, and his *teaching* a διδαχη, or doctrine, whereas the *preacher* is a κηρυξ, and his preaching a κερυγμα, or proclamation. These are works sometimes contrasted, at least distinguished in the New Testament. "They ceased not to *preach* and *teach* Jesus Christ," or to *teach* Christ to the initiated; and to *preach* him to the uninitiated. See also 2 Tim. 1 : 11. There we find κηρυξ και αποστολος εθνων, και διδασκαλος concentrated in one man. Paul was a "*preacher*, and a *teacher*, and an apostle," sent to the nations.

We now have preachers many, and teachers many, and often in the same persons; but no apostles save "The Twelve" and Paul, who, though dead, are still speaking to us.

ᵗ Εξιστατο δε παντες—εξιστημι—ισταμαι, obstupesco, obstupefacio. Ad verbum declarat—they were *extra se esse*, Beza, whence the word *extacy quasi extra se sit raptus*. So *percellor* or *obstupesco;* for the Greek word signifieth, mentem alicujus veluti loco commovere, which the Latin *percello* doth, Beza. See 2 Cor. 5 : 13. Transported. And they were *amazed*, Acts 2 : 7; 8 : 13; 9 : 21; 10 : 45; and 12 : 16. *Amazed, astonished, bewitched—beside one's self, wondered.* So it is rendered in the com. ver., in its 17 occurrences.

ᵘ "Disputed with those Jews who understood Greek." Syriac Version, ch. 6 : 1. The Grecian disciples murmured against the Hebrews.

ᵛ "Proving that this person is the Christ," is better than proving that this one is the true Christ.

ʷ Ανελειν, to put him aside. To kill him was their scheme.

ˣ Επιβουλη, conspiracy. Wiles—*lying in wait* is obsolete.

But their conspiracy was known. See Helian 3 : 5, 9. Χεν., Hell. 3 : 3, 4, 5. Also Sept. Hist. 2 : 22. And παρε τηρουν, imp. They watched the gates narrowly, both day and night. *Τε και οπως, in order that*, ανελωσε—they might put him aside. *Αναιρεω*—here found Aor. 2d Sub., ανελω, 3d per. plur.—that they might *abolish* or destroy him.

ʸ Authorities for both are about equal, known to, or known by, Saul. We prefer the former. It was not known by him as the means, but to him as the end.

ᶻ Then the disciples, λαβοντες, "taking him by night, let him down *through the wall* in a basket," Dodd., Wakefield; "*by the side of the wall*," Bloomfield; through the wall—by an aperture, Ols.; by the side of the wall, Dodd., Wakefield. Δια. By a comparison of 2 Cor. 11 : 33 δια must here mean *through*, i. e., *by an aperture*, Bloom.; "let him down in a basket *through* an opening in the city wall," Ols. Δια θυριδος—sporta, a *basket*, a *pannier*. Some think that *sporta* was a measure twice as large as *cophinus*, because Paul was let down in a *sporta*, Critica Sacra; Christ distinguishes between *cophinos* and *sportas*, Matthew 16 : 9, 10. It is also used Matthew 15 : 37; Mark 8 : 8, 10; Crit. Sacra.—There must have been an opening in the wall—to justify the use of δια. Χαλασαντες, lowering him, or letting him down. This event is more fully detailed by Paul himself—"Through a window in a basket was I let down by the wall," 2 Cor. 11 : 33. Such windows in walls are noted in the East, Jos. 11 : 15. See Aristoph. Vesp. p. 354–379. Athen. p. 214.—There is an engraving of a part of the present wall of Dam. in C. and H. i, p. 110. See also Aristoph. Ves. p. 354 and 379. Athen. p. 214.

him by night, and let *him* down by the wall in a basket.

26 And when Saul was come to Jerusalem, he assayed to join himself to the disciples : but they were all afraid of him, and believed not that he was a disciple.

27 But Barnabas took him, and brought *him* to the apostles, and declared unto them how he had seen the Lord in the way, and that he had spoken to him, and how he had preached boldly at Damascus in the name of Jesus.

28 And he was with them coming in and going out at Jerusalem.

29 And he spake boldly in the name of the Lord Jesus, and disputed against the Grecians : but they went about to slay him.

30 *Which* when the brethren knew, they brought him down to Cesarea, and sent him forth to Tarsus.

31 Then had the churches rest throughout all Judea, and

νυκτὸς, καθῆκαν διὰ τοῦ τείχους, χαλάσαντες ἐν σπυρίδι. ²⁶ Παραγενόμενος δὲ ὁ Σαῦλος εἰς Ἱερουσαλὴμ, ἐπειρᾶτο κολλᾶσθαι τοῖς μαθηταῖς· καὶ πάντες ἐφοβοῦντο αὐτὸν, μὴ πιστεύοντες ὅτι ἐστὶ μαθητής. ²⁷ Βαρνάβας δὲ ἐπιλαβόμενος αὐτὸν, ἤγαγε πρὸς τοὺς ἀποστόλους, καὶ διηγήσατο αὐτοῖς πῶς ἐν τῇ ὁδῷ εἶδε τὸν Κύριον, καὶ ὅτι ἐλάλησεν αὐτῷ, καὶ πῶς ἐν Δαμασκῷ ἐπαρρησιάσατο ἐν τῷ ὀνόματι τοῦ Ἰησοῦ. ²⁸ καὶ ἦν μετ' αὐτῶν εἰσπορευόμενος καὶ ἐκπορευόμενος ἐν Ἱερουσαλὴμ, καὶ παρρησιαζόμενος ἐν τῷ ὀνόματι τοῦ Κυρίου Ἰησοῦ, ²⁹ ἐλάλει τε καὶ συνεξήτει πρὸς τοὺς Ἑλληνιστάς· οἱ δὲ ἐπεχείρουν αὐτὸν ἀνελεῖν. ³⁰ ἐπιγνόντες δὲ οἱ ἀδελφοὶ κατήγαγον αὐτὸν εἰς Καισάρειαν, καὶ ἐξαπέστειλαν αὐτὸν εἰς Ταρσόν. ³¹ Αἱ μὲν οὖν ἐκκλησίαι καθ' ὅλης τῆς

by night, and let him down through the wall in a basket. But [a]coming into Jerusalem, 26 he was attempting to attach himself to the disciples ; but they were all fearing him, not believing him to be a disciple. But Barnabas took him 27 and brought him to the Apostles, and fully declared to them, how he had seen the Lord in the way, and that he had spoken to him, and how he had boldly preached at Damascus, in the name of Jesus.

And he was with them, coming in and going out in Jerusalem, and preaching boldly in the name of the Lord [b]Jesus, and was talking and [c]disputing with the Hellenists ; but they undertook to kill him. The 30 brethren, having [d]ascertained this, conducted him into Cæsarea, and sent him out into Tarsus. Then the [e]congregations 31 had peace, throughout all Ju-

---

[a] But παραγομενος, Aor. Part. coming (εις) into Jerusalem. Επειρατο, *he was attempting*, (the imperfect shows a continuous attempt). Ὁ Σαυλος is omitted by Gb., Sch., Ln., Tf. Καλλασθαι—attach himself—τοις μαθηταις, to the disciples, and they *were* all *fearing* him (imp. mid. following acc.), not, πιστευοντες, believing him to be a disciple—or that he *is* a disciple.

[b] Jesus is omitted by Ln., Tf.

[c] "And was disputing with the Hellenists." These were the Jewish converts who spake the Greek language. The Palestine Jews were called Hebrews. They spoke the Syro-Chaldaic—the Aramaen—προς more properly *with* than *against*, and more frequently *to* than either.

"And he spake and disputed with the *Judaising* Greeks," Penn. A murmuring arose against the Hebrews on the part of the Greek converts," 6 : 1, Penn. Translators have thus varied, for the sake of placing the same people before the reader in various attitudes. And so did the Apostles in presenting the same Gospel facts. Still this is a matter of taste and not of authority.

[d] Δε, "but come to a knowledge of it," is in our day and style, better represented by *ascertained*—for "brought him down to"—*conducted him into Cæsarea.*

[e] The term εκκλησια is not found in this book in the singular number applied to a plurality of churches or communities scattered over one or more provinces or cities, we, therefore, in this case prefer the com. reading to the reading of Ln. and Tf. We have the church of God, the church of Christ, but we have not a *church of churches*, in apostolic currency.

Paul's conversion is here alluded to, as possessing great influence on the churches—both on their peace and prosperity.

Εκκλησιαι—επληθυνοντος—congregations were multiplied. The idea of national, imperial, or provincial churches is without one vestige of authority in all the handprints and footprints of the Apostolic writings or labors. The Church of Galatia, the Church of Asia, the Church of Galilee, Samaria, or Judea—of the Jews or of the Gentiles—occurs not once in the Acts, or in any other book in the N. Testament ; but we often read of the *churches* in numerous districts. Such as the churches of Judea, Samaria, Syria, Cilicia. "*Churches* of Christ"—CHURCHES of the Gentiles, Churches of Asia, churches of Macedonia, "churches of God," &c., &c. In all such cases, as already intimated, it is not *Church* in Greek but εκκλησια, "congregation" or "assembly." The Church of Rome, of

KING JAMES' VERSION.	GREEK TEXT.	REVISED VERSION.

Galilee, and Samaria, and were edified : and walking in the fear of the Lord, and in the comfort of the Holy Ghost, were multiplied.

32 And it came to pass, as Peter passed throughout all *quarters*, he came down also to the saints which dwelt at Lydda.

33 And there he found a certain man named Eneas, which had kept his bed eight years, and was sick of the palsy.

34 And Peter said unto him, Eneas, Jesus Christ maketh thee whole : arise, and make thy bed. And he arose immediately.

35 And all that dwelt at Lydda and Saron saw him, and turned to the Lord.

36 Now there was at Joppa a certain disciple named Tabitha, which by interpretation is called Dorcas ; this woman was full of good works and almsdeeds which she did.

37 And it came to pass in those days, that she was sick,

Ἰουδαίας καὶ Γαλιλαίας καὶ Σαμαρείας εἶχον εἰρήνην, οἰκοδομούμεναι καὶ πορευόμεναι τῷ φόβῳ τοῦ Κυρίου, καὶ τῇ παρακλήσει τοῦ Ἁγίου Πνεύματος ἐπληθύνοντο.

32 ΕΓΕΝΕΤΟ δὲ Πέτρον διερχόμενον διὰ πάντων, κατελθεῖν καὶ πρὸς τοὺς ἁγίους τοὺς κατοικοῦντας Λύδδαν. 33 εὗρε δὲ ἐκεῖ ἄνθρωπόν τινα Αἰνέαν ὀνόματι, ἐξ ἐτῶν ὀκτὼ κατακείμενον ἐπὶ κραββάτῳ, ὃς ἦν παραλελυμένος. 34 καὶ εἶπεν αὐτῷ ὁ Πέτρος, Αἰνέα, ἰᾶταί σε Ἰησοῦς ὁ Χριστός· ἀνάστηθι καὶ στρῶσον σεαυτῷ. Καὶ εὐθέως ἀνέστη· 35 καὶ εἶδον αὐτὸν πάντες οἱ κατοικοῦντες Λύδδαν καὶ τὸν Σαρωνᾶν, οἵτινες ἐπέστρεψαν ἐπὶ τὸν κύριον.

36 Ἐν Ἰόππῃ δέ τις ἦν μαθήτρια ὀνόματι Ταβιθὰ, ἣ διερμηνευομένη λέγεται Δορκάς· αὕτη ἦν πλήρης ἀγαθῶν ἔργων καὶ ἐλεημοσυνῶν ὧν ἐποίει· 37 ἐγένετο δὲ ἐν ταῖς ἡμέραις ἐκείναις

dea, and Galilee, and Samaria, being edified ; and, walking in the fear of the Lord, and in the consolation of the Holy Spirit, they were multiplied.

[f]Now it happened that 32 Peter, while passing through among all, came down also to the [g]saints that dwelt at Lydda : and there he found a 33 certain man, named Æneas, who had kept his bed [h]eight years, and was sick of the palsy. And Peter said to him, 34 Æneas, Jesus, the Christ, heals you. Arise and make your bed. And he arose immediately. And all who dwelt at 35 Lydda, and Saron, beheld him, and turned to the Lord.

Now there was, in Joppa, a 36 certain disciple, named Tabitha ([i]which by [j]interpretation is called, Dorcas) : this woman was full of good works, and of alms [k]which she did. [l]Now it 37 came to pass in those days that

---

England, of France, of Germany, &c., &c., ought to be regarded as solecisms. A national Church is as foreign to the Bible and reason as a national priest, a national prophet, or a national bride. Still more incongruous to speak of a national congregation, as the congregation of Judea, Samaria, Asia, France, England, or the United States.

[f] Δε and και here should be represented by two words in our language—*now* and *also*—and especially as commencing a new subject.

[g] Προς τους αγιους, not ηγιασμενους, ch. 20 : 32, *sanctified ones*, but αγιους, *saints*.

It has been questioned by some, whether δια παντων does refer to τοπων or to αγιων understood. We prefer the former, because in Luke's currency, in some twenty occurrences in this book, it uniformly refers to places.

[h] Εξ ετων οκτω—out of eight years—*from eight years before*, during eight years.

Επι κραββατῳ, upon a *cot* or small bed ; but, for sick and

infirm persons, a *couch* is more appropiate, as indicating a state of infirmity—a softer bed. He was paralytic.

[i] Ἡ, relating to the name and not to the person, should be rendered *which*, or *that*, of all genders. The former is more in use. Μαθητρια—disciple—an ἁπαξ λεγομενον.

[j] Διερμηνευομενη, part. pres. pass., *being explained*, too philosophical ; *being expounded*, too didactical. Being *interpreted* is its radical meaning from Ἡρμες—Mercury—messenger of the *gods*, classic. Its family, occurring only seven times in the N. T., is uniformly represented by *interpret*, *interpretation*, i. e., explanation.

[k] Ὡν εποιει—which she *did*, do alms—is not so established as to *give* or *bestow* alms. But this is not the solitary subject of the verb. Good works and alms are comprehended. No term can apply to both so well—we can *give* alms, but not good works, but we can do or practice both.

[l] Εγενετο δε. *Now it came to pass, in those days, that this woman, being enfeebled, died.* This preserves the accusative

KING JAMES' VERSION.	GREEK TEXT.	REVISED VERSION.

KING JAMES' VERSION.

and died: whom when they had washed, they laid *her* in an upper chamber.

38 And forasmuch as Lydda was nigh to Joppa, and the disciples had heard that Peter was there, they sent unto him two men, desiring *him* that he would not delay to come to them.

39 Then Peter arose, and went with them. When he was come, they brought him into the upper chamber: and all the widows stood by him weeping, and shewing the coats and garments which Dorcas made, while she was with them.

40 But Peter put them all forth, and kneeled down, and prayed; and turning *him* to the body, said, Tabitha, arise. And she opened her eyes: and when she saw Peter, she sat up.

41 And he gave her *his* hand, and lifted her up; and when he had called the saints and widows, he presented her alive.

42 And it was known throughout all Joppa: and many believed in the Lord.

43 And it came to pass, that he tarried many days in Joppa with one Simon a tanner.

GREEK TEXT.

ἀσθενήσασαν αὐτὴν ἀποθανεῖν· λούσαντες δὲ αὐτὴν ἔθηκαν ἐν ὑπερῴῳ. ³⁸ ἐγγὺς δὲ οὔσης Λύδδης τῇ Ἰόππῃ, οἱ μαθηταὶ ἀκούσαντες ὅτι Πέτρος ἐστὶν ἐν αὐτῇ, ἀπέστειλαν δύο ἄνδρας πρὸς αὐτὸν, παρακαλοῦντες μὴ ὀκνῆσαι διελθεῖν ἕως αὐτῶν. ³⁹ ἀναστὰς δὲ Πέτρος συνῆλθεν αὐτοῖς· ὃν παραγενόμενον ἀνήγαγον εἰς τὸ ὑπερῷον, καὶ παρέστησαν αὐτῷ πᾶσαι αἱ χῆραι κλαίουσαι καὶ ἐπιδεικνύμεναι χιτῶνας καὶ ἱμάτια ὅσα ἐποίει μετ’ αὐτῶν οὖσα ἡ Δορκάς. ⁴⁰ ἐκβαλὼν δὲ ἔξω πάντας ὁ Πέτρος, θεὶς τὰ γόνατα προσηύξατο· καὶ ἐπιστρέψας πρὸς τὸ σῶμα, εἶπε, Ταβιθά, ἀνάστηθι. Ἡ δὲ ἤνοιξε τοὺς ὀφθαλμοὺς αὐτῆς· καὶ ἰδοῦσα τὸν Πέτρον, ἀνεκάθισε. ⁴¹ δοὺς δὲ αὐτῇ χεῖρα, ἀνέστησεν αὐτήν· φωνήσας δὲ τοὺς ἁγίους καὶ τὰς χήρας, παρέστησεν αὐτὴν ζῶσαν. ⁴² γνωστὸν δὲ ἐγένετο καθ’ ὅλης τῆς Ἰόππης, καὶ πολλοὶ ἐπίστευσαν ἐπὶ τὸν Κύριον· ⁴³ ἐγένετο δὲ ἡμέρας ἱκανὰς μεῖναι αὐτὸν ἐν Ἰόππῃ παρά τινι Σίμωνι βυρσεῖ.

REVISED VERSION.

she, being sick, died. And, having washed her, they placed her in an upper room. And Lydda being near to Joppa, 38 the disciples, having heard that Peter was in that place, sent two men to him, entreating, that he would not delay to come through as far as to them. Then Peter, arising, 39 went with them; whom having come, they led into the upper room; and all the widows stood by him weeping, and shewing vests and mantles, ᵐall which Dorcas made while she was with them. But Peter, putting 40 them all forth, kneeled down and prayed; and turning to the body, said, Tabitha, arise. And she opened her eyes. 41 And when she saw Peter, she sat up, and he gave her his hand, and caused her to stand up; and having called the saints and widows, he presented her alive. And it was 42 known throughout all Joppa, and many believed in the Lord. And he tarried many 43 days in Joppa, with one Simon, a tanner.

CHAP. X.

THERE was a certain man in Cesarea, called Cornelius, a cen-

CHAP. X.

ΑΝΗΡ δέ τις ἦν ἐν Καισαρείᾳ ὀνόματι Κορνήλιος, ἑκατον-

CHAP. X.

ⁿNow a certain man in Cæ- 1 sarea, called Cornelius, a cen-

---

construction and dispenses with the addition of καὶ—and *having washed her, they placed her in an upper room.*

ᵐ "All which."   It is not exactly a *supplement.* Ὅσα is in the copy of the approved Greek text

ⁿ Δε, now—(ην is omitted by Gb., Ln., Tf.). It is unnecessary, and redundant; a certain man in Cæsarea, (ονοματι) by name, Cornelius; εκ σπειρης της καλουμενης Ιταλικης, *ad literam, of a band the called Italian,* or that being called the Italian. But this, too, is not our present vernacular. We would now say, of a *band called the Italian band.*

We have a rule applicable to this case, of high authority, in a very learned tract, called "Constantini Rhodocanacidis Chiensis Tractatus De Articulis"; appended to some editions of Wm. Robertson's "*Thesaurus Græcæ Lingnæ,*" printed Cantabrigiæ A.D. 1676.—Rule 2d. Nomen substantivum seu appellativum si conjunctum habet adjectivum *exigit* articulum; ita tamen ut *si adjectivum preponatur,* unicus articulus ipsi prefixus sufficit. Vide Demosthenes *pro Corona.*

Others resolve this case so as to read, of a band, *that called the Italian,* which would make this *clause* unnecessarily parenthetical, and redundant.

KING JAMES' VERSION.

turion of the band called the Italian *band*,

2 *A* devout *man*, and one that feareth God with all his house, which gave much alms to the people, and prayed to God always.

3 He saw in a vision evidently, about the ninth hour of the day, an angel of God coming in to him, and saying unto him, Cornelius.

4 And when he looked on him, he was afraid, and said, What is it, Lord? And he said unto him, Thy prayers and thine alms are come up for a memorial before God.

5 And now send men to Joppa, and call for *one* Simon, whose surname is Peter:

6 He lodgeth with one Simon a tanner, whose house is by the sea-side: he shall tell thee what thou oughtest to do.

GREEK TEXT.

τάρχης ἐκ σπείρης τῆς καλουμένης Ἰταλικῆς, 2 εὐσεβὴς καὶ φοβούμενος τὸν Θεὸν σὺν παντὶ τῷ οἴκῳ αὐτοῦ, ποιῶν τε ἐλεημοσύνας πολλὰς τῷ λαῷ, καὶ δεόμενος τοῦ Θεοῦ διαπαντός· 3 εἶδεν ἐν ὁράματι φανερῶς, ὡσεὶ ὥραν ἐννάτην τῆς ἡμέρας, ἄγγελον τοῦ Θεοῦ εἰσελθόντα πρὸς αὐτὸν, καὶ εἰπόντα αὐτῷ, Κορνήλιε. 4 Ὁ δὲ ἀτενίσας αὐτῷ καὶ ἔμφοβος γενόμενος εἶπε, Τί ἐστι, κύριε; εἶπε δὲ αὐτῷ, Αἱ προσευχαί σου καὶ αἱ ἐλεημοσύναι σου ἀνέβησαν εἰς μνημόσυνον ἐνώπιον τοῦ Θεοῦ. 5 καὶ νῦν πέμψον εἰς Ἰόππην ἄνδρας, καὶ μετάπεμψαι Σίμωνα ὃς ἐπικαλεῖται Πέτρος· 6 οὗτος ξενίζεται παρά τινι Σίμωνι βυρσεῖ, ᾧ ἐστιν οἰκία παρὰ θάλασσαν· οὗτος λαλήσει σοι τί σε δεῖ ποιεῖν.

REVISED VERSION.

turion of the band, called the
Italian Band, a [o]devout man, 2
and one who feared God,
with all his family, who gave
much [p]alms to the people, and
[q]prayed to God continually;
he distinctly saw in a [r]vision, 3
about the ninth hour of the
day, an angel of God coming in
to him, and saying to him, Cornelius! And when he [s]looked 4
on him he was afraid, and said;
What is it, Lord? And he said
to him, your prayers and your
[t]alms are come up for a memorial of you before God. And 5
now [u]send men to Joppa, and
call for one Simon, whose surname is Peter. He [v]lodges with 6
one Simon, a tanner, whose
house is by the [w]sea-shore. He
will tell you what you ought

---

[o] *Ευσεβης*, a *pious* man, Booth., Thomp. *Religious*, Rheims, Wiclif. *Devout*, Penn, Tyndale, Cranmer, Geneva, Wakef. *Righteous*, Murd. Devoted, or *devout*, is more expressive. It is, in its four occurrences, com. ver., once *godly*, and three times *devout*.

[p] *Ποιων τε ελεημοσυνας πολλας*, *alms* always, com. ver. occurs fourteen times, yet *doing* alms is not in our currency, while *giving* alms is popular.

[q] *Δεομενος του Θεου*, beseeching God, asking of God, and was praying to God. Praying evermore, Wic. Pray'd God, Tynd., Cran., Gen. Always praying, Rheims. Prayed to God, Wes., Booth., Penn, Thomp., Mur., Wakef.

[r] *Εν ὁραματι.* Literally *in vision;* but all versions have *a vision*, and that with propriety, too; inasmuch as a particular vision is referred to—besides, "*in vision*", is generic and absolute, which in this case could not be true. Cornelius! *Vocative simply*, rather than interrogative.

[s] *Ὁ δε ατενισας*, and *steadfastly* looking; or, when he had *fastened his eyes* upon him. Such is its currency in the N. T. When he looked, or earnestly gazed upon him, he became terrified, or was affrighted.

[t] *Αἱ ελεημοσυναι*, alms, or alms deeds, in all versions, except Thompson's, in which "*acts of benevolence*" is used; but this is too general.

[u] *Μεταπεμψαι*, *send*, or *call for*, com. ver.; the former is preferable. In all versions it is represented by one or other.

[v] *Ουτος ξενιζεται*, ind. pass., *is being entertained;* with us, *lodges with*, *ουτος λαλησει σοι τι σε δει ποιειν*, omitted by Gb., Sch., Ln., Tf. It is, however, the end of the mission, the purpose of the call.

Ουτος, *this person*, is more definite and emphatic than *he*, though frequently so rendered. In emphatic cases, this, or this person, is most eligible.

"He shall tell thee what thou oughtest to do"—*ουτος λαλησει σοι τι σε δει ποιειν*—is repudiated from the text by Gb., Sch., Ln., Tf.

[w] *Παρα θαλασσαν*, literally, near a sea.

This appears a very vague direction, especially if *we insert, as a prefix*, our indefinite article. In this case this would seem *inapropos*. Near sea, near lake, near home, near town, are our familiar formulas; not near a sea, near a lake, near a home, near a town. Hypercriticism stands reproved in this, as in some other cases, in the insertion of our indefinite article where the noun is anarthrous in Greek. These are beacons not to be disregarded.

But again, "*near sea*" is idiomatic of "*the sea-shore*" or "*sea-side*," for which we sometimes have *παρα την θαλασσαν*, *near the sea*, that is, of course, a special sea *in every case*.

KING JAMES' VERSION.

7 And when the angel which spake unto Cornelius was departed, he called two of his household servants, and a devout soldier of them that waited on him continually ;

8 And when he had declared all *these* things unto them, he sent them to Joppa.

9 On the morrow as they went on their journey, and drew nigh unto the city, Peter went up upon the house-top to pray, about the sixth hour :

10 And he became very hungry, and would have eaten : but while they made ready, he fell into a trance,

11 And saw heaven opened, and a certain vessel descending unto him, as it had been a great sheet knit at the four corners, and let down to the earth :

12 Wherein were all manner of four-footed beasts of the earth,

GREEK TEXT.

7 Ὡς δὲ ἀπῆλθεν ὁ ἄγγελος ὁ λαλῶν τῷ Κορνηλίῳ, φωνήσας δύο τῶν οἰκετῶν αὐτοῦ, καὶ στρατιώτην εὐσεβῆ τῶν προσκαρτερούντων αὐτῷ, 8 καὶ ἐξηγησάμενος αὐτοῖς ἅπαντα, ἀπέστειλεν αὐτοὺς εἰς τὴν Ἰόππην. 9 Τῇ δὲ ἐπαύριον ὁδοιπορούντων ἐκείνων καὶ τῇ πόλει ἐγγιζόντων, ἀνέβη Πέτρος ἐπὶ τὸ δῶμα προσεύξασθαι, περὶ ὥραν ἕκτην. 10 ἐγένετο δὲ πρόσπεινος, καὶ ἤθελε γεύσασθαι· παρασκευαζόντων δὲ ἐκείνων, ἐπέπεσεν ἐπ᾽ αὐτὸν ἔκστασις, 11 καὶ θεωρεῖ τὸν οὐρανὸν ἀνεῳγμένον, καὶ καταβαῖνον ἐπ᾽ αὐτὸν σκεῦός τι ὡς ὀθόνην μεγάλην, τέσσαρσιν ἀρχαῖς δεδεμένον, καὶ καθιέμενον ἐπὶ τῆς γῆς· 12 ἐν ᾧ ὑπῆρχε πάντα τὰ τετράποδα τῆς γῆς καὶ

REVISED VERSION.

to do. And when the angel 7 who spoke to Cornelius was gone, he called two of his domestics, and a devout soldier of those who waited on him ; and having [x]fully related all 8 these things to them, he sent them to Joppa. [y]Again, on the 9 next day, while they were on their journey, and drew near the city, Peter went up [z]on the house-top to pray, at about the sixth hour. And becoming very 10 hungry, he [a]desired to eat. Now while they were preparing, he fell into a [b]trance, and [c]saw the 11 heaven open, and a [d]certain vessel descending to him like a great white sheet, bound together at four corners, and let down to the earth ; in which 12 were all kinds of four-footed animals, and wild [e]beasts, and

---

Ὡσει αμμος, as sand, not as *a* sand on the sea-shore. The same law that would justify *a* sea-shore would here justify *a* sand, which of course would not be innumerable !

[x] Εξηγησαμενος, *fully* related. Literally, *exegetically* developed.

[y] Δε, *again*, on the next day. Δε is here *continuative*, well represented by, *and*, generally, but when *reiteration* is implied, *again*, with us, is more in our idiom.

[z] Literally "*onto*", but not in our educated currency. It is not found in Webster, but is in Worcester. *Went up upon* is too pleonastic. We prefer *ascended*, ascended the house-top. Septuagint usage is in favor of the term, *building*. Flat roofs were more in use then than now. The term *roof* would be apposite, if more in our currency. *Garret* would be its Scotch representative—*house-top* leaves the *place where*, with us, as the original presents it.

[a] He *was desiring* is too indefinite, too continuative. At the end of his prayer rather than during it, he desired to eat. Δε will suit either rendition. With us, *and* is not necessarily *continuative*, any more than και. Both are sometimes so. The next verse indicates an event of hunger—he *desired* to eat. The sense of hunger greatly awakens the sensorium, and, appositely to the occasion, he fell into a trance, in harmony with the keen demands of appetite.

[b] Εκστασις, an *ecstasy*, literally, *standing out of himself*.

His outward senses were no encumbrance to him. He gazed, as a spirit disembodied, upon the scene before him.

[c] Θεωρει. He, literally, *theorises*, considers with emphatic attention. It is a sort of *historic* present, and might be rendered, he *fully considered*, or *contemplated* the exhibition, the scene. But the action, being *continuative* is properly present to his inspection, but it is told in the *imperfect* tense, and, therefore, *saw* is admissible. Οθονην, sheet or *cloth* ; occurring only *twice* in N. T., and represented by *sheet*, we prefer it to *cloth*. Sheets are often joined at the four corners. This is more definite, and larger than οθονιον, which may be any sort of linen cloth, as used elsewhere, five times referring to the envelopes of the Savior's corpse. In Homer's Od. 7. 107, οθονη indicates *fine white linen* of any size, sheet or sail.

[d] Σκενος τι ως οθονην μεγαλην τεσσαρσιν, omit. by Ln., Tf.

[e] Και τα θηρια is omitted by Ln., Tf., but according to Gb. it is a probable omission, and might be in the text.

Ὑπηρχε, third sing. imp. of ὑπαρχω, to begin, to start, to arise or spring up. Hom. Od. 24–286. Arch. Cho. 1068. Dem. 408. 22. The whole scene represents a new creation, springing into life.

It is remarkable that Wiclif, Tyndale, Cranmer, Geneva, and Rheims, as well as the common version, omit the article four times occurring in this verse. So do Murdock, Wak., Wes.

KING JAMES' VERSION.	GREEK TEXT.	REVISED VERSION.

and wild beasts, and creeping things, and fowls of the air.

13 And there came a voice to him, Rise, Peter; kill, and eat.

14 But Peter said, Not so, Lord; for I have never eaten any thing that is common or unclean.

15 And the voice *spake* unto him again the second time, What God hath cleansed, *that* call not thou common.

16 This was done thrice: and the vessel was received up again into heaven.

17 Now while Peter doubted in himself what this vision which he had seen should mean, behold, the men which were sent from

τὰ θηρία καὶ τὰ ἑρπετὰ καὶ τὰ πετεινὰ τοῦ οὐρανοῦ. ¹³ καὶ ἐγέ- νετο φωνὴ πρὸς αὐτὸν, ᾿Αναστὰς, Πέτρε, θῦσον καὶ φάγε. ¹⁴ ῾Ο δὲ Πέτρος εἶπε, Μηδαμῶς, κύριε· ὅτι οὐδέποτε ἔφαγον πᾶν κοινὸν ἢ ἀκάθαρτον. ¹⁵ Καὶ φωνὴ πά- λιν ἐκ δευτέρου πρὸς αὐτὸν, ῝Α ὁ Θεὸς ἐκαθάρισε, σὺ μὴ κοίνου. ¹⁶ Τοῦτο δὲ ἐγένετο ἐπὶ τρίς· καὶ πάλιν ἀνελήφθη τὸ σκεῦος εἰς τὸν οὐρανόν.

¹⁷ ῾Ως δὲ ἐν ἑαυτῷ διηπόρει ὁ Πέτρος, τί ἂν εἴη τὸ ὅραμα ὃ εἶδε, καὶ ἰδοὺ, οἱ ἄνδρες οἱ ἀπεσταλμέ-

reptiles of the earth, and birds of the air. And there 13 came a voice to him, ᶠRise, Peter; kill and eat. But Peter 14 said, Not so, Lord; for I have never eaten ᵍany thing common or unclean. And the 15 ʰvoice said to him again, a second time; What God has cleansed, that call not you, common. This was ⁱdone 16 thrice, and the vessel was taken up again into the heaven.

Now as Peter was ʲponder- 17 ing in himself, what the vision which he had seen could mean; behold the men who were ᵏsent

---

and Booth. Penn *twice* omits it. Thompson gives it *three* times, omitting it only once. It should have been either always omitted or always given, so far as any relevant reason appears.

ᶠ Αναστας, ανιστημι is a favorite with Luke. He employs it 72 times in his writings, while all other writers in the N. T. employ it only thirty times. It is idiomatically, with him, of the effect of an imperative, when coupled with an imperative, as, having *arisen*, Peter, *slay*, and *eat*. Peter, rise: slay, and eat, It is so translated, arise, or rise, by all the translators from Wiclif to Thompson and Boothroyd.

Γινομαι is of great latitude in sense and currency—*do, make, be, fulfill, come, come to pass, happen, seem, arise, become, befall, perform, wax, being assembled, continue, marry,* &c., &c. It takes its meaning from its *context,* or contact with other words. It seems to be a very general *representative* of its associates, especially in N. T. currency. *Its special meaning is in its special context.* Its *latitude* is equal to our auxiliary *be,* though not its proper representative. In this passage it seems more contextual to understand εγενετο than ειπε, because the voice had not before said, "what God cleansed," but "arise, slay, and eat." It now says, συ μη κοινου—"Do not you account impure," Bloomfield; "as common," Rob. Hesych.: μη κοινον μη ακαθαρτον λεγε. It also means to *pollute, profane,* or desecrate, with an accusative, as in Acts 21 : 28.

ᵍ Παν, *quodvis,* any thing whatever, impure or unclean.

ʰ Και φωνη παλιν, literally *a voice,* as before, yet, with the exception of the Rheims, Wakefield, Thompson, and Murdock, all English versions make it definite on the assumption that it was the same voice before heard. This is our idiom in such cases.

ⁱ Τουτο δε εγενετο επι τρις, *now this happened thrice;* or

was done thrice, in our idiom, exact to the text.—Επι τρις, *to* or *into* three, exactly represented. According to others, "*reproduced* three times," but this is not the fact, for this would be equal to four editions of it, the first reproduction being the second copy.

Ευθυς is, by Ln., Tf. substituted for παλιν, immediately, for again. So Alf.: εις τον ουρανον, into the heaven.

῾Ως δε,—commencing a new paragraph—literally, *now as,* tantamount to *while;* because it was a continuous exercise, not a transient act of his mind.

ʲ Διαπορεω, twice rendered *perplexed,* and three times in this book, *doubt* and *doubted,* com. ver. which is its whole currency in this book. Doubt, and doubting imply deliberation. Διαπορεω is represented by hæsito, ambigo, sed significat *interrogare* seu inquirere cum dubitantione atque admiratione. Lorin in Acts 2 : 12. Critica Sacra. Vox hæc Lucæ attonitam quandam admiratione significat. Acts 2 : 12; 5 : 24; 10 : 17. Grotius in loco. Crit. Sacra. We therefore prefer *pondering,* because of its generic sense, as covering the whole area of Luke's statement, and especially because he was in doubt as to the meaning of his vision.

ᵏ Απεσταλμενοι, part. perf. passive, exegetically *those having been sent,* but with us *those who were sent,* or *those sent,* fully indicate the fact of their previous mission, with regard to their present appearance. Επι τον πυλωνα, atrium vestibulum, porta, janua, with one exception always rendered *gate* in N. T. com. ver., once only *porch.* Πυλη, its radix, is always in N. T. rendered *gate.* In classic Greek, a gate-way, a gate-tower, or a gate-house. Poly. 4. 18. 2. Luc. Hipp. 5 &c. Luc. Nigrin. 23, an antechamber. The 12 gate-houses of the apocalyptic city for the accommodation of the angelic porters, is a representative idea. In Acts 12 : 10 we have την θυραν του πυλωνος, the door of the gate-house, the place of inquiry.

KING JAMES' VERSION.

Cornelius had made inquiry for Simon's house, and stood before the gate,

18 And called, and asked whether Simon, which was surnamed Peter, were lodged there.

19 While Peter thought on the vision, the Spirit said unto him, Behold, three men seek thee.

20 Arise therefore, and get thee down, and go with them, doubting nothing: for I have sent them.

21 Then Peter went down to the men which were sent unto him from Cornelius; and said, Behold, I am he whom ye seek: what is the cause wherefore ye are come?

22 And they said, Cornelius the centurion, a just man, and one that feareth God, and of good report among all the nation of the Jews, was warned from God by an holy angel to send for thee into his house, and to hear words of thee.

23 Then called he them in,

GREEK TEXT.

νοι ἀπὸ τοῦ Κορνηλίου, διερωτή-σαντες τὴν οἰκίαν Σίμωνος, ἐπέ-στησαν ἐπὶ τὸν πυλῶνα· 18 καὶ φωνήσαντες ἐπυνθάνοντο, εἰ Σί-μων ὁ ἐπικαλούμενος Πέτρος ἐν-θάδε ξενίζεται. 19 Τοῦ δὲ Πέ-τρου ἐνθυμουμένου περὶ τοῦ ὁρά-ματος, εἶπεν αὐτῷ τὸ Πνεῦμα, Ἰδοὺ, ἄνδρες τρεῖς ζητοῦσί σε· 20 ἀλλὰ ἀναστὰς κατάβηθι, καὶ πορεύου σὺν αὐτοῖς, μηδὲν δια-κρινόμενος· διότι ἐγὼ ἀπέσταλκα αὐτούς. 21 Καταβὰς δὲ Πέτρος πρὸς τοὺς ἄνδρας τοὺς ἀπεσταλ-μένους ἀπὸ τοῦ Κορηνλίου πρὸς αὐτὸν, εἶπεν, Ἰδοὺ, ἐγώ εἰμι ὃν ζητεῖτε· τίς ἡ αἰτία δι᾿ ἣν πάρε-στε; 22 οἱ δὲ εἶπον, Κορνήλιος ἑκατοντάρχης, ἀνὴρ δίκαιος καὶ φοβούμενος τὸν Θεὸν, μαρτυρού-μενός τε ὑπὸ ὅλου τοῦ ἔθνους τῶν Ἰουδαίων, ἐχρηματίσθη ὑπὸ ἀγγέλου ἁγίου, μεταπέμψασθαί σε εἰς τὸν οἶκον αὐτοῦ, καὶ ἀκοῦ-σαι ῥήματα παρὰ σοῦ. 23 Εἴσκα-

REVISED VERSION.

from Cornelius, having inquired out Simon's [1]house, stood at the gate, and calling, 18 they asked, whether Simon, surnamed [m]Peter, [n]was lodging there. While Peter [o]thought 19 attentively of the vision, the Spirit said to him, Behold three men are [p]seeking you. Arise therefore, go down and 20 accompany them, doubting nothing, for I have sent them. 21 [q]Then Peter went down to the men, and said, Behold, I am he whom you are seeking. What is the reason for which you are come? And they said, Cor- 22 nelius, the centurion, a just man, and one who fears God, and of good report among all the nation of the Jews, was instructed from God, by a holy angel, to send for you into his house, and to hear words of you. [r]Then, calling them 23

---

[1] Simon's house. It is here οικια.—See note t, below.

[m] Surnamed *Peter*. It depends on the translation of Matthew 16:18, what should be the translation of *Petros* here.— If Matthew 16:13–18 be translated, as in my judgment it ought to be, it would read as follows, v. 16—"And Simon Stone answered, and said, Thou art the Christ, the son of the living God.—"And Jesus answered and said to him, Happy are you, Simon, son of Jonas: for flesh and blood has not revealed this to you, but my Father who is in heaven. And I also say to you, that you are called a STONE, and on this ROCK I will build my church, and the gates of death, or the grave, shall not prevail against it." Then, in this case, it should be rendered, "*Surnamed Rock*."

This version would be fatal to popery, to all who read it, with an honest heart, in our vernacular, and in our opinion it would be a faithful expression of the original. And can there be, or should there be, a special law for translating any word in this book? Do not the context and the scope of the passage demand this? We may add, that Jesus may, in all probability, have alluded to the fact of his calling him *stone*, when he was known only by the name, Simon—*In anticipation*

of his confession, he called him Simon *Stone*—or, if any one prefer it, SIMON ROCK.

For *to Cornelius*, Gb., Sch., Ln., Tf. have αυτω, *to him*. This appears preferable, merely because there is no other person introduced. Not was departed, but *departed* = απηλ-θεν.

[n] Ξενιζεται, is *being entertained* there; rather too formal, though in good keeping with modern usage—*resides* there, *dwells* there, is probably more apposite both to ancient and modern use.

[o] For ενθυμουμενος Gb., Sch., Ln., Tf. substitute διεθυ-μουμενον, carefully considering περι, *about* or *concerning* the vision.

[p] Τους απεσταλμενους απο Κορνηλιου προς αυτον, omitted by Gb., Sch., Ln., Tf. Ζητουσι σε, pres. ind. act., are seeking thee. Τις η αιτια δι᾿ ην παρεστε; what is the *motive* through which you are approaching me? Αιτια, *ratio*, reason or motive.

[q] Δε, then, connecting the time and the speech.

[r] Ουν, in this case, is more appositely represented by *then*. Peter is not found in the approved text in this verse. It is

KING JAMES' VERSION.

and lodged *them*. And on the morrow Peter went away with them, and certain brethren from Joppa accompanied him.

24 And the morrow after they entered into Cesarea. And Cornelius waited for them, and had called together his kinsmen and near friends.

25 And as Peter was coming in, Cornelius met him, and fell down at his feet, and worshipped *him*.

26 But Peter took him up, saying, Stand up: I myself also am a man.

27 And as he talked with him, he went in, and found many that were come together.

28 And he said unto them, Ye know how that it is an unlawful thing for a man that is a Jew to keep company, or come unto one of another nation; but God hath shewed me that I should not call any man common or unclean.

29 Therefore came I *unto you* without gainsaying, as soon as I was sent for: I ask therefore for what intent ye have sent for me?

30 And Cornelius said, Four days ago I was fasting until this hour; and at the ninth hour I prayed in my house, and behold,

GREEK TEXT.

λεσάμενος οὖν αὐτοὺς ἐξένισε. Τῇ δὲ ἐπαύριον ὁ Πέτρος ἐξῆλθε σὺν αὐτοῖς, καί τινες τῶν ἀδελφῶν τῶν ἀπὸ τῆς Ἰόππης συνῆλθον αὐτῷ. ²⁴ καὶ τῇ ἐπαύριον εἰσῆλθον εἰς τὴν Καισάρειαν· ὁ δὲ Κορνήλιος ἦν προσδοκῶν αὐτοὺς, συγκαλεσάμενος τοὺς συγγενεῖς αὐτοῦ καὶ τοὺς ἀναγκαίους φίλους.

²⁵ Ὡς δὲ ἐγένετο εἰσελθεῖν τὸν Πέτρον, συναντήσας αὐτῷ ὁ Κορνήλιος, πεσὼν ἐπὶ τοὺς πόδας προσεκύνησεν. ²⁶ ὁ δὲ Πέτρος αὐτὸν ἤγειρε λέγων, Ἀνάστηθι· κἀγὼ αὐτὸς ἄνθρωπός εἰμι· ²⁷ Καὶ συνομιλῶν αὐτῷ εἰσῆλθε, καὶ εὑρίσκει συνεληλυθότας πολλοὺς, ²⁸ ἔφη τε πρὸς αὐτοὺς, Ὑμεῖς ἐπίστασθε ὡς ἀθέμιτόν ἐστιν ἀνδρὶ Ἰουδαίῳ κολλᾶσθαι ἢ προσέρχεσθαι ἀλλοφύλῳ· καὶ ἐμοὶ ὁ Θεὸς ἔδειξε μηδένα κοινὸν ἢ ἀκάθαρτον λέγειν ἄνθρωπον· ²⁹ διὸ καὶ ἀναντιρρήτως ἦλθον μεταπεμφθείς. πυνθάνομαι οὖν, τίνι λόγῳ μετεπέμψασθέ με; ³⁰ Καὶ ὁ Κορνήλιος ἔφη, Ἀπὸ τετάρτης ἡμέρας μέχρι ταύτης τῆς ὥρας ἤμην νηστεύων, καὶ τὴν ἐννάτην ὥραν προσευχόμενος ἐν τῷ οἴκῳ μου·

REVISED VERSION.

in, he entertained them. And on the next day Peter went with them, and certain brethren from Joppa accompanied him. And on the next day, 24 he ·entered into Cæsarea: and Cornelius was waiting for them, having called together his kindred and intimate friends.

Now, as Peter was entering, 25 Cornelius met him, and falling down at his feet, he worshipped him. But Peter rais- 26 ed him up, saying, Stand up. I myself also am a man. And, 27 conversing with him, he went in and found many assembled.

And he said to them, You 28 well know it is unlawful for a man, who is a Jew, to associate with, or to approach one of another nation; and yet God has shewed to me that I should not call any man common or unclean. And there- 29 fore I came without objecting, as soon as I was sent for. I ask then, for what purpose you have sent for me.

And Cornelius said, Four 30 days ago, I was fasting till this hour; and at the ninth hour I prayed in my ·house,

---

εισκαλεσαμενος, *then calling them in, he entertained them.* Lodged *them is not equal to* εξενισε, *from* ξενιζω, *hospitio recipio.*

ᵃ (Εισηλθεν *not* εισηλθον, Ln., Tf.), *he entered into,* etc., and αναγκαιους φιλους, literally *necessary friends.* Littleton, in his celebrated Dictionary, expounds a *necessarius,* a particularly engaged person.

ᵇ Οικος, οικια. These words frequently occur in the Christian Scriptures; both are translated, com. ver., *house, household,* home. Some late writers have assumed that οικος and

οικια denote two distinct institutions. The former a greater, or more respectable house than the latter. Such as a master's house, compared with the dwelling-place of his servants. The former, οικος, as indicating a family of adults and infants; the latter, a family of servants, with or without infants. They contend that both in the Septuagint of the Old, and in the Greek of the New, this distinction in their use obtains. We have found no authority for this difference. On the contrary, we have found that both terms are used in the Christian Oracles to indicate one and the same house, or family. For

KING JAMES' VERSION.	GREEK TEXT.	REVISED VERSION.
a man stood before me in bright clothing,	καὶ ἰδού, ἀνὴρ ἔστη ἐνώπιόν μου ἐν ἐσθῆτι λαμπρᾷ, ³¹ καί φησι, Κορνήλιε, εἰσηκούσθη σου ἡ προσευχὴ, καὶ αἱ ἐλεημοσύναι σου ἐμνήσθησαν ἐνώπιον τοῦ Θεοῦ. ³² πέμψον οὖν εἰς Ἰόππην, καὶ μετακάλεσαι Σίμωνα ὃς ἐπικαλεῖται Πέτρος· οὗτος ξενίζεται ἐν οἰκίᾳ Σίμωνος βυρσέως παρὰ θάλασσαν ὃς παραγενόμενος λαλήσει σοι. ³³ Ἐξαυτῆς οὖν ἔπεμψα πρός σε· σύ τε καλῶς ἐποίησας παραγενόμενος. νῦν οὖν πάντες ἡμεῖς ἐνώπιον τοῦ Θεοῦ πάρεσμεν ἀκοῦσαι πάντα τὰ προστεταγμένα σοι ὑπὸ τοῦ Θεοῦ. ³⁴ Ἀνοίξας δὲ Πέτρος τὸ στόμα εἶπεν, Ἐπ' ἀληθείας καταλαμβάνομαι, ὅτι οὐκ ἔστι προσωπολήπτης ὁ Θεὸς, ³⁵ ἀλλ' ἐν παντὶ ἔθνει ὁ φοβούμενος αὐτὸν καὶ ἐργαζόμενος δικαιοσύνην, δεκτὸς αὐτῷ ἐστι. ³⁶ τὸν λόγον	and behold, a man stood before me, in bright apparel, and 31 said, Cornelius, your prayer is heard, and your alms are had in remembrance before God. Send, therefore, to Joppa, and call here Simon, whose 32 surname is Peter. He is entertained in the ·house of one Simon, a tanner, by the seashore; who, when he is come, will speak to you. Immediately, therefore, I sent to you, 33 and you have done well that you have come. Now then, we are all here present before ᵘGod, to hear all things that are commanded you by God. Then Peter, ᵛopening his 34 mouth, said, In ʷtruth, I perceive that God is not a ˣrespecter of persons; but, in 35 every nation, he that fears him, and works righteousness, is ʸacceptable to him. You know the ᶻmessage, 36
31 And said, Cornelius, thy prayer is heard, and thine alms are had in remembrance in the sight of God.		
32 Send therefore to Joppa, and call hither Simon, whose surname is Peter; he is lodged in the house of *one* Simon a tanner, by the sea-side: who, when he cometh, shall speak unto thee.		
33 Immediately therefore I sent to thee; and thou hast well done that thou art come. Now therefore are we all here present before God, to hear all things that are commanded thee of God.		
34 Then Peter opened *his* mouth, and said, Of a truth I perceive that God is no respecter of persons:		
35 But in every nation, he that feareth him and worketh righteousness, is accepted with him.		
36 The word which *God* sent		

---

example, Paul calls the household, or family of Stephanas both an *οικος,* and an *οικια.*—Luke, in his Gospel, ch. 7 : 6, calls the centurion's house an *οικια,* and in v. 10 it is called an *οικος.* So of Jairus' house. In Luke 8 : 41 he calls it *οικος,* and again v. 51, he calls it *οικια.* Mark, in his Gospel, calls this house an *οικος,* ch. 5 : 38, and Matthew calls it *οικια,* ch. 9 : 23. In the parable concerning a *house* divided against itself, recorded by Matthew, Mark, and Luke, in the two former it is called *οικια,* and by Luke it is called *οικος,* ch. 12 : 39. But stronger still, the same house, in the same verse, is called both *οικος* and *οικια,* Luke 10 : 5. "Into whatever house you enter, say, Peace be to this house." We need not further expose the frailties of some critics, who in the present century have so largely written and justified their dispensation of Christian ordinances on the presumption that these two words represent two distinct households.

ᵘ For *Θεον,* regarded as more probable by Griesbach, Lachmann prefers *κυριον* as the more probable reading. Either of them is equal in authority. *Τα προστεταγμενα,* part. perf. pass., the things which have been prescribed, or commanded by God.

ᵛ Then Peter *ανοιξας το στομα,* opening his mouth, said.

This form is more explicit and direct, and dispenses with the conjunction *and,* which has no representative in the original.

ʷ *Επ' αληθειας.* Literally *upon truth,* as, "*upon my word.*" But this is in bad taste among us. "*Of a truth,*" is obsolete, far-fetched, and incongruous with *επι.* Its more common representatives in our language are *in, on, upon.* In truth, *επ' αληθειας,* is peculiar to Luke in the N. T. *In truth,* is analogous to our, *in fact.* We prefer on all the premises, "*in truth* I perceive."

ˣ *Προσωποληπτης, qui accipit personam.* James 2 : 9. *προσωποληψια,* faciei acceptio. Col. 3 : 25. "The outward state or condition of men, i. e. country, sex, state of life, riches, wisdom, learning." Critica Sacra.

ʸ *Δεκτος αυτω,* acceptable *to him,* Dodd., Thomp., Rheims; *accepte to him,* Wiclif; *accepted by him,* Wakefield, Wes., Penn, Boothr.; *with him,* Murd; *acceptable to him,* Hackett.

ᶻ *Το ρημα, verbum dictum, factum, mandatum, sententia, sermo, res, negotium.* Both in Hebrew and Greek, *word,* is used for, a *thing,* or matter, Crit. Sacra; *res factum, mandatum, sermo,* Rob.; *things,* Acts 5 : 32 com. ver. Luke 1 : 37;

KING JAMES' VERSION.	GREEK TEXT.	REVISED VERSION.
unto the children of Israel, preaching peace by Jesus Christ : (he is Lord of all :)	ὃν ἀπέστειλε τοῖς υἱοῖς Ἰσραὴλ, εὐαγγελιζόμενος εἰρήνην διὰ Ἰησοῦ Χριστοῦ, οὗτός ἐστι πάντων κύριος. ³⁷ ὑμεῖς οἴδατε τὸ γενόμενον ῥῆμα καθ᾽ ὅλης τῆς Ἰουδαίας, ἀρξάμενον ἀπὸ τῆς Γαλιλαίας, μετὰ τὸ βάπτισμα ὃ ἐκήρυξεν Ἰωάννης· ³⁸ Ἰησοῦν τὸν ἀπὸ Ναζαρὲτ, ὡς ἔχρισεν αὐτὸν ὁ Θεὸς Πνεύματι Ἁγίῳ καὶ δυ-	which he sent to the children of Israel, preaching peace through Jesus Christ, he is Lord of all ;—you know that 37 ªmessage which was published throughout all Judea, beginning from Galilee, after the immersion which John preached ;—concerning Jesus 38 of Nazareth ; how God ªanointed him with the ᵇHoly Spirit
37 That word, *I say*, ye know, which was published throughout all Judea, and began from Galilee, after the baptism of John preached ;		
38 How God anointed Jesus of Nazareth with the Holy Ghost		

---

2 : 15–19 ; that message which he sent, Dodd. This I prefer to any other representative of ῥῆμα in this case. We have our *messages* from kings, and councils, and governments, and they are all ῥήματα, *words* of significance, and words of authority. Jesus is the *messenger* of the everlasting covenant, and the Gospel is *the message* of God to a world in rebellion. It is a message of peace, a word, or message of reconciliation, published not to Jews only, but to Jews and Gentiles.

ª *Εχρισεν αυτον*, christed, or anointed him, empowered him.

ᵇ *Πνευματι Ἁγιω και δυναμει*, not with *a* Holy Spirit and *a* power, but with the Holy Spirit and power absolute. A holy spirit and a power are wholly indefinite, therefore incomprehensible. The history of Jesus Christ has been written, but the history of the Holy Spirit has never been written. The Holy Spirit represents not a spirit of God, nor an angel of God, but all Divinity, and Divinity too, in all its grandeur.

But it appears in numerous and various manifestations, in Creation, in Providence, in moral government, and in redemption. But all these, works one and the same Spirit. "By his Spirit he garnished the heavens, and formed the crooked serpent," or the milky way, Job 26 : 13. "Thou sendest forth thy Spirit and thou renewest the face of the earth," Ps. 104 : 30. But these he consummates by the winds of heaven. So by his word, the breath of the Lord, his Spirit quickens us.

Πνευμα Ἁγιον, in its anarthrous form, is found in the conception of Jesus, Matt. 1 : 18 ; 1 : 20. Again in his promised baptism in *πνευματι και πυρι*, Matt. 3 : 11. He also cast out demons *πνευματι Θεου*, Matt. 14 : 28, etc., etc. In the triune manifestation of God there is a Father, a Son, and a Holy Spirit, and these are, essentially, necessarily, and absolutely, Divine. As there are no degrees in absolute humanity, so are there none in absolute Divinity. These are the elements of all true criticism and interpretation of the oracles of inspiration on this most mysterious and Divine theme, as we conceive of them.

Πνευματι Ἁγιω. See ch. 1 : 2, note e. To our previous remarks on this subject we would add as further exegetical and confirmatory :

In this Book of Acts we find *Πνευμα Ἁγιον twenty-two times*, and in the whole Christian Scriptures *ninety-two times*.—The Book of Acts is, therefore, emphatically the book of the dispensation of the Holy Spirit. It is *ninety times* translated in the common version of the Christian Scriptures *Holy Ghost*, and twice *Holy Spirit*. It should be uniformly Holy Spirit. Luke, in his Gospel, introduces it twelve times—while, in all the other historical books of N. T., it is found only fourteen times. Matthew, in his Gospel, introduces him, and that, too, in reference to the *creation*, or *generation* and baptism of Jesus, in the anarthrous form, ch. 1 : 18, 20 ; 3 : 11. So, also, Mark in his Gospel, ch. 1 : 8. But after this, in the absence of *Ἁγιον*, they both prefix the article, and thus he, who is first introduced as *Πνευμα Ἁγιον*, is immediately designated *το πνευμα*.

Luke also, first introduces him *Πνευμα Ἁγιον*, ch. 1 : 15, and, again, in v. 35, with regard to Christ's conception, he appears as *Πνευμα Ἁγιον*, and, again, in reference to baptism, ch. 3 : 16. John the Baptist says of him, "he will baptize you in *Holy* Spirit and in fire".

And John, too, when he first introduces the *Holy* Spirit, and intimates his baptism, presents him in the same anarthrous form, ch. 1 : 33. So, all the Evangelists in their Gospels introduce him. And, in this Book of Apostolic Acts, when first introduced, both in giving instruction to the Apostles, and in reference to baptism, ch. 1 : 2, 5 ; he is presented as *Πνευμα Ἁγιον*.

After being thus so systematically designated in reference to his birth, baptism, and mission, as simply and absolutely *Πνευμα Ἁγιον*, he is occasionally, indeed often, being now well known, styled *το πνευμα*, *το πνευμα Ἁγιον*, and *το πνευμα το Ἁγιον*. And all this in good taste, and in conformity to the Biographies and Histories of that era. It is, therefore, a gratuitous criticism to assume that *Πνευμα Ἁγιον* does not always indicate, in reference to this glorious personality, the same definite Divine personality into which, or into whose, name, equally with that of the Father and the Son, all Christians are immersed. We thank God that we can have the full

KING JAMES' VERSION.	GREEK TEXT.	REVISED VERSION.
and with power: who went about doing good, and healing all that were oppressed of the devil; for God was with him.	νάμει, ὃς διῆλθεν εὐεργετῶν καὶ ἰώμενος πάντας τοὺς καταδυνα-στευομένους ὑπὸ τοῦ διαβόλου, ὅτι ὁ Θεὸς ἦν μετ᾽ αὐτοῦ· ³⁹ καὶ	and with power; who went about, from place to place, doing good, and healing all that were oppressed by the devil; for God was with him.

assurance of understanding, that Πνευμα Ἁγιον, like Jesus Christ, is the divinely-established designation of the Christian's Advocate and Sanctifier.

We may further say, on all our premises, that Πνευμα Ἁγιον is nowhere in Holy Writ used as applicable to any Christian man, however sanctified and adopted into the family of God. It is an appropriated name—as much as *Jesus* is in the New Testament, or as *Joshua* was in the Old. We have many baptists now-a-days, but no John *the* Baptist. The Hebrews had many *Christs* of the house of David and of the house of Aaron; but now both Jews and Gentiles have but *One* Christ; —and, therefore, he is THE CHRIST—*the* only Christ of God, emphatically, *the Lord's anointed.*

Again, and finally on this topic;—We are never said in the Christian Scriptures to be baptized *in the* Holy Spirit, but uniformly in *Holy Spirit.* We have three baptisms set before us in the Christian oracles:—a baptism in *water*, in *spirit*, and in *fire.* They are in the Greek Scriptures uniformly anarthrous, and not in *the* water, in *the* fire, in *the* Spirit. We may be baptized in Holy Spirit, in water, or in fire; but not in *a* Holy Spirit, in *a* water, or in *a* fire.

Again, every person is said to be baptized *into* something as well as *in* something. Hence the Apostolic commission reads—*immerse* them *into* the name; not *in* the name of the *Theiotes* or Godhead—into "the name of the Father, and of the Son, and of the Holy Spirit." This formula is pregnant with exalted conceptions of a special relation to the Father as now *our* Father; to the Son as *our* kinsman Redeemer; and to the Holy Spirit as *our* Advocate with the Father through the dignity and merit of the Lord Jesus.

To be immersed *in fire* is rather the symbol of destruction. It is, indeed, a symbol of purification of metals, but not of persons. To a promiscuous audience, it may be said, the obedient will be purified and the disobedient consumed. Hence the choice of two baptisms—obey and be purified, disobey and be consumed.

It has been noted that the most sublime operations of the Godhead have been ascribed to the anarthrous Πνευμα Ἁγιον. It was *the* Holy Spirit—or, according to Matthew, Holy Spirit (Πνευμα Ἁγιον) that created the body of Jesus—ευρεθη εν γαστρι εχουσα εκ Πνευματος Ἁγιον. She was pregnant by Holy Spirit, not by *a* Holy Spirit. Again it is affirmed, v. 20,

"*that* conceived in her was by Πνευματος Ἁγιον". And Jesus, too, it is affirmed by John, will immerse in Holy Spirit or in Holy Spirit and in fire—not in *the* Holy Spirit and in *the* fire. He has also promised to give *a* Holy Spirit, but not *the* Holy Spirit, to them that ask him. Appears it not then, that Πνευμα Ἁγιον and το Πνευμα το Ἁγιον, and το Ἁγιον Πνευμα are, in the Christian currency, like the currency—ὁ Ιησους, Ιησους Χριστος, and ὁ Ιησους ὁ Χριστος! We have in Mark 1 : 1, Ιησου Χριστου υιου του Θεου; but when a full confession of faith, the most approved by him, was expressed by Peter, (Matt. 16 : 16,) it is in these words: Συ ει ὁ Χριστος, ὁ υιος του Θεου του ζωντος. Here we find in one affirmation the article *four* times, once for every predicate of the Saviour. *The* Christ *the* Son of the *God*—*the* Living one.

Hence a question arises whether, at any time, or in any case, Πνευμα Ἁγιον does not represent all that is indicated by το Πνευμα το Ἁγιον personally and officially contemplated, especially when this Divine agent is referred to; or whether any personal spirit, angelic or human, is ever represented by Πνευμα Ἁγιον, in any passage in the Christian Scriptures.

To settle this question, another may be propounded. Is there not evidence, full and satisfactory, that the agent that is by one apostle named Πνευμα Ἁγιον is by the same apostle named το Πνευμα το Ἁγιον, while speaking on the same subject? Paul to the Corinthians, in his memorable dissertation on spiritual gifts and on *the* Spirit, whence they emanate, 1st Epistle, ch. 12, thus speaks: περι πνευματικων—Concerning spirituals—on spiritual gifts, states, as prefatory, that no one can say that Jesus is Lord, but by Πνευματι Ἁγιω—by *a* Holy Spirit, or by Holy Spirit, anarthrous.

But this anarthrous Holy Spirit, almost in the same breath, becomes το δε αυτο πνευμα—one and the same Spirit, just as there is ὁ δε αυτος κυριος, and ὁ δε αυτος Θεος, one and the same God; and yet this το αυτο πνευμα is first introduced Πνευμα Ἁγιον—εν Πνευματι Ἁγιω! But if this do not give full satisfaction to the most curious, we have another fact of paramount authority, viz.: that which is ascribed by Paul to Πνευμα Ἁγιον, anarthrous, is by him, again, ascribed to το Πνευμα το Ἁγιον. 1 Cor. 12 : 3. "No one can say that Jesus is Lord, but by Πνευματι Ἁγιω." This, although anarthrous, is construed by *the* Holy Spirit—but literally by Holy Spirit. But logically, as well as grammatically, he reasons thus: There are three διαιρεσεις—one class of gifts, one class of services, and one class of operations. We may admit, if any one calls for it, that there are classes of gifts or offices, classes of services, and classes of operations, subjectively and objectively contemplated. But there is—"το δε αυτο πνευμα", and there is—"ὁ αυτος κυριος", and there is—"ὁ αυτος Θεος". Three Divine agents,

KING JAMES' VERSION.	GREEK TEXT.	REVISED VERSION.

KING JAMES' VERSION.

39 And we are witnesses of all things which he did, both in the land of the Jews, and in Jerusalem; whom they slew and hanged on a tree:

40 Him God raised up the third day, and shewed him openly;

41 Not to all the people, but unto witnesses chosen before of God, *even* to us, who did eat and drink with him after he rose from the dead.

42 And he commanded us to preach unto the people, and to testify that it is he which was ordained of God *to be* the Judge of quick and dead.

43 To him give all the prophets witness, that through his name whosoever believeth in him shall receive remission of sins.

44 While Peter yet spake these words, the Holy Ghost fell on all them which heard the word.

45 And they of the circumcision which believed, were astonished, as many as came with Peter, because that on the Gentiles also was poured out the gift of the Holy Ghost.

46 For they heard them speak with tongues, and magnify God. Then answered Peter,

47 Can any man forbid water,

GREEK TEXT.

ἡμεῖς ἐσμεν μάρτυρες πάντων ὧν ἐποίησεν ἔν τε τῇ χώρᾳ τῶν Ἰουδαίων καὶ ἐν Ἱερουσαλήμ· ὃν ἀνεῖλον κρεμάσαντες ἐπὶ ξύλου. ⁴⁰ τοῦτον ὁ Θεὸς ἤγειρε τῇ τρίτῃ ἡμέρᾳ, καὶ ἔδωκεν αὐτὸν ἐμφανῆ γενέσθαι· ⁴¹ οὐ παντὶ τῷ λαῷ, ἀλλὰ μάρτυσι τοῖς προκεχειροτονημένοις ὑπὸ τοῦ Θεοῦ, ἡμῖν, οἵτινες συνεφάγομεν καὶ συνεπίομεν αὐτῷ, μετὰ τὸ ἀναστῆναι αὐτὸν ἐκ νεκρῶν· ⁴² καὶ παρήγγειλεν ἡμῖν κηρύξαι τῷ λαῷ, καὶ διαμαρτύρασθαι, ὅτι αὐτός ἐστιν ὁ ὡρισμένος ὑπὸ τοῦ Θεοῦ κριτὴς ζώντων καὶ νεκρῶν. ⁴³ τούτῳ πάντες οἱ προφῆται μαρτυροῦσιν, ἄφεσιν ἁμαρτιῶν λαβεῖν διὰ τοῦ ὀνόματος αὐτοῦ πάντα τὸν πιστεύοντα εἰς αὐτόν. ⁴⁴ Ἔτι λαλοῦντος τοῦ Πέτρου τὰ ῥήματα ταῦτα, ἐπέπεσε τὸ Πνεῦμα τὸ Ἅγιον ἐπὶ πάντας τοὺς ἀκούοντας τὸν λόγον. ⁴⁵ καὶ ἐξέστησαν οἱ ἐκ περιτομῆς πιστοὶ ὅσοι συνῆλθον τῷ Πέτρῳ, ὅτι καὶ ἐπὶ τὰ ἔθνη ἡ δωρεὰ τοῦ Ἁγίου Πνεύματος ἐκκέχυται· ⁴⁶ ἤκουον γὰρ αὐτῶν λαλούντων γλώσσαις, καὶ μεγαλυνόντων τὸν Θεόν. τότε ἀπεκρίθη ὁ Πέτρος, ⁴⁷ Μήτι

REVISED VERSION.

39 And we are witnesses of all things which he did, both in the land of the Jews, and in Jerusalem; whom they slew, hanging him on a tree. 40 Him God raised up the third day, and shewed him openly; 41 not to all the people, but to witnesses before chosen by God, even to us who did eat and drink with him after he rose from the dead. 42 And he commanded us to ᶜannounce to the people, and to testify that it is he himself who is ordained by God, to be the judge of the living and the dead. 43 To him all the prophets testify, that whoever believes in him shall, through his name, receive remission of sins. 44 While Peter was yet speaking these words, the ᵇHoly Spirit fell on all those who heard the word. 45 And those of the circumcision, who believed, as many as came with Peter, were astonished because that on the Gentiles also, the gift of the Holy Spirit was poured out. 46 For they heard them speak with other ᵈtongues, and magnify God. 47 Then Peter answer-

---

ᶜ Κηρύξαι καὶ διαμαρτυρασθαι, to herald, or to announce and attest to the people, to proclaim and to testify that it is he who is *ordained*. Ὡρισμενος, ὡριζω, determined, ordained, declared, such are its representatives in com. ver He is both *appointed* and *declared* to be the judge of all.

ᵈ Γλωσσαις, not in one tongue, but in tongues, consequently the ἑτεραις, before employed, is here implied and should be supplied. It is, indeed, more than logically implied, for it is intimated in the words, τοτε απεκριθη ὁ Πετρος, then Peter responded, or answered—their inquiries of course.

---

three Divine functions, and three Divine operations—embracing the personalities of Jehovah—in the Father, in the Son, and in the Holy Spirit, or the Holy Guest of the Christian temple. As for the definitive titles of any one of these Divine personalities, or operations, we should not be hypercritical. The diction of the Spirit is all sufficient, and alone sufficient, for the least and the greatest head or heart in all the ages of the reign of grace. And hence, without any speculative theology or Christology, that which, by one Christian writer under supernatural guidance, is ascribed sometimes to πνευμα, is again ascribed to το πνευμα by himself; and again by others to Πνευμα Ἁγιον—and to το Ἁγιον Πνευμα—and to make it superlative in some cases, το Πνευμα το Ἁγιον, which caps the climax of grammatical precision and of exegetical development. In one sentence Πνευμα Ἁγιον is *tantamount* to το Πνευμα—as ὁ Θεος is to *Jehovah*.

KING JAMES' VERSION.

that these should not be baptized. which have received the Holy Ghost as well as we?

48 And he commanded them to be baptized in the name of the Lord. Then prayed they him to tarry certain days.

CHAP. XI.

And the apostles and brethren that were in Judea, heard that the Gentiles had also received the word of God.

2 And when Peter was come up to Jerusalem, they that were of the circumcision contended with him,

3 Saying, Thou wentest in to men uncircumcised, and didst eat with them.

4 But Peter rehearsed *the matter* from the beginning, and expounded *it* by order unto them, saying,

5 I was in the city of Joppa praying: and in a trance I saw a vision, A certain vessel descend, as it had been a great sheet, let

GREEK TEXT.

τὸ ὕδωρ κωλῦσαι δύναταί τις τοῦ μὴ βαπτισθῆναι τούτους, οἵτινες τὸ Πνεῦμα τὸ Ἅγιον ἔλαβον καθὼς καὶ ἡμεῖς, 48 προσέταξέ τε αὐτοὺς βαπτισθῆναι ἐν τῷ ὀνόματι τοῦ Κυρίου. τότε ἠρώτησαν αὐτὸν ἐπιμεῖναι ἡμέρας τινάς.

CHAP. XI.

ΗΚΟΥΣΑΝ δὲ οἱ ἀπόστολοι καὶ οἱ ἀδελφοὶ οἱ ὄντες κατὰ τὴν Ἰουδαίαν, ὅτι καὶ τὰ ἔθνη ἐδέξαντο τὸν λόγον τοῦ Θεοῦ. 2 καὶ ὅτε ἀνέβη Πέτρος εἰς Ἱεροσόλυμα, διεκρίνοντο πρὸς αὐτὸν οἱ ἐκ περιτομῆς, 3 λέγοντες, Ὅτι πρὸς ἄνδρας ἀκροβυστίαν ἔχοντας εἰσῆλθες, καὶ συνέφαγες αὐτοῖς. 4 Ἀρξάμενος δὲ ὁ Πέτρος ἐξετίθετο αὐτοῖς καθεξῆς λέγων, 5 Ἐγὼ ἤμην ἐν πόλει Ἰόππῃ προσευχόμενος, καὶ εἶδον ἐν ἐκστάσει ὅραμα, καταβαῖνον σκεῦός τι ὡς ὀθόνην μεγάλην, τέσσαρ-

REVISED VERSION.

ed, Can any man ᵉforbid the water, that these should not be immersed, who have ᶠreceived the Holy Spirit, as well as we? And he commanded them to be immersed ᵍin the name of the Lord. Then they requested him to remain some days.   48

CHAP. XI.

And the Apostles and brethren, ʰthroughout Judea, heard that the Gentiles also had received the word of God. And ⁱwhen Peter went up into Jerusalem, they of the circumcision ʲdisputed with him, saying You associated with men who were uncircumcised, and ate with them. But Peter related the matter from the beginning, and set it forth in order to them, saying, I was in the city of Joppa, praying, and I saw, in a trance, a vision, something descend, like a great sheet, let down from   1   2   3   4   5

ᵉ *Κωλῦσαι, forbid, hinder, not suffer, not permit, obstruct, withhold. Τὸ ὕδωρ, the water, not water,* indicative of pre-eminence. The com. ver. gives to this word, *hinder,* as well as to *forbid,* to *withstand.* The primary meaning given by Lidd. and Scott, and Rob., *to cut short,* indicates more than *forbid.* It implies not merely withholding, but hindering, or debarring water. True no Gentiles before had been admitted into the Church, nor were they looked for, or sought after, by the Jews, who had assumed that salvation belonged exclusively to them.

ᶠ They had received, *τὸ Πνεῦμα τὸ Ἅγιον,* that same *τὸ Πνεῦμα τὸ Ἅγιον* of which he had spoken, and they had witnessed.

ᵍ *Ἐν τῷ ὀνόματι,* in the name, or by the authority of the Lord, he *commanded* them to be immersed. *Ἰησοῦ Χριστοῦ* is annexed by Ln., and possesses strong claims in the esteem of Griesbach. *Εἰς τὸ ὄνομα,* and *ἐν τῷ ὀνόματι* are never substituted in Sacred, or Classic Literature, as synonyms. The authority by which any act is performed must never be confounded with the meaning, or intention of it.

ʰ *Κατὰ τὴν Ἰουδαίαν,* "that were in Judea" com. ver. This

version might indicate some place in Judea, as *ἐν Ἰουδαίᾳ.* But *κατα* here ought to be represented by *throughout,* as it is found in com. ver. of Luke's Gospel, and in this book, as well as in classic Greek. In Luke's writings we find it so represented. In his Gospel 8 : 1, 4, 39 ; 23 : 5 ; 9 : 31, 42 ; 10 : 37 ; 24 : 5.

ⁱ *Καὶ ὅτε,* does not indicate " then, when," but, " and when, Peter went up, they of the circumcision ". " Who were " is not in the text, and is redundant. " Thou wentest in," does not, in our style, represent the sense, as well as, *you associated with.* Associate is not found in King James' version of N. T. It was not then in fashion, occurring only twice in the old. But now, no term is more apposite to this and other passages in the New Testament.

ʲ *Διεκρίνοντο,* "contended with him," com. ver. This and Jude, v. 9, are the only places, in the Christian Scriptures, where this word is represented by, *contend.* The Devil *contended* about the body of Moses. *Disputed,* is more apposite to questions of debate, and especially in such a category. We find it thus rendered, Rom. 14 : 1, applied to such cases, as " doubtful disputations."

KING JAMES' VERSION.	GREEK TEXT.	REVISED VERSION.
down from heaven by four corners; and it came even to me:	σιν ἀρχαῖς καθιεμένην ἐκ τοῦ οὐρανοῦ, καὶ ἦλθεν ἄχρις ἐμοῦ·	heaven by four corners, and it came even to me. Upon which, 6
6 Upon the which when I had fastened mine eyes, I considered, and saw four-footed beasts of the earth, and wild beasts, and creeping things, and fowls of the air.	6 εἰς ἣν ἀτενίσας κατενόουν, καὶ εἶδον τὰ τετράποδα τῆς γῆς καὶ τὰ θηρία καὶ τὰ ἑρπετὰ καὶ τὰ πετεινὰ τοῦ οὐρανοῦ. 7 ἤκουσα	when I had kearnestly looked, I considered, and saw four-footed animals of the earth, and wild beasts, and reptiles, and birds of the air. And I heard a voice, 7
7 And I heard a voice saying unto me, Arise, Peter; slay, and eat.	δὲ φωνῆς λεγούσης μοι, Ἀναστὰς, Πέτρε, θῦσον καὶ φάγε.	saying to me, Arise, Peter; kill and eat. But I said, not so, 8
8 But I said, Not so, Lord: for nothing common or unclean hath at any time entered into my mouth.	8 εἶπον δὲ, Μηδαμῶς, κύριε· ὅτι πᾶν κοινὸν ἢ ἀκάθαρτον οὐδέποτε εἰσῆλθεν εἰς τὸ στόμα μου.	Lord; for nothing common or unclean, has, at any time, entered into my mouth. But 9
9 But the voice answered me again from heaven, What God hath cleansed, *that* call not thou common.	9 ἀπεκρίθη δέ μοι φονὴ ἐκ δευτέρου ἐκ τοῦ οὐρανοῦ, Ἃ ὁ Θεὸς ἐκαθάρισε, σὺ μὴ κοίνου.	the voice lanswered me again from heaven; What God has cleansed, that call not you common. And this was done 10
10 And this was done three times: and all were drawn up again into heaven.	10 τοῦτο δὲ ἐγένετο ἐπὶ τρὶς, καὶ πάλιν ἀνεσπάσθη ἅπαντα εἰς τὸν οὐρανόν. 11 καὶ ἰδοὺ, ἐξαυτῆς	three times; and all were drawn up again into heaven. And behold, there were im- 11
11 And behold, immediately there were three men already come unto the house where I was, sent from Cesarea unto me.	τρεῖς ἄνδρες ἐπέστησαν ἐπὶ τὴν οἰκίαν ἐν ᾗ ἤμην, ἀπεσταλμένοι ἀπὸ Καισαρείας πρός με. 12 εἶπε	mediately three men already come to the house where I was, sent from Cæsarea to me.
12 And the Spirit bade me go with them, nothing doubting. Moreover, these six brethren accompanied me, and we entered into the man's house:	δέ μοι τὸ πνεῦμα, συνελθεῖν αὐτοῖς, μηδὲν διακρινόμενον· ἦλθον δὲ σὺν ἐμοὶ καὶ οἱ ἐξ ἀδελφοὶ οὗτοι, καὶ εἰσήλθομεν εἰς τὸν οἶκον τοῦ ἀνδρὸς, 13 ἀπήγγειλέ	And the Spirit bade me go 12 with them, doubting nothing. And, moreover, these six brethren accompanied me; and we entered into the man's house; and he told us, how 13
13 And he shewed us how he had seen an angel in his house, which stood and said unto him, Send men to Joppa, and call for Simon, whose surname is Peter;	τε ἡμῖν πῶς εἶδε τὸν ἄγγελον ἐν τῷ οἴκῳ αὑτοῦ σταθέντα καὶ εἰπόντα αὐτῷ, Ἀπόστειλον εἰς Ἰόππην ἄνδρας, καὶ μετάπεμψαι Σίμωνα τὸν ἐπικαλούμενον Πέτρον, 14 ὃς λαλήσει ῥήματα πρός	he had seen the mmmessenger in his house, who stood and said to him; mSend to Joppa, and call for Simon, whose surname is Peter, who will 14
14 Who shall tell thee words, whereby thou and all thy house shall be saved.	σε, ἐν οἷς σωθήσῃ σὺ καὶ πᾶς ὁ οἶκός σου. 15 ἐν δὲ τῷ ἄρξασθαί	tell you words, by which you and all your nhouse shall be saved. And as I began to 15
15 And as I began to speak, the Holy Ghost fell on them, as on us at the beginning.	με λαλεῖν, ἐπέπεσε τὸ Πνεῦμα τὸ Ἅγιον ἐπ' αὐτοὺς, ὥσπερ καὶ ἐφ' ἡμᾶς ἐν ἀρχῇ. 16 ἐμνέσθην	speak, the Holy Spirit fell on them, as on us in the beginning. Then I remembered 16
16 Then remembered I the		ning. Then I remembered 16

---

k Ατενισας κατενοουν, *I had earnestly looked*, better than "fixed my eyes." Looking steadfastly, Wesley, Mur. Looked earnestly, Wakefield, Boothroyd. I fixed my eyes, Thompson.

l Απεκριθη, were it not that, in its whole currency, (two hundred and forty-seven times), it is represented by *answer, question*, or no question, we would have prefered the word, *responded*.

m Αποστειλον—ανδρας, "men", is omitted, or repudiated by Gr., Sch., Lach., and Tf., Bagster's Imp. Text.

n See Note on ch. 10 : 2.   nn See Note w. p. 83.

o Εν αρχη, fell on them as on us—them, of the Gentiles, and us, of the Jews—"as in the beginning." It is a logical inference from these words, that from the day of Pentecost, to the calling of the Gentiles, no similar display of the Spirit had

KING JAMES' VERSION.	GREEK TEXT.	REVISED VERSION.

word of the Lord, how that he said, John indeed baptized with water; but ye shall be baptized with the Holy Ghost.

17 Forasmuch then as God gave them the like gift as *he did* unto us, who believed on the Lord Jesus Christ, what was I, that I could withstand God?

18 When they heard these things, they held their peace, and glorified God, saying, Then hath God also to the Gentiles granted repentance unto life.

19 Now they which were scattered abroad upon the persecution that arose about Stephen, travelled as far as Phenice, and Cyprus, and Antioch, preaching the word to none but unto the Jews only.

20 And some of them were

δὲ τοῦ ῥήματος Κυρίου, ὡς ἔλεγεν, Ἰωάννης μὲν ἐβάπτισεν ὕδατι, ὑμεῖς δὲ βαπτισθήσεσθε ἐν Πνεύματι Ἁγίῳ. 17 Εἰ οὖν τὴν ἴσην δωρεὰν ἔδωκεν αὐτοῖς ὁ Θεὸς ὡς καὶ ἡμῖν, πιστεύσασιν ἐπὶ τὸν Κύριον Ἰησοῦν Χριστὸν, ἐγὼ δὲ τίς ἤμην δυνατὸς κωλῦσαι τὸν Θεόν; 18 Ἀκούσαντες δὲ ταῦτα ἡσύχασαν, καὶ ἐδόξαζον τὸν Θεὸν, λέγοντες, Ἄραγε καὶ τοῖς ἔθνεσιν ὁ Θεὸς τὴν μετάνοιαν ἔδωκεν εἰς ζωήν.

19 ΟΙ μὲν οὖν διασπαρέντες ἀπὸ τῆς θλίψεως τῆς γενομένης ἐπὶ Στεφάνῳ, διῆλθον ἕως Φοινίκης καὶ Κύπρου καὶ Ἀντιοχείας, μηδενὶ λαλοῦντες τὸν λόγον εἰ μὴ μόνον Ἰουδαίοις. 20 ἦσαν δέ τινες

the declaration of the Lord, how he said, John, indeed, immersed in water, but you shall be immersed in the Holy Spirit. PSince, then, God 17 gave them the ᵠsame gift even as he did to us, when we believed on the Lord Jesus Christ; who was I that I could withstand God? ʳWhen 18 they heard these things they were silent, and glorified ˢGod, saying, God, then, indeed, has also granted to the Gentiles the reformation ᵗto life.

Now they who were scat- 19 tered abroad, upon the persecution that arose about Stephen, travelled as far as Phenicia, and Cyprus, and Antioch, speaking ᵘthe word to none but ᵛJews. And some 20

---

been given, else they would not have gone so far back. The interval between the day of Pentecost, and the calling of the Gentiles, in Cæsarea, is put down, by our best Biblical scholars and commentators, as about seven or eight years. See the chronology of our most approved Polyglott Bibles. Adam Clark makes it some 11 or 12 years. Take the lowest figure, and the Holy Spirit, in its public manifestations of supernatural gifts, descended only twice—at the commencement of the reign of Christ among the Jews, A. D. 33 and among the Gentiles, A. D. 41. Now the Holy Spirit is given to them that believe, as the Holy *Guest*, to dwell in their hearts, as a sanctifier, and a comforter, or an advocate.

This scene in Cæsarea, and that in Jerusalem, are called—and they are the only scenes, that, in Holy Scripture, are called—*the Baptism, or immersion of the Holy Spirit*. They spoke as fluently in foreign tongues, as in their vernacular. The display was sensible, visible.

ᴾ *Εἰ*, if then, rather, *since then*. The premises necessarily conceded. *Τὴν ἴσην δωρεαν, the equal gift*, is the *same gift*. The former is literal, the latter is more familiar and as truthful.

ᵠ *Ἰσην δωρεαν πιστευσασιν*, the same gift. It was only to hem that believed, indicating that only such are the temple of the Holy Spirit—the Holy *Guest*. His miraculous gifts were a sign to those that were out of the Church.

ʳ *Ακουσαντες*, 1st aor. part., on hearing, they were silent—having heard; ησυχασαν, they were quiet.

ˢ *Εδοξαζον*, imp., were glorifying God; αραγε, perhaps then, God εδωκεν has granted also to the nations τὴν μετανοιαν εἰς ζωην. The reformation to life— not μεταμελεια, *pœnitentia*,

but μετανοια, *resipiscentia*, reformation, or *returning to a right understanding = recovery.* Suetonius, *change of life.*

ᵗ *Εἰς, ad, erga*, towards, *on to,* changed to, *into = εἰς ζωην ; on to,* or *into life. A state of mind changing the course of life,* in order to life in its proper intent, enlargement, and enjoyment. God *grants* repentance, or the benefit of repentance into life.

ᵘ *The word, τον λογον*. This formula now becomes a sort of technical term, indicative of *the message*, the last message of God to the world. It is called "the word of the kingdom"— "the word of life"—not the *letter*, or law, but *the word*, or gospel.

This 19th v. resumes the narrative, from the death of Stephen. The 8th, 9th, and 10th chapters, to the 19th verse of the 11th chap., constitute a digression. The 8th chapter gives an account of the conversion of the Samaritans, and the Ethiopian officer; the 9th gives an account of the conversion of Saul of Tarsus ; the 10th the conversion of the Gentiles. The 11th to the 19th v. gives an account of Peter's visit to Jerusalem, and the explanation of his conduct in going to the Gentiles. Here, again, the history of the Acts of the Apostles is resumed, detailing their labors, trials, and success. Paul and Barnabas became prominent actors, and their proper labors engross the principal incidents recorded in this book. They commenced at Antioch, in Syria, to act in concert, under the sanction of a solemn ordination, and mission.

Τον λογον, the word. See ch. 1 : 1, note a, on *λογος. The word, the message,* the *burthen* of the prophets, all, or severally, indicate a *special* message from God—or from man—preceded by the article, in this book, is *specific--the gospel, the word of reconciliation.*

ᵛ *"To none but Jews only."* This is rather a vulgarism. *Only,*

KING JAMES' VERSION.	GREEK TEXT.	REVISED VERSION.

men of Cyprus and Cyrene, which when they were come to Antioch, spake unto the Grecians, preaching the Lord Jesus.

21 And the hand of the Lord was with them: and a great number believed, and turned unto the Lord.

22 Then tidings of these things came unto the ears of the church which was in Jerusalem: and they sent forth Barnabas, that he should go as far as Antioch.

23 Who, when he came, and had seen the grace of God, was glad, and exhorted them all, that with purpose of heart they would cleave unto the Lord.

24 For he was a good man, and full of the Holy Ghost, and of faith: and much people was added unto the Lord.

25 Then departed Barnabas to Tarsus, for to seek Saul:

26 And when he had found him, he brought him unto Antioch. And it came to pass, that a whole year they assembled themselves with the church, and taught much people. And the disciples were called Christians first in Antioch.

ἐξ αὐτῶν ἄνδρες Κύπριοι καὶ Κυρηναῖοι, οἵτινες εἰσελθόντες εἰς Ἀντιόχειαν, ἐλάλουν πρὸς τοὺς Ἑλληνιστὰς, εὐαγγελιζόμενοι τὸν Κύριον Ἰησοῦν. 21 καὶ ἦν χεὶρ κυρίου μετ᾽ αὐτῶν πολύς τε ἀριθμὸς πιστεύσας ἐπέστρεψεν ἐπὶ τὸν κύριον· 22 Ἠκούσθη δὲ ὁ λόγος εἰς τὰ ὦτα τῆς ἐκκλησίας τῆς ἐν Ἱεροσολύμοις περὶ αὐτῶν· καὶ ἐξαπέστειλαν Βαρνάβαν διελθεῖν ἕως Ἀντιοχείας. 23 ὃς παραγενόμενος καὶ ἰδὼν τὴν χάριν τοῦ Θεοῦ ἐχάρη, καὶ παρεκάλει πάντας τῇ προθέσει τῆς καρδίας προσμένειν τῷ κυρίῳ· 24 ὅτι ἦν ἀνὴρ ἀγαθὼς καὶ πλήρης Πνεύματος Ἁγίου καὶ πίστεως. καὶ προσετέθη ὄχλος ἱκανὸς τῷ κυρίῳ. 25 Ἐξῆλθε δὲ εἰς Ταρσὸν ὁ Βαρνάβας ἀναζητῆσαι Σαῦλον, 26 καὶ εὑρὼν αὐτὸν ἤγαγεν αὐτὸν εἰς Ἀντιόχειαν. ἐγένετο δὲ αὐτοὺς ἐνιαυτὸν ὅλον συναχθῆναι ἐν τῇ ἐκκλησίᾳ, καὶ διδάξαι ὄχλον ἱκανὸν, χρηματίσαι τε πρῶτον ἐν Ἀντιοχείᾳ τοὺς μαθητὰς Χριστιανούς. 27 Ἐν

of them were men of Cyprus and Cyrene, who, having come into Antioch, spoke to the Hellenists, ʷpreaching the gospel of the Lord Jesus. And the hand of the Lord was 21 with them, and a great number believed and ˣturned to the Lord. Then tidings of 22 these things came to the ears of the congregation which was in Jerusalem; and they sent forth Barnabas, that he should go ʸthrough to Antioch; who, when he came and beheld the grace of God, was 23 glad, and exhorted them all, that with purpose of heart, they should adhere to the Lord. For he was a good man, 24 and full of ˣˣthe Holy Spirit and of faith. And a great multitude was added to the Lord. Then Barnabas depart- 25 ed to Tarsus to seek Saul. And when he had found him, 26 he brought him to Antioch. And it came to pass that, during a whole year, they were assembled with the congregation, and taught ᶻa great multitude. And the disciples were called ᵃChristians first in Antioch.

---

is wholly redundant. Either, "to Jews only", or, only to Jews, is current English.

ʷ Εὐαγγελιζόμενοι τον Κυριον Ιησουν. Though Ἐυαγγελιζω occurs fifty-six times in N. T., it is only twice presented with a *person* for its burthen. The word is preached, the Gospel is preached, but Jesus is only preached twice, in the import of εὐαγγελιζω. He is here *preached the Lord*, and in ch. 5 : 42, he is preached the Christ. This is an eloquent fact, and gives to the two predicates of Jesus transcendant glory. He is the *anointed* Lord, and the *Christed* Jesus. He is *the* Lord, and *the* Christ of the Universe.

ˣ Επεστρεψεν, turned over upon, cast themselves upon the Lord. ˣˣ See Note on chap. 13. v. 4.

ᶻ Και διδαξαι οχλον ικανον. Ἱκανος, in com., ver., is represented by *worthy, large, great, enough for, many, much, long,*

security, *a good while, long while, sore, sufficient, able, meet.* In forty occurrences it has fourteen representatives. Of these, not one is equal to it. *Sufficient*, most nearly, in *generic* sense, represents it. Beza prefers *dignus*. We have a homely word, or phrase, which well represents it. We say of such a one "he has got", or received, "*what he ought*". It may be good, bad, or indifferent. It was suitable to him—that which he deserved. It was so in this case. He merited "*a great multitude*", and he got it.

ᵃ "The disciples were called Christians first in Antioch." The persecution commenced at the martyrdom of Stephen, and became the means of disseminating the gospel of the grace of God. A large and flourishing church in Antioch, was one of the fruits. The disciples, proving and maintaining that Jesus was the Christ, obtained from them the name of Christians first in Antioch, the capital of Syria, called after Antiochus Epiphanes, a monster of iniquity. It became the seat of a flourishing church, and the occasion of a name, even

KING JAMES' VERSION.	GREEK TEXT.	REVISED VERSION.
27 And in these days came prophets from Jerusalem unto Antioch.	ταύταις δὲ ταῖς ἡμέραις κατῆλθον ἀπὸ Ἱεροσολύμων προφῆται εἰς Ἀντιόχειαν.	And in those days prophets 27 came down from Jerusalem to Antioch. And one of them, 28
28 And there stood up one of them named Agabus, and signified by the Spirit, that there should be great dearth throughout all the world: which came to pass in the days of Claudius Cesar.	28 ἀναστὰς δὲ εἷς ἐξ αὐτῶν ὀνόματι Ἄγαβος, ἐσήμανε διὰ τοῦ Πνεύματος, λιμὸν μέγαν μέλλειν ἔσεσθαι ἐφ' ὅλην τὴν οἰκουμένην· ὅστις καὶ ἐγένετο ἐπὶ Κλαυδίου Καίσαρος.	named Agabus, having stood up [b]made known through the Spirit that there would be a great famine throughout all the land, which occurred in the days of [c]Claudius. Then 29
29 Then the disciples, every man according to his ability, determined to send relief unto the brethren which dwelt in Judea.	29 τῶν δὲ μαθητῶν καθὼς ηὐπορεῖτό τις, ὥρισαν ἕκαστος αὐτῶν εἰς διακονίαν πέμψαι τοῖς κατοικοῦσιν ἐν τῇ Ἰουδαίᾳ ἀδελφοῖς·	[d]the disciples, every one, according to his ability, determined to send relief to the brethren that dwelt in Judea;
30 Which also they did, and sent it to the elders by the hands of Barnabas and Saul.	30 ὃ καὶ ἐποίησαν, ἀποστείλαντες πρὸς τοὺς πρεσβυτέρους διὰ χειρὸς Βαρνάβα καὶ Σαύλου.	which they also did; and sent 30 it to the Elders by the hands of Barnabas and Saul.
CHAP. XII.	CHAP. XII.	CHAP. XII.
Now about that time, Herod the king, stretched forth *his* hands to vex certain of the church.	ΚΑΤ' ἐκεῖνον δὲ τὸν καιρὸν ἐπέβαλεν Ἡρώδης ὁ βασιλεὺς τὰς χεῖρας κακῶσαί τινας τῶν ἀπὸ τῆς ἐκκλησίας.	[e]Now, about that time, Herod, the king, stretched forth his hands to [f]persecute certain persons of the congregation. And he killed James, 2
2 And he killed James the brother of John with the sword.	2 ἀνεῖλε δὲ Ἰάκωβον τὸν ἀδελφὸν Ἰωάννου	the brother of John, [g]with the

---

popular when Luke wrote this book. His allusion to the origin of this name is an evidence of its then extended currency.

[b] Ἀναστας, *having stood up*; εσημανε, *made known*, not merely, *intimated.*—Hack.

[c] Καισαρος, *Cæsar.* Is rejected by Gb., Sch., Ln., and Tf. It is a historic fact that Claudius *Cæsar*, so called in Roman history, is the person here named. He was poisoned by his wife Agrippina, A. D. 54. Being born nine years before Jesus Christ; this event happened A. D. 45, which fact well synchronizes with the details of this book. Another Claudius sat on the same throne, born A. D. 246. He was a great military chieftain, and died A. D. 270. There having been two Claudiuses, one of German, and one of Gothic descent, may have occasioned the insertion in the margin, which finally crept into the text.

[d] Των μαθητων, attracted into the genetive by τις. Instead of οἱ μαθηται καθως ηυπορειτο τις αυτων.—Mey., De Wette, Hack. Βαρναβα, Dor. Gen. 19 : 14 ; Luke 13 : 29 ; John 1 : 43. The disciples, in proportion as (τις) any one was prospered, determined, each of them. See 1 Cor. 16 : 2. Τις, while literally, *any one*, is tantamount in our day and currency to, *every one.* Still as τις, Acts 2 : 45, is, com. ver., *every one*, (yet in that case more pertinently, *any one*), so here, *every one* determined to send relief, according to his ability.

After a long critique on this word, Leigh, in his invaluable Critica Sacra, in allusion to this passage, says :—"Sæpius vero ad animi propositum, seu destinationem ac decretum transfertur. Acts 11 : 29 and 17 : 31". There is here no formal nom. case to ὥρισαν. It is understood to be: "*certain of the brethren*", or every one of the brethren, in prosperous circumstances.

[e] Κατ' εκεινον δε τον καιρον ; δε, *now, secundum, juxta, cum,* καιρος, *opportunitas*; mature and seasonable time. *Tempore enim venire rerum omnium est*, inquit Cornicus. The Greeks make a difference between χρονος, *time*, and καιρος, *season*, if not always, generally ; hence καιρος, opportunitas, mature and seasonable time. Solomon, as well as the Greeks, sometimes placed *season* and *time* in antithesis ; "due season", Luke 12 : 42; Gal. 6 : 10 ; Heb. 11 : 15 ; Acts 24 : 25. Herod, it seems, judged this time of famine, and necessary contribution to the necessities of the poor brethren, a suitable season for him to persecute and oppress them. He laid hands upon the Christians to maltreat, as επεβαλεν τας χειρας intimates. And, seeing it to be αρεστον τοις Ιουδαιοις, pleasing to the Jews, he seized Peter as a feast for them and, having killed Peter with the sword, he intended to present to them another repast.

[f] Κακοω, to hurt, to harm, to vex, to treat evilly, to injure. With us, the word *persecute*, covers the cases here named.

[g] Μαχαιρα, being here anarthrous, would seem to sanction

KING JAMES' VERSION.	GREEK TEXT.	REVISED VERSION.

KING JAMES' VERSION.

3 And because he saw it pleased the Jews, he proceeded further to take Peter also. Then were the days of unleavened bread.

4 And when he had apprehended him, he put *him* in prison, and delivered *him* to four quaternions of soldiers to keep him; intending after Easter to bring him forth to the people.

5 Peter therefore was kept in prison: but prayer was made without ceasing of the church unto God for him.

6 And when Herod would have brought him forth, the same night Peter was sleeping between two soldiers, bound with two chains; and the keepers before the door kept the prison.

7 And behold, the angel of the Lord came upon *him*, and a light shined in the prison; and he smote Peter on the side, and raised him up, saying, Arise up quickly. And his chains fell off from *his* hands.

8 And the angel said unto

GREEK TEXT.

μαχαίρᾳ. ³ καὶ ἰδὼν ὅτι ἀρεστόν ἐστι τοῖς Ἰουδαίοις, προσέθετο συλλαβεῖν καὶ Πέτρον· ἦσαν δὲ ἡμέραι τῶν ἀζύμων. ⁴ ὃν καὶ πιάσας ἔθετο εἰς φυλακὴν, παραδοὺς τέσσαρσι τετραδίοις στρατιωτῶν φυλάσσειν αὐτὸν, βουλόμενος μετὰ τὸ πάσχα ἀναγεῖν αὐτὸν τῷ λαῷ. ⁵ ὁ μὲν οὖν Πέτρος ἐτηρεῖτο ἐν τῇ φυλακῇ· προσευχὴ δὲ ἦν ἐκτενὴς γινομένη ὑπὸ τῆς ἐκκλησίας πρὸς τὸν Θεὸν ὑπὲρ αὐτοῦ.

⁶ Ὅτε δὲ ἔμελλεν αὐτὸν προάγειν ὁ Ἡρώδης, τῇ νυκτὶ ἐκείνῃ ἦν ὁ Πέτρος κοιμώμενος μεταξὺ δύο στρατιωτῶν, δεδεμένος ἁλύσεσι δυσὶ, φύλακές τε πρὸ τῆς θύρας ἐτήρουν τὴν φυλακήν. ⁷ καὶ ἰδοὺ, ἄγγελος κυρίου ἐπέστη, καὶ φῶς ἔλαμψεν ἐν τῷ οἰκήματι· πατάξας δὲ τὴν πλευρὰν τοῦ Πέτρου, ἤγειρεν αὐτὸν λέγων, Ἀνάστα ἐν τάχει. Καὶ ἐξέπεσον αὐτοῦ αἱ ἁλύσεις ἐκ τῶν χειρῶν. ⁸ εἶπέ τε ὁ ἄγγελος πρὸς

REVISED VERSION.

sword. And because he saw 3 that it pleased the Jews, he proceeded further to seize Peter also. (And then were ʰthe days of the unleavened ˡloaves.) And ʲhaving apprehended him, he put him in 4 prison, and delivered him to four ᵏquaternions of soldiers, to guard him, intending, after the passover, to bring him forth to the people. Pe- 5 ter, therefore, was kept in prison, but ˡearnest prayer, without ceasing, was made by the congregation to God for him.

And when Herod would 6 have brought him forth, in that night, Peter was sleeping between two soldiers, bound with two chains; and keepers, before the door, guarded the prison. And behold a mes- 7 senger of the Lord stood near, and a light shone in the prison, and, striking Peter on the side, he raised him up, saying, rise up quickly. And his chains ¹¹fell off from his hands. And the messenger said to him, 8

---

a sword. But this is a special case, because "*the article fails when the idea is general.*" He was slain by the sword; so in our usage we have "the gallows", "the Penitentiary", "the Work-House", not a gallows, a Penitentiary, a Work-House, as *penal* institutions. These are *idiomatic* formulas. See Hackett and others on this passage.

But we have in this context another such case:

ʰ Ησαν δε ημεραι των αζυμων, ad verbum, "*now were days of the unleavened.*" But idiomatically *Now*, or, *then*, (as the case may be), were *the* days of unleavened bread.

These are valuable examples, that supersede the ordinary rules of Greek syntax and etymology, when applied to Hebrew idioms; and in some very grave cases, such as the anarthrous *Πνευμα*, when qualified by *αγιον*. Though to us apparent anomalies, they are not to be disregarded, much less to be annihilated. *Loaves*, in the above case, is a more serious suppression than the article *ἡ*, in the case of *μαχαιρα*, though it indicates several instruments. Literally, *And the days of the unleavened were.*

ˡ *Των αζυμων, of the unleavened.* The article is here used to direct attention to *the feast* of unleavened bread, and should be translated: It was not in *days of unleavened bread*, in a general sense, but of *the unleavened* bread, in a specific sense.

ʲ *Πιασας*, aor. part., having seized; *παραδους*, part., having given him over to four detachments of four soldiers, *φυλασσειν αυτον.*

ᵏ *Τετραδιον*, occurring but once in the Christian Scriptures, should be rendered according to Roman usage. A quaternion was a company of four soldiers. There were, therefore, *sixteen* soldiers on duty, four at each time, in turns, keeping guard.

ˡ *Εκτενης, intentus, assiduus.* It is indicative of extended or protracted and earnest prayer. —Crit. Sacr. *Περι*, Ln., Tf., Gb., prefer to *ὑπερ.*

¹¹ *Εξεπεσον—εκ των χειρων,* not *out of*, but *from* his hands. They could not have fallen *out of*, unless he had held them *in* his hands. *Χειρ*, in Greek currency, includes the whole forearm, or any part of it.

KING JAMES' VERSION.

him, Gird thyself, and bind on thy sandals: and so he did. And he saith unto him, Cast thy garment about thee, and follow me.

9 And he went out, and followed him, and wist not that it was true which was done by the angel; but thought he saw a vision.

10 When they were past the first and the second ward, they came unto the iron gate that leadeth unto the city; which opened to them of his own accord: and they went out, and passed on through one street; and forthwith the angel departed from him.

11 And when Peter was come to himself, he said, Now I know of a surety, that the Lord hath sent his angel, and hath delivered me out of the hand of Herod, and *from* all the expectation of the people of the Jews.

12 And when he had considered *the thing*, he came to the house of Mary the mother of John, whose surname was Mark, where many were gathered together, praying.

13 And as Peter knocked at the door of the gate, a· dam-

GREEK TEXT.

αὐτὸν, Περίζωσαι, καὶ ὑπόδησαι τὰ σανδάλιά σου. Ἐποίησε δὲ οὕτω. καὶ λέγει αὐτῷ Περιβαλοῦ τὸ ἱμάτιόν σου, καὶ ἀκολούθει μοι. ⁹ Καὶ ἐξελθὼν ἠκολούθει αὐτῷ· καὶ οὐκ ᾔδει ὅτι ἀληθές ἐστι τὸ γινόμενον διὰ τοῦ ἀγγέλου, ἐδόκει δὲ ὅραμα βλέπειν. ¹⁰ διελθόντες δὲ πρώτην φυλακὴν καὶ δευτέραν, ἦλθον ἐπὶ τὴν πύλην τὴν σιδηρᾶν, τὴν φέρουσαν εἰς τὴν πόλιν, ἥτις αὐτομάτη ἠνοίχθη αὐτοῖς· καὶ ἐξελθόντες προῆλθον ῥύμην μίαν, καὶ εὐθέως ἀπέστη ὁ ἄγγελος ἀπ' αὐτοῦ. ¹¹ καὶ ὁ Πέτρος γενόμενος ἐν ἑαυτῷ, εἶπε, Νῦν οἶδα ἀληθῶς ὅτι ἐξαπέστειλε κύριος τὸν ἄγγελον αὐτοῦ, καὶ ἐξείλετό με ἐκ χειρὸς Ἡρώδου καὶ πάσης τῆς προσδοκίας τοῦ λαοῦ τῶν Ἰουδαίων. ¹² συνιδών τε ἦλθεν ἐπὶ τὴν οἰκίαν Μαρίας τῆς μητρὸς Ἰωάννου τοῦ ἐπικαλουμένου Μάρκου, οὗ ἦσαν ἱκανοὶ συνηθροισμένοι καὶ προσευχόμενοι. ¹³ Κρούσαντος δὲ τοῦ Πέτρου

REVISED VERSION.

Gird yourself and bind on your sandals. And he did so. And he said to him, Cast your garment around you, and ᵐfollow me. And Peter went out and fol- 9 lowed him, and ⁿhad not ᵒperceived that what was done by the messenger was ᵖreal, but thought that he saw a vision.

When they had passed the 10 ᵠfirst and the second watch, they came to the iron gate, that leads into the city; which opened ʳspontaneously to them; and they went out, and passed on through one street. And forthwith the messenger departed from him. Then Peter, having come to 11 himself, said, Now I ᵗcertainly know that the Lord has sent his messenger, and has delivered me out of the hands of Herod, and from all the expectation of the people of the Jews.

And when he had consid- 12 ered the matter, he went to the house of Mary, the mother of John, whose surname was Mark, where many were assembled, praying. And ᵘwhen 13 he knocked at the door of

---

ᵐ Ακολουθει, not *go with me* nor *come with me*, but *follow me*, such is its almost universal import.

ⁿ Και ουκ ηδει οτι αληθες, pluperfect, he had not perceived that the scene, through which he had passed, was real.

ᵒ Ουκ ηδει, "wist not," is obsolete; *knew not*, is its representative.

ᵖ Αληθες, literally *true*; here, more appositely to the case, it should be, *real*.

ᵠ Πρωτην και δευτεραν, both are *anarthrous*, because, in such cases, it would be pleonastic. There could not be two *first* and two *second* watches, hence a first watch and a second watch, being stationed, all versions, ancient and modern, refer to them as *the first* and *the second*.

ʳ Αυτοματη, *automaton* like, that is "of itself." The word *spontaneously* with us happily represents it. "Of its own accord," may be more familiar to most ears, but too periphrastic.

ᵗ It may be a matter wholly of taste, which is somewhat arbitrary, but so it is with me—"I certainly know," is more forcible, than I know certainly.

ᵘ Now (δε) he—for του Πετρου we read αυτον, on the authority of Gb., Sch., Ln., and Tf. And when he knocked at the door, etc. Την θυραν του πυλωνος—*the door of the gate-way*, Thomp.; *the gate of the court*, Murd.; *the door of the gate*, Penn, Wesley; *entry door*, Rheims, Tyndale, Cranmer. *the door of the porch*, Wakefield; *the door of the outer gate*, Dodd.

KING JAMES' VERSION.	GREEK TEXT.	REVISED VERSION.

sel came to hearken, named Rhoda.

14 And when she knew Peter's voice, she opened not the gate for gladness, but ran in, and told how Peter stood before the gate.

15 And they said unto her, Thou art mad. But she constantly affirmed that it was even so. Then said they, It is his angel.

16 But Peter continued knocking. And when they had opened *the door*, and saw him, they were astonished.

17 But he beckoning unto them with the hand to hold their peace, declared unto them how the Lord had brought him out of the prison. And he said, Go shew these things unto James, and to the brethren. And he departed, and went into another place.

18 Now as soon as it was day, there was no small stir among the soldiers, what was become of Peter.

19 And when Herod had sought for him, and found him not, he examined the keepers, and commanded that *they* should be put to death. And he went

---

τὴν θύραν τοῦ πυλῶνος, προσῆλθε παιδίσκη ὑπακοῦσαι, ὀνόματι Ῥόδη· 14 καὶ ἐπιγνοῦσα τὴν φωνὴν τοῦ Πέτρου, ἀπὸ τῆς χαρᾶς οὐκ ἤνοιξε τὸν πυλῶνα, εἰσδραμοῦσα δὲ ἀπήγγειλεν ἑστάναι τὸν Πέτρον πρὸ τοῦ πυλῶνος. 15 οἱ δὲ πρὸς αὐτὴν εἶπον, Μαίνῃ. Ἡ δὲ διϊσχυρίζετο οὕτως ἔχειν. οἱ δ᾽ ἔλεγον, Ὁ ἄγγελος αὐτοῦ ἐστιν. 16 Ὁ δὲ Πέτρος ἐπέμενε κρούων· ἀνοίξαντες δὲ εἶδον αὐτόν, καὶ ἐξέστησαν. 17 κατασείσας δὲ αὐτοῖς τῇ χειρὶ σιγᾷν, διηγήσατο αὐτοῖς πῶς ὁ κύριος αὐτὸν ἐξήγαγεν ἐκ τῆς φυλακῆς. εἶπε δέ, Ἀπαγγείλατε Ἰακώβῳ καὶ τοῖς ἀδελφοῖς ταῦτα. Καὶ ἐξελθὼν ἐπορεύθη εἰς ἕτερον τόπον. 18 Γενομένης δὲ ἡμέρας, ἦν τάραχος οὐκ ὀλίγος ἐν τοῖς στρατιώταις, τί ἄρα ὁ Πέτρος ἐγένετο. 19 Ἡρώδης δὲ ἐπιζητήσας αὐτὸν καὶ μὴ εὑρών, ἀνακρίνας τοὺς φύλακας, ἐκέλευσεν ἀπαχθῆναι· καὶ κατελθὼν ἀπὸ

---

the gate, a maid servant, named Rhoda, went to hearken. And recognizing Peter's 14 voice, she did not open the gate, for gladness; but ran in and told them that Peter was standing before the gate. And 15 they said to her, You are crazy. But she ᵛconfidently affirmed that it was even so. Then they said, It is his ʷmessenger. But Peter continued 16 knocking. And when they had opened the door, and saw him, they were astonished. But he, beckoning to them 17 with the hand to be quiet, declared to them how the Lord had brought him out of the prison. And he said, Go tell these things to James, and to the brethren. And he departed and went to another place.

Now, as soon as it was day, 18 there was no small stir among the soldiers, as to what had ˣbecome of Peter. And when 19 Herod had sought for him, and did not find him, he examined the keepers, and commanded that they should be put to death. And he went from

---

ᵛ Μαίνῃ, μαινομαι, you are crazy, 2d sing. pres., ind. Ἡ δε διϊσχυριζετο ουτως εχειν, but she pertinaciously continued to affirm that it was even so.

ʷ His messenger, αγγελος. This word so often occurring in the Christian Scriptures, sometimes indicates a heavenly, and sometimes an earthly messenger. The notion that every one, especially every good man, has a guardian angel in constant attendance, is older than the N. T., and still cherished in many minds. In this place, it might be supposed to indicate a messenger sent by Peter, rather than Peter himself in person. But amongst the Jews, it was generally a cherished idea, that every good man had a guardian angel. Luke simply narrates, but comments not on the occasion. Neither shall we.

On weighing all that I have read and thought on the propriety of translation in general, and the word *angel* in particular, I feel a preponderance of reason and propriety, in favor of translating rather than of transferring words of this class. This more especially obtains in this word, and

in those indicative of office in the Christian Church. The abuse of such terms in popular currency, is, with me, a preponderating argument. The ideal forms entertained of angels especially of their personalities, is an additional argument in their case. Coleridge says, "After much thought on the subject of angels as a divine kind of finite beings, I find no sufficing reason to hold it for a revealed doctrine, and assuredly it is no truth of philosophy, which, as I have elsewhere remarked, can conceive but three kinds—1st. The infinite reason; 2nd. The finite rational; and 3d. The finite irrational—that is, God, man, and beast. What, indeed, even for the vulgar, is, or can an archangel be, but a man with wings, better or worse, than the wingless species, according as the feathers are white or black? I would that the word had been translated instead of Anglicized in our English Bible." New Edition, Notes in Hackett: vol. 5, p. 125.

ˣ It might be, in modern style, *not a little agitation as to what Peter came to be.* Too stiff and formal! *Ταραχος* is well represented by *commotion*, indicating both *inquiry* and *alarm.*

KING JAMES' VERSION.

down from Judea to Cesarea, and *there* abode.

20 And Herod was highly displeased with them of Tyre and Sidon. But they came with one accord to him, and having made Blastus the king's chamberlain their friend, desired peace, because their country was nourished by the king's *country*.

21 And upon a set day, Herod arrayed in royal apparel, sat upon his throne, and made an oration unto them.

22 And the people gave a shout, *saying*, *It is* the voice of a god, and not of a man.

23 And immediately the angel of the Lord smote him, because he gave not God the glory: and he was eaten of worms, and gave up the ghost.

24 But the word of God grew and multiplied.

25 And Barnabas and Saul returned from Jerusalem, when they had fulfilled *their* ministry, and took with them John, whose surname was Mark.

CHAP. XIII.

Now there were in the church that was at Antioch certain prophets and teachers; as Barnabas, and Simeon that was called Ni-

GREEK TEXT.

τῆς Ἰουδαίας εἰς τὴν Καισάρειαν διέτριβεν. 20 ⁷Ἦν δὲ ὁ Ἡρώδης θυμομαχῶν Τυρίοις καὶ Σιδωνίοις· ὁμοθυμαδὸν δὲ παρῆσαν πρὸς αὐτὸν, καὶ πείσαντες Βλάστον τὸν ἐπὶ τοῦ κοιτῶνος τοῦ βασιλέως, ᾐτοῦντο εἰρήνην, διὰ τὸ τρέφεσθαι αὐτῶν τὴν χώραν ἀπὸ τῆς βασιλικῆς. 21 Τακτῇ δὲ ἡμέρᾳ ὁ Ἡρώδης ἐνδυσάμενος ἐσθῆτα βασιλικὴν, καὶ καθίσας ἐπὶ τοῦ βήματος, ἐδημηγόρει πρὸς αὐτούς. 22 ὁ δὲ δῆμος ἐπεφώνει, Θεοῦ φωνὴ καὶ οὐκ ἀνθρώπου. 23 παραχρῆμα δὲ ἐπάταξεν αὐτὸν ἄγγελος κυρίου, ἀνθ᾽ ὧν οὐκ ἔδωκε τὴν δόξαν τῷ Θεῷ· καὶ γενόμενος σκωληκόβρωτος ἐξέψυξεν. 24 ὁ δὲ λόγος τοῦ Θεοῦ ηὔξανε καὶ ἐπληθύνετο. 25 Βαρνάβας δὲ καὶ Σαῦλος ὑπέστρεψαν ἐξ Ἱερουσαλὲμ, πληρώσαντες τὴν διακονίαν, συμπαραλαβόντες καὶ Ἰωάννην τὸν ἐπικληθέντα Μάρκον.

CHAP. XIII.

ἨΣΑΝ δέ τινες ἐν Ἀντιοχείᾳ κατὰ τὴν οὖσαν ἐκκλησίαν προφῆται καὶ διδάσκαλοι, ὅ τε Βαρνάβας καὶ Συμεὼν ὁ καλού-

REVISED VERSION.

Judea to Cæsarea, and abode there.

And Herod ⁷being enraged 20 at those of Tyre and Sidon, they came with one accord to him, and, having made Blastus, the king's chamberlain, their friend, desired peace; because their country was supported by the king's country. And, on an appointed day, 21 Herod, arrayed in royal apparel, sat on his throne, and made a speech to them. And 22 the people shouted, saying, It is the voice of a God, and not of a man. And immediately a 23 ᶻmessenger of the Lord smote him because he did not give God the glory. And, having been eaten by worms, he expired.

But the word of God ᶻcon- 24 tinued to grow, and extend. And Barnabas and Saul re- 25 turned from Jerusalem, when they had fulfilled their ministry, and took with them John, whose surname was Mark.

CHAP. XIII.

Now there were in the con- 1 gregation that existed in Antioch, certain prophets and ᵃteachers, as Barnabas and Sim-

---

⁷ Θυμομαχων, part. pres., being enraged at them, &c. (ὁ Ηρωδης, is rejected by Gb., Sch., Ln., Tf.)

ᶻ And the word of God continued to grow ηυξανε. Και επληθυνετο, imp., pass., and was extended. It grew in the accession of the people, and extended over the territory, or among the people. The word of God, or the Gospel of God, was proclaimed and made progress.—Murd. The word of God increased and multiplied.—Penn, Thomp. "Grew and multiplied."—Tyndale, Cranmer, Geneva. Increased and multiplied. —Rheims. There are pleonasms in sacred as well as in common style. Λογος, says Hackett, suggests the complex idea of doctrine and disciples, and the verbs, that follow, divide the idea into parts.

ᵃ *Certain prophets and teachers.* Τινες is rejected by Ln.,

Tf., but by Gb. is regarded as a probable omission. It is, indeed, redundant, placed, as it is, in apposition to the words προφηται και διδασκαλοι, now there were prophets and teachers.

In Antioch, κατα την ουσαν. Κατα is a preposition of great latitude, and is represented by the following words: *according to*, *against*, *apart*, *at*, *aside*, *after*, *by*, *of*, *concerning*, *touching*, *in*, *in every*, *down*. By the annexation of *ly*, it is used adverbially, as in the following cases: dai*ly*, for every day; Acts 3 : 2; 16 : 5; 17 : 11, 17; 19 : 9; private*ly*, Gal. 2 : 2; charitab*ly*, Rom. 14 : 15, etc.

These prophets and teachers were *in* Antioch, not necessarily *of* Antioch; yet they were really *of* the Church, as the Ευαγγελιον κατα Ματθαιον, κατα Μαρκον, κατα Λουκαν, κατα Ιωαννην, were *of* them, as writers, or reporters.

KING JAMES' VERSION.	GREEK TEXT.	REVISED VERSION.
ger, and Lucius of Cyrene, and Manaen, which had been brought up with Herod the tetrarch, and Saul.	μενος Νίγερ, καὶ Λούκιος ὁ Κυρηναῖος, Μαναήν τε Ἡρώδου τοῦ τετράρχου σύντροφος, καὶ Σαῦλος. ² λειτουργούντων δὲ αὐτῶν τῷ κυρίῳ καὶ νηστευόντων, εἶπε τὸ Πνεῦμα τὸ Ἅγιον, Ἀφορίσατε δή μοι τόν τε Βαρνάβαν καὶ τὸν Σαῦλον εἰς τὸ ἔργον ὃ προσκέκλημαι αὐτούς. ³ Τότε νηστεύσαντες καὶ προσευξάμενοι, καὶ ἐπιθέντες τὰς χεῖρας αὐτοῖς, ἀπέλυσαν. ⁴ Οὗτοι μὲν οὖν ἐκπεμφθέντες ὑπὸ τοῦ Πνεύματος τοῦ Ἁγίου, κατῆλθον εἰς	eon, who is called Niger, and Lucius the Cyrenian, and Manaen, ᵇwho had been brought up with Herod the Tetrarch, and Saul. While they were 2 ᶜministering to the Lord, and fasting, the Holy Spirit said, ᵈSeparate for me Barnabas and Saul to the work, for which I have called them. ᵉAnd when 3 they had fasted, and prayed, and laid their hands on them, they ᶠsent them away. So they, 4 being sent forth ᵍby the Holy

But in what sense, *of* them? By election, or by the mission of Christ, or from Jerusalem, or any other place, is not to be inferred from the grammatical construction. This must be learned from history, not from grammar. Barnabas and Paul, we know, were not of Antioch, though, in their travels, they may have been there, once and again. And here, too, was Simeon *the black*, according to Adam Clark; "because", says he, "of skin or hair". But neither did the Greeks, nor do we Americans call any man black, or white, because of his hair, or his coat, but because of his skin. The Roman, *Niger*, is derived from the Greek, *νεκρος, mortuus, dead*. We have not, in the Greek tongue, a common noun that radicates in, or that commences with, *Neg*, long vowel, or short. Hence *negro* has no representative in Greek; nor, indeed, in Latin. *Niger*, in Latin, *μελας*, in Greek, and שחר (*niger fuit*), in Hebrew, represent the *color* called *black*: so Job 30 : 30 says: "My skin is black upon me".

ᵇ *Συντροφος, una educatus.* An infant nourished by the same mother, Hdt. 1 : 99; one coeval, and of the same origin, Id. 2 : 65. We have no phrase more apposite than, "Who had been brought up with Herod". or, was educated with Herod.

ᶜ *Λειτουργουντων δε αυτων τῳ κυριῳ.* Cum ministrarent; id est *cum munere* suo fungerentur docendi, viz., ac prophetandi; nam Paulo ante, doctores ac prophetas fuisse dixerat : itaque Chrysostomus recte interpretatus est *λειτουργουντων, ministrantibus*; id est *prædicantibus*, Syrus et Arabs præcantibus; nom *λειτουργειν*, retulerunt ad publicas preces propter adjunctam jejunii mentionem.—Crit. Sac. This *λειτουργειν* refers exclusively to what is called public service; from *λειτος, public*, and *εργον, work*. The *Mass* in Rome, and the *Communion Service* in England, are properly called, *Liturgy*. The performance of the *ritual* of public worship, is, however, its general scope and intent. For these the State, or body ecclesiastic. is responsible.

Casauban, of the highest reputation for sound learning in this, as in other departments of literature, affirms that this word *λειτουργια* properly indicates, and represents, all religious services; that private, or public prayer, or any religious service, is represented as Liturgy. The verb occurs but three times, and the substantive six times in the Christian Scriptures, represented by *ministration*, or *service* of a public character; sometimes, indeed, personal and private, 2 Cor. 9 : 12; Heb. 10 : 11. This public service, offered to the Lord, is ordained for our good and for his glory. It is, indeed, our honor and happiness to perform it in spirit and in truth.

ᵈ *Αφορισατε δη μοι*, separate to me truly. *In prosa δη semper postponitur et vertitur sane.* It is redundant, Acts 13 : 2 —Crit. Sac. In the Christian Scriptures *δη* is found but six times. It is not represented at all in this case, Com. Ver. *Δη* strengthens the command, ch. 15 : 36; Luke 2 : 15.—Hack.

ᵉ *Επιθεντες* preceded by *νηστευσαντες και προσευξαμενοι*, aorist participles—and having fasted, and prayed, and imposed hands on them, or, *when they had fasted, and prayed, and laid their hands on them*, are equally grammatical. The latter is, perhaps, more popular in the living age. *Their* is supplemental, and, to some minds, necessary as definitive of the coöperants in this work.

ᶠ *They sent them away*, or, dismissed them. The former we prefer, because the latter is, in our forensic currency, to discard from office, to discontinue.—Webster.

ᵍ *Εκπεμφθεντες υπο του Πνευματος του Ἁγιου, by the Holy Spirit.* This specific formula occurs in this book *sixteen* times, the formula *το Ἁγιον Πνευμα seven* times, and *Πνευμα Ἁγιον*, anarthrous, or indefinite, occurs *nineteen* times, always indicative of the same Spirit, uniformly in capital initials, in Bagster's text. But, to classify them under the species of definite, and indefinite, of the former, in this single book, we have *twenty-three* occurrences, and of the latter *nineteen*, in all

KING JAMES' VERSION.	GREEK TEXT.	REVISED VERSION.
Seleucia; and from thence they sailed to Cyprus.	τὴν Σελεύκειαν, ἐκεῖθέν τε ἀπέπλευσαν εἰς τὴν Κύπρον. ⁵ καὶ	Spirit, went down into Seleucia; and thence they sailed into

forty-two occurrences. In all the other books of the Christian Scriptures, we have, of the definite form, *eighteen*, and of the indefinite, *thirty-two* occurrences. We are, from a strict analysis of all these cases, confirmed in the judgment that *Πνευμα Ἅγιον*, whether with, or without the article, uniformly represents *the Holy Spirit*. In the com. ver., it is represented, in the *Christian* Scriptures, by *Holy Ghost*, eighty-two times, and by *Holy Spirit*, only four times. Such is its history.

Both Theology, and Christology, have suffered no little from *ultra*, or hypercriticism on this third personality of Jehovah. New Testament usage is our safest index, or guide, in ascertaining the current value, or import of its most prominent terms, and forms of expression. Our special code, if we either need, or have such a code, is simply New Testament usage.

Be it then noted, that every proper name found in the *nominative*, or, properly, the *naming* case, in the first chapter of Matthew, on its first presentation, is *anarthrous*, or indefinite. It reads: *ΒΙΒΛΟΣ γενεσεως ΙΗΣΟΥ Χριστου, υἱον Δαβιδ υἱον Αβρααμ*. On certain theories these eight anarthrous nouns should be translated: *A book of a generation of a Jesus, a Christ, a son of a David, a son of an Abraham*.

To illustrate farther, a primordial principle, we shall select a prominent case of the same category, found in the Gospel history. It is that of Pontius Pilate, a public and an ostensible actor in the drama of Christian history. He first appears anarthrous, but is made definite by the addition of *τῷ ἡγεμονι*, Pontius Pilate, *the governor*. So is *Πνευμα*, Matt. 1 : 18–20, made definite by *Ἅγιον*. Holy Spirit being known to the Jews as the Divine Spirit—the Spirit of God—it was enough for them to say, that Jesus was begotten by Holy Spirit. This was as much a *personal* name as Pontius Pilate, there being no other spirit so introduced in Jewish or Christian history. There never was but one *Πνευμα Ἅγιον*, since the apostasy of Adam, known, or recognized in the Patriarchal, or Jewish oracles. This is a highly important and suggestive fact.

But to return to Pilate. After his introduction he is seven times named by Matthew without his surname, Pontius, but being a conspicuous personage, a representative of Cesar, he has the article prefixed six of these seven times. It is only once omitted, and that is the appeal made to him by certain Pharisees, (Matt. 27 : 62), instead of which they substitute *κυριε* in the vocative.

The same style occurs in Mark. He names him ten times in chap. 15. In nine of these occurrences, the article is prefixed, yet he never calls him *governor*. In the Acts, his name occurs, ch. 3 : 13; 4 : 27; 13 : 28, only once preceded by Pontius. Paul, too, names him once, 1 Tim. 6 : 13, when speaking of Christ's confession to, or before, Pontius Pilate.

Now, with, or without the article, does not Pilate, in every instance, indicate Governor Pilate? And, with equal, or superior assurance of faith, and of understanding, may we not affirm, (no particular designated spirit being in the premises), that *the Spirit of God*, or the *Πνευμα του Θεου*, the *Πνευμα Ἅγιον*, the *το Πνευμα Ἅγιον*, and the *το Πνευμα το Ἅγιον*, severally do, in Apostolic usage and currency, uniformly indicate one and the self-same Spirit of God, or the Holy Spirit?

No logic, no metaphysics can, as we conceive, entrench upon this position, that will not shake the whole basis of the hitherto well-sustained and documented science of Hermeneutics in general, and of Bible Hermeneutics in particular.

But, to some minds, there is a plausible objection, and, as far as known to us, but one objection found in Matthew 3 : 11. It is: *αυτος ὑμας βαπτισει εν Πνευματι Ἅγιῳ και πυρι*. Being indefinite, it is presumed that it cannot indicate the Holy Spirit, personally contemplated, but officially, or in some special influence.

Paul says: All our fathers were baptized into Moses in the Cloud, and in the Sea. And here some have assumed a parallelism between "*in holy Spirit*," and "*in fire*," that, as the Israelites were baptized into Moses, in the cloud, and in the sea, so Christians are immersed into Christ, in the Holy Spirit and in fire. This, to some minds, may appear plausible. But will the facts sustain, or justify it? We presume not. Fire is not a symbol of any spiritual blessing. On the contrary it is the symbol of a fearful calamity. And so our Lord interprets it. A baptism in fire is destruction. So the winnowing shovel separates the chaff from the wheat, that, while the latter is preserved in the garner, "the chaff is to be consumed in an unquenchable fire". Salvation, and damnation, are the alternatives presented by Jesus Christ. John baptized in water, *into repentance*. His commission reached no farther. But he warned those who repudiated his ministry, that his successor would baptize in the Holy Spirit, and in fire—not the same subjects in both, but one class in the Holy Spirit, afterwards to be poured out; and the other class, in the fire, afterwards to be poured out. No preacher, who preceded Jesus, ever preached of the baptism of fire—"the damnation of hell", of the burning lake, "the unquenchable fire", as did the Prophet whom John immersed in the Jordan. The sum of John's preaching was the last chapter of Malachi. He baptized his converts in the Jordan, and directed them to his Master, assuring them that, if they obeyed him, they should receive his Holy Spirit. If not, he would consume them in an unquenchable fire.

There were then two immersions, in his eye: one for purification, and one for destruction—an immersion in spirit, and an immersion in fire. Both are figurative, or at least metaphorical. Neither spirit, nor fire, can be sprinkled upon us, nor can we be poured, or sprinkled into them. But there is life in Spirit, and destruction in fire, and we can be immersed in, or subjected to them.

KING JAMES' VERSION.	GREEK TEXT.	REVISED VERSION.

KING JAMES' VERSION.

5 And when they were at Salamis, they preached the word of God in the synagogues of the Jews. And they had also John to *their* minister.

6 And when they had gone through the isle unto Paphos, they found a certain sorcerer, a false prophet, a Jew, whose name *was* Bar-jesus:

7 Which was with the deputy of the country, Sergius Paulus, a prudent man; who called for Barnabas and Saul, and desired to hear the word of God.

8 But Elymas the sorcerer (for so is his name by interpretation) withstood them, seeking to turn away the deputy from the faith.

9 Then Saul, (who also *is called* Paul,) filled with the Holy Ghost, set his eyes on him,

10 And said, O full of all subtilty, and all mischief, *thou child*

GREEK TEXT.

γενόμενοι ἐν Σαλαμῖνι, κατήγγελλον τὸν λόγον τοῦ Θεοῦ ἐν ταῖς συναγωγαῖς τῶν Ἰουδαίων· εἶχον δὲ καὶ Ἰωάννην ὑπηρέτην. ⁶ διελθόντες δὲ τὴν νῆσον ἄχρι Πάφου, εὑρόν τινα μάγον ψευδοπροφήτην Ἰουδαῖον, ᾧ ὄνομα Βαριῆσους, ⁷ ὃς ἦν σὺν τῷ ἀνθυπάτῳ Σεργίῳ Παύλῳ, ἀνδρὶ συνετῷ. οὗτος προσκαλεσάμενος Βαρνάβαν καὶ Σαῦλον, ἐπεζήτησεν ἀκοῦσαι τὸν λόγον τοῦ Θεοῦ. ⁸ ἀνθίστατο δὲ αὐτοῖς Ἐλύμας, ὁ μάγος· οὕτω γὰρ μεθερμηνεύεται τὸ ὄνομα αὐτοῦ· ζητῶν διαστρέψαι τὸν ἀνθύπατον ἀπὸ τῆς πίστεως. ⁹ Σαῦλος δὲ, ὁ καὶ Παῦλος, πλησθεὶς Πνεύματος Ἁγίου, καὶ ἀτενίσας εἰς αὐτὸν ¹⁰ εἶπεν, Ὦ πλήρης παντὸς δόλου καὶ πάσης ῥᾳδιουργίας,

REVISED VERSION.

Cyprus. And [h]when they were 5 in Salamis, they preached the word of God in the synagogue of the Jews, and [i]they had also John as their attendant. And 6 when they had gone through the [j]whole island as far as Paphos, they found a certain sorcerer, a false prophet, a Jew, whose name was Bar-Jesus—who was with the proconsul 7 of the country, Sergius Paulus, [k]a prudent man ; who called for Barnabas and Saul, and desired to hear the word of God. But 8 Elymas, the sorcerer, (for so is his name, [l]being translated), opposed them, seeking to turn aside the proconsul from the faith. Then Saul, (also 9 called Paul), [m]filled with the [n]Holy Spirit, [o]having looked earnestly upon him, said, O 10 full of all [p]subtilty and all

---

[h] Γενομενοι, aor. part., equal to οντες, and when they were there ; or, being there, they announced ; or, were announcing τον λογον του Θεου, the word of God, the word of the God.

[i] Ειχον, imp., *were accustomed to have*, we say : They had John &c.

[j] Διελθοντες, add ὁλην, Gb., Sch., Ln., Tf. Ὁλην την νησον, the whole Island of Paphos. Ευρον, they found, ανδρα, a certain man, μαγος. After ευρον, Ln. and Tf. add, ανδρα. "They found a certain magician, a Jew, named Barjesus."—Wakefield. "A certain sorcerer, a Jewish false prophet, whose name was Barjesus."—Penn. "A magian, a false prophet, a Jew, whose name was Barjesus."—Thomp. "A certain man, a sorcerer, a Jew, who was a false prophet, and whose name was Barsuma."—Murd., Syr. Admitting *man* into the text, Murdock's version is exact. It is, however, redundant, like men, brethren, and fathers, the two last implying, or containing the first.

[k] Ανθυπατῳ, deputy governor ; συνετῳ, a man of *understanding*, Wakef, Thomp., *Wiseman*, Mur. ; a well informed man, Boothr. Prudent man, Penn. It is, in its four occurrences in com. vers. represented by, *prudent*. He appears to have been a person of *good understanding, intelligent*, with us ; yet prudence being the attribute most conspicuous in this case, we give it preference.

[l] Μεθερμηνευεται, pres. ind. pass., his name *being translated*,

or, *being interpreted* which, in com. ver. in its seven occurrences, is its representative.

[m] Πλησθεις Πνευματος Ἁγιου. See note on v. 4.

[n] Πνευματας Ἁγιου is, in the selected text of the Bagsters', a misprint. It should be here Πνευματος Ἁγιου ; we correct it gramatically, and find we are sustained in their Hexapla of 1841.

[o] Ατενισας εις αυτον, *having looked*, or *looked intensely upon him, said*. Ῥᾳδιουργια is an ἁπαξ λεγομενον, found in this place only. We found of the same family, ῥᾳδιουργημα, Acts 18 : 14, there rendered, *lewdness*, here, *mischief, maleficentia*. Beza, Pisc. It indicates a propensity to perpetrate all sorts of wickedness. Crit. sac.

[p] Δολου—ῥᾳδιουργητας. The former occurs twelve times in N. T., represented by subtilty, deceit, craft, guile ; the latter seven times in N. T., com. ver.

Ῥᾳδιουργιας, found only in this place. Another member of this family occurs once ; viz. ῥᾳδιουργημα, Acts 18 : 14, "wicked lewdness," com. ver. The former, δολος, denotes all kinds of dissimulation, Rom. 1 : 29, *exquisita diligentia ad insidiandum*.—Basil, Calvin. He feigns one thing, and does another.—Crit. Sac. The latter, ῥᾳδιουργια, is represented by maleficentia, and, according to Beza and Piscator, denotes a person prepense to perpetrate any wicked deed.—Vatablus. Erasmus derives it from ῥᾳδιον, *facile*, and εργαζομαι, *operor*. One who is easily induced to perpetrate crime.

KING JAMES' VERSION.	GREEK TEXT.	REVISED VERSION.

of the devil, *thou* enemy of all righteousness, wilt thou not cease to pervert the right ways of the Lord?

11 And now behold, the hand of the Lord *is* upon thee, and thou shalt be blind, not seeing the sun for a season. And immediately there fell on him a mist and a darkness; and he went about seeking some to lead him by the hand.

12 Then the deputy, when he saw what was done, believed, being astonished at the doctrine of the Lord.

13 Now when Paul and his company loosed from Paphos, they came to Perga in Pamphylia: And John departing from them, returned to Jerusalem.

14 But when they departed from Perga, they came to Antioch in Pisidia, and went into the synagogue on the sabbath-day, and sat down.

15 And after the reading of

υἱὲ διαβόλου, ἐχθρὲ πάσης δικαιοσύνης, οὐ παύσῃ διαστρέφων τὰς ὁδοὺς κυρίου τὰς εὐθείας; ¹¹ καὶ νῦν ἰδοὺ, χεὶρ τοῦ κυρίου ἐπὶ σὲ, καὶ ἔσῃ τυφλὸς μὴ βλέπων τὸν ἥλιον ἄχρι καιροῦ. Παραχρῆμα δὲ ἐπέπεσεν ἐπ᾽ αὐτὸν ἀχλὺς καὶ σκότος, καὶ περιάγων ἐζήται χειραγωγούς. ¹² τότε ἰδὼν ὁ ἀνθύπατος τὸ γεγονὸς ἐπίστευσεν, ἐκπλησσόμενος ἐπὶ τῇ διδαχῇ τοῦ κυρίου.

¹³ Ἀναχθέντες δὲ ἀπὸ τῆς Πάφου οἱ περὶ τὸν Παῦλον, ἦλθον εἰς Πέργην τῆς Παμφυλίας. Ἰωάννης δὲ ἀποχωρήσας ἀπ᾽ αὐτῶν, ὑπέστρεψεν εἰς Ἱεροσόλυμα. ¹⁴ αὐτοὶ δὲ διελθόντες ἀπὸ τῆς Πέργης, παρεγένοντο εἰς Ἀντιόχειαν τῆς Πισιδίας, καὶ εἰσελθόντες εἰς τὴν συναγωγὴν τῇ ἡμέρᾳ τῶν σαββάτων, ἐκάθισαν. ¹⁵ Μετὰ δὲ τὴν ἀνάγνωσιν

mischief, ᴾᴾson of the Devil, enemy of all righteousness, will you not cease to ᑫpervert the ʳright ways of the Lord? And now behold ˢthe hand of 11 the Lord is upon you, and you shall be blind, not seeing the sun for a season. And immediately there fell on him a mist, and a darkness; and he went about seeking some persons to lead him by the hands. Then 12 the proconsul, ᵗhaving seen what was done, believed, ᵘbeing astonished at the doctrine of the Lord.

And, loosing from Paphos, 13 they who were ᵛwith Paul came into Perga of Pamphilia; and John, departing from them, returned into Jerusalem.

But they themselves, de- 14 parting from Perga, came into Antioch of Pisidia, and went into the synagogue on ᵂthe Sabbath day, and sat down. And, after the reading of the 15

ᴾᴾ *υιε*, anarthrous.

ᑫ *Διαστρεφω* always "pervert." or "perverse." Com. ver. Here, by circumlocution, "*turn away, to pervert the mind.* *Διαστρεφων*, part. pres. active. Perverting the right ways = the straight ways of the Lord.

ʳ *Ευθειας, οδους. Ευθυς* is found eight times in N. T., rendered both *straight*, and *right*, in com. vers. The former is figurative of the latter.

ˢ *Χειρ του κυριου.* Literally, a hand, a stroke, of the Lord = the Lord's hand is upon you. It is not a prayer for it, but a judgment announced. So the event declares. The article prefixed to both *οδους* and *ευθειας* is awfully definitive—*the ways of the Lord*, THE RIGHT WAYS. Yet the judgment was limited *αχρι καιρου, for a time*, not perpetually.

ᵗ *Ιδων*, part. aor., *having seen*. The governor, or deputy, believed *επιστευσεν εκπλησσομενος*, indicative of great moral force. In its fourteen occurrences in N. T. *εκπλησσω* is represented, in com. ver., by *amaze* and *astonish*. It is only used by Matt., Mark., and Luke. The cause, or instrument of this astonishment is found in *τη διδαχη του κυριου. Διδαχη* is found in N. T. twenty-nine times represented by *doctrine*, and once by "*what is taught*," Titus, 1 : 9. In the plural number only once found, and then it is *human opinions*, or *human teachings*. It is frequently mistranslated by the word *doctrine*, instead of

teaching. Instances, Matt. 7 : 28; 22 : 33; Mark 1 : 22; 4, 2; 12 : 38; Luke 4 : 32; Acts 2 : 42; Cor. 14 : 6; 2 Tim. 4 : 2; and probably in other passages. It is, in these cases, the act of teaching, and not the lesson taught.

ᵘ *Εκπλησσομενος επι τη διδαχη*, Matt., Mark, and Luke, only use this term in the Christian Scriptures; ten times translated by *astonished*, twice by *amazed*. *Struck with amazement*, is perhaps, to most minds, most expressive of the mind, or the feelings of the proconsul, always translated *deputy*, com. ver. which is not specific, but generic. We, therefore, prefer *proconsul*. Governor.—Wakefield. Deputy-governor.—Penn. Proconsul.—Thomp., Wes., Murd., Dodd.; found only four times in this book.

Οἱ περι τον Παυλον, those about Paul; his pupils, or persons attending him, or upon him ; *ηλθον εις Περγην*, came into Perga.

ᵂ *Τη ημερα των Σαββατων*, literally, on the first of the Sabbaths. In Luke 13 : 14 and 14 : 5, we have the gen. sing. In Acts 16 : 13, we have, as here, the gen. plural, most probably indicative of one of the consecrated weeks of the Jewish year. The same formula occurs, Acts 20 : 7, translated the first *day* of the week. See Cruden's Concordance on the second Sabbath after the first.

KING JAMES' VERSION.	GREEK TEXT.	REVISED VERSION.
the law and the prophets, the rulers of the synagogue sent unto them, saying, *Ye* men *and* brethren, if ye have any word of exhortation for the people, say on.	τοῦ νόμου καὶ τῶν προφητῶν, ἀπέστειλαν οἱ ἀρχισυνάγωγοι πρὸς αὐτοὺς, λέγοντες, Ἄνδρες ἀδελφοὶ, εἰ ἔστι λόγος ἐν ὑμῖν παρακλήσεως πρὸς τὸν λαὸν, λέ-	Law and the Prophets, the rulers of the synagogue sent to them, saying, Brethren, if you have a ˣword of exhortation for the people, speak it.
16 Then Paul stood up, and beckoning with *his* hand, said, Men of Israel, and ye that fear God, give audience.	γετε. 16 Ἀναστὰς δὲ Παῦλος, καὶ κατασείσας τῇ χειρὶ, εἶπεν, Ἄνδρες Ἰσραηλῖται, καὶ οἱ φο- βούμενοι τὸν Θεὸν, ἀκούσατε.	Then Paul stood up, and 16 waving with his hand, he said: Israelites, and you who fear God, hearken. The God 17
17 The God of this people of Israel chose our fathers, and exalted the people when they dwelt as strangers in the land of Egypt, and with an high arm brought he them out of it.	17 ὁ Θεὸς τοῦ λαοῦ τούτου Ἰσρα- ὴλ ἐξελέξατο τοὺς πατέρας ἡμῶν· καὶ τὸν λαὸν ὕψωσεν ἐν τῇ παροι- κίᾳ ἐν γῇ Αἰγύπτῳ, καὶ μετὰ βραχίονος ὑψηλοῦ ἐξήγαγεν αὐ-	of this ʸpeople chose our Fa- thers and ᶻexalted the people, when they ᵃdwelt as strangers ᵇin the land of Egypt, and with a ᶜhigh arm he brought them out of it. And for ᵈabout the 18
18 And about the time of forty years suffered he their manners in the wilderness.	τοὺς ἐξ αὐτῆς· 18 καὶ ὡς τεσσα- ρακονταετῆ χρόνον ἐτροποφόρη- σεν αὐτοὺς ἐν τῇ ἐρήμῳ· 19 καὶ	period of forty years he nour- ished them in the wilderness.

ˣ *Ει εστι λογος εν υμιν.* If there be in you a word. An idiom similar to *est pro habeo*, governing the dative. If you have a word, say it.

ʸ *Ισραηλ* is rejected by Gb., Sch., and Tf. after *τουτου.*

ᶻ *Βραχιονος υψηλου—υψωσεν.* "He elevated the people—and with an elevated arm." These words are used with great uniformity in the Christian Scriptures, com. ver., *υψηλος,* in its *eleven* occurrences, is uniformly rendered *high,* com. ver., and *υψοω,* in its *twenty* occurrences, is represented thirteen times by *exalt,* and seven times by *lift up.* We can find no more apposite representatives in our vernacular.

ᵃ *Εν τη παροικια, commoratio.* This term, occurring twice in the N. T., indicates *delay,* or, *sojourn* in a country. *Κατοι- κια* denotes fixed residence, so Crit. Sacra, and so classic use. It properly signifies the neighborhood of some persons. *Signifi- cat proprie viciniam aliquorum hominum qui simul in aliquo loco cohabitant.* Bucer on Ecclesiastic Government, p. 9.

ᵇ *Εν γη Αιγυπτω,* literally, *in a land,* in Egypt. Had the writer intended an Egyptian land, he could have found the adjective, *Αιγυπτιος,* occurring four times in this book of Acts, and once in Hebrews 11 : 29. This is the only instance, out of six cases, where the dative form is used. It is a pure Latinism. The dative is sustained by manuscripts, CDEGH, Chrysostom, Theophylact, and Œcumenius. The gen. has A.B. 13; 133, 137, and all ancient versions.

ᶜ *Μετα βραχιονος υψηλου,* a *high arm.*—Murd., Penn. *Up- lifted arm.*—Wes., Thomp., Wake., Dodd. This is more grand, and apropos.

ᵈ *Ὡς,* as, when, since, about, as soon as, after, while, when, &c., &c. ; *when,* and *while,* in respect of time. are common re- presentatives of *ὡς,* in com. ver., Acts 1 : 15. We have, in

harmony with very many translations, preferred *about.* The number of the names were *about* one hundred and twenty ; and here, he endured their manners *about* the space of forty years.

ᵉ *Ετροποφορησεν* is repudiated by Gb., Schott, and Tf., and *ετροφοφορησεν* substituted; *he provided nourishment,* or, *bore them as a nurse.* Deut. 1 : 31, 2 Mac. 7 : 27. So the Syriac, Sclavonic, Arabic, Copt. and Ethiopic. "Fed them in the wil- derness."—Wake. He fed them.—Murd. Tremellius, than whom of his age we have few superior Biblical critics, says, *Τρο- ποφορεω,* est instar nutricis ferre et educare. *Τροποφορι- ζειν,* dicitur cum melior pejores fert mores, quos tamen non approbat, ut bonus maritus cogitur mores uxoris morosæ ferre. Aretas, Crit. Sac. Doddrige says; "The Syriac renders this by a word which signifies to *nourish,* or, *educate,* so that Beza conjectures, they read, *ετροφοφορησεν* ;" and while preferring the common reading, he admits that Dr. Hammond thinks this to have been the true reading. Compare Deut. 1 : 31 and Ezek. 16 : 4, 5, 8. Most of the later editors prefer this word to *ετροποφορησεν,* "endured their manners." It is well at- tested and better suits the connection, since what the apostle would here bring to view, is not so much the forbearance of God to his people, as his interpositions in their behalf.— Hackett. "*He nourished*", this reading is better supported and agrees with fact, as well as with the conciliatory designs of the speaker.—Gr., Boothr. Some of the fathers also, with the Syriac, Arabic, Coptic, and Ethiopic, give this reading. This reading, says Adam Clark, confirms the marginal conjec- ture and excellently, agrees with the scope of the place, and is, at least, a reading of equal value with that in the commonly- received text. This fact superadded, we judge, gives it para- mount claims in the proposed revision.

KING JAMES' VERSION.

19 And when he had destroyed seven nations in the land of Chanaan, he divided their land to them by lot.

20 And after that, he gave *unto them* judges, about the space of four hundred *if*. years, until Samuel the prophet

21 And afterward they desired a king: and God gave unto them Saul the son of Cis, a man of the tribe of Benjamin, by the space of forty years.

22 And when he had removed him, he raised up unto them David to be their king: to whom also he gave testimony, and said, I have found David the *son* of Jesse, a man after mine own heart, which shall fulfil all my will.

23 Of this man's seed hath God, according to *his* promise, raised unto Israel a Saviour, Jesus:

24 When John had first

GREEK TEXT.

καθελὼν ἔθνη ἑπτὰ ἐν γῇ Χαναὰν, κατεκληροδότησεν αὐτοῖς τὴν γῆν αὐτῶν. 20 καὶ μετὰ ταῦτα, ὡς ἔτεσι τετρακοσίοις καὶ πεντήκοντα, ἔδωκε κριτὰς ἕως Σαμουὴλ τοῦ προφήτου· 21 κἀκεῖθεν ᾐτήσαντο βασιλέα, καὶ ἔδωκεν αὐτοῖς ὁ Θεὸς τὸν Σαοὺλ υἱὸν Κὶς, ἄνδρα ἐκ φυλῆς Βενιαμὶν, ἔτη τεσσαράκοντα· 22 καὶ μεταστήσας αυτὸν, ἤγειρεν αὐτοῖς τὸν Δαβὶδ εἰς βασιλέα, ᾧ καὶ εἶπε μαρτυρήσας, Εὗρον Δαβὶδ τὸν τοῦ Ἰεσσαὶ, ἄνδρα κατὰ τὴν καρδίαν μοῦ, ὃς ποιήσει πάντα τὰ θελήματά μου. 23 Τούτου ὁ Θεὸς ἀπὸ τοῦ σπέρματος κατ' ἐπαγγελίαν ἤγειρε τῷ Ἰσραὴλ σωτῆρα Ἰησοῦν, 24 προκηρύξαντος Ἰωάννου πρὸ προσώπου τῆς

REVISED VERSION.

And when he had [f]subjected 19 seven nations, in the land of Canaan, he [g]divided their land to them by lot. And after 20 these things, during about four hundred and fifty years, he gave them judges until Samuel, the Prophet.

And after that they [h]asked 21 a king for themselves. And God [i]granted to them Saul the son of Kish, a man of the tribe of Benjamin, during forty years. And having re- 22 moved him, he raised up for them David, to be king; to whom also he testified, saying, "I have found David, the son of Jesse, a man after my own heart," who shall perform all my [j]desires. Of this 23 man's seed, has God, according to promise, [k]brought up for Israel a saviour—Jesus; John having [l]first preached, 24

---

[f] And καθελων, part. aor., *having put down, subjected;* "destroyed" is too strong.

[g] For κατεκληροδοτησεν, Gr., Schol., Ln., Tf., substitute κατεκληρονομησεν, assigned—αυτοις, to them as a possession. Hellenistic for the *Hiphil* of נָחַל—την γην αυτων, their land, by promise. Hack. In behalf of this substitution, we have MSS. ABCDEGH and over *fifty cursive manuscripts.* So depose Chrysostom, Tf., and others.

With Kuinœl we say, Utraque lectio eundem gignit sensum, sed κατεκληρονομησεν, utpote difficilior est preferenda, et *jure hanc lectionem in textum receperunt,* Matthæius et Griesbachius. Scilicet κατακληρονομειν non tantum notat, possidere, obtinere sed etiam sensu Hiphilico possidendum tradere. Judd. 11 : 24 Παντα (τα εθνη scilicet) ὁσα κατεκληρονομησεν ὑμιν κυριος, omnes gentes quas vobis possidendas dedit dominus. Deut. 12 : 1 ; Num. 34 : 18 ; Deut. 3 : 29. See Kuinœl in loco, Acts 13. Lond. ed. A. D. 1835.

[h] Ητησαντο βασιλεα, aor. mid., "They asked a king for themselves," better, we think, than desired. A desire expressed = asked.

[i] God gave them τον Σαουλ υιον Κις. Literatim, *the Saul, son of a Kish. Ανδρα εκ φυλης Βενιαμιν, ετη τεσσαρακοντα,* literatim, *a man, of a tribe, of a Benjamin.* Such a version is an ultraism so evident, as to constitute a reproof to those who imagine that

the presence of the article, is, *in all cases,* necessary to indicate definiteness. It might be rendered, less *definitely,* thus, *a man of Benjamin's tribe.* In contrast with this indefiniteness, we place the most important and the most emphatic proposition in the Christian Scriptures, found in *Matt.* 16 : 16, συ ει ὁ Χριστος, ὁ υιος του Θεου του ζωντος. Ad verbum, *Thou art the Christ, the son of the God, the Living One.* In precision and definiteness, this is not surpassed in any language; nor in any oracular proposition known to me.

[j] Το θελημα, com. ver., *will,* in the *plural,* it cannot be *wills.* We must, therefore, substitute *desires.* In this we are sustained by the editors of the Englishman's Greek concordance.

[k] Ηγειρε. Ηγαγε is here substituted by Gb., Sch., Ln., Tf., and with good reason. He has brought a Savior to Israel. Ad verbum, Of this person's seed, God, etc.

Αγω is a favorite with Luke. He uses it forty times in his Gospel and Acts. All other writers in N. T. use it only thirty times. The style of every inspired writer, or penman, in N. T., is as peculiar as his personality. Their faces, we presume, were not better marked than are their respective styles.

[l] Προκηρυξαντος Ιωαννου, John having previously announced, etc.; "Before whose appearance John proclaimed a baptism of reformation to all the people of Israel", Thomp. "John first preached a baptism of repentance to all the people of Israel", Wakefield. "When John had first preached

KING JAMES' VERSION.	GREEK TEXT.	REVISED VERSION.
preached, before his coming, the baptism of repentance to all the people of Israel. 25 And as John fulfilled his course, he said, Whom think ye that I am? I am not *he*. But behold, there cometh one after me, whose shoes of *his* feet I am not worthy to loose. 26 Men *and* brethren, children of the stock of Abraham, and whosoever among you feareth God, to you is the word of this salvation sent. 27 For they that dwell at Jerusalem, and their rulers, because they knew him not, nor yet the voices of the prophets which are read every sabbath-day, they have fulfilled *them* in condemning *him*. 28 And though they found no cause of death *in him*, yet desired they Pilate that he should be slain.	εἰσόδου αὐτοῦ βάπτισμα μετανοίας παντὶ τῷ λαῷ Ἰσραήλ. 25 ὡς δὲ ἐπλήρου ὁ Ἰωάννης τὸν δρόμον, ἔλεγε, Τίνα με ὑπονοεῖτε εἶναι; οὐκ εἰμὶ ἐγώ, ἀλλ᾽ ἰδού, ἔρχεται μετ᾽ ἐμέ, οὗ οὐκ εἰμὶ ἄξιος τὸ ὑπόδημα τῶν ποδῶν λῦσαι. 26 Ἄνδρες ἀδελφοί, υἱοὶ γένους Ἀβραάμ, καὶ οἱ ἐν ὑμῖν φοβούμενοι τὸν Θεόν, ὑμῖν ὁ λόγος τῆς σωτηρίας ταύτης ἀπεστάλη. 27 οἱ γὰρ κατοικοῦντες ἐν Ἰερουσαλὴμ καὶ οἱ ἄρχοντες αὐτῶν, τοῦτον ἀγνοήσαντες, καὶ τὰς φωνὰς τῶν προφητῶν τὰς κατὰ πᾶν σάββατον ἀναγινωσκομένας, κρίναντες ἐπλήρωσαν· 28 καὶ μηδεμίαν αἰτίαν θανάτου εὑρόντες, ᾐτήσαντο Πιλάτον ἀναιρεθῆναι αὐτόν. 29 ὡς δὲ ἐτέ-	before his ᵐentrance on *his work*, an immersion of reformation to all the people of Israel. Now while John was 25 completing his course, he said, Whom do you suppose me to be? ⁿI am not he. But behold, one is coming after me, the shoes of whose feet I am not worthy to loose. Brethren, 26 sons of the °race of Abraham, and those among you who fear God, to you is the word of this salvation sent. For 27 they who dwell in Jerusalem, and their rulers, not ᵖknowing him, and the ᑫutterances of the prophets, which are read every sabbath, have, in condemning him, fulfilled them. And although they found 28 ʳnot the least cause of death in him, yet they desired Pilate ˢto put him to death. And 29

---

before his appearance, the baptism of repentance to all Israel", Boothr. "John having preached to all the people of Israel, before his coming," etc., Penn. "And *before his advent* he sent John to proclaim the Baptism of repentance to all the people of Israel", Murd. "John having first preached, *before his coming*, the baptism of repentance to all the people of Israel", Wes. These may serve to show how many diverse arrangements of words, there may be in the taste or style of translators, without materially changing the sense; of these, however, Thompson and Wakefield are, in our judgement, most truthful and apposite to the Original.

ᵐ Προσωπον της εισοδου αυτου. Εισοδος is found five times in N. T., represented by *coming, entering*, and *entrance—to enter into*. Προσωπον, *face, countenance, appearance, person*, presence, in com. ver. seventy-four times. Προ προσωπου, *positum est pro simplici προ == before*, Heb. לפני, vide Mal. 3 : 1 ; Matt. 11 : 10. Εισοδος, *ingressus aditus*, John 1 : 19, ss. 27 ; Matt. 3 : 11. In our idiom, as "*John was fulfilling his course*". Kuinœl, in loco, vol. 3, p. 209. "Before whose appearance John first preached a *Baptism of repentance*" (or, an immersion of reformation) to all people of Israel ", Wakefield. "John having preached, to all the people of Israel, before his coming, the baptism of repentance ", Penn.

ⁿ Ουκ ειμι εγω—ὁ σωτηρ. I am not the one promised, τῳ Ισραηλ, v. 24. This elliptical form, his attitude and general appearance, indicated his humble conceptions of himself, and accords with ου ουκ ειμι αξιος το υποδημα των ποδων λυσαι.

° Ὑιοι γενους Αβρααμ. Γενος, in its twenty-one occurrences, com. vers., is represented by *kind, nation, kindred, country, stock, offspring, born, generation, countrymen, diversities*. "*Descendants of Abraham's offspring*"—γενος, rather descendants of the *race* of Abraham. Wakefield prefers it, and it is more, in our idiom, used to denote the lineage of a family. *Stock* applies to *parent*, race to the series of discendants : εξ is prefixed to απεσταλη by Ln. and Tf., and ABD. The *Textus Recep. Gb*., Sch.—was sent out.

ᵖ "This one not having known (*failed to recognize*), *and the declarations of the prophets* (governed by the same participle), by having condemned him to death, *they fulfilled* them, i. e. *the declarations*." "This is the most approved translation." Hackett.

ᑫ Και τας φωνας, the utterances of the prophets ; επληρωσαν, they fulfilled ; τας κατα παν σαββατον αναγινωσκομενας, which are read, *according to the sabbath* ; that is, *each*, or *every* Sabbath-day. Κατα, in its *five hundred* occurrences, in N. T. is represented by a larger suit of connectives than any preposition in the language.

ʳ Εὑροντες, part. aor., having found, μηδεμιαν ; *no cause—not the least cause* of death. This gives to μηδεμιαν its entire force.

ˢ Αναιρεθηναι, infin., *to put him to death*. It indicates either private or public execution. Luk. 23 : 32 ; Acts 2 : 23 ; 10 : 39 ; 12 : 2 ; 22 : 20 ; 26 : 10 ; Septuagint Exod. 21 : 29, here it represents המית. In 2 Sam. 10 : 18, הרג. See also Hdian 2 : 1. Plato seqq. 876, d.

KING JAMES' VERSION.

29 And when they had fulfilled all that was written of him, they took *him* down from the tree, and laid *him* in a sepulchre.

30 But God raised him from the dead:

31 And he was seen many days of them which came up with him from Galilee to Jerusalem, who are his witnesses unto the people.

32 And we declare unto you glad tidings, how that the promise which was made unto the fathers,

33 God hath fulfilled the same unto us their children, in that he hath raised up Jesus again; as it is also written in the second psalm, Thou art my Son, this day have I begotten thee.

34 And as concerning that he raised him up from the dead,

GREEK TEXT.

λεσαν ἅπαντα τὰ περὶ αὐτοῦ γεγραμμένα, καθελόντες ἀπὸ τοῦ ξύλου, ἔθηκαν εἰς μνημεῖον. ³⁰ ὁ δὲ Θεὸς ἤγειρεν αὐτὸν ἐκ νεκρῶν, ³¹ ὃς · ὤφθη ἐπὶ ἡμέρας πλείους τοῖς συναναβᾶσιν αὐτῷ ἀπὸ τῆς Γαλιλαίας εἰς Ἱερουσαλὴμ, οἵτινές εἰσι μάρτυρες αὐτοῦ πρὸς τὸν λαόν. ³² καὶ ἡμεῖς ὑμᾶς εὐαγγελιζόμεθα τὴν πρὸς τοὺς πατέρας ἐπαγγελίαν γενομένην, ³³ ὅτι ταύτην ὁ Θεὸς ἐκπεπλήρωκε τοῖς τέκνοις αὐτῶν ἡμῖν, ἀναστήσας Ἰησοῦν· ὡς καὶ ἐν τῷ ψαλμῷ τῷ δευτέρῳ γέγραπται, Υἱός μου εἶ σὺ, ἐγὼ σήμερον γεγέννηκά σε. ³⁴ Ὅτι δὲ ἀνέστησεν αὐτὸν ἐκ νεκρῶν, μηκέτι μέλλοντα ὑπο-

REVISED VERSION.

when they had fulfilled all that was written of him, they took him down from the 'tree, and laid him in a sepulchre. But God raised him "from the 30 dead; and he was seen many 31 days by 'those who came up with him from Galilee into Jerusalem, who are his witnesses to the people. And 32 "we are declaring to you glad tidings, how that the promise, which was made to the fathers, God has completely 33 fulfilled the same to us their children, he having raised up Jesus; as it is also written in the ˣsecond Psalm, " Thou art my Son, to-day I have begotten thee." And that 34 he raised him up from ʸthe dead, no more to return to

---

ᵗ *Ξυλον, staff, tree, wood, stock*, constitute its representatives, in the N. T. It may be remarked, that *σταυρος*, occurring twenty-eight times, and *σταυροω* forty-four times, in N. T., are immutably represented by *cross* and *crucify*, and *illustrate*, if not *prove*, that words of *mood*, or *specific action*, have but one meaning; a fact when fully contemplated, and weighed, settles many a controversy in the subject of ordinances, human and Divine.

ᵘ *Ηγειρεν αυτον εκ νεκρων.* It is worthy of note that we find not *in any case* in all Luke's writings, *των νεκρων,* used to indicate a class of persons, raised from the dead, *just or unjust!* Even in Paul to the Corinthians, chap. 15, in saying so much of the resurrection, it is six times out of seven *anarthrous*—a resurrection of the dead. The philosophy of this may, perhaps, be found in the fact that in Corinth, and some other cities, the doctrine of a resurrection of *the* dead, or of *certain* dead persons, was treated by the Greeks with much contempt. It was called " the hope of worms".

In 1 Cor. chap. 15, when argued by Paul, he first meets the objection, or rather, the *denial* of the fact in these words, *αναστασις νεκρων ουκ εστιν; a resurrection of dead persons there is not.* It was not *the* resurrection of the dead, for a long time after the promulgation of Jesus as the Christ. It was the question of *a* resurrection of the dead. The main objections to this oracle are met and refuted, 1 Cor. 15 chap.

Some interpret, v. 30, thus "God *raised him up from among dead persons*", not *των νεκρων,* as *a* class, but *νεκρων,* as a *kind,* or *quality* in the abstract. Hence the omission of the article.

ᵛ *Οίτινες,* to this, add *νυν,* by authority of Sch., Ln., Tf., Gb., who are now his witnesses; *αυτου,* said to be " the genitive objective", not of possession.

ʷ *Και ἡμεις ὑμας ευαγγελιζομεθα.* " And we are declaring to you the glad tidings of the promise made to the fathers, how God hath performed," etc., Wakefield. "And lo! we also announce to you that the promise which was made to our fathers, God has fulfilled it to us their children," Murd. " And we declare the glad tidings of the promise which was made to the fathers; for God has fulfilled it," Penn. "And we declare unto you glad tidings concerning the promise," Boothr. *Ευαγγελιζομεθα* has a double accusative only here. *Επαγγελιαν* stands, in the first clause, with the usual effect of that attraction; Hackett, *in loco.*

And now we announce to you, as joyful tidings, the promise made to the Fathers, which God has fulfilled to us their children; having raised up for us Jesus: as also in the first Psalm. It has been written, γεγραπ. perf. ind. pass.; first Psalm, πρωτῳ for δευτερῳ, Gb., Ln., Tf.

ˣ It has been alledged, though apparently incorrect now, yet nevertheless true, that what we call the *second* Psalm *was anciently the first*; or what is now called the first was originally *not numbered* with the Psalms, but contemplated as an introduction. Both the Syriac and the Septuagint, it is admitted, differ from our notation and enumeration of the Psalms.

ʸ *Ὅτι δε ανεστησεν αυτον εκ νεκρων.* And that he raised him up from the dead, no more to return to corruption, he says, etc.; *εκ νεκρων, persons* are understood. The living and the dead include all mankind, from Adam till the last-born, in human

KING JAMES' VERSION.	GREEK TEXT.	REVISED VERSION.
now no more to return to corruption, he said on this wise, I will give you the sure mercies of David. 35 Wherefore he saith also i.. another *psalm*, Thou shalt not suffer thine Holy One to see corruption. 36 For David, after he had served his own generation by the will of God, fell on sleep, and was laid unto his fathers, and saw corruption: 37 But he, whom God raised again, saw no corruption. 38 Be it known unto you therefore, men *and* brethren, that through this man is preached unto you the forgiveness of sins; 39 And by him all that believe are justified from all things, from which ye could not be justified by the law of Moses.	στρέφειν εἰς διαφθορὰν, οὕτως εἴρηκεν, Ὅτι δώσω ὑμῖν τὰ ὅσια Δαβὶδ τὰ πιστά. 35 διὸ καὶ ἐν ἑτέρῳ λέγει, Οὐ δώσεις τὸν ὅσιόν σου ἰδεῖν διαφθοράν. 36 Δαβὶδ μὲν γὰρ ἰδίᾳ γενεᾷ ὑπηρετήσας τῇ τοῦ Θεοῦ βουλῇ, ἐκοιμήθη, καὶ προσετέθη πρὸς τοὺς πατέρας αὐτοῦ, καὶ εἶδε διαφθοράν· 37 ὃν δὲ ὁ Θεὸς, ἤγειρεν, οὐκ εἶδε διαφθοράν. 38 Γνωστὸν οὖν ἔστω ὑμῖν ἄνδρες ἀδελφοὶ, ὅτι διὰ τούτου ὑμῖν ἄφεσις ἁμαρτιῶν καταγγέλλεται· 39 καὶ ἀπὸ πάντων ὧν οὐκ ἠδυνήθητε ἐν τῷ νόμῳ Μωσέως δικαιωθῆναι, ἐν τούτῳ πᾶς ὁ πιστεύων δικαιοῦται. 40 βλέπετε	ᵃcorruption, ᵃhe said thus, "I will give to you the ᵇfaithful mercies of David." Wherefore he says also, in another *psalm*, "Thou wilt not ᶜgive up thy Holy One to see corruption." For David, indeed, after he ᵈhad served his own generation by the will of God, ᵉfell asleep, and was ᶠadded to his fathers, and saw corruption. But he whom God ᵍraised again, did not see corruption. Be it known to you therefore, brethren, that through this ʰperson is announced to you the forgiveness of sins. And by him all that believe are justified from all things from which you could not be justified by the law of Moses.

chronology. Μηκετι, no longer *in time.* Μελλοντα, pres. part., μελλω, to be about to be. Ὑποστρεφειν, in its thirty-five occurrences in N. T., is represented by *return, turn back, to turn back again;* com. ver., *come again,* Acts 22 : 17. We do not think that any one can ever return to that place, or condition, in which he never was before. Jesus could not return to corruption.

ᶻ Διαφθοραν, found in N. T. only in this book of Acts, and only six times in it, and always translated *corruption;* and of these *six* times, *four* are in this chapter, v. 34, 35, 36, 37. In the classics, nor in the Septuagint, does it ever indicate corruption as the effect of putrescence. (See Rob. Lex., διαφ.).

ᵃ Ειρηκεν, pres. ind., he has said. Οὕτως, thus, (in this wise obsolete). "I will give to you τα ὁσια Δαβιδ τα πιστα, the sure mercies of David."

ᵇ Ὁσιος is found but seven times in the approved Greek text of N. T. In this passage alone, it is translated "*sure mercies*", *faithful mercies.* David's name being connected with ὁσια, and τα πιστα, gives us the key of interpretation. We find the true, the covenanted, mercies guaranteed to David. 2 Sam. 7 : 12, 17. These *sure mercies* were not his son Solomon's fortunes; nor those of any other king descended from him, antecedent to *Jesus* of Nazareth, who was finally crowned the Divine and human autocrat of all creatures. We have, then, an immense interest in these *covenanted mercies* to our elder brother David, even, THE BELOVED, in whom we inherit all things. If Christ's, we are Abraham's seed, and David's seed, and heirs according to these sure, or covenanted mercies. Is.

55 : 3, 4; Heb. and Sept. Ὁσιος respondet τῷ חסיד, apud Hebræos ut ἁγιος τῷ קדוש, Drusius, Acts 2 : 27.

ᶜ Wherefore, also, in another psalm = ψαλμῳ, he says, Thou will not give (δωσεις) τον ὁσιον, the Holy one, to see, or suffer corruption.

ᵈ David μεν, indeed, ὑπηρετησας τη του Θεου βουλη—και ειδε διαφθοραν. We have here ὑπερετεω, whence ὑπηρετης, an *officer, minister,* and *servant.* The verb occurs *three* times in this book of Acts, and the noun *four* times. Διακονος, thirty times, *minister, deacon, servant,* are its representatives. Δουλος occurs one hundred and twenty times, and the verb δουλευω twenty-four times. This family indicates all sorts of servants: from the Lord Jesus, down to the meanest servant, or slave, in any age or country.

ᵉ Εκοιμηθη, was laid down to sleep; the sleep of death, Homer, Od. 3 : 397; compare Od. 12 : 372. In this form it is tantamount to death, "he *fell asleep*"—ne died.

ᶠ Προσετεθη, not *gathered,* but *added* to his fathers in the unseen world, indicative of his spirit returning to God, rather than his body returning to dust.

ᵍ He whom God raised, ηγειρεν, third sing. first aor. ind. act. of εγειρω, *excitavit,* "did not see *corruption*". *Destruction* and *corruption* are not constitutional synonyms, as some versions seem to indicate. Etymology is not an infallible guide. The *corrupting* force is generally from within, the *destructive,* from without.

ʰ Δια τουτου belongs to αφεσις rather than the verb. "*Through this one the forgiveness of sins is announced to you.*" Comp. 10 : 36 ; Luke 24 : 47. Hackett.

KING JAMES' VERSION.

40 Beware therefore, lest that come upon you which is spoken of in the prophets;

41 Behold, ye despisers, and wonder, and perish: for I work a work in your days, a work which ye shall in no wise believe, though a man declare it unto you.

42 And when the Jews were gone out of the synagogue, the Gentiles besought that these words might be preached to them the next sabbath.

43 Now when the congregation was broken up, many of the Jews and religious proselytes followed Paul and Barnabas; who speaking to them, persuaded them to continue in the grace of God.

44 And the next sabbath-day came almost the whole city together to hear the word of God.

45 But when the Jews saw the multitudes, they were filled with envy, and spake against those things which were spoken by Paul, contradicting and blaspheming.

46 Then Paul and Barnabas

GREEK TEXT.

οὖν μὴ ἐπέλθῃ ἐφ᾽ ὑμᾶς τὸ εἰρημένον ἐν τοῖς προφήταις, 41 Ἴδετε, οἱ καταφρονηταί, καὶ θαυμάσατε καὶ ἀφανίσθητε· ὅτι ἔργον ἐγὼ ἐργάζομαι ἐν ταῖς ἡμέραις ὑμῶν, ἔργον ᾧ οὐ μὴ πιστεύσητε, ἐάν τις ἐκδιηγῆται ὑμῖν.

42 Ἐξιόντων δὲ ἐκ τῆς συναγωγῆς τῶν Ἰουδαίων, παρεκάλουν τὰ ἔθνη εἰς τὸ μεταξὺ σάββατον λαληθῆναι αὐτοῖς τὰ ῥήματα ταῦτα 43 λυθείσης δὲ τῆς συναγωγῆς, ἠκολούθησαν πολλοὶ τῶν Ἰουδαίων καὶ τῶν σεβομένων προσηλύτων τῷ Παύλῳ καὶ τῷ Βαρνάβᾳ· οἵτινες προσλαλοῦντες αὐτοῖς, ἔπειθον αὐτοὺς ἐπιμένειν τῇ χάριτι τοῦ Θεοῦ.

4 Τῷ δὲ ἐρχομένῳ σαββάτῳ σχεδὸν πᾶσα ἡ πόλις συνήχθη ἀκοῦσαι τὸν λόγον τοῦ Θεοῦ. 45 ἰδόντες δὲ οἱ Ἰουδαῖοι τοὺς ὄχλους, ἐπλήσθησαν ζήλου, καὶ ἀντέλεγον τοῖς ὑπὸ τοῦ Παύλου λεγομένοις, ἀντιλέγοντες καὶ βλασφημοῦντες. 46 παρρησιασάμενοι δὲ ὁ Παῦλος καὶ ὁ Βαρ-

REVISED VERSION.

Beware, then, lest that come 40 upon you which is written in the prophets; [1]Behold, you de- 41 spisers, and wonder and perish. For I execute a work in your days, a work which you will not believe, though any one should fully declare it to you. And as they [1]were going out, 42 the Gentiles besought them, that these words might be spoken to them the next Sabbath. Now when the [k]con- 43 gregation was dispersed, many of the Jews and religious proselytes followed Paul and Barnabas, who, [1]addressing them, persuaded them to persevere in the grace of God. And on the [m]next Sabbath, al- 44 most the whole city assembled to hear the word of God. But 45 [n]when the Jews saw the multitudes, they were filled with [o]zeal, and spoke against those things which were spoken by Paul, contradicting and reviling. Then Paul and Barnabas 46

---

[1] Pro verbis, ראו בגוים Alexandrini interpretes ita expresserunt. Ιδετε, οι καταφρονηται—και εμβλεψατε και θαυμασατε θαυμασια, και αφανισθητε, etc. The Hebrew original, in our alphabet, is in the following words: Reu baggoyim vehabbitu vehitta mehu temahu ki poal poel bimeycem lo taaminu ki yesuppar. Com. ver. is not greatly dissimilar. "Behold you among the heathen people, and regard, and be astonished; be astonished, for I am working a work in your days; which, when it shall be told you, you will not credit." See Kuinoel, in loco.

[1] Εξιοντων δε αυτων παρεκαλουν, Gb., Sch., Ln., Tf., instead of εξιοντων δε εκ της συναγωγης των Ιουδαιων, com. reading. Then, having gone out, of their own accord, they besought, or, entreated. Luke uses this word more than any of the Christian historians, and Paul more than Luke and all other New Test. writers.

[k] Λυθεισης, part. aor. pass. The synagogue having been dismissed. The word "synagogue", like our word "church", was then indicative of the house, and of the people that met in it for worship, and was used occasionally to indicate both.

[1] Προσλαλεω is found only in this chapter, and in ch. 28:20 in the Christian Scriptures. It indicates speaking to, or with, one; and that with earnestness.

[m] On the next Sab., Gb., Sch., Ln., and Tf. read εχομενω, for the Textus Receptus, ερχομενω. The sense is the same, σχεδον πασα η πολις συνηχθη ακουσαι; almost the whole city were assembled, or brought together.

[n] But the Jews having seen, ιδοντες, (part. aor.), the crowds, were full of zeal, and they contradicted the things, λεγομενοις, spoken by Paul—βλασφημουντες—αντιλεγοντες—και; omitted by Ln., Gb., but highly probable.

[o] Indignation, or, zeal, not, envy, as some would have it. Αντιλεγοντες is neither superfluous nor Hebraistic, but, like the participle united with its finite verb in the classics, emphasizes αντελεγον, Mey., Hackett. I think the term, zeal, is, in its ancient and modern acceptation, its most obvious representative with us. It is, according to knowledge, a virtue, but otherwise a vice. "Envy," Mur., Booth., Wakef. "Jealousy," Penn. "Zeal," Wesley, Dodd., Thomp.

KING JAMES' VERSION.	GREEK TEXT.	REVISED VERSION.
waxed bold, and said, It was necessary that the word of God should first have been spoken to you: but seeing ye put it from you, and judge yourselves unworthy of everlasting life, lo, we turn to the Gentiles: 47 For so hath the Lord commanded us, *saying*, I have set thee to be a light of the Gentiles, that thou shouldest be for salvation unto the ends of the earth. 48 And when the Gentiles heard this, they were glad, and glorified the word of the Lord: and as many as were ordained to eternal life, believed. 49 And the word of the Lord was published throughout all the region. 50 But the Jews stirred up the devout and honourable women, and the chief men of the city, and raised persecution against Paul and Barnabas, and expelled them out of their coasts. 51 But they shook off the dust of their feet against them, and came unto Iconium. 52 And the disciples were filled with joy and with the Holy Ghost.	νάβας εἶπον, Ὑμῖν ἦν ἀναγκαῖον πρῶτον λαληθῆναι τὸν λόγον τοῦ Θεοῦ· ἐπειδὴ δὲ ἀπωθεῖσθε αὐτόν, καὶ οὐκ ἀξίους κρίνετε ἑαυτοὺς τῆς αἰωνίου ζωῆς, ἰδοὺ στρεφόμεθα εἰς τὰ ἔθνη. 47 οὕτω γὰρ ἐντέταλται ἡμῖν ὁ κύριος, Τέθεικά σε εἰς φῶς ἐθνῶν, τοῦ εἶναί σε εἰς σωτηρίαν ἕως ἐσχάτου τῆς γῆς. 48 Ἀκούοντα δὲ τὰ ἔθνη ἔχαιρον, καὶ ἐδόξαζον τὸν λόγον τοῦ κυρίου, καὶ ἐπίστευσαν ὅσοι ἦσαν τεταγμένοι εἰς ζωὴν αἰώνιον. 49 διεφέρετο δὲ ὁ λόγος τοῦ κυρίου δι᾽ ὅλης τῆς χώρας. 50 οἱ δὲ Ἰουδαῖοι παρώτρυναν τὰς σεβομένας γυναῖκας καὶ τὰς εὐσχήμονας καὶ τοὺς πρώτους τῆς πόλεως, καὶ ἐπήγειραν διωγμὸν ἐπὶ τὸν Παῦλον καὶ τὸν Βαρνάβαν, καὶ ἐξέβαλον αὐτοὺς ἀπὸ τῶν ὁρίων αὐτῶν. 51 οἱ δὲ ἐκτιναξάμενοι τὸν κονιορτὸν τῶν ποδῶν αὐτῶν ἐπ᾽ αὐτούς, ἦλθον εἰς Ἰκόνιον. οἱ δὲ μαθηταὶ ἐπληροῦντο χαρᾶς καὶ Πνεύματος Ἁγίου.	became bold, and said; It was necessary that the word of God should first have been spoken to you. But seeing you put it from you, and judge yourselves unworthy of the everlasting life, behold we turn to the Gentiles. For so has 47 the Lord commanded us, saying; I have ᴾplaced you for a light of nations that you might be for salvation even to the ends of the earth. On hearing 48 this the Gentiles rejoiced. and glorified the word of the Lord. and as many, as were ᑫdetermined for everlasting life, believed. And the word of the 49 Lord was published throughout all the region. But the 50 Jews stirred up the devout and honorable women, and the chief men of the city, and raised a persecution against Paul and Barnabas, and expelled them out of their borders. But 51 they shook off the dust of their feet against them, and went into Iconium. And the dis-52 ciples were filled with joy and with the Holy Spirit.

ᴾ *Τεθεικα σε εις φως εθνων, I have placed you for a light of nations:* so spoke the Lord, and such were, and are, the Apostles. *Εις σωτηριαν εως εσχατου της γης; I have ordained you, for salvation to the end of the earth. Τον ειναι σε,* infin. pres., *Telic* sense, that thou mayest be for salvation to the end of the earth.

ᑫ *Και επιστευσαν οσοι ησαν τεταγμενοι εις ζωην αιωνιον.*

Τασσω is found only eight times in the Christian Scriptures; Luke employs it *five* times, Paul *twice*, and Mathew *once*. In Luke's writings, it is represented by "set" = *placed*; "ordained", "determined", and "appointed". Paul speaks of magistrates as "ordained" of God, and of the Christians in Corinth, that "they had *addicted themselves* to the ministry of saints". Of Jesus it is said, he "*appointed* his friends to meet him at a certain place." Such is its current value in the Christian Scriptures. As many, then, as were resolved, or *determined* for eternal life, were attentive hearers of the word; and, therefore, believed. "But all things are of God, who has reconciled us to himself," by the means so ordained. Dr Doddridge says, I cannot think with Sir Norton Knatchbull, that *τεταγμενοι* is tantamount, in this place, to *συνηγμενοι*, as many as were met together = the Gentiles, believed; nor, with the great Joseph Mede's interpretation, that *τεταγμενοι εις ζωην αιωνιον* is a *periphrasis* to express "*proselytes of the gate*" In Rom. 13: 1, it is properly rendered, in the margin of some Testaments *ordered*, with Dodd. we prefer *determined*, because as ambiguous as the original.

We cannot but approve the conclusion of a considerable dissertation of the learned and judicious Kuinœl on this passage. His words are: *Iam additus ex gentilibus fidem habuisse ϑϑοι ησαν, κ. τ. λ. Unde consequitur, veram causam, cur a Deo vitæ æternæ destinati fuerint gentiles fuisse ipsorum fidem ob quam Judæi se felicitate illa indignos reddiderunt.* Of which, the sum is: It is now added, that some of the Gentiles believed; from which fact it follows, *that the true cause why the Gentiles were by God ordained to eternal life was their faith; as the rejection of his Divine doctrine was the cause, on account of which the Jews rendered themselves unworthy of this felicity.*

KING JAMES' VERSION.	GREEK TEXT.	REVISED VERSION.
CHAP. XIV.	CHAP. XIV.	CHAP. XIV.

KING JAMES' VERSION.

CHAP. XIV.

AND it came to pass in Iconium, that they went both together into the synagogue of the Jews, and so spake, that a great multitude, both of the Jews, and also of the Greeks, believed.

2 But the unbelieving Jews stirred up the Gentiles, and made their minds evil-affected against the brethren.

3 Long time therefore abode they speaking boldly in the Lord, which gave testimony unto the word of his grace, and granted signs and wonders to be done by their hands.

4 But the multitude of the city was divided: and part held with the Jews, and part with the apostles.

GREEK TEXT.

CHAP. XIV.

ΈΓΕΝΕΤΟ δὲ ἐν Ἰκονίῳ, κατὰ τὸ αὐτὸ εἰσελθεῖν αὐτοὺς εἰς τὴν συναγωγὴν τῶν Ἰουδαίων, καὶ λαλῆσαι οὕτως ὥστε πιστεῦσαι Ἰουδαίων τε καὶ Ἑλλήνων πολὺ πλῆθος. ² οἱ δὲ ἀπειθοῦντες Ἰουδαῖοι ἐπήγειραν καὶ ἐκάκωσαν τὰς ψυχὰς τῶν ἐθνῶν κατὰ τῶν ἀδελφῶν. ³ ἱκανὸν μὲν οὖν χρόνον διέτριψαν παρρησιαζόμενοι ἐπὶ τῷ κυρίῳ τῷ μαρτυροῦντι τῷ λόγῳ τῆς χάριτος αὐτοῦ, καὶ διδόντι σημεῖα καὶ τέρατα γίνεσθαι διὰ τῶν χειρῶν αὐτῶν. ⁴ ἐσχίσθη δὲ τὸ πλῆθος τῆς πόλεως· καὶ οἱ μὲν ἦσαν σὺν τοῖς Ἰουδαίοις, οἱ δὲ σὺν τοῖς ἀποστόλοις. ⁵ Ὡς δὲ

REVISED VERSION.

CHAP. XIV.

AND it occurred in Iconium, that they, ʳat the same time, went into the synagogue of the Jews, and ˢspoke so that a great multitude, both of the Jews, and also of the Hellenists, believed. But the unbelieving Jews ᵘstirred up the Gentiles, and ᵛdisaffected their ʷminds against the brethren. For ˣa long time, therefore, they continued there, speaking boldly respecting the Lord who ʸattested the word of his grace, granting signs and wonders to be done by their hands.

But the multitude of the city was divided. Some were with the Jews, and the others with the Apostles. And 5

ʳ Κατα το αυτο, analogous to, επι το αυτο, ch. 3 : 1, together.

ˢ Και λαλησαι ουτως, and they so spake. So Hackett and others. Wakefield supplies Paul and Barnabas, because named at the close of the preceding chapter. This seems to be unnecessary. "And so spake." Spake is obsolete, or nearly so.—Webster.

ᵗ Απειθουντες, απειθησαντες.—Ln., Tf. The unbelieving Jews. Απειθεω is found three times in this book, associated with the Jews. Paul to the Hebrews, and to the Romans uses it more frequently than any other inspired writer; and, in the sense of disobedient, he and Peter use it seven times.

ᵘ Επεγειραν, found only in this and in the preceding chapter in the Christian Scriptures, raised persecution, ch. 13 : 50. Here "stirred up". This is more than "over-excited", as sometimes found in classic use.

ᵛ Εκακωσαν. With one exception, (Pet. 3 : 13), this word is confined to this Book of Acts. "Made evil affected" their minds, com. ver.; "evil entreated", "vexed", "hurt", not much better. "Harmed", 1 Pet. 3 : 13, no better.

ʷ Of one hundred and fifteen occurrences in N. T. ψυχη is only twice represented by mind. Life and soul are its almost universal representatives. Beza on this passage says: Male affectos reddiderunt. Cum alioquin hoc vocabulum alibi soleat usurpari pro opprimere seu affligere, seu damnum aliquod inferre; ut Acts 12 : 1; 14 : 2. Crit. Sacra. נֶפֶשׁ cum sex punctis est anima, animus. (1) Halitus oris, anhelitus, spiritus, flatus, ventus, Gen. 1 : 20. Sic animæ nomen Latinis et Græcis pro anhelitu sumitur, pulmo animæ prælargus anhelat. (2) VITA, cujus anima fons est et origo. Job 2 : 6; Ps. 7 : 2, 3.

Conceiving it important to discriminate between the soul and the spirit, the anima and the animus, we have here, as occasionally before, drawn liberally on Leigh's Critica Sacra. London ed. A. D. 1650.

ˣ Ἱκανον, χρονον, διετριψαν. Ικανος is a favorite term in Luke's style. He employs it twenty-nine times, while all the other N. T. writers use it only twelve times. In his writings it is represented by worthy, large, great, enough for, many, much, long, security, good while, long while, sore. It is, in some of the other N. T. writers, represented by the word meet, able, and three times in Paul's second Letter to the Corinthians, by the word sufficient. This last representative is broad enough for its whole currency in the Christian Scriptures. Still it appears not exactly apposite in this place. It would be rather an ambiguous epithet to affirm of speaking upon the Lord. They spoke a sufficient time upon the Lord! Sufficient for the theme? or sufficient for the people? Connected with time, as it is here, we may try it in other places. A certain man had demons for a sufficient time; of a sufficient season; of sufficient time Simon had bewitched them with sorceries; Paul talked a sufficient time "till break of day". In such associations it would be more apposite to say for a long time. See Acts 8 : 11; 14 : 3; 18 : 18; 20 : 11; 27 : 7, &c.

ʸ We would have preferred was testifying to the word of his grace, being a continuative testimony, were it not, that it is followed by διδοντι, a dative of the manner, by granting signs and wonders to be done through their hands.

KING JAMES' VERSION.

5 And when there was an assault made both of the Gentiles, and also of the Jews, with their rulers, to use *them* despitefully, and to stone them,

6 They were ware of *it*, and fled unto Lystra and Derbe, cities of Lycaonia, and unto the region that lieth round about:

7 And there they preached the gospel.

8 And there sat a certain man at Lystra, impotent in his feet, being a cripple from his mother's womb, who never had walked.

9 The same heard Paul speak: who steadfastly beholding him, and perceiving that he had faith to be healed,

10 Said with a loud voice, Stand upright on thy feet. And he leaped and walked.

11 And when the people saw what Paul had done, they lifted up their voices, saying in the speech of Lycaonia, The gods

GREEK TEXT.

ἐγένετο ὁρμὴ τῶν ἐθνῶν τε καὶ Ἰουδαίων σὺν τοῖς ἄρχουσιν αὐτῶν, ὑβρίσαι καὶ λιθοβολῆσαι αὐτούς, ⁶ συνιδόντες κατέφυγον εἰς τὰς πόλεις τῆς Λυκαονίας, Λύστραν καὶ Δέρβην, καὶ τὴν περίχωρον, ⁷ κἀκεῖ ἦσαν εὐαγγελιζόμενοι.

⁸ Καί τις ἀνὴρ ἐν Λύστροις ἀδύνατος τοῖς ποσὶν ἐκάθητο, χωλὸς ἐκ κοιλίας μητρὸς αὐτοῦ ὑπάρχων, ὃς οὐδέποτε περιεπεπατήκει. ⁹ οὗτος ἤκουε τοῦ Παύλου λαλοῦντος· ὃς ἀτενίσας αὐτῷ, καὶ ἰδὼν ὅτι πίστιν ἔχει τοῦ σωθῆναι, ¹⁰ εἶπε μεγάλῃ τῇ φωνῇ, Ἀνάστηθι ἐπὶ τοὺς πόδας σου ὀρθός. Καὶ ἥλλετο καὶ περιεπάτει. ¹¹ Οἱ δὲ ὄχλοι ἰδόντες ὃ ἐποίησεν ὁ Παῦλος, ἐπῆραν τὴν φωνὴν αὐτῶν Λυκαονιστὶ

REVISED VERSION.

when there was a ᵃrush, both by the Gentiles, and also by the Jews with their rulers, ᵃto use them spitefully, and to stone them, they, being 6 aware of it, fled down into Lystra and Derbe, cities of Lycaonia, and into the surrounding country. And there 7 they ᵇannounced the gospel.

And, a certain man in Ly- 8 stra was sitting, ᶜimpotent in his feet, a cripple from his birth; who had never walked. The same heard Paul speak; 9 who, looking intently upon him, and ᵈperceiving that he had faith to be healed, said 10 with ᵉa loud voice, ᶠStand upright on your feet. And he ᵍleaped and walked. And when 11 the people saw what Paul had done, they raised their voices, saying in the ʰLycaonian,

---

ᶻ Ὁρμη των εθνων, τε και Ιουδαιων. A violent attempt of the Gentiles, as well as of Jews. Ὁρμη is once rendered, com. ver., *assault*; and the verb, ὁρμαω, to *rush*, to *run violently*. In classic use, ὁρμη is represented by *rush, assault, violent attempt*, impulse.

ᵃ Ὑβρισαι και λιθοβολησαι, to outrage, and to stone them, "to insult them, and to stone them."—Murd., Booth. "To use them despitefully and to stone them."—Wes. "To assault, and stone them."—Thomp.

ᵇ Κἀκει ησαν ευαγγελιζομενοι. And there they were announcing the Gospel. Such is its appropriated meaning, literally, *evangelizing*.

ᶜ Περιεπεπατηκει. Some editors write this pluperfect without an augment.—Hackett. Ὑπαρχων, *being*, appears redundant, and is, therefore, rejected by Gr., Sch., Ln., and Tf. It does not correspond with τις—τις ανηρ χωλος, a certain man, αδυνατος τοις ποσιν, imbecile, or, *impotent in his feet*. Χωλος, *claudus*, in classic usage, is represented by *lame*, halting, crippled, feeble. Its Hebrew representative is אֲשֶׁר רַד *claudus manu*. Hence the name Appius Claudius who was first called "*Appius the lame*". On this case Webster gives, "primarily, one who creeps, halts, or limps; one who has lost, or never enjoyed the use of his limbs", and refers to the Acts of Apostles in proof. This was a splendid miracle, and won for Paul the title of Mercury among the Greeks.

ᵈ Και ιδων ότι πιστιν εχει του σωθηναι, literally thus rendered, "and having perceived that he had faith of being healed", or *confidence of being healed* (unquestionably appropriated to his own case), Paul, with a bold, or a loud voice, said: *stand up straight upon your feet*.

ᵉ Μεγαλη τη φωνη. The manner in which he exerted his voice, not to the power or volume of it.—Hackett.

ᶠ "I say to you, in the name of the Lord Jesus," is not in the *Textus Receptus* published by the Bagsters. It is omitted on the authority of the Uncial and most cursive manuscripts—the Vulgate, Æthiopic, Chrysostom, Theop., and Occ. See Alford. The proper force of the presence, or absence, of the article before a noun, is well illustrated in this case. This was a special faith in a special case. We may have faith in the Christ of God, and not faith in being cured by him of any particular disease of mind, or body, under which we may be languishing. The patient, before us, had not only faith in Jesus the Christ, but also faith that, on his own special appeal to him, he would, through this Apostle, be healed.

ᵍ Ἡλατο rather than ἤλλετο, denoting a single act. Saltavit, 3d sing. 1 aor. mid. of ἁλλομαι, salio, he bounded.

ʰ Saying in the Lycaonian, or in the speech of Lycaonia. Lycaonic, Hackett. The speech of Lycaonia, is more properly Lycaonian; not, according to the dialects of the nations, Lycaonic. As the Persian, Grecian, Roman, are the appropriate

KING JAMES' VERSION.	GREEK TEXT.	REVISED VERSION.
are come down to us in the likeness of men.	λέγοντες, Οἱ θεοὶ ὁμοιωθέντες ἀνθρώποις κατέβησαν πρὸς ἡμᾶς·	The gods are come down to us, in the likeness of men.
12 And they called Barnabas, Jupiter; and Paul, Mercurius, because he was the chief speaker.	12 ἐκάλουν τε τὸν μὲν Βαρνάβαν, Δία· τὸν δὲ Παῦλον, Ἑρμῆν, ἐπειδὴ αὐτὸς ἦν ὁ ἡγούμενος τοῦ λόγου.	And they called Barnabas, 12 ᵢZeus, and Paul, ᵢHermes, because he was ʲthe chief speaker.
13 Then the priest of Jupiter, which was before their city, brought oxen and garlands unto the gates, and would have done sacrifice with the people.	13 ὁ δὲ ἱερεὺς τοῦ Διὸς τοῦ ὄντος πρὸ τῆς πόλεως αὐτῶν, ταύρους καὶ στέμματα ἐπὶ τοὺς πυλῶνας ἐνέγκας, σὺν τοῖς ὄχλοις ἤθελε θύειν. 14 Ἀκούσαντες δὲ	ᵏThen the priest of the 13 Zeus ʲthat was before the city, brought oxen and garlands to the gates, and, with the people, wished to offer sacrifices ᵐto them. Which 14

names of the tongues of Persia, Greece, and Rome, so should the language of the people of Lycaonia be denominated, or distinguished from the tongues of other countries. Its classic root is *Lukos, a wolf.*

ⁱ And they called Barnabas, *Zeus,* and Paul, *Hermes.* These were the facts; but not so the common version of them. The question thence arises: Why *translate* these proper names, or adopt a Roman version of them, and in similar cases not translate Abraham, Isaac, Jacob, Melchizedeck, Moses, Samuel, David, Daniel, Peter, &c., &c.

Jupiter and Mercury are merely a substitution of a Roman currency for a Greek currency. We would, in such cases, prefer the retention of the original name, especially when a historical fact is involved.

ʲ Ὁ ἡγουμενος τοῦ λογου. *The leader of the discourse,* is equivalent to the chief, or leading speaker. It is by some supposed, that, as Paul spoke more than Barnabas, and more officially, the audience were led to think that Barnabas was a Divinity, and Paul his interpreter, or oracle. This view of the subject enhances the courteousness, and the most honorable port and bearing of this most Divinely accomplished ambassador to the Gentile world, towards his fellow-laborer Barnabas, and will everywhere pass at par value.

ᵏ Δε, in this attitude, is rather continuative than adversative, and is, therefore, by most revisers and translators rendered *then,* or *and.*—Dodd., Wes., Thomp., Wake., Penn, Booth., Wic., Tyn., Cran., &c. There are, however, those who prefer *but,* which is sometimes slightly adversative as well as continuative. We think, however, that, in harmony with all the honors conferred, this is named as the consummation, and, though in bad taste, and in worse theology, it is the consummation of the climax of honors conferred on Paul and Barnabas by a polytheistic population.

ˡ It should be here noted, that αυτων, as connected with πολεως, city, is repudiated as a spurious reading by Gb., Sch., Ln., Tf.

Του οντος, after του Διος, stands in apposition with it. Many cities were placed under the protection of some particular deity, and the image of that deity placed at the entrance, to signify that he was the guardian and protector. To

this, Luke everywhere, as accurate as he is circumstantial, refers. Lystra, it appears, was under the guardianship of Jupiter Propuleius, which Luke translates: *Τον Διος του οντος προ της πολεως, the Jupiter that was before the city;* which is another term for Jupiter *Custos,* the guardian. All these deities had their *priests, rites,* and *sacrifices,* and each a peculiar service and priest for the office that he bore; so that Jupiter *Brontes,* Jupiter *the Thunderer,* had a different service from Jupiter *Custos, Jove the Guardian.* Hence we see with what accuracy Luke wrote. The person, who was to offer them sacrifice, was the priest of Jupiter *Custos;* under whose guardianship the city of Lystra was; and who, the priest supposed, had visited the city in a human form; and Barnabas (probably, for the reasons already assigned), he imagined to be the person. And as Mercury, the god of eloquence, was the general *attendant* of Jupiter, the people and the priest supposed that Paul, who had a powerful commanding eloquence, was *that* God also disguised. A beautiful figure of such an impersonation of Jupiter, as, is supposed, formerly stood before the gate of Lystra, still remains; and a fine engraving of it may be seen in Gruter's Inscriptions, Vol. 1, p. 20. Adam Clark, in loco.

Concerning these garlands, both Ovid and Virgil sing.

The former says:—

"Rich curling fumes of incense feast the skies,
A hecatomb of voted victims dies,
With *gilded horns* and *garlands* on their head,
In all the pomp of death to th' altar led."

TATE.

And Virgil sings:—

"The victim ox, that was for altars prest,
Trimm'd with white ribbons and with garlands drest,
Sunk of himself, without the gods' command,
Preventing the slow sacrificer's hand."

DRYDEN's *Virgil.*

ᵐ *To them* is a supplement essential to the proper conception of the discourse of Paul and Barnabas, reported in verses 14–18, which every reflecting reader must keep in his mind, as necessary to his apprehension of the point and drift of the address of Paul and Barnabas, and the rending of their own garments.

KING JAMES' VERSION.

GREEK TEXT.

REVISED VERSION.

14 *Which* when the apostles, Barnabas and Paul, heard *of*, they rent their clothes, and ran in among the people, crying out,

15 And saying, Sirs, why do ye these things? We also are men of like passions with you, and preach unto you, that ye should turn from these vanities unto the living God, which made heaven, and earth, and the sea, and all things that are therein:

16 Who in times past suffered all nations to walk in their own ways.

17 Nevertheless he left not himself without witness, in that he did good, and gave us rain from heaven, and fruitful seasons, filling our hearts with food and gladness.

18 And with these sayings scarce restrained they the people, that they had not done sacrifice unto them.

19 And there came thither *certain* Jews from Antioch, and Iconium, who persuaded the

οἱ ἀπόστολοι Βαρνάβας καὶ Παῦλος, διαρρήξαντες τὰ ἱμάτια αὐτῶν εἰσεπήδησαν εἰς τὸν ὄχλον, κράζοντες 15 καὶ λέγοντες, Ἄνδρες, τί ταῦτα ποιεῖτε; καὶ ἡμεῖς ὁμοιοπαθεῖς ἐσμεν ὑμῖν ἄνθρωποι, εὐαγγελιζόμενοι ὑμᾶς ἀπὸ τούτων τῶν ματαίων ἐπιστρέφειν ἐπὶ τὸν Θεὸν τὸν ζῶντα, ὃς ἐποίησε τὸν οὐρανὸν καὶ τὴν γῆν καὶ τὴν θάλασσαν καὶ πάντα τὰ ἐν αὐτοῖς· 16 ὃς ἐν ταῖς παρῳχημέναις γενεαῖς εἴασε πάντα τὰ ἔθνη πορεύεσθαι ταῖς ὁδοῖς αὐτῶν· 17 καί τοι γε οὐκ ἀμάρτυρον ἑαυτὸν ἀφῆκεν, ἀγαθοποιῶν, οὐρανόθεν ἡμῖν ὑετοὺς διδοὺς καὶ καιροὺς καρποφόρους, ἐμπιπλῶν τροφῆς καὶ εὐφροσύνης τὰς καρδίας ἡμῶν. 18 Καὶ ταῦτα λέγοντες, μόλις κατέπαυσαν τοὺς ὄχλους τοῦ μὴ θύειν αὐτοῖς. 19 Ἐπῆλθον δὲ ἀπὸ Ἀντιοχείας καὶ Ἰκονίου Ἰουδαῖοι, καὶ

when the Apostles, Barnabas and Paul, heard, they rent their clothes, [n]and leaped forth into the crowd, crying out; and saying, Why do you do 15 these things? We are [o]men of like nature with yourselves, declaring to you glad tidings, that you should turn from these vanities to the living God, who made the heaven, and the earth, and the sea, and [p]all things that are in them; who, in [q]the ages 16 past, suffered all the nations [r]to go on in their own ways. Nevertheless, he did not leave 17 himself without [s]testimony, in that he did good, and gave you rain from heaven, and fruitful seasons, filling your hearts with [t]food and gladness. And 18 [u]with these sayings they scarcely restrained the people, that they did not offer sacrifice to them. [v]Then Jews 19 came over from Antioch and Iconium; and having persua-

---

[n] For εισεπηδησαν, Gb., Sch., Ln., Tf., substitute εξεπηδησαν. They leaped out into the crowd exclaiming and saying: Men! why do you do these things?

[o] We are men, εσμεν ανθρωποι—ὁμοιοπαθεις ὑμιν, of passions similar to yourselves, ευαγγελιζομενοι, announcing to you glad tidings, that you should turn away from these vanities to the living God, who has made the heaven, and the earth, and the sea, and all things that are in them.

[p] Το παν, was an abbreviated formula representing the whole Universe, in the Aristotelian age. Τα παντα, and παντα τα, are not always identical in sense; the latter τα has sometimes the position and power of a relative pronoun, which is the case here. Therefore, in this case, we prefer " all things *that* are in them, to all things in them ".

[q] Παρῳχημεναις, from παροιχομαι, preteritus, found only in this place N. T., indicative of ages long since, or fully passed away.

[r] Πορευεσθαι, not properly " to *walk* in their own way," rather *to go on* in their own course.

[s] Και τοι γε ουκ αμαρτυρον, etc. And yet, indeed, he did not leave himself *unattested*.

Γε, enclitic, gives point and pungency to this expression. Αμαρτυρος, is an ἁπαξ λεγομενον, in this book, but in this sense it is found in Josephus Antiq. 14 : 7, 2; Plutarch de Solent Anim. 23; Thuc. 2 : 41. Doing good, &c. Better collocated in English thus: "And yet, indeed, doing good, giving (ὑμιν instead of ἡμιν, Gb., Sch., Ln.—Tf. omits both) to you rain from heaven and fruitful seasons, filling your (ὑμων not ἡμων) hearts with food and gladness."

[t] The heart receives not food; but, rhetorically, the heart is the receptacle of all comfort; hence the fullest expression of the satisfied desires of every category.

[u] Ταυτα λεγοντες, saying these things they, with difficulty (μολις from μολος, labor), restrained the multitude from offering sacrifice to them.

[v] Then (δε) Jews (επηλθον) came over from Antioch and Iconium, και πεισαντες, and having persuaded τους οχλους, the multitudes. Translators are almost equally divided in presenting this in singular and plural, *multitude* and *multitudes*. Being plural in all the best texts, we deem it proper to appear in the same number in the version, as in the original.

KING JAMES' VERSION.

people, and having stoned Paul, drew *him* out of the city, supposing he had been dead.

20 Howbeit, as the disciples stood round about him, he rose up, and came into the city : and the next day he departed with Barnabas to Derbe.

21 And when they had preached the gospel to that city, and had taught many, they returned again to Lystra, and *to* Iconium, and Antioch,

22 Confirming the souls of the disciples, *and* exhorting them to continue in the faith, and that we must through much tribulation enter into the kingdom of God.

23 And when they had ordained them elders in every church, and had prayed with fasting, they commended them to the Lord, on whom they believed.

24 And after they had passed throughout Pisidia, they came to Pamphilia.

25 And when they had preached the word in Perga, they went down into Attalia :

26 And thence sailed to Antioch, from whence they had been recommended to the grace of God, for the work which they fulfilled.

27 And when they were come, and had gathered the church together, they rehearsed all that God had done with them, and how he had opened the door of faith unto the Gentiles.

28 And there they abode long time with the disciples.

GREEK TEXT.

πείσαντες τοὺς ὄχλους, καὶ λιθάσαντες τὸν Παῦλον, ἔσυρον ἔξω τῆς πόλεως, νομίσαντες αὐτὸν τεθνάναι. 20 κυκλωσάντων δὲ αὐτὸν τῶν μαθητῶν, ἀναστὰς εἰσῆλθεν εἰς τὴν πόλιν· καὶ τῇ ἐπαύριον ἐξῆλθε σὺν τῷ Βαρνάβᾳ εἰς Δέρβην. 21 εὐαγγελισάμενοί τε τὴν πόλιν ἐκείνην, καὶ μαθητεύσαντες ἱκανοὺς, ὑπέστρεψαν εἰς τὴν Λύστραν καὶ Ἰκόνιον καὶ Ἀντιόχειαν· 22 ἐπιστηρίζοντες τὰς ψυχὰς τῶν μαθητῶν παρακαλοῦντες ἐμμένειν τῇ πίστει, καὶ ὅτι διὰ πολλῶν θλίψεων δεῖ ἡμᾶς εἰσελθεῖν εἰς τὴν βασιλείαν τοῦ Θεοῦ. 23 χειροτονήσαντες δὲ αὐτοῖς πρεσβυτέρους κατ᾽ ἐκκλησίαν, προσευξάμενοι μετὰ νηστειῶν, παρέθεντο αὐτοὺς τῷ κυρίῳ εἰς ὃν πεπιστεύκεισαν. 24 καὶ διελθόντες τὴν Πισιδίαν, ἦλθον εἰς Παμφυλίαν· 25 καὶ λαλήσαντες ἐν Πέργῃ τὸν λόγον, κατέβησαν εἰς Ἀττάλειαν· 26 κἀκεῖθεν ἀπέπλευσαν εἰς Ἀντιόχειαν, ὅθεν ἦσαν παραδεδομένοι τῇ χάριτι τοῦ Θεοῦ εἰς τὸ ἔργον ὃ ἐπλήρωσαν. 27 παραγενόμενοι δὲ καὶ συναγαγόντες τὴν ἐκκλησίαν, ἀνήγγειλαν ὅσα ἐποίησεν ὁ Θεὸς μετ᾽ αὐτῶν, καὶ ὅτι ἤνοιξε τοῖς ἔθνεσι θύραν πίστεως. 28 διέτριβον δὲ ἐκεῖ χρόνον οὐκ ὀλίγον σὺν τοῖς μαθηταῖς.

REVISED VERSION.

ded ᵛthe multitudes, and having stoned Paul, they were dragging him out of the city, supposing that he ʷwas dead. But, while the disciples were 20 standing about him, rising up, he entered into the city. And the next day he went out with Barnabas into Derbe. And when they had 21 announced the glad tidings to that city, and made many disciples, they returned into Lystra, and Iconium, and Antioch, confirming the souls 22 of the disciples, exhorting them to continue in the faith, *saying* that we must, through much tribulation, enter into the kingdom of God. And, 23 having appointed for them elders in every congregation, and having prayed with fastings, they commended them to the Lord, in whom they believed. And, having passed 24 through Pisidia, they came to Pamphylia. And when they 25 had spoken the word in Perga, they went down into Attalia; and thence they sail- 26 ed to Antioch, whence they had been commended to the grace of God, for the work which they performed.

And when they came, and 27 had assembled the congregation, they rehearsed all that God had done with them, and that he had opened a door of faith to the nations. And they continued no little 28 time with the disciples.

ʷ " *That he had been dead,*" is not only ambiguous, but reckless of all the texts, ancient and modern, that we have seen. They had not dragged, but, according to the text, were dragging him out of the city, when he revived.

KING JAMES' VERSION.

CHAP. XV.

AND certain men which came down from Judea, taught the brethren, *and said,* Except ye be circumcised after the manner of Moses, ye cannot be saved.

2 When therefore Paul and Barnabas had no small dissension and disputation with them, they determined that Paul and Barnabas, and certain other of them, should go up to Jerusalem unto the apostles and elders about this question.

3 And being brought on their way by the church, they passed through Phenice and Samaria, declaring the conversion of the Gentiles : and they caused great joy unto all the brethren.

4 And when they were come to Jerusalem, they were received of the church, and *of the* apostles and elders, and they declared all things that God had done with them.

GREEK TEXT.

CHAP. XV.

ΚΑΙ τινες κατελθόντες ἀπὸ τῆς Ἰουδαίας, ἐδίδασκον τοὺς ἀδελφοὺς, Ὅτι ἐὰν μὴ περιτέμνησθε τῷ ἔθει Μωϋσέως, οὐ δύνασθε σωθῆναι. ² Γενομένης οὖν στάσεως καὶ συζητήσεως οὐκ ὀλίγης τῷ Παύλῳ καὶ τῷ Βαρνάβᾳ πρὸς αὐτοὺς, ἔταξαν ἀναβαίνειν Παῦλον καὶ Βαρνάβαν καί τινας ἄλλους ἐξ αὐτῶν πρὸς τοὺς ἀποστόλους καὶ πρεσβυτέρους εἰς Ἱερουσαλὴμ, περὶ τοῦ ζητήματος τούτου. ³ οἱ μὲν οὖν προπεμφθέντες ὑπὸ τῆς ἐκκλησίας, διήρχοντο τὴν Φοινίκην καὶ Σαμάρειαν, ἐκδιηγούμενοι τὴν ἐπιστροφὴν τῶν ἐθνῶν· καὶ ἐποίουν χαρὰν μεγάλην πᾶσι τοῖς ἀδελφοῖς. ⁴ παραγενόμενοι δὲ εἰς Ἱερουσαλὴμ, ἀπεδέχθησαν ὑπὸ τῆς ἐκκλησίας καὶ τῶν ἀποστόλων καὶ τῶν πρεσβυτέρων, ἀνήγγειλάν τε ὅσα ὁ Θεὸς ἐποί-

REVISED VERSION.

CHAP. XV.

AND certain ˣpersons that 1 came down from Judea, taught the brethren, *saying;* Unless you are circumcised after the custom of Moses, you cannot be saved. When, therefore, 2 Paul and Barnabas had no little ʸdissension and discussion with them, they determined that Paul and Barnabas and certain others of them, should go up into Jerusalem to the Apostles and elders about this question. And being brought on their 3 way by the ᶻcongregation, they passed through Phenicia and Samaria, declaring the conversion of the Gentiles ; and caused great joy to all the brethren.

And when they were come 4 into Jerusalem, ᵃthey were received by the congregation, and by the Apostles and elders, and they declared all things that God had done by them.

ˣ *Τις, aliquis, τινες,* certain persons. The masculine gender is most worthy in all such cases. We sometimes substitute *persons. Τινες κατελθοντες,* Certain men coming down, Wes. ; "Some who came down," Wakef. ; "Had gone down," Penn. ; "Came down," Murd., Thomp. ; "Came," Dodd. *Απο της Ιουδαιας,* from Judea (to Antioch understood), εδιδασκον τους αδελφους—λεγοντες, after εδιδασκον must be supplied, in the sense, that the following ὅτι may redound, Kuinœl. *Τῳ εθει Μωϋσεως,* in the manner Moses prescribed, or, prescribed by Moses.

Περιτμηθητε is preferred by Ln. and Tf. to *περιτεμνησθε.* Griesbach regards it as supported by good authorities. *Τῳ εθει,* according to the custom. Dative of the manner.

ʸ *Γενομενης ουν στασεως—αυτους—controversia et disputatione acri.* In ch. 14 : 4, we find a schism amongst the citizens ; and in Acts 23 : 7, a similar one between the Pharisees and the Sadducees. *Στασις* occurs four times in the book of Acts, and only four times in all other portions of the Christian Scriptures. In com. ver. it is represented by *insurrection, sedition, dissension, uproar ;* and once by *standing.* Hence its special meaning, in any given case, depends upon its context.

Συζητησις occurs twice in this chapter, and only once beside in the Christian Writings, Acts ch. 28 : 29 ; in this last in-

stance it is represented by *reasoning,* and in this chapter by *disputation* and *disputing.*

The verb *συζητεω* is in favor with John Mark, occurring *six* times in his gospel, and only four times in Luke's writings. In Mark, com. ver., it is five times represented by *question,* and once by *reason.* But for *συζητησεως,* in this place, and in v. 7, in some manuscripts, it is *ζητησεως,* which occurs in this sense, at least six times in the Christian Scriptures.

ᶻ *Οἱ μεν ουν προπεμφθεντες ὑπο της εκκλησιας.* Some, as Hammond, on 1 Cor. 16 : 11, interpret these words thus: *Hi igitur ab ecclesia honorifice deducti.* Morus and Heinrichsius so interpret them, i. e. "*they were sent away with all necessary provisions for the journey.*" But no passage can be adduced from any writer of respectability to sustain such an interpretation. *Προπεμπω,* in its eight other occurrences in N. T., is represented by *accompany, conduct,* or *bring forward,* a person on a journey, Xen. Cyr. I. 4, 25 ; Homer's Odys. E. 37, 146, are quoted to sustain this interpretation. But their poetry, or their prose, is quite out of place in Luke's horizon.

ᵃ *Απεδεχθησαν,* they were kindly, or benignantly received. In ch. 2 : 41, and in ch. 21 : 17, we find *ασμενως* before *εδεξαντο,* rather *απεδεξαντο,* according to Ln., Tf.

KING JAMES' VERSION.	GREEK TEXT.	REVISED VERSION.

KING JAMES' VERSION.

5 But there rose up certain of the sect of the Pharisees, which believed, saying, That it was needful to circumcise them, and to command *them* to keep the law of Moses.

6 And the apostles and elders came together for to consider of this matter.

7 And when there had been much disputing, Peter rose up and said unto them, Men *and* brethren, ye know how that a good while ago, God made choice among us, that the Gentiles, by my mouth, should hear the word of the gospel, and believe.

GREEK TEXT.

ησε μετ᾽ αὐτῶν. ⁵ ἐξανέστησαν δέ τινες τῶν ἀπὸ τῆς αἱρέσεως τῶν Φαρισαίων πεπιστευκότες, λέγοντες, Ὅτι δεῖ περιτέμνειν αὐτοὺς, παραγγέλλειν τε τηρεῖν τὸν νόμον Μωϋσέως.

⁶ Συνήχθησαν δὲ οἱ ἀπόστολοι καὶ οἱ πρεσβύτεροι ἰδεῖν περὶ τοῦ λόγου τούτου. ⁷ πολλῆς δὲ συζητήσεως γενομένης, ἀναστὰς Πέτρος εἶπε πρὸς αὐτοὺς, Ἄνδρες ἀδελφοὶ, ὑμεῖς ἐπίστασθε ὅτι ἀφ᾽ ἡμερῶν ἀρχαίων ὁ Θεὸς ἐν ἡμῖν ἐξελέξατο διὰ τοῦ στόματός μου ἀκοῦσαι τὰ ἔθνη τὸν λόγον τοῦ εὐαγγελίου, καὶ πι-

REVISED VERSION.

But ᵇsome of the sect of 5 the Pharisees, who believed, rose up, saying, that it was necessary to ᶜcircumcise them, and to command them to keep the law of Moses.

And the Apostles and 6 elders came together to consider of this matter. And 7 when there had been much discussion, ᵈPeter rose up and said to them; Brethren, you know that at first God made choice ᵉamong us, that the Gentiles, by my mouth, should hear the word of the

---

ᵇ Ἐξανεστησαν δε τινες των απο της αἱρεσεως των Φαρισαιων; But there arose some of the sect of the Pharisees; or— But certain persons of the sect of the Pharisees who believed, arose; or, with Hackett, "But there arose some of those from the sect of the Pharisees." "Thereupon some of the sect of the Pharisees who believed, rose up, and said," Thomp. "But some of the sect of the Pharisees that believed, rose up and said," Dodd. "And they related how certain believers of the sect of the Pharisees had risen up, and said," Wakef. "But there rose up, said they, certain of the sect of the Pharisees who believed," Wesley. "And some who from the sect (or doctrine) of the Pharisees, had believed, rose up, and said," Murd. "But some of the sect of the Pharisees who had believed, arose, saying," Penn. "And there arose certaine of the heresie of the Pharisees that believed, saying," Rheims. "But sayed they, certaine of the secte of the Pharises rose up, which dyd beleue, saying," Geneva. "Then rose up certayne of the Secte of the Pharises which did beleue, saying," Cranmer. "Then arose ther op certayne that were of the secte of the Pharises and dyd beleve sayinge," Tyndale. "But summe of the eresie of farisies that bileuden, risen up and seiden," Wickliffe. Such is the scale-descending of thirteen English versions, as quoted, upon one of the most transparent verses in the Christian Scriptures. The changes in orthography are not much greater than the changes in the sense, so far as perspicuity, precision, and force are considered.

Are those *of* a sect that believed, and those *from* a sect that believed equivalent, or exactly equivalent, alike definite and perspicuous? Are "believers of the sect of the Pharisees," and "some of the Pharisees that believed," tantamount and equally definite indications of position? Is currency coin, or are currency and coin convertible terms? Literally, the Pharisees

thought that it was necessary to command them to circumcise, and to keep the law of Moses.

Αἱρεσης. The Pharisees and the Sadducees constituted each an *heresy* or an αἱρεσις. Hence, in v. 5, we read of certain persons of the *heresy* or *sect* of the Pharisees. Converted Pharisees constituted the first *heretics* or heresiarchs in the Christian Church; or translated from the synagogue to the church their respective theories. Like all HERETICS, in all ages, they were sensitive and tenacious of their respective peculiarities. Hence their tenacity of certain Jewish rites and ceremonies. They had the honor of occasioning the first Christian convention. They were punctiliously sensitive of the claims of Moses, and his law of ceremonies. Thus, in Jerusalem, they placed themselves under the shield of Moses and Abraham.

ᶜ Their central dogma is in the following words: ὅτι δει περιτεμνειν αυτους, παραγγελλειν τε τηρειν τον νομον Μωϋσεως. It behooved them first to be circumcised, and then to keep the law of Moses. They must be subjected to circumcision, and keep the law. Such was the issue—circumcision and the law of Moses.

ᵈ Αναστας Πετρος. In possession of the floor, Peter opens. Ανδρες αδελφοι. More implicated than any other man in that assembly, having immersed the Gentiles by a special command, without any conference, or agreement with any other Apostle. Hence his apology, ὁ Θεος εν ἡμιν εξελεξατο δια του στοματος μου ακουσαι τα εθνη τον λογον του ευαγγελιου, και πιστευσαι.

ᵉ Εν ἡμιν, is better sustained in this passage than εν ὑμιν, preferred by Ln., Tf. Peter modestly uses the plural. It is, indeed, a Hebraism. (Hebræi enim verbo בחר comitem addere solent præpositionem ב; Nehemiah 9 : 7, אֲשֶׁר בָּחַרְתָּ בְּאַבְרָם cui placuit probatus fuit Abrahamus. Add 1 Chronicles 28 : 4, 5. The Septuagint renders it thus: εξελεξατο εν εμοι—

KING JAMES' VERSION.	GREEK TEXT.	REVISED VERSION.

KING JAMES' VERSION.

8 And God, which knoweth the hearts, bare them witness, giving them the Holy Ghost, even as *he did* unto us:

9 And put no difference between us and them, purifying their hearts by faith.

10 Now therefore why tempt ye God, to put a yoke upon the neck of the disciples, which neither our fathers nor we were able to bear?

11 But we believe, that through the grace of the Lord Jesus Christ, we shall be saved, even as they.

12 Then all the multitude kept silence, and gave audience to Barnabas and Paul, declaring what miracles and wonders God had wrought among the Gentiles by them.

13 And after they had held their peace, James answered, saying, Men *amd* brethren, hearken unto me.

14 Simeon hath declared how God at the first did visit the

GREEK TEXT.

στεῦσαι. ⁸ καὶ ὁ καρδιογνώστης Θεὸς ἐμαρτύρησεν αὐτοῖς, δοὺς αὐτοῖς τὸ Πνεῦμα τὸ Ἅγιον, καθὼς καὶ ἡμῖν· ⁹ καὶ οὐδὲν διέκρινε μεταξὺ ἡμῶν τε καὶ αὐτῶν, τῇ πίστει καθαρίσας τὰς καρδίας αὐτῶν. ¹⁰ νῦν οὖν τί πειράζετε τὸν Θεὸν, ἐπιθεῖναι ζυγὸν ἐπὶ τὸν τράχηλον τῶν μαθητῶν, ὃν οὔτε οἱ πατέρες ἡμῶν οὔτε ἡμεῖς ἰσχύσαμεν βαστάσαι; ¹¹ ἀλλὰ διὰ τῆς χάριτος Κυρίου Ἰησοῦ Χριστοῦ πιστεύομεν σωθῆναι, καθ᾽ ὃν τρόπον κἀκεῖνοι. ¹² Ἐσίγησε δὲ πᾶν τὸ πλῆθος, καὶ ἤκουον Βαρνάβα καὶ Παύλου ἐξηγουμένων ὅσα ἐποίησεν ὁ Θεὸς σημεῖα καὶ τέρατα ἐν τοῖς ἔθνεσι δι᾽ αὐτῶν. ¹³ Μετὰ δὲ τὸ σιγῆσαι αὐτοὺς, ἀπεκρίθη Ἰάκωβος, λέγων, Ἄνδρες ἀδελφοὶ, ἀκούσατέ μου. ¹⁴ Συμεὼν ἐξηγήσατο, καθὼς πρῶτον ὁ Θεὸς

REVISED VERSION.

Gospel, and believe. And ᶠGod, 8 who knows the hearts, bore them testimony, giving them the Holy Spirit, even as to us; and put no difference 9 between us and them, having purified their hearts by the faith. Now, therefore, why 10 do you try God by putting a yoke upon the neck of the disciples, which neither our fathers, nor we, were able to bear? But, ᵍthrough the grace 11 of the Lord Jesus, we believe that we shall be saved, even as they.

Then all the multitude 12 were silent, and heard Barnabas and Paul declaring what ʰsigns and wonders God had wrought among the Gentiles by them.

And after they were si- 13 lent, James addressed them, saying; ⁱBrethren, hearken to me. Simeon has declar- 14 ed how God first visited

---

εἶναι βασιλέα. Ἐξελέξατο ἐν Σολομῶν τῷ υἱῷ καθῖσαι (αὐτὸν) ἐπὶ θρόνον. Vide Vorstius de Hebraism. N. T., p. 662. See also Kuinœl in loco.

ᶠ Καὶ ὁ καρδιογνώστης Θεος—δοὺς αὐτοῖς τὸ Πνεῦμα τὸ Ἅγιον. Confessing judgment, he pleads his justification on the basis of a Divine *oracle*, and of a Divine *gift* to the Gentiles, even the το Πνευμα το Ἁγιον, in its greatest, largest amplitude. It is not only the Holy Spirit in all the amplitude of his grace, but as more definite and exegetical he adds, καθως και ἡμιν, even as to us, Jews; and still more pleonastically, he adds, τῃ πιστει καθαρισας τας καρδιας αυτων, *having purified their hearts by the faith*.

ᵍ Χριστου is here omitted by Gb., Sch. and Tf. Lord Jesus is all sufficient. Δια της χαριτος, the *charity*. This word has obtained a very latitudinarian currency in the N. T., com. ver.; being represented by *ten* words: *favor, grace, thank, pleasure, liberality, benefit, joy, thankworthy, gift, acceptable;* while from the same root, χαρισμα, occuring seventeen times, is uniformly represented by *gift;* and χαριζομαι by *give, frankly forgive, grant, deliver.* Were we at liberty to select any one term, to the exclusion of every other, we should give our suffrage for *favor.* In our present currency, it would be adequate to the scope of the original. We should not place

sovereign, or *special* before it, because all *grace* is necessarily *sovereign, special,* and *free.* It may, in degrees, be great, greater, and greatest; but, uniformly, it is *free* and *sovereign.*

ʰ Σημεια και τερατα. Not convertible terms; all *signs* are not *wonders,* nor are all *wonders, signs;* neither are all miracles, signs, nor all signs, miracles. Σημειον, in some eighty occurrences in N. T., is some *fifty* times represented by *sign;* by miracle more than twenty times, and occasionally by *token,* tantamount to *sign,* and sometimes by *wonder.*

ⁱ Ανδρες αδελφοι. Αδελφοι, in some three hundred and fifty occurrences in N. T. is represented by *brother,* or *brethren.* Ανηρ is, some two hundred and twenty times, represented by *man;* and, in reference to married men, by *husband,* some fifty times.

When ανδρες αδελφοι occur, as they do only in this book of Acts, and in it some *twelve* times, we represent them together by the word *brethren.* Peter introduced this formula, and on Pentecost the converts caught it and used it. Stephen used it, but with the addition of the word *fathers*—"*Brethren and Fathers.*" Because ανδρες equally applies to both, and is absorbed alike in both, we prefer, "*Brethren and Fathers.*" So Paul uses them Acts 13:15; 22:21; 13:26, 38; 23:1, 6; 28:17.

KING JAMES' VERSION.	GREEK TEXT.	REVISED VERSION.
Gentiles, to take out of them a people for his name. 15 And to this agree the words of the prophets; as it is written, 16 After this I will return, and will build again the tabernacle of David which is fallen down; and I will build again the ruins thereof, and I will set it up: 17 That the residue of men might seek after the Lord, and all the Gentiles, upon whom my name is called, saith the Lord, who doeth all these things. 18 Known unto God are all	ἐπεσκέψατο λαβεῖν ἐξ ἐθνῶν λαὸν ἐπὶ τῷ ὀνόματι αὐτοῦ. 15 καὶ τούτῳ συμφωνοῦσιν οἱ λόγοι τῶν προφητῶν, καθὼς γέγραπται, 16 Μετὰ ταῦτα ἀναστρέψω καὶ ἀνοικοδομήσω τὴν σκηνὴν Δαβὶδ τὴν πεπτωκυῖαν· καὶ τὰ κατεσκαμμένα αὐτῆς ἀνοικοδομήσω, καὶ ἀνορθώσω αὐτήν· 17 ὅπως ἂν ἐκζητήσωσιν οἱ κατάλοιποι τῶν ἀνθρώπων τὸν Κύριον, καὶ πάντα τὰ ἔθνη, ἐφ᾽ οὓς ἐπικέκληται τὸ ὄνομά μου ἐπ᾽ αὐτούς· λέγει κύριος ὁ ποιῶν ταῦτα πάντα. 18 Γνωστὰ ἀπ᾽	the Gentiles, ʲto take out of them, a people for his name. And with this the words of 15 the prophets agree; as it is written, After this I will re- 16 turn, and will rebuild the ᵏtabernacle of David ˡwhich is fallen down, and I will rebuild its ruins, and I will set it up; that ᵐthe rest 17 of men may seek after the Lord, even all the nations, upon whom my name is called, says the Lord, who does all these things. ⁿKnown to 18

ʲ Λαβειν εξ εθνων λαὸν επι τῳ ονοματι αυτου. To take out of the nations a people *for* his name. επι is redundant. Rejected by Ln., Tf., Gb.

Upon his name, is a literal version of επι τῳ ονοματι αυτου—"To take from among them a people for his name," Thomp. "To take out of them a people for his name," Wakef. "To elect a people for his name out of the Gentiles," Murd. "To take out from them a people for his name," Penn. "To take out of them a people for his name," Wes., Booth. "To take from among them a people *for the honor of* his name," Dodd. So, substantially, are all the versions that we have seen. For the glory of his name, being the God of the Gentiles as well as of the Jews, he commanded his Gospel to be announced to all nations, intending thereby, as a means to an end, to collect out of all the tribes and nationalities of earth one new community.

This amounts to no more than his commission to the Apostles indicates : "Preach the gospel to every creature," the whole human race. The question here is upon επι, which is repudiated by Ln., Tf.; and is by Gb. regarded as a probable omission, which, indeed, very little affects the sense—a people for his name is, without επι, fairly indicated.

Επι, with the dative, is, in the com. ver., translated *by, at, unto, in, of.* In its more than one thousand two hundred occurrences in the N. T. it is frequently, *with the dative,* represented by *in.* In the single book of the Acts, in a hundred and seventy five occurrences, it is found in construction with the genitive, accusative, and dative, and is frequently represented, com. ver., by *in, on,* or *upon. Deus inter Gentiles sibi collegit cœtum, qui esset populus Dei peculiaris sicut olim Iudæi,*" Kuin. In this view, we fully concur. Vigerus on Grecian idioms, De prepositione, επι, p. 612. London ed. 1824.

ᵏ Τὴν σκηνὴν Δαβὶδ. Σκηνή answers to Hebrew סֻכָּה indicating *a tent* woven of leaves or reeds, in use among shepherds, Ro-

senmüller, Amos 1 : 2. But σκηνη is put for any sort of house. Here it is an image of the kingdom of David, as in other places an image of mount Zion, on which David's palace stood. Virtually, it represents the original political state of the nation. See Kuinœl on this passage.

ˡ Κατεσκαμμενα—κατασκαπτω, found here, and in Rom. 11 : 3, perf. part. pas. = *ruins.* Its root is σκαπτω, *diruo, fodio,* that which has fallen to the ground and which is dug up. Τα κατεσκαμμενα, *diruta,* is found in the Alexandrian ver., Amos 9 : 1, 12. "I will restore its ruins," Wakef. Some recognize here, the Hebraism which converts the first of two verbs into an adverb, qualifying the second. "I will again rebuild," Meyer. De Wette and Winer reject that explanation. Hackett also ; and so do we. "I will build again its ruins," Penn. "Restore its ruins," Wakef. Too ambiguous, or elliptical. "I will build again the ruins thereof," Wesley. "That which was in ruins in it," Murd.

ᵐ Οἱ καταλοιποι των ανθρωπων τον Κυριον, και παντα τα εθνη, εφ᾽ οὓς επικεκληται το ονομα μου επ᾽ αυτους—"The residue of men." Καταλοιποι is found only in this place in the N. T., representing all the world beyond the Jews. This passage represents the whole Gentile world, and intimates their participation in this salvation in common with the Jews. "God is immutable, and hath decreed απ᾽ αιωνος, *olim, antiquissimis temporibus, regnum condere, in quod non tantum Judæi sed etiam Gentiles, sine legis ritualis observatione reciperentur.* In other words, he willed that not only the Jews, but also uncircumcised Gentiles, should belong to his peculiar people, Kuinœl, *in loco.*

ⁿ Γνωστα απ᾽ αιωνος, textus receptus, (εστι τῳ Θεῳ παντα τα εργα αυτου)—Griesbach's reading, Kuin. "To God are known all his works from eternity," Thomp. "Known unto

KING JAMES' VERSION.

his works from the beginning of the world.

19 Wherefore my sentence is, that we trouble not them, which from among the Gentiles are turned to God:

20 But that we write unto them that they abstain from pollutions of idols, and *from* fornication, and *from* things strangled, and *from* blood.

21 For Moses of old time hath in every city them that preach him, being read in the synagogues every sabbath-day.

22 Then pleased it the apostles and elders, with the whole church, to send chosen men of their own company to Antioch, with Paul and Barnabas; *namely*, Judas surnamed Barsabas, and Silas, chief men among the brethren:

23 And they wrote *letters* by them after this manner; The apostles, and elders, and brethren, *send* greeting unto the brethren which are of the Gen-

GREEK TEXT.

αἰῶνός ἐστι τῷ Θεῷ πάντα τὰ ἔργα αὐτοῦ. ¹⁹ διὸ ἐγὼ κρίνω μὴ παρενοχλεῖν τοῖς ἀπὸ τῶν ἐθνῶν ἐπιστρέφουσιν ἐπὶ τὸν Θεόν· ²⁰ ἀλλὰ ἐπιστεῖλαι αὐτοῖς τοῦ ἀπέχεσθαι ἀπὸ τῶν ἀλισγημάτων τῶν εἰδώλων καὶ τῆς πορνείας καὶ τοῦ πνικτοῦ καὶ τοῦ αἵματος. ²¹ Μωσῆς γὰρ ἐκ γενεῶν ἀρχαίων κατὰ πόλιν τοὺς κηρύσσοντας αὐτὸν ἔχει ἐν ταῖς συναγωγαῖς κατὰ πᾶν σάββατον ἀναγινωσκόμενος.

²² Τότε ἔδοξε τοῖς ἀποστόλοις καὶ τοῖς πρεσβυτέροις σὺν ὅλῃ τῇ ἐκκλησίᾳ, ἐκλεξαμένους ἄνδρας ἐξ αὐτῶν πέμψαι εἰς Ἀντιόχειαν σὺν τῷ Παύλῳ καὶ Βαρνάβᾳ, Ἰούδαν τὸν ἐπικαλούμενον Βαρσαβᾶν, καὶ Σίλαν, ἄνδρας ἡγουμένους ἐν τοῖς ἀδελφοῖς, ²³ γράψαντες διὰ χειρὸς αὐτῶν τάδε, Οἱ ἀπόστολοι καὶ οἱ πρεσβύτεροι καὶ οἱ ἀδελφοί, τοῖς κατὰ τὴν Ἀντιόχειαν καὶ

REVISED VERSION.

God from everlasting are all his works. Wherefore my 19 judgment is, not to trouble those who from among the Gentiles turn to God; but to 20 write to them, that they abstain from pollutions of the idols, and [p]fornication, and things strangled, and blood. For, [q]from ancient times, Mo- 21 ses has, in every city, those who preach him, being read in the synagogues every sabbath.

Then it pleased the Apos- 22 tles and the elders, with the whole congregation, to send [r]chosen men, from among themselves, to Antioch, with Paul and Barnabas;—Judas, surnamed Barsabas, and Silas, leading men among the brethren. And they wrote by 23 them these *words*:—The Apostles, and elders, and [s]brethren, greeting—To the brethren of the Gentiles in An-

God are all his works from eternity," Wes. "Who made these things known from the beginning," Penn. "Known from of old are the works of God," Murd. "Known—from the beginning of the world," Wakef. "Known, etc., from the beginning of the world," Dodd. Εστι τω Θεω παντα τα εργα αυτον, omitted by Gb., and Tf. To me, of doubtful authority. It is a true oracle, but here unnecessary.

[o] Διο εγω κρινω. "Wherefore I judge," Wes. "Therefore I say to you," Mur. "My opinion is," Wakef. "My judgment is," Penn. "I judge," Hack. 'Therefore' it is my judgment," Thomp. "Wherefore my judgment is," Dodd.

[p] Πορνεια, fornication. Various substitutes for this word have been proposed. See Kuinœl. M. L'Enfant explains this of victims offered by prostitutes out of their scandalous hire (Deut. 23 : 18) which, he says, makes a beautiful sense. Heinsius, at large, vindicates this interpretation, and shows that Athanasius uses πορνεια for πορνικη θυσια, Doddridge. Kuinœl gives some six columns of dissertations on the acceptations of this word, backed by eminent names. With Rosenmüller, Morus, and other distinguished names, we concur, that this word is not to be taken in any private inter-

pretation, but in its full amplitude, or generic acceptation in sacred literature.

[q] Moses—has them that (κηρυσσοντας αυτον—) are *preaching* him, not διδασκοντας—*teaching* him. The words are never confounded, nor substituted the one for the other, in the Christian Scriptures. *Preaching* and *teaching* Christ are as distinct as *making* or gaining disciples is from *teaching* them. The *preacher's* work and the *teacher's* work are frequently contradistinguished in the Apostolic currency. In the case of the synagogues in opposition to Jesus, they proclaimed the divine mission of Moses, and claimed authority for him against the claims of Jesus the Nazarene. Hence we are informed that "daily in the temple, and from house to house, they ceased not to *teach* and to *preach* Jesus, the Christ," διδασκοντες και ευαγγελιζομενοι Ιησουν τον Χριστον.

[r] Εκλεξαμενους passes into the accusative, because the object of the governing verb; αποστολοις serves, at the same time, "as the subject of the infinitive," Hackett. "For Silas, in the Acts, we have always *Silvanus* in the Epistles." Σιλας, Σιλουανος ; the former his Jewish, the latter his Gentile name.

[s] Και οι before αδελφοι is omitted by Ln. (Gb. marks it as a probable omission).

KING JAMES' VERSION.

tiles in Antioch, and Syria, and Cilicia.

24 Forasmuch as we have heard, that certain which went out from us, have troubled you with words, subverting your souls, saying, *Ye must* be circumcised, and keep the law; to whom we gave no *such* commandment:

25 It seemed good unto us, being assembled with one accord, to send chosen men unto you, with our beloved Barnabas and Paul:

26 Men that have hazarded their lives for the name of our Lord Jesus Christ.

27 We have sent therefore Judas and Silas, who shall also tell *you* the same things by mouth.

28 For it seemed good to the Holy Ghost, and to us, to lay upon you no greater burden than those necessary things;

29 That ye abstain from meats offered to idols, and from blood, and from things strangled, and from fornication: from which if ye keep yourselves, ye shall do well. Fare ye well.

30 So when they were dismissed, they came to Antioch; and when they had gathered the multitude together, they delivered the epistle.

31 *Which* when they had read, they rejoiced for the consolation.

32 And Judas and Silas, being prophets also themselves, exhorted the brethren with many words, and confirmed *them*.

33 And after they had tarried *there* a space, they were let go in peace from the brethren unto the apostles.

GREEK TEXT.

Συρίαν καὶ Κιλικίαν ἀδελφοῖς τοῖς ἐξ ἐθνῶν, χαίρειν. 24 Ἐπειδὴ ἠκούσαμεν ὅτι τινὲς ἐξ ἡμῶν ἐξελθόντες ἐτάραξαν ὑμᾶς λόγοις, ἀνασκευάζοντες τὰς ψυχὰς ὑμῶν, λέγοντες περιτέμνεσθαι καὶ τηρεῖν τὸν νόμον, οἷς οὐ διεστειλάμεθα· 25 ἔδοξεν ἡμῖν γενομένοις ὁμοθυμαδόν, ἐκλεξαμένους ἄνδρας πέμψαι πρὸς ὑμᾶς, σὺν τοῖς ἀγαπητοῖς ἡμῶν Βαρνάβᾳ καὶ Παύλῳ, 26 ἀνθρώποις παραδεδωκόσι τὰς ψυχὰς αὐτῶν ὑπὲρ τοῦ ὀνόματος τοῦ κυρίου ἡμῶν Ἰησοῦ Χριστοῦ. 27 ἀπεστάλκαμεν οὖν Ἰούδαν καὶ Σίλαν, καὶ αὐτοὺς διὰ λόγου ἀπαγγέλλοντας τὰ αὐτά. 28 ἔδοξε γὰρ τῷ Ἁγίῳ Πνεύματι καὶ ἡμῖν, μηδὲν πλέον ἐπιτίθεσθαι ὑμῖν βάρος, πλὴν τῶν ἐπάναγκες τούτων, 29 ἀπέχεσθαι εἰδωλοθύτων καὶ αἵματος καὶ πνικτοῦ καὶ πορνείας· ἐξ ὧν διατηροῦντες ἑαυτοὺς, εὖ πράξετε. ἔρρωσθε. 30 Οἱ μὲν οὖν ἀπολυθέντες ἦλθον εἰς Ἀντιόχειαν· καὶ συναγαγόντες τὸ πλῆθος, ἐπέδωκαν τὴν ἐπιστολήν. 31 ἀναγνόντες δὲ, ἐχάρησαν ἐπὶ τῇ παρακλήσει. 32 Ἰούδας δὲ καὶ Σίλας, καὶ αὐτοὶ προφῆται ὄντες, διὰ λόγου πολλοῦ παρεκάλεσαν τοὺς ἀδελφοὺς, καὶ ἐπεστήριξαν. 33 Ποιήσαντες δὲ χρόνον, ἀπελύθησαν μετ' εἰρήνης ἀπὸ τῶν ἀδελφῶν πρὸς τοὺς ἀποστόλους. 34 ἔδοξε

REVISED VERSION.

tioch, and Syria, and Cilicia. Since we have heard, 24 that some persons who went out from us, have troubled you with words, subverting your souls, ᵗsaying, You must be circumcised, and keep the law; to whom we gave no commandment; it seem- 25 ed good to us, being assembled with one accord, to send ᵘchosen men to you, with our beloved Barnabas and Paul; men who have hazarded their 26 lives for the name of our Lord Jesus Christ. We have sent, 27 therefore, Judas and Silas, who also themselves will tell you the same things by word of mouth. For it seemed good to 28 the Holy Spirit, and to us, to lay on you no greater burden than these necessary things; To abstain from meats offer- 29 ed to idols, and from blood, and from things strangled, and from fornication; from which, if you keep yourselves, you will do well. Fare-well. So, then, having been 30 dismissed, they ᵛcame into Antioch: and when they had assembled the multitude, they delivered the epistle; and 31 having read *it*, they rejoiced over the consolation. And 32 Judas and Silas, being also themselves prophets, exhort-ed the brethren with many words, and established *them*. And after they had made some 33 stay, they were dismissed, with ᵂpeace from the breth-ren to the ˣApostles. ʸBut it 34

ᵗ Δεγοντες περιτεμνεσθαι και τηρειν τον νομον is omitted by Ln., Tf., and by Gb., is regarded as a probable omission.

ᵘ For εκλεξαμενους, Ln. would substitute εκλεξαμενοις, which Gb. marks as a reading not quite so strongly supported.

ᵛ For ηλθον, Ln. would substitute κατηλθον, which Griesb. thinks probable.

ᵂ Μετ ειρηνης, with peace. Judas and Silas now return to Jerusalem. Silas next appears with Paul at Antioch.

ˣ For αποστολους Gb., Sch., Ln., Tf. substitute αποστειλαντας αυτους, with much authority.

ʸ This verse is repudiated by Gb., Ln., Tf., and others Verba hujus versus in multis Codd. desunt. In others, it

KING JAMES' VERSION.	GREEK TEXT.	REVISED VERSION.

KING JAMES' VERSION.

34 Notwithstanding, it pleased Silas to abide there still.

35 Paul also and Barnabas continued in Antioch, teaching and preaching the word of the Lord, with many others also.

36 And some days after, Paul said unto Barnabas, Let us go again and visit our brethren, in every city where we have preached the word of the Lord, *and see* how they do.

37 And Barnabas determined to take with them John, whose surname was Mark.

38 But Paul thought not good to take him with them, who departed from them from Pamphylia, and went not with them to the work.

39 And the contention was so sharp between them, that they departed asunder one from the other: and so Barnabas took Mark, and sailed unto Cyprus.

40 And Paul chose Silas, and departed, being recommended by the brethren unto the grace of God.

41 And he went through Syria and Cilicia, confirming the churches.

GREEK TEXT.

δὲ τῷ Σίλᾳ ἐπιμεῖναι αὐτοῦ. ³⁵ Παῦλος δὲ καὶ Βαρνάβας διέτριβον ἐν Ἀντιοχείᾳ, διδάσκοντες καὶ εὐαγγελιζόμενοι, μετὰ καὶ ἑτέρων πολλῶν, τὸν λόγον τοῦ κυρίου. ³⁶ ΜΕΤΑ δέ τινας ἡμέρας εἶπε Παῦλος πρὸς Βαρνάβαν, Ἐπιστρέψαντες δὴ ἐπισκεψώμεθα τοὺς ἀδελφοὺς ἡμῶν κατὰ πᾶσαν πόλιν, ἐν αἷς κατηγγείλαμεν τὸν λόγον τοῦ κυρίου, πῶς ἔχουσι. ³⁷ Βαρνάβας δὲ ἐβουλεύσατο συμπαραλαβεῖν τὸν Ἰωάννην τὸν καλούμενον Μάρκον· ³⁸ Παῦλος δὲ ἠξίου, τὸν ἀποστάντα ἀπ' αὐτῶν ἀπὸ Παμφυλίας, καὶ μὴ συνελθόντα αὐτοῖς εἰς τὸ ἔργον, μὴ συμπαραλαβεῖν τοῦτον. ³⁹ ἐγένετο οὖν παροξυσμὸς, ὥστε ἀποχωρισθῆναι αὐτοὺς ἀπ' ἀλλήλων, τόν τε Βαρνάβαν παραλαβόντα τὸν Μάρκον ἐκπλεῦσαι εἰς Κύπρον· ⁴⁰ Παῦλος δὲ ἐπιλεξάμενος Σίλαν ἐξῆλθε, παραδοθεὶς τῇ χάριτι τοῦ Θεοῦ ὑπὸ τῶν ἀδελφῶν. ⁴¹ διήρχετο δὲ τὴν Συρίαν καὶ Κιλικίαν, ἐπιστηρίζων τὰς ἐκκλησίας.

REVISED VERSION.

pleased Silas to remain there still. Paul and Barnabas, also, 35 continued in Antioch, teaching and preaching the word of the Lord, with many others also.

And some days after, Paul 36 said to Barnabas, Let us visit ᶻthe brethren in every city, in which we have preached the word of the Lord, *to see* how they do. And Barnabas ᵃdetermined to take John with 37 them, whose surname was Mark. But Paul thought it 38 not ᵇproper to take him with them, who departed from them in Pamphylia, and did not go with them into the work. And there arose a 39 ᶜcontention so that they separated one from the other; and Barnabas took Mark, and sailed into Cyprus. But 40 Paul ᵈchose Silas, and departed, being commended by the brethren to the favor of God. And he went through 41 Syria and Cilicia, ᵉestablishing the congregations.

---

reads μονος δε Ιουδας επορευθη. The Syriac, Arab., Polyglott, Copt., Sclavonic, Chrysostom, Theophylact, omit it.

ᶻ Ἡμων is rejected by Gb., Sch., Ln., and Tf. It appears, indeed, redundant.

ᵃ Εβουλευσατο, determined: not as in some editions, εβουλετο, wished, Hack.

ᵇ Ηξιον, thought it not just, worthy of him, or, thought it not right. Of seven occurrences of this verb in N. T., and of forty of the adjective, αξιος, it is, with some five or six exceptions, rendered *worthy*.

ᶜ Εγενετο παροξυσμος, literally, a paroxysm of feeling arose between them, or a contention indicative of Paul's intense interest in his mission. But neither yielded; and so they parted. This controversy occurred in the first year of the second half of the first century.

ᵈ Επιλεξαμενος occurs but twice in N. T., John 5 : 2, com. ver., "*which is called.*" "Having chosen," Thomp., Penn., and Wes. "Chose," Murd., Booth., Wakef. "Made choice of," Dodd. "Having chosen for himself," Hack.

ᵉ Επιστηριζων τας εκκλησιας, establishing the congregations. Εκκλησια occurs some one hundred and sixteen times in N. T.; one hundred and thirteen times rendered by the word *church*, and three times by *assembly*. In Ephesus there was a regularly constituted Christian *assembly*, or εκκλησια, the word here used and represented by the word *assembly*, when applied to a *mob*; but when to a Christian meeting for worship, in com. ver. is represented by the word *church*. This ought not grammatically nor historically so to be. This word, or any one representative of it, is not found in the Christian Scriptures. We have κυριοτης, kuriotes, four times, translated by *dominion* three times, and once by *government*; we have neither *kyrke*

KING JAMES' VERSION.

CHAP. XVI.

Then came he to Derbe and Lystra: and behold, a certain disciple was there, named Timotheus, the son of a certain woman which was a Jewess, and believed, but his father *was* a Greek:

2 Which was well reported of by the brethren that were at Lystra and Iconium.

3 Him would Paul have to go forth with him; and took and circumcised him, because of the Jews which were in those quarters: for they knew all that his father was a Greek:

4 And as they went through the cities, they delivered them the decrees for to keep, that were ordained of the apostles

GREEK TEXT.

CHAP. XVI.

Κατήντησε δὲ εἰς Δέρβην καὶ Λύστραν· καὶ ἰδοὺ, μαθητής τις ἦν ἐκεῖ, ὀνόματι Τιμόθεος, υἱὸς γυναικός τινος Ἰουδαίας πιστῆς, πατρὸς δὲ Ἕλληνος· ² ὃς ἐμαρτυρεῖτο ὑπὸ τῶν ἐν Λύστροις καὶ Ἰκονίῳ ἀδελφῶν. ³ τοῦτον ἠθέλησεν ὁ Παῦλος σὺν αὐτῷ ἐξελθεῖν, καὶ λαβὼν περιέτεμεν αὐτὸν, διὰ τοὺς Ἰουδαίους τοὺς ὄντας ἐν τοῖς τόποις ἐκείνοις· ᾔδεισαν γὰρ ἅπαντες τὸν πατέρα αὐτοῦ, ὅτι Ἕλλην ὑπῆρχεν. ⁴ ὡς δὲ διεπορεύοντο τὰς πόλεις, παρεδίδουν αὐτοῖς φυλάσσειν τὰ δόγματα τὰ κεκριμένα ὑπὸ τῶν ἀποστόλων καὶ τῶν πρεσβυτέρων

REVISED VERSION.

CHAP. XVI.

Then Paul came to Derbe 1 and ʳLystra; and, behold, a disciple was there, named Timothy, (the ,son of a woman who was a Jewess and a believer, but his father was a Greek,) who was ᵍwell at- 2 tested by the brethren in Lystra and Iconium. Paul 3 wished him to go forth with him, and took and circumcised him, because of the Jews who were in those quarters; for they all knew that his father was a Greek. And as they went through 4 the cities, they delivered to them, for their observance, the ʰdecrees that had been ¹ordained by the Apostles and elders

---

nor *curate* in the original *tongues*, and, of course, not in the original Christian *Scriptures*.

In North Britain they have a *kyrke*, made of the first syllable of κυριος, and οικος, contracted into *kuriok*, now written *kyrk* in Scotland, and *church* in England. But these, originally of *stone* or *brick*, cannot represent a Christian community.

The εκκλησια family occurs in N. T. some one hundred and fifteen times, *three* times translated, com. ver., *assembly*, and one hundred and twelve times *church*. This has been, and yet is, a very unfortunate fact. Brick and stone may be *culled* out, but can never be *called* out, as the word εκκλησια intimates. The *called out* are thinking, willing, moving, acting agents, such as men and women; and such only can constitute the living temple—the living, acting, moving, body of Christ—the real *house* of God on this earth—the positive living "*pillar* and support of the truth," to be seen, known, and read by all men. We have been obliged to continue this word *church*, and with it a perpetual conflict. According to the Constitution of the Bible Union, I presume we are bound to translate where it can be done, and not to transfer Hebrew, Greek, or even Roman terms, susceptible of translation, unless, indeed, such terms are almost universally, and, without litigation, admitted. We, therefore, expect to see this word *church* repudiated, and the word congregation, or assembly, substituted for it. We are aware of the difficulty of effecting such a change. Time, however, can and will accomplish it.

We find the word εκκλησια used three times in the 19th chapter of this same book, to represent what we now call a *mob*, a *tumultuous assemblage* of the people. Out of one hundred and fifteen occurrences in the Christian Scripture it is, with the exception of these *three* cases, uniformly rendered *church*; in these three exceptions, *assembly*.

Συναγωγη is found fifty-seven times in N. T., and with *two* exceptions it is transferred *synagogue*, because, like our word "*church*", it *fifty-five times* represents *stone* and *lime buildings*. It is twice applied to the people—once in this book, ch. 13 : 43, "*congregation*"; and once, James 2 : 2, "*assembly*". It is expedient, indeed, important, to state that the verb συναγω, which occurs in N. T. some sixty-three times, is *fifty* times represented by "*gather*", "*gather together*"; by *assembly, took in, bestow fruits*, or "*stow away fruits*", "*resort*".—In all, *thirteen* times.

ᶠ Δερβην και Λυστραν. In ch. 14 : 16, Λυστραν και Δερβην, because the journey now is from East to West, formerly from West to East. Τινος is here omitted by Gb., Sch., Ln., and Tf. There is, indeed, no need for it.

ᵍ Ὅς εμαρτυρειτο, well attested, by brethren in Lystra. Timothy was not circumcised, because his father was a Gentile. Nor was it allowed a mother to circumcise a son, his father not concurring in the act. So teach the writers of the Talmud, as quoted by Kuin., vol. 3, p. 243.

ʰ Τα δογματα τα κεκριμενα υπο των αποστολων. Δογμα occurs three times in Luke's writings, and only twice in Paul's. In Luke's writings, N. T., always represented by *decrees*; in Paul's, by *ordinances*. This is its whole currency in N. T.

¹ Τα κεκριμενα υπο των αποστολων και πρεσβυτερων των εν Ἱερουσαλημ. The elders here are those of the church of

KING JAMES' VERSION.	GREEK TEXT.	REVISED VERSION.
and elders which were at Jerusalem.	τῶν ἐν Ἱερουσαλήμ. ⁵ αἱ μὲν οὖν ἐκκλησίαι ἐστερεοῦντο τῇ πίστει, καὶ ἐπερίσσευον τῷ ἀριθμῷ καθ᾽ ἡμέραν.	who were in Jerusalem. And 5 so were the congregations established in the faith, and daily increased in number.

King James' Version.

and elders which were at Jerusalem.

5 And so were the churches established in the faith, and increased in number daily.

6 Now when they had gone throughout Phrygia, and the region of Galatia, and were forbidden of the Holy Ghost to preach the word in Asia;

7 After they were come to Mysia, they assayed to go into Bithynia: but the Spirit suffered them not.

8 And they passing by Mysia, came down to Troas.

9 And a vision appeared to Paul in the night: There stood a man of Macedonia, and prayed him, saying, Come over into Macedonia, and help us.

10 And after he had seen the vision, immediately we endeavoured to go into Macedonia, assuredly gathering, that the Lord had called us for to preach the gospel unto them.

11 Therefore loosing from Troas, we came with a straight

Greek Text.

τῶν ἐν Ἱερουσαλήμ. ⁵ αἱ μὲν οὖν ἐκκλησίαι ἐστερεοῦντο τῇ πίστει, καὶ ἐπερίσσευον τῷ ἀριθμῷ καθ᾽ ἡμέραν.

⁶ Διελθόντες δὲ τὴν Φρυγίαν καὶ τὴν Γαλατικὴν χώραν, κωλυθέντες ὑπὸ τοῦ Ἁγίου Πνεύματος λαλῆσαι τὸν λόγον ἐν τῇ Ἀσίᾳ, ⁷ ἐλθόντες κατὰ τὴν Μυσίαν ἐπείραζον κατὰ τὴν Βιθυνίαν πορεύεσθαι· καὶ οὐκ εἴασεν αὐτοὺς τὸ πνεῦμα. ⁸ παρελθόντες δὲ τὴν Μυσίαν, κατέβησαν εἰς Τρωάδα. ⁹ καὶ ὅραμα διὰ τῆς νυκτὸς ὤφθη τῷ Παύλῳ· Ἀνήρ τις ἦν Μακεδὼν ἑστὼς, παρακαλῶν αὐτὸν καὶ λέγων, Διαβὰς εἰς Μακεδονίαν, βοήθησον ἡμῖν. ¹⁰ Ὡς δὲ τὸ ὅραμα εἶδεν, εὐθέως ἐζητήσαμεν ἐξελθεῖν εἰς τὴν Μακεδονίαν, συμβιβάζοντες ὅτι προσκέκληται ἡμᾶς ὁ κύριος εὐαγγελίσασθαι αὐτούς. ¹¹ Ἀναχθέντες οὖν ἀπὸ τῆς Τρωάδος, εὐθυδρομήσαμεν

Revised Version.

who were in Jerusalem. And 5 so were the congregations established in the faith, and daily increased in number.

Now when they had gone 6 throughout Phrygia, and the region of Galatia, and (being ʲforbidden by the Holy Spirit to speak the word in Asia) after they came to Mysia, they 7 attempted to go into Bithynia; but the ᵏSpirit suffered them not. So passing along 8 Mysia, they came to Troas. ˡAnd a vision appeared to Paul 9 in the night. There stood a man, a Macedonian, who besought him, saying, come over into Macedonia, and help us. And after he had seen the 10 vision, we immediately ᵐendeavored to go forth into Macedonia, being assured that the Lord had called us to preach the gospel to them. Therefore, loosing from Tro- 11 as, we ran by a ⁿstraight

---

Jerusalem. They enacted τὰ κεκριμενα, the judgments, "that were ordained," com. ver. This word, in this single book of Acts, is, in com. ver., represented by "sentence," "that which is determined," "concluded," "question," "condemning." "The determinations," Thom.; "the injunctions," Mur.; "the decrees," Penn, Wakef., Boothr., Dodd., Wes.; "instituta," the institutions, Beza. A judgment of the human mind may become any one of these; in its development and execution, we have, with much propriety, transferred this word dogmata into our language, and here it might, in our currency, with all propriety, read, "they delivered to them the dogmata of the apostles and elders to keep." But their dogmata were always infallible, while ours are always fallible.

ʲ Κωλυθεντες ὑπο του Ἁγιου Πνευματος. Prohibiti sunt a Spiritu Sancto ne in Asia doctrinam evangelii traderent. "By Asia here we must understand Ionia, as in ch. 2 : 9," Kuinœl. The prohibition to proceed into Bythinia, was only the directing of Paul's course into Europe.

ᵏ Το Πνευμα Ιησου, "the Spirit which he sends," Hackett. This appears somewhat anomalous. There is no parallel passage in the Christian Scriptures. So, however, read the Vatican, Eph., Beza, and Alex. MSS. See Wetstein and

Birch. "Nomen Jesus in omnibus novis bibliis deletum invenitur per Nestorianos falsarios, ut claret ex bibliis tum Latinis tum Græcis ante schisma et scriptis et translatis." John Faber (Malleus Hæreticorum), ap. West. not. Penn, p. 311.

ˡ Ὁραμα δια της νυκτος ωφθη τω Παυλω. Ὁραμα is, with one exception, confined to the Acts of Apostles, being eleven times in this single book, and only once out of it, in the Christian Scriptures. Acts 7 : 31, it is rendered, com. ver., sight, in all other cases, vision. Ὁρασις once occurs in this book Acts, 2 : 17, also rendered vision. Visions are the boldest relief dreams. The eyes of the understanding are, indeed, illuminated, and the object stands out in alto relievo.

ᵐ Εξητησαμεν. Being in the first person plural, Luke for the first time informs us, that he was one of the company that first carried the gospel into Europe. Paul alone saw the vision; the Macedonian entreating them, saying, "Cross over into Macedonia, and help us;" but they were all invited to enter into Europe.

ⁿ Ευθυδρομησαμεν, we ran in a straight course, nautically, before the wind. Neapolis, here named, was a city of Thrace, having a harbor on the Strymonic Gulf.

KING JAMES' VERSION.

course to Samothracia, and the next *day* to Neapolis;

12 And from thence to Philippi, which is the chief city of that part of Macedonia, *and* a colony: and we were in that city abiding certain days.

13 And on the sabbath we went out of the city by a river side, where prayer was wont to be made; and we sat down, and spake unto the women which resorted *thither*.

14 And a certain woman named Lydia, a seller of purple, of the city of Thyatira, which worshipped God, heard *us*: whose heart the Lord opened, that she attended unto the things which were spoken of Paul.

15 And when she was baptized, and her household, she besought *us*, saying, If ye have

GREEK TEXT.

εἰς Σαμοθρᾴκην, τῇ τε ἐπιούσῃ εἰς Νεάπολιν, [12] ἐκεῖθέν τε εἰς Φιλίππους, ἥτις ἐστὶ πρώτη τῆς μερίδος τῆς Μακεδονίας πόλις κολώνια.

Ἦμεν δὲ ἐν ταύτῃ τῇ πόλει διατρίβοντες ἡμέρας τινάς, [13] τῇ τε ἡμέρᾳ τῶν σαββάτων ἐξήλθομεν ἔξω τῆς πόλεως παρὰ ποταμὸν, οὗ ἐνομίζετο προσευχὴ εἶναι, καὶ καθίσαντες ἐλαλοῦμεν ταῖς συνελθούσαις γυναιξί. [14] Καί τις γυνὴ ὀνόματι Λυδία, πορφυρόπωλις πόλεως Θυατείρων, σεβομένη τὸν Θεὸν, ἤκουεν· ἧς ὁ κύριος διήνοιξε τὴν καρδίαν, προσέχειν τοῖς λαλουμένοις ὑπὸ τοῦ Παύλου. [15] ὡς δὲ ἐβαπτίσθη, καὶ ὁ οἶκος αὐτῆς, παρεκάλεσε λέγουσα, Εἰ κεκρίκατέ με

REVISED VERSION.

course to Samothrace, and the
next day to Neapolis; and 12
thence to [o]Philippi, which is a
chief city of that part of Macedonia, and a colony. And
we abode in that city some
days. And on the sabbath, 13
we went out of the city by the
side of a [p]river, where there was
a customary place of [q]prayer;
and we sat down, and spoke
to [r]the women that resorted
there. And a woman, named 14
[s]Lydia, a seller of purple, of
the city of Thyatira, who worshiped God, heard us; whose
heart the Lord opened, to
attend to the things spoken
by Paul. And when she was 15
immersed, and her [t]household, she besought us, saying, [u]Since you have judged

---

[o] Philippi lay ten miles farther west, located on the bank of the river Gangitas. *Ἡτις—κολωνια.* On this river was a *προσευχη,* an inclosure for prayer and meditation.

[p] Gangas was then its name.

[q] *Προσευχη* was not always a synagogue, or a building. It here appears to have been an inclosure in the open air, set apart to this use; lustrations were performed here, which at that time were usual amongst the Jews. Neander, Kuinœl, Hackett.

[r] *Ταις συνελθουσαις γυναιξι.* The probability is, that this was a temporary substitute for a synagogue, a meeting place for worship. Hence Paul spoke to *ταις συνελθουσαις γυναιξι,* the women assembled.

[s] *Και τις γυνη, κ. τ. λ.* Lydia was a very common name among the Greeks and Romans. It coincides admirably with the name of her country.—Hackett.

Lydia seems to have been a proselyte to the Jews' religion. She was a Greek, according to her name; Lydia being a common name amongst the Greeks. The Lord had opened her heart, so that she *attended* to the preaching of the word. Therefore she believed, and was immersed, and also her household, in like manner. She was, it seems, also the head of a family. The *οικος αυτης,* as Meyer remarks, consisted probably of women who assisted her in business. Hackett. Pious Jews and proselytes had *places* of prayer as well as *hours* for prayer.

"A seller of purple cloths", from Thyatira, on the confines of Lydia and Mysia. *Ηκουε,* third pers. sing. imp., ind. of *ακουω.* In this, and in numerous other cases, the imperfect should be rendered in exact harmony with the time which it denotes—*was hearing*, or *was listening* to Paul; whose heart *διηνοιξε,* first sing. first aor., *the Lord had opened,* so that *she attended* to the preacher. It was the Lord that had arrested her attention, and opened her heart; hence she readily and joyfully received the word of the Lord, then and there announced. *Προσεχειν,* to attend, or to *hearken*, to the words uttered.

[t] *Ὁ οικος* is found more than one hundred times in N. T., and *οικια* nearly one hundred times; both are used not merely to indicate the *building*, but also the *family*. This is a very common figure in all languages ancient and modern, more prevalent, however, amongst the Jews, whose tribes and families, because of the *mitre* and the *sceptre*, were so religiously registered and kept. The *οικος αυτης,* as Meyer well observes, probably consisted of females who assisted her in business.

[u] *Ει κεκρικατε* is, by Hackett and others, rendered "*if ye have judged*," rather, *since* you have *judged*. *If* and *since* are equally the representatives of *ει*. Frequently it would be much more intelligibly represented by *since*, than by *if*. "Since you have *risen* with Christ in baptism, set your affections on things *above*, and not on things on the earth," is much more intelligible and pointed than *if*,—as though it were a doubtful matter.

KING JAMES' VERSION.

judged me to be faithful to the Lord, come into my house, and abide *there:* And she constrained us.

16 And it came to pass as we went to prayer, a certain damsel possessed with a spirit of divination, met us, which brought her masters much gain by soothsaying;

17 The same followed Paul and us, and cried, saying, These men are the servants of the most high God, which shew unto us the way of salvation.

18 And this did she many days. But Paul being grieved, turned and said to the spirit, I command thee in the name of Jesus Christ to come out of her. And he came out the same hour.

19 And when her masters saw that the hope of their gains was gone, they caught Paul and Silas, and drew *them* into the market-place unto the rulers,

20 And brought them to the

GREEK TEXT.

πιστὴν τῷ κυρίῳ εἶναι, εἰσελθόντες εἰς τὸν οἶκόν μου, μείνατε· καὶ παρεβιάσατο ἡμᾶς. ¹⁶ Ἐγένετο δὲ πορευομένων ἡμῶν εἰς προσευχὴν, παιδίσκην τινὰ ἔχουσαν πνεῦμα Πύθωνος ἀπαντῆσαι ἡμῖν, ἥτις ἐργασίαν πολλὴν παρεῖχε τοῖς κυρίοις αὐτῆς, μαντευομένη. ¹⁷ αὕτη κατακολουθήσασα τῷ Παύλῳ καὶ ἡμῖν, ἔκραζε λέγουσα, Οὗτοι οἱ ἄνθρωποι δοῦλοι τοῦ Θεοῦ τοῦ ὑψίστου εἰσὶν οἵτινες καταγγέλλουσιν ἡμῖν ὁδὸν σωτηρίας. ¹⁸ Τοῦτο δὲ ἐποίει ἐπὶ πολλὰς ἡμέρας. διαπονηθεὶς δὲ ὁ Παῦλος, καὶ ἐπιστρέψας, τῷ πνεύματι εἶπε, Παραγγέλλω σοι ἐν τῷ ὀνόματι Ἰησοῦ Χριστοῦ, ἐξελθεῖν ἀπ᾽ αὐτῆς. Καὶ ἐξῆλθεν αὐτῇ τῇ ὥρᾳ. ¹⁹ Ἰδόντες δὲ οἱ κύριοι αὐτῆς, ὅτι ἐξῆλθεν ἡ ἐλπὶς τῆς ἐργασίας αὐτῶν, ἐπιλαβόμενοι τὸν Παῦλον καὶ τὸν Σίλαν, εἵλκυσαν εἰς τὴν ἀγορὰν ἐπὶ τοὺς ἄρχοντας· ²⁰ καὶ προσ-

REVISED VERSION.

me to be faithful to the Lord, come into my house, and there remain. And she ᵛconstrained us.

And as we went to prayer, 16 a certain ʷmaid, having a spirit of divination, met us, who brought her masters much gain by soothsaying. The same ˣfollowed Paul and 17 us, and cried, saying, These men are the servants of the most high God, who show to us the way of salvation. And 18 this she did many days; but Paul, ʸoutraged, turned and said to the spirit, I command you in the name of Jesus Christ to come out of her. And he came out tne same hour. And when the masters 19 saw that the hope of their gain was gone, they caught Paul and Silas, and drew them into the market-place, before the ᶻmagistrates. And brought 20

ᵛ Καὶ παρεβιασατο ἡμας, *atque adeo nos coëgit,* nempe *precibus.* A similar use of παραβιαζομαι is found Luke 14 : 23, "compel them to come in". Socrates when urging his disciples to enter upon the arduous path of virtue, uses a similar phrase, εγω δε επι την αρετην ἱκειν βιαζομαι. Priċæus and Elsner on Luke 24 : 29.

ʷ Παιδισκην τινα, represented by *damsel, maid, maiden,* and five times in Paul to the Galatians, *bond maid, bond woman.* Πνευμα Πυθωνος, a Pythonic spirit; δαιμονιον μαντικον, a fortune-telling spirit. This name is given to those persons who were believed to be able, by some Divine inspiration, to foretell future events. Plutarch on the eclipse of the oracles, p. 414, says, τους εγγαστριμυθους Ευρυκλειας παλαι, νυνι Πυθωνας προσαγορευομενοι. They were formerly called Euryclean Ventriloquists (from Eurycle, the inventor of this form of divination), but now they are called Pythians.

ˣ Αὕτη κατακολουθησασα τῳ Παυλῳ, κ. τ. λ., *followed after,* Luke 23 : 35, and here followed Paul, is its whole currency in N. T. Its root is κολλα, gluten, glue, hence κολλαω glutino,

I adhere like glue, pres. pass. κολλαομαι, agglutino, *adhæreo,* adhere with persevering assiduity. Thus was Paul and his fellow-laborers haunted with this hypocritical demon, the most odious one reported in the Christian Scriptures.

ʸ But Paul, outraged with this demon, said, Παραγγελλω σοι εν τῳ ονοματι Ιησου Χριστου, εξελθειν απ᾽ αυτης. And in an instant the command was obeyed. In the name of Jesus Christ come out of her. Here, we find Jesus, and Christ, both anarthrous, not the Jesus, the Christ. This would have been, at this time and place, wholly redundant.

ᶻ These greedy dogs, seeing their demon gains forever fled, enraged, laid violent hands on Paul and Silas, and carried them before τους αρχοντας, the magistrates. These senators or magistrates of free towns were free of the city of Rome, and were eligible to all citizen privileges there. Paul and Silas were brought before the prætors, or city judges—magistrates, or mayors, as then understood—; one was chief or president. Cicero, speaking (Agrar. Il., c. 34) of the *duumviri, or quatuorviri,* says, "Cum in cæteris coloniis duumviri

KING JAMES' VERSION.	GREEK TEXT.	REVISED VERSION.
magistrates, saying, These men, being Jews, do exceedingly trouble our city, 21 And teach customs which are not lawful for us to receive, neither to observe, being Romans. 22 And the multitude rose up together against them: and the magistrates rent off their clothes, and commanded to beat *them*. 23 And when they had laid many stripes upon them, they cast *them* into prison, charging the jailer to keep them safely: 24 Who having received such a charge, thrust them into the inner prison, and made their feet fast in the stocks. 25 And at midnight Paul and Silas prayed, and sang praises unto God: and the prisoners heard them.	ἀγαγόντες αὐτοὺς τοῖς στρατηγοῖς, εἶπον, Οὗτοι οἱ ἄνθρωποι ἐκταράσσουσιν ἡμῶν τὴν πόλιν, Ἰουδαῖοι ὑπάρχοντες· 21 καὶ καταγγέλλουσιν ἔθη ἃ οὐκ ἔξεστιν ἡμῖν παραδέχεσθαι οὐδὲ ποιεῖν, Ῥωμαίοις οὖσι. 22 Καὶ συνεπέστη ὁ ὄχλος κατ' αὐτῶν καὶ οἱ στρατηγοὶ περιρρήξαντες αὐτῶν τὰ ἱμάτια, ἐκέλευον ῥαβδίζειν· 23 πολλάς τε ἐπιθέντες αὐτοῖς πληγὰς, ἔβαλον εἰς φυλακὴν, παραγγείλαντες τῷ δεσμοφύλακι, ἀσφαλῶς τηρεῖν αὐτούς· 24 ὃς παραγγελίαν τοιαύτην εἰληφὼς, ἔβαλεν αὐτοὺς εἰς τὴν ἐσωτέραν φυλακὴν, καὶ τοὺς πόδας αὐτῶν ἠσφαλίσατο εἰς τὸ ξύλον. 25 Κατὰ δὲ τὸ μεσονύκτιον Παῦλος καὶ Σίλας προσευχόμενοι ὕμνουν τὸν θεόν· ἐπηκροῶντο δὲ αὐτῶν οἱ δέσμιοι. 26 ἄφνω δὲ	them to the magistrates, saying, These men, being Jews, do ᵃexceedingly trouble our city, and teach ᵇcustoms, which are 21 not lawful for us to receive, or to observe, being Romans. And the multitude rose up 22 together against them, and the magistrates, ᶜhaving torn off their garments, commanded to beat them. And when 23 they had laid many stripes on them, they cast them into prison, charging the jailer to keep them safely; who, 24 having received such a charge, thrust them into the inner prison, and made their feet fast in the ᵈstocks. And at mid- 25 night Paul and Silas ᵉprayed and sung praises to God; and the prisoners heard them; and 26

appellentur, hi se prætores appellari volebant." This explains why the Roman prætors held the rank of the Grecian στρατηγοι, the title assumed by the Philippian magistrates. It is the only case in which Luke gives this name to the rulers of a city.

ᵃ *Εκταρασσουσιν.* This word is found in the Christian Scriptures only in this passage. *Ταρασσω*, or *ταραττω*, its root, is found seventeen times, and is always represented by the word *trouble*. Jerusalem and its petty prince were awfully troubled when Jesus was born, as supposed, in their political sense, the predicted *king of the Jews.*

ᵇ "And teach customs", *εθη.* Every form of Paganism, or Polytheism, was tolerated in Rome. The gospel and its institutions alone were interdicted. It was a privilege claimed by every Roman to worship whatever god, or goddess, he pleased. Foreigners, indeed, were occasionally inhibited from introducing foreign divinities. Romans, it is said, were positively inhibited circumcision.

ᶜ *Οἱ στρατηγοι*, the magistrates, *περιρρηξαντες αντων τα ἱματια, having torn off their garments*—those of Paul and Silas—, commanded to beat them. "The imperfect tense," as well observed by Prof. Hackett, and others, "in narration stands instead of the aorist, *when the writer would represent the act as passing under his own eye.*" This is presumed to be one of the instances to which Paul alludes when he says, "*Thrice* was I beaten with rods."

ᵈ *Εις το ξυλον—ειληφως*, perf. part. act. *λαμβανω*, having received this command, carried and immured them in the inner part of the prison. "And *confined* their feet in the stocks," Murd. ; "*fastened* their feet in the stocks," Wakef. ; "*secured* their feet in the stocks," Penn, Thomp., Wes., Dodd., Boothr. How definite the command, and how precise the obedience ! The jailer, in the first place, conducted them *into* (*εις*) prison, the *innermost* prison. In the second place, he secured them *into* (*εις*) the block. He appears to have been a very conscientious and law-abiding character. The sequel, indeed, developes and consummates this characteristic.

ᵉ *Προσευχομενοι ὑμνουν τον Θεον.* We find *προσευχομαι* eighty-seven times in N. T., always translated *pray* in some of the flections of that word. Its associate, *ὑμνεω*, is found only four times in N. T., twice translated, *sing praise to* God, and twice, *sung a hymn.* *Ὑμνεω*, Latinized *hymno*, also represented by *ago gratias*, I give thanks ; *laudo*, I praise ; *celebro*, I celebrate. This was a rare occurrence. At midnight Paul and Silas praying (*hymned*), praised God. *Επακροαομαι.* This word is found nowhere else in the N. T. *Exaudio = επι* and *ακροαομαι*, to hear perfectly, to listen. This is most apposite to the occasion. *Listened to them* while they sung. Hackett, "The imperfect *describes* the act, the aorist would have merely *related* it."

26 And suddenly there was a great earthquake, so that the foundations of the prison were shaken: and immediately all the doors were opened, and every one's bands were loosed.

27 And the keeper of the prison awaking out of his sleep, and seeing the prison-doors open, he drew out his sword, and would have killed himself, supposing that the prisoners had been fled.

28 But Paul cried with a loud voice, saying, Do thyself no harm: for we are all here.

29 Then he called for a light, and sprang in, and came trembling, and fell down before Paul and Silas;

30 And brought them out, and said, Sirs, what must I do to be saved?

31 And they said, Believe on the Lord Jesus Christ, and thou shalt be saved, and thy house.

32 And they spake unto him

σεισμὸς ἐγένετο μέγας, ὥστε σαλευθῆναι τὰ θεμέλια τοῦ δεσμωτηρίου· ἀνεῴχθησάν τε παραχρῆμα αἱ θύραι πᾶσαι, καὶ πάντων τὰ δεσμὰ ἀνέθη. 27 ἔξυπνος δὲ γενόμενος ὁ δεσμοφύλαξ, καὶ ἰδὼν ἀνεῳγμένας τὰς θύρας τῆς φυλακῆς, σπασάμενος μάχαιραν, ἔμελλεν ἑαυτὸν ἀναιρεῖν, νομίζων ἐκπεφευγέναι τοὺς δεσμίους. 28 ἐφώνησε δὲ φωνῇ μεγάλῃ ὁ Παῦλος λέγων, Μηδὲν πράξῃς σεαυτῷ κακόν· ἅπαντες γάρ ἐσμεν ἐνθάδε. 29 Αἰτήσας δὲ φῶτα εἰσεπήδησε. καὶ ἔντρομος γενόμενος προσέπεσε τῷ Παύλῳ καὶ τῷ Σίλᾳ· 30 καὶ προαγαγὼν αὐτοὺς ἔξω, ἔφη, Κύριοι, τί με δεῖ ποιεῖν ἵνα σωθῶ; 31 Οἱ δὲ εἶπον, Πίστευσον ἐπὶ τὸν κύριον Ἰησοῦν Χριστὸν, καὶ σωθήσῃ σὺ καὶ ὁ οἶκός σου. 32 Καὶ ἐλάλησαν αὐτῷ τὸν λόγον τοῦ κυρίου,

suddenly there was a great earthquake, so that the foundations of the prison were shaken, and immediately all the doors were opened, and every one's [f]bands were loosed. And the keeper of the prison, 27 awaking out of his sleep, and seeing the prison-doors open, drew his sword, and would have killed himself, supposing that the prisoners [g]had fled. But Paul cried with a loud 28 voice, saying, [h]Do yourself no harm: for we are all here. Then he called for [i]lights, and 29 sprung in, and came trembling, and fell down before Paul and Silas, and brought 30 them out, and said, Sirs, what must I do, in order to be [j]saved? And they said, Believe 31 on the Lord Jesus Christ, and you shall be saved, and your family. And they spoke to 32 him the word of the Lord,

---

[f] Καὶ πάντων τὰ δεσμα ανεθη. The opening of the doors is rather to be ascribed to the power which caused the earthquake, than to the earthquake itself.—Hackett. But the climax of the miracle is found in the last item, "*the bands of every one* (of every prisoner) *were loosed*." Ανεθη is first aor. act. of ανιημι.

[g] Εκπεφευγεναι is here found in the perfect, because the *act*, though past, is connected with the present: "supposing the prisoners *to have fled*," or, to have escaped.

[h] Not a few, critics and others, have perplexed themselves no little, on the question,—How could Paul, in the darkness of the prison, have known the jailer's intention? Or, how, in such circumstances, could he exclaim, "*we are all here?*" Doddridge supposes that Paul might have heard him exclaim, and, benevolently intending to compose his mind, addressed him. To explain miracles is not the province or work of a translator or commentator; and to compare the conceptions of a person possessing a spiritual gift, with the conceptions of any one not possessing such a gift, is quite as unphilosophic, illogical, and unsafe. "Tum Paulus alta voce acclamavit; Noli vim tibi inferre (E vocibus hominis Paulus hoc cognoverat), omnes enim hic sumus." "Then Paul, with a loud voice, said to him, *Do yourself no harm, for we are all here.*"

Paul, it is assumed, by most commentators, knew his voice. So Kuinœl remarks on this passage. But Morus, Rosenmüllerus, Stolzius, and others thus explain it: What must be done by me that the gods may not punish me, because I have so harshly treated men so acceptable to them? Or, to use his own words: *Quid faciendum ne dii me puniant, quia viros diis adeo gratos tam duriter tractavi?* But Kuinœl, and most of the more learned translators into the living tongues, thus render it: *Quid mihi faciendum ut salutem æternum consequor?* Col. v. 31, *What must be done by me; or, What shall I do, that I may obtain eternal safety?* In practical response, we read, v. 33, καὶ εβαπτισθη αυτος και οἱ αυτου παντες παραχρημα. This last word *immediately* is necessarily connected in the context with the words *exegetical of it,* εν εκεινη τη ὡρᾳ της νυκτος, the jailer washed the prisoners' stripes; after which refreshment, he himself and all his household were immersed *in the same hour of the night.*

[i] Φωτα. The noun is plural; whether generic or specific, it should be represented in such a case as plural.

[j] The Apostle understood him as inquiring, not for any temporal protection from the civil powers, but from the sins of his life. The answer indicates a generous and ample salvation tendered equally to himself and family. The development of this answer we have in the next verse.

KING JAMES' VERSION.

the word of the Lord, and to all that were in his house.

33 And he took them the same hour of the night, and washed *their* stripes; and was baptized, he and all his, straightway.

34 And when he had brought them into his house, he set meat before them, and rejoiced, believing in God with all his house.

35 And when it was day, the magistrates sent the sergeants, saying, Let those men go.

36 And the keeper of the prison told this saying to Paul, The magistrates have sent to let you go: now, therefore, depart, and go in peace.

37 But Paul said unto them, They have beaten us openly uncondemned, being Romans, and have cast *us* into prison; and now do they thrust us out privily? nay, verily; but let them come themselves and fetch us out.

3S And the sergeants told these words unto the magistrates: and they feared when

GREEK TEXT.

καὶ πᾶσι τοῖς ἐν τῇ οἰκίᾳ αὐτοῦ. [33] καὶ παραλαβὼν αὐτοὺς ἐν ἐκείνῃ τῇ ὥρᾳ τῆς νυκτὸς ἔλουσεν ἀπὸ τῶν πληγῶν, καὶ ἐβαπτίσθη αὐτὸς καὶ οἱ αὐτοῦ πάντες παραχρῆμα. [34] ἀναγαγών τε αὐτοὺς εἰς τὸν οἶκον αὐτοῦ, παρέθηκε τράπεζαν, καὶ ἠγαλλιάσατο πανοικὶ πεπιστευκὼς τῷ Θεῷ.

[35] Ἡμέρας δὲ γενομένης ἀπέστειλαν οἱ στρατηγοὶ τοὺς ῥαβδούχους λέγοντες, Ἀπόλυσον τοὺς ἀνθρώπους ἐκείνους. [36] Ἀπήγγειλε δὲ ὁ δεσμοφύλαξ τοὺς λόγους τούτους πρὸς τὸν Παῦλον, Ὅτι ἀπεστάλκασιν οἱ στρατηγοὶ, ἵνα ἀπολυθῆτε· νῦν οὖν ἐξελθόντες, πορεύεσθε ἐν εἰρήνῃ. [37] Ὁ δὲ Παῦλος ἔφη πρὸς αὐτοὺς, Δείραντες ἡμᾶς δημοσίᾳ, ἀκατακρίτους, ἀνθρώπους Ῥωμαίους ὑπάρχοντας, ἔβαλον εἰς φυλακὴν, καὶ νῦν λάθρα ἡμᾶς ἐκβάλλουσιν; οὐ γάρ· ἀλλὰ ἐλθόντες αὐτοὶ ἡμᾶς ἐξαγαγέτωσαν. [38] Ἀνήγγειλαν δὲ τοῖς στρατηγοῖς οἱ ῥαβδοῦχοι τὰ ῥήματα ταῦτα· καὶ ἐφοβήθησαν ἀκού-

REVISED VERSION.

and to all who were in his house. And he took them 33 the same hour of the night, and washed their stripes, and was immediately immersed, he and all his family. And 34 when he had [k]brought them into his house, he set food before them, and rejoiced, believing in God with all his family. And when it was 35 day, the magistrates sent the [l]officers, saying, Release those men. And the [m]keeper of the 36 prison told Paul, The [n]magistrates have sent to release you; now, therefore, depart, and go in peace. But Paul 37 said to them, They [o]have beaten us openly uncondemned, being Romans, and have cast us into prison, and now do they cast us out privately? Nay, indeed, but let them come themselves, and lead us out. And the officers told 38 these words to the magistrates, and they feared when

---

[k] Ἀναγαγὼν τε αυτους εις τον οικον αὐτου, παρεθηκε τραπεζαν, he brought them up into his house, spread his table, had a joyful feast *with all his family* (πανοικι), πεπιστευκως τῳ Θεῳ, himself believing in God with his household. Hesychius et ex eo Phavorinus πανοικει (ita quoque scribitur) συν ὁλω τῳ οικῳ. This definition is sustained by Kuinœl, *in loco*, note on vv. 33, 34, vol. 3, pp. 252, 253.

[l] Ῥαβδουχοι, *lictores*, who preceded the chief magistrates in their processions, clearing the way and securing to them the respect of the multitude. They also apprehended and punished criminals. *Twenty-four* attended a *dictator*, *twelve* preceded a *consul*, and *six* a *master of the horse*.

[m] Δεσμοφυλαξ. In the Christian Scriptures this word occurs only in this chapter, vv. 23, 27, 36, translated, v. 23, the *jailer*, vv. 27 and 36, the *keeper of the prison*.

[n] Στρατηγος, in the Christian Scriptures, is exclusively Luke's word. It is found *twice* in his gospel, and *eight* times in his Acts. In the former it is translated *captain*, in the latter by both *captain* and *magistrate;* from this chapter to the end of the Acts it is represented by *magistrate*, com. ver. "Properly it is one *who leads an army*," but in the course of time it was extended to the *magistracy—præfectus, prætor—proprie qui exercitum ducat*. Beza on Acts 16 : 20. Græcis scriptoribus στρατηγοι dicti sunt, que Romæ *prætores*. Beza, *in loc*. Syrus, Luke 22 : 4. *Vertit* principes exercitus templi. Critica Sacra.

[o] Δειραντες ἡμας δημοσια, ακατακριτους. Δειρας, first aor. part. act., verbi δερω, *excorio;* whence *excoriate*, to *flay*, or to *wear off the skin*. Such is, and such was, the current value of this word, *being Romans, too!* Every Roman citizen was free from stripes and every kind of torture, which was inflicted upon slaves. Kuinœl abounds with examples of this fact, vol. 3, p. 253, *in loco*.

KING JAMES' VERSION.	GREEK TEXT.	REVISED VERSION.

they heard that they were Romans.

39 And they came and besought them, and brought *them* out, and desired *them* to depart out of the city.

40 And they went out of the prison, and entered into *the house of* Lydia: and when they had seen the brethren, they comforted them, and departed.

σαντες ὅτι Ῥωμαῖοί εἰσι, 39 καὶ ἐλθόντες παρεκάλεσαν αὐτοὺς, καὶ ἐξαγαγόντες ἠρώτων ἐξελθεῖν τῆς πόλεως. 40 ἐξελθόντες δὲ ἐκ τῆς φυλακῆς εἰσῆλθον εἰς τὴν Λυδίαν· καὶ ἰδόντες τοὺς ἀδελφοὺς, παρεκάλεσαν αὐτοὺς, καὶ ἐξῆλθον.

they heard that they were Romans. And they came and 39 ᴾbesought them, and led them out, and desired them to depart out of the city. And 40 they went out of the prison, and entered into the ᵠhouse of Lydia, and when they had seen the brethren, they exhorted them, and departed.

CHAP. XVII.

Now when they had passed through Amphipolis, and Apollonia, they came to Thessalonica, where was a synagogue of the Jews.

2 And Paul, as his manner was, went in unto them, and three sabbath-days reasoned with them out of the scriptures,

3 Opening and alleging, that Christ must needs have suffered, and risen again from the dead: and that this Jesus, whom I preach unto you, is Christ.

4 And some of them believed, and consorted with Paul and Si-

CHAP. XVII.

ΔΙΟΔΕΥΣΑΝΤΕΣ δὲ τὴν Ἀμφίπολιν καὶ Ἀπολλωνίαν, ἦλθον εἰς Θεσσαλονίκην, ὅπου ἦν ἡ συναγωγὴ τῶν Ἰουδαίων. 2 κατὰ δὲ τὸ εἰωθὸς τῷ Παύλῳ εἰσῆλθε πρὸς αὐτοὺς, καὶ ἐπὶ σάββατα τρία διελέγετο αὐτοῖς ἀπὸ τῶν γραφῶν, 3 διανοίγων καὶ παρατιθέμενος, ὅτι τὸν Χριστὸν ἔδει παθεῖν καὶ ἀναστῆναι ἐκ νεκρῶν, καὶ ὅτι οὗτός ἐστιν ὁ Χριστὸς Ἰησοῦς, ὃν ἐγὼ καταγγέλλω ὑμῖν. 4 Καί τινες ἐξ αὐτῶν ἐπείσθησαν, καὶ προσεκλη-

CHAP. XVII.

Now when ʳ*Paul and Silas* 1 had passed through Amphipolis and Apollonia, they came to Thessalonica, where there was the ˢsynagogue of the Jews. And Paul, as his ᵗcustom 2 was, went in to them, and three sabbaths reasoned with them ᵘfrom the Scriptures, ᵛopening them and setting 3 forth that the Christ must suffer, and rise again from the dead; and that this Jesus, whom I announce to you, is the Christ. And some of them 4 believed and ʷadhered to Paul

---

ᴾ Παρεκάλεσαν αυτους, και εξαγαγοντες ηρωτων. Παρακαλεω, in its more than hundred occurrences in N. T., is represented by *beseech* and *entreat* more frequently than by any other word.

ᵠ Εισηλθον εις την Λυδιαν is put for εις την Λυδιας οικον. The preposition εις, prefixed to the names of persons, *indicates* the place in which the person is, and that to such an extent that εις την Λυδιαν is placed for εις την Λυδιας οικον. Kœnius Wesselingius ad Herod., p. 161. For εις την Λυδιαν, many books have, προς την Λυδιαν, which reading is preferred by Bengelius, Griesbachius, and Matthæius, and argued at considerable length; for no higher reason, as it seems to me, than a proof of scholarship: for there appears not the slightest difference between them.

ʳ For *they*, Paul and Silas is substituted by Wakefield, as a supplement, especially due at the beginning of a new chapter, or paragraph.

ˢ Ἡ συναγωγη. Definite, we presume there was but one synagogue in that district. With the exception of Hackett, it is generally *a* synagogue. But why, through this book, in all other cases, translate the article in our language, and in this

same chapter, v. 10 and 17, translate it, and omit it here! This appears rather more arbitrary than philological.

Articulus emphasin habet et indicat Thessalonicæ tantum celebriorem synagogam fuisse, in reliquis Macedoniæ oppidis nonnisi proseuchas (v. ad 16, 13) at recte monuerunt. Grotius, Wetsteinius, Heumanus, Rosenmüllerus, Heinrichsius, Kuinœl.

ᵗ Κατα δε το εισωθος τῳ Παυλῳ εισηλθε. Paul's custom was, first to visit the Jewish synagogues, before he preached the gospel to the Gentiles.

ᵘ Not εκ, but απο, from the Scriptures; not shewing, but *propounding*.

ᵛ Διανοιγων και παρατιθεμενος. In the judgment of sound critics, αντας must here be understood as representing γραφας. We have, in this assumption, the concurrence of Grotius, Pricæus, Elsnerus, Morus, Rosenmüllerus, and others of minor fame, cited by Kuinœl, vol. 3, p. 258. *Opening* and *setting forth*, that the Messiah, or *the Christ, must suffer.*

ʷ Προσεκληρωθησαν τῳ Παυλῳ, they adhered—sectari aliquem—or, to join ones'self to another. Philo, de Decal., p. 760, quoted by Kuinœl. So Olshausen, Wahl, Robinson, Hackett, Sectatores Pauli et Silæ factæ sunt. Προσκληροεσθαι, adhærere, *adjungere se aliqui, to join ones'self to any one.*

KING JAMES' VERSION.	GREEK TEXT.	REVISED VERSION.

las: and of the devout Greeks a great multitude, and of the chief women not a few.

5 But the Jews which believed not, moved with envy, took unto them certain lewd fellows of the baser sort, and gathered a company, and set all the city on an uproar, and assaulted the house of Jason, and sought to bring them out to the people.

6 And when they found them not, they drew Jason and certain brethren unto the rulers of the city, crying, These that have turned the world upside down, are come hither also;

7 Whom Jason hath received: and these all do contrary to the decrees of Cesar, saying, that there is another king, *one* Jesus.

8 And they troubled the people, and the rulers of the city, when they heard these things.

9 And when they had taken security of Jason and of the other, they let them go.

10 And the brethren immediately sent away Paul and Silas by night unto Berea: who com-

ρώθησαν τῷ Παύλῳ καὶ τῷ Σίλᾳ, τῶν τε σεβομένων Ἑλλήνων πολὺ πλῆθος, γυναικῶν τε τῶν πρώτων οὐκ ὀλίγαι. 5 ζηλώσαντες δὲ οἱ ἀπειθοῦντες Ἰουδαῖοι, καὶ προσλαβόμενοι τῶν ἀγοραίων τινὰς ἄνδρας πονηροὺς, καὶ ὀχλοποιήσαντες, ἐθορύβουν τὴν πόλιν· ἐπιστάντες τε τῇ οἰκίᾳ Ἰάσονος, ἐζήτουν αὐτοὺς ἀγαγεῖν εἰς τὸν δῆμον· 6 μὴ εὑρόντες δὲ αὐτοὺς, ἔσυρον τὸν Ἰάσονα καί τινας ἀδελφοὺς ἐπὶ τοὺς πολιτάρχας, βοῶντες, Ὅτι οἱ τὴν οἰκουμένην ἀναστατώσαντες, οὗτοι καὶ ἐνθάδε πάρεισιν, 7 οὓς ὑποδέδεκται Ἰάσων· καὶ οὗτοι πάντες ἀπέναντι τῶν δογμάτων Καίσαρος πράττουσι, βασιλέα λέγοντες ἕτερον εἶναι, Ἰησοῦν. 8 Ἐτάραξαν δὲ τὸν ὄχλον καὶ τοὺς πολιτάρχας ἀκούοντας ταῦτα· 9 καὶ λαβόντες τὸ ἱκανὸν παρὰ τοῦ Ἰάσονος καὶ τῶν λοιπῶν, ἀπέλυσαν αὐτούς. 10 Οἱ δὲ ἀδελφοὶ εὐθέως διὰ τῆς νυκτὸς ἐξέπεμψαν τόν τε Παῦλον καὶ τὸν Σίλαν εἰς Βέροιαν· οἵτινες

and Silas; and of the devout Greeks a great multitude, and of the principal women not a few.

But the Jews who did not 5 ˣbelieve, moved with envy, gathered some vile men of the street ʸidlers, and raised a mob, and set all the city in an uproar, and assaulted the house of Jason, and sought to bring them out to the people; but 6 not finding them, they dragged Jason and certain brethren ᶻbefore the ᵃcity rulers, exclaiming, These men, who have turned the world upside down, are come hither also; whom Jason has received; and all 7 these act contrary to the ᵇdecrees of Cæsar, saying, That there is another king,—Jesus. And they troubled the 8 people, and the rulers of the city, when they heard these things. And having 9 taken ᶜsecurity of Jason and the others, they dismissed them. And the brethren im- 10 mediately sent away Paul and Silas ᵈby night to Berea, who

---

ˣ Ἀπειθοῦντες, omitted by Gb., Sch., Ln. It is nevertheless implied, for certainly they were unbelieving Jews, if Jews at all. We should, indeed, rather regard it due to the nation of Jews, that ἀπειθοῦντες should be a genuine reading, inasmuch as only a portion of that people acted in this affair, and to specify this class was due to the nation as a whole.

ʸ Τῶν ἀγοραιων, "those street, or *market-house loungers,* were wont to crowd about the city gates," Hackett; "disorderly *rabble,*" Wakef.; "*mischievous* men," Penn; "a mob," Murd., Thomp.; "*multitude,*" Boothr.

ᶻ Ἐπι, occasionally in the com. ver. of this book, is rendered *before;* and in cases of this sort, it is preferable to the com. ver. *to.*

ᵃ Τοὺς πολιτάρχας, the *prefects of the city,* or civil magistrates. "Ἔσυρον violently dragged Iason before the *magistrates,*" Thomp., Wak.; "the *rulers of the city,*" Boothr., Penn; "*chiefs of the city,*" Murd.

ᵇ Δογματων. Dogmata is a mere transference of this word, and indicates its true import, then and now, a *settled opinion:* but when uttered by civil or ecclesiastic lords, it becomes magisterial, authoritative. Hence, in v. 7, it becomes *the decree* of Cesar, that is, an *opinion* demanding acquiescence, *under a penalty.* Hence, v. 8, ἐταραξαν, the statement alarmed them. Their character, interest, and honor were all imperilled. Hence, v. 9, λαβοντες το ἱκανον, having taken *security,* or enough to satisfy, "that the peace should not be violated, and that the alledged authors of the disturbance should leave the city." Neander. But some restrict the stipulation to the first point (Meyer); others to the last. Kuinœl. Τῶν λοιπων, *the others* who, with Jason, had been brought before the tribunal. See v. 6. Hack.

ᶜ Λαβοντες το ἱκαχον, we call "bail," or "security." Τῶν λοιπων, "These others had been brought before the tribunal with Jason." Hackett.

ᵈ Δια της νυκτος. This indicates, *impending danger ap-*

KING JAMES' VERSION.

ing *thither*, went into the synagogue of the Jews.

11 These were more noble than those in Thessalonica, in that they received the word with all readiness of mind, and searched the scriptures daily, whether those things were so.

12 Therefore many of them believed; also of honourable women which were Greeks, and of men not a few.

13 But when the Jews of Thessalonica had knowledge that the word of God was preached of Paul at Berea, they came thither also, and stirred up the people.

14 And then immediately the brethren sent away Paul, to go as it were to the sea: but Silas and Timotheus abode there still.

GREEK TEXT.

παραγενόμενοι, εἰς τὴν συναγωγὴν τῶν Ἰουδαίων ἀπῄεσαν. ¹¹ οὗτοι δὲ ἦσαν εὐγενέστεροι τῶν ἐν Θεσσαλονίκῃ, οἵτινες ἐδέξαντο τὸν λόγον μετὰ πάσης προθυμίας, τὸ καθ᾽ ἡμέραν ἀνακρίνοντες τὰς γραφὰς, εἰ ἔχοι ταῦτα οὕτως. ¹² πολλοὶ μὲν οὖν ἐξ αὐτῶν ἐπίστευσαν, καὶ τῶν Ἑλληνίδων γυναικῶν τῶν εὐσχημόνων καὶ ἀνδρῶν οὐκ ὀλίγοι. ¹³ ὡς δὲ ἔγνωσαν οἱ ἀπὸ τῆς Θεσσαλονίκης Ἰουδαῖοι, ὅτι καὶ ἐν τῇ Βεροίᾳ κατηγγέλη ὑπὸ τοῦ Παύλου ὁ λόγος τοῦ Θεοῦ, ἦλθον κἀκεῖ σαλεύοντες τοὺς ὄχλους. ¹⁴ εὐθέως δὲ τότε τὸν Παῦλον ἐξαπέστειλαν οἱ ἀδελφοὶ πορεύεσθαι ὡς ἐπὶ τὴν θάλασσαν· ὑπέμενον δὲ ὅ τε Σίλας καὶ ὁ Τιμόθεος ἐκεῖ. ¹⁵ Οἱ δὲ

REVISED VERSION.

coming thither went into the synagogue of the Jews. Now 11 these were *more noble-minded than those of Thessalonica, in that they received the word with all *readiness of mind, *searching the Scriptures daily to see if these things were so. Therefore many of 12 them believed; also of honorable women, who were Greeks, and men, not a few. But 13 when the Jews of Thessalonica knew that the word of God was preached by Paul in Berea, they came thither also, and *stirred up the rabble. And then the brethren, imme- 14 diately sent away Paul *even to the sea. But Silas and Timothy abode there still.

---

prehended. Εἰς Βεροιαν, Berœa, now known as Verria, a day's journey south-west of Thessalonica.

ᵉ Εὐγενεστεροι, "more *noble*," Boothr., Dodd.; "more *generous*," Thomp.; "more *liberal*," Murd.; "more *ingenuous*;" Penn, Wes. More *noble minded*, not in the factitious nobility of earth, but in the generous sympathies of piety and humanity with the Divine will.

ᶠ Προθυμιας, readiness of mind. Readiness to will, 2 Cor. 8 : 11 ; a willing mind, 8 : 12 ; ready mind, 8 : 19 ; forwardness of mind, 9 : 2. Such is the N. T. currency. Alacrity, promptness of mind. Critica Sacra, "voluntarily;" Vulgate, "ex toto corde." "From the whole heart," Luther.

ᵍ Αναχρινοντες. Αναχρινω is found five times in this book, represented by examine and search, once in Luke's gospel. In Paul's epistles it is used ten times, and is represented by discern, examine, asking a question, and judge six times. It indicates in its composition strict discriminating inquiry, examination. Κρινω, κρισις, κριτηριον, κριτης, κριτικος are its family, and crime too, which it alone decides, is by affinity amongst its legalized descendants, because by it detected and exposed.

ʰ Σαλευοντες, to which is added by Ln., και ταρασσοντες. With two exceptions, σαλευω is represented by shake, com. ver. The exceptions are move, and stir. It is a favorite with Luke. Of its fifteen occurrences in N. Test. he uses it eight

times. "They shook the people" is quite as apposite as, "they stirred up the people," their minds of course. But that excitement was their object, and excitement against Paul, its specific object, is not unlikely, nay, indeed, most probable; it is thought expedient to express that conception of the movement. Still if it were so, to decide the matter by a special translation is of doubtful propriety. While a license in this case may be allowed, there are not a few cases in which it would be intolerable.

ⁱ Ὡς επι την θαλασσαν. Not a few interpreters—such as Beza, Grotius, Erasmus, Schmidius, Hezellius, Eckermanus, and others—think that Paul was carried to the sea-coast, as if from that region, on board of ship, he would sail to Athens; while, in fact, by a journey on foot, he would hasten on through Macedonia and Thessaly to Athens. We quote from Kuinœl the following exposition of it, "Alii putant, Paulum deductum esse ad oram maris, ut illum Judæi persequi desinerent, quasi navi conscensa ex illo regione enavigasset, mox autem cum reipsa, terrestri itinere, per Macedoniam et Thessaliam Athenas contendisse. Itaque ὡς επι την θαλασσαν vertunt: quasi, velut ad mare." Vol. 3, p. 261. Acts 17 : 14. Ὡς επι, in this place, denotes usque ad mare, even to the sea. The Syriac, Arabic, and Æthiopic interpreters so understand this word. The particle ὡς, when accompanied by the preposition επι, is equal to ἑως, equivalent to the Roman usque ad, vel recte ad. Kuinœl, in loco.

15 And they that conducted Paul brought him unto Athens: and receiving a commandment unto Silas and Timotheus for to come to him with all speed, they departed.

16 Now while Paul waited for them at Athens, his spirit was stirred in him, when he saw the city wholly given to idolatry.

17 Therefore disputed he in the synagogue with the Jews, and with the devout persons, and in the market daily with them that met with him.

18 Then certain philosophers of the Epicureans, and of the Stoics, encountered him. And some said, What will this babbler say? other some, He seemeth to be a setter forth of strange gods: because he preached unto them Jesus, and the resurrection.

19 And they took him, and brought him unto Areopagus,

καθιστῶντες τὸν Παῦλον, ἤγαγον αὐτὸν ἕως Ἀθηνῶν· καὶ λαβόντες ἐντολὴν πρὸς τὸν Σίλαν καὶ Τιμόθεον, ἵνα ὡς τάχιστα ἔλθωσι πρὸς αὐτὸν, ἐξῄεσαν.

16 Ἐν δὲ ταῖς Ἀθήναις ἐκδεχομένου αὐτοὺς τοῦ Παύλου, παρωξύνετο τὸ πνεῦμα αὐτοῦ ἐν αὐτῷ θεωροῦντι κατείδωλον οὖσαν τὴν πόλιν. 17 διελέγετο μὲν οὖν ἐν τῇ συναγωγῇ τοῖς Ἰουδαίοις καὶ τοῖς σεβομένοις, καὶ ἐν τῇ ἀγορᾷ κατὰ πᾶσαν ἡμέραν πρὸς τοὺς παρατυγχάνοντας. 18 τινὲς δὲ τῶν Ἐπικουρείων καὶ τῶν Στωϊκῶν φιλοσόφων συνέβαλλον αὐτῷ· καί τινες ἔλεγον, Τί ἂν θέλοι ὁ σπερμολόγος οὗτος λέγειν; Οἱ δὲ, Ξένων δαιμονίων δοκεῖ καταγγελεὺς εἶναι· ὅτι τὸν Ἰησοῦν καὶ τὴν ἀνάστασιν αὐτοῖς εὐηγγελίζετο. 19 ἐπιλαβόμενοί τε αὐτοῦ, ἐπὶ τὸν Ἄρειον πάγον ἤγαγον

And they who conducted 15 Paul, brought him to Athens; and having received a command-mandment to Silas and Timothy to come to him, as soon as possible, they departed.

Now while Paul was wait- 16 ing for them at Athens, his spirit was ʲroused in him, when he saw the city ᵏwholly devoted to idols. Therefore 17 he disputed in the ˡsynagogue, with the Jews, and with the devout persons, and in the market, daily, with those who met with him.   Then 18 certain philosophers of the ᵐEpicureans and of the Stoics encountered him; and some said, what would this ⁿchatterer say; and others, he seems to be a publisher of °foreign gods, because he announced to them Jesus and the Resurrection. Now they 19 took him and brought him to the ᵖAreopagus, saying, Can

---

¹ Παροξυνετο το πνευμα. Παροξυνομαι, found here and once 1 Cor. 13:5, his spirit was *provoked* (as the word is rendered com. ver., 1 Cor. 13:5), *excited, stirred up, εν αυτῳ, in him.* It was, however, suppressed. He addressed them very courteously.

ᵏ Κατειδωλον. One of the many ἅπαξ λεγομενα of this book of Acts. "Wholly *addicted*," or "wholly *given*," is *pleonastic*, but no more than called for. Petronius, a contemporary of Paul, in his 17th Satire, makes Quartilla say of Athens, "*You can more easily find a god than a man in Athens.*"

ˡ Paul found a synagogue in Athens, and a way into the *Agora*, or *Forum*. There was no *called* auditory. He spoke προς τους παρατυγχανοντας, to those *who happened* to be there. Cicero, de oratore, 1:4, calls the Athenians the inventers of all learning. His words are, "*Athenæ omnium doctrinarum inventrices.*" And in his oration for Flaccus, c. 26, he says: "*humanity, religion, learning, institutions and laws*, whose monuments are known and diffused throughout the world, all originated in Athens."

There were many Forums in Athens. Of these two were most celebrated, called *Vetus* et *Novum*, the OLD and the NEW.

ᵐ Τινες δε Επικουρειων και των Στοϊκων φιλοσοφων συνε-

βαλον αυτῳ, *certain ones*, or, some of the Epicurean and Stoic philosophers encountered Paul.

Like the Jewish Sadducees, these Epicureans were very great triflers, or frivolous persons. "Dum vivimus, vivamus," was their oracle.

ⁿ A babbler, one uttering scraps on any subject. So they understood his quotations from the Jewish Scriptures.

Ὁ σπερμολογος, *garrulus*. "Non απο του σπειρειν τους λογους, but rather παρα το λεγειν σπερματα, *quasi seminilegas dicas, quod sata in agris depascantur; metaphora a passerculis, aliisque aviculis sumpta*, quæ neque magnopere sunt esui, neque cantu delectant, sed *garritu perpetuo* sunt molestæ." Beza. "Demosthenes addressed Æschines by the same name, *three hundred years* before Paul was there." Broughton on the Revelation, quoted in *Critica Sacra*.

° Foreign gods, and new gods, unknown before, are supposed by them to have been indicated by τον Ιησουν και την αναστασιν. These words, in their polytheistic ears, sounded as though a male and female Divinity were intended.

ᵖ Αρειον παγον, a rocky eminence, west of the Acropolis. Επι is often represented by *to* and *upon*. They placed him

KING JAMES' VERSION.

saying, May we know what this new doctrine, whereof thou speakest, *is?*

20 For thou bringest certain strange things to our ears; we would know therefore what these things mean.

21 (For all the Athenians and strangers which were there, spent their time in nothing else, but either to tell, or to hear some new thing.)

22 Then Paul stood in the midst of Mars-hill, and said, *Ye* men of Athens, I perceive that in all things ye are too superstitious.

23 For as I passed by, and beheld your devotions, I found an altar with this inscription, TO THE UNKNOWN GOD. Whom therefore ye ignorantly worship, him declare I unto you.

24 God that made the world, and all things therein, seeing that he is Lord of heaven and earth, dwelleth not in temples made with hands;

25 Neither is worshipped with men's hands, as though he need-

GREEK TEXT.

λέγοντες, Δυνάμεθα γνῶναι, τίς ἡ καινὴ αὕτη ἡ ὑπὸ σοῦ λαλουμένη διδαχή; [20] ξενίζοντα γάρ τινα εἰσφέρεις εἰς τὰς ἀκοὰς ἡμῶν· βουλόμεθα οὖν γνῶναι, τί ἂν θέλοι ταῦτα εἶναι. [21] Ἀθηναῖοι δὲ πάντες καὶ οἱ ἐπιδημοῦντες ξένοι εἰς οὐδὲν ἕτερον εὐκαίρουν, ἢ λέγειν τι καὶ ἀκούειν καινότερον.

[22] Σταθεὶς δὲ ὁ Παῦλος ἐν μέσῳ τοῦ Ἀρείου πάγου, ἔφη, Ἄνδρες Ἀθηναῖοι, κατὰ πάντα ὡς δεισιδαιμονεστέρους ὑμᾶς θεωρῶ. [23] διερχόμενος γὰρ καὶ ἀναθεωρῶν τὰ σεβάσματα ὑμῶν, εὗρον καὶ βωμὸν ἐν ᾧ ἐπεγέγραπτο, Ἀγνώστῳ Θεῷ. ὃν οὖν ἀγνοοῦντες εὐσεβεῖτε, τοῦτον ἐγὼ καταγγέλλω ὑμῖν. [24] ὁ Θεὸς ὁ ποιήσας τὸν κόσμον καὶ πάντα τὰ ἐν αὐτῷ, οὗτος οὐρανοῦ καὶ γῆς κύριος ὑπάρχων, οὐκ ἐν χειροποιήτοις ναοῖς κατοικεῖ, [25] οὐδὲ ὑπὸ χειρῶν ἀνθρώπων θεραπεύε-

REVISED VERSION.

we know what this new doctrine is, of which you speak?
For you bring some strange 20
things to our ears. We wish, therefore, to know what these things mean.
For all Athenians and stran- 21
gers who were there, spent their time in nothing else, but either in telling or hearing
some new thing. Then Paul 22
stood up in [q]the midst of the Areopagus, and said; Athenians! I perceive that, [r]in every respect, you are [s]exceedingly devotional.
For as I 23
passed along and observed [t]the objects of your worship, I found an altar with this inscription, To AN UNKNOWN GOD: him, therefore, whom you, not knowing, worship I declare to you.
God who [u]made the world 24
and all things in it, seeing that he is Lord of heaven and of earth, dwells not in temples
made with hands; neither is 25
ministered to by men's hands,

upon, or brought him to, the Areiopagus, or Mars Hill, not to the court so called.

Concurring in opinion with Doddridge, Calvin, Neander, De Wette, Kuinœl, Winer, Hackett, and sundry other scholars and critics, that Paul is not standing on trial before the Areiopagus, or supreme court of Athens, but standing in sight of its temple of justice, we regard his discourse as a *popular address*, and not as a *defense* before a civil or judicial tribunal.

[q] *Εν μεσῳ του Αρειου παγου*, the highest court of justice in Athens, which had specially the cognizance of whatever respected religion. But in the judgment of our most sober critics, it remains uncertain whether *Αρειου παγου* here represents a *place*, or an *assembly*, the *hill*, or the *court* assembled on it.

[r] *Κατα παντα* is well rendered, "*in every respect*", by Hackett. "*From every thing I see*," Thomp.; "*in all things*," Murd.; "*altogether*," Wakef.; "*by all things*," Penn; "*in all places*," Boothr.

[s] We quote the following judicious exposition of this word from Leigh's Crit. Sacra. *Δεισιδαιμονεστερος*, "Too full of demons already, I shall not need to bring any more among you —a worshiper of demon gods. *Δεισιδαιμονια*, superstition. *Timor Dei inanis*, Cicero. This word is found Acts 25 : 19. Superstitiosior, Vulgate. Per trope, *dévotieux*, French vulgate. In the margin, "*Le mot signifie, qui est exposé envers, afin qu'on y rende quelque service de religion.*" See Critica Sacra. More religious than others. "He (Paul) announced himself as one that would guide their *δεισιδαιμονια*, not rightly conscious of its object and aim, by a revelation of *the object* to which it thus ignorantly tended." Neander.

[t] *Αναθεωρων τα σεβασματα ὑμων*, they had gone beyond their contemporaries in erecting an altar to "the *unknown* God." This justified the ingratiatory manner in which Paul addressed them. No other city, or people, had thus confessed their ignorance and their devotion. It was a grand conception, to erect an altar to the GREAT UNKNOWN in the centre of Grecian civilization!

[u] *Ουκ εν χειροποιητοις ναοις κατοικει.* Stephen, in Acts 7 : 48, uses the same phrase which Paul here uses, having for its subject, *ὁ ὑψιστος—εν χειροποιητοις ναοις κατοικει.* Luke is, doubtless, the author, as well as the reporter of these words.

KING JAMES' VERSION.

ed any thing, seeing he giveth to all life, and breath, and all things;

26 And hath made of one blood all nations of men for to dwell on all the face of the earth, and hath determined the times before appointed, and the bounds of their habitation;

27 That they should seek the Lord, if haply they might feel after him, and find him, though he be not far from every one of us:

28 For in him we live, and move, and have our being; as certain also of your own poets have said, For we are also his offspring.

29 Forasmuch then as we are the offspring of God, we ought not to think that the Godhead is like unto gold, or silver, or stone, graven by art and man's device.

30 And the times of this ignorance God winked at; but now commandeth all men every where to repent:

GREEK TEXT.

ται προσδεόμενός τινος, αὐτὸς διδοὺς πᾶσι ζωὴν καὶ πνοὴν κατὰ πάντα· 26 ἐποίησέ τε ἐξ ἑνὸς αἵματος πᾶν ἔθνος ἀνθρώπων, κατοικεῖν ἐπὶ πᾶν τὸ πρόσωπον τῆς γῆς, ὁρίσας προτεταγμένους καιροὺς καὶ τὰς ὁροθεσίας τῆς κατοικίας αὐτῶν· 27 ζητεῖν τὸν κύριον, εἰ ἄρα γε ψηλαφήσειαν αὐτὸν καὶ εὕροιεν, καίτοιγε οὐ μακρὰν ἀπὸ ἑνὸς ἑκάστου ἡμῶν ὑπάρχοντα. 28 ἐν αὐτῷ γὰρ ζῶμεν καὶ κινούμεθα καί ἐσμεν· ὡς καί τινες τῶν καθ᾽ ὑμᾶς ποιητῶν εἰρήκασι, Τοῦ γὰρ καὶ γένος ἐσμέν. 29 Γένος οὖν ὑπάρχοντες τοῦ Θεοῦ, οὐκ ὀφείλομεν νομίζειν χρυσῷ ἢ ἀργύρῳ ἢ λίθῳ, χαράγματι τέχνης καὶ ἐνθυμήσεως ἀνθρώπου, τὸ θεῖον εἶναι ὅμοιον. 30 Τοὺς μὲν οὖν χρόνους τῆς ἀγνοίας ὑπεριδὼν ὁ Θεὸς, τανῦν παραγγέλλει τοῖς ἀνθρώποις πᾶσι πανταχοῦ μετα-

REVISED VERSION.

as though he needed anything, seeing he gives to all, life and breath, and all things; and 26 has made of one blood every nation of men, to dwell on all the face of the earth, ʳhaving determined the appointed seasons and limits of their abode; that they should seek the 27 Lord, if, perhaps, they might feel after him and find him; although, indeed, he is not far from any one of us; for by 28 him we live, and move, and have our being; as even some of your own poets have said; ʷFor we, indeed, his offspring are.

Since, then, ˣwe are the off- 29 spring of God, we ought not to think that the Godhead is like to gold or silver, graved by art or man's device. And 30 the times of this ignorance God ʸoverlooked, but now commands all men every where,

---

ᵛ Ὁρίσας προτεταγμενους—or, προστεταγμενους, Gb., Sch., Ln., Tf.; a more approved reading, καιρους, etc. "Having determined the appointed times, and the boundaries of their habitations," Penn. "Having fixed from the first the appointed times and boundaries of their habitations," Wakef. "And he ʼhath separated the seasons by his ordinance: and hath set bounds to the residence of men," Murd. "Having marked out times previously arranged in order, and the boundaries of their habitations for them to seek the Lord," Thomp. "And hath determined their appointed times, and the bounds of their habitations, that they might seek God," Boothr. "Having marked out the times fore-allotted, and boundaries of their habitations," Dodd. We see nothing gained or lost to rival theorists in their controversies on these words. According to Adam Clark, instead of προστεταγμενους καιρους, the times before appointed, ABDE and more than forty other MSS., with the Syriac, all the Arabic, the Coptic, Aethiopic, Slavonian, Vulgate, and Itala, read προστεταγμενους καιρους, the appointed times. The difference is, προτασσειν is to "place before others," but προστασσειν is to "command, decree, or appoint."

Προστεταγμενοι καιροι are constituted, or "decreed times,"

and "the bounds of their habitation." Dr. Clark adds, "Every nation had its lot thus appointed of God, as truly as Israel had its land. But the removal of the Jews by the Saracens, the Saracens by the Turks, the Greeks by the Romans, the Romans by the Goths and Vandals, and so of others, show, that a people may forfeit their original inheritance." This, we presume, is a conceded point. The approved reading, I concur with Dr. Hackett, is, προστεταγμενους, rather than προτεταγμενους, common Text.

ʷ Του γαρ και γενος εσμεν, For we, indeed, his offspring are. These words are the first half of a hexameter found in Aratus, a Cicilian poet, whose poem antedates Christ some 270 years.

ˣ Paul concedes its truth. The same idea is also found in other Greek writers. Prof. Hackett quotes from the hymn of Cleanthus, addressed to Jupiter Tonans, almost the same words, "εκ σου γαρ γενος εσμεν." Paul, in his manner of quotation, generalizes the idea, using the words, τινες ειρηκασι, certain Greeks have said, etc.

ʸ Ὑπεριδων. In the Septuagint its most common import is, "contemn, permitted, suffered," Kuin. "Overlooked," Boothr.; "condemning," Wakef.

KING JAMES' VERSION.

31 Because he hath appointed a day, in the which he will judge the world in righteousness, by *that* man whom he hath ordained: *whereof* he hath given assurance unto all *men*, in that he hath raised him from the dead.

32 And when they heard of the resurrection of the dead, some mocked: and others said, We will hear thee again of this *matter*.

33 So Paul departed from among them.

34 Howbeit, certain men clave unto him, and believed: among the which *was* Dionysius the Areopagite, and a woman named Damaris, and others with them.

CHAP. XVIII.

AFTER these things, Paul departed from Athens, and came to Corinth;

2 And found a certain Jew named Aquila, born in Pontus, lately come from Italy, with his wife Priscilla, (because that Claudius had commanded all Jews to depart from Rome) and came unto them.

3 And because he was of the

GREEK TEXT.

νοεῖν· 31 διότι ἔστησεν ἡμέραν, ἐν ᾗ μέλλει κρίνειν τὴν οἰκουμένην ἐν δικαιοσύνῃ. ἐν ἀνδρὶ ᾧ ὥρισε, πίστιν παρασχὼν πᾶσιν, ἀναστήσας αὐτὸν ἐκ νεκρῶν. 32 Ἀκούσαντες δὲ ἀνάστασιν νεκρῶν, οἱ μὲν ἐχλεύαζον· οἱ δὲ εἶπον, Ἀκουσόμεθά σου πάλιν περὶ τούτου. 33 Καὶ οὕτως ὁ Παῦλος ἐξῆλθεν ἐκ μέσου αὐτῶν. 34 τινὲς δὲ ἄνδρες κολληθέντες αὐτῷ, ἐπίστευσαν· ἐν οἷς καὶ Διονύσιος ὁ Ἀρεοπαγίτης, καὶ γυνὴ ὀνόματι Δάμαρις, καὶ ἕτεροι σὺν αὐτοῖς.

CHAP. XVIII.

ΜΕΤΑ δὲ ταῦτα χωρισθεὶς ὁ Παῦλος ἐκ τῶν Ἀθηνῶν ἦλθεν εἰς Κόρινθον· 2 καὶ εὑρών τινα Ἰουδαῖον ὀνόματι Ἀκύλαν, Ποντικὸν τῷ γένει, προσφάτως ἐληλυθότα ἀπὸ τῆς Ἰταλίας, καὶ Πρίσκιλλαν γυναῖκα αὐτοῦ, διὰ τὸ διατεταχέναι Κλαύδιον χωρίζεσθαι πάντας τοὺς Ἰουδαίους ἐκ τῆς Ῥώμης, προσῆλθεν αὐτοῖς· 3 καὶ διὰ τὸ ὁμότεχνον εἶναι,

REVISED VERSION.

to reform. Because he has 31 [z]appointed a day, in which he will judge the world in righteousness, by that man whom he has appointed, giving assurance to all, having raised him from the dead. And when 32 they heard of a resurrection of the dead, some mocked; and others said, we will hear you again concerning this matter. So Paul departed from 33 among them. But ⋅certain 34 persons adhered to him and believed: among whom, was Dionysius the [b]Areopagite, and a woman named Damaris, and others with them.

CHAP. XVIII.

AFTER these things [c]Paul 1 left Athens, and went to Corinth. And having found a 2 certain Jew named [d]Aquila, born in Pontus, lately come from Italy, with his wife Priscilla, (because Claudius had commanded all the Jews to depart from Rome), he came to them. And because he was 3

---

[z] *Ἐν ανδρι ᾧ ὥρισε*, by the man whom he has appointed. Because a definite clause follows *ανδρι*, he omits the article. Stuart's Gram., § 88, 3. *ᾧ* stands by *attraction* for the accusative.

Κρινειν την οικουμενην. *Οικουμενην* occurs eighteen times in N. T., represented by *world* fourteen times, and *earth* once. "Judge all the earth," Murd.; "The world," Thomp., Wes., Penn, Boothr., cum multis aliis.

Ὥρισε, appointed, or decreed; *define* is its most exact representative. So decides Crit. Sacra, "*definio*, Heb. 4: 7, item *definire certo scopo destinare.*"

⋅ *Τινες δε ανδρες κολληθεντες*, aliquot autem viri se ei adjunxerunt.

Κολλαω, in its ten occurrences, N. Test., is six times represented by *join*, three times by *cleave*, and once, to "*keep company.*" These are all, more or less, antiquated, for which

we now substitute the word *associate*, in all cases of companionship; "*associated with him*" is only tolerable, and does not quite express the full sense.

[b] Areopagite, one of the judges of the court at the Areopagus. Tradition says, by Eusebius, that he was afterwards bishop of the church in Athens, and died as a martyr.

[c] Ὁ Παυλος is rejected by Ln., Tf. Paul is, however, the subject of the narrative. His name is, therefore, found in almost all the versions, Wiclif, Tynd., Cran., Geneva, Dodd., Thomp., Wakef., Wes., Murd., Boothr. Ηλθεν εις Κορινθον —χωρισθεις, having left, or removed from, Athens, came to Corinth.

[d] Ονοματι Ακυλαν. Ακυλας is a Latin name. He was a Jew, a σκηνοποιος, a tent-maker; τινα Ιουδαιον, a Jew by birth, now a Christian; exiled, indeed, as a Jew, not as a Christian, as reads the decree of Claudius.

KING JAMES' VERSION.

same craft, he abode with them, and wrought, (for by their occupation they were tent-makers.)

4 And he reasoned in the synagogue every sabbath, and persuaded the Jews and the Greeks.

5 And when Silas and Timotheus were come from Macedonia, Paul was pressed in the spirit, and testified to the Jews, *that* Jesus *was* Christ.

6 And when they opposed themselves, and blasphemed, he shook *his* raiment, and said unto them, Your blood *be* upon your own heads: I *am* clean: from henceforth I will go unto the Gentiles.

7 And he departed thence, and entered into a certain man's house, named Justus, *one* that worshipped God, whose house joined hard to the synagogue.

8 And Crispus, the chief ruler of the synagogue, believed on the Lord with all his house: and many of the Corinthians hearing, believed, and were baptized.

9 Then spake the Lord to Paul in the night by a vision,

GREEK TEXT.

ἔμενε παρ' αὐτοῖς καὶ εἰργάζετο· ἦσαν γὰρ σκηνοποιοὶ τὴν τέχνην. [4] διελέγετο δὲ ἐν τῇ συναγωγῇ κατὰ πᾶν σάββατον, ἔπειθέ τε Ἰουδαίους καὶ Ἕλληνας. [5] Ὡς δὲ κατῆλθον ἀπὸ τῆς Μακεδονίας ὅ τε Σίλας καὶ ὁ Τιμόθεος, συνείχετο τῷ πνεύματι ὁ Παῦλος, διαμαρτυρόμενος τοῖς Ἰουδαίοις τὸν Χριστὸν Ἰησοῦν. [6] ἀντιτασσομένων δὲ αὐτῶν καὶ βλασφημούντων, ἐτιναξάμενος τὰ ἱμάτια, εἶπε πρὸς αὐτούς, Τὸ αἷμα ὑμῶν ἐπὶ τὴν κεφαλὴν ὑμῶν· καθαρὸς ἐγὼ, ἀπὸ τοῦ νῦν εἰς τὰ ἔθνη πορεύσομαι. [7] Καὶ μεταβὰς ἐκεῖθεν ἦλθεν εἰς οἰκίαν τινὸς ὀνόματι Ἰούστου, σεβομένου τὸν Θεόν, οὗ ἡ οἰκία ἦν συνομοροῦσα τῇ συναγωγῇ. [8] Κρίσπος δὲ ὁ ἀρχισυνάγωγος ἐπίστευσε τῷ κυρίῳ σὺν ὅλῳ τῷ οἴκῳ αὐτοῦ· καὶ πολλοὶ τῶν Κορινθίων ἀκούοντες ἐπίστευον καὶ ἐβαπτίζοντο. [9] Εἶπε δὲ ὁ κύριος δι' ὁράματος ἐν νυκτὶ τῷ Παύλῳ, Μὴ φοβοῦ,

REVISED VERSION.

of the same trade, he abode with them, and [e]worked: for by occupation they were tent-makers. And he reasoned in 4 the synagogue every sabbath, and endeavored to [f]persuade both Jews and Greeks. But 5 when Silas and Timothy were [g]come from Macedonia, Paul was constrained in spirit, earnestly testifying to the Jews, that Jesus was the Christ.

And when they resisted and 6 reviled, he shook his raiment, and said to them, Your blood be on your own heads. I am clean. Henceforth I will go to the Gentiles. And he 7 departed thence, and entered into the house of a certain man named Justus, who worshiped God, whose house was adjacent to the synagogue. But Crispus, the chief 8 ruler of the synagogue, believed on the Lord with all his [h]family: and many of the Corinthians, hearing, believed, and were immersed. Then 9 the Lord said to Paul in a vision by night, Be not afraid,

---

[e] Εἰργαζετο, worked for his subsistence. Ὁμοτεχνος, practised the same art or trade. Την τεχνην, a limiting accusative like τον—τροπον, in Jude, v. 7. Hackett. The Jewish law, after their exile, held that a father who taught not his son a trade, taught him to be a thief. So the latter Rabbis taught.

[f] Ἑλληνας, Greek proselytes; επειθε, persuaded, or was persuading, tried to persuade the Jews. "Persuaded the Jews and Gentiles," Murd.; "conciliated the affections," Thomp.; "striving to persuade," Penn; "endeavored to persuade," Boothr.

[g] Κατηλθον, came down (Silas and Timothy). Συνειχετο τῳ πνευματι ὁ Παυλος, Paul was pressed in spirit. For πνευματι Gb., Sch., Ln., Tf. prefer λογῳ. "The evidence decides for τῳ λογῳ as the original word, Griesbach, Mey., Tf." Hack. Our text prefers, τῳ πνευματι. Should we prefer Gb., Sch., Ln., and Tischendorf's selected readings, we should read it, "Paul was engrossed with the word." With our text, we render it, "was impelled by the Spirit," or, his own spirit.

Hackett, the Vulgate, Kuinœl, Olshausen, De Wette, and Robinson, prefer, "*the word*," and so do we. But we follow copy, in this case, however, doubtfully. Paul was, no doubt, much stirred up by the presence of Silas and Timothy, and became more fervent in spirit.

Συνεχω occurs twelve times in N. T. In nine of these it is used by Luke, translated, com. ver., by *taken with, thronged, straitened, kept in, held, stopped their ears*, that is, "*held them*." "*Lay sick* of a fever," or, *seized* by a fever. Elsewhere by *straiten, constrain, taken with*, or seized. Murdock's version of the Syriac renders this passage, "Paul was impeded in discourse, because the Jews stood up against him and reviled, as he testified to them that Jesus is the Messiah." This indicates that it was *word*, and not *spirit*, in his understanding of the Peshito Syriac version, the oldest known.

[h] Συν ὁλῳ τῳ οικῳ αὐτου, with all his family. Such is the frequent acceptation of οικος in the Christian Scriptures, indicating the parents and the children, the masters and the servants, as it does in the Septuagint of O. Test.

KING JAMES' VERSION.	GREEK TEXT.	REVISED VERSION.

KING JAMES' VERSION.

Be not afraid, but speak, and hold not thy peace:

10 For I am with thee, and no man shall set on thee, to hurt thee: for I have much people in this city.

11 And he continued *there* a year and six months, teaching the word of God among them.

12 And when Gallio was the deputy of Achaia, the Jews made insurrection with one accord against Paul, and brought him to the judgment-seat.

13 Saying, This *fellow* persuadeth men to worship God contrary to the law.

14 And when Paul was now about to open *his* mouth, Gallio said unto the Jews, If it were a matter of wrong, or wicked lewdness, O *ye* Jews, reason would that I should bear with you:

GREEK TEXT.

ἀλλὰ λάλει καὶ μὴ σιωπήσῃς· 10 διότι ἐγώ εἰμι μετὰ σοῦ, καὶ οὐδεὶς ἐπιθήσεταί σοι τοῦ κακῶσαί σε· διότι λαός ἐστί μοι πολὺς ἐν τῇ πόλει ταύτῃ. 11 Ἐκάθισέ τε ἐνιαυτὸν καὶ μῆνας ἓξ, διδάσκων ἐν αὐτοῖς τὸν λόγον τοῦ Θεοῦ.

12 Γαλλίωνος δὲ ἀνθυπατεύοντος τῆς Ἀχαΐας, κατεπέστησαν ὁμοθυμαδὸν οἱ Ἰουδαῖοι τῷ Παύλῳ, καὶ ἤγαγον αὐτὸν ἐπὶ τὸ βῆμα 13 λέγοντες, Ὅτι παρὰ τὸν νόμον οὗτος ἀναπείθει τοὺς ἀνθρώπους σέβεσθαι τὸν Θεόν. 14 Μέλλοντος δὲ τοῦ Παύλου ἀνοίγειν τὸ στόμα, εἶπεν ὁ Γαλλίων πρὸς τοὺς Ἰουδαίους, Εἰ μὲν οὖν ἦν ἀδίκημά τι ἢ ῥᾳδιούργημα πονηρόν, ὦ Ἰουδαῖοι, κατὰ λόγον ἂν ἠνεσχόμην ὑμῶν·

REVISED VERSION.

but speak, and be not [i]silent; for I am with you, and no 10 man shall assail [j]you to hurt you: for I have many people in this city. And he con- 11 tinued there a year and six months, teaching the word of God among them.

And when Gallio was gov- 12 erning Achaia as [k]proconsul, the Jews, with one consent, made insurrection against Paul, and brought him to the judgment-seat, saying, This [l]fellow persuades 13 men to worship God contrary to the law.

And as Paul was about 14 to open his mouth, Gallio said to the Jews, Were it, indeed, a matter of [m]wrong, or a wicked act, Jews, it would be reasonable that I should bear with you. But if 15

---

[i] *Μη σιωπησης, do not be silent,* or, *be not silent.* The latter is more imperative than the former, and less persuasive.

[j] *Επιθησεται σοι,* and no one shall attack thee, *telic, to injure* thee. "No one shall attempt it with success, or, ecbatic, *so as to injure thee,*" De Wette, Hackett. *Διοτι λαος εστι μοι πολυς,* "I have much people," i. e., "many who are appointed to be such. See ch. 13 : 48." Hack.

The passage here referred to is, ὅσοι ησαν τεταγμενοι εις ζωην αιωνιον. The *orthodoxy* of Prof. Hackett is unquestionably apparent, we know it well. Still "*the many who are appointed to be such,*" is unnecessarily exegetical of what is not in the text, nor in the context. We know no passage in Luke's writings in which he presumes to draw upon the secrets of a volume in the cabinet of heaven, that has not a transcript in any library in our planetary system which can be consulted by man. One thing is *historically* and *critically* plain, that the Lord had all the people in Corinth. They were all his, and it was a large population. Hence in the ratio of population should all Christian efforts be made.

[k] Ανθυπατευοντος της Αχαια, "was governing Achaia as proconsul," Hackett. *Ανθυπατευω, Proconsul sum,* I govern as proconsul. Gallio, brother of Seneca the moralist, formerly called Novatus, was exceedingly bland and kind to all. "Nemo mortalium uni tam dulcis quam hic omnibus," said Seneca, his brother. Does not Luke here corroborate Seneca, and Seneca Luke? No man so agreeably affable to one man, as he was to every one.

Ὁμοθυμαδον, unanimously, with one mind, with one accord, com. ver. Κατεπεστησαν—κατεφιστημι, an ἅπαξ λεγομενον, insurgo, made insurrection, *rose up against.*

[l] The indictment against Paul was, this person, *fellow,* as implied in the word οὑτος, literally, *this one.* In the vocative it is used for *heus tu*—alas for you! Littleton, "scornfully." "*This one,*" "*this fellow,*" Dodd., Wes., Tynd., Cran., Gen. Αναπειθει, persuades men to worship God contrary to law. All persecutions are prompted and defended on such allegations. Persuadeo—whence comes Pitho, the goddess of eloquence—Latin *suada unde suadæ, medulla.* Crit. Sacra.

[m] Αδικημα, here only found, and in ch. 24 : 20; Apoc. 18 : 5, *matter of wrong, evil doing,* iniquity. Such is its whole currency in N. T., connected with ῥαδιουργημα, an ἅπαξ λεγομενον. Ῥαδιουργια, ch. 13 : 10, com. ver., mischief, a reckless wicked deed. Here it is represented by *facinus, malum.* Crit. Sacra. "*Injury,* or *evil practice,*" Penn; "*injustice,* or wicked heinousness," Wes.; "*fraud,* or base act," Murd.; "*legally,* or *ethically,*" Hack. Any gross enormity, outrage. Λογος indicates any communication, *word, doctrine, saying, question, matter, fame, account, treatise, thing, intent, tidings, speech, reason, utterance, preaching, act of injustice,* or *wicked mischief.* Dodd. *Matter of wrong,* or *wicked act,* concentrates both ideas, as we presume.

KING JAMES' VERSION.

15 But if it be a question of words and names, and *of* your law, look ye *to it:* for I will be no judge of such *matters.*

16 And he drave them from the judgment-seat.

17 Then all the Greeks took Sosthenes, the chief ruler of the synagogue, and beat *him* before the judgment-seat. And Gallio cared for none of those things.

18 And Paul *after this* tarried *there* yet a good while, and then took his leave of the brethren, and sailed thence into Syria, and with him Priscilla, and Aquila; having shorn *his* head in Cenchrea: for he had a vow.

19 And he came to Ephesus, and left them there: but he himself entered into the synagogue, and reasoned with the Jews.

20 When they desired *him* to tarry longer time with them, he consented not:

21 But bade them farewell, saying, I must by all means keep this feast that cometh in Jerusalem: but I will return again unto you, if God will. And he sailed from Ephesus.

GREEK TEXT.

15 εἰ δὲ ζήτημά ἐστι περὶ λόγου
καὶ ὀνομάτων καὶ νόμου τοῦ καθ'
ὑμᾶς, ὄψεσθε αὐτοί· κριτὴς γὰρ
ἐγὼ τούτων οὐ βούλομαι εἶναι.
16 Καὶ ἀπήλασεν αὐτοὺς ἀπὸ τοῦ
βήματος. 17 ἐπιλαβόμενοι δὲ
πάντες οἱ Ἕλληνες Σωσθένην
τὸν ἀρχισυνάγωγον ἔτυπτον ἔμ-
προσθεν τοῦ βήματος· καὶ οὐδὲν
τούτων τῷ Γαλλίωνι ἔμελεν.
18 Ὁ ΔΕ Παῦλος ἔτι προσ-
μείνας ἡμέρας ἱκανὰς, τοῖς ἀδελφοῖς ἀποταξάμενος, ἐξέπλει εἰς
τὴν Συρίαν, καὶ σὺν αὐτῷ Πρίσκιλλα καὶ Ἀκύλας, κειράμενος
τὴν κεφαλὴν ἐν Κεγχρεαῖς· εἶχε
γὰρ εὐχήν. 19 κατήντησε δὲ εἰς
Ἔφεσον, κἀκείνους κατέλιπεν
αὐτοῦ· αὐτὸς δὲ εἰσελθὼν εἰς τὴν
συναγωγὴν, διελέχθη τοῖς Ἰουδαίοις. 20 ἐρωτώντων δὲ αὐτῶν
ἐπὶ πλείονα χρόνον μεῖναι παρ'
αὐτοῖς, οὐκ ἐπένευσεν· 21 ἀλλ'
ἀπετάξατο αὐτοῖς, εἰπὼν, Δεῖ με
πάντως τὴν ἑορτὴν τὴν ἐρχομέ-
νην ποιῆσαι εἰς Ἱεροσόλυμα·
πάλιν δὲ ἀνακάμψω πρὸς ὑμᾶς,
τοῦ Θεοῦ θέλοντος. Καὶ ἀνήχθη

REVISED VERSION.

it be a question concerning
a doctrine, and names, and
your law, look you to it: for
I will not be a [n]judge of these
matters. And he [o]drove them 16
from the judgment-seat. Then 17
all the [p]Greeks took Sosthenes,
the ruler of the synagogue,
and beat him before the judgment-seat: and Gallio cared
for none of these things.
And Paul tarried yet many 18
[q]days, and, having bid adieu
to the brethren, sailed forth
into Syria, and with him
Priscilla and Aquila; having
shorn his head in Cenchrea:
for he had a vow. And 19
he came into Ephesus, and
left them there. But he himself, entering into the synagogue, reasoned with the
Jews, and though they re- 20
quested him to remain longer
time with them, he did not consent: but bade them farewell, 21
saying, I must by all means
keep the approaching feast at
Jerusalem: but I will return
to you again, if God will;
and he [s]sailed from Ephesus.

[n] *Ου βουλομαι, I will not be a judge. Ει δε ζητημα εστι περι λογου και ονοματων και νομου του καθ' υμας, οψεσθε αυτοι.* To translate this climax of Gallio in the spirit of it, without impinging upon the letter of it, is a desideratum. As we conceive of it, spirit and letter, we prefer the following, *If it be a question concerning a word, and of names, and of the law amongst you, look to it yourselves: for I will not be a judge of such matters.* It will not materially affect the spirit, or the import of it, should we adopt the marginal reading in the text, according to Ln., Tf. and Gb., and make it plural instead of singular, *If it be questions concerning a word* (or even of a *doctrine*). We prefer *word*, as more apposite to his conceptions and spirit on the occasion.

[o] *Απηλασεν,* from *απηλαω*, an *ἁπαξ λεγομενον* in this book. He drove them away, compelling their departure.

[p] *Οἱ Ἑλληνες,* omitted by Ln., Tf., Gb., a probable omission. This omission conceded, it would read, And they all beat Sosthenes the president, or ruler of the synagogue.

"Sosthenes was probably the successor of Crispus, v. 8, or, as Briscoe conjectures, may have belonged to another synagogue in the city. The Greeks, always ready to manifest their hatred to the Jews, singled him out as the object of their personal resentment." Hack.

Ουδεν τουτων, the dispute between the Jews and Gentiles.

[q] *Ετι—ἡμερας ἱκανας.* See note on *ἱκανος*, ch. 19:26.

[r] *Παρ' αυτοις,* omitted by Ln., Tf. Its presence or absence affects not the sense.

[s] *Ανηχθη—αναγω,* 1st aor. 3d pers., and he *sailed* from Ephesus. *Αναγω* is represented by *led up, brought, launched forth, loosed, offered,* and by *sailed,* in com. ver., three times. Its meaning is often made contingent upon its associations. Here, being connected with traveling on water, it is represented by *sailed.*

KING JAMES' VERSION.	GREEK TEXT.	REVISED VERSION.

KING JAMES' VERSION.

22 And when he had landed at Cesarea, and gone up and saluted the church, he went down to Antioch.

23 And after he had spent some time *there*, he departed and went over *all* the country of Galatia and Phrygia in order, strengthening all the disciples.

24 And a certain Jew, named Apollos, born at Alexandria, an eloquent man, *and* mighty in the scriptures, came to Ephesus.

25 This man was instructed in the way of the Lord: and being fervent in the spirit, he spake and taught diligently the things of the Lord, knowing only the baptism of John.

26 And he began to speak boldly in the synagogue: whom, when Aquila and Priscilla had heard, they took him unto *them*, and expounded unto him the way of God more perfectly.

27 And when he was disposed to pass into Achaia, the brethren wrote, exhorting the disciples to receive him: who, when he was come, helped them much which had believed through grace.

GREEK TEXT.

ἀπὸ τῆς Ἐφέσου· 22 καὶ κατελθὼν εἰς Καισάρειαν, ἀναβὰς καὶ ἀσπασάμενος τὴν ἐκκλησίαν, κατέβη εἰς Ἀντιόχειαν. 23 καὶ ποιήσας χρόνον τινὰ, ἐξῆλθε, διερχόμενος καθεξῆς τὴν Γαλατικὴν χώραν καὶ Φρυγίαν, ἐπιστηρίζων πάντας τοὺς μαθητάς. 24 Ἰουδαῖος δέ τις Ἀπολλὼς ὀνόματι, Ἀλεξανδρεὺς τῷ γένει, ἀνὴρ λόγιος, κατήντησεν εἰς Ἔφεσον, δυνατὸς ὢν ἐν ταῖς γραφαῖς. 25 οὗτος ἦν κατηχημένος τὴν ὁδὸν τοῦ κυρίου, καὶ ζέων τῷ πνεύματι, ἐλάλει καὶ ἐδίδασκεν ἀκριβῶς τὰ περὶ τοῦ κυρίου, ἐπιστάμενος μόνον τὸ βάπτισμα Ἰωάννου· 26 οὗτός τε ἤρξατο παρρησιάζεσθαι ἐν τῇ συναγωγῇ. ἀκούσαντες δὲ αὐτοῦ Ἀκύλας καὶ Πρίσκιλλα, προσελάβοντο αὐτὸν, καὶ ἀκριβέστερον αὐτῷ ἐξέθεντο τὴν τοῦ Θεοῦ ὁδόν. 27 βουλομένου δὲ αὐτοῦ διελθεῖν εἰς τὴν Ἀχαΐαν, προτρεψάμενοι οἱ ἀδελφοὶ ἔγραψαν τοῖς μαθηταῖς ἀποδέξασθαι αὐτόν· ὃς παραγενόμενος συνεβάλετο πολὺ τοῖς πεπιστευκόσι

REVISED VERSION.

And after he had gone down 22 to Cesarea, and gone up and ᵗsaluted the congregation, he went down to Antioch.

And having spent some 23 time there, he departed, passing through all the country of Galatia and Phrygia in order, ᵘestablishing all the disciples.

And a certain Jew, named 24 Apollos, born at Alexandria, an ᵛeloquent man, and mighty in the Scriptures, came down to Ephesus. This man was 25 instructed in the way of the Lord, and being ʷfervent in spirit, he spoke and taught diligently the things concerning the Lord, though he knew only the immersion of John. And 26 he began to speak boldly in the synagogue: whom, when Aquila and Priscilla had heard, they took him to them, and expounded to him the way of God more ˣaccurately. And 27 when he was disposed to pass into Achaia, the brethren wrote, exhorting the disciples to receive him: who, when he had come, afforded much aid to them who had ʸbelieved through the gift

---

ᵗ Ἀσπασαμενος. Ἀσπαζομαι, in its more than fifty occurrences in N. T., is represented by *salute, greet, embrace*, on meeting and parting with brethren, indicative of the highest natural and Christian affection. The whole εκκλησια was, in this case, saluted with a Christian adieu.

ᵘ Ἐπιστηριζων, found only in this book, and only four times, is three times represented by *confirming*, and once by *strengthening*, associated always with the church, or disciples.

ᵛ Ἀνηρ λογιος. This adjective is found only in this place in the Christian Scriptures, literally a *verbose* man, a man of eloquence. In its highest acceptation of eloquence it was applicable to Apollos His association with Paul was intimate. Paul *planted* the Church in Corinth, and Apollos *watered* it. His eloquence was based upon his power in

using the Christian gospel and the Jewish prophets, so far as Paul distinguishes it.

ʷ "Instructed in the doctrine of the Lord, and being *fervent in spirit*, he spoke and taught exactly the things of the Lord," Boothr. Bible intelligence, fervor in spirit, and his knowledge of John's mission and baptism were the constituents of his eloquence, sustained by a candid and inquisitive temper. At this time he only knew the baptism of John.

ˣ Ἀκυλας και Πρισκιλλα—εξεθεντο την του Θεου ὁδον, "expounded to him more perfectly the way of God," Penn; "expounded accurately the passages concerning the Lord," Thomp.; "laid before him the way of God more exactly," Wakef.; "fully showed him the way of the Lord," Murd. Παρρησιαζεσθαι, "to speak boldly," Hack.

ʸ Συνεβαλετο κ. τ. λ., "contributed much to those who

KING JAMES' VERSION.	GREEK TEXT.	REVISED VERSION.
28 For he mightily convinced the Jews, *and that* publicly, shewing by the scriptures, that Jesus was Christ.	διὰ τῆς χάριτος· ²⁸ εὐτόνως γὰρ τοῖς Ἰουδαίοις διακατηλέγχετο δημοσίᾳ, ἐπιδεικνὺς διὰ τῶν γραφῶν, εἶναι τὸν Χριστὸν Ἰησοῦν.	which he had; for he powerfully and thoroughly in public convinced the Jews, clearly showing by the Scriptures, that Jesus was the Christ. 28

CHAP. XIX.

AND it came to pass, that while Apollos was at Corinth, Paul having passed through the upper coasts, came to Ephesus; and finding certain disciples,	ἘΓΕΝΕΤΟ δὲ ἐν τῷ τὸν Ἀπολλὼ εἶναι ἐν Κορίνθῳ, Παῦλον διελθόντα τὰ ἀνωτερικὰ μέρη, ἐλθεῖν εἰς Ἔφεσον· καὶ εὑρών τινας μαθητὰς,	AND while ᶻApollos was at Corinth, Paul having passed through the upper parts, came into Ephesus; and finding certain disciples there, he 2
2 He said unto them, Have ye received the Holy Ghost since ye believed? And they said unto him, We have not so much as heard whether there be any Holy Ghost.	² εἶπε πρὸς αὐτοὺς, Εἰ Πνεῦμα Ἅγιον ἐλάβετε πιστεύσαντες; Οἱ δὲ εἶπον πρὸς αὐτὸν, Ἀλλ᾽ οὐδὲ εἰ Πνεῦμα Ἅγιόν ἐστιν, ἠκούσαμεν.	said to them, Did you on believing receive the Holy ᵃSpirit? And they said to him, we have not, indeed, heard, that there is a Holy Spirit. And he said to them, 3
3 And he said unto them, Unto what then were ye baptized? And they said, Unto John's baptism.	³ Εἶπέ τε πρὸς αὐτοὺς, Εἰς τί οὖν ἐβαπτίσθητε; Οἱ δὲ εἶπον, Εἰς τὸ Ἰωάννου βάπτισμα.	ᵇInto what then were you immersed? And they said, Into John's immersion. Then said 4
4 Then said Paul, John verily baptized with the baptism of repentance, saying unto the people, that they should believe on him which should come after him, that is, on Christ Jesus.	⁴ Εἶπε δὲ Παῦλος, Ἰωάννης μὲν ἐβάπτισε βάπτισμα μετανοίας, τῷ λαῷ λέγων, εἰς τὸν ἐρχόμενον μετ᾽ αὐτὸν ἵνα πιστεύσωσι, τουτέστιν εἰς τὸν Χριστὸν Ἰησοῦν.	Paul, John, indeed, ᶜadministered an immersion of reformation, saying to the people, that they should believe on him who would come after him, that is, on Jesus the Christ. Having ᵈheard this, 5
5 When they heard *this*, they	⁵ Ἀκούσαντες δὲ ἐβαπτίσθησαν	

---

have believed," Hack.; "he greatly assisted all them that believed," Murd.

Δια της χαριτος, "through grace," Hack., Wes., Penn; to say the least, is a very ambiguous rendering in this place. "By his gift," Thomp., Wakef. "Alii exponant, 'In dextritate quadam gratiosa, quæ et jucunditatem et utilitatem auditoribus,'" Crit. Sacra. The gift of Apollos seems to me the *grace* here indicated. All men who believe, believe through grace. That was not peculiar to those in Ephesus. But the *gift of Apollos* is that noted here. *Χαρις*, though generally rendered *grace*, in com. ver., cannot always be so rendered. It is, therefore, in the com. ver. represented by *favor, thank, thanks, pleasure, liberality, joy, thank-worthy, benefit, gift*.

That the Christ was Jesus, and that Jesus was the Christ, is an evangelical *metastasis*. The eloquent Apollos, well versed in the Jewish Scriptures, knew that if he proved that the promised Christ was Jesus, he proved that Jesus was the Christ.

ᶻ *Εγενετο δε εν τῳ*, "and it came to pass," or, *it happened*, are common versions of *εγενετο*, in such historic connections as this. The latter is equivalent to, *it chanced*, as in profane usage; not to be allowed here. "While Apollos was at Corinth" it occurred, or came to pass; but there is

nothing meant but this, "While Apollos was in Corinth," and, therefore, with Wakef., Murd., Wes., Thomp., Hack., we prefer this.

ᵃ *Ελαβετε πιστευσαντες; Did you on believing receive the Holy Spirit?* This indicates that John's baptism was not Christian baptism; for in the latter they could not have been baptized without hearing of it.

The context indicates that the anarthrous *Πνευμα Ἁγιον* here represents *the* Holy Spirit, not as yet fully revealed to them; for soon as immersed, and Paul had laid his hands on them, *the Holy Spirit* came upon them, and they were endowed with the Holy Spirit, in gifts of tongues and prophesy, v. 6.

ᵇ *Εις*, in its more than 1800 occurrences in N. T., is, in the com. ver., generally represented by *to, into, unto, for*, and very seldom by *in*, which, indeed, ought never to be done. The Greeks having *εν, in*, as well as *εις, into*, and *for*.

ᶜ *Χριστον* is here omitted by Gb., Ln., Tf., for which *Ιησουν* is substituted. *Τουτεστιν*, not *τουτον εστιν*, but *τουτο εστι = hoc est*—that is, on Jesus.

Εβαπτισε βαπτισμα. Literally, *immersed an immersion*.

ᵈ *Δε, and having heard*, or, *having heard*.

KING JAMES' VERSION.	GREEK TEXT.	REVISED VERSION.

KING JAMES' VERSION.

were baptized in the name of the Lord Jesus.

6 And when Paul had laid *his* hands upon them, the Holy Ghost came on them; and they spake with tongues, and prophesied.

7 And all the men were about twelve.

8 And he went into the synagogue, and spake boldly for the space of three months, disputing and persuading the things concerning the kingdom of God.

9 But when divers were hardened, and believed not, but spake evil of that way before the multitude, he departed from them, and separated the disciples, disputing daily in the school of one Tyrannus.

10 And this continued by the space of two years; so that all they which dwelt in Asia heard the word of the Lord Jesus, both Jews and Greeks.

11 And God wrought special miracles by the hands of Paul:

12 So that from his body were brought unto the sick handkerchiefs, or aprons, and the dis-

GREEK TEXT.

εἰς τὸ ὄνομα τοῦ Κυρίου Ἰησοῦ. ⁶ καὶ ἐπιθέντος αὐτοῖς τοῦ Παύλου τὰς χεῖρας, ἦλθε τὸ Πνεῦμα τὸ Ἅγιον ἐπ' αὐτούς, ἐλάλουν τε γλώσσαις καὶ προεφήτευον. ⁷ ἦσαν δὲ οἱ πάντες ἄνδρες ὡσεὶ δεκαδύο. ⁸ Εἰσελθὼν δὲ εἰς τὴν συναγωγὴν, ἐπαρρησιάζετο, ἐπὶ μῆνας τρεῖς διαλεγόμενος καὶ πείθων τὰ περὶ τῆς βασιλείας τοῦ Θεοῦ. ⁹ Ὡς δέ τινες ἐσκληρύνοντο καὶ ἠπείθουν, κακολογοῦντες τὴν ὁδὸν ἐνώπιον τοῦ πλήθους, ἀποστὰς ἀπ' αὐτῶν ἀφώρισε τοὺς μαθητάς, καθ' ἡμέραν διαλεγόμενος ἐν τῇ σχολῇ Τυράννου τινός. ¹⁰ Τοῦτο δὲ ἐγένετο ἐπὶ ἔτη δύο, ὥστε πάντας τοὺς κατοικοῦντας τὴν Ἀσίαν ἀκοῦσαι τὸν λόγον τοῦ Κυρίου Ἰησοῦ, Ἰουδαίους τε καὶ Ἕλληνας. ¹¹ Δυνάμεις τε οὐ τὰς τυχούσας ἐποίει ὁ Θεὸς διὰ τῶν χειρῶν Παύλου, ¹² ὥστε καὶ ἐπὶ τοὺς ἀσθενοῦντας ἐπιφέρεσθαι ἀπὸ τοῦ χρωτὸς αὐτοῦ σουδάρια

REVISED VERSION.

they were immersed into the name of the Lord Jesus. And 6 when Paul had laid his hands on them, the Holy Spirit came on them, and they spoke with tongues, and prophesied. Now all the men were about 7 twelve. And he went into 8 the synagogue, and spoke boldly for about three months, ᵉdiscussing and persuading as to things concerning the kingdom of God. But when some 9 were hardened, and believed not, but spoke evil of the ᶠway, in the presence of the multitude, he departed from them, and separated the disciples, discussing daily in the school of one Tyrannus And this 10 continued during two ᵍyears; so that all those who dwelt in Asia heard the word of the Lord Jesus, both Jews and Greeks. And God worked 11 ʰspecial miracles by the hands of Paul: So that from his body 12 were carried to the sick, handkerchiefs, or ⁱaprons, and the

---

Διαλεγομενος is found in "Acts" ten times, represented, com. ver., by *reasoning, disputing, preaching,* and *preaching unto.* Διαλεγομενος και πειθων, "disputing and persuading,", A. Clark, Wakef.; "*discoursing and persuading,*" Wes.; "*reasoning and recommending,*" Thomp.; "*seeking to persuade them,*" Hack. "The first accusative specifies the aim of the act, *in hoc loco, τα βασιλειας,*" Kuinœl. After much consideration, we would, in our age and country, prefer, *discussing and pleading the things pertaining to the kingdom of God.*

Πειθων αυτους τα περι τον Κυριον Ιησου Χριστον, "he delivered to them the doctrine of the kingdom," Kuin., in loco. "*Discussing and persuading,*" though literal, is not in our idiom. In a summary of three months' labor, allusion is had to the debates, discussions, and pleadings had upon the person, claims, character, and kingdom of Jesus, and to the earnestness of the preachers.

ᶠ Κακολογουντες, speaking evil of the way. Την οδον, the way, the faith, and the practice, "not concretely, *the* sect, or party," Hackett. Αφωρισε τους μαθητας, separated the disciples from the synagogue, εν τη σχολη—rather in the schoolhouse than in the school. Τυραννου τινος, some think, is justly reprobated as an interpolation. It is not, they say, in Luke's style, and is redundant. We are of a different opinion. This word τις is a peculiar favorite of Luke, and is found more frequently occurring in his writings in an indefinite sense, than in all the other evangelists, or in all the epistles of Paul.

ᵍ Επι ετη δυο, exclusive of the three months referred to v. 8; for τουτο "expressly opposes the preaching in the school of Tyrannus, to that in the synagogue," Hack. Ὥστε —Ασιαν. This is not the continent of Asia, but a Roman province of which the capital was Ephesus.

ʰ Ου τας τυχουσας well represented by extraordinary, or, special. All miracles are equally supernatural, but do not all appear alike supernatural. Of these there may be great, greater, and greatest.

ⁱ Σουδαρια η σιμικινθια. Common handkerchiefs and

KING JAMES' VERSION.	GREEK TEXT.	REVISED VERSION.
eases departed from them, and the evil spirits went out of them. 13 Then certain of the vagabond Jews, exorcists, took upon them to call over them which had evil spirits, the name of the Lord Jesus, saying, We adjure you by Jesus whom Paul preacheth. 14 And there were seven sons of *one* Sceva a Jew, *and* chief of the priests, which did so. 15 And the evil spirit answered and said, Jesus I know, and Paul I know; but who are ye?	ἢ σιμικίνθια, καὶ ἀπαλλάσσεσθαι ἀπ᾽ αὐτῶν τὰς νόσους, τά τε πνεύματα τὰ πονηρὰ ἐξέρχεσθαι ἀπ᾽ αὐτῶν. ¹³ Ἐπεχείρησαν δέ τινες ἀπὸ τῶν περιερχομένων Ἰουδαίων ἐξορκιστῶν ὀνομάζειν ἐπὶ τοὺς ἔχοντας τὰ πνεύματα τὰ πονηρὰ τὸ ὄνομα τοῦ Κυρίου Ἰησοῦ, λέγοντες, Ὁρκίζομεν ὑμᾶς τὸν Ἰησοῦν ὃν ὁ Παῦλος κηρύσσει. ¹⁴ Ἦσαν δέ τινες υἱοὶ Σκευᾶ Ἰουδαίου ἀρχιερέως ἑπτὰ οἱ τοῦτο ποιοῦντες. ¹⁵ ἀποκριθὲν δὲ τὸ πνεῦμα τὸ πονηρὸν εἶπε, Τὸν Ἰησοῦν γινώσκω, καὶ τὸν Παῦλον ἐπίσταμαι· ὑμεῖς δὲ τίνες ἐστέ; ¹⁶ Καὶ	diseases departed from them, and the evil spirits went out of them. Then certain of the 13 Jewish ʲexorcists, who went about from place to place, also attempted to pronounce the name of the Lord Jesus upon those who had evil spirits, saying, We adjure you by the Jesus whom Paul preaches. And there were 14 seven sons of one ᵏSceva, a Jew and chief of the priests, who did so. And the evil spirit 15 answered and said, Jesus I ˡacknowledge, and Paul I know: but who are you?

aprons, taken from persons at work, as these terms indicate, became the vehicles of omnipotence.

Tas νοσους, τα—πνευματα. Two kinds of diseases are here indicated, physical and spiritual, or those the fruits of material nature or of physical causes, and those of evil spirits. *Απ᾽ αντων* is omitted by Gb., Sch., Ln., Tf.

ʲ *Τινες απο των περιερχομενων, κ. τ. λ.,* com. ver. *Τινες και των.* Gb., Tf., Mey. give this more approved reading. *Και* joins *τινες* with Paul, in the act expressed in *ονομαζειν,* they also attempted to call. *Περιερχομενων,* not opprobriously *vagabond,* but *wandering* Jews, *εξορκιστης, exorcista.* "Qui tanquam Dei nomine adigit ad veri confessionem aut factum aliquod. Augustinus adjuratorem vertit." Crit. Sacra. "Expellers of demons," Dr. Whitby. Mr. Biscoe (at Boyle's Lecture, ch. 7, § 6, p. 281, et seq.) has produced many passages from Iren., Origen, Epiph., and Josephus, showing that several Jews at this time pretended to a power of casting out demons. See Dodd., in loco. "Such as used magical arts, adjuring demons, etc.," Boothr.

Ὁρκιζομεν is substituted by *ὁρκιζω,* on the authority of Gb., Sch., Ln., Tf., we adjure you, for, I adjure you. We must, in this case, prefer the Received Text for the amended, inasmuch as it conflicts with the antecedent and subsequent context, and with the judgment of the great majority of critics, ancient and modern. It is seldom we feel more assurance than in this case, in dissenting from these distinguished critics. The seven sons of Sceva, a Jew, we learn in the subsequent verse, were coöperants in this case; hence, and for other reasons, we prefer the received text to that of Gb., Sch., Ln., and Tf.

ᵏ *Σκευα,* Doric genitive, similar to *Βαρναβα,* ch. 11 : 30; *βορρα,* Luke 13 : 29; *Ιωνα,* John 1 : 43.

ˡ *Τον Ιησουν γινωσκω, και τον Παυλον επισταμαι.* This demon was a *critic,* and well versed in the import of Greek terms. "I *know* Jesus, and *have some acquaintance* with Paul," Murd.; "Jesus, indeed, I know, and Paul I know," Penn; "*Jesus I know to my cost,* and Paul I know as his servant," Dodd.; "Jesus I know, and I have some knowledge of Paul," Thomp.; "I acknowledge Jesus, and am acquainted with Paul," Adam Clark. "Jesus I know, i. e., his authority and power, *επισταμαι, I know fully;* stronger than the other verb, and applied to Paul in opposition to them," Hack.

We have fanciful critics, and those of more profound judgment. This appears to good advantage in the contrasts here given. We institute no invidious comparisons. We all look at objects from different standpoints. Where two inspired men use a word in different acceptations, it may be resolved by ascertaining their scope, design, or the special cases to which they refer. *Επισταμαι,* ab *επι* and *ισταμαι,* to stand *upon* a thing, whereas to *understand* is to stand *under* it, as *υποστασις, persona,* Heb. 1 : 3. Yet this *standing upon* a subject, or this *standing under* it, may in different attitudes indicate the same knowledge of it. In either case there must be a very particular and intimate acquaintance with it. I feel a distinction in these terms difficult to define exactly. I am disposed upon all my premises to acquiesce with Critica Sacra. The Latins borrowed their *nosco* and *cognosco* from *γινωσκο.* *Non nuda et simplex notitia, sed affectiva cum desiderio, approbatione et dilectione conjuncta.* 1 John 4 : 8; Matt. 7 : 23, and 25 : 12. *Not a naked and simple notion, but associated with affection, desire, and approbation, terminating in delight.* It is an Hebraism.

Το πνευμα το πονηρον. Emphatically, the wicked the

KING JAMES' VERSION.

16 And the man in whom the evil spirit was, leaped on them, and overcame them, and prevailed against them, so that they fled out of that house naked and wounded.

17 And this was known to all the Jews and Greeks also dwelling at Ephesus: and fear fell on them all, and the name of the Lord Jesus was magnified.

18 And many that believed came, and confessed, and shewed their deeds.

19 Many of them also which used curious arts, brought their books together, and burned them before all *men*; and they counted the price of them, and found *it* fifty thousand *pieces* of silver.

20 So mightily grew the word of God, and prevailed.

21 After these things were ended, Paul purposed in the spirit, when he had passed through Macedonia, and Achaia, to go to Jerusalem, saying, After I have been there. I must also see Rome.

22 So he sent into Macedonia

GREEK TEXT.

ἐφαλλόμενος ἐπ᾽ αὐτοὺς ὁ ἄνθρωπος ἐν ᾧ ἦν τὸ πνεῦμα τὸ πονηρὸν, καὶ κατακυριεύσας αὐτῶν, ἴσχυσε κατ᾽ αὐτῶν, ὥστε γυμνοὺς καὶ τετραυματισμένους ἐκφυγεῖν ἐκ τοῦ οἴκου ἐκείνου. 17 τοῦτο δὲ ἐγένετο γνωστὸν πᾶσιν Ἰουδαίοις τε καὶ Ἕλλησι τοῖς κατοικοῦσι τὴν Ἔφεσον, καὶ ἐπέπεσε φόβος ἐπὶ πάντας αὐτοὺς, καὶ ἐμεγαλύνετο τὸ ὄνομα τοῦ Κυρίου Ἰησοῦ. 18 Πολλοί τε τῶν πεπιστευκότων ἤρχοντο ἐξομολογούμενοι καὶ ἀναγγέλλοντες τὰς πράξεις αὐτῶν. 19 ἱκανοὶ δὲ τῶν τὰ περίεργα πραξάντων, συνενέγκαντες τὰς βίβλους κατέκαιον ἐνώπιον πάντων· καὶ συνεψήφισαν τὰς τιμὰς αὐτῶν, καὶ εὗρον ἀργυρίου μυριάδας πέντε. 20 οὕτω κατὰ κράτος ὁ λόγος τοῦ κυρίου ηὔξανε καὶ ἴσχυεν. 21 ΩΣ δὲ ἐπληρώθη ταῦτα, ἔθετο ὁ Παῦλος ἐν τῷ πνεύματι, διελθὼν τὴν Μακεδονίαν καὶ Ἀχαΐαν πορεύεσθαι εἰς Ἱερουσαλὴμ, εἰπὼν, Ὅτι μετὰ τὸ γενέσθαι με ἐκεῖ, δεῖ με καὶ Ῥώμην ἰδεῖν. 22 Ἀποστείλας δὲ εἰς τὴν

REVISED VERSION.

And the man in whom the 16 evil spirit was, leaped on ᵐthem, and overcame them, and prevailed against them; so that they fled out of that house naked and wounded. And this was known to all 17 the Jews and Greeks dwelling at ⁿEphesus; and fear fell on them all, and the name of the Lord Jesus was magnified. And many who believed 18 came, and ᵒconfessed, and declared their deeds. Many of 19 them also, who practiced magic arts, brought together their books, and burnt them in the presence of all, and they counted the price of them, and found it fifty thousand pieces of silver. So 20 powerfully grew the word of God, and ᵖprevailed.

When these things were 21 ended, Paul firmly purposed in ᵠspirit, when he had passed through Macedonia, and Achaia, to go to Jerusalem, saying, after I have been there, I must also see Rome. So he sent into Macedonia 22

---

spirit, the evil spirit. This is as emphatic as τὸ Πνεῦμα τὸ Ἅγιον, the Spirit the Holy, the Holy Spirit. This emphatic form is again presented τὸ πνεῦμα τὸ πονηρὸν, v. 16. The analogy is remarkably striking. The master spirit of all evil, and the master spirit of all goodness, while often anarthrous, are, on prominent occasions, presented before us as equally conspicuous, the one as *the fountain* of all evil, the other as *the fountain* of all good.

ᵐ Ἐφαλλόμενος, leaping upon them; κατακυριευσας, having overpowered them, Wakef., Murd. Αὐτῶν, in this place, is substituted by αμφοτερον, Ln., Tf., regarded by Gb. as of much authority, and marked as probable.

ⁿ Τοῖς κατοικουσι την Εφεσον, to those inhabiting or dwelling in Ephesus.

ᵒ Ἐξομολογουμενοι, openly confessed; αναγγελλοντες τας

πραξεις, and reported their practices, superstitious practices. Ols., Mey., De Wette. Sins in general, Kuin., Hack.

ᵖ Ηυξανε και ισχυεν = not only *extended*, but *augmented* in its power.

ᵠ Ἐθετο—εν τω πνευματι, strongly *purposed*; with us, *decided*. Paul and his spirit are sometimes distinguished as God and his spirit are spoken of in Holy Writ. He. Paul, purposed in his mind—not in his soul, but in his *spirit*—to visit Rome. Δει με και Ῥωμην ιδειν, it behooves me to see Rome, after I have visited Jerusalem; not to fulfill any decree, "or revealed purpose of God." Hack.

The Apostle Paul never intended to say, that he, or any one else, *must* do anything merely to fulfill a Divine purpose, unless a Divine oracle had enjoined it. He certainly believed that God had purposes to accomplish by him; but until revealed to him, he felt no obligation to consummate them.

KING JAMES' VERSION.	GREEK TEXT.	REVISED VERSION.
two of them that ministered unto him, Timotheus and Erastus; *but* he himself stayed in Asia for a season.	Μακεδονίαν δύο τῶν διακονούντων αὐτῷ, Τιμόθεον καὶ Ἔραστον, αὐτὸς ἐπέσχε χρόνον εἰς τὴν Ἀσίαν.	two of those who ministered to him, Timothy and Erastus: but he himself stayed in Asia for a season. And the same 23
23 And the same time there arose no small stir about that way.	²³ Ἐγένετο δὲ κατὰ τὸν καιρὸν ἐκεῖνον τάραχος οὐκ ὀλίγος περὶ τῆς ὁδοῦ. ²⁴ Δη	time there arose no small stir about the ʳway. For a certain 24
24 For a certain *man* named Demetrius, a silver-smith, which made silver shrines for Diana, brought no small gain unto the craftsmen;	μήτριος γάρ τις ὀνόματι, ἀργυροκόπος, ποιῶν ναοὺς ἀργυροῦς Ἀρτέμιδος, παρείχετο τοῖς τεχνίταις ἐργασίαν οὐκ ὀλίγην·	man, named Demetrius, a silver-smith, who made silver shrines for ˢArtemis, brought no small gain to the artisans;
25 Whom he called together with the workmen of like occupation, and said, Sirs, ye know that by this craft we have our wealth:	²⁵ οὓς συναθροίσας, καὶ τοὺς περὶ τὰ τοιαῦτα ἐργάτας, εἶπεν, Ἄνδρες, ἐπίστασθε ὅτι ἐκ ταύτης τῆς ἐργασίας ἡ εὐπορία ἡμῶν ἐστι·	whom he called together, with 25 the workmen of like occupation, and said, Sirs, you know well, that by this employment we have our ᵗprosperity.
26 Moreover, ye see and hear, that not alone at Ephesus, but almost throughout all Asia, this Paul hath persuaded and turned away much people, saying, that they be no gods which are made with hands.	²⁶ καὶ θεωρεῖτε καὶ ἀκούετε ὅτι οὐ μόνον Ἐφέσου, ἀλλὰ σχεδὸν πάσης τῆς Ἀσίας ὁ Παῦλος οὗτος πείσας μετέστησεν ἱκανὸν ὄχλον, λέγων ὅτι οὐκ εἰσὶ θεοὶ οἱ διὰ χειρῶν γινόμενοι.	Moreover, you see and ᵘhear, 26 that not only at Ephesus, but almost throughout Asia, this Paul has persuaded and turned aside many people, saying, that they are no gods which are made with hands; so that 27
27 So that not only this our craft is in danger to be set at nought; but also that the temple of the great goddess Diana should be despised, and her magnificence should be destroyed,	²⁷ οὐ μόνον δὲ τοῦτο κινδυνεύει ἡμῖν τὸ μέρος εἰς ἀπελεγμὸν ἐλθεῖν, ἀλλὰ καὶ τὸ τῆς μεγάλης θεᾶς Ἀρτέμιδος ἱερὸν εἰς οὐδὲν λογισθῆναι, μέλλειν δὲ καὶ καθαιρεῖσθαι τὴν μεγαλειότητα αὐ	not only this our ᵛtrade is in danger of coming into contempt; but also that the temple of the great goddess Artemis will be despised, and her magnificence destroyed,

---

ʳ Περι της οδου—κατα τον καιρον εκεινον. About the time of accomplishing his purpose of visiting Rome, there arose some opposition, some new difficulties concerning *the way*; not the way to Rome, nor the journey thither; but *the way*, "every where then spoken against."

Ὁδος frequently occurs in this book, "the *way* of God;" and, in other books of the Holy Scriptures, such as "the *way* of Cain," "the *way* of Balaam." Paul, when persecuting Christ, demanded letters of authority, against any of "*this way*" that he might find.

ˢ Artemis, from Ἀρτεμης, integer. ob virginitatis illibatæ laudem—Diana.

Ἀρτεμις, com. ver., Diana, occurs five times in this chapter. Nowhere else found in N. Test. We know no good reason for changing the name of this goddess. These silver shrines were mere images of the temple at Ephesus, of which the manufacture in that city was very great.

ᵗ Οὓς συναθροισας, και τους περι τα τοιαυτα εργατας κ. τ. λ. Artizans, so-called, and laborers in attendance, mechanics and common hands. His argument was, ἡ ευπορια ἡμων, our prosperity arises from this employment.

ᵘ Θεωρειτε και ακουετε, a true *argumentum ad hominem:* you see and know, therefore. Some would render it, *see* and *know;* but this assumes their ignorance of their own interests, which would be inapposite to the occasion.

Ἱκανος was a favorite with Luke. He employs it twenty-nine times in his book of Acts and Gospel, while all the other writers of the N. Test. only employ it twelve times. It is necessarily a vague term, having not less than *fourteen* representatives; consequently much depends on its connections. It is one of a small class of words that is so sympathetic as to assume the gesture of every associate. Thus it is, *worthy, great, large, many, enough, long, alike, security, good while, while, sore, meet, able, sufficient.* It is like the Scotch *unco.*

ᵛ Ου μονον δε τουτο κινδυνευει ἡμιν το μερος, "*this business,*" as some interpret it; others, "*this part* of our religion." We presume, their business was more in their hearts than their religion.

KING JAMES' VERSION.

whom all Asia, and the world worshippeth.

28 And when they heard *these sayings*, they were full of wrath, and cried out, saying, Great *is* Diana of the Ephesians.

29 And the whole city was filled with confusion: and having caught Gaius and Aristarchus, men of Macedonia, Paul's companions in travel, they rushed with one accord into the theatre.

30 And when Paul would have entered in unto the people, the disciples suffered him not.

31 And certain of the chief of Asia, which were his friends, sent unto him desiring *him* that he would not adventure himself into the theatre.

32 Some therefore cried one thing, and some another: for the assembly was confused, and the more part knew not wherefore they were come together.

33 And they drew Alexander out of the multitude, the Jews putting him forward. And Alex-

GREEK TEXT.

τῆς, ἣν ὅλη ἡ Ἀσία καὶ ἡ οἰκουμένη σέβεται. 28 Ἀκούσαντες δὲ καὶ γενόμενοι πλήρεις θυμοῦ, ἔκραζον λέγοντες, Μεγάλη ἡ Ἄρτεμις Ἐφεσίων. 29 Καὶ ἐπλήσθη ἡ πόλις ὅλη συγχύσεως· ὥρμησάν τε ὁμοθυμαδὸν εἰς τὸ θέατρον, συναρπάσαντες Γάϊον καὶ Ἀρίσταρχον Μακεδόνας, συνεκδήμους τοῦ Παύλου. 30 τοῦ δὲ Παύλου βουλομένου εἰσελθεῖν εἰς τὸν δῆμον, οὐκ εἴων αὐτὸν οἱ μαθηταί. 31 τινὲς δὲ καὶ τῶν Ἀσιαρχῶν ὄντες αὐτῷ φίλοι, πέμψαντες πρὸς αὐτὸν, παρεκάλουν μὴ δοῦναι ἑαυτὸν εἰς τὸ θέατρον. 32 ἄλλοι μὲν οὖν ἄλλο τι ἔκραζον· ἦν γὰρ ἡ ἐκκλησία συγκεχυμένη, καὶ οἱ πλείους οὐκ ᾔδεισαν, τίνος ἕνεκεν συνεληλύθεισαν. 33 ἐκ δὲ τοῦ ὄχλου προεβίβασαν Ἀλέξανδρον, προβαλόντων αὐτὸν τῶν Ἰουδαίων· ὁ δὲ Ἀλέξανδρος

REVISED VERSION.

whom all Asia and the world worship.

And when they heard this, 28 they were full of wrath, and cried out, saying, Great is Artemis of the Ephesians. And the whole [w]city was filled 29 with tumult, and having caught Gaius and Aristarchus, Macedonians, Paul's companions in travel, they rushed with one accord into the theatre. And when Paul would 30 have gone in to the people, the disciples suffered him not. And some of the chief men of 31 Asia, who were his friends, sent to him, entreating him not to venture himself into the theatre. Some, therefore, 32 cried one thing, and some another: for the [x]assembly was confused, and the greater part knew not wherefore they were come together. And they 33 drew Alexander out of the crowd, the Jews urging him [y]forward. And Alexander, wav-

---

[w] Ἡ πόλις ὅλη. Ὅλη is rejected by Ln., Tf., omitted on the authority of AB 13, 40, and Coptic, Arm. Ὁμοθυμαδον, *concorditer—uno animo*, with one consent.

[x] Ἦν γαρ ἡ εκκλησια συγκεχυμενη. Εκκλησια here represents a *mob*, a tumultuous assembly, concourse of people. In N. Test. it is appropriated to a Christian congregation, or the whole Christian community. Literally and appropriately, in N. T. currency, it is represented by the word *congregation*, or *assembly*, a meeting of a people, always communicating the idea of *calling out*, or of *their being called out* of the world. The root, εκκαλεω, *evoco, I call out*, is not found in the Christian Scriptures. Εκκλησια, in its one hundred and fourteen occurrences, is only three times translated *assembly*. In every other case it is *misrepresented* by the word *church*, an abbreviation of κυριον οικος, contracted into *kuriok*, or *kyrke*. It answers to, or it responds to the Hebrew *kahal et edah*, from *yaad*, that is, *to assemble*, or, to congregate. Critica Sacra. It is added by the same high authority, εκκλησια, *proprie cœtum aliquem, a superiori aliquo convocatum in finem polliticum vel ecclesiasticum denotat*. The same high authority says, "The English word *church* is ambiguously taken by the people for *the place of the assembly, and for the assembly itself*." It is as lawful for us to call it *congregation*, as for the Papists to call it *assembly*. See ch. 7 : 38; 1 Cor. 1 : 2, ἡγιασμενοις εν Χριστω Ιησου, κλητοις αγιοις, συν πασι τοις επικαλουμενοις το ονομα του Κυριου ἡμων Ιησου Χριστου, εν παντι τοπω αυτων τε και ἡμων, "to the sanctified in Christ Jesus, called saints, with all that call upon the name of our Lord Jesus Christ in every place, both their Lord and ours." Such is Paul's exegetical development of a particular church of Christ, and of the church universal as he understood the genius, relation, and character of that institution.

The definition of a thing is the true philosophy of its name. So God himself gave names to his own operations in the drama of creation. And so taught he his son Adam. Hence whatever significant names Adam gave were appropriate names; and God himself approved them giving to him a diploma, so that whatsoever name he gave to any living creature that became the name thereof."

[y] Προεβιβασαν, "*prodire, faciebant*," Kuin.; "*they thrust forward*," Wes., Dodd.; "*they dragged him*," Penn; "*putting him forward*," Wakef.; "*urged forward*," Hack. In this verse we have προβαλλω, and προβιβαζω, each found only *twice* in the Christian Scriptures, and used by Luke, the

KING JAMES' VERSION.	GREEK TEXT.	REVISED VERSION.

ander beckoned with the hand, and would have made his defence unto the people.

34 But when they knew that he was a Jew, all with one voice about the space of two hours cried out, Great *is* Diana of the Ephesians.

35 And when the town-clerk had appeased the people, he said *Ye* men of Ephesus, what man is there that knoweth not how that the city of the Ephesians is a worshipper of the great goddess Diana, and of the *image* which fell down from Jupiter?

36 Seeing then that these things cannot be spoken against, ye ought to be quiet, and to do nothing rashly.

37 For ye have brought hither these men, which are neither robbers of churches, nor yet blasphemers of your goddess.

38 Wherefore, if Demetrius, and the craftsmen which are with him, have a matter against any man, the law is open, and there are deputies: let them implead one another.

39 But if ye inquire any thing concerning other matters, it shall be determined in a lawful assembly.

κατασείσας τὴν χεῖρα, ἤθελεν ἀπολογεῖσθαι τῷ δήμῳ. 34 ἐπιγνόντων δὲ ὅτι Ἰουδαῖός ἐστι, φωνὴ ἐγένετο μία ἐκ πάντων ὡς ἐπὶ ὥρας δύο κραζόντων, Μεγάλη ἡ Ἄρτεμις Ἐφεσίων. 35 Καταστείλας δὲ ὁ γραμματεὺς τὸν ὄχλον, φησὶν, Ἄνδρες Ἐφέσιοι, τίς γάρ ἐστιν ἄνθρωπος ὃς οὐ γινώσκει τὴν Ἐφεσίων πόλιν νεωκόρον οὖσαν τῆς μεγάλης θεᾶς Ἀρτέμιδος καὶ τοῦ Διοπετοῦς; 36 ἀναντιρρήτων οὖν ὄντων τούτων, δέον ἐστὶν ὑμᾶς κατεσταλμένους ὑπάρχειν, καὶ μηδὲν προπετὲς πράττειν. 37 ἠγάγετε γὰρ τοὺς ἄνδρας τούτους, οὔτε ἱεροσύλους οὔτε βλασφημοῦντας τὴν θεὰν ὑμῶν. 38 εἰ μὲν οὖν Δημήτριος καὶ οἱ σὺν αὐτῷ τεχνῖται πρός τινα λόγον ἔχουσιν, ἀγοραῖοι ἄγονται, καὶ ἀνθύπατοί εἰσιν· ἐγκαλείτωσαν ἀλλήλοις. 39 εἰ δέ τι περὶ ἑτέρων ἐπιζητεῖτε, ἐν τῇ ἐννόμῳ ἐκκλησίᾳ ἐπιλυθήσεται. 40 καὶ

ing the hand, would have made his defense to the people. But when they knew 34 that he was a Jew, all with one voice, about the space of two hours, cried out, Great is Artemis of the Ephesians.

And when the [z]city-clerk 35 had appeased the people, he says, Ephesians, what man is there who knows not that the city of the Ephesians is a worshipper of the great Artemis, and of the image which fell down from Jupiter? Seeing then that these things 36 cannot be spoken against, you ought to be quiet, and to do nothing rashly. For you have 37 brought hither these men, who are neither robbers of temples, nor yet revilers of your [a]goddess. Therefore, if 38 Demetrius, and the artisans that are with him, have a complaint against any man, the law is [b]open, and there are proconsuls: let them accuse one another. But if you in- 39 quire any thing concerning other matters, it shall be determined in the lawful [c]assem-

---

former exclusively, and the latter once by Matt. 14 : 8. "Then was Alexander advanced out of the multitude, the Jews having put him forward," Boothr.; "but when they had thrust Alexander out of the crowd, the Jews pushing him forward, and he, waving his hand, wished to make a defense to the people," Thomp.; "Waved his hand, and wished to make a defense," Murd, Penn.

[z] Ὁ γραμματευς, "scriba in multis Asiæ civitatibus magistratus erat et personam primariam in senatu agebat, leges in tabulas referebat earumque conservator et custos erat prælegebat etiam, quæ in concione populi prælegenda erant, ut adeo commode voc. γραμματευς etiam reddi possit *prefectus* tabularii, archivarius, *Canzler*, cf. de scribis veterum, eorumque diversis ordinibus Trotzius ad calcem Hermani Hugonis libri de prima scribendi origine, p. 436, seq." Kuinœl, in loco, p. 298, Tom. 3.

"In Asia Minor, as coins and inscriptions show, such was the title of the heads or chiefs of the municipal government;

their duties being to register the public acts and laws, and to keep the records," Winer, Hack.

Νεωκορον, literally *temple-sweeper*, was an honorary title granted to certain Asiatic cities, because of their care and expense bestowed on the temple and worship of their elect deities. Kuinœl, 311. 4. There was a similar tradition in regard to a statue of Artemis in Tauris (Eurip., Iph., T. 977), and also one of Pallas at Athens (Pausan., I., 26. 6). Hack., p. 276.

[a] Ἱεροσυλους οντε βλασφημουντας την θεαν υμων. Ὑμων rejected by Gb., Sch., Ln., Tf., as is "θεας" in v. 35. Τουτους, Gaius and Aristarchus.

[b] Αγοραιοι = ἡμεραι αγονται = αγοραιοι, courts are held, = the law is open, ch. 16 : 19; 17 : 5. Και ανθυπατοι εισι, the class is referred to; there being but one in every province.

[c] Εν τη εννομω εκκλησια. This indicates that their *meeting* or assemblage was an illegal one. There may be a syna-

KING JAMES' VERSION.	GREEK TEXT.	REVISED VERSION.
40 For we are in danger to be called in question for this day's uproar, there being no cause whereby we may give an account of this concourse.	γὰρ κινδυνεύομεν ἐγκαλεῖσθαι στάσεως περὶ τῆς σήμερον, μηδενὸς αἰτίου ὑπάρχοντος περὶ οὗ δυνησόμεθα ἀποδοῦναι λόγον τῆς συστροφῆς ταύτης. ⁴¹ Καὶ ταῦτα εἰπὼν, ἀπέλυσε τὴν ἐκκλησίαν.	bly. For we are in danger 40 of being called in question for this day's ᵈuproar, there being no cause in reference to which we shall be able to give an account of this concourse. And when he had thus spoken, 41 he dismissed the assembly.
41 And when he had thus spoken, he dismissed the assembly.		
CHAP. XX.	CHAP. XX.	CHAP. XX.
AND after the uproar was ceased, Paul called unto *him* the disciples, and embraced *them*, and departed for to go into Macedonia.	ΜΕΤΑ δὲ τὸ παύσασθαι τὸν θόρυβον, προσκαλεσάμενος ὁ Παῦλος τοὺς μαθητὰς, καὶ ἀσπασάμενος, ἐξῆλθε πορευθῆναι εἰς τὴν Μακεδονίαν. ² διελθὼν δὲ τὰ μέρη ἐκεῖνα, καὶ παρακαλέσας αὐτοὺς λόγῳ πολλῷ, ἦλθεν εἰς τὴν Ἑλλάδα· ³ ποιήσας τε μῆνας τρεῖς, γενομένης αὐτῷ ἐπιβουλῆς ὑπὸ τῶν Ἰουδαίων μέλλοντι ἀνάγεσθαι εἰς τὴν Συρίαν, ἐγένετο γνώμη τοῦ ὑποστρέφειν διὰ Μακεδονίας. ⁴ συνείπετο δὲ αὐτῷ ἄχρι τῆς Ἀσίας Σώπατρος Βεροιαῖος· Θεσσαλονικέων δὲ, Ἀρίσταρχος καὶ Σεκοῦνδος, καὶ Γάϊος Δερβαῖος καὶ Τιμόθεος· Ἀσιανοὶ δὲ, Τυχικὸς καὶ Τρόφιμος. ⁵ οὗτοι προελθόντες ἔμενον ἡμᾶς ἐν Τρωάδι· ⁶ ἡμεῖς δὲ ἐξεπλεύσαμεν μετὰ τὰς ἡμέρας	AND after the ᵉdisturbance 1 had ceased, Paul called to him the disciples, and embracing them, departed to go into Macedonia. And when 2 he had gone over those parts, and had given them much ᶠexhortation, he came into Greece, and having spent three 3 months there, he resolved to return through Macedonia, the Jews having laid ᵍwait for him, as he was about to embark for Syria. And there 4 ʰaccompanied him to Asia, Sopater of Berea, and of the Thessalonians, Aristarchus and Secundus; and Gaius of Derbe, and Timothy; and of Asia, Tychicus and Trophimus. And these going before, 5 tarried for us at Troas. And 6 we sailed away from Philippi,
2 And when he had gone over those parts, and had given them much exhortation, he came into Greece,		
3 And *there* abode three months. And when the Jews laid wait for him, as he was about to sail into Syria, he purposed to return through Macedonia.		
4 And there accompanied him into Asia, Sopater of Berea; and of the Thessalonians, Aristarchus and Secundus; and Gaius of Derbe, and Timotheus; and of Asia, Tychicus and Trophimus.		
5 These going before, tarried for us at Troas.		
6 And we sailed away from		

gogue of Satan, as well as a synagogue of Jews—so of the church—a church of Christ, and a church of Antichrist.

ᵈ Ἐγκαλεισθαι στασεως περι, to be summoned, called to account, concerning this *riot*. So would we designate such an assemblage. *Riot* "at common law is a tumultuous disturbance of the peace by three or more persons." Webster.

ᵉ Τον θορυβον, ex θροος et βοη, clamor, also *pugna, battle, contention*. In its whole currency in N. T., com. ver., it is represented by *tumult, uproar*. The verb θορυβεομαι is also found *twice* in this book, ch. 17 : 5, *set on an uproar*. With us the word *disturbance*, being *generic*, rather than *specific*, is, we think, preferable in this place.

Εξηλθε πορευθηναι. This is quite pleonastic. *Departed to go, departed for*, is our present formula. We presume not to improve Luke's style by our provincialisms.

ᶠ Παρακαλεσας αυτους λογῳ πολλῳ. This παρακαλεω is one of Luke and Paul's favorites. They almost monopolize its use in the Christian Scriptures. Of more than *one hundred* occurrences in N. T., they use it over *eighty* times. To *exhort*, to *comfort*, to *beseech*, are its most popular representatives.

ᵍ Επιβουλης. This is exclusively one of Luke's words, and found only in this single book of Acts. *Laying*, or *lying in wait*, are its only representatives, com. ver. Insidiæ, *snares, stratagems*, would be sometimes more definite. It is of επι and βουλη, because those that *lie in wait* for one another *take counsel* together. Crit. Sacra.

ʰ Συνειπετο δε αυτῳ. Συνεπομαι is an ἅπαξ λεγομενον, found only in this place in the N. T.—*comitor*, to accompany. We have επω and επομαι, *operor* and *sequor*, as well as επω, *dico*, now out of use in the present tense. Instead of an augment, ι is inserted after ε through all modes.

Philippi, after the days of unleavened bread, and came unto them to Troas in five days; where we abode seven days.

7 And upon the first *day* of the week, when the disciples came together to break bread, Paul preached unto them, (ready to depart on the morrow) and

τῶν ἀζύμων ἀπὸ Φιλίππων, καὶ ἤλθομεν πρὸς αὐτοὺς εἰς τὴν Τρωάδα ἄχρις ἡμερῶν πέντε, οὗ διετρίψαμεν ἡμέρας ἑπτά. 7 Ἐν δὲ τῇ μιᾷ τῶν σαββάτων, συνηγμένων τῶν μαθητῶν τοῦ κλάσαι ἄρτον, ὁ Παῦλος διελέγετο αὐτοῖς, μέλλων ἐξιέναι τῇ ἐπαύ-

after the days of unleavened bread, and came to them to Troas, in five days, where we abode seven days.

And on the first day of the ¹week, when we came together for the breaking a ¹loaf, Paul discoursed with them, ready to depart on

---

¹ "And on the first day of the week, we being assembled to break bread;" not τῶν μαθητῶν, but ἡμῶν, as in the com. ver. Hackett. This is based on the authority of Griesbach, Scholz, Lachmann, and Tischendorf, followed by Wesley, who has it, "And on the first day of the week, when we were met together, to break bread.'

"Upon the first day of the week which was called the Lord's day, the Christian sabbath, to break bread." "The Eucharist as the Syriac has it, intimating by this, that they were accustomed to receive the holy sacrament on each Lord's day." Adam Clark.

"And on the first day of the week, when we assembled to break the Eucharist," Murd. Syr. ver. "And on the first day of the week, when the disciples met together to break bread, to celebrate the Eucharist," Doddridge. He adds, "it is well-known that the primitive Christians administered the Eucharist every Lord's day."

Ἐν δε τῇ μιᾷ των σαββάτων. The force, or import, of the definitive article is forcibly indicated here. Before Θεος, in the Christian Scriptures, it uniformly represents *the* God of all *the* Israel of God, whether in blood, Jew or Gentile. It distinguishes Jesus, God, and Christ always as the subject of a proposition from every other God, Jesus, or Christ. There were many Gods, Jesuses, and Christs in the days of the Apostles; but they were not honored by any inspired man with the article ὁ. See Acts 7 : 45 ; Heb. 4 : 8 ; Col. 4 : 11, etc.

The article before μια ἡμερα, or before μια, without ἡμερα, in the New Test., is always indicative of one and the same day. It therefore indicates, in this connection, *the day* of the meetings of the first Christians, to remember and honor the day of the Lord's resurrection. On this day the Holy Spirit descended, in Jerusalem, on the first Christian church in full assembly met. For των μαθητων του, ἡμων is substituted by Gb., Sch., Ln., Tf. We met—we met "to break bread," or to *break a loaf.*

Κλασις, *fractio,* Luke 24 : 35 ; Acts 2 : 42, is its whole currency in the N. Test. The meeting *of,* or *on,* the first day of the week, alluded to here, and in the Epistle of Paul to the Corinthians, was for this purpose; hence their contributions were, on this day, to be made by special requirement from Paul. 1 Cor. 16 : 2. This also indicates Christian offerings to the Lord, in behalf of his cause and people. There is no specific reason assigned for this assembling, but *communion in worship,* and *communion in contributing* to the Lord's cause and people. Paul to the Corinthians commands the latter, and the practice of the Christian church at Troas is commendatory of the former.

If Bagster's Greek text must in all cases be preferred, we should then read it, "And on the first day of the week, the disciples having assembled to break a loaf."

And on the first of the week, εν δε τη μια των σαββατων.

Εις is here tantamount to πρωτος. See Matt. 28 : 1, οψε δε σαββατων, *the end of the sabbath. Οψε, vespera, serum diei*—late of the day. The period of the day sunset and midnight. It ceased at midnight; only used by Matthew and Mark. The οψε, or end of the sabbath, was the επιφωσκουση —the dawning—εις μιαν σαββατων, of the first of the week. In the instance before us, ἡμερα is understood as indicated by μια—the *day* of the week, and not the *time* of the day.

The first day of the week and the first day of creation are solemnly associated in the memory of the Christian. *Light,* in the drama of creation, was the first offspring of creative power. "Hail! holy light, of heaven *first born!*" Thus by his bidding God made darkness the mother of light. Light sprang from eternal darkness at the bidding of God, and Jesus from the night of the grave brought immortality to light. Hence Christ's first communion with his disciples was upon this day. Hence its consecration to the memory of that event. Hence it became the day of solemn and joyful assemblies. Conventibus Christianorum sacris et eucharistice celebratum fuisse ex hoc loco patet. Vide Mosheimius, de rebus Christi, ante Constantini Mosh., p. 116, Kuin., cum multis aliis.

¹ Αρτος occurs some ninety times in the N. T. In com. ver. it is always translated *loaves* in the plural number; but in the singular number, one case excepted, always *bread.* In the case excepted there was a sort of necessity for translating it *loaf,* because a whole ship's company had but one loaf. In that case to have translated it one *bread,* would have been wholly inapposite. Such laxity is peculiarly faulty, in a case, where Paul argues the unity of the church from the fact that in its assemblies they had but " *one loaf,*" of which they all partook. In this case the argument makes *loaf,* and not *bread,* indispensable. See ch. 2 : 42.

KING JAMES' VERSION.

continued his speech until midnight.

8 And there were many lights in the upper chamber, where they were gathered together.

9 And there sat in a window a certain young man named Eutychus, being fallen into a deep sleep: and as Paul was long preaching, he sunk down with sleep, and fell down from the third loft, and was taken up dead.

10 And Paul went down, and fell on him, and embracing *him*, said, Trouble not yourselves; for his life is in him.

11 When he therefore was come up again, and had broken bread, and eaten, and talked a long while, even till break of day, so he departed.

12 And they brought the young man alive, and were not a little comforted.

13 And we went before to ship, and sailed unto Assos, there

GREEK TEXT.

ριον, παρέτεινέ τε τὸν λόγον μέχρι μεσονυκτίου· 8 ἦσαν δὲ λαμπάδες ἱκαναὶ ἐν τῷ ὑπερῴῳ ν̔ ἦσαν συνηγμένοι. 9 καθήμενος δέ τις νεανίας ὀνόματι Εὔτυχος ἐπὶ τῆς θυρίδος, καταφερόμενος ὕπνῳ βαθεῖ, διαλεγομένου τοῦ Παύλου ἐπὶ πλεῖον, κατενεχθεὶς ἀπὸ τοῦ ὕπνου, ἔπεσεν ἀπὸ τοῦ τριστέγου κάτω, καὶ ἤρθη νεκρός. 10 καταβὰς δὲ ὁ Παῦλος ἐπέπεσεν αὐτῷ, καὶ συμπεριλαβὼν εἶπε, Μὴ θορυβεῖσθε· ἡ γὰρ ψυχὴ αὐτοῦ ἐν αὐτῷ ἐστιν. 11 Ἀναβὰς δὲ καὶ κλάσας ἄρτον καὶ γευσάμενος, ἐφ' ἱκανόν τε ὁμιλήσας ἄχρις αὐγῆς, οὕτως ἐξῆλθεν. 12 ἤγαγον δὲ τὸν παῖδα ζῶντα, καὶ παρεκλήθησαν οὐ μετρίως. 13 Ἡμεῖς δὲ προελθόντες ἐπὶ τὸ πλοῖον, ἀνήχθημεν εἰς τὴν Ἄσσον, ἐκεῖθεν

REVISED VERSION.

the morrow, and continued his speech till midnight. And 8 there were many lamps in the upper ᵏchamber, where we were assembled together. And 9 there sat in the open window a certain young man, named Eutychus, who had fallen into a deep sleep: and as Paul was long ˡdiscoursing, he sunk down with sleep, and fell from the third story, and was taken up dead. And 10 Paul went down, and fell upon him, and embracing him, said, Be not troubled, for his ᵐlife is in him. And when he 11 had come up, and had broken the ⁿloaf, and eaten, and talked a long while, even till daybreak, so he departed. And 12 they brought the young man °alive, and were not a little comforted. And we went for- 13 ward to the ᵖship, and sailed to

---

ᵏ For ησαν read ημεν, Gb., Sch., Ln., Tf. *Ησαν δε λαμπαδες ικαναι—εν τω υπερωω*, in the upper room.

ˡ Διαλεγομενον του Παυλου επι πλειον, while Paul was long *discoursing*, not *preaching*. In modern times, we confound *preaching*, *discoursing*, and *teaching*. This is a frequent source of confusion and error, in many minds. When and where the Apostles, once and again, use two words in the same connection, we ought also to use two. See ch. 5 : 42, where both words occur in the same period as indicating two distinct works, preaching and teaching.

For των μαθητων του, Gb., Sch., Ln., Tf. substitute ημων; making it read, *We having assembled to break bread, Paul discoursed with them*, instead of, "The disciples came together 'to break a loaf,' or 'to break bread,' and Paul discoursed to them." We cannot make it *preached* to them; for, in com. ver., in no other passage than this, is διαλεγομαι rendered to *preach*. In its thirteen occurrences in the Christian Scriptures, ten of which are in this book, it is represented by *dispute* six times, by *reason* four times, and once by "*speaketh*." The distinctions which etymology would suggest, are not always regarded with minute accuracy in the Hellenistic dialect. It seems certain that this dialect has been much influenced in its forms and significations by the ordinary use of the Hebrew, or, to speak more correctly, the Syro-Chaldaic.

Διαλεγομαι is better rendered by *dissero* than by any other

Roman word. Dissero, to *discourse*, to *declare*. "*Dissere cum aliquo de re aliquá, in utramque partem.*" Cicero. To discourse with any one concerning anything on either side, *pro* or *con*.

ᵐ Ψυχη—for his life is in him—*soul*, or *life*, are equally its representatives.

ⁿ Τον αρτον, Tf., Ln., Mey., Hack., not *a* loaf, but *the* loaf. Γευσαμενος, v. 11, *and having eaten*. Love-feasts were usual, in connection with the Eucharist, or Lord's supper generally preceding it. Here, as they sat very late, it may have been a refreshment before separating.

Κλασας αρτον και γευσαμενος. This was an ordinary meal for refreshment. The same formula, κλασας αρτον, breaking bread, or, breaking a loaf at that day, and amongst that people, intimated any refreshment by food, special, or common.

° Ηγαγον—they brought him into the assembly ζωντα, *living*, alive; παρεκληθησαν ου μετριως, and were not a little comforted.

ᵖ "And we went before him to the ship," Penn. "We went before to the ship," Thomp. "We going before into ship," Wes. "Then we went forward to the vessel," Wakef. "But we went before into the ship," Dodd. "And we went on board the ship," Murd. "And we went before to the ship," Boothr. Doctors differ in small, as well as in great,

intending to take in Paul: for so had he appointed, minding himself to go afoot.

14 And when he met with us at Assos, we took him in, and came to Mitylene.

15 And we sailed thence, and came the next *day* over against Chios; and the next *day* we arrived at Samos, and tarried at Trogyllium; and the next *day* we came to Miletus.

16 For Paul had determined to sail by Ephesus, because he would not spend the time in Asia: for he hasted, if it were possible for him, to be at Jerusalem the day of Pentecost.

17 And from Miletus he sent to Ephesus, and called the elders of the church.

18 And when they were come to him, he said unto them, Ye know, from the first day that I came into Asia, after what manner I have been with you at all seasons,

19 Serving the Lord with all humility of mind, and with many tears and temptations, which be-

μέλλοντες ἀναλαμβάνειν τὸν Παῦλον· οὕτω γὰρ ἦν διατεταγμένος, μέλλων αὐτὸς πεζεύειν. [14] ὡς δὲ συνέβαλεν ἡμῖν εἰς τὴν Ἄσσον, ἀναλαβόντες αὐτὸν ἤλθομεν εἰς Μιτυλήνην· [15] κἀκεῖθεν ἀποπλεύσαντες, τῇ ἐπιούσῃ κατηντήσαμεν ἀντικρὺ Χίου· τῇ δὲ ἑτέρᾳ παρεβάλομεν εἰς Σάμον· καὶ μείναντες ἐν Τρωγυλλίῳ, τῇ ἐχομένῃ ἤλθομεν εἰς Μίλητον. [16] ἔκρινε γὰρ ὁ Παῦλος παραπλεῦσαι τὴν Ἔφεσον, ὅπως μὴ γένηται αὐτῷ χρονοτριβῆσαι ἐν τῇ Ἀσίᾳ· ἔσπευδε γὰρ, εἰ δυνατὸν ἦν αὐτῷ, τὴν ἡμέραν τῆς Πεντηκοστῆς γενέσθαι εἰς Ἱεροσόλυμα. [17] Ἀπὸ δὲ τῆς Μιλήτου πέμψας εἰς Ἔφεσον, μετεκαλέσατο τοὺς πρεσβυτέρους τῆς ἐκκλησίας. [18] ὡς δὲ παρεγένοντο πρὸς αὐτὸν, εἶπεν αὐτοῖς, Ὑμεῖς ἐπίστασθε, ἀπὸ πρώτης ἡμέρας ἀφ' ἧς ἐπέβην εἰς τὴν Ἀσίαν, πῶς μεθ' ὑμῶν τὸν πάντα χρόνον ἐγενόμην, [19] δουλεύων τῷ κυρίῳ μετὰ πάσης ταπεινοφροσύνης καὶ πολλῶν δακρύων καὶ πειρασμῶν,

Assos, there intending to take in Paul: for so he had [q]appointed, intending himself to go on foot. And when he met us 14 at Assos, we took him in, and came to Mitylene. And hav- 15 ing sailed thence, we came the next day over against Chios; and the next day we arrived at Samos, and remained at Trogyllium; and the next day we came to Miletus; for 16 Paul had determined to sail past Ephesus, that he might not spend the time in Asia; for he hastened, if it were possible for him, to be at Jerusalem on the day of Pentecost. And from Miletus he 17 sent to Ephesus, and called for the [r]elders of the congregation. And when they 18 were come to him, he said to them: You well know from the first day that I came into Asia, [rr]in what manner I have always been with you, serving 19 the Lord with all humility of mind, and with many tears

---

matters. We most incline to Wakefield; though we had so rendered it, before we consulted him. As confirmatory of our version of it, we find in Mark 14 : 35, it is so rendered com. ver.

[q] *Οὕτω γαρ εν διατεταγμενος. Τασσω, διατασσω, προτασσομαι, διατεταγμενος*, are of one family in their root and more frequently used by Luke than any other N. T. writer; *τασσω* five times used by Luke, and four times by all other inspired writers.

Προτασσομαι—only by Luke, and only once—*before appointed*, ch. 17 : 26; and *διατασσω* sixteen times in N. T., nine of which by Luke, translated. com. ver., by *command, appoint, ordain, set in order*, here appointed; *ordained* to eternal life, ch. 13 : 48. The civil magistrates are *ordained* of God, Rom. 13 : 1, yet inaugurated by man. *Ταττω*, or

τασσω—ch. 13 : 48—as many as were ordained to eternal life, believed—as were disposed, or determined for eternal life. "Determined," Boothr., Dodd.; "so disposed," Wakef. Luke is not speculating or philosophizing on the subject. It is declared as a fact, a Divine and glorious fact. God granted to the Gentiles the benefit of repentance even to everlasting life.

[r] *Πρεσβυτερους*. The word, occurring sixty-seven times in New Testament, is, with one exception, represented by elders, once *old*, and once *eldest*, in the plural.

[rr] *Πως*, "how," "after what manner," "by what means." It is both *declarative* and *interrogative* in N. Test. currency, in our idiomatic style. *In what manner* is, with us, as we judge, in better taste.

KING JAMES' VERSION.	GREEK TEXT.	REVISED VERSION.
fell me by the lying in wait of the Jews: 20 *And* how I kept back nothing that was profitable *unto you,* but have shewed you, and have taught you publicly, and from house to house, 21 Testifying both to the Jews, and also to the Greeks, repentance toward God, and faith toward our Lord Jesus Christ. 22 And now behold, I go bound in the spirit unto Jerusalem, not knowing the things that shall befall me there: 23 Save that the Holy Ghost witnesseth in every city, saying, that bonds and afflictions abide me. 24 But none of these things move me, neither count I my life dear unto myself, so that I might finish my course with joy, and the ministry which I have received of the Lord Jesus, to testify the gospel of the grace of God.	τῶν συμβάντων μοι ἐν ταῖς ἐπιβουλαῖς τῶν Ἰουδαίων· 20 ὡς οὐδὲν ὑπεστειλάμην τῶν συμφερόντων, τοῦ μὴ ἀναγγεῖλαι ὑμῖν καὶ διδάξαι ὑμᾶς δημοσίᾳ καὶ κατ᾽ οἴκους, 21 διαμαρτυρόμενος Ἰουδαίοις τε καὶ Ἕλλησι τὴν εἰς τὸν Θεὸν μετάνοιαν, καὶ πίστιν τὴν εἰς τὸν Κύριον ἡμῶν Ἰησοῦν Χριστόν. 22 καὶ νῦν ἰδοὺ ἐγὼ δεδεμένος τῷ πνεύματι, πορεύομαι εἰς Ἱερουσαλὴμ, τὰ ἐν αὐτῇ συναντήσοντά μοι μὴ εἰδὼς, 23 πλὴν ὅτι τὸ Πνεῦμα τὸ Ἅγιον κατὰ πόλιν διαμαρτύρεται λέγον, ὅτι δεσμά με καὶ θλίψεις μένουσιν. 24 ἀλλ᾽ οὐδενὸς λόγον ποιοῦμαι, οὐδὲ ἔχω τὴν ψυχήν μου τιμίαν ἐμαυτῷ, ὡς τελειῶσαι τὸν δρόμον μου μετὰ χαρᾶς, καὶ τὴν διακονίαν ἣν ἔλαβον παρὰ τοῦ Κυρίου Ἰησοῦ, διαμαρτύρασθαι τὸ εὐαγγέλιον τῆς χάριτος τοῦ Θεοῦ. 25 καὶ	and trials, which befell me by the plots of the Jews: and that I have kept back 20 nothing that was profitable, but have declared to you, and have taught you both publicly, and from house to house, testifying both to the 21 Jews and Greeks, ⁸reformation ⁹⁹toward God, and faith toward our Lord Jesus Christ. And now behold, I go bound 22 in spirit to Jerusalem, not knowing the things which will befall me there: except 23 that the Holy Spirit testifies in every city, saying, that bonds and afflictions await me. But none of these things move 24 me, neither count I my life dear to myself, so that I may finish my course with joy, and the ministry which I have received from the Lord Jesus, to ⁱtestify the gospel of the grace of God. And now be- 25

Μετανοια. See ch. 2 : 38.

Why God should be the special object of *repentance*, or *reformation*, and our Lord Jesus Christ the special object of *faith* in the Apostolic teachings, is an interesting question, on which one remark at present must suffice. Sin terminates upon God in its dishonoring him, and faith upon Jesus Christ as honoring him in expiating it.

⁸⁸ Εις τον Κυριον—εις τον Θεον—εις. In the philosophy of this preposition there is *motion, progress;* not *repose,* not absolute rest. Whereas εν is indicative of *repose, rest, quiescence.*

Repentance, or reformation, *toward* God, is, to say the least, awkward and clumsy; and faith *toward* the Lord Jesus is no better. It is, however, so consecrated and familiar that we realize not its dissonance with either reason or taste. *Ward, toward,* from the Saxon *weard,* and this from the radix of the Roman *verto, versus* to turn—*toward. Motion to* is the incipient idea. Motion *to, into, unto,* or *on to.* Hence the splendidly awkward conception, *from glory to glory*—an eternal ascent. Repentance, or reformation, *toward* God, and · faith *toward* our Lord Jesus Christ. Godward, Christward, are equally proper, *n* and *of* themselves. *Froward* is only from*ward,* or *turning from.*

ⁱ Διαμαρτυρασθαι το ευαγγελιον της χαριτος του Θεου. Of fifteen occurrences of this word in N. Test., ten are found in Luke's narratives; to *witness,* to *testify,* to *charge,* are its representatives in his writings, com. ver. Three times *charge,* in Paul's Epistles to Timothy and Titus. "*Testificor, obtestor, pergens testificari,*" Beza. "*Exprimitur vis prepositionis δια,* vel potius exacte *testificans* ut præpositio δια notet penetrationem," Piscator. In the Septuagint it is in all cases the representative of הֵעִיד. Leigh's Crit. Sacra. It properly indicates, *I call God to witness that the following words indicate the truth.* It indicates to us the solemn and earnest manner in which the apostle Paul preached the gospel.

KING JAMES' VERSION.	GREEK TEXT.	REVISED VERSION.

KING JAMES' VERSION.

25 And now behold, I know that ye all, among whom I have gone preaching the kingdom of God, shall see my face no more.

26 Wherefore I take you to record this day, that I *am* pure from the blood of all *men*;

27 For I have not shunned to declare unto you all the counsel of God.

28 Take heed therefore unto yourselves, and to all the flock over the which the Holy Ghost hath made you overseers, to feed the church of God, which he hath purchased with his own blood.

29 For I know this, that after my departing shall grievous wolves enter in among you, not sparing the flock.

30 Also of your own selves shall men arise, speaking perverse things, to draw away disciples after them.

GREEK TEXT.

νῦν ἰδοὺ ἐγὼ οἶδα, ὅτι οὐκέτι ὄψεσθε τὸ πρόσωπόν μου ὑμεῖς πάντες, ἐν οἷς διῆλθον κηρύσσων τὴν βασιλείαν τοῦ Θεοῦ. 26 διὸ μαρτύρομαι ὑμῖν ἐν τῇ σήμερον ἡμέρᾳ, ὅτι καθαρὸς ἐγὼ ἀπὸ τοῦ αἵματος πάντων· 27 οὐ γὰρ ὑπεστειλάμην τοῦ μὴ ἀναγγεῖλαι ὑμῖν πᾶσαν τὴν βουλὴν τοῦ Θεοῦ. 28 προσέχετε οὖν ἑαυτοῖς καὶ παντὶ τῷ ποιμνίῳ, ἐν ᾧ ὑμᾶς τὸ Πνεῦμα τὸ Ἅγιον ἔθετο ἐπισκόπους, ποιμαίνειν τὴν ἐκκλησίαν τοῦ Θεοῦ, ἣν περιεποιήσατο διὰ τοῦ ἰδίου αἵματος. 29 ἐγὼ γὰρ οἶδα τοῦτο, ὅτι εἰσελεύσονται μετὰ τὴν ἄφιξίν μου λύκοι βαρεῖς εἰς ὑμᾶς, μὴ φειδόμενοι τοῦ ποιμνίου· 30 καὶ ἐξ ὑμῶν αὐτῶν ἀναστήσονται ἄνδρες λαλοῦντες διεστραμμένα, τοῦ ἀποσπᾶν τοὺς μαθητὰς ὀπίσω αὐ-

REVISED VERSION.

hold, I know that you all, among whom I have gone preaching the kingdom of God, will see my face no more, wherefore I take you 26 to "witness this day, that I am clear from the blood of all. For I have kept nothing back, 27 but have declared to you the whole "counsel of God. Take 28 heed, therefore, to yourselves, and to all the flock in which the Holy Spirit has constituted you ""overseers, to feed the congregation of the Lord, which he has purchased with his own blood. For I 29 know this, that after my departure fierce wolves will enter in among you, not sparing the flock. Also from 30 among your ownselves, men will arise, speaking "perverse things, to draw away disciples

---

^u Ὅτι καθαρος εγω απο του αἱματος παντων. Εγω καθαρος—in apposition—no verb intervening, always imply the substantive verb. It seems most probable that εγω—probably from the Bœotian Ιωγα—gave to us the pronoun *I*, which, in the absence of every verb, indicates *I am*. Here, then, associated only with an adjective, ειμι is essentially understood.

Του αιματος, literally, the *blood,* but, substantively, the *life;* for the blood is the scabbard of the life of every earthly animated being. Παντων, of course, in this same sentential oracle, implies ανθρωπων.

Εν τη σημερον ἡμερα, in the Attic style, or dialect, is tantamount to τηδε ἡμερα, *hoc die,* this very day, *hodiernus dies.* This is superlatively formal and impressive.

^u *Την βουλην—βουλη* is one of Luke's favorites. In its twelve occurrences in the Christian Scriptures, he employs it nine times. In arguing the internal evidences of the Christian records, one who is attentive to the peculiar style of the inspired writers, could testify to their respective style, as we testify to the faces of men. The man that wrote the Acts of the Apostles, could not have written the testimonies of Matthew, Mark, or John; nor could any one of them, by any possibility, have written the two books of Luke.

The *counsel* of God is not the *advice, opinion, consultation, prudence,* or *deliberation,* but the *purpose, design, will, direction, command* of God. It is used in these different shades, all comprehended in his revealed will.

^{uu} *Επισκοπους, bishops,* overseers. Instead of one bishop to

a whole diocess, the church at Ephesus had a plurality of bishops over it.

For Θεου, Gb., Ln., Tf. have, I judge, with more propriety, if not with more authority, substituted κυριον. Davidson's Lectures on Biblical Criticism. Hack.

Ἣν περιεποιησατο δια του ιδιου αιματος. Περιποιεομαι, found only here and 1 Tim. 3 : 13, *purchase;* "purchased by his blood," "purchased a good degree," (1 Tim. 3 : 13), whence is derived the word περιποιησις.

This word, περιποιησις, is found *five* times only in N. Test.; and, in com. ver., is represented by *purchased possession,* Eph. 1 : 14; *obtain salvation,* 1 Thess. 5 : 9; *obtaining glory,* 2 Thess. 2 : 14; *saving the soul,* Heb. 10 : 39; a *peculiar* people; a *people of acquirement.* Greek Concordance. Such is the entire history of the inspired use and currency of this litigated word. Like all other words of much consecrated currency, it has passed through a fiery furnace.

According to the Critica Sacra, *peculium,* Ep. 1 : 14; *acquisitio,* 1 Thess. 5 : 9; ecclesia—the church of God is so called, which Peter calls (1 Ep. 2 : 9) *populus acquisitionis,* his *acquired* or *purchased* people. *Acquisivit per sanguinem suum; id est, per mortem cruentem Filii sui.* Grotius. *Conservatio,* Heb. 10 : 39; 1 Pet. 2 : 9. Λαος εις περιποιησιν; a *peculiar* people; "a people for purchasing." According to the Greek, for so the verb is used, Acts 20 : 28; also 2 Thess. 2 : 14. Crit. Sacr., p. 207.

^v Διεστραμμενα. This is also one of Luke's words: of its seven occurrences, it is five times employed by him. He

KING JAMES' VERSION.	GREEK TEXT.	REVISED VERSION.

KING JAMES' VERSION.

31 Therefore watch, and remember, that by the space of three years I ceased not to warn every one night and day with tears.

32 And now, brethren, I commend you to God, and to the word of his grace, which is able to build you up, and to give you an inheritance among all them which are sanctified.

33 I have coveted no man's silver, or gold, or apparel.

34 Yea, ye yourselves know, that these hands have ministered unto my necessities, and to them that were with me.

35 I have shewed you all things, how that so labouring ye ought to support the weak, and to remember the words of the Lord Jesus, how he said, It is more blessed to give than to receive.

36 And when he had thus spoken, he kneeled down, and prayed with them all.

37 And they all wept sore, and fell on Paul's neck, and kissed him.

38 Sorrowing most of all for the words which he spake, that they should see his face no more. And they accompanied him unto the ship.

GREEK TEXT.

τῶν. 31 διὸ γρηγορεῖτε, μνημονεύοντες ὅτι τριετίαν νύκτα καὶ ἡμέραν οὐκ ἐπαυσάμην μετὰ δακρύων νουθετῶν ἕνα ἕκαστον. 32 καὶ τανῦν παρατίθεμαι ὑμᾶς, ἀδελφοὶ, τῷ Θεῷ καὶ τῷ λόγῳ τῆς χάριτος αὐτοῦ, τῷ δυναμένῳ ἐποικοδομῆσαι καὶ δοῦναι ὑμῖν κληρονομίαν ἐν τοῖς ἡγιασμένοις πᾶσιν. 33 ἀργυρίου ἢ χρυσίου ἢ ἱματισμοῦ οὐδενὸς ἐπεθύμησα· 34 αὐτοὶ δὲ γινώσκετε ὅτι ταῖς χρείαις μου καὶ τοῖς οὖσι μετ' ἐμοῦ ὑπηρέτησαν αἱ χεῖρες αὗται. 35 πάντα ὑπέδειξα ὑμῖν, ὅτι οὕτω κοπιῶντας δεῖ ἀντιλαμβάνεσθαι τῶν ἀσθενούντων, μνημονεύειν τε τῶν λόγων τοῦ Κυρίου Ἰησοῦ, ὅτι αὐτὸς εἶπε, Μακάριόν ἐστι διδόναι μᾶλλον ἢ λαμβάνειν. 36 Καὶ ταῦτα εἰπὼν θεὶς τὰ γόνατα αὐτοῦ, σὺν πᾶσιν αὐτοῖς προσηύξατο. 37 Ἱκανὸς δὲ ἐγένετο κλαυθμὸς πάντων· καὶ ἐπιπεσόντες ἐπὶ τὸν τράχηλον τοῦ Παύλου, κατεφίλουν αὐτόν· 38 ὀδυνώμενοι μάλιστα ἐπὶ τῷ λόγῳ ᾧ εἰρήκει, ὅτι οὐκέτι μέλλουσι τὸ πρόσωπον αὐτοῦ θεωρεῖν. προέπεμπον δὲ αὐτὸν εἰς τὸ πλοῖον.

REVISED VERSION.

after them. Therefore watch, 31 and remember, that during three years I ceased not to warn every one night and day with tears. And now, breth- 32 ren, I commend you to God. and to the word of his grace, which is able to build you up, and to give you an inheritance among all them who are sanctified. I have coveted no 33 man's silver, or gold, or apparel. You yourselves know, 34 that these hands have ministered to my necessities, and to those that were with me. I have shown you in all re- 35 spects that by so laboring you ought to support the weak, and to remember the words of the Lord Jesus, that he himself said, It is more blessed to give than to receive. And 36 when he had said this, he kneeled down, and prayed with them all. And they all wept 37 much, and having fallen on Paul's neck, they kissed him, sorrowing especially for the 38 words which he had spoken, that they would see his face no more. And they accompanied him to the ship.

---

quotes it once from the Saviour. Literally the verb διαστρεφω, perverto, distorqueo. Herè it is perversa et depravata. Viæ impiorum dicuntur perversæ. Crit. Sacra. Distorqueo, to distort, is its most literal representative.

☞ Αδελφοι, omitted by Ln., Tf., as also ὑμιν, after δοῦναι. Both are, indeed, implied. Εν τοις ἡγιασμενοις πασιν, amongst all the sanctified. Αγη is the root of a large family, a negative of γη—not of the earth—the sin-polluted earth. Sanctification as well as justification and adoption, indicate both an act and a state. There is one that justifies, sanctifies, adopts and saves, as well as pardons a fallen man. There is a state of justification, of sanctification, of adoption and of sulvation. In states there are no degrees, in character there is an indefinite variety.

KING JAMES' VERSION.	GREEK TEXT.	REVISED VERSION.
CHAP. XXI.	CHAP. XXI.	CHAP. XXI.

KING JAMES' VERSION.

CHAP. XXI.

AND it came to pass, that after we were gotten from them, and had launched, we came with a straight course unto Coos, and the *day* following unto Rhodes, and from thence unto Patara:

2 And finding a ship sailing over unto Phenicia, we went aboard, and set forth.

3 Now when we had discovered Cyprus, we left it on the left hand, and sailed into Syria, and landed at Tyre: for there the ship was to unlade her burden.

4 And finding disciples, we tarried there seven days: who said to Paul through the Spirit, that he should not go up to Jerusalem.

5 And when we had accomplished those days, we departed, and went our way; and they all brought us on our way, with wives and children, till *we were* out of the city: and we kneeled down on the shore, and prayed.

6 And when we had taken our leave one of another, we

GREEK TEXT.

CHAP. XXI.

ὩΣ δὲ ἐγένετο ἀναχθῆναι ἡμᾶς ἀποσπασθέντας ἀπ᾿ αὐτῶν, εὐθυδρομήσαντες ἤλθομεν εἰς τὴν Κῶν, τῇ δὲ ἑξῆς εἰς τὴν Ῥόδον, κἀκεῖθεν εἰς Πάταρα. 2 καὶ εὑρόντες πλοῖον διαπερῶν εἰς Φοινίκην, ἐπιβάντες ἀνήχθημεν. 3 ἀναφάναντες δὲ τὴν Κύπρον, καὶ καταλιπόντες αὐτὴν εὐώνυμον, ἐπλέομεν εἰς Συρίαν, καὶ κατήχθημεν εἰς Τύρον· ἐκεῖσε γὰρ ἦν τὸ πλοῖον ἀποφορτιζόμενον τὸν γόμον. 4 καὶ ἀνευρόντες τοὺς μαθητὰς, ἐπεμείναμεν αὐτοῦ ἡμέρας ἑπτά· οἵτινες τῷ Παύλῳ ἔλεγον διὰ τοῦ πνεύματος, μὴ ἀναβαίνειν εἰς Ἱερουσαλήμ. 5 ὅτε δὲ ἐγένετο ἡμᾶς ἐξαρτίσαι τὰς ἡμέρας, ἐξελθόντες ἐπορευόμεθα, προπεμπόντων ἡμᾶς πάντων σὺν γυναιξὶ καὶ τέκνοις ἕως ἔξω τῆς πόλεως, καὶ θέντες τὰ γόνατα ἐπὶ τὸν αἰγιαλὸν προσηυξάμεθα. 6 καὶ ἀσπασάμενοι ἀλλήλους, ἐπέβημεν εἰς

REVISED VERSION.

CHAP. XXI.

WHEN now it came to pass, 1 that we put to sea, having departed from ʸthem, we came with a straight course to Cos, and the day following to Rhodes, and thence to Patara. And having found a ship cross- 2 ing ᶻover to Phenicia, we went on board, and set sail. Now 3 having had a view of Cyprus, and having left it behind on the ᵃleft hand, we sailed to Syria, and landed at Tyre: for there the ship was to unlade her cargo. And having sought 4 out the ᵇdisciples, we remained there seven days; who said to Paul, through the Spirit, that he should not go up to Jerusalem. But having ᶜcomplet- 5 ed the days, we went on our way; and they all with their wives and children conducted us on our way, till we were out of the city; and having kneeled down on the shore, we prayed. And hav- 6 ing embraced one another,

---

ʸ Ἀποσπασθέντας. Ἀποσπαω is, with one exception, found only in Luke, represented, com. ver., by *draw, withdraw, draw away;* here, *after we were gotten away.* "Separated from them," Dodd., Wakef.; "having departed from them," De Wette, Rob., Murd.; "*torn away,*" Wes., Penn; *separated from,*" Boothr. "*Having torn ourselves from them*" is too violent; we prefer, having *departed from* them.

ᶻ Διαπερῶν. Διαπεραω, in its six occurrences in N. T., is represented by *passed over, gone over,* only here *sailing over,* com. ver. This is an implied use of the word, for which we see no propriety. We might as well say, in speaking of one *passing over* a country, that *he walked over it,* which is not implied in διαπερων; better say *crossing over,* leaving the manner to the discretion of the reader.

ᵃ Καταλιποντες αυτην ενωνυμον, on the left, an *adjective,* not an adverb. "Proprie αριστερος est sinister," Kuinœl, Hack.; " sed cum dextræ partes apud veteres boni habebantur ominis; sinistræ autem infelicis, inde factum ut Græci

ipsius nominis mentionem formidarent, et pro, αριστερος frequenter dicerent ενωνυμον, quasi dicas bene nominatum," Kuin., in loco. Αναφαναντες δε την Κυπρον, "and having had a view of Cyprus." Αναφαινω is found only here, and in Luke 19 : 11. There it is translated *appear,* literally, *having had Cyprus brought up to sight.*

ᵇ Και ανευροντες τους μαθητας. The article and the preposition in these words are untranslated in com. ver.; fully expressed it should be read, *and having sought out the disciples.* Ανευρισκω, employed only by Luke, and by him but twice, is translated by *found,* Luke 2 : 16, and here by *finding.* Had it been ευρισκω, this would have sufficed; but the preposition is thereby regarded as redundant, and untranslated; a license of dangerous precedent.

ᶜ Εξαρτιζω, in its second occurrence, 2 Tim. 3 : 17, is rendered *thoroughly furnished,* here, *fully accomplished;* with us, " completed," Boothr.; " the days were *ended,*" Thompson, Wakef.; "*finished,*" Wes.

KING JAMES' VERSION.	GREEK TEXT.	REVISED VERSION.

KING JAMES' VERSION.

took ship; and they returned home again.

7 And when we had finished *our* course from Tyre, we came to Ptolemais, and saluted the brethren, and abode with them one day.

8 And the next *day* we that were of Paul's company departed, and came unto Cesarea; and we entered into the house of Philip the evangelist, which was *one* of the seven; and abode with him.

9 And the same man had four daugthers, virgins, which did prophesy.

10 And as we tarried *there* many days, there came down from Judea a certain prophet, named Agabus.

11 And when he was come unto us, he took Paul's girdle, and bound his own hands and feet, and said, Thus saith the Holy Ghost, So shall the Jews at Jerusalem bind the man that owneth this girdle, and shall deliver *him* into the hands of the Gentiles.

12 And when we heard these things, both we, and they of that place, besought him not to go up to Jerusalem.

GREEK TEXT.

τὸ πλοῖον, ἐκεῖνοι δὲ ὑπέστρεψαν εἰς τὰ ἴδια. ⁷ Ἡμεῖς δὲ τὸν πλοῦν διανύσαντες ἀπὸ Τύρου κατηντήσαμεν εἰς Πτολεμαΐδα, καὶ ἀσπασάμενοι τοὺς ἀδελφοὺς ἐμείναμεν ἡμέραν μίαν παρ᾽ αὐτοῖς. ⁸ τῇ δὲ ἐπαύριον ἐξελθόντες οἱ περὶ τὸν Παῦλον ἦλθον εἰς Καισάρειαν· καὶ εἰσελθόντες εἰς τὸν οἶκον Φιλίππου τοῦ εὐαγγελιστοῦ, τοῦ ὄντος ἐκ τῶν ἑπτὰ, ἐμείναμεν παρ᾽ αὐτῷ. ⁹ τούτῳ δὲ ἦσαν θυγατέρες παρθένοι τέσσαρες προφητεύουσαι. ¹⁰ ἐπιμενόντων δὲ ἡμῶν ἡμέρας πλείους, κατῆλθέ τις ἀπὸ τῆς Ἰουδαίας προφήτης ὀνόματι Ἄγαβος· ¹¹ καὶ ἐλθὼν πρὸς ἡμᾶς, καὶ ἄρας τὴν ζώνην τοῦ Παύλου, δήσας τε αὐτοῦ τὰς χεῖρας καὶ τοὺς πόδας εἶπε, Τάδε λέγει τὸ Πνεῦμα τὸ Ἅγιον, Τὸν ἄνδρα οὗ ἐστιν ἡ ζώνη αὕτη, οὕτω δήσουσιν ἐν Ἱερουσαλὴμ οἱ Ἰουδαῖοι, καὶ παραδώσουσιν εἰς χεῖρας ἐθνῶν. ¹² Ὡς δὲ ἠκούσαμεν ταῦτα, παρεκαλοῦμεν ἡμεῖς τε καὶ οἱ ἐντόπιοι, τοῦ μὴ ἀναβαίνειν αὐτὸν εἰς Ἱερουσαλήμ.

REVISED VERSION.

we went on board the ship, and they returned home. Now we, 7 having completed the voyage, came down from Tyre to Ptolemais, and ᵈsaluted the brethren, and remained with them one day. And the next day 8 we ᵉdeparted, and came to Cesarea; and entering into the house of Philip the evangelist, who was one of the seven, we remained with him. Now the 9 same man had four daughters, virgins, who prophesied. And 10 as we remained there several days, there came down from Judea a certain prophet, named ᶠAgabus. And when he 11 came to us, he took Paul's girdle, and binding his own hands and feet, said, Thus, says the Holy Spirit, So shall the Jews at Jerusalem bind the man who owns this girdle, and shall deliver him into the hands of the Gentiles.

Now when we heard these 12 things, both we, and they of that place, besought Paul not to go up to Jerusalem. Then 13

ᵈ Ἀσπασαμενοι, *osculor, amplector,* to salute. Rom. 16 : 16, "Salute one another with an holy kiss." Paul uses this word very often—nineteen times in the sixteenth chapter of the Romans—indicative of the most cordial greetings and salutations. This being a very solemn and affectionate adieu, it is presumed that no word in our currency so fully expresses it, as the word *embraced.* This gives the fullest latitude to the reader, to infer the manner of the adieu.

ᵉ The phrase, οἱ περι τον Παυλον, after εξελθοντες, is repudiated, by some of our best critics, as an interpolation. Prof. Hackett affirms it to be untenable. It is retained in Bagster's text. But that is not sufficient authority against the testimony of collators, Elz., Gb., Sch., Ln., and Tf.

For ελθον, ελθομεν is substituted by the Elz., Gb., Sch., Ln., Tf.

Φιλιππου του ευαγγελιστου, *Philip the Evangelist.* "This title appears to have been given to those who had no stated pastoral charge, but who traveled from place to place, and preached as they had opportunity," Hack. "Evangelists in the Apostolic age were not the regular and constant teachers of the church, but were sent by the apostles into various cities; *ut vel elementa religionis Christiana traderint vel institutionem Apostolorum continuarent,*" Kuin., as referred to by Professor Hackett, vol. 3, p. 316. It is only found here in the book of Acts, and twice in Paul's epistles, Eph. 4 : 11; 2 Tim. 4 : 5.

ᶠ Αγαβος—τις προφητας, a certain prophet, first named ch. 11 : 28, and again in this place. He is known to us only as a Christian prophet.

13 Then Paul answered, What mean ye to weep, and to break mine heart? for I am ready not to be bound only, but also to die at Jerusalem for the name of the Lord Jesus.

14 And when he would not be persuaded, we ceased, saying, The will of the Lord be done.

15 And after those days we took up our carriages, and went up to Jerusalem.

16 There went with us also *certain* of the disciples of Cesarea, and brought with them one Mnason of Cyprus, an old disciple, with whom we should lodge.

17 And when we were come to Jerusalem, the brethren received us gladly.

18 And the *day* following Paul went in with us unto James: and all the elders were present.

19 And when he had saluted them, he declared particularly what things God had wrought among the Gentiles by his ministry.

20 And when they heard *it*, they glorified the Lord, and said unto him, Thou seest, brother, how many thousands of Jews

13 ἀπεκρίθη δὲ ὁ Παῦλος, Τί ποιεῖτε κλαίοντες καὶ συνθρύπτοντές μου τὴν καρδίαν; ἐγὼ γὰρ οὐ μόνον δεθῆναι, ἀλλὰ καὶ ἀποθανεῖν εἰς Ἱερουσαλὴμ ἑτοίμως ἔχω ὑπὲρ τοῦ ὀνόματος τοῦ Κυρίου Ἰησοῦ. 14 Μὴ πειθομένου δὲ αὐτοῦ, ἡσυχάσαμεν εἰπόντες, Τὸ θέλημα τοῦ κυρίου γενέσθω.

15 Μετὰ δὲ τὰς ἡμέρας ταύτας ἀποσκευασάμενοι ἀνεβαίνομεν εἰς Ἱερουσαλήμ. 16 συνῆλθον δὲ καὶ τῶν μαθητῶν ἀπὸ Καισαρείας σὺν ἡμῖν, ἄγοντες παρ' ᾧ ξενισθῶμεν, Μνάσωνί τινι Κυπρίῳ, ἀρχαίῳ μαθητῇ.

17 ΓΕΝΟΜΕΝΩΝ δὲ ἡμῶν εἰς Ἱεροσόλυμα, ἀσμένως ἐδέξαντο ἡμᾶς οἱ ἀδελφοί. 18 τῇ δὲ ἐπιούσῃ εἰσῄει ὁ Παῦλος σὺν ἡμῖν πρὸς Ἰάκωβον, πάντες τε παρεγένοντο οἱ πρεσβύτεροι. 19 καὶ ἀσπασάμενος αὐτοὺς, ἐξηγεῖτο καθ' ἓν ἕκαστον ὧν ἐποίησεν ὁ Θεὸς ἐν τοῖς ἔθνεσι διὰ τῆς διακονίας αὐτοῦ. 20 οἱ δὲ ἀκούσαντες ἐδόξαζον τὸν κύριον· εἶπόν τε αὐτῷ, Θεωρεῖς ἀδελφέ, πόσαι μυριάδες εἰσὶν Ἰουδαίων

Paul answered, What do you, weeping and breaking my [g]heart? for I am ready not only to be bound, but also to die at Jerusalem for the name of the Lord Jesus. And when 14 he could not be persuaded, we ceased, saying, The will of the Lord be done!

And after those days we 15 packed up our [h]baggage, and went up to Jerusalem. There 16 went with us certain of the disciples of Cesarea, bringing us to Mnason a Cyprian, an old disciple, with whom we should [i]lodge.

Now when we were come 17 to [j]Jerusalem, the brethren gladly received us. And the 18 day [k]following Paul went in with us to James, and all the elders were present. And 19 when he had saluted [l]them, he related particularly what things God had wrought among the Gentiles through his ministry. And when they 20 heard it, they glorified the Lord, and said to Paul, You see, brother, what [m]myriads of Jews there are who have be-

---

[g] Συνθρυπτιοντες μου την καρδιαν; breaking my heart? Their distress was unnecessary. Ετοιμως εχω. We have a bold oxymoron, equal to this, chap. 5 : 41, κατηξιωθησαν ατιμασθηναι, were accounted worthy to be disgraced, to suffer shame for his name. Hack., Kuin. Elegans oxymorum inesse observarunt, Cassaubonus et Wolfius.

[h] Επισκευασαμενοι is here preferable to αποσκευασαμενοι, Ln., Tf., Gb. Hack., "*having packed up our baggage*, and prepared for the journey;" "making up our baggage," Dodd.; "we have put our goods upon," Penn. Dr. Bloomfield asks, why αποσκευασαμενοι should not mean to pack up baggage, as the same verb signifies *exonerare alvum*. I apprehend the reason to be, because *to pack up* signifies *onerare*, and is the reverse of *exonerare*. Matthæi reads, επισκ., Scholz, αποσκ. Penn.

[i] Αγοντες—Μνασωνι stands by attraction for αγοντες παρα Μνασωνι παρ' ᾧ ξενισθωμεν, bringing us to Mnason, with whom we should lodge. (Ols., Mey., De Wette, Hackett.)

Αρχαιῳ μαθητη = μαθητη απ' αρχης, an ancient, not an aged disciple. We more familiarly say, *an old* disciple. He may have been converted on the day of Pentecost. Hack.

[j] This seems to be the *fifth* time the apostle visited Jerusalem, since he set out against the brethren at Damascus. For εδεξαντο, απεδεξαντο is preferred by Ln., Tf.

[k] Τη—επιουσια, on, or immediately after, their arrival.

[l] Ασπασαμενος αυτους. In N. T. currency it is generally represented by *salute, embrace, greet.*

Δια της διακονιας αυτου, through his ministry.

[m] Ποσαι μυριαδες, what myriads, multitudes, believe. Ζηλωται του νομου, zealots *for the law*, an objective genitive.

KING JAMES' VERSION.	GREEK TEXT.	REVISED VERSION.

KING JAMES' VERSION.

there are which believe; and they are all zealous of the law.

21 And they are informed of thee, that thou teachest all the Jews which are among the Gentiles to forsake Moses, saying, that they ought not to circumcise *their* children, neither to walk after the customs.

22 What is it therefore? the multitude must needs come together: for they will hear that thou art come.

23 Do therefore this that we say to thee: We have four men which have a vow on them;

24 Them take, and purify thyself with them, and be at charges with them, that they may shave *their* heads: and all may know that those things whereof they were informed concerning thee, are nothing; but *that* thou thyself also walkest orderly, and keepest the law.

25 As touching the Gentiles which believe, we have written *and* concluded that they observe no such thing, save only that they keep themselves from *things* offered to idols, and from blood, and from strangled, and from fornication.

26 Then Paul took the men, and the next day purifying himself with them, entered into the temple, to signify the accomplishment of the days of purification, until that an offering

GREEK TEXT.

τῶν πεπιστευκότων. καὶ πάντες ζηλωταὶ τοῦ νόμου ὑπάρχουσι. 21 κατηχήθησαν δὲ περὶ σοῦ, ὅτι ἀποστασίαν διδάσκεις ἀπὸ Μωσέως τοὺς κατὰ τὰ ἔθνη πάντας Ἰουδαίους, λέγων μὴ περιτέμνειν αὐτοὺς τὰ τέκνα, μηδὲ τοῖς ἔθεσι περιπατεῖν. 22 τί οὖν ἐστι; πάντως δεῖ πλῆθος συνελθεῖν· ἀκούσονται γὰρ ὅτι ἐλήλυθας. 23 τοῦτο οὖν ποίησον ὅ σοι λέγομεν· εἰσὶν ἡμῖν ἄνδρες τέσσαρες εὐχὴν ἔχοντες ἐφ᾽ ἑαυτῶν· 24 τούτους παραλαβὼν ἁγνίσθητι σὺν αὐτοῖς, καὶ δαπάνησον ἐπ᾽ αὐτοῖς, ἵνα ξυρήσωνται τὴν κεφαλὴν, καὶ γνῶσι πάντες ὅτι ὧν κατήχηνται περὶ σοῦ οὐδέν ἐστιν, ἀλλὰ στοιχεῖς καὶ αὐτὸς τὸν νόμον φυλάσσων. 25 περὶ δὲ τῶν πεπιστευκότων ἐθνῶν ἡμεῖς ἐπεστείλαμεν, κρίναντες μηδὲν τοιοῦτον τηρεῖν αὐτούς, εἰ μὴ φυλάσσεσθαι αὐτοὺς τό τε εἰδωλόθυτον καὶ τὸ αἷμα καὶ πνικτὸν καὶ πορνείαν. 26 Τότε ὁ Παῦλος παραλαβὼν τοὺς ἄνδρας, τῇ ἐχομένῃ ἡμέρᾳ σὺν αὐτοῖς ἁγνισθεὶς εἰσῄει εἰς τὸ ἱερὸν, διαγγέλλων τὴν ἐκπλήρωσιν τῶν ἡμερῶν τοῦ ἁγνισμοῦ, ἕως οὗ

REVISED VERSION.

lieved; and they are all zealous for the law; now they have 21 been informed concerning you, that you teach all the Jews who are among the Gentiles [n]apostasy from Moses, saying, that they ought not to circumcise their children, neither to walk after the customs. What then is [o]it? 22 The multitude must needs come together; for they will hear that you have come. Do 23 this, therefore, which we say to you: We have four men who have a [p]vow on themselves; [q]taking these with 24 yourself, purify yourself with them, and bear the charges for them, that they may shave their heads: and all will know that those things of which they were informed concerning you, are nothing, but that you yourself also walk orderly, and keep the law.

[r]But as respects the Gen- 25 tiles who have believed, we have already written and concluded, that they observe no such thing; only that they abstain from things offered to idols, and from blood, and from things strangled, and from all kinds of lewdness.

Then Paul [s]took the men, 26 and the next day purifying himself with them, entered into the temple, announcing the fulfillment of the days of purification, till the offer-

---

[n] *Ἀποστασια, standing off*, not merely, *standing off*, but *standing off from*. This term, now transferred into our language, needs no representative. *Παντας,* omitted by Ln., Gb., as somewhat doubtful.

[o] *Τι ουν εστι; what then, is it?* more familiar than, what, therefore, is it?

[p] Jews alone made such vows. This settled their nationality.

[q] *Τουτους παραλαβων ἁγνισθητι συν αυτοις, και δαπανησον επ᾽ αυτοις, taking these with thyself, purify thyself with them.*

[r] *Περι δε των πεπιστευκοτων εθνων,* but, with respect to the Gentiles who have believed, *ἡμεις, we* (the apostles and brethren at Jerusalem), comprehends the whole assembly convened at Jerusalem, reported, "The apostles, the elders, and the brethren," ch. 15 : 23, Antiochian, Syrian, and Cilician Gentiles, constituted the brethren addressed.

[s] *Παραλαβων* refers to his connecting himself with them, as in v. 24, not to his taking them to the temple. *Συν αυτοις* belongs to *ἁγνισθεις*, not to *εισῃει*, Mey. Hack., "announcing the fulfillment of the days of the purification."

KING JAMES' VERSION.	GREEK TEXT.	REVISED VERSION.

should be offered for every one of them.

27 And when the seven days were almost ended, the Jews, which were of Asia, when they saw him in the temple, stirred up all the people, and laid hands on him,

28 Crying out, Men of Israel, help. This is the man that teacheth all *men* every where against the people, and the law, and this place: and further, brought Greeks also into the temple; and hath polluted this holy place.

29 (For they had seen before with him in the city, Trophimus, an Ephesian, whom they supposed that Paul had brought into the temple.)

30 And all the city was moved, and the people ran together: and they took Paul and drew

προσηνέχθη ὑπὲρ ἑνὸς ἑκάστου αὐτῶν ἡ προσφορά. ²⁷ ὡς δὲ ἔμελλον αἱ ἑπτὰ ἡμέραι συντελεῖσθαι, οἱ ἀπὸ τῆς Ἀσίας Ἰουδαῖοι θεασάμενοι αὐτὸν ἐν τῷ ἱερῷ, συνέχεον πάντα τὸν ὄχλον, καὶ ἐπέβαλον τὰς χεῖρας ἐπ᾽ αὐτὸν, ²⁸ κράζοντες, Ἄνδρες Ἰσραηλῖται, βοηθεῖτε. οὗτός ἐστιν ὁ ἄνθρωπος ὁ κατὰ τοῦ λαοῦ καὶ τοῦ νόμου καὶ τοῦ τόπου τούτου πάντας πανταχοῦ διδάσκων· ἔτι τε καὶ Ἕλληνας εἰσήγαγεν εἰς τὸ ἱερόν, καὶ κεκοίνωκε τὸν ἅγιον τόπον τοῦτον. ²⁹ Ἦσαν γὰρ προεωρακότες Τρόφιμον τὸν Ἐφέσιον ἐν τῇ πόλει σὺν αὐτῷ, ὃν ἐνόμιζον ὅτι εἰς τὸ ἱερὸν εἰσήγαγεν ὁ Παῦλος. ³⁰ ἐκινήθη τε ἡ πόλις ὅλη, καὶ ἐγένετο συνδρομὴ τοῦ λαοῦ· καὶ ἐπιλαβόμενοι τοῦ Παύλου, εἷλ-

ing should be offered for each one of them.

Now as the seven ᵗdays were 27 about to be completed, the Jews who were of Asia, when they saw him in the temple, stirred up all the people, and laid hands on him, crying out, 28 Israelites, help! This is the man who teaches all men every where against this people, and the law, and this place: and further ᵘalso has brought Greeks into the temple, and has polluted this holy place. For they had for- 29 merly seen with him in the city, ᵛTrophimus, an Ephesian, whom they supposed that Paul had brought into the temple. And all the city was moved, 30 and the people ran ᵂtogether, and seizing Paul, they dragged

---

ᵗ Αἱ ἑπτα ἡμεραι refers to ἡμερων του ἁγνισμου, v. 26.

Οἱ απο της Ασιας Ιουδαιοι, the Asiatic Jews—proconsular Asia—not the continent so called.

Two opinions have been entertained of the bearing of the import of these *seven days*, whether in reference to the completion of *the vow* itself, or in reference to the *period* when the vow would cease—the first being the vow itself, and the other the completion of its time. The last is, in our judgment, preferable to the first; for the first is opposed to εὑρον με ἡγνισμενον εν τῳ ἱερῳ, ch. 24 : 18. The vow was yet upon him at the time of his arrest.

Ὡς δε εμελλον, now as the seven days were about to be completed, i. e., according to the views generally entertained, the seven days during which the vow of these Nazarites was still to continue, after Paul became a party to it (Beng., Kuin., Olsh., De W.). Αἱ, in this case, refers to the days mentioned v. 26. "Αἱ, before ἑπτα ἡμερων, in this connection most naturally recalls the ἡμερων του ἁγνισμου just spoken of," Hack. "When the seven days were almost ended," Wakef.; "as the seven days were to be completed," Thomp.; "and when the seventh day arrived," Murd.; "were about to be accomplished," Wes., Dodd.; "when the seven days were almost ended," Boothr.

ᵘ Ετι τε και, and further also. This with Luke is a common phrase. In this book, chs. 1 : 1; 2 : 26; 9 : 1, etc., *and,*

further also, moreover. Τε is found above one hundred and fifty times in this single book of Acts, and but seven times in his gospel.

ᵛ Trophimus the Ephesian first appears in ch. 20 : 4, and again in 2 Tim. 4 : 20. Paul left him sick at Miletus. We hear no more of him.

ᵂ Συνδρομη, an ἁπαξ λεγομενον, found only in this place. It indicates a *concourse*, especially a *crowd* rushing together, or hastily assembled. Its family sprang from τρεχω, I run— συντρεχω, I run together with others. Hence, in classic currency, it represents any crowd of persons suddenly called together, or assembled; even a mob. Συνδρομος, from συντρεχω, any tumultuous crowd, hastily gathered for any intent, or purpose, constitutes a *concourse*. It is composed of those who, from passion, or excitement, convene.

Εἱλκον—ἱερον, they dragged him out of the temple; and εκλεισθησαν αἱ θυραι, the doors were closed. *Drew him out* is too mild, too tame for this scene, and this language. Some opine, intending to kill him, but fearing that his blood would pollute and desecrate the sanctuary. Levites alone could lawfully enter the holy place. The altar of burnt-offerings, possessing horns, was the only canonized and conservative refuge of the blood-stained sinner. They dragged him out, and immediately the gates were closed.

KING JAMES' VERSION.	GREEK TEXT.	REVISED VERSION.
him out of the temple. And forthwith the doors were shut.	κον αὐτὸν ἔξω τοῦ ἱεροῦ· καὶ εὐθέως ἐκλείσθησαν αἱ θύραι.	him out of the ᵃtemple : and immediately the doors were shut.
31 And as they went about to kill him, tidings came unto the chief captain of the band, that all Jerusalem was in an uproar ;	³¹ ζητούντων δὲ αὐτὸν ἀποκτεῖ-ναι, ἀνέβη φάσις τῷ χιλιάρχῳ τῆς σπείρης, ὅτι ὅλη συγκέχυ-ται Ἱερουσαλήμ·	And ᵇas they were seeking to kill him, ᶜword came up ᵈto the chiliarch ᵉof the cohort, that all Jerusalem ᶠwas in confusion ; who immediately took 31
32 Who immediately took soldiers and centurions, and ran down unto them. And when they saw the chief captain and the soldiers, they left beating of Paul.	³² ὃς ἐξαυτῆς παραλαβὼν στρατιώτας καὶ ἑκα-τοντάρχους, κατέδραμεν ἐπ᾽ αὐ-τούς. οἱ δὲ ἰδόντες τὸν χιλίαρ-χον καὶ τοὺς στρατιώτας, ἐπαύ-σαντο τύπτοντες τὸν Παῦλον.	soldiers and centurions, and ran down ᵍupon them. And when they saw the chiliarch and the soldiers, they ʰceased from beating Paul. Then ⁱthe chiliarch 33 ʲdrew near and took him, and 32
33 Then the chief captain came near and took him, and commanded *him* to be bound with two chains : and demanded who he was, and what he had done.	³³ τότε ἐγγίσας ὁ χιλίαρχος ἐπε-λάβετο αὐτοῦ, καὶ ἐκέλευσε δε-θῆναι ἀλύσεσι δυσί· καὶ ἐπυν-θάνετο τίς ἂν εἴη, καὶ τί ἐστι πεποιηκώς.	commanded him to be bound with two chains and inquired who ᵏhe might be, and what he had done. ˡBut some ᵐin the 34 ⁿcrowd ᵒwere shouting one
34 And some cried one thing, some another, among the multitude : and when he could not know the certainty for the tumult, he commanded him to be carried into the castle.	³⁴ ἄλλοι δὲ ἄλλο τι ἐβόων ἐν τῷ ὄχλῳ· μὴ δυνάμε-νος δὲ γνῶναι τὸ ἀσφαλὲς διὰ τὸν θόρυβον, ἐκέλευσεν ἄγεσθαι αὐτὸν εἰς τὴν παρεμβολήν.	thing, and some another : and when he could not know the certainty, ᵖon account of the tumult, he commanded him ᑫto be led into the castle. And 35
35 And when he came upon the stairs, so it was that he was borne of the soldiers, for the violence of the people.	³⁵ ὅτε δέ ἐγένετο ἐπὶ τοὺς ἀναβαθμοὺς, συνέβη βαστάζεσθαι αὐτὸν ὑπὸ τῶν στρατιωτῶν διὰ τὴν βίαν τοῦ ὄχλου.	when ʳhe was ˢon the stairs, ᵗit came to pass that he was borne by the soldiers, ᵘon account of the violence of the ᵛcrowd. For the multitude 36
36 For the multitude of the people followed after, crying, Away with him.	³⁶ ἠκολούθει γὰρ τὸ πλῆ-θος τοῦ λαοῦ κράζον, Αἶρε αὐτόν.	of the people followed, crying out, Away with him!
37 And as Paul was to be led into the castle, he said unto the	³⁷ Μέλλων τε εἰσάγεσθαι εἰς τὴν παρεμβολὴν ὁ Παῦλος λέγει	And as Paul was ʷabout to 37 be led into the castle, he said

ᵃ In accordance with the text, a colon is placed after " temple." So Wesley, Wakef., Penn, Scarlett.

ᵇ Ζετουντων, " as they were seeking." Penn. Eras., " querentibus illis ;" S. Fr., " ils cherchaient."

ᶜ Ανεβη φασις, " word came up." So Rob., Lex. (αναβαινω.) The propriety of giving ανα its proper force " up," is obvious; the commander was stationed in the tower of Antonia, to which there was an ascent by steps. See αναβαθμους, in v. 35.

ᵈ Τῷ χιλιαρχῳ, " to the chiliarch." This word, which literally signifies " the commander of a thousand men," is transferred, as we have no single term corresponding to it.

ᵉ Της σπειρης, " of the cohort." Wesley, Dick., Dodd., Scarlett, Murdock.

ᶠ Συγκεχυται, " was in confusion." Penn, Wakef., Dick. S. Fr., " était en confusion." See Rob. Lex. on this verb.

ᵍ Επ᾽ αυτους, " upon them." Rob., Lex., επι (cum accus.) " with accus. pl. of persons, upon."

ʰ Επαυσαντο τυπτοντες, " ceased from beating." Wesley, Penn, Dodd., Scarlett.

ⁱ " The chiliarch." See v. 31, note.

ʲ Εγγισας, " drew near." Wakef., Dodd., Rob. (Lex.)

ᵏ Αν ειη, " he might be." This optative should not be rendered as an indicative. It is to be distinguished from the indicative which follows it, τι εστι. See Trollope (Gram.), p. 142. Beza, Vulg., Eras., " esset."

ˡ Δε, " but." This particle is adversative. So Wakef. De Wette, " aber ;" Schott, " vero ;" Vulg., Eras., Beza, " autem."

ᵐ Εν, " in." The primary signification of εν is appropriate.

ⁿ Οχλῳ, " crowd." Rob. (Lex.), a crowd, throng ;" Vulg., Mont., Eras., Beza, " turbâ ;" G. and S. Fr., De Sacy, " foule ;" De Wette, " Volke." This word should be distinguished from πληθος in translating. See v. 36.

ᵒ Εβοων, " were shouting." Liddell and Scott's Lex. The imperfect should have its usual continuative force here. So Vulg., Mont., Eras., Beza, Schott, " clamabant."

ᵖ Δια (with accus.), " on account of." Rob. (Lex.)

ᑫ Αγεσθαι, " to be led." See this verb in Rob. and Liddell's Lex. Vulg., Mont., Eras., Beza, Castal., " duci ;" Schott, " deduci." So (E. V.) Mark 13 : 11. Luke 4 : 1, 29 ; 22 : 54.

ʳ Εγενετο, " he was." Dodd., Penn, Sharpe, Wakef., (" Paul was ;") S. Fr., " il fut."

ˢ Επι τους αναβαθμους. After neuter verbs, " on is the appropriate preposition.

ᵗ Συνεβη, " it came to pass." Dodd. Beza, " evenit ;" S. Fr., " il arriva." See this verb, Rob. (Lex.)

ᵘ Δια, " on account of." See v. 34, note. So Penn, Kend.

ᵛ " Crowd." See v. 34, note.

ʷ " Μελλων—εισαγεισθαι, " about to be led." Penn, Kend. Schott, " introducendus ;" Mont., " Futurus—induci ;" S. Fr., " on allait faire entrer Paul."

KING JAMES' VERSION.	GREEK TEXT.	REVISED VERSION.
chief captain, May I speak unto thee? Who said, Canst thou speak Greek?	τῷ χιλιάρχῳ, Εἰ ἔξεστί μοι εἰπεῖν τι πρός σε; Ὁ δὲ ἔφη, Ἑλληνιστὶ γινώσκεις;	to the chiliarch, May I speak to you? Who said, Do you know [d]Greek?
38 Art thou not that Egyptian, which before these days madest an uproar, and leddest out into the wilderness four thousand men that were murderers?	38 οὐκ ἄρα σὺ εἶ ὁ Αἰγύπτιος ὁ πρὸ τούτων τῶν ἡμερῶν ἀναστατώσας καὶ ἐξαγαγὼν εἰς τὴν ἔρημον τοὺς τετρακισχιλίους ἄνδρας τῶν σικαρίων;	Are you not 38 then that Egyptian, who before these days made an uproar, and led out into the wilderness the four thousand [e]assassins?
39 But Paul said, I am a man *which am* a Jew of Tarsus, *a city* in Cilicia, a citizen of no mean city: and I beseech thee suffer me to speak unto the people.	39 Εἶπε δὲ ὁ Παῦλος, Ἐγὼ ἄνθρωπος μέν εἰμι Ἰουδαῖος Ταρσεὺς, τῆς Κιλικίας οὐκ ἀσήμου πόλεως πολίτης· δέομαι δέ σου, ἐπίτρεψόν μοι λαλῆσαι πρὸς τὸν λαόν.	But Paul said, I am, 39 indeed, a Jew from [f]Tarsus, a city in Cilicia, a citizen of no mean city; and I beseech you to permit me to speak to the people.
40 And when he hath given him license, Paul stood on the stairs, and beckoned with the hand unto the people. And when there was made a great silence, he spake unto *them* in the Hebrew tongue, saying,	40 Ἐπιτρέψαντος δὲ αὐτοῦ, ὁ Παῦλος ἑστὼς ἐπὶ τῶν ἀναβαθμῶν κατέσεισε τῇ χειρὶ τῷ λαῷ· πολλῆς δὲ σιγῆς γενομένης, προσεφώνησε τῇ Ἑβραΐδι διαλέκτῳ λέγων,	And when he had 40 permitted him, Paul stood on the stairs, and waved with his hand to the people; and when there was made a great silence, he spoke to them in the Hebrew [g]tongue, saying,
CHAP. XXII.	CHAP. XXII.	CHAP. XXII.
MEN, brethren, and fathers, hear ye my defence *which I make* now unto you.	Ἄνδρες ἀδελφοὶ καὶ πατέρες, ἀκούσατέ μου τῆς πρὸς ὑμᾶς νῦν ἀπολογίας.	BRETHREN, and [h]fathers! 1 Hear my defense which I now make to you. And when they 2
2 (And when they heard that he spake in the Hebrew tongue to them, they kept the more silence: and he saith,)	2 Ἀκούσαντες δὲ ὅτι τῇ Ἑβραΐδι διαλέκτῳ προσεφώνει αὐτοῖς, μᾶλλον παρέσχον ἡσυχίαν. καί φησιν, 3 Ἐγὼ	heard that he spoke the Hebrew tongue, they kept the greater silence. And he says,

[d] Ἑλληνιστὶ γινώσκεις, do you know Greek? "The adverb stands in place of the object, and λαλεῖν is not to be supplied," Kuin., Hack. Τοὺς Συριστὶ ἐπισταμένους, Xen., Cyr., 7. 5. 31, and in Latin, *Græce nescire.* Mey., De Wette, Hack.

[e] Οὐκ ἄρα σὺ εἶ ὁ Αἰγύπτιος ὁ πρὸ τούτων τῶν ἡμερῶν, κ. τ. λ., "art thou not that Egyptian who formerly led out into the wilderness the four thousand of the assassins?" Thomp. Εἰς τὴν ἐρημον, viz. between Egypt and Palestine, as he came from that direction. Τοὺς τετρακισχιλίους, the four thousand. Tholuck as quoted by Hackett. "The event seems to have been quite recent, the precise number being so well known. Felix—when procurator of Judea—was familiar with this fact, occurring as it did during his administration of its affairs. They were called the Sicarii, taking their name, or receiving it, from the Roman *sica*, a curved dagger, adapted by its form to be concealed beneath the clothes. They could use it

for striking a fatal blow, in a crowd, without being observed." Hackett.

[f] Ἐγὼ ἄνθρωπος μὲν εἰμι Ἰουδαῖος Ταρσεὺς, τῆς Κιλικίας οὐκ ἀσήμου πόλεως πολίτης, I am, indeed, a Tarsion Jew. Ταρσεὺς and Ταρεὺς, *nomen urbis Syriæ*—Ταρσεὺς and Ταρσος —are both found in the original Scriptures—a Jew of Tarsos, or Ταρσεὺς.

[g] Τῇ Ἑβραΐδι διαλέκτῳ, in the Syro-Chaldaic. See John 5: 2; 19: 13.

[h] Ἀδελφοὶ καὶ πατερες. Here, as in ch. 7: 2, ανδρες is a mere qualification of αδελφοι και πατερες. Some, however, suppose that ανδρες represents those present, who were neither Jewish brethren nor Sanhedrists, nor civil rulers. It is more, however, in consonance with the Jewish idiom to regard it as above, inasmuch as Paul appeals only to the Jews, speaking in the Hebrew tongue. See Wakef., Wesley, Penn, Murdock.

KING JAMES' VERSION.

3 I am verily a man *which am* a Jew, born in Tarsus, *a city* in Cilicia, yet brought up in this city at the feet of Gamaliel, *and* taught according to the perfect manner of the law of the fathers, and was zealous toward God, as ye all are this day.

4 And I persecuted this way unto the death, binding and delivering into prisons both men and women.

5 As also the high priest doth bear me witness, and all the estate of the elders; from whom also I received letters unto the brethren, and went to Damascus, to bring them which were there bound unto Jerusalem, for to be punished.

6 And it came to pass, that, as I made my journey, and was come nigh unto Damascus about noon, suddenly there shone from heaven a great light round about me.

7 And I fell unto the ground, and heard a voice saying unto me, Saul, Saul, why persecutest thou me?

8 And I answered, Who art thou, Lord? And he said unto me, I am Jesus of Nazareth, whom thou persecutest.

GREEK TEXT.

μέν εἰμι ἀνὴρ Ἰουδαῖος, γεγεννημένος ἐν Ταρσῷ τῆς Κιλικίας, ἀνατεθραμμένος δὲ ἐν τῇ πόλει ταύτῃ παρὰ τοὺς πόδας Γαμαλιὴλ, πεπαιδευμένος κατὰ ἀκρίβειαν τοῦ πατρῴου νόμου, ζηλωτὴς ὑπάρχων τοῦ Θεοῦ, καθὼς πάντες ὑμεῖς ἐστε σήμερον· ⁴ ὃς ταύτην τὴν ὁδὸν ἐδίωξα ἄχρι θανάτου, δεσμεύων καὶ παραδιδοὺς εἰς φυλακὰς ἄνδρας τε καὶ γυναῖκας, ⁵ ὡς καὶ ὁ ἀρχιερεὺς μαρτυρεῖ μοι, καὶ πᾶν τὸ πρεσβυτέριον· παρ᾽ ὧν καὶ ἐπιστολὰς δεξάμενος πρὸς τοὺς ἀδελφοὺς, εἰς Δαμασκὸν ἐπορευόμην, ἄξων καὶ τοὺς ἐκεῖσε ὄντας, δεδεμένους εἰς Ἱερουσαλὴμ, ἵνα τιμωρηθῶσιν. ⁶ ἐγένετο δέ μοι πορευομένῳ καὶ ἐγγίζοντι τῇ Δαμασκῷ περὶ μεσημβρίαν ἐξαίφνης ἐκ τοῦ οὐρανοῦ περιαστράψαι φῶς ἱκανὸν περὶ ἐμέ· ⁷ ἔπεσόν τε εἰς τὸ ἔδαφος, καὶ ἤκουσα φωνῆς λεγούσης μοι, Σαοὺλ, Σαοὺλ, τί με διώκεις; ⁸ Ἐγὼ δὲ ἀπεκρίθην, Τίς εἶ κύριε; Εἶπέ τε πρός με, Ἐγώ εἰμι Ἰησοῦς ὁ Ναζωραῖος ὃν σὺ διώκεις. ⁹ Οἱ δὲ

REVISED VERSION.

I am indeed a Jew, born in 3 Tarsus in Cilicia, yet brought ¹up in this city, and taught at the feet of Gamaliel, according to the perfect law of our fathers, and was as zealous toward God, as you all are this day. And I persecuted those 4 of this ʲway to death, binding and delivering into prison both men and woman, as also the 5 high priest and the whole body of the elders can bear me testimony; from whom also I received letters to the brethren, and went to Damascus, to bring those that were bound there to Jerusalem, to be punished. And as I was on my 6 ᵏjourney, and was come nigh to Damascus about noon, suddenly there shone from heaven a great light around me: and I ˡfell to the ground, and 7 heard a voice saying to me, Saul, Saul, why do you persecute ᵐme? And I answered, 8 Who art thou, Lord? And he said to me, I am Jesus of Nazareth, whom you persecute. And they who were 9

---

¹ *Ἀνατεθραμμενος—ανατρεφω*, to nourish, to bring up. In our country and currency, *to raise, raised up*—a provincialism to be avoided. We *raise* live stock, and we *raise* families. We nourish children. We supply the means of support, of growth, and physical and mental development.

Πεπαιδευμενος has respect to his education, but *ανατεθραμμενος* to his physical development. While born at Tarsus, he was both brought up to manhood and educated in Jerusalem.

ʲ *Ταυτην την ὁδον, those of this way*. It is with us, in this age and country, to say A is of "*this way* of thinking," and B of "*that way* of thinking." These we regard as *provincialisms* which should not have any place in *the book* which every man should read, and whose style must, more or less, enter into that of all who love to read it. Its formative influence is observed in all who make it a study.

Αχρι θανατου. The result, not the aim, as well observed

by Grotius and Hackett. To persecute Christians to death, however irreligious, on the part of persecutors, is nevertheless a legible and conspicuous monument on their part, in attestation of the value which they profess to cherish for true religion. In the very act of persecution, all persecutors confess that true religion is of transcendent importance. And even infidels hate it, because it threatens eternal ruin to all those who oppose its claims and pretensions. To banish, to kill, or even to imprison any one for his faith, is a tribute paid to the faith which he professes, indicative of the impotency of those who war against it. No infidel can be a martyr in its proper sense.

ᵏ Not "*event*," *επορευομην*—was journeying. We say in our idiom, was on his journey.

ˡ *Επεσα* is, in our text, changed into *επεσον*. The former is an Alexandrian form. Hackett.

ᵐ See ch. 9 : 4, note z.

KING JAMES' VERSION.

9 And they that were with me saw indeed the light, and were afraid; but they heard not the voice of him that spake to me.

10 And I said, What shall I do, Lord? And the Lord said unto me, Arise, and go unto Damascus, and there it shall be told thee of all things which are appointed for thee to do.

11 And when I could not see for the glory of that light, being led by the hand of them that were with me, I came into Damascus.

12 And one Ananias, a devout man according to the law, having a good report of all the Jews which dwelt *there*,

13 Came unto me, and stood, and said unto me, Brother Saul, receive thy sight. And the same hour I looked up upon him.

14 And he said, The God of our fathers hath chosen thee, that thou shouldest know his

GREEK TEXT.

σὺν ἐμοὶ ὄντες τὸ μὲν φῶς ἐθεάσαντο, καὶ ἔμφοβοι ἐγένοντο· τὴν δὲ φωνὴν οὐκ ἤκουσαν τοῦ λαλοῦντός μοι. 10 εἶπον δὲ, Τί ποιήσω κύριε; Ὁ δὲ κύριος εἶπε πρός με, Ἀναστὰς πορεύου εἰς Δαμασκόν. κἀκεῖ σοι λαληθήσεται περὶ πάντων ὧν τέτακταί σοι ποιῆσαι. 11 Ὡς δὲ οὐκ ἐνέβλεπον ἀπὸ τῆς δόξης τοῦ φωτὸς ἐκείνου, χειραγωγούμενος ὑπὸ τῶν συνόντων μοι, ἦλθον εἰς Δαμασκόν. 12 Ἀνανίας δέ τις, ἀνὴρ εὐσεβὴς κατὰ τὸν νόμον, μαρτυρούμενος ὑπὸ πάντων τῶν κατοικούντων Ἰουδαίων, 13 ἐλθὼν πρός με καὶ ἐπιστὰς εἶπέ μοι, Σαοὺλ ἀδελφὲ, ἀνάβλεψον. Κἀγὼ αὐτῇ τῇ ὥρᾳ ἀνέβλεψα εἰς αὐτόν. 14 ὁ δὲ εἶπεν, Ὁ Θεὸς τῶν πατέρων ἡμῶν προεχειρίσατό σε γνῶναι τὸ θέλημα αὐ-

REVISED VERSION.

with me, saw indeed the light,
and were afraid: but they
understood not the [n]voice of
him that spake to me. And 10
I said, What shall I do, Lord?
And the Lord said to me,
Arise, and go into Damascus;
and there it shall be told you
concerning all the things
which are appointed you to
do. And as I could not see 11
for the splendor of that light,
I was led by the hand by
those who were with me, and
came into Damascus. And 12
one Ananias, a [o]devout man according to the law, well spoken of among all the Jews who
dwelt there, came to me, and
stood, and said to me, Brother 13
Saul, receive your sight, and
the same hour I looked up
upon [p]him. And he said, The 14
God of our fathers has chosen
[q]you, that you should know his

---

[n] *Την δε φωνην ουκ ηκουσαν.* Wakef., Wes., Penn, Murd., Thompson have "*hear;*" Boothroyd has "*distinctly heard.*" In Hebrew usage it is often equivalent to *understand* and *obey.* And as they *saw* the light, we must suppose they *heard;* for why should one sense be paralyzed, and not the other? It is, therefore, more consonant, to employ the figurative sense, *understand*, than the literal, *hear.* *Ακουει* sometimes passes into *οἱ δε.* So we find it in Mark 14 : 11. Robinson's Greek Lex. This is a Hebraism very common in the gospels; to *hear* is to *understand*, and sometimes to *obey*, in Hebrew usage. See Gesenius.

Και εμφοβοι εγενοντο. Omitted by Ln., Tf.; a probable omission by Gb.

[o] *Ευσεβης,* not *ευλαβης,* is the true reading in this place. Hack., "cum multis aliis."

[p] Not *αναβλεψον,* as chap. 9 : 12, but *αναβλεψα εις αυτον,* I looked *up*, upon him.

[q] *Προεχειρισατο σε γνωναι — προχειριζωμαι*; found only here and in ch. 26 : 16. "*Hath chosen thee,*" com. ver., and in ch. 26. We have again in this book, ch. 10 : 41, *προχειροτονεομαι* rendered "*chosen before.*"

These two words, *προχειριζομαι* and *προχειροτονεομαι*, are not precise equivalents. The former is rendered, in the Vulgate, *præordinavit te*, has *foreordained* thee; by Erasmus, *preparavit te*, he has *prepared* thee; by Beza, *designavit te*, he has *designed* thee; by the Syriac, Arabic, and Æthiopic, *constituit te*, he has *constituted* thee, or *appointed you. Non gravate verto.* "I do not with regret," says Edward Leigh, author of the "*Critica Sacra,*" *the sacred criticisms*, on both Testaments, Hebrew and Greek, "translate *προεχειρισατο*, in this place, *sumpsit te ut cognoscas voluntatem ejus, he has taken you, chosen you*, or *drawn you.* By the Greek classic writers, *αιρουμαι*, representative of בחר, may indicate, to *choose*, to *claim*, to *elect.* See Phil. 1 : 22; 2 Thess. 2 : 1, 3; Hebrews 11 : 25. *Αιρεομαι, eligo*, is tantamount to "I have chosen thee." *Choosing rather to suffer affliction*, com. ver. of Heb. 11 : 25. "*Chosen thee,*" in this place, covers the whole area of this word, so far as we can trace its history in holy and classic writings.

Προχειροτονεομαι, prius designor, Acts 10 : 41. It is found nowhere else in holy writ; and here, in its participial form, *προ χειροτονημενοις*—the longest word in the Christian Scriptures—a composite term of three words, *προ, ante*, before; *χειρ, hand*, and *τεινω, tendo, extendo*, in its elements, *I before stretched out my hand;* tantamount, in miniature, to, *I choose.* The etymological history of the word *choose*, as given by Webster and Richardson, in its Anglo-Saxon origin, is: *ceosan, cisan, chese, choice*, anciently written *chose*; to cull out one thing before another; tantamount to *eligo, elect*, or *choose out*

KING JAMES' VERSION.	GREEK TEXT.	REVISED VERSION.
will, and see that Just One, and shouldest hear the voice of his mouth.	τοῦ, καὶ ἰδεῖν τὸν δίκαιον, καὶ ἀκοῦσαι φωνὴν ἐκ τοῦ στόματος αὐτοῦ· ¹⁵ ὅτι ἔσῃ μάρτυς αὐτῷ	will, and see that Just One, and hear the voice of his mouth. For you shall be his 15 ʳwitness to all men, of what
15 For thou shalt be his witness unto all men of what thou hast seen and heard.	πρὸς πάντας ἀνθρώπους, ὧν ἑώρακας καὶ ἤκουσας. ¹⁶ καὶ νῦν τί μέλλεις; ἀναστὰς βάπτισαι	you have seen and heard. And now why do you delay? 16 Arise, and be immersed, and
16 And now why tarriest thou? arise, and be baptized, and wash away thy sins, calling on the name of the Lord.	καὶ ἀπόλουσαι τὰς ἁμαρτίας σου, ἐπικαλεσάμενος τὸ ὄνομα τοῦ κυρίου. ¹⁷ Ἐγένετο δέ μοι ὑπο-	wash away your sins, invoking the name of the ˢLord. And when I returned to Je- 17
17 And it came to pass, that, when I was come again to Je-	στρέψαντι εἰς Ἱερουσαλὴμ, καὶ προσευχομένου μου ἐν τῷ ἱερῷ,	rusalem, even while I prayed

of, to *prefer*, to *select from others of the same class, tribe*, or *condition*. For some reason, from *coesan*, Saxon, up to קבץ, to *collect, select*, or to *choose*, intimates a class *from* which, and a class *to* which, the person or thing to which *preference* is given, is assigned. Indeed, all this is implied and expressed in the word *preference*, which we have taken from the Romans of ancient pagan Rome. *Preference*, in its etymology and in our currency, is placing one thing or person before another. This appears equally true in *creation, providence, moral government*, and in *redemption*.

Προσχειροτονεομαι, prius designor. But why the word χειρ, hand! and that, too, as the central idea in the radix of this word! Its philosophy and philology is thus given by plenary authority. *Græca vox dicta est a porrigindis digitis-quo gestro* suffragabatur *olim populus*. So Erasmus and Beza. In former or ancient times, the people gave their suffrage by stretching out their fingers; what we laconically call *a shew of hands*, or fingers. See *Critica Sacra, ad verbum,*

ʳ *Ὁτι εσῃ μαρτυς. Μαρτυς* and *μαρτυρ* always have in them the full orbed idea of a *witness*. The *slain witnesses* have had the posthumous honor of having this word, almost if not altogether, appropriated to them. They constitute, in the minds of the multitude, the only martyrs. But it is a superlative mistake.

Paul and the original twelve were all *martyrs*, in its proper sense, from the day of Pentecost to the last verse, and to the last word of John at the close of the Apocalypse. All other martyrs, so called, are unworthy of the name, as used in the *Christian* Scriptures. Webster, in his Dictionary, says, "a martyr is one who by his death bears witness to the truth of the Gospel." This is true lexicographically, or in the currency of English and other modern languages. But currency is not always gold; and, in this case, it is base coin. No one could be a *witness* of Christ's death, burial, resurrection, or ascension, who did not witness, or see, *with his own eyes*, these events; and this is precisely tantamount to saying, that no one could be a martyr on any other testimony than on

that of one, or more of his five senses. This is the reason why Paul was born out of due time, and never could have been a martyr, had not Jesus Christ visibly appeared to him, and so spoke that he both *saw* him, and *heard* his voice. Hence the declaration, you shall be his *witness*, or *martyr* to all men, *of what you have seen and heard*.

ˢ *Αναστας βαπτισαι και απολυσαι τας αμαρτιας σου.* We have here three imperatives in fact, and two in form. *Αναστας.* This verse is felicitously exegetically developed by Professor Hackett. We shall quote the whole of it:

"*Αναστας* stands opposed to *μελλεις*, that is, *without delay.* See on ch. 9 : 18. *Βαπτισαι, be baptized;* or, with a stricter adherence to the form, *have thyself baptized* (De Wette). One of the uses of the middle voice is to express an act which a person procures another to perform for him. This is the only instance in which the verb occurs, in this voice, with reference to Christian baptism.

"*Και απολουσαι τας αμαρτιας σου, and wash away your sins.* This clause states a result of the immersion, in language derived from the nature of that ordinance. It answers to *εις αφεσιν αμαρτιων*, in ch. 2 : 38. Immersion is represented as having this importance or efficacy because it is the sign of the repentance and faith which are the conditions of salvation. *Επικαλεσαμενος το ονομα αυτου* supplies, essentially, the place of *επι τῳ ονοματι Ιησου Χριστου*, in ch. 2 : 38. See the note on that clause. *Του Κυριου*, after *ονομα*, has much less support than *αυτου*. It is rejected by Gb., Sch., Ln., Tf. The pronoun can refer only to Christ. Comp. ch. 9 : 14."

Prof. Hackett sustains the com. ver. of this verse. His words are: "This clause states a result of baptism in language derived from the nature of that ordinance. It answers to *εις αφεσιν αμαρτιων*, in Acts 2 : 38, i. e., submit to the rite in order to be forgiven. In both passages baptism is represented as having this importance or efficacy, because it is the sign of the repentance and faith, which are the conditions of this salvation." See Hackett, 22 : 10.

KING JAMES' VERSION.

rusalem, even while I prayed in the temple, I was in a trance;

18 And saw him saying unto me, Make haste, and get thee quickly out of Jerusalem; for they will not receive thy testimony concerning me.

19 And I said, Lord, they know that I imprisoned, and beat in every synagogue them that believed on thee:

20 And when the blood of thy martyr Stephen was shed, I also was standing by, and consenting unto his death, and kept the raiment of them that slew him.

21 And he said unto me, Depart: for I will send thee far hence unto the Gentiles.

22 And they gave him audience unto this word, and *then* lifted up their voices, and said, Away with such a *fellow* from the earth: for it is not fit that he should live.

23 And as they cried out, and

GREEK TEXT.

γενέσθαι με ἐν ἐκστάσει, [18] καὶ ἰδεῖν αὐτὸν λέγοντά μοι, Σπεῦσον καὶ ἔξελθε ἐν τάχει ἐξ Ἱερουσαλήμ· διότι οὐ παραδέξονταί σου τὴν μαρτυρίαν περὶ ἐμοῦ. [19] Κἀγὼ εἶπον, Κύριε, αὐτοὶ ἐπίστανται, ὅτι ἐγὼ ἤμην φυλακίζων καὶ δέρων κατὰ τὰς συναγωγὰς τοὺς πιστεύοντας ἐπὶ σέ· [20] καὶ ὅτε ἐξεχεῖτο τὸ αἷμα Στεφάνου τοῦ μάρτυρός σου, καὶ αὐτὸς ἤμην ἐφεστὼς καὶ συνευδοκῶν τῇ ἀναιρέσει αὐτοῦ, καὶ φυλάσσων τὰ ἱμάτια τῶν ἀναιρούντων αὐτόν. [21] Καὶ εἶπε πρός με, Πορεύου, ὅτι ἐγὼ εἰς ἔθνη μακρὰν ἐξαποστελῶ σε.

[22] Ἤκουον δὲ αὐτοῦ ἄχρι τούτου τοῦ λόγου, καὶ ἐπῆραν τὴν φωνὴν αὐτῶν λέγοντες, Αἶρε ἀπὸ τῆς γῆς τὸν τοιοῦτον· οὐ γὰρ καθῆκον αὐτὸν ζῆν. [23] Κραυγαζόντων δὲ αὐτῶν, καὶ ῥιπτούν-

REVISED VERSION.

in the temple, I was in a 'trance; and beheld him say- 18 ing to me, Make haste, and go quickly out of Jerusalem; for they will not receive your testimony concerning me. And 19 I said, Lord, they know that I imprisoned, and beat in every synagogue those who believed on thee: And when the blood 20 of Stephen thy "witness, was shed, I also was standing by consenting, and kept the raiment of them who slew him. And he said to me, Depart; 21 for I will send you out far 'hence to the Gentiles.

And they heard him up to 22 this word, and then raised their voices, and said, Away with such a fellow from the earth: for it is not fit that he should "live. And as they 23 shouted, and threw up their ×clothes, and cast dust into

---

[t] Εκστασις. Literally, an ecstasy. This word occurs eight times in the N. T., four times translated *trance*, twice *amazement*, and twice *astonishment*. *Trance*, in Luke's style, four times indicates an ecstasy, or suspension of the senses. It is such a paroxysm as suspends the action of all the senses for a time, and places the mind beyond the control of the physical laws of our being.

Με accompanies γενεσθαι, though εγενετο has the same logical subject.

[u] See v. 15, note r.

Τη αναιρεσι omitted by Gb., Sch., Ln., Tf.

[v] Εξαποστελλω. Στελλω, I send ; απο, from me ; εξ, out ; or, I send out from me. Αποστελλω whence αποστολος, and whence αποστολη. This is a very peculiar word. It is first found in N. Test., Matt. 10 : 2 ; but it is of higher antiquity. It was used by the Greeks from a very high antiquity. It was first indicative of any one sent out with power, or authority—*mittere cum potestate et autoritate aliqua.* *The captains of ships*, long before the Christian era, were by the ancients called *apostles.* Chamier, quoted by Leigh, in his Crit. Sacra, says, "*Significat cursum navis dirigere et de dirigendis navibus disponere et constituere.*" Indeed, στολος classem significat; hence the commander of a fleet, or *navy*

was called, by the ancient Greeks, an *apostle*, or *apostolos.*

Jesus Christ, the great captain of salvation, is called an *apostle*, rather *the* apostle, as well as the *high priest* of our religion, Heb. 3 : 1; certain brethren, 2 Cor. 8 : 23, are called the *apostles* of the churches—messengers, com. ver. Epaphroditus is called an apostle of the church at Philippi. All persons commissioned by an individual, a city, a government, and sent with any message, or on any errand, is entitled to the full import and meaning of the word *apostle.* But those whom Jesus Christ himself educated, inspired, and commissioned, are the only apostles clothed with his authority, and entitled to all obedience, respect, and honor by all the disciples of the Lord Jesus Christ, emphatically himself called *the apostle*, as well as *the high priest* of our religion.

Εξαποστελλω, I will send you out as an apostle. This phrase cannot be exactly rendered in our language.

[w] Αχρι τουτου του λογου. This is specially definitive of the very word on the utterance of which he was interrupted. We have a similar instance of such definiteness in the narrative, in ch. 19 : 25. Ου γαρ καθηκον αυτον ζην, for it was inexpedient, or, it was not fit that he should live.

[x] Ριπτουντων τα ιματια, "not *throwing off their garments* as a preparation for stoning Paul," (Grotius, Hack.) being

KING JAMES' VERSION.	GREEK TEXT.	REVISED VERSION.
cast off *their* clothes, and threw dust into the air,	τῶν τὰ ἱμάτια, καὶ κονιορτὸν βαλλόντων εἰς τὸν ἀέρα,	the air, the chiliarch com- 24 manded him to be brought into the castle, and ordered
24 The chief captain commanded him to be brought into the castle, and bade that he should be examined by scourging; that he might know wherefore they cried so against him.	24 ἐκέλευσεν αὐτὸν ὁ χιλίαρχος ἄγεσθαι εἰς τὴν παρεμβολὴν, εἰπὼν μάστιξιν ἀνετάζεσθαι αὐτὸν, ἵνα ἐπιγνῷ δι' ἣν αἰτίαν οὕτως ἐπεφώνουν αὐτῷ.	that he should be examined by ʸscourging, that he might ascertain wherefore they cried out against him. And as they 25
25 And as they bound him with thongs, Paul said unto the centurion that stood by, Is it lawful for you to scourge a man that is a Roman, and uncondemned?	25 ὡς δὲ προέτεινεν αὐτὸν τοῖς ἱμᾶσιν, εἶπε πρὸς τὸν ἑστῶτα ἑκατόνταρχον ὁ Παῦλος, Εἰ ἄνθρωπον Ῥωμαῖον καὶ ἀκατάκριτον ἔξεστιν ὑμῖν μαστίζειν;	were binding him with ᶻthongs, Paul said to the centurion who stood by, Is it lawful for you to scourge a man who is a Roman, and uncondemned? When the 26
26 When the centurion heard *that*, he went and told the chief captain, saying, Take heed what thou doest; for this man is a Roman.	26 Ἀκούσας δὲ ὁ ἑκατόνταρχος, προσελθὼν ἀπήγγειλε τῷ χιλιάρχῳ λέγων, Ὅρα τί μέλλεις ποιεῖν· ὁ γὰρ ἄνθρωπος οὗτος Ῥωμαῖός ἐστι.	centurion heard that, he went and told the chiliarch, saying, Take ᵃheed what you are about to do; for this man is a Roman. Then the chiliarch came, and 27
27 Then the chief captain came, and said unto him, Tell me, art thou a Roman? He said, Yea.	27 Προσελθὼν δὲ ὁ χιλίαρχος εἶπεν αὐτῷ, Λέγε μοι, εἰ σὺ Ῥωμαῖος εἶ; Ὁ δὲ ἔφη, Ναί.	said to him, Tell me, are you a Roman? He said, Yes. And 28
28 And the chief captain answered, With a great sum obtained I this freedom. And Paul said, But I was *free*-born.	28 Ἀπεκρίθη τε ὁ χιλίαρχος, Ἐγὼ πολλοῦ κεφαλαίου τὴν πολιτείαν ταύτην ἐκτησάμην. Ὁ δὲ Παῦλος ἔφη, Ἐγὼ δὲ καὶ γεγέννημαι.	the chiliarch answered, With a great sum I obtained this citizenship; and Paul said, But I was born *with it*. Then 29
29 Then straightway they departed from him which should have examined him: and the chief captain also was afraid, after he knew that he was a Roman, and because he had bound him.	29 Εὐθέως οὖν ἀπέστησαν ἀπ' αὐτοῦ οἱ μέλλοντες αὐτὸν ἀνετάζειν. καὶ ὁ χιλίαρχος δὲ ἐφοβήθη, ἐπιγνοὺς ὅτι Ῥωμαῖός ἐστι, καὶ ὅτι ἦν αὐτὸν δεδεκώς.	immediately they departed from him who were about to have examined him; and the chiliarch also was afraid after he knew that he was a Roman, and because he had bound him.
30 On the morrow, because he would have known the cer-	30 Τῇ δὲ ἐπαύριον βουλόμενος γνῶναι τὸ ἀσφαλὲς, τὸ τί κατη-	On the next day, being de- 30 sirous to know with certainty

now a prisoner—rather tossing them in a frenzied mood into the air—at the same time casting dust into the air. This is usually done by mobs and infuriate persons, to excite the passions of those around them.

ʸ Ὁ χιλιαρχος—εκελευσεν—μαστιξιν ανεταζεσθαι αυτον, *the chiliarch gave orders that he should be examined by scourging.* Such was Roman civilization compared with ours, or rather with Christian civilization. Ειπων, *directing; saying* is too tame for such an oracle at such a time. Επω is sometimes represented by *command*, Luke 4 : 3; 9 : 54; 2 Cor. 4 : 6, etc.

ᶻ Ὁς δε προετεινεν αυτον τοις ἱμασιν, "as they stretched him

forth for the thongs," De Wette, Meyer, Rob. Others say, "stretched him forth with *the thongs,*" consisting of a plurality. It would appear *with those in use,* according to law. This seems to be indicated by the fact that the chiliarch commanded him to be unbound, as soon as he understood that he was a Roman citizen. Hack.

Binding him as a prisoner was not illegal, but binding him for scourging was illegal, and, therefore, the centurion feared the law, and released him.

ᵃ "Take heed," lacks authority, and is rejected by Gb., and others. It is merely a supplement. The most approved reading is simply, "*What do you?*" This man is a Roman!

KING JAMES' VERSION.	GREEK TEXT.	REVISED VERSION.
tainty wherefore he was accused of the Jews, he loosed him from *his* bands, and commanded the chief priests and all their council to appear, and brought Paul down, and set him before them.	γορεῖται παρὰ τῶν Ἰουδαίων, ἔλυσεν αὐτὸν ἀπὸ τῶν δεσμῶν, καὶ ἐκέλευσεν ἐλθεῖν τοὺς ἀρχιερεῖς καὶ ὅλον τὸ συνέδριον αὐτῶν· καὶ καταγαγὼν τὸν Παῦλον ἔστησεν εἰς αὐτούς.	on what account he was accused by the Jews, he loosed him from his bonds, and commanded the chief priests and all their council to appear, and having brought down Paul, he placed him before them.

CHAP. XXIII.	CHAP. XXIII.	CHAP. XXIII.
AND Paul, earnestly beholding the council, said, Men *and* brethren, I have lived in all good conscience before God until this day. 2 And the high priest Ananias commanded them that stood by him, to smite him on the mouth. 3 Then said Paul unto him, God shall smite thee, *thou* whited wall: for sittest thou to judge me after the law, and commandest me to be smitten contrary to the law? 4 And they that stood by,	ΑΤΕΝΙΣΑΣ δὲ ὁ Παῦλος τῷ συνεδρίῳ εἶπεν, Ἄνδρες ἀδελφοὶ, ἐγὼ πάσῃ συνειδήσει ἀγαθῇ πεπολίτευμαι τῷ Θεῷ ἄχρι ταύτης τῆς ἡμέρας. 2 Ὁ δὲ ἀρχιερεὺς Ἀνανίας ἐπέταξε τοῖς παρεστῶσιν αὐτῷ, τύπτειν αὐτοῦ τὸ στόμα. 3 τότε ὁ Παῦλος πρὸς αὐτὸν εἶπε, Τύπτειν σε μέλλει ὁ Θεὸς, τοῖχε κεκονιαμένε· καὶ σὺ κάθῃ κρίνων με κατὰ τὸν νόμον, καὶ παρανομῶν κελεύεις με τύπτεσθαι; 4 Οἱ δὲ	AND Paul, earnestly beholding the council, said, [b]Brethren, I have lived to God with all good conscience until this day. And the high priest Ananias commanded them who stood by him, to strike him on the mouth. Then Paul said to him, God will strike you, you whited wall: for do you sit to judge me according to the law, and command me to be struck contrary to the law? And they

[b] *Ατενισας δε ὁ Παυλος τῳ συνεδιον.* Earnestness in oratory is well defined, and recommended in this case. *Ατενιζω,* occulos in aliquem defigo, *to fasten, to fix,* with a *piercing, penetrating gaze, the eyes upon a person or object.* Something of excitement, or of intensity of feeling, is unambiguously indicated by Paul in his exordium on this occasion. There is much of argument and eloquence in a look. There is an all-puissant, all-subduing glance of the eye; and Paul, in his earnestness and point on this occasion, affords us a fine specimen of it.

Τῳ συνεδριῳ—συνεδριον, Sanhedrim council. Luke, in this single book, refers to it fourteen times, and once in his gospel. All the other writers in the N. T. refer to it only seven times. Its etymology is fully indicative of its distinctive character— *συν, together, εδρα, sedes—a sitting together.* Moses and his *seventy elders* gave it a local habitation and a name, in both sacred and profane history. *Συνεδριον,* in Grecian history, indicates a *council,* a *court—et locus in quem conveniunt senatores. Thesaurus Græcæ Linguæ.* Num. ch. 11; Deut. 27 : 1; 31 : 9; Ezekiel 8 : 11. In one acceptation of it, " An assembly of prelates and doctors convened to regulate matters of discipline in Church affairs."

Looking in the face of the whole tribunal, he, with an intrepid countenance, affirms *εγω πασῃ συνειδησει αγαθῃ.*

Ego optima gaudens conscientia voluntatis divinæ ad hunc usque diem. Activum, *πολιτευιν,* et medium, *πολιτευεσθαι,* notat rempublicam administrare, publicum in civitate munus administrare. Thucyd. viii. 97. Kuin. vol. 3, p. 330. Conscience, in this case, is well defined. It is a judge, whose verdict upon our own acts, in thought, in volition, in word, or in action, creates within us pleasing or unpleasing associations or feelings, as contemplated in reference to a perfect law of perfect happiness, and an omniscient Judge.

Συνειδησει αγαθῃ πεπολιτευμαι. It is worthy of notice, that in some thirty-two occurrences of this word *συνειδησις,* in the Christian Scriptures, it is always, in com. ver., translated *conscience.*

Πολιτευομαι is found only twice, and *πολιτευμα* once, in the N. Test. Both words are, com. ver., translated *conversation;* the latter, literally, *enfranchisement,* or *community.* Greek Concordance of N. Test. ; the former, " *I have lived,*" Acts 23 : 1; and Phil. 1 : 27, *conversation.* But this is *obsolete.* Webster, " *familiar intercourse.*" Behavior, in general, is intended; and such was its currency at the date of the com. ver.

The natural or syntactic order of this sentence is as follows, and ought, in my judgment, to be preferred: " Brethren, I have lived to God, with all good conscience, until this day."

KING JAMES' VERSION.

said, Revilest thou God's high priest?

5 Then said Paul, I wist not, brethren, that he was the high priest: for it is written, Thou shalt not speak evil of the ruler of thy people.

6 But when Paul perceived that the one part were Sadducees, and the other Pharisees, he cried out in the council, Men *and* brethren, I am a Pharisee, the son of a Pharisee: of the hope and resurrection of the dead I am called in question.

7 And when he had so said, there arose a dissension between

GREEK TEXT.

παρεστῶτες εἶπον, Τὸν ἀρχιερέα τοῦ Θεοῦ λοιδορεῖς; 5 Ἔφη τε ὁ Παῦλος, Οὐκ ᾔδειν ἀδελφοὶ, ὅτι ἐστὶν ἀρχιερεύς· γέγραπται γὰρ, Ἄρχοντα τοῦ λαοῦ σου οὐκ ἐρεῖς κακῶς. 6 Γνοὺς δὲ ὁ Παῦλος ὅτι τὸ ἓν μέρος ἐστὶ Σαδδουκαίων, τὸ δὲ ἕτερον Φαρισαίων, ἔκραξεν ἐν τῷ συνεδρίῳ, Ἄνδρες ἀδελφοὶ, ἐγὼ Φαρισαῖός εἰμι, υἱὸς Φαρισαίου· περὶ ἐλπίδος καὶ ἀναστάσεως νεκρῶν ἐγὼ κρίνομαι. 7 Τοῦτο δὲ αὐτοῦ λαλήσαντος, ἐγένετο στάσις τῶν Φα-

REVISED VERSION.

who stood by, said, Do you revile God's ᶜhigh priest? Then said Paul, ᵈI knew not, 5 brethren, that he was the high priest; for it is written, You shall not speak evil of the ruler of your people.

But when Paul perceived 6 that the one part were Sadducees, and the other Pharisees, he cried out in the council, Brethren, I am a ᵉPharisee, the son of a Pharisee: ᶠconcerning a hope and a resurrection of the dead I am now judged. And 7 when he had so said, there

---

ᶜ Ὁ ἀρχιερεα τοῦ Θεου, *pontificem, qui jussu et auctoritate Dei agit, vicem Dei gerit. Conviciis proscindere.* Kuin. The high priest Ananias, not the Annas or Ananus named 4 : 6; Luke 3 : 2; John 18 : 13. "He, unquestionably," says Winer, "is the son of Nebedæus, who obtained the office of high priest under procurator Tiberius Alexander, A. D. 48, the immediate successor of Camidus or Camithus." (Josep. Ant. 20 : 5, 2. Hack.)

A pontiff, who by the command and authority of God acts for God, most certainly stands in his place; and we must approach to God and commune with God through him, while through him God communes with us. Such a dignitary is not to be contemned.

Ουκ ηδειν αδελφοι, οτι εστιν αρχιερευς. These words have long been in debate. Cameranus, Marnixius, Thiessius and Heinrichius regard these words as used ironically; equivalent to, that *he did not execute the office.* Others interpret them, that he did not acknowledge him to be high priest, but as usurping this dignity. But, as well observed by others, if the apostle did not wish this dignity to enure to him, he would not have said that he did not know. *Ουκ ηδειν,* but rather *ουκ οιδα τουτον αρχιερεα.* I do not know, or acknowledge, this person as high priest of this people. Kuin. Ananias had been dispossessed of this office, and Jonathan raised to that dignity. On the death of Jonathan, it continued for some time vacant; and, in this interval, Ananias undertook to fill it, but without proper authority. Boothr. "I was not aware that he was the high priest," *Ουκ ηδειν οτι εστιν αρχιερευς,* cannot be fairly translated, *I do not acknowledge him* to be high priest. Nor is it probable that Paul would enter into a discussion of the legality of his claim. He simply declares his own ignorance of the fact, having been some time absent from the country. He, however, apologizes

for his charge or allegation of hypocrisy, and more especially as Ananias was, at least, a magistrate in authority.

ᵈ "I did not know." This might not be *literally* true, and yet, in the Hebrew license of this verb, it was true. It is equivalent, in Hebrew currency, to *perceive,* to *know,* to *make known,* to *acknowledge,* and to *consider.* At the moment the idea of the *judge,* absorbed the idea of the high priest, so that Paul did not consider, or regard him as acting the high priest but the civil judge.

ᵉ "I am a Pharisee," was true, in one sense, so far as he was *the son of a Pharisee.* But this is an *oratorical* argument, on the principle—*Divide and conquer.* It was as *lawful* as *rhetorical.*

ᶠ Περι ελπιδος και αναστασεως νεκρων εγω κρινομαι, *de spe et resurrectione mortuorum ego in judicium vocor.* Beza, Biblia Sacra, I. Tremellio et Francisco Junio, London. 1581. Literally, according to the text, *concerning a hope and a resurrection of the dead, I am judged.* "Concerning the hope," Boothr., Wakefield. They supply *the.* "For hope's sake and a resurrection of the dead," Meyer, De Wette. Or, by Hendiadys, "*the hope of the resurrection,*" Kuin., Ols., quoted by Hack. "For a hope even of a resurrection of the dead," Thomp. "The hope and resurrection of the dead," Dodd. "The hope of a resurrection," Penn. So many theories of the resurrection of the dead, extant and obsolete, we prefer to be strictly literal. Hence, according to Bagster's Improved and Corrected Text, we render it, "concerning a hope and a resurrection of the dead I am now judged." Other reasons give to this an importance greater than the then existing controversy between the Pharisees and the Sadducees. Instead of *Φαρισαιου, Φαρισαιων* is regarded as a better reading by Ln., Tf., Gb.

KING JAMES' VERSION.	GREEK TEXT.	REVISED VERSION.
the Pharisees and the Sadducees: and the multitude was divided. 8 For the Sadducees say that there is no resurrection, neither angel, nor spirit: but the Pharisees confess both. 9 And there arose a great cry: and the scribes *that were* of the Pharisees' part arose, and strove, saying, We find no evil in this man: but if a spirit or an angel hath spoken to him, let us not fight against God. 10 And when there arose a	ρισαίων καὶ τῶν Σαδδουκαίων, καὶ ἐσχίσθη τὸ πλῆθος. ⁸ Σαδδουκαῖοι μὲν γὰρ λέγουσι μὴ εἶναι ἀνάστασιν, μηδὲ ἄγγελον μήτε πνεῦμα· Φαρισαῖοι δὲ ὁμολογοῦσι τὰ ἀμφότερα. ⁹ ἐγένετο δὲ κραυγὴ μεγάλη· καὶ ἀναστάντες οἱ γραμματεῖς τοῦ μέρους τῶν Φαρισαίων διεμάχοντο λέγοντες, Οὐδὲν κακὸν εὑρίσκομεν ἐν τῷ ἀνθρώπῳ τούτῳ· εἰ δὲ πνεῦμα ἐλάλησεν αὐτῷ ἢ ἄγγελος, μὴ θεομαχῶμεν. ¹⁰ Πολλῆς δὲ γε-	arose a [g]dissension between the Pharisees and the Sadducees; and the multitude was divided. For the Sadducees say 8 that there is no resurrection nor angel, nor spirit; but the Pharisees confess [h]both. And 9 there arose a great clamor; and the scribes who were of the Pharisees' party arose, and strove, saying, We find no evil in this man: but, if an angel or spirit spoke to him,—[i] And when there arose 10

---

[g] Στασις, *insurrection, sedition, dissension, uproar, standing.* Such is the whole currency of σχιζω, in N. Test. Its usual representatives in the N. Test. are: *rend, divide, open, break.* It is, with one exception, only found in the historical books. In Hebrews, ch. 9 : 8, it is literally and properly rendered *standing;* because, applied to the tabernacle, indicating its mere continuance; literally, *having a standing.* This word is a valuable monument of the fact, that often the *subject* and the *context* must decide the sense or meaning of a word, especially when it has a liberal currency.

[h] Μηδε αγγελον μητε πνευμα, are often represented by *neque, neither,* but when, as here, in conjunction, in one member of a sentence, they stand to each other as *neither* and *nor,* in our vernacular. But in certain cases, as in the one before us, when preceded by a negative absolute, we extend it to the whole category—no resurrection, no angel, no spirit. Μηδε adds a second denial to the first, while μητε expands this denial into its parts. See Matt. 5 : 34, 35, 36, Hack., Winer, Stuart. Here are four specifications.

Τα αμφοτερα, *both.* Yet there are *three* specifications of the Sadducean infidelity—αναστασις, αγγελος, πνευμα, no resurrection, nor *angel,* nor *spirit.* Boothroyd gets out of this grammatical difficulty by translating it, " *no resurrection nor angel or spirit.*" Also Hack. But Penn has it, " *there is no resurrection, nor angel, nor spirit;*" and instead of " the Pharisees *confess both,*" he gives it, " *confess all these.*" This difficulty has occurred to many thinkers. It occurred to Chrysostom. But it is found in the oldest Greek poets and philosophers. Hence Kuinœl decides " vocabulum αμφοτερα de duobus usurpari solet, sed tria nominata sunt, quæ Sadducæi infelicitata esse dicuntur, tenendum igitur est αμφοτερον etiam de pluribus dici." Chrysostomus, vol. 3, p. 334.

It is, indeed, found in Homer's Odys. 15, 78, αμφοτερον, κυδος τε και αγλαϊη, και ονειαρ. We regard it as indicative of only two distinct ideas, giving two specifications of the

second—*angel* and *spirit*—as representative of a future state —and a spiritual universe—a literal resurrection, and a literal spiritual universe, both which were denied by the Sadducees, and affirmed by the Pharisees. Τα αμφοτερα—Prof. Hackett has it, according to the above analysis, " a resurrection, and the reality of spiritual existences, whether angels, or the souls of the departed." There yet appears a cloud in the horizon of many on the *true analysis of man,* as to the true constituency of man. Man, in Holy Writ, is contemplated as a miniature *trinity* in his nature, the " *likest image*" of God in the universe. Hence the grand reason for his redemption. The word *angel* necessarily denotes no personality in the universe. It is essentially and exclusively an *official* name. It applies to *men, winds, lightnings, pestilence.* These are scripturally called God's *angels,* Psalm 78 : 49. It is applied to men—even *the spies,* entertained by the innkeeper Rahab, are called *angels,* James 2 : 25. Acts 12 : 15. Fire and lightning are God's *angels,* Heb. 1 : 7. They are called *ministering* spirits, *officially.* They are in *nature* spirits, but in *office* and employment *ministers.* Man has a body, a house. He has also a ψυχη, a *soul,* a *life animal.* He has also a πνευμα, a *spirit.* These three make one man. 1 Thess. 5 : 23. To draw the lines of distinction, though somewhat palpable, is not a task to be undertaken here. We can only say that the *spirit* is from God; the *animal soul* is the seat and centre of the animal instincts. In the *lapsus* of humanity it predominates over the spirit, the reason and conscience of man. Hence the necessity of a spiritual new birth. That which is born of the flesh is *flesh,* and that which is born of the spirit is *spirit.*

[i] Οι γραμματεις. The Σαδδουκαιοι μεν and the Φαρισαιοι δε stand in contraposition; hence we have ανασταντες οι γραμματεις, and hence the κραυγη μεγαλη, the great clamor and the favor shown to the apostles by the Pharisees, because of their more cogent evidence of a resurrection in the asser-

KING JAMES' VERSION.

great dissension, the chief captain, fearing lest Paul should have been pulled in pieces of them, commanded the soldiers to go down, and to take him by force from among them, and to bring *him* into the castle.

11 And the night following the Lord stood by him, and said, Be of good cheer, Paul: for as thou hast testified of me in Jerusalem, so must thou bear witness also at Rome.

12 And when it was day, certain of the Jews banded together, and bound themselves under a curse, saying, that they would neither eat nor drink till they had killed Paul.

13 And they were more than

GREEK TEXT.

νομένης στάσεως, εὐλαβηθεὶς ὁ χιλίαρχος μὴ διασπασθῇ ὁ Παῦλος ὑπ᾽ αὐτῶν, ἐκέλευσε τὸ στράτευμα καταβὰν ἁρπάσαι αὐτὸν ἐκ μέσου αὐτῶν, ἄγειν τε εἰς τὴν παρεμβολήν.

11 ΤΗ δὲ ἐπιούσῃ νυκτὶ ἐπιστὰς αὐτῷ ὁ κύριος εἶπε, Θάρσει Παῦλε· ὡς γὰρ διεμαρτύρω τὰ περὶ ἐμοῦ εἰς Ἱερουσαλὴμ, οὕτω σε δεῖ καὶ εἰς Ῥώμην μαρτυρῆσαι. 12 Γενομένης δὲ ἡμέρας, ποιήσαντές τινες τῶν Ἰουδαίων συστροφὴν, ἀνεθεμάτισαν ἑαυτοὺς, λέγοντες μήτε φαγεῖν μήτε πιεῖν ἕως οὗ ἀποκτείνωσι τὸν Παῦλον· 13 ἦσαν δὲ πλείους

REVISED VERSION.

a great dissension, the [1]chiliarch, fearing that Paul would have been pulled in pieces by them, commanded the soldiery to go down, and take him by force from among them, and to bring him into the castle. And the night following, the 11 Lord stood by him, and said, Take courage, for as you have testified of me in Jerusalem, so must you also bear [k]testimony in Rome.

And when it was day, the 12 Jews, having formed a [1]combination, bound themselves under a curse, saying, that they would neither eat nor drink, till they had killed Paul: and 13

---

tion of the real ἀνάστασις τῶν νεκρῶν, in the case and person of the Lord Jesus. The literal resurrection of the dead, in the person of the son of Mary and the son of God, was the omnipotent argument, wielded with irresistable power by the eye-witnesses of the fact, against Sadduceeism and every form of materialism and infidelity which any form of philosophy, falsely so called, has ever obtruded upon mankind.

Μὴ θεομαχῶμεν is, we think, justly repudiated by Gb., Sch., Ln., and Tf. It is nowhere else found in the Christian Scriptures. We have θεομάχος once only in the Christian Scriptures, Acts 5 : 39; but the verb θεομαχέω never, but in this place ; and that, without adequate evidence, from ancient manuscripts or versions.

While Bagster's text retains, "let us not fight against God," it must be conceded that it is without satisfactory authority. Sundry critics repudiate it, and the evidences are against it.

[j] Εὐλαβηθεὶς is somewhat of doubtful authority in this place ; for which, φοβηθεὶς is substituted by Ln., but by Gb. regarded as not so strongly supported. We, therefore, give our suffrage for εὐλαβηθεὶς, and retain the com. ver.

[k] Παῦλε, deservedly, as we think, is repudiated by Gb., Ln., Tf., Sch. Διεμαρτύρω, 2d per. sing. 1st aor. mid., from διαμαρτύρομαι, *etiam atque etiam obtestor. You must again and again witness for me.* "So must thou testify," Boothr., Wes. "*So thou must bear witness,*" Thomp. "So must thou bear testimony," Penn. "So also art thou to testify," Murd. "So must thou also testify," Wake. "So shall thou also bear testimony," Dodd. *Sic et oportet etiam Romæ testificare*—Beza—So it behooves you also to bear witness at Rome.

Διαμαρτύρομαι is, etymologically, more than μαρτυρέω—εομαι, yet are they frequently represented by the same word, in the com. ver., as well as in others. The prefix δια to μαρτυρέω, extends, or intensifies, its value or import. It is more continuative in its operations and activities. It is clumsily expressed by *thoroughly testify*, or *fully* or *completely testify*. Yet this is only expressive of its full signification. This is one of the cases, or instances, wherein the Greek language excels our language. In this case, it contemplates a continuous effort.

[1] For τινες τῶν Ἰουδαίων συστροφὴν, are substituted συστροφὴν οἱ Ἰουδαῖοι by Gb., Ln., Sch., Tf. "Some of the Jews combined together and bound themselves under a curse, saying: that they would neither eat nor drink till they had killed Paul." Boothr. "Certain of the Jews banded together and bound themselves under a curse."

Συστροφή, *concursus, seditio,* Arabs bene, *seditio.* Tumultuarium enim et *seditionum concursum significat:* ut συστρέφειν est populum factiose cogere—sic συστροφή est factiosus cœptus. Crit. Sacra, *in loco.* So the Septuagint, on Judges 14 : 8, συστροφὴ τοῦ λαοῦ—is, *seditio coitio populi.* Hence they use it for *conjuratione,* קשר, σύστασις, a confederacy, a conspiracy. The Romans, in their patriotic mood, would say, on any ominous movement of conspirators, *Qui rempublicam vult salvam esse me sequatur.* Such was the σύστασις, the συνωμοσία, of the Greeks. "Having formed a combination," Mey., Rob., Hack.

This combination, literally, said, "We anathematize ourselves that we will neither eat nor drink till we have killed Paul."

KING JAMES' VERSION.

forty which had made this conspiracy.

14 And they came to the chief priests and elders, and said, We have bound ourselves under a great curse, that we will eat nothing until we have slain Paul.

15 Now therefore ye with the council signify to the chief captain, that he bring him down unto you to-morrow, as though ye would inquire something more perfectly concerning him: and we, or ever he come near, are ready to kill him.

16 And when Paul's sister's son heard of their lying in wait, he went and entered into the castle, and told Paul.

17 Then Paul called one of the centurions unto *him*, and said, Bring this young man unto the chief captain; for he hath a certain thing to tell him.

18 So he took him, and brought *him* to the chief captain, and said, Paul the prisoner called me unto *him*, and prayed me to bring this young man

GREEK TEXT.

τεσσαράκοντα οἱ ταύτην τὴν συνωμοσίαν πεποιηκότες· ¹⁴ οἵτινες προσελθόντες τοῖς ἀρχιερεῦσι καὶ τοῖς πρεσβυτέροις εἶπον, Ἀναθέματι ἀνεθεματίσαμεν ἑαυτούς, μηδενὸς γεύσασθαι ἕως οὗ ἀποκτείνωμεν τὸν Παῦλον. ¹⁵ νῦν οὖν ὑμεῖς ἐμφανίσατε τῷ χιλιάρχῳ σὺν τῷ συνεδρίῳ, ὅπως αὔριον αὐτὸν καταγάγῃ πρὸς ὑμᾶς, ὡς μέλλοντας διαγινώσκειν ἀκριβέστερον τὰ περὶ αὐτοῦ· ἡμεῖς δὲ, πρὸ τοῦ ἐγγίσαι αὐτὸν, ἕτοιμοί ἐσμεν τοῦ ἀνελεῖν αὐτόν. ¹⁶ Ἀκούσας δὲ ὁ υἱὸς τῆς ἀδελφῆς Παύλου τὸ ἔνεδρον, παραγενόμενος καὶ εἰσελθὼν εἰς τὴν παρεμβολὴν, ἀπήγγειλε τῷ Παύλῳ. ¹⁷ προσκαλεσάμενος δὲ ὁ Παῦλος ἕνα τῶν ἑκατοντάρχων, ἔφη, Τὸν νεανίαν τοῦτον ἀπάγαγε πρὸς τὸν χιλίαρχον· ἔχει γάρ τι ἀπαγγεῖλαι αὐτῷ. ¹⁸ Ὁ μὲν οὖν παραλαβὼν αὐτὸν ἤγαγε πρὸς τὸν χιλίαρχον, καί φησιν, Ὁ δέσμιος Παῦλος προσκαλεσάμενός με ἠρώτησε, τοῦτον τὸν

REVISED VERSION.

there were more than forty who had formed this conspiracy. And they went to 14 the chief priest and elders, and said, We have bound ourselves under a great ᵐcurse, that we will eat nothing till we have slain Paul. Now, 15 therefore, you with the ⁿcouncil, signify to the chiliarch that he bring him down to you to-morrow, as though you would inquire something more exactly concerning him: and we, before he can come near, will be ready to kill him.

And when Paul's sister's 16 son heard of the ambush, he went and entered into the castle, and told Paul. Then 17 Paul called one of the ᵒcenturions to him, and said, Bring this young man to the chiliarch; for he has a certain thing to tell him. And so he 18 took him, and brought him to the chiliarch, and says, Paul the ᵖprisoner called me to

---

ᵐ Ἀνεθεματισαμεν ἑαυτους. *We have cursed ourselves*—as explained, v. 13, συνωμοσιαν πεποιηκοτες, *conjuratio*. Crit. Sacr., *in loco*. The reflexive of the third person (as in v. 12) may follow a subject of the first or second person. Kuhner's Greek Gram. and Buttman; Hackett.

ⁿ Συνεδριω—συνεδριον, *consessus*, always, in N. Test., translated *council*. Com. ver.,—it was called the court of *the seventy and two*, and was held only in Jerusalem; from which the Jews retained this word, calling the judges the Sanhedrim. None might appeal to any other. Num. 11 : 26. Critica Sacra. Synagogues are ecclesiastic conventions. Synedria are conventions of civil judges, more frequently alluded to, and named, in this book of Acts, than in all the other Christian Scriptures, *but never once applied to any Christian assembly, summoned or convened for any act of Christian discipline, legislation, or judgment.* It always refers to a pagan or a Jewish institution; never to any Christian assembly.

Χιλιαρχω συν τω συνεδριω—χιλιαρχος, seventeen times occurring in this book, always rendered *chief captain*. Com. ver. The *chiliarch*, often called a *tribune*, had, as his name indicates, the command of a thousand men. Tribunus militum—John 8 : 12—vertendum fuit praefectus cohortis. *A military tribune*, called the *prefect* of a cohort; for so the Latins called him whom the Greeks called a *chiliarch*. But adds Crit. Sacra, a tribune is he who presides over a legion. These, among the Jews, were called *chiliarchs*. Grotius, Leigh.

ᵒ Ἐνα των ἑκατονταρχων—του ανελειν depends on ετοιμοι as a genitive construction. Hack. Εκατανταρχος is often rendered *centurion*; because, in fact, he was the captain or commander of one hundred men; and such is its etymology.

ᵖ Ὁ δεσμιος indicates that Paul was still a prisoner, and that by a chain. The Roman custom was to attach the chain, on the person of the prisoner, to the arm of a Roman soldier.

KING JAMES' VERSION.	GREEK TEXT.	REVISED VERSION.
unto thee, who hath something to say unto thee.	νεανίαν ἀγαγεῖν πρός σε, ἔχοντά τι λαλῆσαί σοι. ¹⁹ Ἐπιλαβό-	him, and requested me to bring this young man to you. Then 19

unto thee, who hath something to say unto thee.

19 Then the chief captain took him by the hand and went *with him* aside privately, and asked *him*, What is that thou hast to tell me?

20 And he said, The Jews have agreed to desire thee, that thou wouldest bring down Paul to-morrow into the council, as though they would inquire somewhat of him more perfectly.

21 But do not thou yield unto them: for there lie in wait for him of them more than forty men, which have bound themselves with an oath, that they will neither eat nor drink till they have killed him: and now are they ready, looking for a promise from thee.

22 So the chief captain *then* let the young man depart, and charged *him*, *See thou* tell no man that thou hast shewed these things to me.

23 And he called unto *him* two centurions, saying, Make ready two hundred soldiers to go to Cesarea, and horsemen threescore and ten, and spearmen two hundred, at the third hour of the night;

24 And provide *them* beasts, that they may set Paul on, and bring *him* safe unto Felix the governor.

νεανίαν ἀγαγεῖν πρός σε, ἔχοντά τι λαλῆσαί σοι. ¹⁹ Ἐπιλαβό-μενος δὲ τῆς χειρὸς αὐτοῦ ὁ χι-λίαρχος, καὶ ἀναχωρήσας κατ᾽ ἰδίαν ἐπυνθάνετο, Τί ἐστιν ὃ ἔχεις ἀπαγγεῖλαί μοι; ²⁰ Εἶπε δὲ, Ὅτι οἱ Ἰουδαῖοι συνέθεντο τοῦ ἐρωτῆσαί σε, ὅπως αὔριον εἰς τὸ συνέδριον καταγάγῃς τὸν Παῦ-λον, ὡς μέλλοντές τι ἀκριβέσ-τερον πυνθάνεσθαι περὶ αὐτοῦ. ²¹ σὺ οὖν μὴ πεισθῇς αὐτοῖς· ἐνεδρεύουσι γὰρ αὐτὸν ἐξ αὐτῶν ἄνδρες πλείους τεσσαράκοντα, οἵτινες ἀνεθεμάτισαν ἑαυτοὺς μήτε φαγεῖν μήτε πιεῖν ἕως οὗ ἀνέλωσιν αὐτόν· καὶ νῦν ἕτοιμοί εἰσι προσδεχόμενοι τὴν ἀπὸ σοῦ ἐπαγγελίαν. ²² Ὁ μὲν οὖν χι-λίαρχος ἀπέλυσε τὸν νεανίαν, παραγγείλας μηδενὶ ἐκλαλῆσαι, ὅτι ταῦτα ἐνεφάνισας πρός με. ²³ Καὶ προσκαλεσάμενος δύο τινὰς τῶν ἑκατοντάρχων εἶπεν, Ἑτοιμάσατε στρατιώτας διακο-σίους, ὅπως πορευθῶσιν ἕως Καισαρείας, καὶ ἱππεῖς ἑβδομή-κοντα, καὶ δεξιολάβους διακο-σίους, ἀπὸ τρίτης ὥρας τῆς νυκ-τός· ²⁴ κτήνη τε παραστῆσαι, ἵνα ἐπιβιβάσαντες τὸν Παῦλον διασώσωσι πρὸς Φήλικα τὸν

him, and requested me to bring this young man to you. Then 19 the chiliarch took him by the hand, and went with him aside privately, and asked him, What is that you have to say to me? And he said, The 20 Jews have agreed to request you, that you would bring down Paul to-morrow into the council, as though they would inquire something about him more perfectly. But do not 21 you yield to them: for there lie in wait for him more than forty men of them, who have bound themselves with an oath, that they will neither eat nor drink till they have killed him; and now are they ready, ᵠlooking for the promise from you. So the chiliarch let 22 the young man depart, and charged him, Tell no person that you have showed these things to me. And he call- 23 ed to him some two of the ʳcenturions, saying, Make ready two hundred soldiers, and seventy horsemen, and two hundred spearmen, to go to Cesarea, at the third hour of the night; and let them pro- 24 vide beasts on which they may place Paul, and bring him safe to Felix the governor. And he 25

ᵠ *Προοδεχομενοι την—επαγγελιαν—Looking for, expecting, waiting for—the promise.* No word, of the same frequency of occurrence in this book, is more uniformly represented by one word than this is—by the word *promise.* Its only exception is found, I. John 1 : 5, in the word *message* ; and in this case alone does it extend beyond one idea. A *message*, indeed, generally, in the *evangelical* economy, is a promise. A message, however, is more general, including a promise, or a threatening. In John's first epistle, it indicates an *annunciation* or *message*, and not simply a promise.

ʳ *Δυο τινας των ἑκατονταρχων—τις* is indefinite—it may be doubtful whether two or more ; but two, at least. *Τις,* joined with numerals, renders them indefinite. So Winer, Kuinoel, Hack., Stuart, etc., regard it.

Δεξιολαβους "occurs only here, and in two obscure writers of the iron age. Its meaning is a riddle," De Wette. The proposed explanations are these : *παραφυλακες*, military lictors who guarded prisoners ; so called from their taking the right-hand side (Suid., Beza, Kuinoel). *Lancers* (Vulg., Eng. ver.), a species of light-armed troops (Meyer), since they are mentioned once in connection with archers and peltasts. Codex A reads, *δεξιοβολους*. Jaculantes dextra. Syr., Hack.

KING JAMES' VERSION.	GREEK TEXT.	REVISED VERSION.

KING JAMES' VERSION.

25 And he wrote a letter after this manner:

26 Claudius Lysias, unto the most excellent governor Felix, *sendeth* greeting.

27 This man was taken of the Jews, and should have been killed of them: then came I with an army, and rescued him, having understood that he was a Roman.

28 And when I would have known the cause wherefore they accused him, I brought him forth into their council:

29 Whom I perceived to be accused of questions of their law, but to have nothing laid to his charge worthy of death, or of bonds.

30 And when it was told me how that the Jews laid wait for the man, I sent straightway to thee, and gave commandment to his accusers also, to say before thee what *they had* against him. Farewell.

31 Then the soldiers, as it was commanded them, took Paul,

GREEK TEXT.

ἡγεμόνα· 25 γράψας ἐπιστολὴν περιέχουσαν τὸν τύπον τοῦτον· 26 Κλαύδιος Λυσίας τῷ κρατίστῳ ἡγεμόνι Φήλικι χαίρειν. 27 Τὸν ἄνδρα τοῦτον συλληφθέντα ὑπὸ τῶν Ἰουδαίων, καὶ μελλοντα ἀναιρεῖσθαι ὑπ᾽ αὐτῶν, ἐπιστὰς σὺν τῷ στρατεύματι ἐξειλόμην αὐτὸν, μαθὼν ὅτι Ῥωμαῖός ἐστι. 28 βουλόμενος δὲ γνῶναι τὴν αἰτίαν δι᾽ ἣν ἐνεκάλουν αὐτῷ, κατήγαγον αὐτὸν εἰς τὸ συνέδριον αὐτῶν· 29 ὃν εὗρον ἐγκαλούμενον περὶ ζητημάτων τοῦ νόμου αὐτῶν, μηδὲν δὲ ἄξιον θανάτου ἢ δεσμῶν ἔγκλημα ἔχοντα. 30 μηνυθείσης δέ μοι ἐπιβουλῆς εἰς τὸν ἄνδρα μέλλειν ἔσεσθαι ὑπὸ τῶν Ἰουδαίων, ἐξαυτῆς ἔπεμψα πρός σε, παραγγείλας καὶ τοῖς κατηγόροις λέγειν τὰ·πρὸς αὐτὸν ἐπὶ σοῦ. Ἔρρωσο. 31 Οἱ μὲν οὖν στρατιῶται, κατὰ τὸ διατεταγμένον αὐτοῖς,

REVISED VERSION.

wrote a letter after this ·manner: Claudius Lysias, to the 26 most excellent governor Felix, sends greeting. This man was 27 taken by the Jews, and was about to be killed by them; but I came with the soldiery, and rescued him, having learned that he was a Roman. And when I wished to know 28 the cause for which they accused him, I brought him forth into their council: and 29 found him to be accused about questions of their law, but to have nothing laid to his charge worthy of death, or of bonds. And when it was told 30 me how the Jews laid wait for the man, I sent him ·immediately to you, and gave commandment to his accusers also, to say before you what they had against him. Farewell.

Then the soldiers, as it was 31 commanded them, took Paul,

---

* *Περιεχουσαν τον τυπον τουτον.* "*Containing this outline.*" Τυπος, represented by *print, figure, fashion, example, ensample, pattern,* in com. ver. *Proprie significat notam insculptam pulsatione.*

t *Μελλειν,* omitted by Ln. Ὑπο των Ιουδαιων, omitted by Ln. and Tf. Το μελλειν εσεσθοι, Kuin. objects, as an anacoluthon, indicating a want of sequence, not correspondent with the remainder of the sentence; and, therefore, should be written μηνοθεισης μελλουσης εσεσθαι, or μηνοθεντος δε μοι—επιβουλην μελλειν εσεσθαι. "The writer falls out of his construction here. He says μηνυθεισης at the beginning of the sentence, as if he would have added της μελλουσης; but, in the progress of the thought, adds μελλειν, as if he had commenced with μηνυσαντων . . . εφιβουλην. The idea of the thing disclosed, yields to that of the persons who disclose it." Hack. "And when it was made known to me that the Jews laid wait for the man, I sent him immediately to you, and commanded his accusers also to say before you what they

had against him. Farewell." Booth. "But having been informed of a plot laid against the man by the Jews." Wake. "And when it was shown me that an ambush was about to be laid for the man by the Jews." Wes. "But when it was signified to me that an ambush would be laid by the Jews." Dodd. "But receiving intelligence of a plot against the man which the Jews were in act to execute." Thomp. "*Indicatis autem mihi insidiis quæ a Judæis ei struerentur, statim eum ad te misi, et accusatoribus ejus præcepi, ut accusationes suas coram te proferrent.*" Kuin. "*Quum autem mihi indicatum esset insidias huic viro factum iri a Judæis eo ipso momento misi eum ad te: et denuntiavi quoque accusatoribus ut quæ habent adversus eum dicant apud te. Vale.*" This we presume to be a full expression of the original text, and would render it: *But soon as it was indicated to me that an ambush was about to be laid by the Jews, against this man, I immediately sent him to you, having given orders to his accusers to state to you whatsoever they have against him.*" Ἔρρωσο. *Farewell.* Om., Ln., Tf.

KING JAMES' VERSION.	GREEK TEXT.	REVISED VERSION.
and brought *him* by night to Antipatris.	ἀναλαβόντες τὸν Παῦλον, ἤγαγον διὰ τῆς νυκτὸς εἰς τὴν Ἀντιπατρίδα. ³² τῇ δὲ ἐπαύριον ἐάσαντες τοὺς ἱππεῖς πορεύεσθαι σὺν αὐτῷ, ὑπέστρεψαν εἰς τὴν παρεμβολήν· ³³ οἵτινες εἰσελθόντες εἰς τὴν Καισάρειαν, καὶ ἀναδόντες τὴν ἐπιστολὴν τῷ ἡγεμόνι, παρέστησαν καὶ τὸν Παῦλον αὐτῷ. ³⁴ ἀναγνοὺς δὲ ὁ ἡγεμὼν, καὶ ἐπερωτήσας ἐκ ποίας ἐπαρχίας ἐστὶ, καὶ πυθόμενος ὅτι ἀπὸ Κιλικίας, ³⁵ Διακούσομαί σου, ἔφη, ὅταν καὶ οἱ κατήγοροί σου παραγένωνται. Ἐκέλευσέ τε αὐτὸν ἐν τῷ πραιτωρίῳ τοῦ Ἡρώδου φυλάσσεσθαι.	and brought him by night to Antipatris; and on the mor-³² row they left the horsemen to go with him ᵘ(and returned to the castle): who, when they ³³ came to Cesarea, and delivered the epistle to the governor, presented Paul also before him. And when the governor ³⁴ had read the letter, he asked of what province he was.ᵛ And when he understood that he was of Cilicia, he said, I will hear ³⁵ you, ᵂwhen your accusers are also come. And he commanded him to be kept under guard in the ˣpretorium of Herod.
32 On the morrow they left the horsemen to go with him, and returned to the castle:		
33 Who, when they came to Cesarea, and delivered the epistle to the governor, presented Paul also before him.		
34 And when the governor had read *the letter*, he asked of what province he was. And when he understood that *he was* of Cilicia;		
35 I will hear thee, said he, when thine accusers are also come. And he commanded him to be kept in Herod's judgment-hall.		
CHAP. XXIV.	CHAP. XXIV.	CHAP. XXIV.
AND after five days, Ananias the high priest descended with the elders, and *with* a certain orator *named* Tertullus, who informed the governor against Paul.	ΜΕΤΑ δὲ πέντε ἡμέρας κατέβη ὁ ἀρχιερεὺς Ἀνανίας μετὰ τῶν πρεσβυτέρων καὶ ῥήτορος Τερτύλλου τινὸς, οἵτινες ἐνεφάνισαν τῷ ἡγεμόνι κατὰ τοῦ Παύλου. ² κληθέντος δὲ αὐτοῦ, ἤρξατο κατηγορεῖν ὁ Τέρτυλλος λέγων, ³ Πολλῆς εἰρήνης τυγχάνοντες διὰ σοῦ, καὶ κατορθω-	Now after ᵃfive days, Ana-¹ nias the high priest came down to Cesarea with the elders, and with a certain orator named Tertullus, who appeared before the governor against Paul. And when he ² was called, Tertullus ᵇproceeded to accuse him, saying, Seeing that through you we enjoy much ᶜpeace, and that many
2 And when he was called forth, Tertullus began to accuse *him*, saying, Seeing that by thee we enjoy great quietness, and that very worthy deeds are done		

ᵘ Ἐάσαντες τοὺς ἱππεῖς, having left or permitted the horsemen to go with him, they returned to the castle; *relictis equitatibus qui cum eo irent, reversi sunt in castra.* Beza. For πορευεσθα, απερχεσθαι is substituted by Ln., Tf., and thought probable by Gb.

ᵛ Ὁ ἡγεμων is repudiated by Gb., Sch., Ln., Tf. It is, however, an appropriate supplement. Ἐπερωτησας, κ. τ. λ., having asked from what province he is. This suggests his profession of being a Roman citizen.

ᵂ Διακουσομαι σου. *I will hear you fully.*

ˣ Ἐν τῷ πραιτωριῳ τοῦ Ἡρωδου, in Herod's *prætorium.* The residence of the Roman procurators. A palace built by him at Cæsarea; then occupied as the residence of Roman procurators. Hack.

ᵃ Μετα δε πεντε ἡμερας, *post quinque dies advenit* Ananias, *potius die quinto—on the fifth day,* Kuin. Michaelis, Dindorfius, Rosenmüllerus count these days from the captivity of Paul in Jerusalem, as cited by Kuin., in which view Meyer De Wette, and Hackett agree.

ᵇ Ἡρξατο κατηγορειν, *began to accuse,* or, *proceeded to accuse.* Tertullus instituted, if not in form, in fact, three distinct *counts,* or charges—*sedition, heresy, profanation* of the temple, vv. 5, 6. Instead of κατορθωματων, some copies read διορθωματων, which reading Grotius, Griesbach, and Valckenarius approve. Kuin.

ᶜ Πολλῆς ειρηνης, "much peace," rather than "great quietness;" "many worthy deeds," rather than "very worthy deeds."

KING JAMES' VERSION.	GREEK TEXT.	REVISED VERSION.

KING JAMES' VERSION.

unto this nation by thy providence,

3 We accept *it* always, and in all places, most noble Felix, with all thankfulness.

4 Notwithstanding, that I be not further tedious unto thee, I pray thee, that thou wouldest hear us of thy clemency a few words.

5 For we have found this man *a* pestilent *fellow*, and a mover of sedition among all the Jews throughout the world, and a ring-leader of the sect of the Nazarenes:

6 Who also hath gone about to profane the temple: whom we took, and would have judged according to our law:

GREEK TEXT.

μάτων γινομένων τῷ ἔθνει τούτῳ διὰ τῆς σῆς προνοίας πάντῃ τε καὶ πανταχοῦ, ἀποδεχόμεθα, κράτιστε Φῆλιξ, μετὰ πάσης εὐχαριστίας. ⁴ ἵνα δὲ μὴ ἐπὶ πλεῖόν σε ἐγκόπτω, παρακαλῶ ἀκοῦσαί σε ἡμῶν συντόμως τῇ σῇ ἐπιεικείᾳ. ⁵ εὑρόντες γὰρ τὸν ἄνδρα τοῦτον λοιμὸν, καὶ κινοῦντα στάσιν πᾶσι τοῖς Ἰουδαίοις τοῖς κατὰ τὴν οἰκουμένην, πρωτοστάτην τε τῆς τῶν Ναζωραίων αἱρέσεως· ⁶ ὃς καὶ τὸ ἱερὸν ἐπείρασε βεβηλῶσαι, ὃν καὶ ἐκρατήσαμεν καὶ κατὰ τὸν ἡμέτερον νόμον ἠθελήσαμεν κρίνειν.

REVISED VERSION.

very worthy ᵈdeeds are done this nation through your prudent administration; we 3 receive it in every way, and ᵉevery where, most ᶠnoble Felix, with all thankfulness. But 4 that I may not weary you longer, I pray you of your clemency to hear a few words from us. For we have found this 5 man a pest, and exciting disturbance among all the ᵍJews throughout the world, a chief-leader of the sect of the Nazarenes: who also has gone about 6 to profane the temple: whom we took, and would have judged according to our ʰlaw: but

---

ᵈ Πολλων being understood.

Δια της σης προνοιας. Προνοιας is found only here and in Rom. 13 : 14; here *providence*, there *provision*.

The verb προνοεω is found three times, and is uniformly translated *provide*, com. ver. Providing for good and against evil, classifies all the duties of civil government. *Prudence* is itself a species of providence.

Ευχαριστια is a favorite with Paul. With two exceptions, found in the Apocalypse, he engrosses its whole currency in the Christian Scriptures. His use of the verb ευχαριστεω is quite as remarkable. Tertullus the orator justifies his use of it.

ᵉ We concur with Robinson and others, in preferring "every way, and everywhere," to "always, and in all places," as being more apposite to the use of παντη.

ᶠ Κρατιστε Φηλιξ, most noble, most excellent. Tertullus, Claudius Lysias, Luke, and Paul are alike courteous in their use of this complimentary term. In the same style he uses the phrase, τη ση επιεικεια, gentleness, clemency. *Gentile, gentle*, and *genteel* are of the same family, and in Latin, French, Spanish, and Italian of the same radical orthography. Gentleness is one of the most conspicuous fruits of the Holy Spirit, and, therefore, he alone creates a *true* gentleman. The language of Tertullus is heartless flattery. Felix, according to Tacitus, Josephus, and hoary tradition, was one of the most corrupt and corrupting governors ever sent from Rome into Judea.

ᵍ Λοιμον, pro λοιμωδης, vel λοιμικος, ut Lat. *pestis* pro *pestifer*. Kuin. *A pest*, for a pestilent fellow, "exciting disturbance *among*" or *unto* all the Jews, amongst themselves, not amongst the Romans. Ναζωραιων, a term of reproach. Ols., Hack.

ʰ Ος και το ιερον επειρασε βεβηλωσαι, ον και εκρατησαμεν. The following words connected with these are omitted by Ln., Tf., (Gb.,—a probable omission)—"και κατα τον ημετερον νομον ηθελησαμεν κρινειν. (V. 7.) παρελθων δε Λυσιας ο χιλιαρχος μετα πολλης βιας εκ των χειρων ημων απηγαγε, (V. 8.) κελευσας τους κατηγορους αυτου ερχεσθαι επι σε." They are, indeed, repudiated by Ln. and Tf., thought doubtful by Gb., regarded as an interpolation by Mill, Beng., Morus, Heinr. But with Kuinœl, after considerable vacillation, I concur. His conclusion is: "*After weighing the objections of Mill, Beng., Mor., and Heinr., and their motion to have them striken out of the text—equidem tamen verba textus genuina existimanda puto—notwithstanding I am of the opinion that they are to be regarded as the genuine words of the text.*" They are rejected by De Wette, Mill, Bengel, Lachmann, and some others. But inasmuch as they are reported as found in different forms in a *majority* of extant manuscripts, I must vote for their retention.

The following are the popular versions of this passage: "*And having seized him, we wished to judge him according to our law. But Lysias the chiliarch came, and with great violence took him out of our hands.*" Syriac Peshito. "*Qui templum quoque tentavit profanari: quem etiam prehensum volumus secundum Legem nostram indicare sed interveniens tribunus Lysias cum magna vi abducit eum e manibus nostriis.*" Beza, edition of Junius and Tremellius, Old and New Testament, London, A.D. 1581. "*Who attempted to profane the temple, and whom we, therefore, seized : by examining whom thou canst obtain knowledge of the things of which we accuse him.*" Penn. "*Who attempted to profane even the temple, we apprehended him, and would have judged him according to our law.*" Thomp. To the same effect, Boothr., Dodd., Wes., Wakef. See ch. 21 : 31, 33.

KING JAMES' VERSION.	GREEK TEXT.	REVISED VERSION.

KING JAMES' VERSION.

7 But the chief captain Lysias came *upon us*, and with great violence took *him* away out of our hands,

8 Commanding his accusers to come unto thee: by examining of whom, thyself mayest take knowledge of all these things whereof we accuse him.

9 And the Jews also assented, saying, That these things were so.

10 Then Paul, after that the governor had beckoned unto him to speak, answered, Forasmuch as I know that thou hast been of many years a judge unto this nation, I do the more cheerfully answer for myself:

11 Because that thou mayest understand, that there are yet but twelve days since I went up to Jerusalem for to worship.

12 And they neither found me in the temple disputing with any man, neither raising up the people, neither in the synagogues, nor in the city:

13 Neither can they prove the things whereof they now accuse me.

GREEK TEXT.

7 παρελθὼν δὲ Λυσίας ὁ χιλίαρχος μετὰ πολλῆς βίας ἐκ τῶν χειρῶν ἡμῶν ἀπήγαγε, 8 κελεύσας τοὺς κατηγόρους αὐτοῦ ἔρχεσθαι ἐπὶ σέ· παρ' οὗ δυνήσῃ αὐτὸς ἀνακρίνας περὶ πάντων τούτων ἐπιγνῶναι ὧν ἡμεῖς κατηγοροῦμεν αὐτοῦ. 9 Συνέθεντο δὲ καὶ οἱ Ἰουδαῖοι, φάσκοντες ταῦτα οὕτως ἔχειν.

10 Ἀπεκρίθη δὲ ὁ Παῦλος, νεύσαντος αὐτῷ τοῦ ἡγεμόνος λέγειν, Ἐκ πολλῶν ἐτῶν ὄντα σε κριτὴν τῷ ἔθνει τούτῳ ἐπιστάμενος, εὐθυμότερον τὰ περὶ ἐμαυτοῦ ἀπολογοῦμαι. 11 δυναμένου σου γνῶναι ὅτι οὐ πλείους εἰσί μοι ἡμέραι ἢ δεκαδύο, ἀφ' ἧς ἀνέβην προσκυνήσων ἐν Ἱερουσαλήμ· 12 καὶ οὔτε ἐν τῷ ἱερῷ εὗρόν με πρός τινα διαλεγόμενον ἢ ἐπισύστασιν ποιοῦντα ὄχλου, οὔτε ἐν ταῖς συναγωγαῖς, οὔτε κατὰ τὴν πόλιν· 13 οὔτε παραστῆσαί με δύνανται περὶ ὧν νῦν κατηγοροῦσί μου. 14 ὁμολο-

REVISED VERSION.

the chiliarch Lysias came upon 7 us, and with great violence took him away out of our [i]hands, commanding his accusers to 8 come to you: by examining of whom you yourself may obtain knowledge of all these things whereof we accuse [j]him. And 9 the Jews also assailed [k]him, saying that these things were so.

Then Paul, after that the gov- 10 ernor had beckoned to him to speak, answered:—[l]Knowing that you have been for many years a judge for this nation, I do the more cheerfully answer for myself; it being in your power 11 to know that there are yet but twelve [m]days since I went up to Jerusalem to worship. And 12 they neither found me in the temple disputing with any man, neither stirring up the people, neither in the synagogue, nor in the [n]city: nei- 13 ther can they prove the things of which they now accuse me.

---

[i] In μετα πολλης βιας, Tertullus mistates the fact. On the appearance of Lysias, the Jews released Paul without any struggle.

[j] Επι σε, *before thee.* Hack. Ανακρισις indicates any form of inquisition.

[k] For συνεθεντο, Gb., Sch., Ln., Tf. substitute συνεπεθεντο. They did more then *assent*, they *assailed him* at the same time. It is again found in ch. 23 : 30.

[l] Εκ πολλων ετων, *since many years.* Κριτην governs εθνει. The relation was for their benefit. Hence the dative.

[m] Δυναμενου σου γνωναι, *while*, or *since*, you *are able to know*, you *may know*, it being in your power to know. Η δεκαδυο later editions omit. "The best mode of reckoning the *twelve* days is the following—beginning with the day of their arrival at Jerusalem (ch. 21 : 17); second, their interview with James (21 : 18); third, the assumption of the vow (21 : 26); fourth, fifth, sixth, and seventh, the vow continued, to have been kept seven days, being interrupted on the fifth;

eighth, Paul before the sanhedrim (22 : 30; 23 : 1-10); ninth, the plot of the Jews, and the journey to Antipatris (23 : 12-31); tenth, eleventh, twelfth and thirteenth, the days at Cæsarea (24 : 1), on the last of which the trial was then taking place. The number of complete days would, therefore, be twelve; the day in progress at the time of speaking is not counted. So Wetstein Augm., Meyer, De Wette, and others." Hackett.

Αφ' ης, an abbreviation for απο της ημερας ης. Προσκυνησων, *worshiping*, or, in order to worship. Αφ' ης *elliptice positum est pro* αφ' ημερας ης ανεβην, *et in* Jerusalem *positum pro* εις Ιερουσαλημ. Kuinœl, *in loco*.

[n] For επισυστασιν some read επιστασιν, substituted by Ln., Gb., not so well sustained. *Vox rarior occurrit apud Joseph. C. Apion* 1. 20. Οντι εκ της αυτης επισυστασεως, *qui in eadem seditione fuerat.* Esr. V, 70. Και επιβουλας και δημαγωγιας και επιστασεις ποιουμενο-, *verbum* επισυνιστασθαι *concursum facere legitur ap. Joseph. Ant.* 14, 1, 3. Kuin.

KING JAMES' VERSION.

14 But this I confess unto
thee, that after the way which
they call heresy, so worship I
the God of my fathers, believing
all things which are written in
the law and in the prophets:
15 And have hope toward
God, which they themselves also
allow, that there shall be a resurrection of the dead, both of
the just and unjust.
16 And herein do I exercise
myself, to have always a conscience void of offence toward
God, and *toward* men.
17 Now, after many years, I
came to bring alms to my nation, and offerings.
18 Whereupon certain Jews
from Asia found me purified in
the temple, neither with multitude, nor with tumult:
19 Who ought to have been
here before thee, and object, if
they had aught against me.
20 Or else let these same *here*
say, if they have found any evil

GREEK TEXT.

γῶ δὲ τοῦτο σοι, ὅτι κατὰ τὴν
ὁδὸν ἣν λέγουσιν αἵρεσιν, οὕτω
λατρεύω τῷ πατρῴῳ Θεῷ, πι-
στεύων πᾶσι τοῖς κατὰ τὸν νόμον
καὶ τοῖς προφήταις γεγραμμένοις,
15 ἐλπίδα ἔχων εἰς τὸν Θεὸν, ἣν
καὶ αὐτοὶ αὗτοι προσδέχονται,
ἀνάστασιν μέλλειν ἔσεσθαι νεκρῶν, δικαίων τε καὶ ἀδίκων·
16 ἐν τούτῳ δὲ αὐτὸς ἀσκῶ, ἀπ-
ρόσκοπον συνείδησιν ἔχειν πρὸς
τὸν Θεὸν καὶ τοὺς ἀνθρώπους
διαπαντός. 17 δὶ ἐτῶν δὲ πλειόνων παρεγενόμην ἐλεημοσύνας
ποιήσων εἰς τὸ ἔθνος μου καὶ
προσφοράς· 18 ἐν οἷς εὗρόν με
ἡγνισμένον ἐν τῷ ἱερῷ, οὐ μετὰ
ὄχλου οὐδὲ μετὰ θορύβου, τινὲς
δὲ ἀπὸ τῆς Ἀσίας Ἰουδαῖοι,
19 οὓς δεῖ ἐπὶ σοῦ παρεῖναι καὶ
κατηγορεῖν εἴ τι ἔχοιεν πρός με.
20 ἢ αὐτοὶ οὗτοι εἰπάτωσαν, εἴ τι
εὗρον ἐν ἐμοὶ ἀδίκημα, στάντος

REVISED VERSION.

But this I confess to you, that 14
after the way which they call
a [o]sect, so I worship the God
of my fathers, believing all
things which are written in
the law and in the prophets:
and have a hope towards God, 15
which they themselves also
[p]entertain, that there is to be
a resurrection of the dead,
both of the just and also of
the unjust. And in this do 16
[q]I exercise myself, to have
always a conscience void of
offense towards God and men.
Now, after many years, 17
I came in order to bring
alms to my nation, and to
make [r]offerings; on which 18
[s]occasion certain Jews from
Asia found me purified in the
temple, but neither with a
crowd, nor with tumult: who 19
ought to have been here before you [t]to accuse me, had
they any charge against me; or 20
else let these themselves say,

---

[o] *Κατα την ὁδον ἣν λεγουσιν αἱρεσιν*, which they call *a sect*—literally, *heresy*. At the beginning it was a word of middle signification, and, in general, signified any opinion good or bad. *Non sum in eadem cum illo hæresi*, i. e. *sententiam*—*I am not of the same opinion with him*. Tull. Paradox. *Secta odiosus est vocabulum quam hæresis: a secundo dicitur. Hæresis* Græcis dicitur ab *elegendo*. Ecclesiastical writers take it for an error in religion, and so it may be defined. *Heresy* is, however, regarded rather as a fundamental error taught and defended with obstinacy. Two things are regarded as essential to heresy. 1st, it must respect and concern *the articles of our faith;* 2dly, there must be a stubborn and a pertinacious affirmation of it: there must be error *in ratione, et pertinacia in voluntate*. Taken in Scripture, *malem partem*. Leigh's Crit. Sacra. The word is found ch. 5 : 17; 15 : 5; for a sect, ch. 24 : 5, and 28 : 22.

Αἱρετικος, Titus 3 : 5, indicates one who takes pleasure in sectarisms. Crit. Sacra.

[p] *Νεκρων*, after *αναστασιν*, is rejected by Ln., Tf., Gb. as a reading not strongly supported. A resurrection of the just and of the unjust.

[p] *Ασκω, I exercise myself*, not in force and compass equal to this term. I use *diligence, skill*, and *constancy*. *Ασκω meditare est et ex exercere se in re aliqua.* Gregorius. It is *constantly to meditate* and *exercise one's self* in any thing *διαπαντος, perpetually, without ceasing.*

[r] *Προσφορας, oblations, offerings*, ch. 21 : 26. Rom. 15 : 16. Heb. 10 : 5, 8, 10, 14, 18. Græci appellabant *προσφοραν*. *When they had finished their social prayers*, bread and wine were presented to the minister who was accustomed to recite the words of the Supper and its institution. This was after, and independent of their contributions to the poor. Crit. Sacra.

[s] *Εν οἱς εὑρον με ἡγνισμενον εν τῳ ἱερῳ. Εν οἱς, in his dum occupor, dum ejusmodi pietatis officia exsequor*, while engaged in these services, or duties, the Jews found me purified—*certain Jews from Asia*—excited a tumult, *not I*, as my accusers allege. The verb is wanting, and the context suggests the supplement. For *εν οἱς*, Sch., Ln., Gb. suggest *εν αἱς*.

[t] *Ει τι εχοειν.*

doing in me, while I stood before the council,

21 Except it be for this one voice, that I cried, standing among them, Touching the resurrection of the dead I am called in question by you this day.

22 And when Felix heard these things, having more perfect knowledge of *that* way, he deferred them, and said, When Lysias the chief captain shall come down, I will know the uttermost of your matter.

23 And he commanded a centurion to keep Paul, and to let *him* have liberty, and that he should forbid none of his acquaintance to minister, or come unto him.

24 And after certain days, when Felix came with his wife Drusilla, which was a Jewess, he sent for Paul, and heard him concerning the faith in Christ.

25 And as he reasoned of

μου ἐπὶ τοῦ συνεδρίου· 21 ἢ περὶ μιᾶς ταύτης φωνῆς, ἧς ἔκραξα ἑστὼς ἐν αὐτοῖς, Ὅτι περὶ ἀναστάσεως νεκρῶν ἐγὼ κρίνομαι σήμερον ὑφ' ὑμῶν.

22 Ἀκούσας δὲ ταῦτα ὁ Φῆλιξ ἀνεβάλετο αὐτούς, ἀκριβέστερον εἰδὼς τὰ περὶ τῆς ὁδοῦ, εἰπών, Ὅταν Λυσίας ὁ χιλίαρχος καταβῇ, διαγνώσομαι τὰ καθ' ὑμᾶς· 23 διαταξάμενός τε τῷ ἑκατοντάρχῃ τηρεῖσθαι τὸν Παῦλον, ἔχειν τε ἄνεσιν, καὶ μηδένα κωλύειν τῶν ἰδίων αὐτοῦ ὑπηρετεῖν ἢ προσέρχεσθαι αὐτῷ.

24 Μετὰ δὲ ἡμέρας τινὰς παραγενόμενος ὁ Φῆλιξ σὺν Δρουσίλλῃ τῇ γυναικὶ αὐτοῦ οὔσῃ Ἰουδαίᾳ, μετεπέμψατο τὸν Παῦλον, καὶ ἤκουσεν αὐτοῦ περὶ τῆς εἰς Χριστὸν πίστεως. 25 διαλεγομένου δὲ αὐτοῦ περὶ δικαιο-

[u]if they found any evil in me, when I stood before the council, except it be for this one 21 [v]expression which I made standing among them, Concerning the resurrection of the dead I am this day called in question.

And when Felix heard these 22 things, knowing more accurately the things in regard to the [w]way, he deferred them, and said, When Lysias the chiliarch shall come down, I will thoroughly examine the matters between you. And he com- 23 manded the centurion that Paul should be kept, and that he should have a [x]relaxation, and that he should forbid none of his acquaintance to minister, or come to him. And, after some 24 days, when Felix came with his wife Drusilla (who was a Jewess), he sent for Paul, and heard him concerning the faith in [y]relation to Christ. And as he reasoned concern- 25

---

[u] Εἰ τι εὗρον, *If they have any thing against me,* if they *found anything* in me. Ἀδικημα, *anything unjust,* anything *wicked.* Σταντος μου επι του συνεδριου, *when I appeared,* or, *while I was standing* επι, *before.* This versatile preposition freely takes the condition, color, or sense of its associates, or associations in the Christian Scriptures. When in connection with magistrates, courts, or councils, it is generally in the Christian Scriptures, com. ver., represented by *before.*

[v] Επι, in this case, is the prefix to του συνεδριου, and indicates the attitude of trial before a court. Περι is equally latitudinarian in its currency, and in cases of this sort it answers to our word *concerning.* The trial here is περι αναστασεως.

[w] Αναβαλλομαι, here Φηλιξ ανεβαλετο, he deferred them. It is an ἁπαξ λεγομενον, found only in this one case N. T. Ακριβεστερον, found only in this book in the Christian Scriptures—*more perfectly,* thrice; *more perfect,* once. Διαγνωσομαι, διαγνωσις. This is one of Luke's special words, and is indicative that he was a *physician.* The διαγνωσις of disease is as old as Æsculapius, deified after his death for his διαγνωσις and his προγνωσις, *precognition* of disease. Luke, Acts 2 : 23, has also this word. Besides Luke, Peter

only once uses it. Its use indicates a thorough knowledge. Felix is distinguished for a full developed inquisitiveness in all cases brought before him. Therefore he trembled before the logic and rhetoric of Paul (v. 25). He promised to hear him thoroughly, and to examine the case of Paul when chief captain Lysias had come down.

[x] Εχειν τε ανεσιν. Ανεσις, *liberty, relaxation, rest, take off his chains.* After Paul, αυτον is added by Gb., Sch., Ln., Tf.; η προσερχεσθαι rejected by Ln., Tf., and doubtful by Gb. Τηρεισθαι αυτον, being passive, and not mid. voice, should not be, *to keep him,* but, *that he should be kept.* Ανεσις means a *relaxation.* This is, in a case, the only word in our language that represents its acceptation in this passage. Our *jail* limits more than indicate ανεσις, and our word *liberty* transcends it. This is a special relaxation of the rigors of the law, in Paul's favor, amounting to a release, and yet it was not legally a release. "To keep Paul at rest," Murd. ; "without confinement," Wakef.

[y] Felix with Drusilla his wife were curious to hear Paul while in Judea, and sent for him. They heard him on the thrilling theme, περι της εις Χριστον πιστεως, *the faith into,* or *towards Christ,* in relation to Christ.

KING JAMES' VERSION.	GREEK TEXT.	REVISED VERSION.

righteousness, temperance, and judgment to come, Felix trembled, and answered, Go thy way for this time; when I have a convenient season, I will call for thee.

26 He hoped also that money should have been given him of Paul, that he might loose him: wherefore he sent for him the oftener, and communed with him.

27 But after two years Porcius Festus came into Felix' room: and Felix, willing to shew the Jews a pleasure, left Paul bound.

CHAP. XXV.

Now when Festus was come into the province, after three days he ascended from Cesarea to Jerusalem.

2 Then the high priest and

σύνης καὶ ἐγκρατείας καὶ τοῦ κρίματος τοῦ μέλλοντος ἔσεσθαι, ἔμφοβος γενόμενος ὁ Φῆλιξ ἀπεκρίθη, Τὸ νῦν ἔχον πορεύου· καιρὸν δὲ μεταλαβὼν μετακαλέσομαί σε· 26 ἅμα δὲ καὶ ἐλπίζων, ὅτι χρήματα δοθήσεται αὐτῷ ὑπὸ τοῦ Παύλου, ὅπως λύσῃ αὐτόν· διὸ καὶ πυκνότερον αὐτὸν μεταπεμπόμενος ὡμίλει αὐτῷ. 27 Διετίας δὲ πληρωθείσης ἔλαβε διάδοχον ὁ Φῆλιξ Πόρκιον Φῆστον· θέλων τε χάριτας καταθέσθαι τοῖς Ἰουδαίοις ὁ Φῆλιξ, κατέλιπε τὸν Παῦλον δεδεμένον.

CHAP. XXV.

ΦΗΣΤΟΣ οὖν ἐπιβὰς τῇ ἐπαρχίᾳ, μετὰ τρεῖς ἡμέρας ανέβη εἰς Ἱεροσόλυμα ἀπὸ Καισαρείας. 2 ἐνεφάνισαν δὲ αὐτῷ ὁ ἀρχιε-

---

ing justice, [1]self-government, and the judgment to come, Felix trembled, and answered, Go your way for this time; when I have a convenient season, I will send for you. [11]At the 26 same time hoping that money would have been given him by Paul, that he might release him, he therefore sent for him the oftener, and conversed with him. But after 27 two years Felix had a successor, Porcius Festus; and Felix, willing to show the Jews a favor, left Paul bound.

CHAP. XXV.

Now when Festus had come 1 into the [a]province, after three days, he went up from Cesarea to Jerusalem. Then the 2 high priest, and the chief of

---

[1] Διαλεγομενου, though represented by *disputing*, com. ver., six times; by *reasoning*, four times; *preaching*, twice; *speaking*, once; *discoursing*, or *discussing*, is its generic sense. Words have their *genera* and *species*, as well as plants and animals. The abstract or generic idea in this word is *dissero*, *dicendo rem diducere*, to deduce a matter, a fact, a cause, or a thing by discussion, or reasoning—the dialectic art. There is neither preaching nor teaching, neither discussing nor exhorting, neither affirming nor denying in the essence or act of reasoning. *It is a simple comparison of objects, and for deduction.*

The faculty of reasoning is exhibited in comparing and deducing. When Paul reasoned on certain topics Felix trembled. His response demonstrated the power of Paul's reasonings in his presence. Εσεσθαι is omitted by Ln., Sch., Gb. It appears redundant or pleonastic, but pleonasms are allowable in such cases.

[11] Ὁπως λυση αυτον omitted by Sch., Ln., Tf., and doubtful by Gb. It naturally occurs from ελπιζων, ὁτι χρηματα δοθησεται, and seems to be a circumstantial inference of much plausibility.

Ὡμιλει αυτῳ, 3d sing. imp. ind. act. of ὁμιλεω, *colloquor*, he conversed with Paul familiarly. This word is found only four times in the Christian Scriptures. It indicates familiar conversation—"*una versari sed hic accipitur pro colloqui*," Beza.

"*Talked together*," "*communed together*," is its currency and import in N. T., the topic may be either good, or evil. It seems to have been conducted on the part of Felix from a mercenary spirit, as the sequel warrants.

[a] Επαρχια, found only twice in this book of Acts, is represented by the word *province*, a verbal from επαρχομαι, *auspicor*, *cœpi*, from which επαρχος, *præfectus*—from επι and αρχω, *incipio*—also επαρχοτης, identical in import with επαρχια, a *province*. Αρχη, the root, does not indicate that which is passive, but that which is active in originating. Αρχη non principium passivum sed activum significat, a *quo* omnes creaturæ principium suum ducunt: quam interpretationem utriusque Testamenti pagina evincit. It is taken for the *magistrate*, Luke 12 : 11. Titus 3 : 1. Αρχαι qui mero imperio utuntur. Those who under God have plenary power, and by that power command, administer justice within their respective dominions. Hence a *province* is a department of an empire placed under the management or government of one, invested with supreme authority, whether it be human or divine, or both. In this view Jesus Christ, Heb. 12 : 2, is called Autorem fidei et consummatorem fidei—the author and founder of the faith; not a particular or special faith, but the faith, *the whole Christian institution*. Crit. Sacra. This is that province assigned to Jesus Christ by the apostles.

KING JAMES' VERSION.	GREEK TEXT.	REVISED VERSION.
the chief of the Jews informed him against Paul, and besought him,	ρεὺς καὶ οἱ πρῶτοι τῶν Ἰουδαίων κατὰ τοῦ Παύλου, καὶ παρεκάλουν αὐτὸν, ³ αἰτούμενοι χάριν κατ' αὐτοῦ, ὅπως μεταπέμψηται αὐτὸν εἰς Ἱερουσαλὴμ, ἐνέδραν ποιοῦντες ἀνελεῖν αὐτὸν κατὰ τὴν ὁδόν. ⁴ ὁ μὲν οὖν Φῆστος ἀπεκρίθη, τηρεῖσθαι τὸν Παῦλον ἐν Καισαρείᾳ, ἑαυτὸν δὲ μέλλειν ἐν τάχει ἐκπορεύεσθαι. ⁵ Οἱ οὖν δυνατοὶ ἐν ὑμῖν, φησὶ, συγκαταβάντες, εἴ τι ἐστὶν ἐν τῷ ἀνδρὶ τούτῳ, κατηγορείτωσαν αὐτοῦ. ⁶ Διατρίψας δὲ ἐν αὐτοῖς ἡμέρας πλείους ἢ δέκα, καταβὰς εἰς Καισάρειαν, τῇ ἐπαύριον καθίσας ἐπὶ τοῦ βήματος, ἐκέλευσε τὸν Παῦλον ἀχθῆναι. ⁷ παραγενομένου δὲ αὐτοῦ, περιέστησαν οἱ ἀπὸ Ἱεροσολύμων καταβεβηκότες Ἰουδαῖοι, πολλὰ καὶ βαρέα αἰτιάματα φέροντες κατὰ τοῦ Παύλου, ἃ οὐκ ἴσχυον ἀποδεῖξαι, ⁸ ἀπολογουμένου αὐτοῦ, Ὅτι οὔτε εἰς τὸν νόμον τῶν Ἰουδαίων, οὔτε	the Jews, informed him against Paul, and besought him, [b]asking for themselves a favor against him, that he would send for him to Jerusalem, preparing an [c]ambush to kill him on the way. But Festus answered that Paul should be kept in [d]custody at Cesarea, and that he himself would shortly depart thither. Let the [e]powerful among you, said he, go down with me and accuse this man, if there is any wickedness in him. And when he had tarried among them more than ten days, he went down to Cesarea; and the next day sitting on the judgment-seat, commanded Paul to be brought. And when he was come, the Jews who came down from Jerusalem stood around [f]him, and laid many and heavy complaints against Paul, which they could not prove; while he answered for himself, Neither against the law of the Jews, [g]nor against the temple,

Verse numbers in Revised Version column: 3, 4, 5, 6, 7, 8.

---

[b] For ὁ ἀρχιερεὺς is substituted οἱ ἀρχιερεῖς by Ln., Tf., a reading not so strongly supported by Gb. The priests and elders were as much as ever enraged against Paul, and nothing but his blood would satisfy their malice. Gb., Boothr.

[c] Ἐνέδραν ποιοῦντες. "Forming a plot to kill him," Penn; "having laid an ambush," Thomp.; "placing an ambush," Murd., "lying in wait to kill him," Wes.; "preparing an ambush," Hack.; "to lie in wait to destroy him," Boothr.

[d] Ἀπεκρίθη—ἐκπορεύεσθαι. This indicates not a refusal, but an intimation that he should be still kept at Cæsarea, inasmuch as Festus was about to return to that place, and would, when there, judge his case.

Τηρεῖσθαι. "That Paul was in custody," Thomp.; "kept in custody," Hack.

[e] Οἱ οὖν δυνατοὶ ἐν ὑμῖν, the powerful, not the able. Not those who are able have it in their power. Cal., Grot., Hack. "Let the chief men among you go down with me," Thomp.; "let those, therefore, among you who are able, said he, come down with me," Penn; "Let those, therefore, among you who are able," Murd. Verba οἱ δυνατοὶ ἐν ὑμῖν Erasmus, Grotius alii explicant: quibus commodum est Cæsarum

venire. Sed ut Pricæus recte monuit, hoc si Lucas voluisset, scripsisset. Josephus uses οἱ δυνατοι in the same sense, and many other writers as indicative of power, whether physical, moral, or ecclesiastical.

[f] Περιέστησαν, "stood around him, not the tribunal," Kuin.; "stood round about," "stood around him," Hack., Penn; "stood around," Thomp.; "Surrounded him," Murd. "Most manuscripts omit κατα του Παυλου, after φεροντες," Hack. Tf. has καταφεροντες, instead of φεροντες, before κατα του Παυλου. Αποδειξαι—αποδεικνυμι, probo, demonstro, Acts 2 : 22. 2 Thess. 2 : 4.

[g] Οντε εις τον νομον—το ιερον—εις Καισαρα. Οντε three times very specific—neither against the law, the temple, nor against Cæsar.

Εις is seldom translated against. For the most part it occurs in cases of trial, charge, or legal prosecution. Relation to, for, or against, is often indicated by it. The context must decide its value. Εις Χριστον may, according to the import of the preceding verb, be either for, or against Christ.

Οντε εις Καισαρα τι ημαρτον, neither have I in any respect sinned against Cæsar.

temple, nor yet against Cesar have I offended any thing at all.

9 But Festus, willing to do the Jews a pleasure, answered Paul, and said, Wilt thou go up to Jerusalem, and there be judged of these things before me?

10 Then said Paul, I stand at Cesar's judgment-seat, where I ought to be judged: to the Jews have I done no wrong, as thou very well knowest.

11 For if I be an offender, or have committed any thing worthy of death, I refuse not to die: but if there be none of these things whereof these accuse me, no man may deliver me unto them. I appeal unto Cesar.

12 Then Festus, when he had conferred with the council, answered, Hast thou appealed unto Cesar? unto Cesar shalt thou go.

13 And after certain days, king Agrippa and Bernice came unto Cesarea, to salute Festus.

14 And when they had been

εἰς τὸ ἱερὸν, οὔτε εἰς Καίσαρά τι ἥμαρτον. 9 Ὁ Φῆστος δὲ τοῖς Ἰουδαίοις θέλων χάριν καταθέσθαι, ἀποκριθεὶς τῷ Παύλῳ εἶπε, Θέλεις εἰς Ἱεροσόλυμα ἀναβὰς, ἐκεῖ περὶ τούτων κρίνεσθαι ἐπ᾽ ἐμοῦ; 10 Εἶπε δὲ ὁ Παῦλος, Ἐπὶ τοῦ βήματος Καίσαρος ἑστώς εἰμι, οὗ με δεῖ κρίνεσθαι. Ἰουδαίους οὐδὲν ἠδίκησα, ὡς καὶ σὺ κάλλιον ἐπιγινώσκεις· 11 εἰ μὲν γὰρ ἀδικῶ καὶ ἄξιον θανάτου πέπραχά τι, οὐ παραιτοῦμαι τὸ ἀποθανεῖν· εἰ δὲ οὐδέν ἐστιν ὧν οὗτοι κατηγοροῦσί μου, οὐδείς με δύναται αὐτοῖς χαρίσασθαι. Καίσαρα ἐπικαλοῦμαι. 12 Τότε ὁ Φῆστος συλλαλήσας μετὰ τοῦ συμβουλίου, ἀπεκρίθη, Καίσαρα ἐπικέκλησαι, ἐπὶ Καίσαρα πορεύσῃ. 13 Ἡμερῶν δὲ διαγενομένων τινῶν, Ἀγρίππας ὁ βασιλεὺς καὶ Βερνίκη κατήντησαν εἰς Καισάρειαν, ἀσπασόμενοι τὸν Φῆστον. 14 ὡς δὲ πλείους ἡμέρας διέτριβον

nor yet against Cesar have I at all offended. But Festus, 9 willing to do the Jews a ʰfavor, answered Paul, and said, Will you go up to Jerusalem, and there be judged of these things before me? Then said Paul, 10 I stand at Cesar's judgment-seat, where I ought to be judged: to the Jews I have done no wrong, as you ʲyourself very well know. For if I 11 am doing wrong, and have committed any thing worthy of death, I refuse not to die; but if there is nothing in these matters of which they accuse me, ʲno man can deliver me up to them: I appeal to Cesar. Then Festus, when 12 he had talked with the council, answered, ᵏYou have appealed to Cesar, to Cesar shall you go.

And after certain days, king 13 Agrippa and Bernice came to Cesarea to ˡsalute Festus. And 14 when they had been there many

---

ʰ Καταθεσθαι, second aor. infin. mid. of κατατιθημι, reponere, to reinstate himself; ch. 24: 27, to ingratiate himself with the Jews, Felix left Paul a prisoner. On ch. 24: 27 Kuinœl makes the following remark: "Χαριν, χαριτα, χαριτας κατατι θεσθαι τινι denotat, gratiam inire apud aliquem, ut suo tempore vicissim res grata expectari vel etiam posci possit," of which examples from Demosthenes, Plato, Diodorus are adduced; and further refers to Kypkius, Elsner, Wetstein. It is an act of prudent selfishness to confer a favor upon a person, in expectation that in some emergency it may redound to our advantage; nay, that it may be demanded as a right. "To do the Jews a pleasure," com. ver.

ⁱ Επι του βηματος, κ. τ. λ. Επι, followed by a genitive, occurs Matt. 27: 19. In connection with judges and tribunals, and in appearing before them, connected with a genitive, επι is often represented by the word before. 23: 30; 24: 19; 25: 26; 26: 2.

ʲ Χαριζομαι, to give, to give frankly, to grant, to forgive. Here alone, in com. ver., it is represented by to deliver up;

forensically, to deliver, to give up; in our currency, to deliver into custody. "No one can give me up to them, merely to gratify," Dodd.; "no one has power to deliver me up to them," Penn; "no one should deliver me up to gratify them," Boothr.; "no one can gratify them at my expense," Wakef.; "no one may sacrifice me to their pleasure," Murd. —a very free translation—; "no man can give me up to gratify them," Thomp.

Καισαρα επικαλουμαι — επικαλεομαι, ουμαι — cognominor, modo passive, modo active sumitur, et utroque, to call upon another for help in extremity, sometimes merely to call, to name, Heb. 11: 16. 1 Pet. 3: 15. Crit. Sacra.

ᵏ Συλλαλησας, communing with, talking with, conferred with, is its current value, N. T. μετα—συμβουλιον, in its currency five times, N. T., counsel, twice council. Επικεκλησαι; hast thou appealed to Cæsar? Frequently surnamed call on, or upon.

ˡ Ασπασομενοι. Salute, greet, and embrace are its representatives in N. T., com. ver. Here salute is most apropos.

KING JAMES' VERSION.	GREEK TEXT.	REVISED VERSION.

there many days, Festus declared Paul's cause unto the king, saying, There is a certain man left in bonds by Felix:

15 About whom, when I was at Jerusalem, the chief priests and the elders of the Jews informed *me*, desiring *to have* judgment against him.

16 To whom I answered, It is not the manner of the Romans to deliver any man to die, before that he which is accused have the accusers face to face, and have license to answer for himself concerning the crime laid against him.

17 Therefore, when they were come hither, without any delay on the morrow I sat on the judgment-seat, and commanded the man to be brought forth;

18 Against whom, when the accusers stood up, they brought none accusation of such things as I supposed:

19 But had certain questions against him of their own superstition, and of one Jesus, which

ἐκεῖ, ὁ Φῆστος τῷ βασιλεῖ ἀνέθετο τὰ κατὰ τὸν Παῦλον λέγων, Ἀνήρ τις ἐστὶ καταλελειμμένος ὑπὸ Φήλικος δέσμιος, ¹⁵ περὶ οὗ, γενομένου μου εἰς Ἱεροσάλυμα, ἐνεφάνισαν οἱ ἀρχιερεῖς καὶ οἱ πρεσβύτεροι τῶν Ἰουδαίων, αἰτούμενοι κατ᾽ αὐτοῦ δίκην. ¹⁶ πρὸς οὓς ἀπεκρίθην, ὅτι οὐκ ἔστιν ἔθος Ῥωμαίοις χαρίζεσθαί τινα ἄνθρωπον εἰς ἀπώλειαν, πρὶν ἢ ὁ κατηγορούμενος κατὰ πρόσωπον ἔχοι τοὺς κατηγόρους, τόπον τε ἀπολογίας λάβοι περὶ τοῦ ἐγκλήματος. ¹⁷ συνελθόντων οὖν αὐτῶν ἐνθάδε, ἀναβολὴν μηδεμίαν ποιησάμενος, τῇ ἑξῆς καθίσας ἐπὶ τοῦ βήματος, ἐκέλευσα ἀχθῆναι τὸν ἄνδρα· ¹⁸ περὶ οὗ σταθέντες οἱ κατήγοροι οὐδεμίαν αἰτίαν ἐπέφερον ὧν ὑπενόουν ἐγώ· ¹⁹ ζητήματα δέ τινα περὶ τῆς ἰδίας δεισιδαιμονίας εἶχον πρὸς αὐτόν, καὶ περί τινος Ἰησοῦ

days, Festus ᵐset forth to the king the facts concerning Paul, saying, There is a certain man left prisoner by Felix; about 15 whom, when I was at Jerusalem, the chief priests and the elders of the Jews brought an information, asking for themselves justice against him; to 16 whom I answered: It is not the custom of the Romans to deliver any man to die before he that is accused ⁿhave his accusers face to face, and have an opportunity to answer for himself concerning the charge. Therefore, when they had come 17 hither, without any °delay on the morrow, I sat on the judgment-seat, and commanded the man to be brought; against ʷhom, 18 ᵖwhen the accusers stood up, they brought no accusation of such things as I surmised: but had certain questions 19 against him respecting their own ᵍreligion, and of one Je-

---

ᵐ Ανεθετο, "laid *the case* of Paul before the king" Penn, Wakef.; laid the *business*," Dodd.

ⁿ Εις απωλειαν omitted by Gb., Ln., Tf.

Χαριζεσθαι τινα ανθρωπον, "to gratify any man with the condemnation of another," Wakef.; "to give up any man to destruction," Thomp., Dodd.; "to give up a man gratuitously to be slain," Murd.; "to give up any man," Penn; "to deliver up any man to die," Boothr.

° Αναβολην—an ἅπαξ λεγομενον—delay.

ᵖ Ὑπενοουν εγω, imperfect active of ὑπονοεω, suspicor. "Against whom, when his accusers stood up, they brought no accusation of such things as I supposed," Dodd. "And his accusers stood up with him, and they were not able to substantiate any criminal charge against him as I had expected," Wakef. "They advanced no charge of such things as I expected," Thomp.

After ὑπενοουν εγω, πονηραν is added by Ln., doubtful by Gb.

Ὑπενοουν, "which is *suspected*," Hackett; "*expected*," Wakef., Thomp.; "*supposed*," Wes., Penn.

ᵍ Δεισιδαιμονιας, and δεισιδαιμονεστερος, ch. 17 : 22, are

the only occurrences of this word in the N. T., rendered, com. ver., *superstition*, and *superstitious*.

Not *too superstitious*, some say, because Paul would not have aroused their prejudices. This is doubtful. "Much given to Divine worship," not too superstitious, as our translators have expressed. "*Veyne worshiperes*," Wiclif; "more than others attentive to religious matters," Bloomfield. This is sufficiently paraphrastic. Pollux has assigned δεισιδαιμων to the pious. It is by some supposed that Paul used it in this favorable sense, to propitiate the ears of the Athenians. None doubt that Paul found a true bill when he charged the Athenians of being exceedingly devoted to the worship of the shades or spirits of dead hero-men.

"Δεισιδαιμονεστερους, a vox medio, may signify also, more superstitious," Hack., who on ch. 17 : 21–23 adds: "It is improbable, as a matter of just rhetoric, that the apostle employed it in that reproachful sense at the outset of his remarks." He proceeds to deduce their seeking after God (which Paul, doubtless, considered as something good) from this δεισιδαιμονια, or religious propensity, so prevalent among the Athenians. He announces himself as one who would guide their δεισιδαιμονια, not rightly conscious of its object

KING JAMES' VERSION.	GREEK TEXT.	REVISED VERSION.
was dead, whom Paul affirmed to be alive. 20 And because I doubted of such manner of questions, I asked *him* whether he would go to Jerusalem, and there be judged of these matters. 21 But when Paul had appealed to be reserved unto the hearing of Augustus, I commanded him to be kept till I might send him to Cesar. 22 Then Agrippa said unto Festus, I would also hear the man myself. To-morrow, said he, thou shalt hear him. 23 And on the morrow, when Agrippa was come, and Bernice, with great pomp, and was entered into the place of hearing, with the chief captains and principal men of the city, at Festus' commandment Paul was brought forth. 24 And Festus said, King Agrippa, and all men which are here present with us, ye see this man about whom all the multi-	τεθνηκότος, ὃν ἔφασκεν ὁ Παῦλος ζῆν. ²⁰ ἀπορούμενος δὲ ἐγὼ εἰς τὴν περὶ τούτου ζήτησιν, ἔλεγον, εἰ βούλοιτο πορεύεσθαι εἰς Ἱερουσαλὴμ, κἀκεῖ κρίνεσθαι περὶ τούτων. ²¹ τοῦ δὲ Παύλου ἐπικαλεσαμένου τηρηθῆναι αὐτὸν εἰς τὴν τοῦ Σεβαστοῦ διάγνωσιν, ἐκέλευσα τηρεῖσθαι αὐτὸν, ἕως οὗ πέμψω αὐτὸν πρὸς Καίσαρα. ²² Ἀγρίππας δὲ πρὸς τὸν Φῆστον ἔφη, Ἐβουλόμην καὶ αὐτὸς τοῦ ἀνθρώπου ἀκοῦσαι. Ὁ δὲ, Αὔριον, φησὶν, ἀκούσῃ αὐτοῦ. ²³ Τῇ οὖν ἐπαύριον ἐλθόντος τοῦ Ἀγρίππα καὶ τῆς Βερνίκης μετὰ πολλῆς φαντασίας, καὶ εἰσελθόντων εἰς τὸ ἀκροατήριον, σύν τε τοῖς χιλιάρχοις καὶ ἀνδράσι τοῖς κατ' ἐξοχὴν οὖσι τῆς πόλεως, καὶ κελεύσαντος τοῦ Φήστου, ἤχθη ὁ Παῦλος. ²⁴ καὶ φησιν ὁ Φῆστος, Ἀγρίππα βασιλεῦ, καὶ πάντες οἱ συμπαρόντες ἡμῖν ἄνδρες, θεωρεῖτε τοῦτον	sus, who had died, whom Paul affirmed to be alive. And be- 20 cause I doubted how to investigate such questions, I asked him whether he would go to Jerusalem, and be judged concerning these matters: but Paul having appealed, to 21 be kept as a prisoner, with a view to the examination of Augustus, I commanded him to be kept till I shall send him to Cæsar. Then Agrippa 22 said to Festus, I myself also would wish to hear the man. To-morrow, said he, you shall hear him. And on the morrow, when 23 Agrippa had come, and Bernice, with much pomp, and had entered into the place of audience, with the chiliarchs and principal men of the city, at the command of Festus, Paul was brought forth. Then 24 Festus says, King Agrippa, and all men who are present with us, you see this

---

and aim, to a state of clear self-consciousness, by a revelation of the object to which it thus ignorantly tended. Neander, Hackett.

Θρησκεια is the word used by James and Paul to indicate religion in its Jewish and Christian sense and currency, and much more in concert with its object and design than δεισιδαιμονια.

ʳ *Διαγνωσομαι—διαγνωσις.* The latter term occurs but once in the Christian Scriptures, and is here rendered, in com. ver., *hearing,* the *hearing of Augustus.* Coguition is its most appropriate representative in our vernacular. The judgment, or hearing of a cause—a *trial,* or an *investigation,* or examination—presents it in its full import. Any one of these, indeed, answers the present occasion. This is a striking instance of the freedom of interpretation of metaphorical language. *Cognosco* instead of *connosco,* or of *con* and *nosco.*

Cicero uses this word as equivalent to *make inquiry,* and Suetonius, to *judge,* or *determine* a matter. Physicians have introduced this word into their science and art, and now we

have the *διαγνωσις—diagnosis* of disease, or its symptoms—as an English word naturalized and nationalized.

ˢ *Εβουλομην και αυτος. Εβουλομαι,* was minded, willing, intended, *disposed, would.* Such is the variety of its renderings, com. ver. *I myself was willing,* quite analogous to Paul's style, Rom. 9 : 3, ηυχομην γαρ αυτος. Like the Jews, said Paul, *For I too myself was wishing* to be accursed from Christ, αναθημα ειναι—not when he wrote to the Romans, but comparing himself to them in his former state, as if he had said, "As they are now so once was I," wishing to be accounted accursed from Christ. So Agrippa said to Festus, *Εβουλομην και αυτος,* I also myself am wishing to hear him, I desire to hear him. Agrippa ad cujus aures plura de Jesu et Christianorum secta pervenerant. Vide 26 : 28. Kuin.

ᵗ *Μετα πολλης φαντασιας,* cum ingenti pompa—with great pomp—εισελθοντων εις το ακροατηριον, having entered with great pomp into *το ακροατηριον,* the Hall of audience—the place of hearing—found only in this place N. T., *Auditorium.*

KING JAMES' VERSION.

tude of the Jews have dealt with me, both at Jerusalem, and *also* here, crying that he ought not to live any longer.

25 But when I found that he had committed nothing worthy of death, and that he himself hath appealed to Augustus, I have determined to send him.

26 Of whom I have no certain thing to write unto my lord. Wherefore I have brought him forth before you, and specially before thee, O king Agrippa, that after examination had, I might have somewhat to write.

27 For it seemeth to me unreasonable to send a prisoner, and not withal to signify the crimes *laid* against him.

CHAP. XXVI.

Then Agrippa said unto Paul, Thou art permitted to speak for thyself. Then Paul stretched forth the hand, and answered for himself:

2 I think myself happy, king Agrippa, because I shall answer for myself this day before thee, touching all the things whereof I am accused of the Jews:

GREEK TEXT.

περὶ οὗ πᾶν τὸ πλῆθος τῶν Ἰουδαίων ἐνέτυχόν μοι ἔν τε Ἱεροσολύμοις καὶ ἐνθάδε, ἐπιβοῶντες μὴ δεῖν ζῆν αὐτὸν μηκέτι. ²⁵ ἐγὼ δὲ καταλαβόμενος μηδὲν ἄξιον θανάτου αὐτὸν πεπραχέναι, καὶ αὐτοῦ δὲ τούτου ἐπικαλεσαμένου τὸν Σεβαστὸν, ἔκρινα πέμπειν αὐτόν. ²⁶ περὶ οὗ ἀσφαλές τι γράψαι τῷ κυρίῳ οὐκ ἔχω· διὸ προήγαγον αὐτὸν ἐφ' ὑμῶν, καὶ μάλιστα ἐπὶ σοῦ, βασίλευ Ἀγρίππα, ὅπως τῆς ἀνακρίσεως γενομένης σχῶ τι γράψαι. ²⁷ ἄλογον γάρ μοι δοκεῖ, πέμποντα δέσμιον, μὴ καὶ τὰς κατ' αὐτοῦ αἰτίας σημᾶναι.

CHAP. XXVI.

ΑΓΡΙΠΠΑΣ δὲ πρὸς τὸν Παῦλον ἔφη, Ἐπιτρέπεταί σοι ὑπὲρ σεαυτοῦ λέγειν. Τότε ὁ Παῦλος ἀπελογεῖτο, ἐκτείνας τὴν χεῖρα, ² Περὶ πάντων ὧν ἐγκαλοῦμαι ὑπὸ Ἰουδαίων, βασιλεῦ Ἀγρίππα, ἥγημαι ἐμαυτὸν μακάριον μέλλων ἀπολογεῖσθαι ἐπὶ σοῦ σήμερον· ³ μάλιστα γνώ-

REVISED VERSION.

man about whom "all the multitude of the Jews have interceded with me, both at Jerusalem, and also here, crying out that he ought not to live any longer. But when I found 25 that he had committed nothing worthy of death, and he himself having appealed to Augustus, I determined to send him: of whom I have 26 ʷnothing certain to write to my sovereign, wherefore I have brought him forth before you; and especially before you, king Agrippa, that after examination, I may have something to write. For it 27 seems to me ʷunreasonable to send a prisoner, and not also to signify the charges against him.

CHAP. XXVI.

Then Agrippa says to Paul, 1 You are ᵃpermitted to speak for yourself. Then Paul stretched forth his hand, and answered for himself: I think 2 myself happy, king Agrippa, because I shall answer for myself this day before you, concerning all the things of which I am accused by ᵇJews:

ᵈ The procurator could say, παν το πληθος των Ιουδαιων, "all the whole multitude of the Jews." A very vague charge, επιβοωντες μη δειν ζην αυτον μηκετι.

Ενετυχον μοι, in malem partem, interceded with me. "Some manuscripts read, ζην αυτον, others, αυτον ζην—and so in the next verse some read, θανατου αυτον, and others, αυτον θανατου." Hack.

ᵛ Περι ου, concerning whom I have nothing sure, definite to write to the sovereign. "In σχω τι γραψαι the pronoun belongs to the first verb, not to the second," Kuin., Hack. "Some repeat ασφαλες after τι (Mey.), which is not necessary," Hack. For γραψαι Ln., Tf. γραψω, Gb. doubtful.

ʷ "For it is unsuitable when we send up a prisoner, not to designate his offense," Murd.; "*unreasonable* in sending a prisoner, not to signify the charges against him," Wes., Penn; "without specifying the charge," Thomp.; "signifying the charge," Wakef.; "the charges," Boothr.

ᵃ Ἐπιτρεπεται σοι ὑπερ σεαυτου λεγειν. For ὑπερ, Ln., Tf., Gb. would substitute περι. Nothing important in deciding this case; whether *concerning* himself, or *for* himself, is quite equal in law, or equity. And whether we represent επιτρεπω by *suffer*, or *permit*, or *have leave*, or *license*, or *liberty*, is wholly a matter of taste, as it is, indeed, in a hundred other cases. In our taste, we would prefer, "*you are permitted to speak for yourself*," or, *thou* art permitted to speak for *thyself*. *You* should be followed by *yourself*, and *thou* by *thyself*, a *congruity* which is not always appreciated, or even perceived.

ᵇ Grammatically, there is a difference between *Jews*, and *the Jews*. The former may be only a *clique*; the latter is the whole nation. We appreciate the difference between, Americans have taken Cuba, and, *the* Americans have taken Cuba. As a *scribe*, or even as a *prudent* man, Paul would not have represented himself before King Agrippa as having the whole

KING JAMES' VERSION.	GREEK TEXT.	REVISED VERSION.
3 Especially, *because I know* thee to be expert in all customs and questions which are among the Jews: wherefore I beseech thee to hear me patiently.	στην ὄντα σε πάντων τῶν κατὰ Ἰουδαίους ἐθῶν τε καὶ ζητημάτων. διὸ δέομαί σου, μακροθύμως ἀκοῦσαί μου. ⁴ τὴν μὲν οὖν βίωσίν μου τὴν ἐκ νεότητος, τὴν	because I know you to be especially ᶜskilled in all customs and questions which are among Jews; wherefore I beseech you to hear me patiently. 3
4 My manner of life from my youth, which was at the first among mine own nation at Jerusalem, know all the Jews,	ἀπ' ἀρχῆς γενομένην ἐν τῷ ἔθνει μου ἐν Ἱεροσολύμοις, ἴσασι πάντες οἱ Ἰουδαῖοι, ⁵ προγινώ-	My manner of life from my youth, which was at the first among my own nation at Jerusalem, all the Jews know, 4
5 Which knew me from the beginning, (if they would testify,) that after the most straitest sect of our religion, I lived a Pharisee.	σκοντές με ἄνωθεν, ἐὰν θέλωσι μαρτυρεῖν, ὅτι κατὰ τὴν ἀκρι- βεστάτην αἵρεσιν τῆς ἡμετέρας θρησκείας ἔζησα Φαρισαῖος·	who have ᵈknown me from the beginning, if they would testify, that after the strictest sect of our religion, I lived a Pharisee. And now I stand, 5
6 And now I stand, and am judged for the hope of the promise made of God unto our fathers:	⁶ καὶ νῦν ἐπ' ἐλπίδι τῆς πρὸς τοὺς πατέρας ἐπαγγελίας γενο- μένης ὑπὸ τοῦ Θεοῦ ἕστηκα κρι- νόμενος, ⁷ εἰς ἣν τὸ δωδεκάφυ-	and am judged for the hope of the promise made by God to our fathers: to *the accomplishment* of which promise 6
7 Unto which *promise* our twelve tribes, instantly serving *God* day and night, hope to come. For which hope's sake, king Agrippa, I am accused of the Jews.	λον ἡμῶν ἐν ἐκτενείᾳ νύκτα καὶ ἡμέραν λατρεῦον ἐλπίζει καταν- τῆσαι· περὶ ἧς ἐλπίδος ἐγκαλοῦ- μαι, βασιλεῦ Ἀγρίππα, ὑπὸ τῶν	our twelve tribes, earnestly serving God day and night, hope to attain; on account of which hope, king Agrippa, I am accused by Jews. What! 7
8 Why should it be thought	Ἰουδαίων. ⁸ τί; ἄπιστον κρίνε-	8

---

nation of the Jews combined against him; he very legally and judiciously says, Jews, *certain Jews.*

On this *ὑπὸ Ἰουδαίων* Professor Hackett says—"without the article (comp. 22 : 30), because he would represent the accusation as purely *Jewish* in its character." Very good, indeed; but not quite enough. *Purely Jewish* may include the whole nation of the Jews; but that was still too formidable for the occasion. To have the Jewish people all in combination against him, was, indeed, greatly enhancing the argument against himself. But Paul, still more prudently, gives the bald indefinite word *Jews*, indicating a mere clique, and neither a tribe, nor a nation, nor a whole people. It is not often that we find an illustration, so unambiguous and forcible, of the grammatical power of the presence or absence of the article. The power of its absence can only be valued by the power of its presence. "The head and front of his offending" extends only to an indefinite class of Jews. We, therefore, prefer, "I am accused by *Jews*," to, "I am accused by *the Jews.*"

ᶜ *Μάλιστα γνώστην, especially intelligent,* is good; but we think, *skilled, especially skilled,* is better.

Wisdom, skill, and *knowledge,* are not synonymous, but often confounded. There is no writer known to us that does not often confound these terms. And, indeed, our lexico-graphers are perplexed in defining them. Webster himself is bewildered in his efforts to discriminate and clearly distinguish them. Our very best writers and orators confound them. *Knowledge* is both speculative and practical. *Wisdom* is the maximum of knowledge, prudence, and discretion combined. We may have much knowledge, and no wisdom. We sometimes find intelligent fools, and comparatively ignorant wise men. "I *wisdom* dwell with *prudence,* and find out the knowledge of artful devices," said the wisest and the most intelligent man of Bible history. Knowledge is theoretic and speculative; wisdom is discriminating and practical. "The *Sophia* of the Greeks, and the *Chachemah* of the Hebrews, are indicative of that prudence and discretion which enable men to perceive what is fit or suitable to be done, according to the knowledge they may possess of the circumstances of time, place, persons, manners, and end of doing." So defines Alexander Cruden in his Concordance; and in this definition he excels all the lexicographers that come within my horizon.

ᵈ *Προγινώσκοντες με ἄνωθεν.* "Who knew me from the first," Wes.; "who were acquainted with me many years ago," Wakef.; they have a prior knowledge of me, from an early period," Thomp.; "Who have known me from the beginning," Penn.

KING JAMES' VERSION.

a thing incredible with you, that God should raise the dead?

9 I verily thought with myself, that I ought to do many things contrary to the name of Jesus of Nazareth.

10 Which thing I also did in Jerusalem: and many of the saints did I shut up in prison, having received authority from the chief priests; and when they were put to death, I gave my voice against *them*.

11 And I punished them oft in every synagogue, and compelled *them* to blaspheme; and being exceedingly mad against them, I persecuted *them* even unto strange cities.

12 Whereupon, as I went to Damascus, with authority and commission from the chief priests,

13 At mid-day, O king, I saw in the way a light from heaven, above the brightness of the sun, shining round about me, and them which journeyed with me.

14 And when we were all fallen to the earth, I heard a voice speaking unto me, and saying in the Hebrew tongue, Saul, Saul, why persecutest thou me? *It is* hard for thee to kick against the pricks.

15 And I said, Who art thou, Lord? And he said, I am Jesus whom thou persecutest.

16 But rise, and stand upon thy feet: for I have appeared unto thee for this purpose, to

GREEK TEXT.

ται παρ᾽ ὑμῖν, εἰ ὁ Θεὸς νεκροὺς ἐγείρει; ⁹ ἐγὼ μὲν οὖν ἔδοξα ἐμαυτῷ πρὸς τὸ ὄνομα Ἰησοῦ τοῦ Ναζωραίου δεῖν πολλὰ ἐναντία πρᾶξαι· ¹⁰ ὃ καὶ ἐποίησα ἐν Ἱεροσολύμοις, καὶ πολλοὺς τῶν ἁγίων ἐγὼ φυλακαῖς κατέκλεισα, τὴν παρὰ τῶν ἀρχιερέων ἐξουσίαν λαβών· ἀναιρουμένων τε αὐτῶν κατήνεγκα ψῆφον. ¹¹ καὶ κατὰ πάσας τὰς συναγωγὰς πολλάκις τιμωρῶν αὐτοὺς, ἠνάγκαζον βλασφημεῖν· περισσῶς τε ἐμμαινόμενος αὐτοῖς, ἐδίωκον ἕως καὶ εἰς τὰς ἔξω πόλεις. ¹² ἐν οἷς καὶ πορευόμενος εἰς τὴν Δαμασκὸν μετ᾽ ἐξουσίας καὶ ἐπιτροπῆς τῆς παρὰ τῶν ἀρχιερέων, ¹³ ἡμέρας μέσης, κατὰ τὴν ὁδὸν εἶδον, βασιλεῦ, οὐρανόθεν ὑπὲρ τὴν λαμπρότητα τοῦ ἡλίου, περιλάμψαν με φῶς καὶ τοὺς σύν ἐμοὶ πορευομενους. ¹⁴ πάντων δὲ καταπεσόντων ἡμῶν εἰς τὴν γῆν, ἤκουσα φωνὴν λαλοῦσαν πρός με καὶ λέγουσαν τῇ Ἑβραΐδι διαλέκτῳ, Σαοὺλ, Σαοὺλ, τί με διώκεις; σκληρόν σοι πρὸς κέντρα λακτίζειν. ¹⁵ Ἐγὼ δὲ εἶπον, Τίς εἶ κύριε; Ὁ δὲ εἶπεν, Ἐγώ εἰμι Ἰησοῦς ὃν σὺ διώκεις. ¹⁶ ἀλλὰ ἀνάστηθι, καὶ στῆθι ἐπὶ τοὺς πόδας σου· εἰς τοῦτο γὰρ ὤφθην

REVISED VERSION.

Is it judged incredible with you [e]that God raises the dead? I, indeed, thought with myself 9 that I ought to do many things against the name of Jesus of Nazareth. Which things I also 10 did in Jerusalem: and many of the saints I shut up in prisons, having received authority from the chief priests; and when they were put to death, I gave my vote against them. And 11 punishing them often throughout all the synagogues, I compelled them to revile [f]Jesus, and being exceedingly mad against them, I persecuted them even to foreign cities. In doing this, as I went to Da- 12 mascus, with authority and commission from the chief priests, at mid-day, O king, I saw along 13 the [g]way a light from heaven, above the brightness of the sun, shining round about me, and those that journeyed with me. And when we had all fallen to 14 the earth, I heard a voice speaking to me, and saying in the Hebrew tongue, Saul, Saul, why do you persecute me? It is hard for you to kick against [h]goads. And I said, Who art 15 thou, Lord? And he said, I am Jesus whom you persecute. But rise, and stand upon 16 your feet: for I have appeared to you for this purpose, to make you a minister and a wit-

---

[e] Εἰ is very generally translated by *if*: by *that*, in the com. ver. Τι, interrogative, what? indicative of surprise. According to punctuation in Bagster's selected readings, we punctuate and render it, What? Is it judged, etc.

[f] To revile *Jesus*. Jesus, in this place, is a necessary supplement to ordinary readers. Indeed, it is contextually the sense of the passage. It was not as some, if not many, of the uneducated imagine, to blaspheme God. To speak against Christ, or to speak disparagingly of him, is blasphemy.

[g] Κατα την ὁδον, "on the way," De Wette, (Mey., Rob.); "along the way," Hack.

[h] Instances of this formula are given, from Greek and Roman writers.

"Nam quæ inscita est,
Adversum stimulum calces."—TERENCE.

KING JAMES' VERSION.	GREEK TEXT.	REVISED VERSION.

make thee a minister and a witness both of these things which thou hast seen, and of those things in the which I will appear unto thee;

17 Delivering thee from the people, and *from* the Gentiles, unto whom now I send thee,

18 To open their eyes, *and* to turn *them* from darkness to light, and *from* the power of Satan unto God, that they may receive forgiveness of sins, and inheritance among them which are sanctified by faith that is in me.

19 Whereupon, O king Agrippa, I was not disobedient unto the heavenly vision:

20 But shewed first unto them of Damascus, and at Jerusalem, and throughout all the coasts of Judea, and *then* to the Gentiles,

σοι, προχειρίσασθαι σε ὑπηρέτην καὶ μάρτυρα ὧν τε εἶδες ὧν τε ὀφθήσομαί σοι, [17] ἐξαιρούμενός σε ἐκ τοῦ λαοῦ καὶ τῶν ἐθνῶν, εἰς οὓς νῦν σε ἀποστέλλω, [18] ἀνοῖξαι ὀφθαλμοὺς αὐτῶν, τοῦ ἐπιστρέψαι ἀπὸ σκότους εἰς φῶς καὶ τῆς ἐξουσίας τοῦ Σατανᾶ ἐπὶ τὸν Θεόν, τοῦ λαβεῖν αὐτοὺς ἄφεσιν ἁμαρτιῶν, καὶ κλῆρον ἐν τοῖς ἡγιασμένοις, πίστει τῇ εἰς ἐμέ. [19] Ὅθεν βασιλεῦ Ἀγρίππα, οὐκ ἐγενόμην ἀπειθὴς τῇ οὐρανίῳ ὀπτασίᾳ, [20] ἀλλὰ τοῖς ἐν Δαμασκῷ πρῶτον καὶ Ἱεροσολύμοις, εἰς πᾶσάν τε τὴν χώραν τῆς Ἰουδαίας, καὶ τοῖς ἔθνεσιν,

ness both of those things you have seen, and of those things in which I will appear to you; delivering you from the peo- 17 ple, and from the Gentiles, to whom I now send ⁱyou, to 18 open their eyes, that they may turn from darkness to light, and from the power of Satan to God, that they may ʲreceive forgiveness of sins, and an inheritance among them that are sanctified, by the faith respecting ᵏme.

Whence, king Agrippa, I 19 was not disobedient to the heavenly vision, but showed 20 first to those of Damascus, and at Jerusalem, and throughout all the region of Judea, and then to the Gentiles, that

---

ⁱ For νυν, Gb., Ln., Tf. substitute εγω.

ʲ *Του λαβειν, κ. τ. λ.*, expresses the direct object of the second infinitive, and the alternate object of the first. Hack.

This is an impressive, as well as a most perspicuous and connected summary of *means* and *ends.* Paul's work is sententiously expressed under the figure of *"opening"* closed eyes, or *blind* eyes. This was *his* work, being declared in this place as the end of his mission. *Their* work, whose eyes were enlightened, is also explicitly declared. It is distinctly, 1st, turning from darkness to light; 2dly, and, consequently, that they might receive, first, a *"remission of sins;"* and, in the next place, *"an inheritance* amongst the sanctified; and then again *the means* are proposed—*"through* faith," or *" by* faith." It is πιστει τη εις εμε.

ᵏ *Πιστει τη εις εμε.* "Our English translators, and some others, join with ἡγιασμενος; but the words specify evidently the condition by which believers obtain the pardon of sin, and an interest in the heavenly inheritance." Hackett. *Εις* is seldom represented by *upon*, and even in those cases it may be, if not more, intelligibly rendered *"in regard to,"* in reference to," or, *in order to* some end, or object.

Εις = πιστει τη. This is the distinctive and most characteristic *instrument* in the Evangelical dispensation, or the present existing administration of the remedial system, consummated in the person, the mission, and the work of the Lord Jesus Christ. Faith is, however, but an instrument. It is never an ultimate end, but a means to the attainment of ultimate ends.

The translators of the Received Version were quite arbitrary in their respect to the presence of the article. Some *forty* times they have annihilated it in their version, when the apostles wrote it as all important to the proper and profitable understanding of the mind of the Spirit.

Πιστις, faith, and *η πιστις, the faith,* are very distinct ideas. We have this most important common noun in the apostolic writings in two very different, distinct, and clearly appreciable attitudes; *subjectively* and *objectively* contemplated. When used *subjectively,* in reference to a *person,* unless it become itself the subject of a proposition, it is anarthrous; when objectively, with the article always, or with some other distinguishing connective, indicative of its special significance and association. On turning to Paul's splendid development of the renowned "cloud of witnesses," he summons the mighty men of faith to demonstrate his own definition of it. He first defines faith, and gives *twenty-three* cases of it, illustrative of it as a principle of action in its subject. In each and every one of these cases it is *anarthrous.* In conclusion (Heb. 11 : 39) he says, οὗτοι παντες μαρτυρηθεντες δια της πιστεως. Thus distinguishing *the faith* objectively, from *faith* subjectively contemplated;—an inheritance *through the faith.*

Εις εμε, towards me, *into* me, are awkward and clumsy formulas of speech. *With regard to* me, or *respecting* me, are not only good English, but as fashionable as *unto* me, *toward* me, *concerning* me, *upon* me, *at* me, all of which, and many similar are, in com. ver., constituted representatives of εις, in its numerous and various associations.

KING JAMES' VERSION.	GREEK TEXT.	REVISED VERSION.
that they should repent and turn to God, and do works meet for repentance.	ἀπαγγέλλων μετανοεῖν, καὶ ἐπιστρέφειν ἐπὶ τὸν Θεὸν, ἄξια τῆς μετανοίας ἔργα πράσσοντας.	they should ¹reform and turn to God, and do works proper for reformation. For these 21
21 For these causes the Jews caught me in the temple, and went about to kill *me*.	21 ἕνεκα τούτων με οἱ Ἰουδαῖοι συλλαβόμενοι ἐν τῷ ἱερῷ, ἐπειρῶντο διαχειρίσασθαι.	causes the Jews seized me in the temple, and tried to kill me. Having, however, ob- 22
22 Having therefore obtained help of God, I continue unto this day, witnessing both to small and great, saying none other things than those which the prophets and Moses did say should come:	22 ἐπικουρίας οὖν τυχὼν τῆς παρὰ τοῦ Θεοῦ, ἄχρι τῆς ἡμέρας ταύτης ἕστηκα, μαρτυρούμενος μικρῷ τε καὶ μεγάλῳ, οὐδὲν ἐκτὸς λέγων ὧν τε οἱ προφῆται ἐλάλησαν μελλόντων γίνεσθαι καὶ Μωσῆς,	tained the help of God, I continue to this day, testifying both to small and great, saying no other things than those which the prophets and Moses did say would come: that 23 the Christ ᵐwas to suffer, and
23 That Christ should suffer, *and* that he should be the first that should rise from the dead, and should shew light unto the people, and to the Gentiles.	23 εἰ παθητὸς ὁ Χριστὸς, εἰ πρῶτος ἐξ ἀναστάσεως νεκρῶν φῶς μέλλει καταγγέλλειν τῷ λαῷ καὶ τοῖς ἔθνεσι.	that he first, by his resurrection from the dead, would show light to the people, and to the Gentiles.
24 And as he thus spake for himself, Festus said with a loud voice, Paul, thou art beside thyself; much learning doth make thee mad.	24 Ταῦτα δὲ αὐτοῦ ἀπολογουμένου, ὁ Φῆστος μεγάλῃ τῇ φωνῇ ἔφη, Μαίνῃ Παῦλε· τὰ πολλά σε γράμματα εἰς μανίαν περιτρέπει.	And as he thus spoke for 24 himself, Festus said with a loud voice, Paul, you are mad, much learning has made you mad. But he says, I am not mad, 25
25 But he said, I am not mad, most noble Festus; but speak forth the words of truth and soberness.	25 Ὁ δὲ, Οὐ μαίνομαι, φησὶ, κράτιστε Φῆστε, ἀλλ' ἀληθείας καὶ σωφροσύνης ῥήματα ἀποφθέγγομαι.	most excellent Festus; but speak the words of truth and of a sound mind. For the 26
26 For the king knoweth of these things, before whom also I speak freely. For I am persuaded that none of these things are hidden from him; for this thing was not done in a corner.	26 ἐπίσταται γὰρ περὶ τούτων ὁ βασιλεὺς, πρὸς ὃν καὶ παρρησιαζόμενος λαλῶ· λανθάνειν γὰρ αὐτόν τι τούτων οὐ πείθομαι οὐδέν· οὐ γάρ ἐστιν ἐν γωνίᾳ πεπραγμένον	king well knows concerning these things, before whom, therefore, I speak boldly; for I am persuaded that none of these things are hidden from him: for this thing has not been done in a ⁿcorner. King 27

---

¹ We are still more penetrated with the conviction that μετανοεω and μετανοια should be represented in all cases by *reform* and *reformation*. They are not equivalents to μεταμελομαι and μεταμελεια. When and where the Holy Spirit uses two words, we should not use only one. *Pœnitentia* is not *reformatio*. A change of views is not a change of conduct, nor a change of life. That sinners should not only be *penitent*—regret, and mourn over the past—not merely *profess* reformation, but *do works meet*, or suitable to such profession of reformation. Μεταμελεια is mere *painful* and *sorrowful* reminiscences of the past, pregnant with fearful forebodings of the future; but a change of views, a change of mind and purpose, a change of heart and of life are represented by μετανοια. There are works meet and suitable to a change of views and a change of heart which are called *works meet for repentance*.

ᵐ Ει παθητος ὁ Χριστος, might otherwise be rendered, whether the Christ can suffer. De Wette, Mey. "Not whether he must suffer in order to fulfill the Scripture." Hackett. "Some make ει = ὁτι, i. e., the sign of a moderated assertion." Hack. "That the Christ *would* suffer death," Wakef., Penn; "*should* suffer," Thomp., Boothr. According to Hackett, the Apostle "approaches the question on the *Jewish* side of it, not on the *Christian*, and that was, whether the Messiah being such as many of the Jews expected, *could suffer*." Others make ει equal ὁτι, that, = that he would suffer, and that he would rise, etc. He is, indeed, the προτοτοκος εκ των νεκρων with Christians. But such was not the Messiah expected by the Jews. And, therefore, the point in debate was whether, according to prophecy, the Messiah *could* suffer death. Paul proved that he *could* die, and did die, according to the Scriptures.

ⁿ Σωφροσυνη, *sobriety*. So rendered in its two other occurrences in Paul's writings. It is an antithesis of μανια ου μαινομαι—αληθειας, of truth, "as opposed not merely to falsehood, but to the fancies and hallucinations of a disordered intellect." Hackett.

KING JAMES' VERSION.	GREEK TEXT.	REVISED VERSION.
27 King Agrippa, believest thou the prophets? I know that thou believest. 28 Then Agrippa said unto Paul, Almost thou persuadest me to be a Christian.	τοῦτο. ²⁷ πιστεύεις βασιλεῦ Ἀγρίππα τοῖς προφήταις; οἶδα ὅτι πιστεύεις. ²⁸ Ὁ δὲ Ἀγρίπ- πας πρὸς τὸν Παῦλον ἔφη, Ἐν ὀλίγῳ με πείθεις Χριστιανὸν	Agrippa, do you believe the prophets? I know that you be- lieve them. Then Agrippa said 28 to Paul, You in a little time per- suade me to become a °Chris-

° Ἐν ὀλιγῳ—χρονῳ, *in a little time.* *At this rate* you per- suade me to be a Christian. By taking *εν ολιγω* as *quanti- tative* instead of *temporal*, Meyer brings out this sense from the expression, "with little effort you persuade me to become a Christian." In other words (said sarcastically), "you ap- peal to me as if you thought me an easy convert to your faith." "Should *εν μεγαλῳ*, according to Mey. and Tf., be adopted as the current reading in Paul's reply, instead of *εν πολλῳ*, this would be correct; but the testimony for the com- mon text outweighs that against it," Hack., Neander, De Wette. It is at present held to be unphilological to translate *εν ολιγω* almost (Beza, Grotius, Eng. Ver.). "The Greek for that sense would have been *ολιγου δει*, or *παρ' ολιγον*. Agrippa appears to have been moved by the apostle's earnest manner, but attempts to conceal his emotion under the form of a jest," Hack.

Whatever may have been his motives or convictions, sin- cerely or insincerely expressed, he gives conspicuity and emphasis to the Christian name as then of some notoriety. As to the *origin* of this name, the consideration of which we deferred to this place though occurring ch. 11 : 26, we are called upon to notice. The word Χριστιανος is found only three times in the Christian Scriptures, Acts 11 : 26 ; 26 : 28 ; 1 Pet. 4 : 16. Whether this name was self-imposed, or im- posed on the disciples of Christ by their enemies, is even yet a litigated question. The com. ver. makes the disciples *pas- sive* in receiving this name; so does Wakef., Murd., Dodd., Thomp., Boothr., Wiclif, Tynd., Cranmer, the Genevan, the Rheims, all lying before me. I have before me also the London Polyglott, published by Bagster and Sons, under the super- vision of the distinguished Dr. Lee. In this admirable work at one opening, we have the Hebrew, Greek, Latin, German, French, Spanish, Italian, and English Old Testament and New; and in all these, so far as we understand them, we find them unanimous and uniform in presenting the disciples at Antioch not as *active*, but as *passive*, in receiving the name *Christian.* Superadded to these authorities the impressive fact that every creature in the universe is *passive*, in receiving a name, confirms our convictions that neither Paul nor Barna- bas, nor any inspired man, then and there, *first called* the dis- ciples of Christ at Antioch *Christians.* Sacred history, from its first to its last page, presents this view. God himself gave the first man a name. Adam gave to his wife the name *Eve*, or *life*, and to the whole animal creation around him. He did this work so appropriately that God confirmed it all; for Moses says, " The Lord God brought every beast of the

field, and every fowl of the air to Adam to see what he would call them. And whatsoever Adam called every living creature, that became the name thereof." Gen. 2 : 19. Adam was, therefore, the most learned zoologist that ever lived.

But we must hear the profound Kuinœl on this verb *chree- matizoo.* Χρηματιζω (*chreematizoo*) among the Greeks in Attica indicated *to transact anything,*, or so to transact a matter *that* it should thence obtain a name. His own words are: "*Atticis erat res agere; apud recensiores res ita agere ut nomen inde adispicaris hinc significatione intransitiva.*" In consulting *Thesaurus Grœcœ Linguœ, secundum Constan- tini methodum et Schrevellii, Reseratus, concinnatus, et adorna- tas, studio et industria Guilelmi Robertson, Cantabrigiœ,* A. D. 1676, we find this name dilated upon in the words following, to wit: "Χρηματισαι τους μαθητας Χριστιανους, nam cogno- menta hominibus imponi solebant ex negotio quod tractabant, vel ex efficio quo fungebantur; item oraculo reddo. *Respon- sum do at postulata, ut* πρεσβειας χρηματιζειν. Diodorus." To this high authority we shall only add that of Leigh's Crit. Sacra, London, A. D. 1650: "Χρηματιζω, ομαι, nominor, Divi- nitas *nuncior.* Rom. 7 : 3, χρηματισει, vocabitur scil. adultera —she shall be called an adulteress." Acts 11 : 26 it indicates "*to be called,*" "to be named," not to call themselves. Let us hear Kuinœl a little further. "*Quæritur, imposuerintne Christi Sectatores sibi ipsi hoc nomen, an illud* acceperint ab aliis. Christi cultores ipsos primum usos esse Christianorum appellatione non modo probari nequit, sed etiam gravibus ne- gari potest argumentis. Primum enim, si sibi ipsi peculiare nomen vindicassent, invidiam adversus se graviorem excitas- sent, et magis magisque aluissent." "*That the Christian wor- shipers placed this name upon themselves is not only void of all scriptural evidence; but can be denied with weighty ar- guments. If they had asserted, or vindicated a right to the name, they would have only excited a more grievous enmity against themselves, and more and more nourished it.*" So reasoned Kuinœl. Besides, the Greek text, fairly interpreted, affords no authority for such an idea. That it may with all propriety, and with little or no reasonable offense, *now* be as- sumed and worn by the disciples of Christ everywhere, is not to be questioned, at least, comes not within our present horizon.

But it may be said, Does not the word χρηματιζω in He- brew style intimate a Divine oracle? Does it not in the Christian currency imply or involve a Divine *communication*, or suggestion? We can positively say that while this may sometimes be the case, it does not necessarily indicate such an

KING JAMES' VERSION.	GREEK TEXT.	REVISED VERSION.
29 And Paul said, I would to God, that not only thou, but also all that hear me this day, were both almost, and altogether such as I am, except these bonds.	γενέσθαι. ²⁹ Ὁ δὲ Παῦλος εἶπεν, Εὐξαίμην ἂν τῷ Θεῷ, καὶ ἐν ὀλίγῳ καὶ ἐν πολλῷ οὐ μόνον σε, ἀλλὰ καὶ πάντας τοὺς ἀκούοντάς μου σήμερον, γενέσθαι τοιούτους ὁποῖος κἀγώ εἰμι, παρεκτὸς τῶν δεσμῶν τούτων. ³⁰ Καὶ ταῦτα εἰπόντος αὐτοῦ, ἀνέστη ὁ βασιλεὺς καὶ ὁ ἡγεμὼν, ἥ τε Βερνίκη, καὶ οἱ συγκαθήμενοι αὐτοῖς. ³¹ καὶ ἀναχωρήσαντες ἐλάλουν πρὸς ἀλλήλους λέγοντες, Ὅτι οὐδὲν θανάτου ἄξιον ἢ δεσμῶν πράσσει ὁ ἄνθρωπος αὗτος. ³² Ἀγρίππας δὲ τῷ Φήστῳ ἔφη, Ἀπολελύσθαι ἐδύνατο ὁ ἄνθρωπος οὗτος, εἰ μὴ ἐπεκέκλητο Καίσαρα.	tian. And Paul said, ᵖI would to God, that not only you, but also all that hear me this day, were, in a little or much time, such as I am, except these bonds. 29 And when he had said these things, the king rose ᵠup, and the governor, and Bernice, and they who sat with them, and when they had gone aside, they talked among themselves, saying, This man does nothing worthy of death, or of bonds. Then Agrippa said to Festus, This man might have been set at liberty, if he had not appealed to Cesar. 30 31 32
39 And when he had thus spoken, the king rose up, and the governor, and Bernice, and they that sat with them:		
31 And when they were gone aside, they talked between themselves, saying, This man doeth nothing worthy of death, or of bonds.		
32 Then said Agrippa unto Festus, This man might have been set at liberty, if he had not appealed unto Cesar.		

idea. Its use in the Christian Scriptures does not always indicate such an idea. For example, in its nine occurrences it is fully exhausted by the words, *called, admonished, spoke.* Rom. 7 : 3, she shall be *called an adulteress,* according to law, not according to a Divine suggestion, or impulse. "It was *revealed,*" Luke 2 : 26, and it is once represented by the mere term *spoke,* Heb. 12 : 25, and by the Romans translated in their own currency to *name, named—appellor, nominor.* Χρῆμα, its root in Greek, is, *negotium res, consilium, necessitas.* They assume too much who say it necessarily involves the idea of a Divine oracle in this connection. It *may,* or it *may not,* is the most that can be philologically and truthfully said of it. It would, indeed, be assuming too much, to affirm that it here indicates a special Divine communication. It is quite as possible and as probable, that because the disciples of Jesus spoke so much of his being *the Christ,* that their enemies indignantly called them *Christians.* This becomes more plausible from an allusion to the sufferings of the early Christians on the part of Peter, 1st Ep. ch. 4 : 16, "If any

man suffer *as a Christian,* let him not be ashamed, but let him glorify God in that name;" or, "*on account of that name,*" Penn. It is the most probable presumption, that being the custom in all the sects of philosophy to call the school after its founder—Platonists, Pythagoreans, Aristotelians; or as the Christian sects, Lutherans, Calvinists, Arminians, etc., glorify their founders. So did the disciples either voluntarily, or by constraint, the author and the founder of the faith. "If any man suffer *as a Christian,* let him not be ashamed, but let him glorify God on that account."

ᵖ Ευξαιμην αν τω Θεω, *I could pray to God,* according to my feelings. Αν, with the optative, intensifies the idea, και εν ολιγω και εν πολλω. Εφη (v. 28) omitted by Ln., Tf., Gb. For πολλω, Ln., Tf., Gb. substitute, as a better reading, μεγαλω.

ᵠ After ανεστη, τε is properly inserted before ὁ βασιλευς, both the king and the governor, etc. *Then the king rose up* is in better taste.

KING JAMES' VERSION.	GREEK TEXT.	REVISED VERSION.
CHAP. XXVII.	CHAP. XXVII.	CHAP. XXVII.

AND when it was determined, that we should sail into Italy, they delivered Paul and certain other prisoners unto *one* named Julius, a centurion of Augustus' band.

2 And entering into a ship of Adramyttium, we launched, meaning to sail by the coasts of Asia, *one* Aristarchus, a Macedonian of Thessalonica, being with us.

3 And the next *day* we touched at Sidon. And Julius courteously entreated Paul, and gave *him* liberty to go unto his friends to refresh himself.

4 And when we had launched from thence, we sailed under

ΏΣ δὲ ἐκρίθη τοῦ ἀποπλεῖν ἡμᾶς εἰς τὴν Ἰταλίαν, παρεδίδουν τόν τε Παῦλον καί τινας ἑτέρους δεσμώτας ἑκατοντάρχῃ, ὀνόματι Ἰουλίῳ, σπείρης Σεβαστῆς. ² ἐπιβάντες δὲ πλοίῳ Ἀδραμυττηνῷ, μέλλοντες πλεῖν τοὺς κατὰ τὴν Ἀσίαν τόπους, ἀνήχθημεν, ὄντος σὺν ἡμῖν Ἀριστάρχου Μακεδόνος Θεσσαλονικέως. ³ τῇ τε ἑτέρᾳ κατήχθημεν εἰς Σιδῶνα· φιλανθρώπως τε ὁ Ἰούλιος τῷ Παύλῳ χρησάμενος, ἐπέτρεψε πρὸς φίλους πορευθέντα ἐπιμελείας τυχεῖν. ⁴ κἀκεῖθεν ἀναχθέντες ὑπεπλεύσαμεν

AND when it was determin-1 ed that we should sail to Italy, they delivered Paul and certain other prisoners to a centurion of the Augustan ᵃcohort, named Julius. And entering 2 into a vessel of Adramyttium, ᵇwe put to sea, being about to sail by the coasts of Asia, Aristarchus, a Macedonian of Thessalonica, being with us. And the next day we landed 3 at Sidon: and Julius courteously treated Paul, and gave him liberty to go to the ᶜfriends, to partake of their kindness. And when we had 4 ᵈloosed from thence, we sailed

---

ᵃ Ἐκριθη του αποπλειν ημας. Not their departure, but the time of it, *that we* (*Luke* and company) *should sail.* The infinitive with του is generally indicative of purpose. Τινας ἑτερους δεσμωτας, *certain other prisoners;* ἑτερος, *other;* tantamount to αλλος—σπειρης Σεβαστης, of the Augustan band or cohort—called Italian—generally composed of Italians.

ᵇ Πλοιῳ Αδραμυττηνῳ, a ship of Adramyttium, a sea-port of Mysia. Μελλοντι, by Gb., Tf. and Meyer, is preferred to μελλοντες—ambiguous according to De Wette. Πλειν τους κατα την Ασιαν τοπους; εις after πλειν seems to be wanting, and is in some texts supplied. By what authority we know not.

ᶜ Κατηχθημεν εις Σιδωνα, first per. plur. aor. 1. ind. pass., of καταγω, deduco. We landed at Sidon, εκ κατα, deorsum, downwards, et αγω, duco; literally, *we were borne down into Sidon,* a Phœnician city. Our Saviour had visited the confines of Tyre and Sidon; reported Matt. 15 : 21. Τους φιλους, not *his* friends, but *the* friends, i. e., the brethren. This title, οἱ φιλοι, of *the brethren,* occurs 3d John, v. 15, twice.

Φιλανθρωπως τε ὁ Ιουλιος τω Παυλω χρησαμενος. Χραω, *commodato do,* quasi *e manu in manum;* *I benignantly place my hand in yours.* Captain Julius treated benignantly, *philanthropically;* *courteously,* is not enough; *most benignantly.* Captain Julius was a true Roman gentleman. Ἡμερας ἑπτα may be indefinite; *about a week.* Hack., ch. 20 : 6, "Means probably about a week.

ᵈ Αναχθεντες υπεπλευσαμεν την Κυπρον—εναντιους. Αναγω, *subduco, adduco, produco, reduco;* αναγειν, *proficere, ascendere.*—Crit. Sacra. This is a word of special favor with Luke. In the Christian Scriptures αναγω is found *twenty-four* times;

and of these, *out of Luke's writings, only three are found.* So largely in the use of this word, he gives much latitude to its import, as well as a very free circulation. Our translators found themselves obliged to give no less a variety in their version of it. On examining it with much care, we find they have given to it the following variety of representatives: *lead, lead up, bring, bring up, bring up again, take up, launch, launch forth, offer, loose, sail, set forth, depart.* Here are *thirteen* distinct and distinguishable acts represented in the currency of one man by one and the same word; and these occurring in only *two* of the *twenty-seven* documents that constitute the Christian Scriptures !

How much, then, depends upon the subject, and the context, and the discrimination of the interpreter or translator.

As further developing the progress of our language and of the literature, the taste and science of the age we live in, and more especially the marvelous change that has silently and progressively come upon our language and our taste, we shall give a few versions of the 4th and 5th verses of this 27th ch. "And whanne we remoueden fro thennes we vndirsaileden to Cipre, for that Wyndis werun contrarie. V. 5, And we seileden in the see of Silici, and Panfili: and camen to Listris that is Licie." Wiclif, A. D. 1380. V. 4, "And from thence lanched we, and sayled harde by Cypers because the wyndes were contrarye. V. 5, Then sayled we over the sea of Cilicia and Pamphilia and came to Myra a cite in Lyciia." Tyndale, A. D. 1534. V. 4, "And whan we had launched from thence, we sayled hard by Cypers, because the Wyndes were contrarye. V. 5, And whan we had sayled over the see of Cylicia and Pamphilia we cam to Myra which is in Lycia." Cranmer,

KING JAMES' VERSION.	GREEK TEXT.	REVISED VERSION.
Cyprus, because the winds were contrary. 5 And when we had sailed over the sea of Cilicia and Pamphylia, we came to Myra, *a city* of Lycia. 6 And there the centurion found a ship of Alexandria sailing into Italy; and he put us therein. 7 And when we had sailed slowly many days, and scarce were come over against Cnidus, the wind not suffering us, we sailed unto Crete, over against Salmone: 8 And hardly passing it, came unto a place which is called, The Fair Havens; nigh whereunto was the city *of* Lasea.	τὴν Κύπρον, διὰ τὸ τοὺς ἀνέμους εἶναι ἐναντίους. ⁵ τό τε πέλαγος τὸ κατὰ τὴν Κιλικίαν καὶ Παμφυλίαν διαπλεύσαντες, κατήλθομεν εἰς Μύρα τῆς Λυκίας. ⁶ Κἀκεῖ εὑρὼν ὁ ἑκατόνταρχος πλοῖον Ἀλεξανδρῖνον πλέον εἰς τὴν Ἰταλίαν, ἐνεβίβασεν ἡμᾶς εἰς αὐτό. ⁷ ἐν ἱκαναῖς δὲ ἡμέραις βραδυπλοοῦντες, καὶ μόλις γενόμενοι κατὰ τὴν Κνίδον, μὴ προσεῶντος ἡμᾶς τοῦ ἀνέμου, ὑπεπλεύσαμεν τὴν Κρήτην κατὰ Σαλμώνην· ⁸ μόλις τε παραλεγόμενοι αὐτὴν, ἤλθομεν εἰς τόπον τινὰ καλούμενον Καλοὺς Λιμένας, ᾧ ἐγγὺς ἦν πόλις Λασαία.	under Cyprus, because the winds were contrary. And 5 when we had sailed over the sea along Cilicia and Pamphylia, we came to Myra, a city of Lycia: and there the cen- 6 turion found a ship of Alexandria sailing into Italy, and he put us on board of ᵉit. And when we had sailed 7 slowly many days, and with ᶠdifficulty came off Cnidus, the wind not permitting us, we sailed ᵍunder Crete, over against Salmone; and ʰcoast- 8 ing along it with difficulty, came to a certain place called, The Fair Havens; near which was the city of Lasea.

A. D. 1539. V. 4, "And from thence we launched, and sayled harde by Cyprus, because the Windes were contrary. V. 5, Then sayled over the sea by Cilicia and Pamphilia, and came to Myra, *a citie* in Lycia." Cranmer, A. D. 1557. V. 4, "And vvhen vve had loosed thence vve sailed vnder Cypres, because the vvindes vvere contrarie. V. 5, And sailing the sea of Cilicia and Pamplia, vve came to Lystra vvhich is in Lycia." Rheims, A. D. 1582. V. 4, "And when we had lanched from thence we sailed vnder Cyprus, because the winds were contrary. V. 5, And when we had sailed over the sea of Cilicia and Pamphylia we came to Myra, a citie of Lysia." Com. Ver. A. D. 1611.

Such was the progress, and such were the changes in our English Sacred Scriptures during 231 years.

It will be observed, that the *proper* names changed less than the *common* nouns. The reason was, the originals from which they were borrowed were substantially the same, being Grecian and Roman. Again, it will be noted in many places, that a few instances only appear in these two verses of a change in the verbiage in our version, compared with the authorized of 1611. These were not made by any assembly recognized in Protestant Christendom, but were made by the unauthorized editors or publishers of them. This is the most convincing argument in vindication of the labors of the Bible Union to have a thorough revision. These selections were made without an election of any place.

ᵉ Literally, "*upon it.*" Luke abounds in nautical expressions, and to do him justice, we ought to translate it, technically, "he put us on board of it.

ᶠ *Πόλις.* The com. ver. supposes their *having sailed so far* for the *difficulties* they had to encounter, which is absolutely the import of *πόλις.* See again v. 8, which, in the com. ver., sustains this change.

ᵍ *Ὑπεπλευσαμεν την Κρητην κατα Σαλμωνην,* we sailed *under* Crete against Salmone. *Under Crete,* not literally! but under its protection against the wind and the swollen waves dashing upon its wind-beaten side. On the leeward, or sheltered side of the island. "We sailed under Crete against Salmone." This promontory is yet recognized, "forming the eastern extremity of that island," and still retaining the original name. The allusions to this island and its wind-beaten side, and its present map, all correspond with the references here found.

ʰ *Μολις τε παραλεγομενοι αυτην. Παραλεγομαι, præter-lego, præternavigo. Proprie significat,* q. d. *legο littus* vel *oram littoris lego,* I scan *the shore* of the sea. The Romans had in their nomenclature *præternavigatio, a παραπλους—a sailing by,* or *along the coast.* "Nautical authorities assure us that this place is the furthest point to which an ancient ship could have attained with northwestwardly winds, because the land turns suddenly to the north." Hack.

ᾧ—Λασαια. ᾧ is here governed as an adverb by εγγυς.

Crete, once covered with its hundred cities in which Christian churches abounded, spread over an area of 270 miles in length, and 50 in breadth, celebrated for its lying poets, according to Epimenides, is now called Candia, and famous only for what it once was.

9 Now, when much time was spent, and when sailing was now dangerous, because the fast was now already past, Paul admonished *them*,

10 And said unto them, Sirs, I perceive that this voyage will be with hurt and much damage, not only of the lading and ship, but also of our lives.

11 Nevertheless, the centurion believed the master and the owner of the ship more than those things which were spoken by Paul.

12 And because the haven was not commodious to winter in, the more part advised to depart thence also, if by any means they might attain to Phenice,

9 Ἱκανοῦ δὲ χρόνου διαγενομένου, καὶ ὄντος ἤδη ἐπισφαλοῦς τοῦ πλοὸς, διὰ τὸ καὶ τὴν νηστείαν ἤδη παρεληλυθέναι, παρῄνει ὁ Παῦλος 10 λέγων αὐτοῖς, Ἄνδρες, θεωρῶ ὅτι μετὰ ὕβρεως καὶ πολλῆς ζημίας οὐ μόνον τοῦ φόρτου καὶ τοῦ πλοίου, ἀλλὰ καὶ τῶν ψυχῶν ἡμῶν μέλλειν ἔσεσθαι τὸν πλοῦν. 11 Ὁ δὲ ἑκατόνταρχος τῷ κυβερνήτῃ καὶ τῷ ναυκλήρῳ ἐπείθετο μᾶλλον ἢ τοῖς ὑπὸ τοῦ Παύλου λεγομένοις. 12 ἀνευθέτου δὲ τοῦ λιμένος ὑπάρχοντος πρὸς παραχειμασίαν, οἱ πλείους ἔθεντο βουλὴν ἀναχθῆναι κἀκεῖθεν, εἴπως δύναιντο καταντήσαντες εἰς Φοίνικα παραχειμά-

Now a [1]long time having 9 elapsed, the navigation being now unsafe (because also the fast was already past), Paul exhorted them, saying, Sirs, I 10 [j]perceive that the voyage will be with violence and much loss, not only of the cargo and ship, but also of our lives. Nevertheless the centurion 11 believed the [k]helmsman and the owner of the ship rather than those things spoken by Paul: and because the haven 12 was [l]incommodious to winter in, the majority also advised to depart thence, if by any means they might attain to Phœnix, to winter, which is a

---

[1] Ἱκανοῦ δὲ χρόνου διαγενομενου, *a long time having now transpired.* Ἱκανος, in a former note, we have shown to be of great latitude, reaching from what is merely *sufficient* or *enough* to that which is *great,* and *worthy,* and *able,* and all potent, *sufficient* for any given purpose, or as a *means* to any proposed end. Τὴν νηστειαν is generally thought here to refer to the great fast observed on the celebrated day of the great national expiation—the tenth of Tisri—about the autumnal equinox. "Philo also says that 'no prudent man thought of puting to sea after this season of the year.'" Jahn's Archæol., § 357. The Greeks and Romans thought that sailing in the Mediterranean was not safe after the middle of October nor till after the middle of March. And this is not far from the figures on the Atlantic.

[j] Θεωρεω. Literally, *to see,* with regard to physical nature, but *to perceive,* with regard to the intellectual, the moral, and the religious. We, however, metaphorically represent the perceptions of the *inner* man by the outward senses of the *animal* man. Hence we *see,* and *hear,* and *feel* internally, as well as externally.

[k] Κυβερνητη—ἑκατονταρχος—ναυκληρῳ. Here stand three officers, the *shipmaster,* the *centurion,* and the *owner* of the ship. The last was most interested; the shipmaster or pilot, most responsible, having persons, and property, and his own life at stake; the centurion least concerned while at sea, but most responsible when on land.

In this book we have two words in the original, representative of the same officer; ἑκατονταρχης, only found in this book of Acts; and ἑκατονταρχος, used by both Matthew and

Luke—the former by Luke only. We can give no reason for it. We have in classic Greek the word αρχος, a *prince,* from which the English word *arch,* a prefix to *bishops* and some political potentates; and we have in classic Greek αρχη of large currency as a constituent of the highest officials in all realms. We observe, once more, that αρχη, *wherever found,* indicates, in the words of the distinguished Edward Leigh, of the first half of the sixteenth century, *non principium passivum; sed activum significat,* a quo omnes creaturæ *principium suum ducunt:* quam interpretationem utriusque Testamenti pagina evincit. Amama, Antibarb. Bib. Lib. 3. *Principium,* John 1 : 1; *height of place,* or superiority of man in his office, 1 Cor. 15 : 24. It is taken for the magistrate, Luke 12 : 11. Titus 3 : 1, αρχαι, *qui mero imperio utuntur*—those who have primary and plenary power under God.

But we must distinguish the κυβερνητης from its two associates. Here the *helmsman,* or the *pilot,* stands first, he is the *master* of the ship. He guides and commands its course, and, in this sense, he is not poetically nor rhetorically, but *in fact* the *governor* and *director* of the ship, and, as such, must be obeyed in his station by all aboard. To this effect says Kuinœl: "Sed κυβερνητης est *gubernator navis,* qui clavum *tenet,* et puppim *dirigit.*" He holds the helm, and directs the ship.

[l] Ανευθετον, was incommodious, inconvenient. The question was, whether they should abide in that harbor or seek another, not whether they should proceed to Italy at that season. "Paul preferred that they should remain there, and the event justified his discernment." Hack. Οἱ πλειους, the

KING JAMES' VERSION.	GREEK TEXT.	REVISED VERSION.

KING JAMES' VERSION.

and there to winter; *which is* an haven of Crete, and lieth toward the south-west and north-west.

13 And when the south wind blew softly, supposing that they had obtained *their* purpose, loosing *thence*, they sailed close by Crete.

14 But not long after there arose against it a tempestuous wind, called Euroclydon.

15 And when the ship was caught, and could not bear up into the wind, we let *her* drive.

16 And running unto a certain island which is called Clauda, we had much work to come by the boat:

17 Which when they had taken up, they used helps, undergirding the ship; and fearing lest they should fall into the quicksands, strake sail, and so were driven.

18 And we being exceedingly tossed with a tempest, the next *day* they lightened the ship;

19 And the third *day* we cast out with our own hands the tackling of the ship.

20 And when neither sun nor stars in many days appeared, and no small tempest lay on *us*, all hope that we should be saved was then taken away.

21 But after long abstinence, Paul stood forth in the midst of them, and said, Sirs, ye should have hearkened unto me, and not have loosed from Crete, and to have gained this harm and loss.

22 And now I exhort you to be of good cheer: for there shall

GREEK TEXT.

σαι, λιμένα τῆς Κρήτης βλέποντα κατὰ λίβα καὶ κατὰ χῶρον. ¹³ ὑποπνεύσαντος δὲ νότου, δόξαντες τῆς προθέσεως κεκρατηκέναι, ἄραντες ἆσσον παρελέγοντο τὴν Κρήτην. ¹⁴ μετ᾽ οὐ πολὺ δὲ ἔβαλε κατ᾽ αὐτῆς ἄνεμος τυφωνικὸς, ὁ καλούμενος Εὐροκλύδων. ¹⁵ συναρπασθέντος δὲ τοῦ πλοίου, καὶ μὴ δυναμένου ἀντοφθαλμεῖν τῷ ἀνέμῳ, ἐπιδόντες ἐφερόμεθα. ¹⁶ νησίον δέ τι ὑποδραμόντες καλούμενον Κλαύδην, μόλις ἰσχύσαμεν περικρατεῖς γενέσθαι τῆς σκάφης· ¹⁷ ἣν ἄραντες, βοηθείαις ἐχρῶντο, ὑποζωννύντες τὸ πλοῖον· φοβούμενοί τε μὴ εἰς τὴν σύρτιν ἐκπέσωσι, χαλάσαντες τὸ σκεῦος, οὕτως ἐφέροντο, ¹⁸ Σφοδρῶς δὲ χειμαζομένων ἡμῶν, τῇ ἑξῆς ἐκβολὴν ἐποιοῦντο· ¹⁹ καὶ τῇ τρίτῃ αὐτόχειρες τὴν σκευὴν τοῦ πλοίου ἐρρίψαμεν· ²⁰ μήτε δὲ ἡλίου, μήτε ἄστρων ἐπιφαινόντων ἐπὶ πλείονας ἡμέρας, χειμῶνός τε οὐκ ὀλίγου ἐπικειμένου, λοιπὸν περιῃρεῖτο πᾶσα ἐλπὶς τοῦ σώζεσθαι ἡμᾶς. ²¹ πολλῆς δὲ ἀσιτίας ὑπαρχούσης, τότε σταθεὶς ὁ Παῦλος ἐν μέσῳ αὐτῶν εἶπεν, Ἔδει μὲν, ὦ ἄνδρες, πειθαρχήσαντάς μοι μὴ ἀνάγεσθαι ἀπὸ τῆς Κρήτης, κερδῆσαί τε τὴν ὕβριν ταύτην καὶ τὴν ζημίαν. ²² καὶ τανῦν παραινῶ ὑμᾶς εὐθυμεῖν·

REVISED VERSION.

haven of Crete, facing southwest and northwest.

Now when a south-wind 13 blew moderately, thinking to have gained their purpose, having weighed *anchor*, they sailed close by Crete. But immediately a ᵐwhirlwind, called 14 Euroclydon, struck against the ship. And when it was 15 borne away, and could not bear up against the wind, giving up, we let it drive. And 16 running under a certain small island, called Clauda, with difficulty we were able to secure the boat: which when 17 they had taken up, they used helps, undergirding the ship; and fearing lest they should be stranded on the sand bank,ⁿ they lowered the sail, and so were driven. Now we being 18 exceedingly tempest tossed, the next day they lightened the ship; and the third day 19 we cast out with our own hands the tackling of the ship. And when neither sun nor 20 stars had for many days appeared, and no small tempest lay on us, at last all hope that we should be saved was utterly taken away.

But after much abstinence, 21 Paul stood in the midst of them, and said, Sirs, you should have hearkened to me, and not have loosed from Crete, and so have ᵒsustained this harm and loss. Yet now 22 I exhort you to be of good cheer; for there shall be no

---

majority. A consultation being had—*the majority* were for proceeding to Phœnice, a port in Crete. Strabo mentions a harbor of this name on the south of Crete, and Ptolemy mentions a town called Phœnix, with a port which he names Phœnicus. On the contrary, Stephanus Byzantinus calls the town Phœnicus, which Hierocles again calls Phenice. *Κατὰ λιβα καὶ κατὰ χωρον,* looking *towards*, facing, rather than looking *to*. Lips and Corus, i. e., the points from which the winds so called blew, viz., the southwest and the northwest. Hackett is very felicitous, as well as laborious in his exposition of the usual terms in this description.

ᵐ *Τυφωνικος,* a whirlwind, called a Typhon, Euroaquilo—Northeastern, Euroclydon.

ⁿ *Την συρτιν,* the syrtis; so called as *drawn* together by currents of the sea. Rob.

ᵒ *Κερδῆσαι.* Literally, *gained*, sustained.

KING JAMES' VERSION.

be no loss of *any man's* life among you, but of the ship.

23 For there stood by me this night the angel of God, whose I am, and whom I serve,

24 Saying, Fear not, Paul; thou must be brought before Cesar: and lo, God hath given thee all them that sail with thee.

25 Wherefore, sirs, be of good cheer: for I believe God, that it shall be even as it was told me.

26 Howbeit, we must be cast upon a certain island.

27 But when the fourteenth night was come, as we were

GREEK TEXT.

ἀποβολὴ γὰρ ψυχῆς οὐδεμία
ἔσται ἐξ ὑμῶν, πλὴν τοῦ πλοίου.
23 παρέστη γάρ μοι τῇ νυκτὶ
ταύτῃ ἄγγελος τοῦ Θεοῦ, οὗ εἰμι,
ᾧ καὶ λατρεύω, 24 λέγων, Μὴ
φοβοῦ Παῦλε, Καίσαρί σε δεῖ
παραστῆναι· καὶ ἰδοὺ κεχάρισταί
σοι ὁ Θεὸς πάντας τοὺς πλέοντας
μετὰ σοῦ. 25 Διὸ εὐθυμεῖτε ἄν-
δρες· πιστεύω γὰρ τῷ Θεῷ ὅτι
οὕτως ἔσται καθ' ὃν τρόπον λε-
λάληταί μοι. 26 εἰς νῆσον δέ
τινα δεῖ ἡμᾶς ἐκπεσεῖν. 27 Ὡς
δὲ τεσσαρεσκαιδεκάτη νὺξ ἐγένετο, διαφερομένων ἡμῶν ἐν τῷ

REVISED VERSION.

loss of any man's life among
you, except the ship.
For there stood by me this 23
night the angel of God, whose
I am, and whom I also [p]wor-
ship, saying, Fear not, Paul; 24
[q]you must be brought before
Cesar: and lo, God has given
to you all those who sail with
you. Wherefore, sirs, be of 25
good cheer: for [r]I believe God,
that it shall be even as it was
told me. But still, we must 26
be cast upon [s]some island.
But when the fourteenth 27
night was come, as we were

[p] *Λατρευω, I worship, I serve.* In its *twenty-one* occurrences in the Christian Scriptures, it is, in com. ver., rendered *four* times *worship*, and seventeen times *serve*. "It is derived," says Erasmus, "of the particle *λα*, which is added (prefixed) for more vehemency, and the word *τρειν*, which signifies, to *tremble*, because it is the use of servants to be much afraid, and *tremble* at the presence of their masters." Suidas says, it is *idem quod mercede servire*, and sustains it out of profane writers, the same as to *serve for wages*. It is specially taken for *sacrifice*, which is a special part of Divine worship, according to both law and gospel, Rom. 12 : 7. "*Θυσια* and *λατρεια* are joined together." Crit. Sacra.

Λατρεια. In its five occurrences in N. T., *four* of which are found in Paul's Epistle to the Hebrews and Romans, it is represented by the word *service*, and *God*, in *every case*, is expressed, or implied.

Προσκυνεω is the word consecrated to *worship* in its highest and most sublime sense, when and where *Jehovah Elohim* is the object, or where persons of great dignity, as his ambassadors, are addressed. Its Roman representative is *adoro*. In the Septuagint it is, indeed, used promiscuously in reference to the homage paid to God and man. "Significat, proprie, capitis inclinati gestum, cum moto a fronte galero, caput submittimus. Erasmus. Adorare est manum ori admovere. It signifieth an outward reverence of bowing down the body to the ground, as well civil as religious homage. It properly signifieth, *in falling down to worship*, by which word Cornelius is represented as to his manner of worshiping Peter, Acts 10 : 25." Crit. Sacra.

"The Hebrew word *Shachah* doth properly signify, *to bow down*, and, therefore, is used of such bowing down, as is not for adoration as Ps. 42 : 5, 6, and in divers other places. This Greek word also signifies to use some gesture of body in worshiping, and sometimes *to fall down*." Dr. Fulk against Gregory Martin.

"It comes from *κυων*, canis, a metaphor from the manner of spaniels, when they couch and crouch on the ground before their masters. Zanchius on the second commandment: or, according to others, from *κυω*, osculor—*to kiss*—because an ancient custom of adoring amongst the Persians was by kissing the hand, the mouth, or the knees, which was the most profound homage, or adoration. Vide Beza, Matt. 2 : 11; Rivet on Ps. 22 : 29; and Grotius on the second commandment." Crit. Sacra.

[q] *Καισαρι σε δει παραστηναι. Δει, it is necessary, it behooveth.*

Κεχαρισται—σου, God has given you all that sail with you. They should be all saved for the sake of Paul, because Paul had prayed for them. Such is the view of Calvin, Bengel, Olshausen, De Wette, Hackett, and others. Bengel here remarks: "*Facilius multi mali cum paucis piis servantur, quam unus pius cum multis reis perit. Navi huic similis mundus.*" "Many wicked persons can be more easily saved with a few pious persons, than one pious person perish with many wicked persons." Or, more sententious, "Many wicked can be more easily saved with a few pious, than one pious perish with many wicked. *The world is like to this ship.*"

[r] *Πιστευω, I believe.* This indicates his consciousness of an authority, of which he felt himself possessed, over the minds of his fellow-passengers.

[s] *Εις νησον—τινα*, upon some island. Such indefiniteness is in good keeping with all the scenes before them. It is also in harmony with the tenor of all Divine responses, or communications to man, as to the future events of his life. Definite in end, indefinite in the means of escape.

KING JAMES' VERSION.	GREEK TEXT.	REVISED VERSION.

driven up and down in Adria, about midnight the shipmen deemed that they drew near to some country;

28 And sounded, and found *it* twenty fathoms: and when they had gone a little further, they sounded again, and found *it* fifteen fathoms.

29 Then fearing lest they should have fallen upon rocks, they cast four anchors out of the stern, and wished for the day.

30 And as the shipmen were about to flee out of the ship, when they had let down the boat into the sea, under colour as though they would have cast anchors out of the foreship,

31 Paul said to the centurion, and to the soldiers, Except these abide in the ship, ye cannot be saved.

32 Then the soldiers cut off

Ἀδρίᾳ, κατὰ μέσον τῆς νυκτὸς ὑπενόουν οἱ ναῦται προσάγειν τινὰ αὐτοῖς χώραν· 28 καὶ βολίσαντες εὗρον ὀργυιὰς εἴκοσι· βραχὺ δὲ διαστήσαντες, καὶ πάλιν βολίσαντες, εὗρον ὀργυιὰς δεκαπέντε· 29 φοβούμενοί τε μήπως εἰς τραχεῖς τόπους ἐκπέσωσιν, ἐκ πρύμνης ῥίψαντες ἀγκύρας τέσσαρας, ηὔχοντο ἡμέραν γενέσθαι. 30 τῶν δὲ ναυτῶν ζητούντων φυγεῖν ἐκ τοῦ πλοίου, καὶ χαλασάντων τὴν σκάφην εἰς τὴν θάλασσαν, προφάσει ὡς ἐκ πρώρας μελλόντων ἀγκύρας ἐκτείνειν, 31 εἶπεν ὁ Παῦλος τῷ ἑκατοντάρχῃ καὶ τοῖς στρατιώταις, Ἐὰν μὴ οὗτοι μείνωσιν ἐν τῷ πλοίῳ, ὑμεῖς σωθῆναι οὐ δύνασθε 32 Τότε οἱ στρατιῶται

borne along in the 'Adriatic sea, about midnight the seamen thought that they drew near to some land; and sounded, and 28 found it "twenty fathoms; and when they had gone a little further, they sounded again, and found it fifteen fathoms. Then fearing lest we should 29 have fallen upon ʳrocks, they cast four anchors out of the stern, and longed for day.

And as the ʷseamen were 30 about to flee out of the ship, when they had let down the boat into the sea, under pretense of carrying anchors out of the foreship, Paul said to 31 the centurion, and to the ˣsoldiers, Unless these abide in the ship, you can not be saved. Then the soldiers cut off the 32

ᵗ Τεσσαρεσκαιδεκατη νυξ, the fourteenth night—since they put to sea—διαφερομενων ἡμων εν τῳ Ἀδρια, we being borne through (the waves) *in the Adriatic.* "It has been said that the modern Malta lies too far south to be embraced in the sea so designated. The statement is erroneous. The Adriatic in our ancient maps was the name of the sea lying between Italy and Greece; but in its wider sense comprehended the Ionian Sea around Sicily; near which stood Melite." Hack.

ᵘ Βραχυ δε διαστησαντες, *a short interval of time,* and a short distance of space. The first sounding was twenty fathoms, the second, fifteen. This rate of decrease, in the depth of the water, on the coasts of Malta, is yet pretty much the same, according to the statements of modern sea-captains. The firmness of the bottom as anchor-ground is yet celebrated. In St. Paul's Bay, the traditionary locality of this shipwreck, every circumstance stated here, as to the entire locality, is in good keeping with every allusion here, as shown in all the modern references to it.

ᵛ Εις τραχεις τοπους, upon rough = rocky places. Strong and fearful apprehensions are inseparable from such a position. [We can confirm this fact from our own experience, having been shipwrecked on the coasts of Scotland in just such a bay, and on such a rocky bottom, that our anchors could not hold against the surges of the sea and the tossings of the tempest.] "By cutting away the anchors, (τας αγκυρας περιελοντες), loosing the bands of the rudders, (ανεντες τας ζευκτηριας), and hoisting the *artemon* (επαραντες

τον αρτεμονα), all of which could be done simultaneously, the ship was immediately under command, and could be directed with precision to any part of the shore which offered a prospect of safety." Ηυχοντο ἡμεραν γενεσθαι, *they desired that day might come.*

ʷ Των δε ναυτων, κ. τ. λ. This movement, so heartless, confirms the idea that the seamen believed that the ship was so seriously damaged as to render uncertain its fortunes for the night. Χαλασαντων την σκαφην, *having lowered down the boat*—so recently hoisted on board—αγκυρας εκτεινειν, *to carry,* not *cast out,* anchors. But for Paul's attention and discrimination, they would most likely have accomplished their purpose, and jeopardized the lives of many.

ˣ Ειπεν στρατιωταις. Paul, apprehending that the officers of the ship were implicated in the plot, addressed himself *to the centurion and the soldiers.* They had charge of the prisoners, as the centurion had particular care of the apostle. Except these (the seamen), said he, abide in the ship, you cannot be saved. Soldiers could not manage the ship, and without the aid of mariners the ship could not be brought to land. This would indicate that the purpose or plan of abandoning the ship was very general, seamen and sailors alike implicated in it. Hence the position taken by Paul, that it was essential to their preservation that the seamen be prohibited from leaving the vessel. Thus means and ends are indissoluble.

KING JAMES' VERSION.	GREEK TEXT.	REVISED VERSION.

KING JAMES' VERSION.

the ropes of the boat, and let her fall off.

33 And while the day was coming on, Paul besought *them* all to take meat, saying, This day is the fourteenth day that ye have tarried, and continued fasting, having taken nothing.

34 Wherefore I pray you to take *some* meat; for this is for your health: for there shall not an hair fall from the head of any of you.

35 And when he had thus spoken, he took bread, and gave thanks to God in presence of them all; and when he had broken *it*, he began to eat.

36 Then were they all of good cheer, and they also took *some* meat.

37 And we were in all in the ship two hundred threescore and sixteen souls.

38 And when they had eaten enough, they lightened the ship, and cast out the wheat into the sea.

GREEK TEXT.

ἀπέκοψαν τὰ σχοινία τῆς σκάφης, καὶ εἴασαν αὐτὴν ἐκπεσεῖν. ³³ ἄχρι δὲ οὗ ἔμελλεν ἡμέρα γίνεσθαι, παρεκάλει ὁ Παῦλος ἅπαντας μεταλαβεῖν τροφῆς, λέγων, Τεσσαρεσκαιδεκάτην σήμερον ἡμέραν προσδοκῶντες, ἄσιτοι διατελεῖτε, μηδὲν προσλαβόμενοι. ³⁴ διὸ παρακαλῶ ὑμᾶς προσλαβεῖν τροφῆς· τοῦτο γὰρ πρὸς τῆς ὑμετέρας σωτηρίας ὑπάρχει· οὐδενὸς γὰρ ὑμῶν θρὶξ ἐκ τῆς κεφαλῆς πεσεῖται. ³⁵ Εἰπὼν δὲ ταῦτα, καὶ λαβὼν ἄρτον, εὐχαρίστησε τῷ Θεῷ ἐνώπιον πάντων, καὶ κλάσας ἤρξατο ἐσθίειν. ³⁶ εὔθυμοι δὲ γενόμενοι πάντες, καὶ αὐτοὶ προσελάβοντο τροφῆς· ³⁷ ἦμεν δὲ ἐν τῷ πλοίῳ αἱ πᾶσαι ψυχαί, διακόσιαι ἑβδομηκονταέξ. ³⁸ κορεσθέντες δὲ τροφῆς, ἐκούφιζον τὸ πλοῖον, ἐκβαλλόμενοι τὸν σῖτον εἰς τὴν θάλασσαν. ³⁹ Ὅτε δὲ

REVISED VERSION.

ʸropes of the boat, and let it fall off. And while the day 33 was coming on, Paul besought them all to take food, saying, ᶻThis is the fourteenth day that you have been waiting, and continue fasting, having taken nothing. Wherefore 34 I pray you to take some food, for this is ᵃnecessary for your preservation: ᵃᵃfor there shall not a hair perish from the head of any of you. And when he 35 had thus spoken, having taken ᵇa loaf, he gave thanks to God in presence of them all; and when he had broken it, he began to eat. Then were they 36 all of ᶜgood cheer, and they also themselves took some food. Now all the souls ᵈto- 37 gether in the ship were two hundred and seventy-six. And 38 when they had eaten enough, they lightened the ship, and cast out the wheat into the sea.

ʸ *Τα σχοινια της σκαφης*, the ropes of the boat, most probably those that fastened it to the vessel, not those by which they were lowering it. Notwithstanding the assurance which Paul cherished of the salvation of all on board, he is as special and particular in the direction and use of means as if he had no such assurance; indeed, as if the event desired were wholly contingent on the proper use of the proper means.

ᶻ *Σημερον ημεραν*, appositional.

ᵃ *Τουτο γαρ προς της υμετερας σωτηριας υπαρχει*, for this is essential to your salvation. This is, in fact, not too strong: means are necessary to every proposed end. Without adequate means, no end can be attained, or obtained. Ὑπαρχω, sum; τα υπεχοντα, *quae quis habet, bona, facultates*; often, "*de bonis et figurative de omnibus quæ in hac vita diligi solent.*" Grotius. *Sum* and *ειμι* are in their respective tongues *absolute*. *Appropriate food* is essential to every form of life, vegetable, animal, spiritual.

ᵃᵃ *Θριξ εκ της κεφαλης πεσειται*. Literally, *for of not one of you a hair from the head shall perish*; or, according to the *textus receptus*: *for of not one of you a hair from the head shall fall*. Πεσειται is repudiated as a false reading by Gb., Sch., Ln., Tf., and for it απολειται is adopted.

ᵇ *Λαβων αρτον*. Literally, having taken *a bread*, properly with us, *a loaf*. Bread is generic, *a loaf* is specific; "our daily bread" is not our *daily loaf*, nor our *daily meat*. Paul argues from *one loaf, one body* of Christ; not, as we think, from one *bread*, or one particle of a loaf. "Αρτον, bread. This word by Hebraistic usage often signifies *food* in the New Test. But κλασας, which follows, appears to exclude that sense here." And this, with equal propriety, applies to the monumental loaf of blessings which commemorates *one Lord, one faith, one immersion*, one God and Father of all, one body, one Spirit, one hope. These are the seven pillars of the Christian temple.

ᶜ *Ευθυμοι*, cheerful—they all became cheerful. The consequence was, προσελαβοντο τροφης. Despair annihilates, *pro tempore*, appetite; but the return of hope creates, or invigorates it.

ᵈ *Αἱ πασαι ψυχαι*, all the souls together. Πας, in this adverbial sense, is seldom found but in connection with numerals, equal to το παν, together. Διακοσιαι εβδομηκονταεξ, two hundred and seventy-six. This, according to calculations made, was quite a large ship, measuring from eleven to twelve hundred tons.

KING JAMES' VERSION.	GREEK TEXT.	REVISED VERSION.
39 And when it was day, they knew not the land: but they discovered a certain creek with a shore, into the which they were minded, if it were possible, to thrust in the ship. 40 And when they had taken up the anchors, they committed *themselves* unto the sea, and loosed the rudder-bands, and hoisted up the mainsail to the wind, and made toward shore. 41 And falling into a place where two seas met, they ran the ship aground; and the fore-part stuck fast, and remained unmoveable, but the hinder part was broken with the violence of the waves. 42 And the soldiers' counsel was to kill the prisoners, lest any of them should swim out, and escape. 43 But the centurion, willing to save Paul, kept them from *their* purpose, and commanded that they which could swim, should cast *themselves* first *into the sea*, and yet to land: 44 And the rest, some on boards, and some on *broken pieces* of the ship. And so it came to pass, that they escaped all safe to land.	ἡμέρα ἐγένετο, τὴν γῆν οὐκ ἀπεγίνωσκον· κόλπον δέ τινα κατενόουν ἔχοντα αἰγιαλὸν, εἰς ὃν ἐβουλεύσαντο, εἰ δύναιντο, ἐξῶσαι τὸ πλοῖον. ⁴⁰ καὶ τὰς ἀγκύρας περιελόντες εἴων εἰς τὴν θάλασσαν, ἅμα ἀνέντες τὰς ζευκτηρίας τῶν πηδαλίων· καὶ ἐπάραντες τὸν ἀρτέμονα τῇ πνεούσῃ κατεῖχον εἰς τὸν αἰγιαλόν. ⁴¹ περιπεσόντες δὲ εἰς τόπον διθάλασσον, ἐπώκειλαν τὴν ναῦν· καὶ ἡ μὲν πρώρα ἐρείσασα ἔμεινεν ἀσάλευτος, ἡ δὲ πρύμνα ἐλύετο ὑπὸ τῆς βίας τῶν κυμάτων. ⁴² τῶν δὲ στρατιωτῶν βουλὴ ἐγένετο ἵνα τοὺς δεσμώτας ἀποκτείνωσι, μήτις ἐκκολυμβήσας διαφύγοι. ⁴³ ὁ δὲ ἑκατόνταρχος βουλόμενος διασῶσαι τὸν Παῦλον, ἐκώλυσεν αὐτοὺς τοῦ βουλήματος, ἐκέλευσέ τε τοὺς δυναμένους κολυμβᾷν, ἀπορρίψαντας πρώτους ἐπὶ τὴν γῆν ἐξιέναι, ⁴⁴ καὶ τοὺς λοιποὺς, οὓς μὲν ἐπὶ σανίσιν, οὓς δὲ ἐπί τινων τῶν ἀπὸ τοῦ πλοίου. καὶ οὕτως ἐγένετο πάντας διασωθῆναι ἐπὶ τὴν γῆν.	And when it was day, they 39 ᵉrecognized not the land, but they perceived a certain inlet having a shore, into which they determined, were it possible, to thrust the ship. And 40 having ᶠentirely cut away the anchors, they abandoned them to the sea, and at the same time having unfastened the rudder-bands, and hoisted up the foresail to the wind, they made toward shore. And 41 having fallen into a place where two currents met, they ran the ship aground; and the prow sticking fast, remained immovable, but the stern was broken by the violence of the waves. And 42 the soldiers' counsel was to kill the prisoners, lest any of them should swim out, and escape. But the captain, 43 willing to save Paul, kept them from their purpose, and commanded that they who could swim should cast themselves first into the sea, and get to land; and the rest, 44 some on ᵍboards, and others on some of the things from the ship. And so they all escaped safe to land.

ᵉ Τὴν γην—επεγινωσκον, *they did not recognize the land in view.* Being shipwrecked on its coasts, probably at a considerable distance from the principal harbor.

Κολπον—αιγιαλον, "*they perceived a certain inlet—creek—having a shore,* on which they could run the ship with a hope of saving their lives. Luke uses here the correct hydrographical term." Hack.

Εις ὁν—πλοιον, *into which* they determined *to thrust forth the ship.* Εξωθεω, found only in this book in N. Test., ch. 7 : 45 ; 27 : 39. *Drove out* is its representative ch. 7 : 45 ; here, *to thrust forth.*

The whole family, in N. T. use, is composed of εξω, foras, foris ; εξωθεν, extra, extrinsic, quod foris est ; το εξωθεν, exterior pars, of frequent occurrence ; and εξωθεω, expello, ch. 7 : 45 ; and here, *to thrust forth in any direction.* Εξω-

σαι, expellere, first aor. inf. act., *to thrust forth, to drive ashore the ship.* "*To force the ship,*" Thomp.; "*to drive the ship,*" Murd. ; "*to have thrust the ship,*" Dodd.

ᶠ Και τας αγκυρας—θαλασσαν, "and having entirely cut away the anchors, they abandoned them to the sea." Our English translators followed the Vulgate in their inaccurate version of this clause. Ἁμα—πηδαλιων, *at the same time having unfastened the bands of the rudders.* Most of the ancient vessels were furnished with two rudders. Hack.

ᵍ "Pieces from the ship." Hack. These of course were *boards ;* and as boards are already specified, it seems to me that some things more movable must have been intended, of which there were then, as now, a variety on which a drowning man, or one apprehensive of being drowned, would gladly seize.

KING JAMES' VERSION.

CHAP. XXVIII.

And when they were escaped, then they knew that the island was called Melita.

2 And the barbarous people shewed us no little kindness: for they kindled a fire, and received us every one, because of the present rain, and because of the cold.

3 And when Paul had gathered a bundle of sticks, and laid *them* on the fire, there came a viper out of the heat, and fastened on his hand.

4 And when the barbarians saw the *venomous* beast hang on his hand, they said among themselves, No doubt this man is a murderer, whom, though he hath escaped the sea, yet vengeance suffereth not to live.

5 And he shook off the beast into the fire, and felt no harm.

6 Howbeit, they looked when

GREEK TEXT.

CHAP. XXVIII.

ΚΑΙ διασωθέντες, τότε ἐπέγνωσαν ὅτι Μελίτη ἡ νῆσος καλεῖται. 2 Οἱ δὲ βάρβαροι παρεῖχον οὐ τὴν τυχοῦσαν φιλανθρωπίαν ἡμῖν· ἀνάψαντες γὰρ πυρὰν, προσελάβοντο πάντας ἡμᾶς, διὰ τὸν ὑετὸν τὸν ἐφεστῶτα, καὶ διὰ τὸ ψύχος. 3 Συστρέψαντος δὲ τοῦ Παύλου φρυγάνων πλῆθος, καὶ ἐπιθέντος ἐπὶ τὴν πυρὰν, ἔχιδνα ἐκ τῆς θέρμης ἐξελθοῦσα καθῆψε τῆς χειρὸς αὐτοῦ. 4 ὡς δὲ εἶδον οἱ βάρβαροι κρεμάμενον τὸ θηρίον ἐκ τῆς χειρὸς αὐτοῦ, ἔλεγον πρὸς ἀλλήλους, Πάντως φονεύς ἐστιν ὁ ἄνθρωπος οὗτος, ὃν διασωθέντα ἐκ τῆς θαλάσσης ἡ δίκη ζῆν οὐκ εἴασεν. 5 Ὁ μὲν οὖν ἀποτινάξας τὸ θηρίον εἰς τὸ πῦρ, ἔπαθεν οὐδὲν κακόν. 6 οἱ δὲ προσεδό-

REVISED VERSION.

CHAP. XXVIII.

1 And when we had fully escaped, then we ascertained that the island was called Melite. 2 And the barbarous people showed us no common philanthropy: for they kindled a fire, and brought us all to it, because of the present rain, and because of the cold.

3 And when Paul had gathered a great number of dry sticks, and laid them on the fire, there came a viper out of the heat, and fastened on his hand. 4 And when the barbarians saw the venomous creature hanging on his hand, they said among themselves, No doubt this man is a murderer, whom, though he has escaped the sea, yet justice permits not to live. 5 And he shook off the creature into the fire, and suffered no harm; but 6

a For επεγνωσαν, Ln., Tf. substitute επεγνωμεν, and with much internal evidence: ἡμιν, in the second verse, and the other two sections of this chapter, each commencing with a first person plural, are all sufficient to justify such a reading. Επιγνωμεν, v. 1; ανηχθημεν, v. 11; and ηλθομεν, v. 16.

Διασωθεντες is more than σωθεντες. In Matt. 14 : 36, it is very happily rendered, *made perfectly whole*, and here it is, *safely escaped*, or *fully escaped*. "And when we had fully escaped." Δια auget significationem, sicut apud Latinos, *per*. This preposition increases the signification of words. Leigh, Crit. Sacra.

b Ου την τυχουσαν φιλανθρωπιαν, *no common philanthropy*. Τυχουσαν, from τυγχανω. Luke and Paul are the only inspired writers that use this word. They were educated men, and are the two most copious writers of the New Testament, having written more than the half of it. In their acceptation and use of this word, they have made it tantamount to the following words, com. ver., "to be," "to obtain," "common," "seeing that," to "meet with," "no little," "may be," "may chance." *Obtain* is most frequently its representative. "*No common kindness*," "*many kindnesses*," Syriac Version. Even amongst miracles, some were extraordinary. Οἱ δε βαρβαροι παρειχον. Βαρβαρος, used only by Luke and Paul in the Christian Scriptures. It it well represeted by *foreigner*, whether civil-

ized or uncivilized. We, nowadays, enhance its import, and make it tantamount to *savage*.

c Συστρεψαντος, from συστρεφω, *converto, convolvo in fascem*—now Paul having gathered, or "when Paul had gathered." "Now Paul having collected" πληθος, a great number of dry sticks. Εχιδνα, a viper. The Greeks applied this term to that reptile in distinction from other serpents, as is evident from Aristotle, lib. I. c. 6, αλλ' οἱ μεν αλλοι ωοτοκουσιν οφεις, ἡ δ' εχιδνα μονον ζωοτοκει, vipers are the only viviparous serpents in Europe. Hack. At present unknown in Malta. Εκ της θερμης, from the heat. "It seems to have been cast into the fire. Επιθεντος επι την πυραν. This latter supposition is required by the second sense of εκ της θερμης, and is entirely consistent with the first." Hack. Απο της θερμης is preferred by Grotius, Pricæus, Bengelius, and Griesbach. Still απο rather appears as a gloss, εκ more generally is preferred, because more frequently indicative than απο of a cause. Εκ της πληγης, *propter plagam*, Apoc. 16 : 21. Εκ σμικρου λογου, *ob levem causum*, Soph., Œd. Col. 612, quoted by Kuin., in loco.

d Παντως. *Surely, by all means, no doubt, in no wise*, are its common currency. Φονευς is always represented, com. ver., by *murderer*, from φονευω, *to kill*, whence φονος, murder, slaughter, ch. 9 : 1.

KING JAMES' VERSION.	GREEK TEXT.	REVISED VERSION.
he should have swollen, or fallen down dead suddenly: but after they had looked a great while, and saw no harm come to him, they changed their minds, and said that he was a god. 7 In the same quarters were possessions of the chief man of the island, whose name was Publius; who received us, and lodged us three days courteously. 8 And it came to pass, that the father of Publius lay sick of a fever, and of a bloody-flux: to whom Paul entered in, and prayed, and laid his hands on him, and healed him. 9 So when this was done, others also which had diseases in the island, came, and were healed: 10 Who also honoured us with many honours; and when we departed, they laded *us* with such things as were necessary.	κων αὐτὸν μέλλειν πίμπρασθαι ἢ καταπίπτειν ἄφνω νεκρόν· ἐπὶ πολὺ δὲ αὐτῶν προσδοκώντων, καὶ θεωρούντων μηδὲν ἄτοπον εἰς αὐτὸν γινόμενον, μεταβαλλόμενοι ἔλεγον θεὸν αὐτὸν εἶναι. 7 Ἐν δὲ τοῖς περὶ τὸν τόπον ἐκεῖνον ὑπῆρχε χωρία τῷ πρώτῳ τῆς νήσου, ὀνόματι Ποπλίῳ, ὃς ἀναδεξάμενος ἡμᾶς τρεῖς ἡμέρας φιλοφρόνως ἐξένισεν. 8 ἐγένετο δὲ τὸν πατέρα τοῦ Ποπλίου πυρετοῖς καὶ δυσεντερίᾳ συνεχόμενον κατακεῖσθαι· πρὸς ὃν ὁ Παῦλος εἰσελθὼν, καὶ προσευξάμενος, ἐπιθεὶς τὰς χεῖρας αὐτῷ, ἰάσατο αὐτόν. 9 τούτου οὖν γενομένου, καὶ οἱ λοιποὶ οἱ ἔχοντες ἀσθενείας ἐν τῇ νήσῳ, προσήρχοντο καὶ ἐθεραπεύοντο· 10 οἳ καὶ πολλαῖς τιμαῖς ἐτίμησαν ἡμᾶς, καὶ ἀναγομένοις ἐπέθεντο τὰ πρὸς τὴν χρείαν.	they expected that he would be ᵉinflamed, or that he would suddenly fall down dead. But after they had looked a great while, and saw no harm come to him, they changed their minds, and said that he was a god. In the same parts 7 were possessions of the ᶠchief of the island, whose. name was Publius; who received us, and lodged us three days courteously. And the father 8 of Publius lay sick of a fever, and of a bloody ᵍflux: to whom Paul went, and prayed, and laid his hands upon him, and healed him. So 9 when this was done, others also who had diseases in the island, came, and were healed; who also honored us with 10 many ʰhonors; and when we departed, they laded us with such things as were necessary.

ᵉ Προσεδοκων—προσδοκαω. *Look for, wait for, expect, tarry for,* com. ver., are its representatives; of these, *expect* is most in keeping with our popular idiom. That he *would*, according to Webster, is preferable to *should*. It frequently denotes simply *an event under a condition, or supposition,*—that he would be inflamed. "That he would suddenly fall down dead," Hack.; "that he would have swollen, or fallen down dead," Boothr., Penn, Wes.; "that he would swell, or fall down dead," Thompson; "would suddenly swell, and fall down on the ground," Murdock. "Illi tamen expectabant, ut vel intumesceret, vel mortuus subito concederet." Kuin.

ᶠ Τῳ πρωτῳ της νησου, the chief, or chief of the island. "In illo autem tractu prædia erant Publio, insulæ primario," Kuin. "And there were lands in that quarter, belonging to a man named Publius, who was the chief man of the island," Murd. "Now in the neighborhood of that place lay the estate of the chief man of the island, whose name was Publius," Thomp., Penn; "of a chief man of the island," Wes. This is not true to the original. It is τῳ πρωτῳ, *the chief.* He was the Roman governor, as Paley, Lardner, Tholuck, and others have alleged. In harmony with our usage, we prefer, *the chief* of the island.

ᵍ Πυρετοις και δυσεντερια, with fevers and a dysentery. "A fever and a dysentery," Thomp., Penn; "a fever and a bloody flux," Wes., Murd., Wakef., Dodd. We lack authority and sometimes reason, for making that which is plural, singular, as in the case before us. The plural has been supposed to describe the fever with reference to its recurrent attacks, or paroxysms. This is one of those expressions in Luke's style that have been supposed to indicate his professional training as a physician. "To whom Paul *entered in*" is not so apposite or truthful as, *to whom Paul went.*

ʰ Πολλαις τιμαις ετιμησαν ημας. We concur with Prof. Hackett, and others, that τιμαις ought not to be rendered *rewards*, as though the apostle received any remuneration for the exercise of his gift of healing the afflicted Publius, or for any cure performed by his spiritual gifts. The acquaintances formed by them during their abode in Melita, were exceedingly courteous: for whatever favors were received by them on their departure, were not received as a reward for their services—"for that would have been at variance with the command of Christ (Matt. 10 : 8)." Hack.

KING JAMES' VERSION.	GREEK TEXT.	REVISED VERSION.
11 And after three months we departed in a ship of Alexandria, which had wintered in the isle, whose sign was Castor and Pollux.	11 Μετὰ δὲ τρεῖς μῆνας ἀνήχθημεν ἐν πλοίῳ παρακεχειμακότι ἐν τῇ νήσῳ, Ἀλεξανδρίνῳ, παρασήμῳ Διοσκούροις· 12 καὶ καταχθέντες εἰς Συρακούσας, ἐπεμείναμεν ἡμέρας τρεῖς· 13 ὅθεν περιελθόντες κατηντήσαμεν εἰς Ῥήγιον, καὶ μετὰ μίαν ἡμέραν ἐπιγενομένου νότου δευτεραῖοι ἤλθομεν εἰς Ποτιόλους· 14 οὗ εὑρόντες ἀδελφοὺς, παρεκλήθημεν ἐπʼ αὐτοῖς ἐπιμεῖναι ἡμέρας ἑπτά.	And after three months[i] we 11 departed in a ship of Alexandria, which had wintered in the isle, whose sign was Castor and Pollux. And landing 12 at Syracuse, we tarried there three days. And thence we 13 coasted[k] round, and came to Rhegium: and after one day, the south wind having risen, we came the next day to Puteoli: where we found breth- 14 ren, and were desired to tarry with them seven days, and
12 And landing at Syracuse, we tarried *there* three days.		
13 And from thence we fetched a compass, and came to Rhegium: and after one day the south wind blew, and we came the next day to Puteoli:		
14 Where we found brethren, and were desired to tarry with		

[i] "At the end of three months," equivalent to, *after three months*, μετα—τρεις μηνας. These three months are the time that they remained on the island, which were, probably, the months of November, December, and January; the season admitted of their putting to sea earlier than usual. Εν πλοιω παρακεχειμακοτι, "*in a ship that had wintered there.*" Luke does not say why this vessel had wintered there. It is a circumstance which shows the consistency of the narrative. The storm which had occasioned the wreck of Paul's vessel, had delayed this one so long that it was necessary, on reaching Melita, to suspend the voyage until spring.

[j] Παρασημω Διοσκουροις, *with the sign*, or distinguished *by the sign of Castor and Pollux.* This sign was usually carved or painted on the prow. These were regarded as the tutelar genii, or divinities, the guardians, or gods of seamen. "The figure that was used for Castor and Pollux," as Dr. Lightfoot says, "was that of two young men on horseback, with each of them holding a javelin in his hand." According to others, the sign of Castor and Pollux was that of a double cross. With others, two fictitious deities, the sons of Jupiter by Leda; with others, *a sign in the zodiac called the twins.*

[k] Περιελθοντες, *having come round or about.* The sense of the preposition it is impossible to determine with accuracy. One supposition is, that it refers to their frequent alteration of the ship's course; in other words, to their tacking, because the wind was unfavorable. Another is, that they were compelled by that cause to follow closely the sinuosities of the coast, to proceed circuitously. De Wette says, which is much less probable, that they may have gone around Sicily, or the southern extremity of Italy. Εις Ρηγιον, unto Rhegium, now Regio, which was an Italian sea-port opposite to the north-eastern point of Sicily. Here they remained a day, when the wind, which had been adverse since their leaving Syracuse, became fair, and they resumed the voyage. Επιγενομενου νοτου, *a south-wind having arisen upon them.* Compare the compound participle in v. 2, and in vv. 27, 20. The dative of

the person is often expressed, after επι, with this force. See Herodotus 8 : 13, δευτεραιοι, *on the second day.* Com. ver. has, John 11 : 39, for he hath been *dead* four days—τεταρταιος. "This adverbial use of the ordinals is classical." Kuin., § 264. 3. 6. Εις Ποτιολους, "Puteoli, now Puzzeoli, was eight miles northwest from Neapolis, the modern Naples. It derived its name from putei, being famous for the baths which abounded there." Hack.

[i] Επʼ αυτοις. Επι is often rendered into Latin by *ad.* In Rom. 2 : 2 it is rendered *against.* "Against those," Vat., Great English Bible. By Tremellius, and Beza, *adversus eos.*" It is so in Wiclif, Tyndale, Cranmer, Geneva, Rheims; indeed, in all the versions quoted in this Revision, with the exception of Wakefield and Murdock; in the former by *upon*, and in the latter by, *in regard to.* In the Apocal. 7 : 15 it is translated, in one clause of a verse, by *upon*, and *among*—"he that sitteth (επι) *upon* the throne shall dwell (επι) *among* them." It is argued in justification of the latter that in the Vulgate it is rendered *super illos*; but it is again argued that the sense is, *cum illis*—*with* them, and this is sustained, because the Hebrew על is used for עם, *cum*—*with.*

In the com. ver. επι is represented by the following words— *at, among, about, against, above, because, beside, by, before, in, into, for the space of, to, upon, on, of, over, unto, toward, with, through, touching, under.* As a *connective*, like one of the natives of our forests and climate, it seems to assume the color of every tree on which it is found; still it has a specific nature of its own, but it has an indefinite power of assimilation, and merely connects *harmoniously* its associates with one another, according to their specific nature, or gravity. Here it is apposite to render it, *with* them, or *among* them.

They stayed *with* the brethren one week. The weekly feast of the primitive church was a great attraction. We learn it from ch. 20 : 7. It was not on *a first day of a week,* but, as Doddridge renders it, on *the first day of the week,* when the disciples as usual met together to break a loaf. This was their spiritual banquet.

KING JAMES' VERSION.

them seven days: and so we went toward Rome.

15 And from thence, when the brethren heard of us, they came to meet us as far as Appii-forum, and The Three Taverns; whom when Paul saw, he thanked God, and took courage.

16 And when we came to Rome, the centurion delivered the prisoners to the captain of the guard: but Paul was suffered to dwell by himself, with a soldier that kept him.

17 And it came to pass, that after three days, Paul called the chief of the Jews together. And when they were come together, he said unto them, Men *and* brethren, though I have committed nothing against the people, or customs of our fathers, yet was I delivered prisoner from Jerusalem into the hands of the Romans:

18 Who when they had examined me, would have let *me* go, because there was no cause of death in me.

19 But when the Jews spake

GREEK TEXT.

καὶ οὕτως εἰς τὴν Ῥώμην ἤλθομεν. 15 κἀκεῖθεν οἱ ἀδελφοὶ ἀκούσαντες τὰ περὶ ἡμῶν, ἐξῆλθον εἰς ἀπάντησιν ἡμῖν ἄχρις Ἀππίου Φόρου καὶ Τριῶν Ταβερνῶν· οὓς ἰδὼν ὁ Παῦλος, εὐχαριστήσας τῷ Θεῷ, ἔλαβε θάρσος.

16 ΟΤΕ δὲ ἤλθομεν εἰς Ῥώμην, ὁ ἑκατόνταρχος παρέδωκε τοὺς δεσμίους τῷ στρατοπεδάρχῃ· τῷ δὲ Παύλῳ ἐπετράπη μένειν καθ᾽ ἑαυτὸν, σὺν τῷ φυλάσσοντι αὐτὸν στρατιώτῃ. 17 Ἐγένετο δὲ μετὰ ἡμέρας τρεῖς συγκαλέσασθαι τὸν Παῦλον τοὺς ὄντας τῶν Ἰουδαίων πρώτους· συνελθόντων δὲ αὐτῶν, ἔλεγε πρὸς αὐτοὺς, Ἄνδρες ἀδελφοὶ, ἐγὼ οὐδὲν ἐναντίον ποιήσας τῷ λαῷ ἢ τοῖς ἔθεσι τοῖς πατρῴοις, δέσμιος ἐξ Ἱεροσολύμων παρεδόθην εἰς τὰς χεῖρας τῶν Ῥωμαίων· 18 οἵτινες ἀνακρίναντές με ἐβούλοντο ἀπολῦσαι, διὰ τὸ μηδεμίαν αἰτίαν θανάτου ὑπάρχειν ἐν ἐμοί. 19 ἀντιλεγόντων δὲ τῶν Ἰουδαίων,

REVISED VERSION.

then we went towards Rome. And from thence, when the 15 brethren heard of us, they came to meet us as far as Appii Forum, and the Three Taverns; whom when Paul saw, he thanked God, and took courage. And when we 16 came to Rome, the [m]centurion delivered the prisoners to the commander of the camp, but it was permitted to Paul to dwell by himself, with a soldier who guarded him. And 17 after three days, [n]he called the chief of the Jews together, and when they were come together, he said to them, Brethren, though I have committed nothing against our people, or the customs of our fathers, yet I was delivered prisoner from Jerusalem into the hands of the Romans; who when they had examined 18 me, would have [nn]released me, because there was no cause of death in me. But when 19 the Jews spoke against it, I

---

[m] Ὁ ἑκατόνταρχος—στρατοπεδάρχῃ, the *centurion* delivered the prisoners to *the commander of the camp,* i. e., the prætorian camp, where the emperor's guard was quartered. See Philip. 1:13. The centurion Julius, when he had brought the prisoners to Rome, delivered them up bound to the prætorian prefect.

In the times of the Roman emperors this custom obtained, that the accused sent from the provinces to Rome, to Cæsar, were delivered up in custody to the prætorian prefect; and that they might be safely kept, and have more liberty, they were bound by a longer chain than that worn upon their journey. Of these there were on hand at that time an unusually large number. By the letters of Festus, and the intercessions of Julius, it came to pass that Paul's liberties were much enlarged, and, though a prisoner, he enjoyed a comparative freedom. He was permitted to have a lodging for himself, with the single soldier that guarded him. "Paulo autem per-

missum est seorsim manere cum milite qui eum custodiret." Kuin., vol. 3. pp. 381, 382. For the received reading in our text (εἰς Ῥωμην, ὁ ἑκατονταρχος παρεδωκε τους δεσμιους τῳ στρατοπεδαρχῃ· τῳ δε Παυλῳ επετραπη), Ln. probably, and possibly Gb., would substitute, εἰς Ῥωμην, επετραπη τῳ Παυλῳ.

[n] For τον Παυλον substitute αυτον, Gb., Sch., Ln., Tf.

Τους πρωτους Ιουδαιων, the chief or principal men of the Jews, of course, of the *unbelieving* Jews. When assembled, he said to them, *Brethren,* not, "men *and* brethren." *Committed,* here, is equal to, *I have perpetrated, I have committed no trespass.*

[nn] Εβουλοντο απολυσαι. Βουλομαι is represented, com. ver., by *mind, will, intend, dispose;* απολυσαι, *to release, set free;* released me, or, *set me at liberty.* They would have released me.

KING JAMES' VERSION.	GREEK TEXT.	REVISED VERSION.

against *it*, I was constrained to appeal unto Cesar; not that I had aught to accuse my nation of.

20 For this cause therefore have I called for you, to see *you*, and to speak with *you*: because that for the hope of Israel I am bound with this chain.

21 And they said unto him, We neither received letters out of Judea concerning thee, neither any of the brethren that came shewed or spake any harm of thee.

22 But we desire to hear of thee, what thou thinkest: for as concerning this sect, we know that every where it is spoken against.

23 And when they had appointed him a day, there came many to him into *his* lodging:

ἠναγκάσθην ἐπικαλέσασθαι Καίσαρα, οὐχ ὡς τοῦ ἔθνους μου ἔχων τι κατηγορῆσαι. 20 διὰ ταύτην οὖν τὴν αἰτίαν παρεκάλεσα ὑμᾶς ἰδεῖν καὶ προσλαλῆσαι· ἕνεκεν γὰρ τῆς ἐλπίδος τοῦ Ἰσραὴλ τὴν ἅλυσιν ταύτην περίκειμαι. 21 Οἱ δὲ πρὸς αὐτὸν εἶπον, Ἡμεῖς οὔτε γράμματα περὶ σοῦ ἐδεξάμεθα ἀπὸ τῆς Ἰουδαίας, οὔτε παραγενόμενός τις τῶν ἀδελφῶν ἀπήγγειλεν ἢ ἐλάλησέ τι περὶ σοῦ πονηρόν. 22 ἀξιοῦμεν δὲ παρὰ σοῦ ἀκοῦσαι ἃ φρονεῖς· περὶ μὲν γὰρ τῆς αἱρέσεως ταύτης γνωστόν ἐστιν ἡμῖν ὅτι πανταχοῦ ἀντιλέγεται. 23 Ταξάμενοι δὲ αὐτῷ ἡμέραν, ἧκον πρὸς αὐτὸν εἰς τὴν ξενίαν

was °compelled to appeal to Cesar; not that I had any thing to charge against my nation. On this account, there- 20 fore, I have invited you, that I might see you, and speak with you: ᴾfor on account of the hope of Israel I am compassed with this chain.

And they said to him, We 21 neither received letters from Judea concerning you, nor has any one of the brethren who came, reported or said any harm of you; but we think it 22 proper to hear from you, what you think: for as it ᑫrespects this sect, we know that it is every where spoken against.

And when they had appoint- 23 ed him a day, there came many to him into his ʳlodging; to

---

° *Ηναγκασθεν επικαλεσασθαι,* I was *necessitated, obliged, compelled* to appeal. This version of *επικαλεομαι* is given to this word in every case (six times) in reference to Paul. To *surname,* and to *call upon,* are more frequently its representatives, com. ver.

*Αναγκαζω—cogo—*always, com. ver., *constrain, compel.* The latter generally denotes *extrinsic* violence; the former *external* and *internal* motives, or reasons of action.

ᴾ *Δια ταυτην ουν την αιτιαν,* on this account; *παρακαλεσα,* I have *besought* you, *invited* you, *desired* you, *exhorted* you. Of these, *invited* seems most apposite from our stand-point. Had it been simply *called, εκαλεσα* would have sufficed. In com. ver. it is represented by *comforted, besought, desired, prayed, exhorted, intreated.*

Ἑνεκεν—Ισραηλ, on account of the hope of Israel; *την ἁλυσιν ταυτην περικειμαι,* I am compassed by this chain. Although an arm only was bound, his liberty was encompassed, was taken away.

There is something exceedingly kind and courteous in this address to his alienated Jewish brethren. In his exordium he disabuses their minds as to his position towards them. They had placed him in the hands of the Romans. He was compelled to appeal to Cæsar, not to prefer charges against them, but in self-defense; not to inculpate them, but to exculpate himself. He touchingly alludes to the hope of Israel, and assures the court and the audience that for this hope's sake he was a prisoner in chains.

ᑫ *Περι—της αιρεσεως. Αιρεσις* is found nine times in N. Test.; com. ver., *sect* five times, and *heresy* four times, represent it. There appears no justifiable reason for this distinction. "Originally *αιρεσις* was a word of middle signification, and generally signified any opinion, good or bad. The Christians constituted a sect amongst the Jews. It is said to have been derived from *secando,* while the Greeks say it is derived from *eligendo.*" Leigh, Crit. Sacra. Every schism is a heresy, whether good or bad, so far as the term *αιρεσις* is concerned.

ʳ *Εις την ξενιαν.* The term implies that it was a place in which he was entertained as a *guest.* (Hesych.) Compare Philemon, v. 22. "Those critics are right who distinguish it from the '*hired house,*' mentioned v. 30."' Hack., Penn, Boothr., Wes. The apostle was, at first, as it would be natural, received into some one of the Christian families; but, after a time, for the sake, probably of greater convenience, or independence, he removed to apartments which would be more entirely subject to his own control. He had now *πλειονες,* more persons than before to hear him. *Οἱς εξετιθετο,* from *εκτιθημι,* to expound—once rendered, *I cast out, to set forth,* found only in this book; once, *to cast out;* thrice, *to expound.*

Διαμαρτυρομενος, used only by Paul and Luke, indicates *testifying* or *witnessing* — exhibiting the facts and documents, and expounding and applying them. Luke employs it ten times, and Paul five times. It is eminently indicative of the apostolic method of exhibiting the claims of Jesus. His documents were the writings of Moses and the

KING JAMES' VERSION.	GREEK TEXT.	REVISED VERSION.

KING JAMES' VERSION.

to whom he expounded and testified the kingdom of God, persuading them concerning Jesus, both out of the law of Moses, and *out of* the prophets, from morning till evening.

24 And some believed the things which were spoken, and some believed not.

24 And when they agreed not among themselves, they departed, after that Paul had spoken one word, Well spake the Holy Ghost by Esaias the prophet unto our fathers,

26 Saying, Go unto this people, and say, Hearing ye shall hear, and shall not understand; and seeing ye shall see, and not perceive.

27 For the heart of this people is waxed gross, and their ears are dull of hearing, and their eyes have they closed; lest they should see with *their* eyes, and hear with *their* ears, and understand with *their* heart, and should be converted, and I should heal them.

GREEK TEXT.

πλείονες· οἷς ἐξετίθετο διαμαρτυρόμενος τὴν βασιλείαν τοῦ Θεοῦ, πείθων τε αὐτοὺς τὰ περὶ τοῦ Ἰησοῦ, ἀπό τε τοῦ νόμου Μωσέως καὶ τῆν προφητῶν, ἀπὸ πρωῒ ἕως ἑσπέρας. 24 καὶ οἱ μὲν ἐπείθοντο τοῖς λεγομένοις, οἱ δὲ ἠπίστουν. 25 ἀσύμφωνοι δὲ ὄντες πρὸς ἀλλήλους ἀπελύοντο, εἰπόντος τοῦ Παύλου ῥῆμα ἓν, Ὅτι καλῶς τὸ Πνεῦμα τὸ Ἅγιον ἐλάλησε διὰ Ἡσαΐου τοῦ προφήτου πρὸς τοὺς πατέρας ἡμῶν, 26 λέγον, Πορεύθητι πρὸς τὸν λαὸν τοῦτον καὶ εἰπὲ, Ἀκοῇ ἀκούσετε, καὶ οὐ μὴ συνῆτε· καὶ βλέποντες βλέψετε, καὶ οὐ μὴ ἴδητε. 27 ἐπαχύνθη γὰρ ἡ καρδία τοῦ λαοῦ τούτου, καὶ τοῖς ὠσὶ βαρέως ἤκουσαν, καὶ τοὺς ὀφθαλμοὺς αὐτῶν ἐκάμμυσαν· μήποτε ἴδωσι τοῖς ὀφθαλμοῖς, καὶ τοῖς ὠσὶν ἀκούσωσι, καὶ τῇ καρδίᾳ συνῶσι, καὶ ἐπιστρέψωσι, καὶ ἰάσωμαι αὐτούς. 28 Γνωστὸν

REVISED VERSION.

whom he expounded and testified the kingdom of God, persuading them of the things concerning Jesus, both out of the law of Moses, and out of the prophets, from morning to evening. And some 24 believed the things that were spoken, and ·others believed them not. So not agreeing 25 among ·themselves, they departed, Paul having said one word, Well spoke the Holy Spirit by Isaiah the prophet to our fathers, saying, Go to 26 this people, and say, Hearing you ꞌwill hear, and will not understand; and seeing you will see, and not perceive; for the heart of this 27 people is become gross, and their ears are dull of hearing, and they have closed their eyes, lest they should see with their eyes, and hear with their ears, and understand with their heart, and should be converted, and I should heal them. Be it 28

---

prophets. His labors were only from morning to evening. Thus he taught in his own lodging, in the capitol of the world, testifying both to the Jews and to the Greeks *repentance* Godward, and *faith* Christward. Some, indeed, believed, but many believed not the things that were spoken.

ᵃ Οἱ μεν, and οἱ δε, indicate two parties, but which constituted the majority we are not informed. The proportion is a matter of inference.

ᵗ Ἀσυμφωνοι δε οντες προς αλληλους, *being discordant with one another*; more in our modern style, *not agreeing among themselves.* Of course, there must have been some controversy. Paul listened to them, doubtless, with an attentive ear. He comprehended the drift and point of all they said. He, therefore, speaks his last words advisedly.

The audience, we presume, were for the most part Jews. This we gather from his last words, rather his ῥημα ἑν, *one word*, a sentence, indeed, in one word. It was spoken by the Holy Spirit through Isaiah the prophet, to *our fathers*, προς τους πατερας ἡμων.

Ἀκοῃ ακουσετε, και ου μη συνητε· και βλεποντες βλεψετε, και ου μη ιδητε, a combination of a verb and noun as necessary

to express the infinitive absolute with a finite verb in Hebrew. Gesenius, Heb. Gram., § 128. 3. "The frequency of this construction in the N. Test. is undoubtedly Hebraistic." Hack. "*Hearing you will hear and will not understand; and seeing you will see, and will not comprehend.*"

Matt. 13 : 14, 15, gives the reason of this ακοῃ ακουσετε, και ου μη συνητε. και βλεποντες βλεψετε, και ου μη ιδητε.

"Ἀκοῃ ακουσετε pro simplici ακουσετε ex hebraismo ut βλεποντες βλεψετε pro βλεψετε." v. Vorstius, de Hebraism, p. 611. "Audietis nec tamen intelligetis, videbebitis, nec tamen perspicietis. Cur nihil intellecturi sint hujus nec rationem hic versus continet—επαχυνθη γαρ, κ. τ. λ., stupida enim facta est mens hujus populi. Παχειν ut השְׁמֵן notat pingue, obesum *reddere*, et proprie ad corpus pertinet, sed deinde transfertur ad mentem ut הִשְׁמֵן לֵב, i. e. ubi paulo post legitur רָבִין συνιεναι intelligere atque usurpatur ut h. l. de iis, que vim eorum qua vident et audiunt quamvis clare sunt atque perspicua, tamen non intelligunt et percipiunt, saltem non recte perspiciunt." Kuinœl, Matt. 13 : 15–17.

ᵘ Ου μη συνητε "may express the future result with more certainty than the future indicative." Hack.

KING JAMES' VERSION.	GREEK TEXT.	REVISED VERSION.
28 Be it known therefore unto you, that the salvation of God is sent unto the Gentiles, and *that* they will hear it.	οὖν ἔστω ὑμῖν, ὅτι τοῖς ἔθνεσιν ἀπεστάλη τὸ σωτήριον τοῦ Θεοῦ, αὐτοὶ καὶ ἀκούσονται. ²⁹ Καὶ ταῦτα αὐτοῦ εἰπόντος, ἀπῆλθον οἱ Ἰουδαῖοι, πολλὴν ἔχοντες ἐν ἑαυτοῖς συζήτησιν.	known, therefore, to you, that the salvation of God is sent to the Gentiles, and they ᵛwill hear it. And when he 29 had said these things, the Jews departed, and had much reasoning among themselves.
29 And when he had said these words, the Jews departed, and had great reasoning among themselves.		
20 And Paul dwelt two whole years in his own hired house, and received all that came in unto him,	³⁰ ΕΜΕΙΝΕ δὲ ὁ Παῦλος διετίαν ὅλην ἐν ἰδίῳ μισθώματι, καὶ ἀπεδέχετο πάντας τοὺς εἰσπορευομένους πρὸς αὐτὸν, ³¹ κηρύσσων τὴν βασιλείαν τοῦ Θεοῦ, καὶ διδάσκων τὰ περὶ τοῦ Κυρίου Ἰησοῦ Χριστοῦ, μετὰ πάσης παῤῥησίας ἀκωλύτως.	And Paul ʷremained in his 30 own hired house during two whole years, and gladly received all who came to him, ˣannouncing the kingdom of 31 God, and teaching the things concerning the Lord Jesus Christ, with all boldness, and without molestation.
31 Preaching the kingdom of God, and teaching those things which concern the Lord Jesus Christ, with all confidence, no man forbidding him.		

ᵛ *Καὶ ακουσονται*, and they also will hear it.

ʷ *Εμεινε, remained.* This, as well observed by sundry critics, indicates that Paul's condition and circumstances, here detailed, had passed away before this book was written; a fact of some importance to the curious inquirers on the subject of the chronology of this book. These two whole years living in his own hired house gave a good opportunity to the disciples of Christ to contribute to his necessities. We know that he was not forgotten by the Philippians.

Again it is a monumental proof of Paul's hospitality. He was living in a rented house, but he kept an open house for all the friends of his Master. We thank Luke for the following memento: *απεδεχετο παντας τους εισπορευομενους προς αυτον.* He *received* all that came to his house, or that came to him; for so intimates *αποδεχομαι*, all that came to him he received.

ˣ We have a perspicuous and most definite statement of the two distinct departments of the Evangelical ministry in the last period of this history—the *κηρυσσων την βασιλειαν του Θεου*, the proclamation, the annunciation, or the *preaching* of the kingdom of God; and the *διδασκων τα περι του Κυριου Ιησου Χριστου*, the *teaching* of the Lord Jesus Christ; and this with the manner of it, *μετα πασης παῤῥησιας ακολυτως—nemine prohibente.* This he might not have enjoyed in Jerusalem, no person hindering or inhibiting him. We are informed that he did this with all boldness; or, with all *confidence* he announced the reign of the Lord Jesus Christ.

We should say that the 29th verse is held doubtful by Ln., Tf., but is by Gb. regarded as of almost equal authority with the other portions of the book. The name of Paul, in v. 30, is omitted by Gb., Sch., Ln., Tf., but for this *he* is all sufficient. And he remained, is quite equal to, Paul remained; he being the subject of the section, and the last person named in the narrative.

ACTS OF THE APOSTLES.

REVISED VERSION

ARRANGED IN PARAGRAPHS.

ACTS OF THE APOSTLES.

REVISED VERSION

ARRANGED IN PARAGRAPHS.

I.—THE former narrative, Theophilus, I composed, of all that Jesus began both to do and 2 to teach, even to the day, on which he was taken up, after that he, through the Holy Spirit had given commandment to the Apostles whom 3 he had chosen; to whom also he showed himself alive, after his suffering, in many convincing proofs, during forty days appearing to them, and speaking of the things pertaining 4 to the Kingdom of God; and having convened them together, he commanded them not to depart from Jerusalem; but to await the gift promised them by the Father, which, says he, 5 you have heard from me: for John indeed immersed in water, but you shall be immersed in the Holy Spirit, not many days hence.

6 They now having come together, asked him, saying, Lord, dost thou at this time restore the 7 kingdom to Israel? And he said to them, It is not for you to know times or occasions, which the Father has reserved for his own disposal. 8 But you shall receive power, after that the Holy Spirit is come upon you: and you shall be witnesses for me, both in Jerusalem, and in all Judea, and in Samaria, and to the uttermost parts of the earth.

9 And when he had spoken these things, while they beheld, he was taken up, and a cloud re- 10 ceived him out of their sight. And while they were gazing into the heaven as he went up, behold, two men stood by them in white apparel; who also said, Galileans, why stand you gazing 11 into the heaven? This same Jesus, who is taken from you into the heaven, shall so come, in like manner, as you have seen him going into the heaven. Then they returned into Jerusa- 12 lem, from a mount called Olivet, from Jerusalem a sabbath-day's journey. And when they 13 had entered, they went up into the upper room, where abode both Peter, and James, and John, and Andrew, Philip and Thomas, Bartholomew and Matthew, James, *son* of Alpheus, and Simon Zelotes, and Judas, *the brother* of James. These 14 were all persevering with one consent, in prayer and supplication, with women, with Mary the mother of Jesus, and with his brothers.

And in those days Peter stood up in the 15 midst of the disciples, and said (the number of the names together being about one hundred and twenty), Brethren, this scripture must needs 16 have been fulfilled, which the Holy Spirit, by the mouth of David, before spoke, concerning Judas, who was guide to them that seized Jesus. For 17 he was numbered with us, and had obtained part of this ministry. (Now a field was pur- 18 chased with the reward of his iniquity, and he, falling headlong, burst asunder in the midst, and all his bowels gushed out. And it was 19 known to all the dwellers in Jerusalem; insomuch as that field is called in their proper

tongue Aceldama, that is to say, the field of
20 blood.) For it is written in the book of
Psalms; Let his habitation be desolate, and let
no man dwell in it, and his episcopate let an-
21 other take. Wherefore, of these men that have
accompanied us all the time that the Lord Jesus
22 went in and out among us, beginning from the
immersion of John, to the day that he was
taken up from us, must one be appointed to be
23 witness with us of his resurrection. And they
appointed two, Joseph, called Barsabas, who
24 was surnamed Justus, and Matthias. And they
praying said: Thou Lord, who knowest the
hearts of all men, show which of these two
25 thou hast chosen, to take a part in this ministry
and an apostleship, from which Judas by transgression fell, that he might go to his own place.
26 And they gave forth their lots; and the lot fell
upon Matthias, and he was numbered together
with the eleven Apostles.

II.—When the day of Pentecost was fully
come, they were all with one accord in one
2 place. And suddenly there came a sound out
of heaven, as of a rushing mighty wind, and
it filled all the house where they were sitting.
3 And there appeared to them tongues distributed, as of fire, and it sat upon every one of
4 them. And they were all filled with the Holy
Spirit, and they began to speak in other tongues,
as the spirit gave them utterance.
5 And there were dwelling in Jerusalem Jews,
devout men, of every nation under heaven.
6 Now when this was noised abroad, the multitude came together, and were confounded, because every one heard them speak in his own
7 tongue. And all were amazed, and marvelled,
saying one to another, Behold, are not all these
8 who speak, Galileans? And how hear we,
every man in our own tongue, in which we
9 were born? Parthians, and Medes, and Elamites, and those inhabiting Mesopotamia,—both
10 Judea and Cappadocia, Pontus and Asia, Phrygia and Pamphilia, and the parts of Lybia
about Cyrene, and Roman strangers,—both
11 Jews and proselytes, Cretes and Arabians,—
we hear them speaking in our own tongues
12 the majestic works of God. And they were all

amazed and perplexed, saying one to another,
What means this? Others (mocking) said, They 13
are full of sweet wine. But Peter, standing up 14
with the eleven, raised his voice, and said to
them, Jews, and all you that reside in Jerusalem, be this known to you, and hearken to my
words: for these men are not drunk,· as you 15
suppose, seeing it is but the third hour of the
day. But this is that which was spoken 16
through the prophet Joel, And it shall come 17
to pass, in the last days, that I will pour out
of my Spirit upon all flesh, and they shall
prophesy. Your young men shall see visions,
and your old men shall dream in dreams: and 18
on my man servants, and my maid servants, in
those days, I will pour out of my Spirit, and
they shall prophesy. And I will show won- 19
ders in the heavens above, and signs on the
earth beneath—blood and fire, and smoky vapor. The sun shall be turned into darkness, 20
and the moon into blood, before that great and
illustrious day of the Lord come. And it shall 21
come to pass, that every one who shall call
upon the name of the Lord, shall be saved.
Israelites, hear these words: Jesus, the Naza- 22
rene, a man approved of God among you, by
miracles, and wonders, and signs, which God
did by him, in the midst of you (as you, yourselves also know)—him having seized, who, by 23
the declared counsel and foreknowledge of God
was yielded up, you have, by wicked hands.
crucified and slain, whom God has raised up, 24
having loosed the bands of death, because it
was impossible that he should be held under it.
For David speaks for him: I have always re- 25
garded the Lord, as before my face; for he is
on my right hand, that I should not be moved.
Therefore did my heart rejoice, and my tongue 26
was glad: moreover my flesh shall rest in
hope, that thou wilt not leave my soul among 27
the dead, neither wilt thou suffer thy Holy One
to see corruption. Thou hast made known to 28
me the ways of life: thou wilt make me full
of joy with thy presence. Brethren, let me 29
freely speak to you of the Patriarch David,
that he is both dead and buried, and his
sepulchre is with us to this day. But being 30
a prophet, and knowing that God had sworn to

him, that of the fruit of his loins he would raise
31 up the Christ, to sit on his throne; he, foreseeing this, spoke of the resurrection of the Christ,
that his soul should not be left among the dead,
32 nor his flesh see corruption. This Jesus has
God raised up, of which we are all witnesses.
33 Therefore, being exalted by the right hand of
God, and having received of the Father the
promise of the Holy Spirit, he was shedding
34 forth this which you now see and hear. For
David is not ascended into the heavens; but
he himself says, The Lord said to my Lord:
35 Sit thou on my right hand, till I make thy foes
36 thy footstool. Let all the house of Israel,
therefore, assuredly know, that God has constituted that same Jesus, whom you have cru-
37 cified, Lord and Christ. Now when they heard
this, they were pierced to the heart, and said
to Peter, and to the other Apostles, Brethren,
38 what shall we do? Then Peter said to them,
Reform and be immersed, every one of you,
in the name of Jesus Christ, for the remission
of sins, and you shall receive the gift of the
39 Holy Spirit. For the promise is to you, and
to your children, and to all those that are
afar off, even as many as the Lord our God
40 shall call. And with many other words he
testified, and exhorted, saying, Save yourselves
from this froward generation.

41 They, therefore, having gladly received the
word, were immersed; and the same day, there
42 were added about three thousand souls. And they
perseveringly continued in the Apostle's teaching, and in the contribution, and in the break-
43 ing of the loaf, and in the prayers. And fear
came upon every soul; and many wonders and
44 signs were done by the Apostles. And all
that believed were together, and had all things
45 common, and sold their possessions and goods,
and distributed them to all, as any one had
46 need. And they, continuing daily with one
accord in the temple, and breaking bread from
house to house, did eat their food with glad-
47 ness and singleness of heart, praising God,
and having favor with all the people. And
the Lord daily added the saved to the congregation.

III.—Now Peter and John went up together
into the temple, at the hour of prayer—the
2 ninth hour. And a certain man, lame from his
birth, was carried thither, whom they daily
laid at the gate of the temple, which is called
Beautiful, to ask alms of those entering into
3 the temple, who, seeing Peter and John about
4 to go into the temple, asked alms. And Peter,
earnestly looking upon him with John, said,
5 Look on us. And he gave heed to them, ex-
6 pecting to receive something from them. Then
Peter said, Silver and gold I have not, but
what I have, I give you. In the name of Jesus
Christ of Nazareth rise up and walk. And
7 seizing him by the right hand, he lifted him
up; and immediately his feet and ankles re-
8 ceived strength. And leaping forth, he stood,
and walked, and entered with them into the
temple, walking, and leaping, and praising God.
9 And all the people saw him walking and prais-
10 ing God: and they well knew that it was he,
who sat for alms, at the Beautiful gate of the
temple: and they were filled with wonder and
amazement at that which had happened to
him.

11 And while the lame man, who was healed,
held fast Peter and John, all the people ran
together to them, upon the porch, called Solo-
12 mon's, greatly wondering. And when Peter
saw it, he addressed the people;—Israelites,
why marvel at this? or why look so earnestly
on us, as though, by our own strength, or piety,
13 we had caused this man to walk? The God
of Abraham, and of Isaac, and of Jacob, the
God of our fathers, glorified his servant Jesus,
whom you delivered up, and disowned, in presence of Pilate, when he was determined to
14 acquit him. But you disowned the Holy and
the Just one, and desired a murderer to be
15 granted to you: and killed the Author of the
Life, whom God raised from the dead: whose
16 witnesses we are. And upon the faith in his
name, he has made this man strong, whom you
behold and know. Yes, his name, and the
faith, which is through him, has given him this
perfect soundness, in presence of you all.

17 And now, brethren, I know that you acted in
18 ignorance, as also did your rulers. But God

has thus accomplished those things which he had formerly announced by the mouth of all his prophets, that the Christ should suffer.

19 Reform, then, and turn, that your sins may be blotted out, and that seasons of refreshing may

20 come from the presence of the Lord : and that he may send Jesus Christ, the one before pre-

21 pared for you, whom the heavens must, indeed, retain until the times of the completion of all things, which God has spoken through the mouth of all his holy prophets, since the world

22 began. For Moses, indeed, said to the Fathers, That a prophet shall the Lord, your God, raise up for you, from among your brethren, as he raised me up ; him shall you hear in all things, whatever he shall say to you.

23 And every soul who will not hear that prophet, shall be destroyed from among the people.

24 And, indeed, all the prophets, from Samuel and those following in order, as many as have

25 spoken, have also foretold these days. You are the sons of the prophets, and of the covenant which God made with our fathers, saying, to Abraham, "And in thy seed shall all the

26 kindreds of the earth be blessed." God having raised up his servant Jesus, sent him first to you, to bless you in turning away, every one of you, from his iniquities.

IV.—AND while they were speaking to the people, the priests, and the captain of the temple guard, and the Sadducees came upon them,

2 being indignant that they taught the people, and preached, that through Jesus is the resur-

3 rection from the dead. And they laid hands on them, and put them in prison, until the next day :

4 for it was already evening. But many of those who heard the word believed ; and the number of the men became about five thousand.

5 And it came to pass, on the morrow, that their

6 rulers, and elders, and scribes, and Annas, the High Priest, and Caiaphas, and John, and Alexander, and as many as were of the pontifical fami-

7 ly, were gathered together in Jerusalem. And placing them in the midst, they asked, In what strength, or in what name, have you done this ?

8 Then Peter, filled with the Holy Spirit, said to them, Rulers of the people, and Elders of Israel,

9 if we be examined this day concerning a good

10 deed done to an infirm man, in what name he is made whole, be it known to you all, and to all the people of Israel, that in the name of Jesus Christ, the Nazarene—whom you crucified—whom God raised from the dead, by him does

11 this man stand before you sound. This is the stone which was set at naught by you, the build-

12 ers, which is made the head of the corner. And the salvation is not in another person ; for there is not another name under the heaven, given among men, by which it behooves us to be saved.

13 Now, considering the freedom of speech, of Peter and John, and having perceived that they were illiterate, and persons in private life, they marveled ; and they knew them well, that they

14 used to be with Jesus. And beholding the man who was healed, standing with them, they had

15 nothing to say against it. But having commanded them to withdraw from the council, they conferred with one another, saying, What

16 shall we do to these men ? for, that, indeed, a notorious miracle has been wrought by them, is manifest to all those who dwell at Jerusalem,

17 and we can not deny it. But, that it may be spread no further among the people, let us strictly threaten them, that they speak, hence-

18 forth, to no man upon this name. And they called them, and commanded them not to speak at all, nor to teach, upon the name of Jesus.

19 But Peter and John answered, and said to them, Whether it be right in the sight of God, to hearken to you, rather than to God, judge.

20 For we can not but speak the things which we

21 have seen and heard. So, when they had further threatened them, they discharged them, finding no means of punishing them, because of the people ; for all were glorifying God, for that

22 which had been done. For the man on whom this miracle of the healing was wrought, was more than forty years old.

23 And now, having been discharged, they went to their own friends, and announced all that the

24 priests and elders had said to them. And they, hearing, raised a voice to God, with one accord, and said, Sovereign Lord, thou art the God who hast made the heavens, and the earth, and the

25 sea, and all that is in them ; who by thy servant David's mouth hast said, Why did nations rage,

26 and people imagine a vain thing ? The kings of the earth presented themselves, and the Princes were gathered together against the

27 Lord, and against his Anointed. For, of a truth, in this city, against thy holy son, Jesus, whom thou hast anointed, both Herod and Pontius Pilate, with the Gentiles and the people of

28 Israel, were assembled, to do whatever thy hand, and thy counsel had before determined to be

29 done. And now, Lord, behold their threatenings, and grant to thy servants, that, with all

30 boldness, they may speak thy word, by stretching out thy hand to heal ; and that signs and wonders may be done, by the name of thy holy son, Jesus.

31 And, they having prayed, the place in which they were assembled together was shaken, and they were all filled with the Holy Spirit, and

32 spoke the word of God with boldness. And the multitude of those that believed were of one heart and of one soul, neither did any of them say, that any of the things which he possessed, was his own ; but they had all things

33 common. And with great power the Apostles gave testimony concerning the resurrection of the Lord Jesus : and great grace was upon them

34 all. For neither was there any among them who lacked ; for as many as were possessors of lands, or of houses, sold them, and brought the prices

35 of the things sold, and laid them down at the Apostles' feet. And it was distributed to every one, according as any one had need.

36 Now Joses, who, by the Apostles, was surnamed Barnabas (which is, being translated, Son of Consolation), a Levite. a Cyprian by birth, having land, sold it, and brought the money, and laid it at the Apostles' feet.

V.—But a certain man named Ananias, with
2 Sapphira, his wife sold a possession and purloined from the price (his wife also being privy to it), and brought a certain part, and laid it
3 at the Apostles' feet. But Peter said, Ananias, why has Satan possessed your heart, to lie to the Holy Spirit, and to purloin from the price
4 of the land ? While it remained, was it not

your own ? and after it was sold, was it not in your own power ? Why have you conceived this thing in your heart ? you have not lied to men only, but to God. And Ananias hearing 5 these words, falling, expired ; and great fear came on all that heard these things. And the 6 young men arose, wrapped him up, and carrying him out; buried him. Now an interval of 7 about three hours occurred, and his wife, not knowing what was done, came in. And Peter 8 said to her, Tell me whether you sold the land for so much ? And she said verily, for so much. Then Peter said to her, Why is it, 9 that you have agreed together, to tempt the Spirit of the Lord ? Behold the feet of these who have buried your husband are at the door, and shall carry you out. Then she instantly 10 fell down at his feet and expired : and the young men came in and found her dead, and carrying her out, buried her by her husband. And great fear came upon all the congregation, 11 and upon all those hearing these things.

And through the hands of the Apostles were 12 many signs and wonders done among the people, (and they were all with one accord in Solomon's porch. And of the rest durst no man join 13 himself to them, but the people magnified them. And believers were still more added to the 14 Lord, multitudes of men and also of women), insomuch that they brought forth their sick into 15 streets, and laid them on beds and couches, that at the least, the shadow of Peter, passing by, might overshadow some of them. And the 16 multitude of the surrounding cities also came together into Jerusalem, bringing the sick and those harassed with unclean spirits, and they were every one healed.

But the High Priest arising, and all who 17 were with him (being the party of the Sadducees), were filled with zeal, and threw their 18 hands upon the Apostles, and put them in public custody. But an angel of the Lord, under 19 cover of the night, opened the prison doors, and bringing them forth, said, Go stand and 20 speak in the temple to the people, all the words of this life.

And when they heard that, they entered into 21 the temple early in the morning, and were teaching. But the High Priest came, and those that were with him, and called the council together, and all the senate of the children of Israel, and sent into the prison to have them brought.

22 But when the officers came and found them not in the prison, they returned and reported,

23 saying : The prison indeed we found shut with all security, and the guards, standing before the entrances ; but on opening, we found not one

24 within. Now when the High Priest, and the Captain of the temple, and the Chief Priests, heard these words, they were in perplexity

25 about them, what this might come to be. But one came and reported, saying, Behold, those whom you placed in the prison are standing in

26 the temple and teaching the people. Then, the Captain went, with the officers, and brought them without force (for they feared the people), that they might not be stoned.

27 And having led them away, they placed them in the council : and the High Priest asked

28 them ;—Did we not strictly command you not to teach upon this name ? and, behold, you have filled up Jerusalem with your doctrine, and are intending to bring the blood of this man upon us.

29 But Peter and the Apostles answering, said,

30 We ought to obey God rather than men. The God of our fathers has raised up Jesus, whom

31 you slew, having hanged him on a tree. This person has God exalted to his right hand, a Prince and a Saviour, to grant repentance to

32 Israel, and forgiveness of sins. And we are his witnesses of these things ; and so is also the Holy Spirit, whom God has given to those

33 who obey him. Now those hearing, were exasperated, and they were making up their mind

34 to slay them. But a certain one, arising in the Sanhedrim, a Pharisee, Gamaliel by name, a teacher of law, honored by all the people, commanded to put the Apostles out, for a little

35 while, and said to them, Israelites, take heed to yourselves, what you execute upon these men.

36 For before these days Theudas arose, declaring himself to be somebody, to whom a number of men, about four hundred, attached themselves ; who was slain ; and all, as many as

obeyed him, were scattered and brought to nothing.

After this man, Judas the Galilean rose up, 37 in the days of the enrollment, and drew away sufficient people after him : and he utterly destroyed himself ; and all, as many as were obedient to him, were dispersed. And now I say 38 to you, Withdraw from these men and let them alone ; for if this purpose, or this work be of men, it will be destroyed ; but if it be of God, 39 you are not able to destroy it, and lest, perhaps, you be found to fight against God. And they were persuaded by him ; and having 40 called the Apostles, and scourged them, they commanded that they should not speak upon the name of Jesus, and released them. So 41 they departed from the presence of the council, rejoicing that they were esteemed worthy to be dishonored for his name. And they did not 42 cease teaching every day, in the temple, and in every house, and proclaiming Jesus the Christ.

VI.—Now, in those days, the number of the disciples being multiplied, a murmuring of the Hellenists against the Hebrews occurred, because their own widows were neglected in the daily ministration. Then the Twelve, having 2 called the multitude of the disciples to them, said : Relinquishing the word of God to serve tables is not pleasing to us. Wherefore, breth- 3 ren, look out among you seven men of attested character, full of the Holy Spirit and of wisdom, whom we may appoint over this business ; but we will give ourselves wholly to prayer, 4 and to the ministry of the word And the 5 speech was pleasing in the mind of all the people ; and they chose Stephen, a man full of faith and of the Holy Spirit, and Philip, and Prochorus, and Nicanor, and Timon, and Parmenas, and Nicholas, a proselyte of Antioch : whom they presented before the Apostles ; and, 6 praying, they laid their hands upon them. And 7 the word of God was increasing, and the number of the disciples in Jerusalem was being greatly multiplied, and a great crowd of the priests was becoming submissive to the faith. And Stephen, full of faith and power, did great 8 wonders and miracles among the people.

9 Then there arose certain of the Synagogue—of that composed of the freedmen—Cyrenians and Alexandrians, and of those from Cilicia, and
10 of Asia, putting questions to Stephen; and they were not able to resist the wisdom and the
11 spirit by which he spoke. And they privately procured men who said, We have heard him speaking reviling words against Moses and against
12 God. And they excited the people, and the elders, and the scribes, and came upon him, and
13 seized, and brought him to the council, and set up false witnesses, saying, This man ceases not to speak words against this holy place, and the
14 law: for we have heard him saying, that this Jesus, the Nazarene, will destroy this place, and change the customs which Moses delivered us.
15 And all who sat in the council, looking steadfastly on him, saw his face, as if it had been the face of an angel.

VII.—THEN the High Priest said, Are these
2 things so? And he said, Brethren and fathers, hearken: The God of the glory appeared to our father Abraham, when he was in Mesopotamia,
3 before he dwelt in Haran, and said to him, " Go forth out of your country, and from your kindred, and come into a country that I will
4 show you." Then he came out of the land of the Chaldeans and dwelt in Haran; and thence, after his father was dead, God caused him to remove into this land, in which you are now
5 dwelling: but he did not give him an inheritance in it, not even a foot breadth. Yet he promised that he would give it to him, for a possession, and to his seed after him, when, as yet, he
6 had no child. Then God spoke thus to him: That his seed should be sojourners in a strange land, and that they should enslave, and oppress
7 them four hundred years. And the nation to whom they shall be in bondage, I will punish, said God, and after this they shall come forth
8 and serve me in this place. And God gave Abraham a covenant of circumcision; and so he begat Isaac, and circumcised him the eighth day. And Isaac begat Jacob, and Jacob begat the
9 twelve patriarchs. And the patriarchs, moved with envy, sold Joseph into Egypt. But God
10 was with him, and delivered him out of all his afflictions, and gave him favor and wisdom in the sight of Pharaoh, king of Egypt: and he made him governor over Egypt, and all his household.

Now there came a famine upon all the land of 11 Egypt and Canaan, and great affliction: and our fathers found no sustenance. But Jacob, 12 having heard that there was grain in Egypt, first sent our fathers. And at the second time, 13 Joseph was made known to his brethren; and Joseph's kindred became well known to Pharaoh.

Then Joseph sent and called his father Jacob 14 to him; and all his kindred, seventy-five souls. So Jacob went down into Egypt, and died, he 15 and our fathers, and were carried over into She- 16 chem, and laid in a sepulchre—that which Abraham purchased with a sum of money of Hamor, *father* of Shechem. But, according as 17 the time of the promise, which God had sworn to Abraham, was drawing near, the people had grown and multiplied in Egypt, till another king 18 arose, who had not known Joseph. The same 19 having treated our race craftily, oppressed our fathers, that they might expose their infants, in order that they might not be preserved alive. At this time Moses was born, and was exceed- 20 ingly beautiful; who was nourished in his father's house, three months. And, he being 21 exposed, Pharaoh's daughter adopted him, and nourished him for her own son. And Moses 22 was educated in all the wisdom of the Egyptians, and was mighty in his words and in his actions.

And when he was full forty years old, it came 23 into his heart to look after his brethren, the children of Israel. And seeing one of them 24 wronged, he defended him, and avenged him who was oppressed, smiting the Egyptian. He 25 supposed, indeed, his brother would have understood that God, by his hand, would deliver them: but they did not understand. And the 26 next day, he showed himself to them as they were quarreling, and would have compelled them to peace, saying, You are brethren; why do you wrong one another? But he who did 27 his neighbor wrong, thrust him away, saying, Who made you a ruler and a judge over us? Will you kill me, as you killed the Egyptian 28

29 yesterday? Then Moses fled at this saying, and was a stranger in the land of Midian, in which

30 he begot two sons. And when forty years were expired, there appeared to him, in the wilderness of the mountain, Sinai, a messenger of the

31 Lord, in a flame of fire in a bush. And when Moses saw it, he wondered at the sight; and, as he drew near to contemplate it, the voice of the

32 Lord came to him, saying, I am the God of your fathers, the God of Abraham, and the God of Isaac, and the God of Jacob. Then Moses trem-

33 bled and durst not look. Then the Lord said to him, Put off your shoes from your feet, for the

34 place on which you stand is holy ground. Truly I have seen the affliction of my people, who are in Egypt, and have heard their groaning, and am come down to deliver them. And now, come, I

35 will send you into Egypt. This Moses, whom they had rejected, saying, Who made you a ruler and a judge? God sent the same to be a ruler and a deliverer, by the hand of the messenger

36 that appeared to him in the bush. He brought them out, after showing wonders and signs, in the land of Egypt, and in the Red Sea, and in

37 the wilderness, forty years. This is the Moses who said to the children of Israel, The Lord your God will raise up a prophet for you, of your brethren, as he raised up me; you shall hear him.

38 This is he who was in the congregation in the wilderness, with the messenger that spoke to him in the mount Sinai, and with our fathers, who received the life-giving oracles to give to

39 us: whom our fathers would not obey, but thrust him from them, and in their hearts turned back again into Egypt, saying to Aaron, Make us gods to go before us: because, as for this Moses, who brought us out of the land of Egypt, we do not know what is become of him.

41 And they made a calf in those days, and offered sacrifice to the idol, and rejoiced in the work of

42 their own hands. Then God turned and gave them up to worship the army of heaven: as it is written in the book of the prophets; O house of Israel, have you offered to me slain beasts and sacrifices, during forty years in the wilderness?

43 You even took up the tabernacle of Moloch, and the star of your god Remphan, images which you made to worship; therefore, I will carry you

away beyond Babylon. Our fathers had the 44 tabernacle of testimony in the wilderness, as he had appointed, speaking to Moses, that he should make it according to the pattern that he had seen: which tabernacle also our fathers having 45 received, they brought in with Joshua, into the possession of the heathen, whom God drove out before the face of our fathers, until the days of David; who found favor before God, and 46 desired to find a tabernacle for the God of Jacob. But Solomon built him a house. Never- 47 theless, the Most High does not dwell in temples 48 made with hands; as the prophet says: The 49 heaven is my throne, and the earth is my footstool. What house will you build for me? says the Lord: or, what is the place of my rest? Did not my hand make all these?   50

Stiffnecked and uncircumcised in heart and 51 ears, you are always resisting the Holy Spirit: as your fathers did, so you are doing. Which 52 of the prophets did not your fathers persecute? They even slew those who had previously announced the coming of the Just One, of whom you have now been the betrayers and murderers —you who have received the law by the minis- 53 tration of angels, and have not kept it. When 54 they heard these things, they were cut to the heart, and they gnashed on him with their teeth. But he, being full of the Holy Spirit, looked up 55 steadfastly into the heaven, and saw the glory of God, and Jesus standing on the right hand of God, and said: Behold, I see the heaven opened, 56 and the Son of man standing on the right hand of God. Then they cried out with a loud 57 voice, and stopped their ears, and ran upon him with one consent, and cast him out of the city, and stoned him. And the witnesses laid off 58 their garments at the feet of a young man, named Saul. And they stoned Stephen, in- 59 voking, and saying, Lord Jesus, receive my spirit. And he kneeled down and cried out, 60 with a loud voice, Lord, lay not this sin to their charge. And when he had said this he fell asleep. Now Saul was consenting to his death.

VIII.—Now on that day there arose a great persecution against the congregation, which was in Jerusalem; and they were all scattered

abroad throughout the districts of Judea and
2 Samaria, except the Apostles. Yet devout men
jointly bore away Stephen to the grave, and
3 made great lamentation over him. But Saul
wasted the congregation, entering into the houses,
and dragging forth men and women, he com-
4 mitted them to prison. Nevertheless, the dis-
5 persed, passed along preaching the word. Philip, indeed, having gone down to a city of
Samaria, was announcing the Christ to them:
6 and the multitudes were, with one accord, giving heed to the things spoken by Philip, when
they heard and saw the miracles which he was
7 doing: for, from many who had unclean spirits,
they were going out, crying with a loud voice;
8 and many palsied and lame were healed. And
there was great joy in that city.
9 But there was there, before, a certain man,
named Simon, who formerly, in the same city,
had practiced sorcery, and astonished the people of Samaria, boasting that he was some great
10 one. To whom they all gave heed, young and
old, saying, This man is the great power of God.
11 And to him indeed they gave heed, because that
for a long time, he had astonished them with
12 his sorceries. But when they believed Philip,
preaching the things concerning the kingdom
of God, and the name of Jesus Christ, they
13 were immersed, both men and women. Also
Simon himself believed; and when he was immersed, he constantly adhered to Philip, and,
beholding the miracles and signs which were
done, he was astonished.
14 Now when the Apostles who were at Jerusalem, heard that Samaria had received the
word of God, they sent to them Peter and
15 John, who, when they had come down, prayed
for them, that they might receive the Holy
16 Spirit. For as yet, he had fallen upon none
of them: only they had been immersed into the
17 name of the Lord Jesus. Then they laid hands
on them, and they received the Holy Spirit.
18 And when Simon saw that, through laying on
of the Apostles' hands, the Holy Spirit was
19 given, he offered them money, saying, Give to
me also this power, that on whomever I lay
20 hands, he may receive the Holy Spirit. But
Peter said to him, May your silver go to de-

struction with you, because you have presumed
to procure the gift of God through money. To 21
you there is no part nor portion in this thing,
for your heart is not right in the sight of God.
Reform, therefore, from this your wickedness, 22
and pray the Lord, if, perhaps, the device of
your heart shall be forgiven you; for I perceive 23
that you are in the gall of bitterness, and in
the bond of iniquity. Then Simon, answering, 24
said, Pray to the Lord for me that none of these
things, which you have spoken, may come upon
me. They therefore, when they had testified and 25
preached the word of the Lord, set out on their
return to Jerusalem, and they preached the
gospel in many villages of the Samaritans.
But an angel of the Lord spoke to Philip, 26
saying, Arise, and go toward the south, to the
the way that goes down from Jerusalem to
Gaza (which is the way through the desert).
And he arose and went; and behold a man of 27
Ethiopia, an officer of great authority, under
Candace, queen of the Ethiopians, who had the
charge of all her treasure, and had come into
Jerusalem to worship; and he was returning, 28
and, sitting upon his chariot, he was reading
Isaiah, the prophet. Moreover the Spirit said 29
to Philip, Go near and join yourself to this
chariot. And Philip having run up to him, and 30
heard him reading Isaiah, the prophet, said, Do
you understand what you are reading? He 31
replied, How can I, except some one should
guide me? And he invited Philip to come up
and sit with him. Now the passage of the 32
Scripture, which he was reading, was this, "He
was led away as a sheep to slaughter: and as a
lamb is silent before the shearer, so he opens
not his mouth. In his humiliation, his con- 33
demnation was extorted; and who shall declare
his generation? for his life is violently taken
from the earth." And the officer, replying to 34
Philip, said, I beg of you, of whom does the
prophet speak this? of himself, or of some
other person? And Philip opened his mouth, 35
and began at the same Scripture, and announced
to him Jesus.
And as they were going along the road, they 36
came upon a certain water: and the officer
said,—Behold water! What hinders my being

37 immersed? And Philip said, If you believe with all your heart, you may. And he answered, and said, I believe that Jesus Christ is
38 the Son of God. And he commanded the chariot to stand still; and they both went down into the water, Philip and the officer, and
39 he immersed him. And when they were come up out of the water, the Spirit of the Lord caught Philip away, that the officer saw him no more; for he went on his journey rejoicing.
40 But Philip was found in Azotus: and, passing along, he announced the tidings in all the cities till his entrance into Cæsarea.

IX.—But Saul yet breathing out threatening and slaughter against the disciples of the Lord,
2 went to the High Priest, and desired from him letters to Damascus, to the Synagogues, that if he found any of that way, whether they were men or women, he might bring them bound to to Jerusalem.
3 Now in the journey, he came near Damascus: and, suddenly, there flashed
4 around him, a light from heaven, and having fallen upon the earth, he heard a voice saying to him, Saul, Saul, why do you persecute me?
5 And he said, Who art thou, Lord? And the the Lord said, I am Jesus, whom you persecute; it is hard for you to kick against the goads.
6 And he, trembling and astonished, said, Lord, what wilt thou have me to do? And the Lord said to him, Arise, and go into the city, and it
7 shall be told you what you must do. And the men who were journeying with him, had stood speechless, hearing, indeed, the voice, but seeing
8 no person. But Saul was raised from the earth; and, though his eyes were opened, he saw no person: but they led him by the hand,
9 and brought him into Damascus. And he was there three days without seeing, and did not eat nor drink.
10 Now, there was a certain disciple at Damascus, named Ananias: and the Lord said to him in a vision, Ananias! And he said, Behold, I am
11 here, Lord. And the Lord said to him, Arise and go upon the street which is called Straight, and inquire in the house of Judas for one called Saul, of Tarsus: for behold he is praying *to*
12 *me*, and has seen in a vision a man named

Ananias coming in, and putting his hand on him, that he might receive his sight. Then Ananias 13 answered, Lord, I have heard, by many, of this man, how much evil he has done to thy saints who are in Jerusalem. And here he has author- 14 ity from the chief Priests, to bind all those invoking thy name. But the Lord said to him, Go, 15 for he is a chosen instrument for me, to bear my name before the Gentiles, and kings, and the children of Israel: for I will indicate to him 16 how great things he must suffer on account of my name.

And Ananias went away and entered into 17 the house, and having laid his hands on him, said, Brother Saul, the Lord, even Jesus, who appeared to you in the way as you came, has sent me, that you may receive sight, and be filled with the Holy Spirit. And immediately there 18 fell from his eyes, as it were scales: and he received sight forthwith, and arose, and was immersed: and having taken food he was strength- 19 ened. Then Saul was some days with the disciples who were at Damascus. And immedi- 20 ately he proclaimed Christ in the synagogues, that this is the Son of God. But all that heard 21 him were amazed, and said, Is not this he who destroyed those who invoked this name in Jerusalem, and came hither for this purpose, that he might bring them bound to the chief Priests? But Saul increased the more in strength, and 22 confounded the Jews who dwelt in Damascus, proving that this person is the Christ. Now 23 when many days were accomplished, the Jews consulted to kill him. But their conspiracy was 24 known to Saul, and they watched the gates, day and night, that they might kill him. Then 25 the disciples took him by night, and let him down through the wall in a basket. But coming 26 into Jerusalem, he was attempting to attach himself to the disciples; but they were all fearing him, not believing him to be a disciple. But Barnabas took him and brought him to the 27 Apostles, and fully declared to them, how he had seen the Lord in the way, and that he had spoken to him, and how he had boldly preached at Damascus, in the name of Jesus.

And he was with them, coming in and going out 28 in Jerusalem, and preaching boldly in the name 29 of the Lord Jesus, and was talking and disputing with the Hellenists; but they undertook to kill

30 him. The brethren, having ascertained this, conducted him into Cæsarea, and sent him out

31 into Tarsus. Then the congregations had peace, throughout all Judea, and Galilee, and Samaria, being edified; and, walking in the fear of the Lord, and in the consolation of the Holy Spirit, they were multiplied.

32 Now it happened that Peter, while passing through among all, came down also to the saints

33 that dwelt at Lydda: and there he found a certain man, named Æneas, who had kept his bed

34 eight years, and was sick of the palsy. And Peter said to him, Æneas, Jesus, the Christ, heals you. Arise and make your bed. And he

35 arose immediately. And all who dwelt at Lydda, and Saron, beheld him, and turned to the Lord.

36 Now there was, in Joppa, a certain disciple, named Tabitha (which by interpretation is called, Dorcas): this woman was full of good

37 works, and of alms which she did. Now it came to pass in those days that she, being sick, died. And, having washed her, they placed her

38 in an upper room. And Lydda being near to Joppa, the disciples, having heard that Peter was in that place, sent two men to him, entreating, that he would not delay to come

39 through as far as to them. Then Peter, arising, went with them; whom having come, they led into the upper room; and all the widows stood by him weeping, and showing vests and mantles, all which Dorcas made while she was with

40 them. But Peter, putting them all forth, kneeled down and prayed; and turning to the body, said, Tabitha, arise. And she opened her

41 eyes. And when she saw Peter, she sat up, and he gave her his hand, and caused her to stand up; and having called the saints and widows,

42 he presented her alive. And it was known throughout all Joppa, and many believed in the

43 Lord. And he tarried many days in Joppa, with one Simon, a tanner.

X.—Now a certain man in Cæsarea, called Cornelius, a centurion of the band, called the

2 Italian Band, a devout man, and one who feared God, with all his family, who gave much alms to the people, and prayed to God continually;

3 he distinctly saw in a vision, about the ninth hour of the day, an angel of God coming in

4 to him, and saying to him, Cornelius! And when he looked on him he was afraid, and said; What is it, Lord? And he said to him, Your prayers and your alms are come up for a memorial of you before God. And now send

5 men to Joppa, and call for one Simon, whose surname is Peter. He lodges with one Simon,

6 a tanner, whose house is by the sea-shore. He will tell you what you ought to do. And

7 when the angel who spoke to Cornelius was gone, he called two of his domestics, and a devout soldier of those who waited on him; and

8 having fully related all these things to them, he sent them to Joppa. Again, on the next

9 day, while they were on their journey, and drew near the city, Peter went up on the house-top to pray, at about the sixth hour.

10 And becoming very hungry, he desired to eat. Now while they were preparing, he fell into a

11 trance, and saw the heaven open, and a certain vessel descending to him like a great white sheet, bound together at four corners, and let

12 down to the earth; in which were all kinds of four-footed animals, and wild beasts, and reptiles

13 of the earth, and birds of the air. And there came a voice to him, Rise, Peter; kill and eat.

14 But Peter said, Not so, Lord; for I have never eaten any thing common or unclean. And the

15 voice said to him again, a second time; What God has cleansed, that call not you common.

16 This was done thrice, and the vessel was taken up again into the heaven.

17 Now as Peter was pondering in himself, what the vision which he had seen could mean; behold the men who were sent from Cornelius, having inquired out Simon's house, stood at

18 the gate, and calling, they asked, whether Simon, surnamed Peter, was lodging there.

19 While Peter thought attentively of the vision,

20 the Spirit said to him, Behold three men are seeking you. Arise, therefore, go down and accompany them, doubting nothing, for I have

21 sent them. Then Peter went down to the men, and said, Behold, I am he whom you are seeking. What is the reason for which you

22 are come? And they said, Cornelius, the centurion, a just man, and one who fears God, and of good report among all the nation of the Jews, was instructed from God, by a holy messenger, to send for you into his house, and to

23 hear words of you. Then, calling them in, he entertained them. And on the next day Peter went with them, and certain brethren from

24 Joppa accompanied him. And on the next day, he entered into Cæsarea: and Cornelius was waiting for them, having called together his kindred and intimate friends.

25 Now, as Peter was entering, Cornelius met him, and falling down at his feet, he wor-

26 shiped him. But Peter raised him up, saying,

27 Stand up. I myself also am a man. And, conversing with him, he went in and found many assembled.

28 And he said to them, You well know that it is unlawful for a man, who is a Jew, to associate with, or to approach one of another nation; and yet God has showed to me that I should not call any man common or unclean.

29 And therefore I came without objecting, as soon as I was sent for. I ask then, for what purpose you have sent for me?

30 And Cornelius said, Four days ago, I was fasting till this hour; and at the ninth hour I prayed in my house, and behold, a man stood

31 before me, in bright apparel, and said, Cornelius, your prayer is heard, and your alms are had

32 in remembrance before God. Send, therefore, to Joppa, and call here Simon, whose surname is Peter. He is entertained in the house of one Simon, a tanner, by the sea-shore; who,

33 when he is come, will speak to you. Immediately, therefore, I sent to you, and you have done well that you have come. Now then, we are all here present before God, to hear all

34 things that are commanded you by God. Then Peter, opening his mouth, said, In truth, I perceive that God is not a respecter of persons;

35 but, in every nation, he that fears him, and

36 works righteousness, is acceptable to him. You know the message, which he sent to the children of Israel, preaching peace through Jesus

37 Christ, he is Lord of all;—you know that message which was published throughout all Judea,

beginning from Galilee, after the immersion which John preached;—concerning Jesus of Nazareth: how God anointed him with the 38 Holy Spirit and with power; who went about, from place to place, doing good, and healing all that were oppressed by the devil; for God was with him. And we are witnesses of all 39 things which he did, both in the land of the Jews, and in Jerusalem; whom they slew, hanging him on a tree. Him God raised up 40 the third day, and showed him openly; not to 41 all the people, but to witnesses before chosen by God, even to us who did eat and drink with him after he rose from the dead. And 42 he commanded us to announce to the people, and to testify that it is he himself who is ordained by God, to be the judge of the living and the dead. To him all the prophets testify, 43 that whoever believes in him shall, through his name, receive remission of sins. While Peter 44 was yet speaking these words, the Holy Spirit fell on all those who heard the word. And 45 those of the circumcision, who believed, as many as came with Peter, were astonished because that on the Gentiles also, the gift of the Holy Spirit was poured out. For they heard 46 them speak with other tongues, and magnify God. Then Peter answered, Can any man for- 47 bid the water, that these should not be immersed, who have received the Holy Spirit, as well as we? And he commanded them to be 48 immersed in the name of the Lord. Then they requested him to remain some days.

XI.—And the Apostles and brethren, throughout Judea, heard that the Gentiles also had received the word of God. And when Peter 2 went up into Jerusalem, they of the circumcision disputed with him, saying, You associated with 3 men who are uncircumcised, and ate with them. But Peter related the matter from the beginning, 4 and set it forth in order to them, saying, I was 5 in the city of Joppa, praying; and I saw, in a trance, a vision, something descend, like a great sheet, let down from heaven by four corners, and it came even to me. Upon which, when I 6 had earnestly looked, I considered, and saw foor-footed animals of the earth, and wild beasts, and

7 reptiles and birds of the air. And I heard a voice,
8 saying to me, Arise, Peter; kill and eat. But I said, Not so, Lord; for nothing common or unclean, has, at any time, entered into my mouth.
9 But the voice answered me again from heaven; What God has cleansed, that call not you common.
10 And this was done three times; and all were
11 drawn up again into heaven. And behold, there were immediately three men already come to the house where I was, sent from Cæsarea to me.
12 And the Spirit bade me go with them, doubting nothing. And, moreover, these six brethren accompanied me; and we entered into the man's
13 house; and he told us, how he had seen the messenger in his house, who stood and said to him; Send to Joppa, and call for Simon, whose
14 surname is Peter, who will tell you words, by which you and all your house shall be saved.
15 And as I began to speak, the Holy Spirit fell on
16 them, as on us in the beginning. Then I remembered the declaration of the Lord, how he said, John, indeed, immersed in water, but you
17 shall be immersed in the Holy Spirit. Since, then, God gave them the same gift even as he did to us, when we believed on the Lord Jesus Christ; who was I that I could withstand
18 God? When they heard these things they were silent, and glorified God, saying, God, then, indeed, has also granted to the Gentiles the reformation to life.
19   Now they who were scattered abroad, upon the persecution that arose about Stephen, traveled as far as Phenicia, and Cyprus, and Antioch,
20 speaking the word to none but Jews. And some of them were men of Cyprus and Cyrene, who, having come into Antioch, spoke to the Hellenists, preaching the gospel of the Lord Jesus.
21 And the hand of the Lord was with them, and a great number believed and turned to the Lord.
22 Then tidings of these things came to the ears of the congregation which was in Jerusalem; and they sent forth Barnabas, that he should go
23 through to Antioch; who, when he came and beheld the grace of God, was glad, and exhorted them all, that with purpose of heart, they should
24 adhere to the Lord. For he was a good man, and full of the Holy Spirit and of faith. And a
25 great multitude was added to the Lord. Then

Barnabas departed to Tarsus to seek Saul. And 26 when he had found him, he brought him to Antioch. And it came to pass that, during a whole year, they were assembled with the congregation, and taught a great multitude. And the disciples were called Christians first in Antioch.

And in those days prophets came down from 27 Jerusalem to Antioch. And one of them, named 28 Agabus, having stood up made known through the Spirit that there would be a great famine throughout all the land, which occurred in the days of Claudius. Then the disciples, every one, 29 according to his ability, determined to send relief to the brethren that dwelt in Judea; which 30 they also did; and sent it to the Elders by the hands of Barnabas and Saul.

XII.—Now, about that time, Herod, the king, stretched forth his hands to persecute certain persons of the congregation. And he killed 2 James, the brother of John, with the sword. And because he saw that it pleased the Jews, he 3 proceeded further to seize Peter also. (And then were the days of the unleavened loaves.) And having apprehended him, he put him in 4 prison, and delivered him to four quarternions of soldiers, to guard him, intending, after the passover, to bring him forth to the people. Pe- 5 ter, therefore, was kept in prison, but earnest prayer, without ceasing, was made by the congregation to God for him.

And when Herod would have brought him 6 forth, in that night, Peter was sleeping between two soldiers, bound with two chains; and keepers, before the door, guarded the prison. And behold a messenger of the Lord stood near, 7 and a light shone in the prison, and, striking Peter on the side, he raised him up, saying, Rise up quickly. And his chains fell off from his hands. And the messenger said to him, Gird 8 yourself and bind on your sandals. And he did so. And he said to him, Cast your garment around you, and follow me. And Peter went 9 out and followed him, and had not perceived that what was done by the messenger was real, but thought that he saw a vision.

10 When they had passed the first and the second watch, they came to the iron gate, that leads into the city; which opened spontaneously to them; and they went out, and passed on through one street. And forthwith the mes-

11 senger departed from him. Then Peter, having come to himself, said, Now I certainly know that the Lord has sent his messenger, and has delivered me out of the hands of Herod, and from all the expectation of the people of the Jews.

12 And when he had considered the matter, he went to the house of Mary, the mother of John, whose surname was Mark, where many were

13 assembled, praying. And when he knocked at the door of the gate, a maid servant, named

14 Rhoda, went to hearken. And recognizing Peter's voice, she did not open the gate, for gladness; but ran in and told them that Peter

15 was standing before the gate. And they said to her, You are crazy. But she confidently affirmed that it was even so. Then they said,

16 It is his messenger. But Peter continued knocking. And when they had opened the

17 door, and saw him, they were astonished. But he, beckoning to them with the hand to be quiet, declared to them how the Lord had brought him out of the prison. And he said, Go tell these things to James, and to the brethren. And he departed and went to another place.

18 Now, as soon as it was day, there was no small stir among the soldiers, as to what had

19 become of Peter. And when Herod had sought for him, and did not find him, he examined the keepers, and commanded that they should be put to death. And he went from Judea to Cæsarea, and abode there.

20 And Herod being enraged at those of Tyre and Sidon, they came with one accord to him, and, having made Blastus, the king's chamberlain, their friend, desired peace; because their country was supported by the king's country.

21 And, on an appointed day, Herod, arrayed in royal apparel, sat on his throne, and made a

22 speech to them. And the people shouted, saying, It is the voice of a God, and not of a man.

23 And immediately a messenger of the Lord smote him because he did not give God the glory. And, having been eaten by worms, he expired.

24 But the word of God continued to grow, and

25 extend. And Barnabas and Saul returned from Jerusalem, when they had fulfilled their ministry, and took with them John, whose surname was Mark.

XIII.—Now there were in the congregation that existed in Antioch, certain prophets and teachers, as Barnabas and Simeon, who is called Niger, and Lucius the Cyrenian, and Manaen, who had been brought up with Herod the Te-

2 trarch, and Saul. While they were ministering to the Lord, and fasting, the Holy Spirit said, Separate for me Barnabas and Saul to the work, for which I have called them. And

3 when they had fasted, and prayed, and laid their hands on them, they sent them away. So

4 they, being sent forth by the Holy Spirit, went down into Seleucia; and thence they sailed into Cyprus. And when they were in Salamis, they

5 preached the word of God in the synagogue of the Jews, and they had also John as their attendant. And when they had gone through

6 the whole island as far as Paphos, they found a certain sorcerer, a false prophet, a Jew, whose name was Bar-Jesus—who was with the

7 proconsul of the country, Sergius Paulus, a prudent man; who called for Barnabas and Saul, and desired to hear the word of God. But

8 Elymas, the sorcerer (for so is his name, being translated), opposed them, seeking to turn aside the proconsul from the faith. Then Saul (also

9 called Paul), filled with the Holy Spirit, having looked earnestly upon him, said, O full of all

10 subtilty and all mischief, son of the Devil, enemy of all righteousness, will you not cease to pervert the right ways of the Lord? And

11 now behold the hand of the Lord is upon you, and you shall be blind, not seeing the sun for a season. And immediately there fell on him a mist, and a darkness; and he went about seeking some persons to lead him by the hands.

12 Then the proconsul, having seen what was done, believed, being astonished at the doctrine of the Lord.

13 And, loosing from Paphos, they who were with Paul came into Perga of Pamphilia; and John, departing from them, returned into Jerusalem.

14 But they themselves, departing from Perga, came into Antioch of Pisidia, and went into the synagogue on the sabbath-day, and sat down.

15 And, after the reading of the Law and the Prophets, the rulers of the synagogue sent to them, saying, Brethren, if you have a word of exhortation for the people, speak it.

16 Then Paul stood up, and waving with his hand, he said: Israelites, and you who fear

17 God, hearken. The God of this people chose our Fathers and exalted the people, when they dwelt as strangers in the land of Egypt, and with a high arm he brought them out of it.

18 And for about the period of forty years he

19 nourished them in the wilderness. And when he had subjected seven nations, in the land of Canaan, he divided their land to them by lot.

20 And after these things, during about four hundred and fifty years, he gave them judges until Samuel, the Prophet.

21 And after that they asked a king for themselves. And God granted to them Saul the son of Kish, a man of the tribe of Benjamin, during

22 forty years. And having removed him, he raised up for them David, to be king; to whom also he testified, saying, "I have found David, the son of Jesse, a man after my own heart,"

23 who shall perform all my desires. Of this man's seed has God, according to promise,

24 brought up for Israel a saviour—Jesus; John having first preached, before his entrance on his work, an immersion of reformation to all the

25 people of Israel. Now while John was completing his course, he said, Whom do you suppose me to be? I am not he. But behold, one is coming after me, the shoes of whose feet I am

26 not worthy to loose. Brethren, sons of the race of Abraham, and those among you who fear God, to you is the word of this salvation sent.

27 For they who dwell in Jerusalem, and their rulers, not knowing him, and the utterances of the prophets, which are read every sabbath,

28 have, in condemning him, fulfilled them. And although they found not the least cause of death in him, yet they desired Pilate to put him to death. And when they had fulfilled all that 29 was written of him, they took him down from the tree, and laid him in a sepulchre. But God 30 raised him from the dead; and he was seen 31 many days by those who came up with him from Galilee into Jerusalem, who are his witnesses to the people. And we are declaring to 32 you glad tidings, how that the promise, which was made to the fathers, God has completely 33 fulfilled the same to us their children, he having raised up Jesus; as it is also written in the second Psalm, "Thou art my Son, to-day I have begotten thee." And that he raised him up 34 from the dead, no more to return to corruption, he said thus, "I will give to you the faithful mercies of David." Wherefore he says also, in 35 another *psalm*, "Thou wilt not give up thy Holy One to see corruption." For David, indeed, 36 after he had served his own generation by the will of God, fell asleep, and was added to his fathers, and saw corruption. But he whom God 37 raised again, did not see corruption.

Be it known to you therefore, brethren, that 38 through this person is announced to you the forgiveness of sins. And by him all that believe 39 are justified from all things from which you could not be justified by the law of Moses. Beware, then, lest that come upon you which is 40 written in the prophets; Behold, you despisers, 41 and wonder and perish. For I execute a work in your days, a work which you will not believe, though any one should fully declare it to you. And as they were going out, the Gentiles 42 besought them, that these words might be spoken to them the next sabbath. Now when 43 the congregation was dispersed, many of the Jews and religious proselytes followed Paul and Barnabas, who, addressing them, persuaded them to persevere in the grace of God. And 44 on the next sabbath, almost the whole city assembled to hear the word of God. But when 45 the Jews saw the multitudes, they were filled with zeal, and spoke against those things which were spoken by Paul, contradicting and reviling. Then Paul and Barnabas became bold, 46 and said; It was necessary that the word of God should first have been spoken to you. But

seeing you put it from you, and judge yourselves unworthy of the everlasting life, behold
47 we turn to the Gentiles. For so has the Lord
commanded us, saying; I have placed you for
a light of nations that you might be for salva-
48 tion even to the ends of the earth. On hearing
this the Gentiles rejoiced, and glorified the
word of the Lord, and as many, as were deter-
49 mined for everlasting life, believed. And the
word of the Lord was published throughout all
50 the region. But the Jews stirred up the devout
and honorable women, and the chief men of the
city, and raised a persecution against Paul and
Barnabas, and expelled them out of their bor-
51 ders. But they shook off the dust of their feet
52 against them, and went into Iconium. And the
disciples were filled with joy and with the Holy
Spirit.

XIV.—AND it occurred in Iconium, that they,
at the same time, went into the synagogue of
the Jews, and spoke so that a great multitude,
both of the Jews, and also of the Hellenists,
2 believed. But the unbelieving Jews stirred up
the Gentiles, and disaffected their minds against
3 the brethren. For a long time, therefore, they
continued there speaking boldly respecting the
Lord who attested the word of his grace, granting signs and wonders to be done by their
hands.
4 But the multitude of the city was divided.
Some were with the Jews, and the others with
5 the Apostles. And when there was a rush, both
by the Gentiles, and also by the Jews with their
rulers, to use them spitefully, and to stone them,
6 they, being aware of it, fled down into Lystra
and Derbe, cities of Lycaonia, and into the sur-
7 rounding country. And there they announced
the gospel.
8 And, a certain man in Lystra was sitting, impotent in his feet, a cripple from his birth; who
9 had never walked. The same heard Paul
speak; who, looking intently upon him, and
perceiving that he had faith to be healed,
10 said with a loud voice, Stand upright on your
11 feet. And he leaped and walked. And when
the people saw what Paul had done, they raised
their voices, saying in the Lycaonian, The gods

are come down to us, in the likeness of men.
And they called Barnabas, Zeus, and Paul, 12
Hermes, because he was the chief speaker.
Then the priest of the Zeus that was before the 13
city, brought oxen and garlands to the gates,
and, with the people, wished to offer sacrifices
to them. Which when the Apostles, Barnabas 14
and Paul, heard, they rent their clothes, and
leaped forth into the crowd, crying out, and 15
saying, Why do you do these things? We are
men of like nature with yourselves, declaring to
you glad tidings, that you should turn from these
vanities to the living God, who made the
heaven, and the earth, and the sea, and all
things that are in them; who, in the ages past, 16
suffered all the nations to go on in their own
ways. Nevertheless, he did not leave himself 17
without testimony, in that he did good, and gave
you rain from heaven, and fruitful seasons, filling
your hearts with food and gladness. And with 18
these sayings they scarcely restrained the people,
that they did not offer sacrifice to them. Then 19
Jews came over from Antioch and Iconium : and
having persuaded the multitudes, and having
stoned Paul, they were dragging him out of the
city, supposing that he was dead. But, while 20
the disciples were standing about him, rising up,
he entered into the city. And the next day he
went out with Barnabas into Derbe. And when 21
they had announced the glad tidings to that city,
and made many disciples, they returned into
Lystra, and Iconium, and Antioch, confirming 22
the souls of the disciples, exhorting them to continue in the faith, saying that we must, through
much tribulation, enter into the kingdom of
God. And, having appointed for them elders 23
in every congregation, and having prayed with
fastings, they commended them to the Lord, in
whom they believed. And, having passed 24
through Pisidia, they came to Pamphylia. And 25
when they had spoken the word in Perga, they
went down into Attalia; and thence they sailed 26
to Antioch, whence they had been commended
to the grace of God, for the work which they
performed.
And when they came, and had assembled the 27
congregation, they rehearsed all that God had
done with them, and that he had opened a door

28 of faith to the nations. And they continued no little time with the disciples.

XV.—And certain persons that came down from Judea, taught the brethren, *saying*, Unless you are circumcised after the custom of

2 Moses, you can not be saved. When, therefore, Paul and Barnabas had no little dissension and discussion with them, they determined that Paul and Barnabas and certain others of them, should go up into Jerusalem to the Apostles

3 and elders about this question. And being brought on their way by the congregation, they passed through Phenicia and Samaria, declaring the conversion of the Gentiles; and caused great joy to all the brethren.

4 And when they were come into Jerusalem, they were received by the congregation, and by the Apostles and elders, and they declared all

5 things that God had done by them. But some of the sect of the Pharisees, who believed, rose up, saying, that it was necessary to circumcise them, and to command them to keep the law of Moses.

6 And the Apostles and elders came together

7 to consider of this matter. And when there had been much discussion, Peter rose up and said to them, Brethren, you know that at first God made choice among us, that the Gentiles, by my mouth, should hear the word of the

8 Gospel, and believe. And God, who knows the hearts, bore them testimony, giving them the

9 Holy Spirit, even as to us; and put no difference between us and them, having purified their

10 hearts by the faith. Now, therefore, why do you try God by putting a yoke upon the neck of the disciples, which neither our fathers, nor

11 we, were able to bear? But, through the grace of the Lord Jesus, we believe that we shall be saved, even as they.

12 Then all the multitude were silent, and heard Barnabas and Paul declaring what signs and wonders God had wrought among the Gentiles by them.

13 And after they were silent, James addressed

14 them, saying, Brethren, hearken to me. Simeon has declared how God first visited the Gentiles, to take out of them, a people for his name.

And with this the words of the prophets agree; 15 as it is written, After this I will return, and 16 will rebuild the tabernacle of David which is fallen down, and I will rebuild its ruins, and I will set it up; that the rest of men may seek 17 after the Lord, even all the nations, upon whom my name is called, says the Lord, who does all these things. Known to God from everlasting 18 are all his works. Wherefore my judgment is, 19 not to trouble those who from among the Gentiles turn to God; but to write to them, that 20 they abstain from pollutions of the idols, and fornication, and things strangled, and blood. For, from ancient times, Moses has, in every 21 city, those who preach him, being read in the synagogues every sabbath.

Then it pleased the Apostles and the elders, 22 with the whole congregation, to send chosen men, from among themselves, to Antioch, with Paul and Barnabas;—Judas, surnamed Barsabas, and Silas, leading men among the brethren. And they wrote by them these *words:*—The 23 Apostles, and elders, and brethren, greeting— To the brethren of the Gentiles in Antioch, and Syria, and Cilicia. Since we have heard, that 24 some persons who went out from us, have troubled you with words, subverting your souls, saying, You must be circumcised, and keep the law; to whom we gave no commandment; it 25 seemed good to us, being assembled with one accord, to send chosen men to you, with our beloved Barnabas and Paul; men who have haz- 26 arded their lives for the name of our Lord Jesus Christ. We have sent, therefore, Judas and 27 Silas, who also themselves will tell you the same things by word of mouth. For it seemed 28 good to the Holy Spirit, and to us, to lay on you no greater burden than these necessary things; to abstain from meats offered to idols, 29 and from blood, and from things strangled, and from fornication; from which, if you keep yourselves, you will do well. Farewell. So, 30 then, having been dismissed, they came into Antioch: and when they had assembled the multitude, they delivered the epistle; and having 31 read *it*, they rejoiced over the consolation. And Judas and Silas, being also themselves 32 prophets, exhorted the brethren with many

33 words, and established *them*. And after they had made some stay, they were dismissed, with

34 peace from the brethren to the Apostles. But

35 it pleased Silas to remain there still. Paul and Barnabas, also, continued in Antioch, teaching and preaching the word of the Lord, with many others also.

36 And some days after, Paul said to Barnabas, Let us visit the brethren in every city, in which we have preached the word of the Lord, *to see*

37 how they do. And Barnabas determined to take John with them, whose surname was Mark.

38 But Paul thought it not proper to take him with them, who departed from them in Pamphylia, and did not go with them into the work.

39 And there arose a contention so that they separated one from the other; and Barnabas

40 took Mark, and sailed into Cyprus. But Paul chose Silas, and departed, being commended by

41 the brethren to the favor of God. And he went through Syria and Cilicia, establishing the congregations.

XVI.—THEN Paul came to Derbe and Lystra; and, behold, a disciple was there, named Timothy (the son of a woman who was a Jewess and

2 a believer, but his father was a Greek), who was well attested by the brethren in Lystra and

3 Iconium. Paul wished him to go forth with him, and took and circumcised him, because of the Jews who were in these quarters: for they all

4 knew that his father was a Greek. And as they went through the cities, they delivered to them, for their observance, the decrees that had been ordained by the Apostles and elders who were

5 in Jerusalem. And so were the congregations established in the faith, and daily increased in number.

6 Now when they had gone throughout Phrygia, and the region of Galatia, and (being forbidden by the Holy Spirit to speak the word in Asia)

7 after they came to Mysia, they attempted to go into Bithynia; but the Spirit suffered them not.

8 So passing along Mysia, they came to Troas.

9 And a vision appeared to Paul in the night. There stood a man, a Macedonian, who besought him, saying, come over into Macedonia, and help

10 us. And after he had seen the vision, we immediately endeavored to go forth into Macedonia, being assured that the Lord had called us to preach the gospel to them. Therefore, loosing 11 from Troas, we ran by a straight course to Samothrace, and the next day to Neapolis; and 12 thence to Philippi, which is a chief city of that part of Macedonia, and a colony. And we abode in that city some days. And on the sab- 13 bath, we went out of the city by the side of a river, where there was a customary place of prayer; and we sat down, and spoke to the women that resorted there. And a woman, 14 named Lydia, a seller of purple, of the city of Thyatira, who worshiped God, heard us; whose heart the Lord opened, to attend to the things spoken by Paul. And when she was immersed, 15 and her household, she besought us, saying, Since you have judged me to be faithful to the Lord, come into my house, and there remain. And she constrained us.

And as we went to prayer, a certain maid, 16 having a spirit of divination, met us, who brought her masters much gain by soothsaying. The 17 same followed Paul and us, and cried, saying, These men are the servants of the most high God, who show to us the way of salvation. And this she did many days; but Paul, outraged, 18 turned and said to the spirit, I command you in the name of Jesus Christ to come out of her. And he came out the same hour. And when 19 the masters saw that the hope of their gain was gone, they caught Paul and Silas, and drew them into the market-place, before the magistrates. And brought them to the magistrates, 20 saying, These men, being Jews, do exceedingly trouble our city, and teach customs, which are 21 not lawful for us to receive, or to observe, being Romans. And the multitude rose up together 22 against them, and the magistrates, having torn off their garments, commanded to beat them. And when they had laid many stripes on them, 23 they cast them into prison, charging the jailer to keep them safely; who, having received such 24 a charge, thrust them into the inner prison, and made their feet fast in the stocks. And at mid- 25 night Paul and Silas prayed and sung praises to God; and the prisoners heard them; and sudden- 26 ly there was a great earthquake, so that the foun-

dations of the prison were shaken, and immediately all the doors were opened, and every one's
27 bands were loosed. And the keeper of the
prison, awaking out of his sleep, and seeing the
prison-doors open, drew his sword, and would
have killed himself, supposing that the prisoners
28 had fled. But Paul cried with a loud voice,
saying, Do yourself no harm : for we are all
29 here. Then he called for lights, and sprung in,
and came trembling, and fell down before Paul
30 and Silas, and brought them out, and said, Sirs,
31 what must I do, in order to be saved? And
they said, Believe on the Lord Jesus Christ, and
32 you shall be saved, and your family. And they
spoke to him the word of the Lord, and to all
33 who were in his house. And he took them the
same hour of the night, and washed their stripes,
and was immediately immersed, he and all his
34 family. And when he had brought them into
his house, he set food before them, and rejoiced,
35 believing in God with all his family. And
when it was day, the magistrates sent the
36 officers, saying, Release those men. And the
keeper of the prison told Paul, The magistrates
have sent to release you ; now, therefore, de-
37 part, and go in peace. But Paul said to them,
They have beaten us openly uncondemned, being Romans, and have cast us into prison, and
now do they cast us out privately? Nay, indeed, but let them come themselves, and lead us
38 out. And the officers told these words to the
magistrates, and they feared when they heard
39 that they were Romans. And they came and
besought them, and led them out, and desired
40 them to depart out of the city. And they went
out of the prison, and entered into the house
of Lydia, and when they had seen the brethren, they exhorted them, and departed.

XVII.—Now when *Paul and Silas* had passed
through Amphipolis and Apollonia, they came
to Thessalonica, where there was the syna-
2 gogue of the Jews. And Paul, as his custom
was, went in to them, and three sabbaths
3 reasoned with them from the Scriptures, opening them and setting forth that the Christ must
suffer, and rise again from the dead ; and that
this Jesus, whom I announce to you, is the

Christ. And some of them believed and adher- 4
ed to Paul and Silas ; and of the devout Greeks
a great multitude, and of the principal women
not a few.

But the Jews who did not believe, moved with 5
envy, gathered some vile men of the street
idlers, and raised a mob, and set all the city in
an uproar, and assaulted the house of Jason,
and sought to bring them out to the people ; but 6
not finding them, they dragged Jason and certain brethren before the city rulers, exclaiming,
These men, who have turned the world upside
down, are come hither also ; whom Jason has 7
received ; and all these act contrary to the decrees of Cæsar, saying, That there is another
king,—Jesus. And they troubled the people, 8
and the rulers of the city, when they heard these
things. And having taken security of Jason 9
and the others, they dismissed them. And the 10
brethren immediately sent away Paul and Silas
by night to Berea, who coming thither went into
the synagogue of the Jews. Now these were 11
more noble-minded than those of Thessalonica,
in that they received the word with all readiness of mind, searching the Scriptures daily, *to
see* if these things were so. Therefore many of 12
them believed ; also of honorable women, who
were Greeks, and men, not a few. But when 13
the Jews of Thessalonica knew that the word of
of God was preached by Paul in Berea, they
came thither also, and stirred up the rabble.
And then the brethren, immediately sent away 14
Paul even to the sea. But Silas and Timothy
abode there still. And they who conducted 15
Paul, brought him to Athens ; and having received a commandment to Silas and Timothy to
come to him, as soon as possible, they departed.

Now while Paul was waiting for them at 16
Athens, his spirit was roused in him, when he
saw the city wholly devoted to idols. There- 17
fore he disputed in the synagogue, with the
Jews, and with the devout persons, and in the
market, daily, with those who met with him.
Then certain philosophers of the Epicureans 18
and of the Stoics encountered him ; and some
said, What would this chatterer say? and
others, He seems to be a publisher of foreign
gods, because he announced to them Jesus and

19 the resurrection. Now they took him and brought him to the Areopagus, saying, Can we know what this new doctrine is, of which you
20 speak? For you bring some strange things to our ears. We wish, therefore, to know what these things mean.
21 For all Athenians and strangers who were there, spent their time in nothing else, but either
22 in telling or hearing some new thing. Then Paul stood up in the midst of the Areopagus, and said, Athenians! I perceive that, in every
23 respect, you are exceedingly devotional. For as I passed along and observed the objects of your worship, I found an altar with this inscription, To AN UNKNOWN GOD: him, therefore, whom you, not knowing, worship, I declare to you.
24 God who made the world and all things in it, seeing that he is Lord of heaven and of earth,
25 dwells not in temples made with hands; neither is ministered to by men's hands, as though he needed anything, seeing he gives to all life and
26 breath, and all things; and has made of one blood every nation of men, to dwell on all the face of the earth, having determined the ap-
27 pointed seasons and limits of their abode; that they should seek the Lord, if, perhaps, they might feel after him and find him; although,
28 indeed, he is not far from any one of us; for by him we live, and move, and have our being; as even some of your own poets have said;

For we, indeed, his offspring are.

29 Since, then, we are the offspring of God, we ought not to think that the Godhead is like to gold or silver, graved by art or man's device.
30 And the times of this ignorance God over-looked, but now commands all men every where,
31 to reform. Because he has appointed a day, in which he will judge the world in righteousness, by that man whom he has appointed, giving assurance to all, having raised him from the
32 dead. And when they heard of a resurrection of the dead, some mocked; and others said, We will hear you again concerning this mat-
33 ter. So Paul departed from among them.
34 But certain persons adhered to him and believed: among whom was Dionysius the Areo-

pagite, and a woman named Damaris, and others with them.

XVIII.—AFTER these things Paul left Athens, and went to Corinth. And having found a 2 certain Jew named Aquila, born in Pontus, lately come from Italy, with his wife Priscilla (because Claudius had commanded all the Jews to depart from Rome), he came to them. And 3 because he was of the same trade, he abode with them, and worked: for by occupation they were tent-makers. And he reasoned in 4 the synagogue every sabbath, and endeavored to persuade both Jews and Greeks. But when 5 Silas and Timothy were come from Macedonia, Paul was constrained in spirit, earnestly testifying to the Jews that Jesus was the Christ.

And when they resisted and reviled, he shook 6 his raiment, and said to them, Your blood be on your own heads. I am clean. Henceforth I will go to the Gentiles. And he departed thence, 7 and entered into the house of a certain man named Justus, who worshiped God, whose house was adjacent to the synagogue. But 8 Crispus, the chief ruler of the synagogue, believed on the Lord with all his family: and many of the Corinthians, hearing, believed, and were immersed. Then the Lord said to Paul, in 9 a vision by night, Be not afraid, but speak, and be not silent; for I am with you, and no man 10 shall assail you to hurt you: for I have many people in this city. And he continued there a 11 year and six months, teaching the word of God among them.

And when Gallio was governing Achaia as 12 proconsul, the Jews, with one consent, made insurrection against Paul, and brought him to the judgment-seat, saying, This fellow persuades 13 men to worship God contrary to the law.

And as Paul was about to open his mouth, 14 Gallio said to the Jews, Were it, indeed, a matter of wrong, or a wicked act, Jews, it would be reasonable that I should bear with you. But 15 if it be a question concerning a doctrine, and names, and your law, look you to it: for I will not be a judge of these matters. And he drove 16 them from the judgment-seat. Then all the 17 Greeks took Sosthenes, the ruler of the synagogue, and beat him before the judgment-seat: and Gallio cared for none of these things.

18 And Paul tarried yet many days, and, having bid adieu to the brethren, sailed forth into Syria, and with him Priscilla and Aquila; having shorn his head in Cenchrea: for he had a vow.

19 And he came into Ephesus, and left them there. But he himself, entering into the synagogue,

20 reasoned with the Jews, and though they requested him to remain longer time with them,

21 he did not consent: but bade them farewell, saying, I must by all means keep the approaching feast at Jerusalem: but I will return to you again, if God will; and he sailed from Ephesus.

22 And after he had gone down to Cesarea, and gone up and saluted the congregation, he went down to Antioch.

23 And having spent some time there, he departed, passing through all the country of Galatia and Phrygia, in order, establishing all the disciples.

24 And a certain Jew, named Apollos, born at Alexandria, an eloquent man, and mighty in the

25 Scriptures, came down to Ephesus. This man was instructed in the way of the Lord, and being fervent in spirit, he spoke and taught diligently the things concerning the Lord, though he knew

26 only the immersion of John. And he began to speak boldly in the synagogue: whom, when Aquila and Priscilla had heard, they took him to them, and expounded to him the way of God

27 more accurately. And when he was disposed to pass into Achaia, the brethren wrote, exhorting the disciples to receive him: who, when he had come, afforded much aid to them who had

28 believed, through the gift which he had: for he powerfully and thoroughly in public convinced the Jews, clearly showing by the Scriptures, that Jesus was the Christ.

XIX.—AND while Apollos was at Corinth, Paul having passed through the upper parts, came into Ephesus; and finding certain disciples there,

2 he said to them, Did you on believing receive the Holy Spirit? And they said to him, we have not, indeed, heard, that there is a Holy Spirit.

3 And he said to them, Into what then were you immersed? And they said, Into John's immersion. Then said Paul, John, indeed, administered

4 an immersion of reformation, saying to the people, that they should believe on him who would come after him, that is, on Jesus the Christ.

5 Having heard this, they were immersed into the name of the Lord Jesus. And when Paul had

6 laid his hands on them, the Holy Spirit came on them, and they spoke with tongues, and prophesied: now all the men were about twelve.

7

8 And he went into the synagogue, and spoke boldly for about three months, discussing and persuading as to things concerning the kingdom

9 of God. But when some were hardened, and believed not, but spoke evil of the way, in the presence of the multitude, he departed from them and separated the disciples, discussing daily in

10 the school of one Tyrannus. And this continued during two years; so that all those who dwelt in Asia heard the word of the Lord Jesus, both

11 Jews and Greeks. And God worked special

12 miracles by the hands of Paul: so that from his body were carried to the sick, handkerchiefs, or aprons and the diseases departed from them, and the evil spirits went out of them. Then

13 certain of the Jewish exorcists, who went about from place to place, also attempted to pronounce the name of the Lord Jesus upon those who had evil spirits, saying, We adjure you by the Jesus whom Paul preaches. And there were seven

14 sons of one Sceva, a Jew and chief of the priests,

15 who did so. And the evil spirit answered and said, Jesus I acknowledge, and Paul I know: but

16 who are you? And the man in whom the evil spirit was, leaped on them, and overcame them, and prevailed against them; so that they fled

17 out of that house naked and wounded. And this was known to all the Jews and Greeks dwelling at Ephesus; and fear fell on them all, and the name of the Lord Jesus was magnified.

18 And many who believed came, and confessed,

19 and declared their deeds. Many of them also, who practiced magic arts, brought together their books, and burnt them in the presence of all, and they counted the price of them, and found

20 it fifty thousand pieces of silver. So powerfully grew the word of God, and prevailed.

21 When these things were ended, Paul firmly purposed in spirit, when he had passed through

Macedonia, and Achaia, to go to Jerusalem, saying, after I have been there, I must also see
22 Rome.   So he sent into Macedonia two of those
who ministered to him, Timothy and Erastus:
23 but he himself stayed in Asia for a season.   And
the same time there arose no small stir about
24 the way.   For a certain man, named Demetrius,
a silversmith, who made silver shrines for Artemis, brought no small gain to the artisans;
25 whom he called together, with the workmen of
like occupation, and said, Sirs, you know well
that, by this employment we have our prosperity.
26 Moreover, you see and hear that, not only at
Ephesus, but almost throughout Asia, this Paul
has persuaded and turned aside many people,
saying that they are no gods which are made
27 with hands; so that not only this our trade is
in danger of coming into contempt; but also
that the temple of the great goddess Artemis
will be despised, and her magnificence destroyed,
whom all Asia and the world worship.
28   And when they heard this, they were full of
wrath, and cried out, saying, Great is Artemis
29 of the Ephesians.   And the whole city was
filled with tumult, and having caught Gaius and
Aristarchus, Macedonians, Paul's companions in
travel, they rushed with one accord into the
30 theatre.   And when Paul would have gone in
to the people, the disciples suffered him not.
31 And some of the chief men of Asia, who were
his friends, sent to him, entreating him not to
32 venture himself into the theatre.   Some, therefore, cried one thing, and some another : for the
assembly was confused, and the greater part
knew not wherefore they were come together.
33 And they drew Alexander out of the crowd, the
Jews urging him forward.   And Alexander,
waving the hand, would have made his defense
34 to the people.   But when they knew that he
was a Jew, all with one voice, about the space
of two hours, cried out, Great is Artemis of the
Ephesians.
35   And when the city-clerk had appeased the
people, he says, Ephesians, what man is there
who knows not that the city of the Ephesians is a worshiper of the great Artemis, and
of the image which fell down from Jupiter?
36 Seeing then that these things can not be spoken

against, you ought to be quiet, and to do
nothing rashly.   For you have brought hither 37
these men, who are neither robbers of temples
nor yet revilers of your goddess.   Therefore, 38
if Demetrius, and the artisans that are with
him, have a complaint against any man, the law
is open, and there are proconsuls : let them
accuse one another.   But if you inquire any 39
thing concerning other matters, it shall be determined in the lawful assembly.   For we are in 40
danger of being called in question for this day's
uproar, there being no cause in reference to
which we shall be able to give an account of
this concourse.   And when he had thus spoken, 41
he dismissed the assembly.

XX.—And after the disturbance had ceased,
Paul called to him the disciples, and embracing
them, departed to go into Macedonia.   And 2
when he had gone over those parts, and had
given them much exhortation, he came into
Greece, and having spent three months there, 3
he resolved to return through Macedonia, the
Jews having laid wait for him, as he was about
to embark for Syria.   And there accompanied 4
him to Asia, Sopater of Berea, and of the Thes-
salonians, Aristarchus and Secundus; and Gaius
of Derbe, and Timothy ; and of Asia, Tychicus
and Trophimus.   And these going before, tar- 5
ried for us at Troas.   And we sailed away 6
from Philippi, after the days of unleavened
bread, and came to them to Troas, in five days,
where we abode seven days.

And on the first day of the week, when we 7
came together for the breaking a loaf, Paul
discoursed with them, ready to depart on the
morrow, and continued his speech till midnight.
And there were many lamps in the upper 8
chamber, where we were assembled together.
And there sat in the open window a certain 9
young man, named Eutychus, who had fallen
into a deep sleep : and as Paul was long discoursing, he sunk down with sleep, and fell
from the third story, and was taken up dead.
And Paul went down, and fell upon him, and 10
embracing him, said, Be not troubled, for his
life is in him.   And when he had come up, 11
and had broken the loaf, and eaten, and talked

a long while, even till day-break, so he depart-
12 ed. And they brought the young man alive,
13 and were not a little comforted. And we went
forward to the ship, and sailed to Assos, there
intending to take in Paul: for so he had
appointed, intending himself to go on foot.
14 And when he met us at Assos, we took him in,
15 and came to Mitylene. And having sailed
thence, we came the next day over against
Chios; and the next day we arrived at Samos,
and remained at Trogyllium; and the next day
16 we came to Miletus; for Paul had determined
to sail past Ephesus, that he might not spend
the time in Asia; for he hastened, if it were
possible for him, to be at Jerusalem on the day
17 of Pentecost. And from Miletus he sent to
Ephesus, and called for the elders of the con-
18 gregation. And when they were come to him,
he said to them: You well know from the first
day that I came into Asia, in what manner I
19 have always been with you, serving the Lord
with all humility of mind, and with many tears
and trials, which befell me by the plots of the
20 Jews: and that I have kept back nothing that
was profitable, but have declared to you, and
have taught you both publicly, and from house
21 to house, testifying both to the Jews and
Greeks, reformation toward God, and faith
22 toward our Lord Jesus Christ. And now behold, I go bound in spirit to Jerusalem, not
knowing the things which will befall me there:
23 except that the Holy Spirit testifies in every
city, saying, that bonds and afflictions await me.
24 But none of these things move me, neither count
I my life dear to myself, so that I may finish my
course with joy, and the ministry which I have
received from the Lord Jesus, to testify the
25 gospel of the grace of God. And now behold,
I know that you all, among whom I have gone
preaching the kingdom of God, will see my
26 face no more; wherefore I take you to witness
this day, that I am clear from the blood of all.
27 For I have kept nothing back, but have declar-
28 ed to you the whole counsel of God. Take
heed, therefore, to yourselves, and to all the
flock in which the Holy Spirit has constituted
you overseers, to feed the congregation of the
Lord, which he has purchased with his own

blood. For I know this, that after my depar- 29
ture fierce wolves will enter in among you, not
sparing the flock. Also from among your own- 30
selves, men will arise, speaking perverse things,
to draw away disciples after them. Therefore 31
watch, and remember, that during three years I
ceased not to warn every one night and day
with tears. And now, brethren, I commend you 32
to God, and to the word of his grace, which is
able to build you up, and to give you an inheritance among all them who are sanctified. I 33
have coveted no man's silver, or gold, or
apparel. You yourselves know, that these 34
hands have ministered to my necessities, and
to those that were with me. I have shown you 35
in all respects that by so laboring you ought
to support the weak, and to remember the
words of the Lord Jesus, that he himself said,
It is more blessed to give than to receive.
And when he had said this, he kneeled down, 36
and prayed with them all. And they all wept 37
much, and having fallen on Paul's neck, they
kissed him, sorrowing especially for the words 38
which he had spoken, that they would see his
face no more. And they accompanied him to
the ship.

XXI.—WHEN now it came to pass that we
put to sea, having departed from them, we came
with a straight course to Cos, and the day following to Rhodes, and thence to Patara. And 2
having found a ship crossing over to Phenicia,
we went on board, and set sail. Now having 3
had a view of Cyprus, and having left it behind
on the left hand, we sailed to Syria, and landed
at Tyre: for there the ship was to unlade her
cargo. And having sought out the disciples, we 4
remained there seven days; who said to Paul,
through the Spirit, that he should not go up to
Jerusalem. But having completed the days, we 5
went on our way; and they all with their wives
and children conducted us on our way, till we
were out of the city; and having kneeled down
on the shore, we prayed. And having embraced 6
one another, we went on board the ship, and
they returned home. Now we, having com- 7
pleted the voyage, came down from Tyre to
Ptolemais, and saluted the brethren, and

8 remained with them one day. And the next day we departed, and came to Cesarea; and entering into the house of Philip the evangelist, who was one of the seven, we remained with
9 him. Now the same man had four daughters,
10 virgins, who prophesied. And as we remained there several days, there came down from Judea
11 a certain prophet, named Agabus. And when he came to us, he took Paul's girdle, and binding his own hands and feet, said, Thus says the Holy Spirit, So shall the Jews at Jerusalem bind the man who owns this girdle, and shall deliver him into the hands of the Gentiles.
12 Now when we heard these things, both we, and they of that place, besought Paul not to go
13 up to Jerusalem. Then Paul answered, What do you, weeping and breaking my heart? for I am ready not only to be bound, but also to die at Jerusalem for the name of the Lord Jesus.
14 And when he could not be persuaded, we ceased, saying, The will of the Lord be done!
15 And after those days we packed up our bag-
16 gage, and went up to Jerusalem. There went with us certain of the disciples of Cesarea, bringing us to Mnason, a Cyprian, an old disciple, with whom we should lodge.
17 Now when we were come to Jerusalem, the
18 brethren gladly received us. And the day following Paul went in with us to James, and all
19 the elders were present. And when he had saluted them, he related particularly what things God had wrought among the Gentiles through
20 his ministry. And when they heard it, they glorified the Lord, and said to Paul, You see, brother, what myriads of Jews there are who have believed; and they are all zealous for the
21 law; now they have been informed concerning you, that you teach all the Jews who are among the Gentiles apostasy from Moses, saying that they ought not to circumcise their children,
22 neither to walk after the customs. What then is it? The multitude must needs come together:
23 for they will hear that you have come. Do this, therefore, which we say to you: We have four
24 men who have a vow on themselves; taking these with yourself, purify yourself with them, and bear the charges for them, that they may shave their heads: and all will know that those

things of which they were informed concerning you, are nothing, but that you yourself also walk orderly, and keep the law.

But as respects the Gentiles who have believ- 25 ed, we have already written and concluded that they observe no such thing; only that they abstain from things offered to idols, and from blood, and from things strangled, and from all kinds of lewdness.

Then Paul took the men, and the next day 26 purifying himself with them, entered into the temple, announcing the fulfillment of the days of purification, till the offerings should be offered for each one of them.

Now as the seven days were about to be 27 completed, the Jews who were of Asia, when they saw him in the temple, stirred up all the people, and laid hands on him, crying out, 28 Israelites, help! This is the man who teaches all men every where against this people, and the law, and this place: and further also has brought Greeks into the temple, and has polluted this holy place. For they had formerly seen 29 with him in the city, Trophimus, an Ephesian, whom they supposed that Paul had brought into the temple. And all the city was moved, and 30 the people ran together, and seizing Paul, they dragged him out of the temple: and immediately the doors were shut. And as they 31 were seeking to kill him, word came up to the chiliarch of the cohort, that all Jerusalem was in confusion; who immediately took soldiers 32 and centurions, and ran down upon them. And when they saw the chiliarch and the soldiers, they ceased from beating Paul. Then the 33 chiliarch drew near and took him, and commanded him to be bound with two chains, and inquired who he might be, and what he had done. But some in the crowd were shouting 34 one thing, and some another: and when he could not know the certainty, on account of the tumult, he commanded him to be led into the castle. And when he was on the stairs, it 35 came to pass that he was borne by the soldiers, on account of the violence of the crowd. For 36 the multitude of the people followed, crying out, Away with him! And as Paul was about to be 37 led into the castle, he said to the chiliarch, May

I speak to you? Who said, Do you know
38 Greek? Are you not then that Egyptian, who
before these days made an uproar, and led out
into the wilderness the four thousand assassins?
39 But Paul said, I am, indeed, a Jew from Tarsus,
a city in Cilicia, a citizen of no mean city; and
I beseech you to permit me to speak to the
40 people. And when he had permitted him, Paul
stood on the stairs, and waved with his hand to
the people; and when there was made a great
silence, he spoke to them in the Hebrew tongue,
saying:

XXII.—BRETHREN, and fathers! Hear my
2 defense which I now make to you. And when
they heard that he spoke the Hebrew tongue,
3 they kept the greater silence. And he says, I am
indeed a Jew, born in Tarsus in Cilicia, yet
brought up in this city, and taught at the feet of
Gamaliel, according to the perfect law of our
fathers, and was as zealous toward God, as you
4 all are this day. And I persecuted those of
this way to death, binding and delivering into
5 prison both men and women, as also the high
priest and the whole body of the elders can
bear me testimony; from whom also I received
letters to the brethren, and went to Damascus,
to bring those that were bound there to Jeru-
6 salem, to be punished. And as I was on my
journey, and was come nigh to Damascus about
noon, suddenly there shone from heaven a great
7 light around me: and I fell to the ground, and
heard a voice saying to me, Saul, Saul, why do
8 you persecute me? And I answered, Who art
thou, Lord? And he said to me, I am Jesus of
9 Nazareth, whom you persecute. And they who
were with me, saw indeed the light, and were
afraid: but they understood not the voice of
10 him that spake to me. And I said, What shall
I do, Lord? And the Lord said to me, Arise,
and go into Damascus; and there it shall be
told you concerning all the things which are
11 appointed you to do. And as I could not see
for the splendor of that light, I was led by the
hand by those who were with me, and came
12 into Damascus. And one Ananias, a devout
man according to the law, well spoken of among
13 all the Jews who dwelt there, came to me, and
stood, and said to me, Brother Saul, receive
your sight, and the same hour I looked up upon
him. And he said, The God of our fathers has 14
chosen you, that you should know his will, and
see that Just One, and hear the voice of his
mouth. For you shall be his witness to all 15
men, of what you have seen and heard. And 16
now why do you delay? Arise, and be immersed, and wash away your sins, invoking the name
of the Lord. And when I returned to Jerusa- 17
lem, even while I prayed in the temple, I was in
a trance; and beheld him saying to me, Make 18
haste, and go quickly out of Jerusalem; for
they will not receive your testimony concerning
me. And I said, Lord, they know that I 19
imprisoned, and beat in every synagogue those
who believed on thee: and when the blood of 20
Stephen thy witness, was shed, I also was standing by, consenting, and kept the raiment of
them who slew him. And he said to me, 21
Depart; for I will send you out far hence to the
Gentiles.

And they heard him up to this word, and 22
then raised their voices, and said, Away with
such a fellow from the earth; for it is not fit
that he should live. And as they shouted, and 23
threw up their clothes, and cast dust into the
air, the chiliarch commanded him to be brought 24
into the castle, and ordered that he should be
examined by scourging, that he might ascertain
wherefore they cried out against him. And as 25
they were binding him with thongs, Paul said
to the centurion who stood by, Is it lawful
for you to scourge a man who is a Roman,
and uncondemned? When the centurion heard 26
that, he went and told the chiliarch, saying,
Take heed what you are about to do; for this
man is a Roman. Then the chiliarch came, and 27
said to him, Tell me, are you a Roman? He
said, Yes. And the chiliarch answered, With 28
a great sum I obtained this citizenship; and
Paul said, But I was born *with it*. Then imme- 29
diately they departed from him who were about
to have examined him; and the chiliarch also
was afraid after he knew that he was a Roman,
and because he had bound him.

On the next day, being desirous to know with 30
certainty on what account he was accused by

the Jews, he loosed him from his bonds, and commanded the chief priests and all their council to appear, and having brought down Paul, he placed him before them.

XXIII.—AND Paul, earnestly beholding the council, said, Brethren, I have lived to God 2 with all good conscience until this day. And the high priest Ananias commanded them who stood by him, to strike him on the mouth. 3 Then Paul said to him, God will strike you, you whited wall: for do you sit do judge me according to the law, and command me to be 4 struck contrary to the law? And they who stood by, said, Do you revile God's high priest? 5 Then said Paul, I knew not, brethren, that he was the high priest; for it is written, You shall not speak evil of the ruler of your people.

6 But when Paul perceived that the one part were Sadducees, and the other Pharisees, he cried out in the council, Brethren, I am a Pharisee, the son of a Pharisee: concerning a hope and a resurrection of the dead I am now judged. 7 And when he had so said, there arose a dissension between the Pharisees and the Sad- 8 ducees; and the multitude was divided. For the Sadducees say that there is no resurrection nor angel, nor spirit; but the Pharisees confess 9 both. And there arose a great clamor; and the scribes who were of the Pharisees' party arose, and strove, saying, We find no evil in this man: but, if an angel or spirit spoke to him,— 10 And when there arose a great dissension, the chiliarch, fearing that Paul would have been pulled in pieces by them, commanded the soldiery to go down, and take him by force from among them, and to bring him into the castle. 11 And the night following, the Lord stood by him, and said, Take courage, for as you have testified of me in Jerusalem, so must you also bear testimony in Rome.

12 And when it was day, the Jews, having formed a combination, bound themselves under a curse, saying that they would neither eat nor 13 drink till they had killed Paul: and there were more than forty who had formed this con- 14 spiracy. And they went to the chief priest and elders, and said, We have bound ourselves under a great curse, that we will eat nothing till we we have slain Paul. Now, therefore, you with 15 the council, signify to the chiliarch that he bring him down to you to-morrow, as though you would inquire something more exactly concerning him: and we, before he can come near, will be ready to kill him.

And when Paul's sister's son heard of the 16 ambush, he went and entered into the castle, and told Paul. Then Paul called one of the 17 centurions to him, and said, Bring this young man to the chiliarch; for he has a certain thing to tell him. And so he took him, and brought 18 him to the chiliarch, and says, Paul the prisoner called me to him, and requested me to bring this young man to you. Then the chiliarch took 19 him by the hand, and went with him aside privately, and asked him, What is that you have to say to me? And he said, The Jews 20 have agreed to request you, that you would bring down Paul to-morrow into the council, as though they would inquire something about him more perfectly. But do not you yield to them: 21 for there lie in wait for him more than forty men of them, who have bound themselves with an oath, that they will neither eat nor drink till they have killed him; and now are they ready, looking for the promise from you. So the 22 chiliarch let the young man depart, and charged him, Tell no person that you have showed these things to me. And he called to him some two 23 of the centurions, saying, Make ready two hundred soldiers, and seventy horsemen, and two hundred spearmen, to go to Cesarea, at the third hour of the night; and let them provide 24 beasts on which they may place Paul, and bring him safe to Felix the governor. And he wrote 25 a letter after this manner: Claudius Lysias, to 26 the most excellent governor Felix, sends greeting. This man was taken by the Jews, and 27 was about to be killed by them; but I came with the soldiery, and rescued him, having learned that he was a Roman. And when I 28 wished to know the cause for which they accused him, I brought him forth into their council: and found him to be accused about 29 questions of their law, but to have nothing laid to his charge worthy of death, or of bonds.

30 And when it was told me how the Jews laid wait for the man, I sent him immediately to you, and gave commandement to his accusers also, to say before you what they had against Farewell.

31 Then the soldiers, as it was commanded them, took Paul, and brought him by night to Antipa-

32 tris; and on the morrow they left the horsemen to go with him (and returned to the castle):

33 who, when they came to Cesarea, and delivered the epistle to the governor, presented Paul also

34 before him. And when the governor had read the letter, he asked of what province he was. And when he understood that he was of Cilicia, he

35 said, I will hear you, when your accusers are also come. And he commanded him to be kept under guard in the pretorium of Herod.

XXIV.—Now after five days, Ananias the high priest came down to Cesarea with the elders, and with a certain orator named Tertullus, who appeared before the governor against

2 Paul. And when he was called, Tertullus proceeded to accuse him, saying, Seeing that through you we enjoy much peace, and that many very worthy deeds are done this nation through

3 your prudent administration; we receive it in every way, and everywhere, most noble Felix,

4 with all thankfulness. But that I may not weary you longer, I pray you of your clemency to hear

5 a few words from us. For we have found this man a pest, and exciting disturbance among all the Jews throughout the world, a chief-leader

6 of the sect of Nazarenes: who also has gone about to profane the temple: whom we took, and would have judged according to our law:

7 but the chiliarch Lysias came upon us, and with great violence took him away out of our hands,

8 commanding his accusers to come to you: by examining of whom you yourself may obtain knowledge of all these thing whereof we accuse

9 him. And the Jews also assailed him, saying that these things were so.

10 Then Paul, after that the governor had beckoned to him to speak, answered:—Knowing that you have been for many years a judge for this nation, I do the more cheerfully answer for

11 myself; it being in your power to know that there are yet but twelve days since I went up to Jerusalem to worship. And they neither found

12 me in the temple disputing with any man, neither stirring up the people, neither in the synagogue,

13 nor in the city: neither can they prove the

14 things of which they now accuse me. But this I confess to you, that after the way which they call a sect, so I worship the God of my fathers, believing all things which are written in the law

15 and in the prophets: and have a hope towards God, which they themselves also entertain, that there is to be a resurrection of the dead, both

16 of the just and also of the unjust. And in this do I exercise myself, to have always a conscience void of offense towards God and men.

17 Now, after many years, I came in order to bring alms to my nation, and to make offerings;

18 on which occasion certain Jews from Asia found me purified in the temple, but neither with a

19 crowd, nor with tumult: who ought to have been here before you to accuse me, had they any

20 charge against me; or else let these themselves say, if they found any evil in me, when I stood

21 before the council, except it be for this one expression which I made standing among them, Concerning the resurrection of the dead I am this day called in question.

22 And when Felix heard these things, knowing more accurately the things in regard to the way, he deferred them, and said, When Lysias the chiliarch shall come down, I will thoroughly

23 examine the matters between you. And he commanded the centurion that Paul should be kept, and that he should have a relaxation, and that he should forbid none of his acquaintance

24 to minister, or come to him. And, after some days, when Felix came with his wife Drusilla (who was a Jewess), he sent for Paul, and heard him concerning the faith in relation to Christ.

25 And as he reasoned concerning justice, self-government, and the judgment to come, Felix trembled, and answered, Go your way for this time; when I have a convenient season, I will

26 send for you. At the same time hoping that money would have been given him by Paul, that he might release him, he therefore sent for him

27 the oftener, and conversed with him. But after two years Felix had a successor, Porcius Festus;

and Felix, willing to show the Jews a favor, left Paul bound.

XXV.—Now when Festus had come into the province, after three days, he went up from 2 Cesarea to Jerusalem. Then the high priest, and the chief of the Jews, informed him against 3 Paul, and besought him, asking for themselves a favor against him, that he would send for him to Jerusalem, preparing an ambush to kill him on 4 the way. But Festus answered that Paul should be kept in custody at Cesarea, and that he him- 5 self would shortly depart thither. Let the powerful among you, said he, go down with me and accuse this man, if there is any wickedness in him.

6 And when he had tarried among them more than ten days, he went down to Cesarea; and the next day sitting on the judgment-seat, com- 7 manded Paul to be brought. And when he was come, the Jews who came down from Jerusalem stood around him, and laid many and heavy complaints against Paul, which they could not 8 prove; while he answered for himself, Neither against the law of the Jews, nor against the temple, nor yet against Cesar have I at all 9 offended. But Festus, willing to do the Jews a favor, answered Paul, and said, Will you go up to Jerusalem, and there be judged of these 10 things before me? Then said Paul, I stand at Cesar's judgment-seat, where I ought to be judged: to the Jews I have done no wrong, as 11 you yourself very well know. For if I am doing wrong, and have committed any thing worthy of death, I refuse not to die; but if there is nothing in these matters of which they accuse me, no man can deliver me up to them: 12 I appeal to Cesar. Then Festus, when he had talked with the council, answered, You have appealed to Cesar, to Cesar shall you go.

13 And after certain days, king Agrippa and Bernice came to Cesarea to salute Festus. 14 And when they had been there many days, Festus set forth to the king the facts concern- ing Paul, saying, There is a certain man left 15 prisoner by Felix; about whom, when I was at Jerusalem, the chief priests and the elders of the Jews brought an information, asking for

themselves justice against him; to whom I 16 answered: It is not the custom of the Romans to deliver any man to die before he that is accused have his accusers face to face, and have an opportunity to answer for himself concerning the charge. Therefore, when they had come 17 hither, without any delay on the morrow, I sat on the judgment-seat, and commanded the man to be brought; against whom, when the accu- 18 sers stood up, they brought no accusation of such things as I surmised: but had certain 19 questions against him respecting their own religion, and of one Jesus, who had died, whom Paul affirmed to be alive. And because I 20 doubted how to investigate such questions, I asked him whether he would go to Jerusalem, and be judged concerning these matters: but 21 Paul having appealed, to be kept as a prisoner, with a view to the examination of Augustus, I commanded him to be kept till I shall send him to Cesar. Then Agrippa said to Festus, I my- 22 self also would wish to hear the man. To-mor- row, said he, you shall hear him.

And on the morrow, when Agrippa had come, 23 and Bernice, with much pomp, and had entered into the place of audience, with the chiliarchs and principal men of the city, at the command of Festus, Paul was brought forth. Then 24 Festus says, King Agrippa, and all men who are present with us, you see this man about whom all the multitude of the Jews have interceded with me, both at Jerusalem, and also here, crying out that he ought not to live any longer. But 25 when I found that he had committed nothing worthy of death, and he himself having appealed to Augustus, I determined to send him: of 26 whom I have nothing certain to write to my sovereign, wherefore I have brought him forth before you; and especially before you, king Agrippa, that after examination, I may have something to write. For it seems to me un- 27 reasonable to send a prisoner, and not also to signify the charges against him.

XXVI.—Then Agrippa says to Paul, You are permitted to speak for yourself. Then Paul stretched forth his hand, and answered for himself: I think myself happy, king Agrippa, 2 because I shall answer for myself this day before you, concerning all the things of which I am 3 accused by Jews: because I know you to be especially skilled in all customs and questions which are among Jews; wherefore I beseech you to hear me patiently.

4 My manner of life from my youth, which was at the first among my own nation at Jerusalem, all the Jews know, who have known me from 5 the beginning, if they would testify, that, after the strictest sect of our religion, I lived a Pharisee. And now I stand, and am judged for the hope 6 of the promise made by God to our fathers: to *the accomplishment* of which promise our twelve 7 tribes, earnestly serving God day and night, hope to attain; on account of which hope, king 8 Agrippa, I am accused by Jews. What! Is it judged incredible with you that God raises the 9 dead? I, indeed, thought with myself that I ought to do many things against the name of 10 Jesus of Nazareth. Which things I also did in Jerusalem: and many of the saints I shut up in prisons, having received authority from the chief priests; and when they were put to death, I gave 11 my vote against them. And punishing them often throughout all the synagogues, I compelled them to revile *Jesus*, and being exceedingly mad against them, I persecuted them even to foreign 12 cities. In doing this, as I went to Damascus, with authority and commission from the chief priests, 13 at mid-day, O king, I saw along the way a light from heaven, above the brightness of the sun, shining round about me, and those that jour- 14 neyed with me. And when we had all fallen to the earth, I heard a voice speaking to me, and saying in the Hebrew tongue, Saul, Saul, why do you persecute me? It is hard for you 15 to kick against goads. And I said, Who art thou, Lord? And he said, I am Jesus whom 16 you persecute. But rise, and stand upon your feet: for I have appeared to you for this purpose, to make you a minister and a witness both of those things you have seen, and of those 17 things in which I will appear to you; delivering you from the people, and from the Gentiles, 18 to whom I now send you, to open their eyes, that they may turn from darkness to light, and from the power of Satan to God, that they may

receive forgiveness of sins, and an inheritance among them that are sanctified, by the faith respecting me.

Whence, king Agrippa, I was not disobedient 19 to the heavenly vision, but showed first to those 20 of Damascus, and at Jerusalem, and throughout all the region of Judea, and then to the Gentiles, that they should reform and turn to God, and do works proper for reformation. For 21 these causes the Jews seized me in the temple, and tried to kill me. Having, however, obtain- 22 ed the help of God, I continue to this day, testifying both to small and great, saying no other things than those which the prophets and Moses did say would come: that the Christ was to 23 suffer, and that he first, by his resurrection from the dead, would show light to the people, and to the Gentiles.

And as he thus spoke for himself, Festus said 24 with a loud voice, Paul, you are mad, much learning has made you mad. But he says, I am 25 not mad, most excellent Festus; but speak the words of truth and of a sound mind. For the 26 king well knows concerning these things, before whom, therefore, I speak boldly; for I am persuaded that none of these things are hidden from him: for this thing has not been done in a corner. King Agrippa, do you believe the 27 prophets? I know that you believe them. Then Agrippa said to Paul, You in a little time 28 persuade me to become a Christian. And Paul 29 said, I would to God, that not only you, but also all that hear me this day, were, in a little or much time, such as I am, except these bonds.

And when he had said these things, the king 30 rose up, and the governor, and Bernice, and they who sat with them, and when they had 31 gone aside, they talked among themselves, saying, This man does nothing worthy of death, or of bonds. Then Agrippa said to Festus, This man might have been set at liberty, if he 32 had not appealed to Cesar.

XXVII.—AND when it was determined that we should sail to Italy, they delivered Paul and certain other prisoners to a centurion of the Augustan cohort, named Julius. And entering 2 into a vessel of Adramyttium, we put to sea, being about to sail by the coasts of Asia, Aristarchus, a Macedonian of Thessalonica, 3 being with us. And the next day we landed at Sidon : and Julius courteously treated Paul, and gave him liberty to go to the friends, to partake 4 of their kindness. And when we had loosed from thence, we sailed under Cyprus, because 5 the winds were contrary. And when we had sailed over the sea along Cilicia and Pamphy- 6 lia, we came to Myra, a city of Lycia : and there the centurion found a ship of Alexandria sailing into Italy, and he put us on board of it. 7 And when we had sailed slowly many days, and with difficulty came off Cnidus, the wind not permitting us, we sailed under Crete, over 8 against Salmone ; and coasting along it with difficulty, came to a certain place called, The Fair Havens ; near which was the city of Lasea. 9 Now a long time having elapsed, the navigation being now unsafe (because also the fast was already past), Paul exhorted them, saying, 10 Sirs, I perceive that the voyage will be with violence and much loss, not only of the cargo 11 and ship, but also of our lives. Nevertheless the centurion believed the helmsman and the owner of the ship rather than those things 12 spoken by Paul : and because the haven was incommodious to winter in, the majority also advised to depart thence, if by any means they might attain to Phœnix, to winter, which is a haven of Crete, facing southwest and northwest. 13 Now when a south-wind blew moderately, thinking to have gained their purpose, having 14 weighed *anchor*, they sailed close by Crete. But immediately a whirlwind, called Euroclydon, 15 struck against the ship. And when it was borne away, and could not bear up against the 16 wind, giving up, we let it drive. And running under a certain small island, called Clauda, with difficulty we were able to secure the boat : 17 which when they had taken up, they used helps, undergirding the ship ; and fearing lest they should be stranded on the sand bank, they 18 lowered the sail, and so were driven. Now we being exceedingly tempest tossed, the next day 19 they lightened the ship ; and the third day we cast out with our own hands the tackling of the ship. And when neither sun nor stars had for 20 many days appeared, and no small tempest lay on us, at last all hope that we should be saved was utterly taken away.

But after much abstinence, Paul stood in the 21 midst of them, and said, Sirs, you should have hearkened to me, and not have loosed from Crete, and so have sustained this harm and loss. Yet now I exhort you to be of good cheer ; for 22 there shall be no loss of any man's life among you, except the ship.

For there stood by me this night the angel 23 of God, whose I am, and whom I also worship, saying, Fear not, Paul ; you must be brought 24 before Cesar : and lo, God has given to you all those who sail with you. Wherefore, sirs, be 25 of good cheer : for I believe God, that it shall be even as it was told me. But still, we must 26 be cast upon some island.

But when the fourteenth night was come, as 27 we were borne along in the Adriatic sea, about midnight the seamen thought that they drew near to some land ; and sounded, and found it 28 twenty fathoms ; and when they had gone a little further, they sounded again, and found it fifteen fathoms. Then fearing lest we should 29 have fallen upon rocks, they cast four anchors out of the stern, and longed for day.

And as the seamen were about to flee out of 30 the ship, when they had let down the boat into the sea, under pretense of carrying anchors out of the foreship, Paul said to the centurion, and 31 to the soldiers, Unless these abide in the ship, you can not be saved. Then the soldiers cut 32 off the ropes of the boat, and let it fall off. And while the day was coming on, Paul 33 besought them all to take food, saying, This is the fourteenth day that you have been waiting, and continue fasting, having taken nothing. Wherefore I pray you to take some food, for 34 this is necessary for your preservation : for there shall not a hair perish from the head of any of you. And when he had thus spoken, 35 having taken a loaf, he gave thanks to God in presence of them all ; and when he had broken it, he began to eat. Then were they all of good 36 cheer, and they also themselves took some food. Now all the souls together in the ship were two 37

38 hundred and seventy-six. And when they had eaten enough, they lightened the ship, and cast out the wheat into the sea.

39 And when it was day, they recognized not the land, but they perceived a certain inlet having a shore, into which they determined,

40 were it possible, to thrust the ship. And having entirely cut away the anchors, they abandoned them to the sea, and at the same time having unfastened the rudder-bands, and hoisted up the foresail to the wind, they made toward

41 shore. And having fallen into a place where two currents met, they ran the ship aground; and the prow sticking fast, remained immovable, but the stern was broken by the violence of the

42 waves. And the soldiers' counsel was to kill the prisoners, lest any of them should swim out,

43 and escape. But the captain, willing to save Paul, kept them from their purpose, and commanded that they who could swim should cast themselves first into the sea, and get to land;

44 and the rest, some on boards, and others on some of the things from the ship. And so they all escaped safe to land.

XXVIII.—AND when we had fully escaped, then we ascertained that the island was called

2 Melite. And the barbarous people showed us no common philanthropy: for they kindled a fire, and brought us all to it, because of the present rain, and because of the cold.

3 And when Paul had gathered a great number of dry sticks, and laid them on the fire, there came a viper out of the heat, and fastened on

4 his hand. And when the barbarians saw the venomous creature hanging on his hand, they said among themselves, No doubt this man is a murderer, whom, though he has escaped the sea,

5 yet Justice permits not to live. And he shook off the creature into the fire, and suffered no

6 harm; but they expected that he would be inflamed, or that he would suddenly fall down dead. But after they had looked a great while, and saw no harm come to him, they changed

7 their minds, and said that he was a god. In the same parts were possessions of the chief of the island, whose name was Publius; who

received us, and lodged us three days courteously. And the father of Publius lay sick of a 8 fever, and of a bloody flux: to whom Paul went, and prayed, and laid his hands upon him, and healed him. So when this was done, others 9 also who had diseases in the island, came, and were healed; who also honored us with many 10 honors; and when we departed, they laded us with such things as were necessary.

And after three months we departed in a ship 11 of Alexandria, which had wintered in the isle, whose sign was Castor and Pollux. And land- 12 ing at Syracuse, we tarried there three days. And thence we coasted round, and came to 13 Rhegium: and after one day, the south wind having risen, we came the next day to Puteoli: where we found brethren, and were desired to 14 tarry with them seven days, and then we went towards Rome. And from thence, when the 15 brethren heard of us, they came to meet us as far as Appii Forum, and the Three Taverns; whom when Paul saw he thanked God, and took courage. And when we came to Rome, 16 the centurion delivered the prisoners to the commander of the camp, but it was permitted to Paul to dwell by himself, with a soldier who guarded him. And after three days, he called 17 the chief of the Jews together, and when they were come together, he said to them, Brethren, though I have committed nothing against our people, or the customs of our fathers, yet I was delivered prisoner from Jerusalem into the hands of the Romans; who when they had 18 examined me, would have released me, because there was no cause of death in me. But when 19 the Jews spoke against it, I was compelled to appeal to Cesar; not that I had any thing to charge against my nation. On this account, there- 20 fore, I have invited you, that I might see you, and speak with you: for on account of the hope of Israel I am compassed with this chain.

And they said to him, We neither received 21 letters from Judea concerning you, nor has any one of the brethren who came, reported or said any harm of you; but we think it proper to 22 hear from you, what you think: for as it respects this sect, we know that it is every where spoken against.

23 And when they had appointed him a day, there came many to him into his lodging; to whom he expounded and testified the kingdom of God, persuading them of the things concerning Jesus, both out of the law of Moses, and out 24 of the prophets, from morning to evening. And some believed the things that were spoken, and 25 others believed them not. So not agreeing among themselves, they departed, Paul having said one word, Well spoke the Holy Spirit by 26 Isaiah the prophet to our fathers, saying, Go to this people, and say, Hearing you will hear, and will not understand; and seeing you will see, 27 and not perceive; for the heart of this people is become gross, and their ears are dull of hearing, and they have closed their eyes, lest they should see with their eyes, and hear with their ears, and understand with their heart, and should be converted, and I should heal them. Be it known, therefore, to you, that the sal- 28 vation of God is sent to the Gentiles, and they will hear it. And when he had said these 29 things, the Jews departed, and had much reasoning among themselves.

And Paul remained in his own hired house 30 during two whole years, and gladly received all who came to him, announcing the kingdom of 31 God, and teaching the things concerning the Lord Jesus Christ, with all boldness, and without molestation.